The Empire State At War

World War II

Compiled and Written for the

NEW YORK STATE WAR COUNCIL

by

KARL DREW HARTZELL, Ph.D.

Published by

THE STATE OF NEW YORK

1949

*Prepared pursuant to action of the War Council and
printed under Chapter 468, Laws of 1948*

DEDICATION

To the Citizens of New York State who fought abroad or labored at home that this country might have peace with freedom, this volume is gratefully dedicated by their government, in the hope that should it ever again become necessary to prepare the State for war, the experiences recorded herein may be drawn upon with confidence in the loyalty and stamina of its people.

Preface

THE NEW YORK STATE WAR COUNCIL authorized the writing of this volume for a number of reasons quite apart from the recognized necessity for preserving a record of the New York home front in World War II. The most practical purpose that a volume of this kind can serve is to provide a blueprint for the organization of the State, should it ever be necessary at some future time to prepare it again for war. It is earnestly hoped that such a use of this volume will never be required. It would be foolhardy, however, to omit an analysis, as well as a description, of the State's collective war experience from 1940 to 1945. Individuals learn from experience; New York State can also. An effort has accordingly been made to point out how, and why, and in what sequence events took place on the home front, as well as their significance for the future welfare of the inhabitants of the State.

Another purpose of the War Council in authorizing this account has been to make it possible for those who played an active part at home to comprehend the exact point at which their efforts fitted into the over-all pattern of the State's war effort. Such an understanding, it is hoped, will contribute to their personal satisfaction with a job well done. The work of one individual, when compared with the total efforts of 13 million people, naturally appears insignificant. Nevertheless, the success of New York State as a whole depended fundamentally upon the willingness of each of its 13 million inhabitants to perform his personal duties to the limit of his ability. Especially in a time of crisis, individual faithfulness in small things becomes the basic social need.

It is also anticipated that this record of the home front will be read by those who were absent from the State while serving in the armed forces of their country. Many veterans while far away from home wondered whether their relatives and neighbors were actually backing them up; whether they really knew "there was a war going on." If read completely and thoughtfully, this book should set at rest all doubts on that score. The vast majority of New Yorkers eagerly and anxiously did what they could to help win the war. When it came to the test, this democratic microcosm proved sound.

In some respects the war history of one state is the war history of all. Consequently, this narrative may prove interesting to Americans generally, for in the experience of the citizens of New York State they will recognize much that was common to their own. Furthermore, the story of events in the Empire State is a vital part of the national record, which itself will not be complete until each state in the union has written an account of its own achievements.

In surveying as crowded a period as that of the war years, it has usually been considered wise to wait until time could furnish the writer with a more accurate perspective. The War Council decided against this policy for a number of reasons. In the first place this volume is intended as a very sincere tribute to the efforts of volunteers and war workers alike. Recognition of their tremendous contributions to the war effort of the State is being accorded them herewith as soon after the event as possible. Second, it seemed wise to compile the record while written sources were still available in large quantity, rather than run the risk of their subsequent dispersal to the four winds. Above all, however, it was intended that the writer should have the unusual advantage, open only to those who write of events immediately following their occurrence, of being able to talk with the wartime leaders of the State. These men and women have not only revealed the flavor of the war years and the spirit which kept them on the job at all hours, but they have frequently filled in gaps in the correspondence and aided the writer in presenting a balanced account. Many have been kind enough to check sections of the manuscript for errors of fact and interpretation. A delay of five or ten years in writing this history would have rendered interviewing and checking on any comparable scale more difficult and far less effective. To all who have assisted in this way the writer is deeply indebted.

In organizing the material for this volume, care has been taken to present the activities on the home front by topics rather than as the work of separate State departments or War Council agencies. This has greatly simplified the design of the book and has furnished a logical synthesis which should enable the average reader to comprehend quickly from the table of contents the main lines along which the war effort of the State proceeded.

K. D. H.

Geneseo, New York

Acknowledgments

A VOLUME OF THIS character is never the work of one man. The amount of information compressed into these pages has been such as to require close dependence upon sources both written and oral. Reliance for written materials has been placed primarily upon the minutes and agenda of the meetings of the State War Council; upon correspondence and reports in the files of the Headquarters Office of the State War Council, and upon those files of the Governor's office which dealt strictly with War Council matters. The files of the individual War Council agencies have also been useful. One circumstance assisted materially in the writing of the manuscript: the writer's original assignment with the State War Council was the classification and preservation of all historically valuable records created under the War Emergency Act, including those of the State and local war councils, of the thirty-odd war council agencies and records created within the regular State Departments as a result of programs operated wholly or in part with War Council funds. The performance of this task required visits to numerous sections of the State and afforded an acquaintance with the nature and extent of available materials. Efforts were made early to secure a file of administrative histories from each of the War Council agencies, from the State Departments involved, and from the local war councils. These reports proved invaluable in the subsequent task of writing.

A substantial amount of additional statistical material, however, had to be secured directly from Federal, State, and municipal departments and agencies. Among these may be cited the Federal Departments of Agriculture, Commerce, the Navy, the Treasury, and War; also the following Federal agencies: The Maritime Commission, the Office of Defense Transportation, the Office of Price Administration, the Petroleum Administration for War, the Selective Service System, the United States Conciliation Service, the United States Employment Service, the War Manpower Commission, the War Production Board, and the War Shipping Administration.

New York State departments and commissions that contributed important information included the Departments of Agriculture and Markets, Commerce, Education; the Divisions of Housing, Military and Naval Affairs, the State Police, the Selective Service System, the State Commission Against Discrimination and the State Youth Commission, all under the Executive Department; the Department of Health; the New York State Mediation Board, the New York State Workmen's Compensation Board, and the Division of Placement and Unemployment Insurance of the Department of Labor; the Department of Mental

Hygiene; the Public Service Commission; the Department of Public Works; and the Department of Social Welfare.

Assistance has also been received from the New York Port of Embarkation, the Second Service Command, the Port of New York Authority, the American Merchant Marine Institute, Incorporated, the Delaware and Hudson Railroad Corporation, the New York Central System, the New York Petroleum Industries Committee, the New York State Automobile Dealers, Incorporated, the American Red Cross, and the United Service Organizations.

For information of a general nature essential to an understanding of the background of events during the war period, the writer is happy to acknowledge his debt to the following individuals who were kind enough to allow him to interview them with a stenographer: The Honorable Herbert H. Lehman, the Honorable Charles Poletti, the Honorable Irving M. Ives, the Honorable Oswald D. Heck, Commissioners M. P. Catherwood and Elmer A. Carter; John M. Hancock, Louis Hollander, Thomas A. Morgan, Lewis A. Wilson, Oakley Furney, Edwin R. Van Kleeck, V. A. Van Volkenburgh, Mrs. Clarice Leavell Pennock, Thomas L. J. Corcoran, Milton Enzer, Arthur K. Getman, F. Wellington Gilcreas, Warren W. Knox, and Maurice F. Neufeld.

Specific assistance for chapters and sections of this volume has been received from a large number of individuals. Some have read parts of the manuscript and offered valuable suggestions and criticism. Others have supplied information upon request of the author. For the sake of the record these will be ennumerated in detail chapter by chapter. It will thus appear that while the organization and actual writing of this volume were the work of one man, its information was drawn from the citizens and public servants of the State whose generous cooperation is deeply appreciated.

Chapter I has been read by the Honorable Herbert H. Lehman, H. McIntyre Grout, Jr., Maurice F. Neufeld, and Walter Tracey.

Chapter II has been read in part by Colonel W. H. Boughton (Selective Service), Maurice F. Neufeld (Rationing), William K. Arnoldy (Salvage), William L. Pfeiffer and Alonzo P. Adams (War Bonds). Additional information has been supplied by Brigadier General Carlton S. Dargusch, Major Carl A. Foss, Colonel George W. Hinman, Jr., Louis Hollander, Dr. Robert E. Plunkett, Paul O. Komora, Dr. Arthur K. Getman, Edward F. McDougal, and John D. Stuart.

Chapter III has been read by Commissioner Harold Keller and by George B. Robinson. It has been read in part by Commissioners M. P. Catherwood and Elmer A. Carter; Miss Mary Donlon, Mrs. Emily Sims Marconnier, Dr. Donald H. Davenport, William N. Fenninger, Richard W. Hill, Jr., Paul Kelley, and Dwyer W. Shugrue. Information has also been furnished by Leonard P. Adams, Thomas B. Bergen, Frederick H. Bullen, Karel F. Ficek, Meredith B. Givens, Edward A. Lutz, David M. Schneider, and Edgar L. Warren.

Chapter IV has been read by Dr. John J. Bourke, John J. Farrell, and Colonel Frank McNamee. It has been read in part by Earl Devendorf, Leon A. Fischel, and Gardner LeRoy. Information has been furnished by William H. Frank, Jr., E. T. Gawkins, J. R. Hawkins, William G. Howard, W. D. Tiedeman, and Lieutenant Colonel Stuart C. Welch.

Chapter V has been read by Mrs. Walter Scott McNab, Mrs. Clarice Leavell Pennock, C. M. Britt, H. McIntyre Grout, Jr., George H. Liddle, and Walter Tracey. Information has been supplied by Mary S. Brumer and Philip Guenther.

Chapter VI has been read by Edward S. Foster, Dr. T. Norman Hurd, and Dr. L. A. Maynard. It has been read in part by Mrs. C. M. McKay, Mrs. Roger W. Straus, Dr. L. R. Simons, and H. C. Thompson. Information has been supplied by Miss Vera A. Caulum, Commissioner Earl C. Foster, Roy L. Gillett, Harry N. Haight, Albert Hoefer, and W. J. Weaver.

Chapter VII has been read in part by R. C. Georger, LeRoy Greenalch, Frederick D. Lonergan, and Guy W. Pinck. Information was supplied by William J. Carey, Harvey C. Mansfield, R. D. Starbuck, and Joseph L. White.

Chapter VIII has been read in part by Miss Elsie M. Bond, Miss Emily L. Creevey, Miss Ruth E. Rives, Miss Florence K. Wilson, A. F. Allen, Dr. John J. Bourke, Donald A. Campbell, Ellis C. Champlin, Earl Devendorf, Leon A. Fischel, Byron T. Hipple, Jr., Leonard F. Horan, Dr. James E. Perkins, Joseph Strack, Edwin R. Van Kleek. Information was furnished by Dr. Ruth Andrus, Mary S. Brumer, and Harry N. Haight.

Chapter IX was read by Hickman Powell, and in part by Commissioner Herman T. Stichman, Dr. John S. Allen, Colonel Colin D. McRae and Lawrence E. Walsh. Commissioner Stichman and Colonel McRae supplied valuable information.

Chapter X was read in an early draft by Charles A. Winding who gave additional information and valuable criticism.

Chapter XI owes practically its entire existence to the individuals and organizations mentioned in the footnotes to the various sections. Further acknowledgment for valuable information supplied the author is due to Frances Cook, Mrs. Paul Nelligan, Zoe B. Fales, Leonard P. Adams, Clement G. Bowers, L. B. Cartwright, W. C. Cameron Edey, John L. Eyre, August E. Gill, Stephen Sheridan, and James L. Smith. The courtesy of Miss Rebecca Rankin in making available the records of the New York City Protective Services and also of its Civilian Defense Volunteer Office is greatly appreciated.

Chapter XII has been read by members of the Albany City Office of Civilian Mobilization, George H. Liddle, and Walter Tracey. Material has also been furnished by Mrs. Edward D. Mulligan, Senator Austin W. Erwin, George J. Clancy, and the Reverend Joseph Sunter.

Milton Alpert, former Counsel to the Executive Secretary, and since September, 1945, Acting Executive Secretary of the New York State War Council has read the entire manuscript including Chapter XIII. His guidance and encouragement have been major factors in bringing the work to completion, and his assistance with those portions of the volume which dealt with legal problems has been absolutely essential. The writer's indebtedness to Mr. Alpert is not easily expressed in words.

Several persons who were in no way connected with the wartime operations of the State have nevertheless assisted materially in the preparation of the text. Dr. Albert B. Corey, State Historian, checked the original plan of organization. Henry H. Eddy, Acting Director of the Division of History and Archives of the State of North Carolina, read, polished, and made valuable suggestions in connection with six of the chapters. William Crocker, Assistant State Archivist, completed the work of Mr. Eddy. These two supplied the very necessary detachment of the layman.

Colonel Thomas C. T. Buckley, of Geneseo, was kind enough to read and comment on the entire manuscript from the viewpoint of a combat soldier absent from the State during the war. At the request of Paul E. Lockwood, Secretary to Governor Dewey, Hickman Powell read the manuscript and made valuable suggestions for improvement.

Finally, the author wishes to express his appreciation of the invaluable technical proficiency and the excellent judgment of his secretary, Mrs. Earl D. Gibbons, to thank Miss Mary Wiechnik, who typed the final manuscript, and to recognize with gratitude the patience and good humor of the watchmen who for a period of eight months ran the elevators in the south tower of the D. and H. Building night after night, Saturdays, Sundays, and holidays.

K. D. H.

Introduction

THE CONTRIBUTIONS of the State of New York to the winning of World War II constitute in themselves a dramatic story well worth preserving for subsequent generations. Taken together in retrospect they comprise a body of experience which in some possible future emergency might well be of tremendous value. Accordingly, it was only logical for the New York State War Council to authorize, at the close of the war, the preparation of a volume recording and analyzing the experiences of the State.

The war efforts of 13 million people are so complex and collectively of such vast scope that only a small segment of the total picture can at any one time be comprehended by a single person. To those who served overseas, as well as to those who took an active part at home, it is hoped this volume will give a clearer understanding of the part their efforts played in the great drama of a democratic society organized for total war.

America's successful part in the winning of the Second World War depended fully as much upon the efforts of the forty-eight states as it did upon the directives of the Federal government. The operations of a country the size of the United States are on too vast a scale to be handled with sureness and finesse from Washington alone. One of the lessons of the war is that governments are no stronger than the spirit and intelligence of those who serve them willingly, and that the foundations of our own democracy rest upon the spirit of individual relationships present in the localities. This was strikingly true in the case of the forty-eight states. Not only did there fall upon these political units a terrific responsibility for implementing the Federal policies, but they were also called upon to supplement these policies with specific war programs of their own. In fact wartime problems involved all levels of government, state, county, city and village as well as national.

If the country were to be mobilized fully for total war, New York, with 10 per cent of the nation's population within its borders, had a tremendous load to carry. Not only was it the most populous state, it was also the wealthiest. The total of war bonds purchased in New York State alone came to 30 per cent of the national figure. New York City was one of the largest manufacturing centers in the country. The city was also the nation's foremost port, handling approximately 25 per cent of the country's total wartime foreign trade. The funneling of freight through its port facilities necessitated a wartime traffic density on New York State's principal railroads far above that of the national average.

Furthermore, because of the State's proximity to the Atlantic seaboard, its more mature industrial economy, and the size of its labor force, New York's volume of war supply contracts, 21.5 billion dollars, was the highest figure for any state in the union.

A war record of such magnitude is the product of many factors. A skilled and educated population, a large number and variety of available plant facilities, proximity to natural resources — all are important. Most important in a crisis, however, is a quality of leadership that can direct and inspire while maintaining under pressure those conditions which best facilitate the translation into action of a people's will to victory.

Leadership in a democracy is like carbon in a steel. Supply too little and the product lacks form and resiliency: too much, and it becomes rigid and will crack or break under strain. To add the right amount of leadership requires a willingness to experiment, a capacity to learn from results, and an ability to keep one eye fixed steadfastly on the main goals of achievement.

One of the principal problems facing democracies in World War II was to discover quickly ways by which large masses of people could function promptly and effectively under pressure. The energies of the entire population had to be mobilized and channeled completely into the struggle for survival. Loss of efficiency from excessive bureaucratic regimentation had to be avoided. Inevitably at this point the age-old problem of the proper balance between freedom and organization—liberty and discipline—came rapidly to the fore.

The capacity of the American political system to improvise new methods to meet problems arising from the strains of war was strikingly illustrated in the political and administrative laboratory which is the State of New York. The principal agency there devised to effect the rapid mobilization of the State's resources was known as the New York State War Council. Its members and the dates of their appointment were:

MEMBERS OF NEW STATE WAR COUNCIL

Date of First
Appointment

August 1, 1940
(Original appointees)

Governor Herbert H. Lehman, Chairman

Lieutenant Governor Charles Poletti, Vice-Chairman

John M. Hancock, Lehman Brothers, New York City (Resigned August 10, 1943)

Dr. Carl E. Ladd, Dean, New York State College of Agriculture (Deceased July 24, 1943)

Thomas J. Lyons, President, New York State Federation of Labor (Deceased, May 6, 1943)

Thomas A. Morgan, President, Sperry Corporation

Mrs. Anna M. Rosenberg, Regional Director, Social Security Board, and War Manpower Commission

Paul Schoellkopf, President, Niagara Falls Power Company

Gustav A. Strebel, President, New York State Industrial Union Council (Resigned July 8, 1943)

Albert F. Sulzer, Vice-President, Eastman Kodak Company (Resigned September 2, 1943)

F. E. Williamson, President, New York Central Railroad (Did not desire reappointment in 1942.)

Charles E. Wilson, President, General Electric Company (Resigned September 24, 1942) Made Vice-Chairman of War Production Board

* * * *

February 20, 1941
Added by Chap. 22,
Laws of 1941

John J. Dunnigan, Minority Leader of State Senate

Joe R. Hanley, President Pro Tem of State Senate

Oswald D. Heck, Speaker of State Assembly

Irwin Steingut, Minority Leader of State Assembly

* * * *

Added by amendment
April 23, 1941
Chap. 457

John J. Bennett, Jr., State Attorney General

* * * *

January 29, 1942

Thomas L. J. Corcoran, Assistant Counsel to the Governor, Executive Secretary and Counsel (Resigned January 16, 1943)

April 21, 1942

Elmer A. Carter, Unemployment Insurance Appeal Board, New York City

May 1, 1942
Added by Chap. 445,
Laws of 1942

Irving M. Ives, Majority Leader of the State Assembly

Nov. 4, 1943   Speaker Oswald D. Heck, War Plans Coordinator, to succeed Lieutenant Governor Thomas W. Wallace, deceased

Nov. 19, 1943   John J. Meegan, Buffalo *Courier Express,* to succeed Albert F. Sulzer, resigned

Jan. 1, 1944   Harold H. Schaff, Executive Secretary to succeed Charles A. Winding, resigned (Mr. Schaff died August 31, 1945.)

Jan. 1, 1944   Benjamin F. Feinberg, President Pro Tem of the Senate, to succeed Joe R. Hanley, recently elected Lieutenant Governor

April 1, 1944   Milton Alpert, Counsel; appointed Acting Executive Secretary September 20, 1945, to succeed Harold H. Schaff, deceased

May 16, 1944   George Z. Medalie, New York City, to succeed John M. Hancock, resigned. Mr. Medalie resigned September 29, 1945, upon appointment to the New York Court of Appeals.

Jan. 3, 1945   Elmer F. Quinn, Minority Leader of the State Senate to succeed John J. Dunnigan

Originally called into being by Governor Herbert H. Lehman as an unofficial group of personal advisers, the Council consisted of representatives from such widely diverse occupations as manufacturing, banking, public utilities, labor, agriculture, and government. Early meetings took place at Governor Lehman's private residence in New York City, but as pressure increased they were transferred to the Executive Mansion, or to the Executive Chamber in the Capitol in Albany. It was in these smoke-filled sessions around a long table that matters of wartime policy were thrashed out in rapid-fire debate. The minutes tell only part of the story, as much discussion was off the record. When agreement was reached and decision made, policies were rarely reversed.

In 1941, by action of the Legislature, the Council became an official body with considerable administrative authority; and the leaders of the Legislature were added to its membership. Following the attack on Pearl Harbor, its functions expanded rapidly, its membership was further increased, and broad legal powers were conferred to enable it to deal effectively with all possible situations. Originally, when new problems were arising thick and fast, and the State had to be organized for the emergency, meetings were held as often as once a week. Gradually, however, especially after Governor Thomas E. Dewey took office in 1943, patterns of policy developed, the Statewide organization crystalized, details were delegated to subordinate agencies, and meetings became less and less frequent.

In furnishing leadership during the war years to 13 million people, members of the New York State War Council exhibited a spirit of nonpartisanship that would be hard to equal. For three years the Republican legislative leaders gave loyal and unstinting support to a Democratic chairman, Governor Lehman. For six years a Republican-dominated Council supported the policies of a Democratic national administration even to the point of reenacting as State law many of the regulations of ODT, OPA, and other Federal agencies. Throughout its existence the Democratic and Republican legislative leaders on the War Council buried the political hatchet and worked harmoniously for the best interests of the war effort. Labor leaders and industrialists developed mutual respect and better understanding while working out details of regulations governing hours and conditions of employment in war plants for women and minors. With everyone, winning the war was paramount.

There were two periods in the wartime political history of New York: the administrations of Governors Herbert H. Lehman and Thomas E. Dewey, two extraordinarily gifted individuals. To Governor Lehman, in the threatening years before Pearl Harbor, fell the task of building up the War Council organization on both State and local levels. To him fortune assigned the role of preparing the people for war and of stimulating the production of war equipment by New York manufacturers. He pushed the formation of a Civilian Protection organization, the Statewide mobilization of volunteers, and the support of such Federal programs as Selective Service, rationing, salvage, and the sale of war bonds. The program for the procurement and assignment of nurses, and the development of physical fitness and recreation facilities, were inaugurated under him. His was a role of initiation prior to Pearl Harbor and, in the country's first year of war, of experimentation in operating the State War Council organization on a war basis. Governor Lehman understood clearly the fundamental issues of the great international struggle, and he did his utmost to convince his fellow citizens that the war would come and that New York must be prepared to wage it. In this he was eminently successful. When Pearl Harbor came, New York was prepared to go into high gear. For such an accomplishment his State and his country owe him a permanent debt of gratitude.

With the inauguration of Thomas E. Dewey, January 1, 1943, the long period of Democratic governors came to an end, and a new era began. In the gubernatorial campaign, Governor Dewey had pledged a progressive, independent, teamwork government which would ensure New York's playing its full part in the war. He pointed out the threatened food shortage, the shortage of farm labor, the shortage of war contracts and industrial jobs in New York City, the loss of doctors and nurses to the armed forces, and declared flatly that although he would support "every constructive step taken by the Federal government to meet these problems," the responsibility of the State government for the health and welfare of its people was primary, and without regard to what Federal officials did or did not do about them.

Concentrating on food, a shortage of which might lose the war, he pointed out the production record of New York farmers up to that time unassisted by the State, and pledged full cooperation and support. This pledge was fulfilled with the creation of the Emergency Food Commission with special appropriations for handling the problems of nutrition, farm machinery repair, and farm labor shortages.

Once firmly established in office, the first administration of Governor Dewey was concerned primarily with the vigorous prosecution of the war, with the maintenance of the efficiency of the individual producer on the home front, whether farmer, war worker, or volunteer, and with preparations for handling inevitable readjustments following the termination of hostilities. With the exception of the Civilian Protection Program, which was gradually reduced as danger of invasion faded, War Council programs initiated under the previous administration were steadily maintained; programs for care for children of working mothers, food production, and nutrition, were rapidly expanded. To meet new situations, additional permanent and temporary agencies were set up outside the purview of the War Council—such as the Veterans' Service Agency, the Commission Against Discrimination, the Youth Commission and the Postwar Reconversion Agency. Emergency programs for veterans in the fields of housing and education were likewise undertaken.

Wartime dislocations had a curious pattern. The earliest, and in some ways the more sudden, were those of housing for war workers, the terrific demand for skilled labor, the need for subcontracting, and the shrinkage of civilian production as a result of priorities on materials. Dislocations such as these arose from the struggle for war production, and fell largely within the period of Governor Lehman's administration.

At the beginning of Governor Dewey's first administration more subtle and more fundamental dislocations were beginning to make themselves felt. Outside of war plants, and the City of New York, the manpower shortage was by this time general. This was true of farms, hospitals, medical services, transportation, the professions — virtually every walk of life. A severe shortage of food was likewise threatened. Rationing failed to disguise fundamental lacks, whether of food, fuel oil, rubber goods, tires, or gasoline. Transportation was a problem. Heavier traffic had to be hauled with a declining amount and quality of available equipment. By the end of 1945, dislocation was general and chronic. To make things worse, on top of this situation was superimposed the rapidly snowballing problem of returning veterans. This became manifest in 1943 and acute in 1946 with the increased rates of demobilization from the armed services. Housing, civilian goods, education, hospital services, all were acute problems by 1946. The reconversion of industry from war contracts to peacetime production revived the earlier headaches in reverse order. On top of everything else came an epidemic of strikes accompanied by inflation, with no over-all war goal this time with which to conjure the selfishness and short-sightedness of men. It took courage to hold the line of honesty and efficiency in war's aftermath.

Thus the problems of the two governors differed, each set in a way unique, each set a challenge to the best that heart and brain could offer. Herbert H. Lehman and Thomas E. Dewey each made his special contribution to the outstanding war record of the State of New York. The average citizen listening to speeches in which everything must be said in fifteen minutes has little idea of the vast amount of effort that goes into the operations of a state the size of New York. If he would know more about the struggles and achievements of 13 million people and their leaders let him continue this story.

Introduction to the Sources

THE collection of material for this volume was undertaken in July, 1945, before the end of World War II when the author was assigned to the New York State War Council to classify and preserve all historically valuable records created under the War Emergency Act.[*] When asked, subsequently, to prepare this manuscript, he was already familiar with much of the source material. He was also in a position to talk with many of the State and local war leaders at a time when the end of hostilities had removed the sense of pressure and there was a general desire to discuss the war period in an analytical and reminiscent mood.

PRIMARY SOURCES

Unwritten Sources

First-hand information was acquired orally in a variety of ways. Stenotype records were made of interviews with the Honorable Herbert H. Lehman, the Honorable Charles Poletti, the Honorable Irving M. Ives, the Honorable Oswald D. Heck, four other members of the New York State War Council, Elmer A. Carter, John M. Hancock, Louis Hollander and Thomas A. Morgan, and the Executive Secretary and Counsel, Charles A. Winding; New York State Commissioners M. P. Catherwood, Lewis A. Wilson, Oakley Furney, Edwin R. Van Kleeck and V. A. Van Volkenburgh; also, Mrs. Clarice Leavell Pennock, Thomas L. J. Corcoran, Milton Enzer, Arthur K. Getman, F. Wellington Gilcreas, Warren W. Knox and Maurice F. Neufeld.

Day to day contacts developed with members of the Headquarters Staff of the State War Council, especially with Milton Alpert, the Acting Executive Secretary, with Acting Director of Civilian Protection, John A. Farrell and with the Director and Field Representatives of the Office of Civilian Mobilization, Mrs. Walter S. McNab, Donald A. Campbell, Claire M. Britt, H. McIntyre Grout, Jr., Philip Guenther, George H. Liddle, and Walter Tracey. Contact with leaders of more than two-score of the local War Councils also proved valuable. Individuals in all fields of war activity, Federal, State and local, contributed from experience judgments of men and events and illustrative anecdotes unavailable in written form. Trips throughout the State with the OCM field men were highly informative, as their knowledge of community activities, other than civilian protection, and of community

---

[*] These records are described in the article, "Home Front Records of New York, 1940-1945; The Problem of Disposition," *American Archivist*, April, 1946.

organization in general was unexcelled. For the purposes of this manuscript, the advantages of becoming acquainted with the Statewide War Council organization before it broke up were priceless, as the men and women who composed it revealed in conversation the flavor of the war years and the spirit which kept them on the job at all hours. Many were kind enough later on to check sections of this volume for errors of fact and interpretation. Approximately one hundred and twenty-five individual contributions were made of specific pieces of information, pertinent suggestions or criticism, while miscellaneous helpful conversations were three to four times that number.

Manuscript Sources

A large portion of the written records of the War are as yet unpublished. The bulk of those on the State level used in the preparation of this work have been official. These consist of:

a) the Minutes and Agenda of the meetings of the State Defense Council, later the State War Council;
b) correspondence and reports from its thirty-three subsidiary agencies, retained in the files of the Headquarters Office of the New York State War Council;
c) correspondence in the files of the Governor's Office relating to the State's contribution to the national war effort, and
d) papers of the Governor and releases from the Governor's Office;
e) correspondence, reports, mimeographed bulletins, memoranda and other releases, occasional personal minutes, card files and other types of special records from each of the War Council agencies created under the authority of the War Emergency Act;
f) similar records of programs operated within the regular State departments, with the help of War Council Funds.

The one hundred and eight local War Councils left records of varying complexity, those of New York City being most voluminous, those of one or two of the smaller Councils being non-existent. Efforts were made in 1945 and 1946 to secure a file of administrative histories from each of the War Council agencies and from the local War Councils. A few of these have been published. These manuscript histories, collections of materials produced by each local Council, a file of war pamphlets, and the bulk of the State records outlined in items (b) and (e) above have been transferred recently from the State Historian's Office to the Manuscript Room of the State Library in Albany.

A substantial amount of additional statistical material was secured directly from Federal, State and municipal departments and agencies through correspondence. Among those supplying information were the Federal Departments of Agriculture, the Navy, the Treasury and War, and the following Federal agencies: the Maritime Commission, the Office of Defense Transportation, the Office of Price Administration, the Petroleum Administration for War, the Selective Service System, the United States Conciliation Service, the United States Employment Service, the War Manpower Commission, the War Production Board, and the War Shipping Administration.

New York State Departments and Commissions contributing special information include the Adjutant General, the Departments of Agriculture and Markets, Commerce, Education; the Divisions of Housing, Military and Naval Affairs, and State Police; the Selective Service System, the State Commission Against Discrimination and the State Youth Commission, — all under the Executive Department; the Department of Health; the New York State Mediation Board, the New York State Workmen's Compensation Board and the Division of Placement and Unemployment Insurance of the Department of Labor; the Department of Mental Hygiene; the Public Service Commission; the Department of Public Works; and the Department of Social Welfare.

Assistance was also received from the New York Port of Embarkation, the Second Service Command, the Port of New York Authority, the American Merchant Marine Institute, Incorporated, the Delaware and Hudson Railroad Corporation, the New York Central System, the New York Petroleum Industries Committee, the American Red Cross and the United Service Organizations.

Printed Sources

Many of these organizations published quarterly or annual reports. With important exceptions, published materials were of less value in the preparation of the manuscript than unpublished materials. Among the exceptions should be mentioned the Official Bulletin of the New York State War Council, the Annual Reports of that organization, the annual compilation of the New York State War Emergency Act, the published papers of the Governor, and reports such as those of the War Manpower Commission and the Port of New York Authority.

Published material was abundant all during the War, especially from the Office of Civilian Defense in Washington. Important publications relating to the war activities of the State appeared from the following departments or agencies: the Child Care Committee, the Office of Civilian Mobilization, the Division of Commerce, the Committee Against Discrimination, the Education Department, the Emergency Food Commission, the Health Department, the Health Preparedness Commission, the Labor Department, the Office of Physical Fitness, the State Council of Defense, the Office of War Training, and the School of Nutrition at Cornell. Some of the local War Councils published periodicals, as did the western district of the State Office of Civilian Protection.

The amount of ephemeral material was staggering. Some of this is preserved in the Pamphlet File in the Manuscript Room of the State

Library in Albany. It is valuable only as an illustration of the way people collected, classified or dispensed information, or as evincing the particular programs and emphases which came along from time to time during the War.

SECONDARY SOURCES

With the exception of newspaper accounts and magazine articles, most of which were as much primary as secondary material, it was still too early in 1945-46 for secondary accounts to be available. A few War Council histories have now appeared, notably the history of New York City's Civilian Volunteer Defense organization by Mrs. Castle, the history of the Buffalo War Council by Dudley Irwin, the history of the Civilian Protection Organization in Syracuse, and the four-volume history of war activities in Westchester County. This history of New York State in World War II constitutes, in itself, one of the first extensive secondary works on the period.

Contents

List of Illustrations for "The Empire State at War"

Photo Sources

General Electric Company, Associated Press, Acme, Wide World, American Locomotive Company, Virginia F. Stern and U. S. Navy.

Governor Thomas E. Dewey

Governor Dewey was the Chief Executive of New York State during three-fourths of the nearly four years the United States took part in World War II.

CHAPTER ONE

Coming Events Cast Their Shadow, 1940-1941: The Organization of New York State for National Defense

IT HAS been demonstrated that no nation, whatever its inclination, can successfully achieve isolation from a war-torn world, and that no state, least of all the wealthiest and most populous of the United States, can ignore circumstances which affect the nation as a whole. It becomes essential in recounting the part played by the State of New York in the National Defense Program to give in rapid review world events of the late thirties and early forties. With the larger sequence freshly in mind, the trend of local events is more easily comprehended and relationships otherwise obscure become significant.

THE TIDE OF BATTLE ABROAD

When Hitler invaded Poland, September 1, 1939, Americans were in some respects relieved that the suspense was over at last. Their hopes, however, that Poland could resist long enough to enable the French and British to come to her aid were soon completely blasted. The temporary breathing spell which followed caused some Americans, as late as March, 1940, to refer to the war as a "phony war." The resumption of the initiative by the Nazis with their surprise invasion of Denmark and Norway in April, 1940, suddenly brought the period of lull to a close. The rapid fall of Denmark and Norway revealed the inability of the British and French to do more than defend themselves, but confidence still remained firm in the Maginot Line and the British Navy. It was the explosion of Hitler's war machine into the Netherlands, May 10, 1940, and the subsequent inability of either the French or the British to bring the panzers and dive bombers to a halt that finally awoke most Americans to a lively sense of danger. The fool's paradise in which many lived during the winter of 1939-1940 was very rudely shattered.

President Roosevelt and his military and naval advisers undoubtedly had foreseen partially what would happen, but until the event actually occurred it was virtually impossible to arouse the country into making military preparations. Even when Italy entered the war on June 10, 1940, it was hoped that the French would be able to hold on; only the signing of the Armistice on June 22 and the complete disappearance of active French resistance in North Africa finally convinced most of us that the sole hope for stopping the Nazis in Europe lay in continued resistance by Britain. Fortunately, as we now know, the rapid success of his armies had not been completely foreseen even by the Fuehrer, with the result that the Nazi air attack on Britain did not gain force until August, 1940. The two months' interval had been so well used that the climax of the Battle of Britain came in October, November and December, with the result that by January 6, 1941, President Roosevelt could say that he felt sure, on the "latest information," that the Axis would not win the war. Few Americans, however, dared to believe him.

Meanwhile, the war in China dragged on. During 1940 our relations with Japan became more and more strained. In September of that year, France was forced to permit Japanese troops to occupy bases in Indo-China. Less than a week later, on September 27, Japan joined the Rome-Berlin Axis by signing at Berlin what came to be called the Anti-Comintern Pact; it was but ten days later that American citizens in the Far East were advised by the State Department to come home.

Had it not been for British successes in Ethiopia and the surprisingly successful Greek resistance to the Italians in Albania during the winter of 1940-1941, the war picture would have looked completely black. Allied hopes that somehow it would be possible to maintain a foothold in the Balkans, after the fashion of Saloniki in the First World War, came to an end in the spring of 1941. In April the Germans came to the aid of the Italians in Greece, overran Yugoslavia, and drove the Greeks and British into the Mediterranean. England lost Crete in June, 1941, and it looked to many as though Russia was doing her best to come to terms with both the Germans and Japanese.

Then came the sudden Nazi attack upon Russia, June 22, 1941, a stroke of unbelievable luck. Americans were stunned, but so great was the fear of the Nazi machine and so complete the general belief in its invincibility, that the Russians were generally expected to hold but from three to six months. Their desperate resistance on into the winter of

1941 and 1942, while foreseen by those few who understood the basis of Soviet strength, was a distinct surprise and a source of encouragement to most Americans.

The German push eastward did little to affect the war in Asia. That struggle was at a stalemate, and the trade treaty between Russia and Japan, signed June 12, 1941, appeared merely to aid the Japanese by guaranteeing their back door against Russian attack. However, encouraged by the accession of Russia to the allied cause, Britain and the United States did freeze Japanese funds on July 25, 1941, and on August 1 the United States placed an embargo on aviation gasoline. There followed, October 16, an embargo on scrap iron and steel to Japan. The State Department was finally taking the action that many Americans had long desired. The announcement, November 5, 1941, of the impending mission of a Japanese diplomat by the name of Kurusu passed almost unnoticed, but in Tokyo war lords had already decided to make the attack on Pearl Harbor.

AMERICAN COUNTERMEASURES IN EUROPE

The national government reacted quickly to events abroad. No sooner had war broken out in Europe than President Roosevelt declared a limited national emergency, on September 8, 1939. On November 3, Congress amended the Neutrality Law by repealing the Arms Embargo, and adopted the principle of cash and carry, allowing foreign countries to buy armaments from us and ship them home at their own risk. There came a slight increase in business following the outbreak of the war, with exports (largely of a military nature) up one-third in the first six months. However, foreign orders for civilian goods took a sharp drop. During the first three months of 1940, since England and France seemed to be in a strong position, little attention was paid to the necessity for building up our national defenses. The deceptive lull in active hostilities made it appear that some form of peace might be possible. In March, Sumner Welles was sent on a mission to the European capitals to observe and report back to the President on the situation. He made no peace proposals and received none.

Following the invasion of Denmark and Norway and the collapse of France, the trend of the war became obvious and alarming. President Roosevelt assumed vigorous leadership of the preparations for defending the United States. In his message to Congress on May 16, 1940, he declared that the American people "must recast their thinking about national protection." The speed of the Nazi advance both on the ground and in the air against what had been regarded as a first-class French army made action necessary. He called for "military implements — not on paper" and the facilities for producing them at top speed. He set for the country the immediate goal of fifty thousand planes with the capacity to produce an equal number annually. When called upon for an immediate appropriation of nearly 900 million dollars, Congress supported him. Invoking a statute passed in 1916, he created, May 28, 1940, a seven-member Advisory Commission to the Council of National Defense, a body which itself consisted of the Secretaries of War, Navy, Interior, Commerce, and Labor, to enable the President "to plan and direct all phases of the defense program." There was also set up within the Executive Department, on May 25, 1940, the Office of Emergency Management. Two days later the President declared the national emergency to be unlimited.

The speed with which the Army and Navy let contracts in June and July was startling: in June, contracts totaled 825 million dollars; in July, 1,137 million dollars. Prior to June, 1940, except for limited manufacture of equipment for the British and French, armament production by American plants was a relatively minor activity. Early in September the President announced the agreement with Great Britain to trade fifty overage destroyers for British bases in the Western Hemisphere. With submarine warfare increasing in intensity, Britain's survival had become to Americans a matter of primary concern. In September, 1940, Congress also passed the Burke-Wadsworth Bill setting up a national system of selective service — peacetime conscription for the first time in American history. Age limits were set from twenty-one to thirty-six with a quota of 800,000 men a year.

The national election campaign was peculiarly influenced by events abroad; apparently the nation decided not to swap horses at a time of national emergency. As the pressure of the *Luftwaffe* appeared to be telling on Britain, the role of America became clearer, and in a fireside chat December 29, 1940, the President declared, "We must be the great arsenal of democracy. For us this is an emergency as serious as war itself." The annual message to Congress delivered January 6, 1941, referred to our national aims as comprising

> . . . A world founded upon four essential human freedoms . . . freedom of speech and expression . . . freedom of every person to worship God in his own way . . . freedom from want . . . freedom from fear.

In the President's view this was "a definite basis for the kind of world obtainable in our own time and generation." The next day an Executive Order pushed the program of preparedness a step farther by creating the Office of Production Management.

That Great Britain could not bear alone the financial burden of the war became apparent early in 1941. Committed though we were to lend assistance, the terms of the Johnson Act forbade loans to nations in default on debts of World War I. To remove this impediment and avoid a repetition of the financial impasse of the twenties, Congress passed the Lend-Lease Act. The main purpose of this act was "to promote the defense of the United States by supplying material aid to those nations whose defense is vital to our defense." Within minutes of its signing by the President, war materials were on their way to Great Britain and Greece. To implement this policy Congress appropriated, on March 27, 7 billion dollars. The effect of America's increasing preparations may be seen in the fact that in the first five months of 1941 we sent to Britain twelve times as many airplanes and ten times as many aircraft engines as were sent to her in the same period of 1940, and in the first four months of 1941 we sent her seventeen times as much explosives and ninety times as much ammunition and firearms as in the same period of 1940. As of May 1, 1941, actual contracts awarded by the Army and Navy amounted to 15.2 billion dollars, not including 3.7 billion dollars of British orders, and on May 17 total appropriations and authorizations for contracts actually passed by Congress came to 37.3 billion dollars.

At the same time, with the object lesson of the bombing of London and other British towns staring us in the face, the President created on May 20, 1941, the Office of Civilian Defense within the Office of Emergency Management.

It is important to note that at no time did the President divorce ultimate aims from immediate action. In practically every speech he made in 1940 and 1941 there was some reference to the goals, whether domestic or international, for which the country was fighting. The need for a basic statement of democratic war aims was met by the signing of the Atlantic Charter in August, 1941. This was soon followed by the declaration, in September, 1941, that American naval vessels and planes would shoot on sight and in

October that "the shooting has started." In addition to the problems of production for lend-lease, America had also assumed the equally serious task of getting the goods safely across the Atlantic.

The events of the previous two years, when viewed in retrospect, lead inevitably to the conclusion that America's defensive measures divided naturally into two distinct categories. One series of moves lay in the field of diplomacy. Such were the various interpretations of the neutrality laws, the regulations governing international trade, the occupation of outlying territories including the British bases Greenland and Iceland, and extensive lend-lease aid to Britain, Russia, China, and Greece. On the other hand, the various efforts of the Roosevelt administration to speed up the processes of national rearmament were primarily of domestic concern. These included the establishment of the Offices of Production Management and Civilian Defense, the rapid increase in the personnel of the Army and Navy, the call for fifty thousand planes and a two-ocean navy, the huge Congressional appropriations for these purposes. The second group of measures intimately affected conditions in the State of New York as early as the summer of 1940. With her 13 million people, her industrial and financial strength, and her proximity to the Atlantic seaboard, it was inevitable that New York should play a leading part in the nation's preparation for war.

NEW YORK STATE PREPARES TO PLAY ITS PART IN NATIONAL DEFENSE

President Roosevelt's speech of May 16, 1940, calling for the production of fifty thousand airplanes and for the development of a capacity to produce a like number annually, anticipated by less than a month the complete surrender of France. These two events, taken with the entrance of Italy into the war, touched off the first active defense preparations within New

York State. The outlook was dark. To Governor Lehman, an active member of the Committee to Defend America by Aiding the Allies, it was obvious that since a permanently satisfactory compromise with Germany was impossible, it was necessary to prepare for ultimate conflict.

The mass of citizens became aroused also, and almost overnight the Governor's mail, which previously ran fifty to seventy-five letters a day, jumped to several hundreds daily. All kinds of people volunteered their services for everything under the sun and warned against "the imminence of the peril to Western civilization." All kinds of crackpot ideas were proposed, such as underground highways between all the larger cities. The total mail for June ran into the thousands and such pressure effectively thrust the Governor's office into the middle of the "defense" problem.

Located on the Atlantic seacoast, with a concentrated population, and a highly industrialized economy, New York was inevitably one of the leaders in developing details of the national defense program. Governor Lehman was quick to support the declared intention of the President to give all-out aid to France and Britain, and was one of the leaders of the Governors' Conference which met June 3 in Duluth, and pledged "that all necessary steps should be taken immediately to provide adequately and extensively for the defense of these United States. . . ."

The fulfillment of this pledge by New York State in the ensuing two years prior to the attack on Pearl Harbor can best be described in four brief sections:

Section 1. May 16 — July 30, 1940, consists of the early moves in defense production and civilian protection undertaken prior to the appointment of the Defense Council on August 1, 1940.

Section 2. August 1, 1940 — January 7, 1941, includes the setting up of the local defense councils on a Statewide basis, the enunciation of a definite defense program by the State Defense Council, the establishment of the machinery of Selective Service, and the creation of the State Guard.

Section 3. January 8 — May 7, 1941, begins with the Governor's message to the 1941 Legislature. It is naturally partly dominated by the legislative session itself, but includes a number of specific efforts to acquaint the localities with the nature of the coming program and the beginning of systematic efforts to coordinate all State and local defense measures in the fields of production, health, recreation, housing, and agriculture.

Section 4. May 8 — December 31, 1941, opens with the appointment of a Director of Civilian Protection and is devoted partly to the efforts to organize a State-wide protective service inclusive of many previously independent programs, and partly to a similar effort to coordinate under a Director of Civilian Mobilization the activities of all volunteers in the field of community service. Within three weeks after Pearl Harbor the entire situation, hitherto in a semifluid condition, rapidly crystallized into permanent form.

A diagram of the expansion of the defense program in New York State would resemble a fan, or perhaps a family tree. It would indicate the successive appearance in 1940 and 1941 of some twenty individual programs. By December, 1941, each was progressing reasonably well, but a certain amount of friction was inevitable, and coordination on the State and local levels was a continuing problem.

1. May 16 — July 30, 1940. In May and June of 1940 a state of excitement prevailed. The Governor was besieged with schemes for doing away with the Fifth Column ranging from one proposal to arm all members of the National Rifle Clubs to another for calling a special session of the State Legislature. Patriotic resolutions against un-American activities poured forth by the hundreds. In compliance with popular sentiment for the protection of property and civilians against possible sabotage, the Governor, on June 3, ordered out a section of the National Guard to protect State armories, arsenals, and National Guard camps. Soon afterward, by agreement with the leaders of the Legislature, he secured a Certificate of Intent for $150,000 for "structural changes and protective additions."

June 7 Governor Lehman announced plans for the formation of a State Guard, when, and if, the President should call the existing National Guard into Federal service. The mission of the Guard would be to "suppress insurrection, tumult, riot, or breach of the peace within the borders of the State of New York." Shortly, he was informed by the War Department that such a military force would conflict with the National Defense Act, which did not provide for the creation in time of peace of state military forces other than the National Guard. New York subsequently led the fight in Congress to iron out these discrepancies, and the Governor was largely responsible for the passage of H. R. 10495 and its signing by the President on October 21. The way was thus cleared for the organization by the states in time of peace of military forces other than the National Guard.

In accordance with directions issued by the War Department, plans were announced on June 24 for the reorganization of the New York National Guard preparatory to its induction into the Federal service. On July 25, following a series of conferences held by the Governor and Lieutenant Governor with representatives of the city police chiefs, county sheriffs, New York City police, State Police, and the mayors of the larger cities, a Statewide plan for the coordination of personnel, equipment, transportation, and communication resources of the various police units of the State was announced. The purpose was to make possible, if ever an emergency should arise, the massing at any given point of collective strength far greater than would be

available through local action alone. The arresting of aliens, however, especially Japanese, was declared by the Attorney General to be entirely a matter for the Federal Bureau of Investigation.

The most urgent problem was that of securing increased industrial production for defense purposes in line with the National Defense Program. On June 13, the Governor directed the Industrial Commissioner, the Board of Standards and Appeals, the State Board of Mediation, the State Labor Relations Board, the Public Service Commission, and the Superintendent of Banks to "assume an even more than usually generous atitude toward industries directly engaged in national defense." Red tape was to be cut to a minimum. Five days later at a conference between leaders of the State Planning Council and the Joint Legislative Committee on Industrial and Labor Conditions, it was proposed to commence a series of inventories of the industrial and labor resources of the state. The Governor's permission to go ahead was secured, and surveys of idle plants, of labor skills available, of all manufacturing industries, and some important nonmanufacturing industries were begun by the State Planning Council. All department heads were instructed to aid in the survey. For the first time the State Planning Council, which had hitherto confined its efforts to the preparation of long-range programs for the development of the State's physical and economic resources, was definitely tied in with the State's defense program. This reorientation of the work of the State Planning Council furnishes a striking example of the way the war emergency gradually drew into its orbit virtually every department and agency of the State that could serve on the home front.

About this same time the production problem was attacked from another angle. In spite of the fact that in May, 1940, 257,153 home relief cases were still on the rolls, a drop of 18,000 since April, and that for every employable person on relief there were three unemployed persons still seeking jobs, a shortage of semi-skilled labor in the essential war industries was considered likely. On June 13, a memorandum was presented by Deputy Commissioner of Education Lewis A. Wilson on the training of approximately 150,000 men for essential war work. New York's plan was the result of nearly two weeks of discussion in Washington and was part of an over-all national drive for the training of 750,000 men, a program estimated to cost approximately 70 million dollars. The plan, which was promptly adopted by the Regents of the University of the State of New York, provided for the use after regular school hours of the State's vocational and engineering schools whose total equipment was valued at over 100 million dollars. On July 1, 1940, at a meeting held in the State Education Building, this plan was presented to representatives of nearly all the communities of the State that had trade or technical high schools or large departments of industrial arts. Within two weeks, national defense vocational schools were opened in twenty-seven cities with an enrollment of almost eleven thousand adults "who desired to be prepared for employment in war industries." This was the beginning of a Statewide program of Vocational Training for National Defense.

Foresight was not confined, however, to those responsible for the development of the industrial defense program. On June 22, and on its own initiative, the Executive Committee of the Agricultural Conference Board met in Ithaca and formed the New York State Emergency Agricultural Defense Committee, composed of leaders from five Statewide agricultural organizations. Representatives of these bodies were immediately designated to serve on similar county agricultural defense committees. The Governor was informed of this action and his approval secured.

Other organizations began to align their activities with the defense efforts. The New York State Nurses Association, the Hospital Association, and the State Commission to Formulate a Long-range Health Program, headed by Assemblyman Lee B. Mailler, became active during June in investigating the public health problems arising from the transition to large-scale war production. On July 5, the New York State Nurses Association announced that it was preparing to take inventory of the available nursing power in the State. The survey was finished in November. Prior to that the Hospital Association had begun a survey of hospital facilities and of the possibilities for their expansion to meet the needs of the defense program. The work was undertaken in cooperation with the New York State Health Preparedness Commission and results were tabulated by county and published in June of the following year.

In addition to the work of Assemblyman Mailler's commission, of the State Nurses Association, and of the State Hospital Association, nurses were being enrolled in the Red Cross Reserve, courses in the training of nurses aides were being offered, and supplementary volunteer work in connection with the care of the sick at home was being carried out by the State's thirteen local Red Cross units.

It soon fell to the lot of Mr. Mailler's Commission to Formulate a Long-range Health Program to become the official Health and Medical Section of the State Council of Defense. As a result of communications from the Governor dated in June, 1940, and from the Lieutenant Governor dated July 17, 1940, the commission called a Statewide Health Mobilization Conference at the Academy of Medicine in New York City for July 30. This conference considered the various health problems which might confront the State in an emergency and one of its recommendations — that county advisory health preparedness committees should be formed — was approved by Lieutenant Governor Charles Poletti on August 26.

A letter of instructions was sent out early in October to establish these county committees in close touch with the county defense councils. Nearly a year later this framework was made the basis of the Emergency Medical Service of the New York State Office of Civilian Protection.

It was recognized that every industrial area which had been successful in securing government contracts would soon be facing a shortage of housing facilities for its increasing numbers of war workers. This problem was being considered by the State Division of Housing as early as July, 1940. Information from Washington showed that, exclusive of New York City, there were in New York State at least thirty-three key centers with industrial defense programs. A survey of these areas was conducted in July and August to ascertain available private housing for unskilled and skilled labor, technicians, and specialists.

These various activities, all stemming from the State's war production efforts, were increasing so rapidly in number and scope that it was felt necessary not only to set up some system of coordination but also to pass on some of the responsibility to local communities. Up to that time, leaders in Albany had borne the brunt of initiating the defense program, and they alone could see the Statewide picture. It was felt that local leaders should also be informed concerning the trend of affairs. With this need in mind, the Governor called a conference of all mayors of cities of over thirty thousand inhabitants to meet in Albany, July 1. Here the problems of defense production and likewise those of social dislocation, which were beginning to appear, were thoroughly covered. The following day, the Lieutenant Governor, Charles Poletti, was made State Coordinator on National Defense to take the burden of administering the defense program from the shoulders of the Governor. Lieutenant Governor Poletti immediately asked

for and received pledges of cooperation from all departments and henceforth remained in constant communication with the Federal government, the Legislature, the Defense Council soon to be appointed, and the localities.

All through July "defense" work in the Governor's office expanded. The variety and urgency of the problems became such that Governor Lehman began to feel the need for an advisory group to help him, and in August appointed a State Council of National Defense, consisting of representatives of industry, agriculture, labor, commerce, and public utilities. Its composition clearly reflected the paramount importance at this time of the economics of defense production. The Governor was to be chairman and the Lieutenant Governor vice-chairman. Council members served in an advisory capacity to the Governor, but their decisions carried no legal weight until the passage of Chapter 22 of the Laws of 1941 on February 20, 1941. The Council's decisions were then given statutory authority and its membership was increased by the addition of the Attorney General, the President and Minority Leader of the Senate, and the Speaker and Minority Leader of the Assembly.

2. August 1, 1940 — January 7, 1941. The period from the appointment of the Defense Council to the opening of the 1941 Legislature in January was characterized primarily by the continuance of the problem of defense production, the setting up of the machinery of Selective Service, the formation of local defense councils, the creation of the State Guard, and tentative discussions of a number of social problems created by the war. From the beginning, however, partly because of its composition and the avowed purpose of its creation, the Defense Council was interested primarily in working out a solution to the problem of defense production. The needs of the allies and the President's call for a drastic rearmament program could not be ignored.

As an outcome of its very first meeting, a three-page memorandum was drawn up declaring that "one of the primary purposes for the creation of the Defense Council is to aid in making available to the Federal government in its preparedness plans all the resources of industry and the people of the State of New York." This early statement mapped the general strategy to be followed by the Council for over a year in its attack on the production problem. It was recognized that until the surveys of idle plants undertaken in July by the State Planning Commission had been completed, the Council would be in no position to promote industrial expansion effectively. Nevertheless, it was already clear that all the existing manufacturing facilities in the State should be fully utilized before new plants were built, and that before additional labor was imported all available labor should be employed as near as possible to where it was then located. If this were done, the resolution continued, it would avoid sudden shifts of population, with their attendant housing shortages and "inadequacies of such public facilities as schools and public utilities." To run into these problems needlessly would be to slow up the tempo of production and compete with the war industries for vitally needed raw materials.

By November, the principal surveys had been completed and an industrial directory had appeared, placing the Governor and the Council in a position to call the attention of the Federal government to the manufacturing resources of the State and to urge their views in detail upon the leaders of the Office of Production Management. This was done on December 26 in a letter to Mr. William S. Knudsen, in which the Governor pointed out the additional speed which could be obtained in production through the process of subcontracting or farming out. This method had been approved by the Defense Council as early as August, several of its members having tried it in

their own plants and found that it worked. To proceed one step farther and get a line on available productive capacity, in October a trial survey of production facilities was conducted in the Buffalo area. Here the State Planning Council worked in conjunction with a private organization, Associated Industries, Inc. In its original form the questionnaire used was not completely successful, demonstrating what could not, as well as what could, be secured by that method of inquiry. The experience, however, proved valuable later on in connection with the survey of metal-working facilities undertaken the following spring.

As had been anticipated in June, and in compliance with a presidential proclamation of September 22, a large part of the National Guard entered the active military service of the United States on October 15. Ten days later, in accordance with a plan previously prepared, Governor Lehman issued orders for the formation of a State Guard under the command of Major General William Ottman. By the middle of December the guard numbered 9582 officers and men, and by November of the following year the Adjutant General reported a total strength of 13,068.

Along with his interest in the creation of a State Guard, Governor Lehman manifested definite interest in the passage of the National Selective Service Act. He kept in touch with the progress of the Burke-Wadsworth Bill and on September 8 announced a Selective Service plan for the State of New York, drawn in line with the provisions of this bill. Local boards of three members each were to be appointed by mayors and county judges for areas with a population of thirty thousand or less. Twenty-four appeal boards were set up — thirteen in New York City. The entire machinery of advisory boards, examining physicians, medical advisory boards and appeal agents was functioning by the end of the year. On October 16, the first day of registration, 1,709,715 men between the ages of twenty-one and thirty-six registered in New York State.

Meanwhile, Governor Lehman and the Defense Council had been considering for some time the creation of city and county defense councils to deal on the local level with problems such as civilian protection, vocational training, inventories of labor and industrial resources, war production, public health, and agricultural readjustments. The defense program was becoming too complex and detailed to be handled entirely from Albany. It was obvious that if the program were to succeed it would have to be taken to the people. On September 22, the Governor requested the mayors of all cities and the boards of supervisors of all counties to appoint defense councils outlining in detail the duties that he would expect them to perform. The principle of decentralization of both responsibility and administration was thus introduced early into the New York State defense organization.

The autumn of 1940 found the Defense Council taking up a number of new problems which had arisen in the field of health and social welfare. As early as September the Commissioner of Education was requested to outline the operation of the department's program of physical education, the request stemming from the report that as high as 20 per cent of the applicants for enlistment in the armed forces of the country were physically unfit. The commissioner's reply of January 4, 1941, reported the appointment of a special committee by the Board of Regents to go into the entire matter. Physical fitness was destined to become a source of considerable anxiety at the outbreak of the war. Also, the first discussion of the problem of discrimination in employment took place in the Defense Council meeting of December 20 as a result of complaints to the State Coordinator that Negroes were not being given a fair share of the opportunities in defense work. This matter was discussed subsequently at

other meetings and on March 29 the Council appointed a Committee on Discrimination in Employment within the Department of Labor, to be headed by the Industrial Commissioner, Frieda S. Miller.

The year closed with the Defense Council at last in possession of information regarding the industrial and labor resources of the State sufficiently specific to enable them to approach the Office of Production Management with definite proposals. It was agreed that the following were needed:

1. Greater speed in defense production
2. The complete utilization of the labor resources of the State
3. An increase in the volume of war contracts in New York State

A short time before, notice was likewise taken of the need for a survey of metal-working capacity. Machine tools were rapidly becoming one of the worst bottlenecks, and Washington was urged to take the lead in straightening out the kinks in the defense production process. On December 26, the Governor addressed an open letter to William S. Knudsen in which he said in part:

The State Defense Council and I are convinced that the time has come when manufacturers who can convert all or part of their facilities now engaged in production of nonessentials to the production of defense needs should do so. In that way, large additional plant and labor facilities can undoubtedly be made available for defense needs, with relatively little delay or fresh capital expenditures.

As you probably know, New York State sometime ago undertook a survey of idle plant facilities and the available labor supply in this State. The primary purpose of this survey was to enable New York concerns, who have Federal Defense contracts, to utilize to the fullest extent existing industrial facilities. The survey has been completed and is now available.

He then went into the whole question of subcontracting in detail, promising that New York State would "push aggressively forward along this line" and offered to discuss the matter in Washington.

3. January — May 8, 1941. At the opening of the State Legislature on January 8, Governor Lehman reported in detail on the accomplishments of the previous year in furthering the National Defense Program. He called attention to the tragedy of Europe and to the existing threat to the foundations of America's way of living. Speed, he said, was vital if the country was to be effectively prepared to defend itself. He reviewed the extent of the State's cooperation with the national government and asked that a specific appropriation for defense purposes be included in the 1941-1942 budget.

The legislation setting up the Council as a temporary State commission was drafted with speed, passed both houses of the Legislature, and was approved by the Governor February 20. Only two other states, Iowa and Nebraska, had previously taken such action. The State Council of Defense was to consist of sixteen members including the Governor as chairman, the Lieutenant Governor as vice-chairman, the temporary President of the Senate, the Speaker of the Assembly, the minority leaders of the Senate and Assembly, and the ten members whose names the Governor had submitted to the Senate for approval, and who were already serving. An amendment in 1941 added the Attorney General as an ex-officio member.

Under Chapter 22 of the Laws of 1941, the powers of the Council were outlined as follows:

1. To undertake, supervise, or direct the making of studies and surveys of all activities, matters, and things which are or may be related to or in the interest of State and national defense.
2. To cooperate with agencies established by or pursuant to laws of the United States and of the several states to promote national defense, and to cooperate with and coordinate the work and activities of all similar councils of defense established by the several political subdivisions of the State and of all other agencies having substantially similar objects and purposes.
3. To create subcommittees, composed of members and/or of nonmembers of the council, to aid and assist in the discharge of one or more of its powers and duties under this act.
4. To request and obtain such cooperation, assistance, and data from any department, board, bureau, commission, agency, or official of the State or any political subdivision thereof as it may reasonably require for the consummation of its work.
5. To make a study and analysis of the laws of the State in the light of its plans and program and to recommend such amendatory or supplemental legislation as may be deemed necessary or appropriate for the prosecution and execution thereof.
6. To do all other acts and things, not inconsistent with law, to further and promote State and national defense.

The act gave mayors and boards of supervisors authority to create local defense councils in the cities and counties, and such municipalities were permitted to borrow funds to defray expenses.

Subsequently, an appropriation of $2,-448,875 for defense purposes passed the State Legislature. The Defense Council itself, however, was not given an additional $500,000 lump sum appropriation which had been requested. The resulting shortage of working funds was recognized at the meeting of the Defense Council on April 23, when it was unanimously agreed that an additional $200,000 for the use of the Defense Council should be made available immediately by Certificates of Intent.

At the end of the session the leaders of the State and Assembly issued a joint statement on the defense measures passed by the 1941 session of the Legislature. They called attention to Chapter 22 which created the State Defense Council of sixteen members, whose duties were "the coordination and promotion of all measures of national defense, within the powers of the state." They emphasized the fact that in dealing successfully with the problem of sabotage prevention they had avoided the incorporation of any clauses that could be used as an antilabor weapon. Provisions for guarding against unlawful entry on property, for the closing of highways and for the punishment for damage done to military or naval equipment, supplies, and stores had been included. Other measures included the cooperation of New York with other states for the purpose of conserving oil resources; the creation of county fire-training schools, provisions for absentee voting by members of the armed forces; the establishment of town recreation centers near military camps; the creation of a commission to survey and facilitate military transportation, and the regulation of the manufacture and sale of explosives. The New York State Health Commission was continued for another year and given additional authority to assist the Governor and the Defense Council in coordinating "the services and skills pertaining to health for state and national defense purposes." The Legislature had cooperated with the Governor virtually 100 per cent in putting through the defense program.

For the first four months of 1941 defense problems were somewhat different from those of the latter part of 1940. While the Governor's preoccupation with the legislative session cut down considerably the progress of the defense program until early in March, to some extent production was an exception. It was still the principal concern of the Council. In the national capital, Knox, Stimson, Knudsen, and Hillman had become definitely worried about the machine-tool shortage. It was to secure the help of the local defense councils for the machine-tool survey and to speed the State-wide subcontracting movement that a conference of local defense-council representatives was held in Albany on January 28, 1941. Officials from the Federal government and repre-

sentatives of private industries and of the State government were in attendance to explain the intricacies of subcontracting and to outline the efforts that the Federal government was making to provide ways of ready contact between manufacturers and the procurement officers of the Army and Navy. The meeting, attended by over two hundred persons, was definitely successful in launching the machine-tool survey and in stimulating the local defense councils. By the end of April, the machine-tool survey was yielding gratifying results. By this time, too, some of the burden of promoting defense production had been shifted definitely from the Defense Council to the State Planning Council under the direction of Dr. M. P. Catherwood. This organization had been doing consistently good work, and on April 1 was expanded and its name changed to the Division of Commerce. Occasionally matters of policy as well as the administrative details of such surveys as that covering machine tools were entrusted to it. The division showed itself more and more capable of assuming primary responsibility for stimulating defense production.

Furthermore, a shift in emphasis was definitely in the making within the Defense Council. The techniques for expanding production were now fairly well developed, and more and more thought was being given to the secondary matter of social problems arising in the so-called war-impact areas. A shortage of adequate housing facilities for war workers at rentals they could afford was one of the earliest bottlenecks to appear in the production program. Although the State Division of Housing had been in touch with the situation since 1940, the rapid increase in the number of war contracts let in New York State early in 1941 created an increasingly difficult situation. On March 29, the Governor wrote to forty-one local defense council chairmen, whose communities were considered war-impact areas, urging them to look carefully into their local housing situations. He also suggested to the State Commissioner of Housing that a survey be made of existing vacancies at different rental levels, estimates secured as to the condition of the dwellings, and a full report written on the subject. This same division was charged "with responsibility for housing matters under the State Council of Defense," and had prepared the necessary forms and procedures for making the studies. Homes Registration Services were suggested for the larger centers and help from Washington was offered in setting them up. The problem was regarded as sufficiently grave to warrant the passage of an amendment to the Public Housing Law giving the Commissioner of Housing the definite right to lend funds to the municipalities of the State, or their housing authorities, for the construction of public housing facilities for defense workers.

The rapid growth of communities with plants engaged in war production and the increasing use of night shifts brought new needs for recreational and health facilities. At its meeting on February 28, the Defense Council considered these subjects. Mr. Charles E. Wilson, President of the General Electric Company, thought the Council should warn the private industries of their obligation to provide additional recreational and health facilities for the large number of men then being engaged for the second and third shifts. Three weeks later a general letter sent to all chairmen of local war councils urged them to supply adequate dispensary and cafeteria services, and recreational facilities such as gymnasiums or bowling alleys for the night shifts. Such matters were primarily the responsibility of plant management, but the councils were urged to communicate with employers and give advice and assistance. Emphasis was placed upon the fundamental need for a comprehensive community recreational and health program as a definite contribution to national defense. Support

for the attack on health problems likewise came from the Health Preparedness Commission which had been continued by the Legislature another year and was designated on June 17 by the Defense Council as its official Health and Medical Section.

Although as late as April, 1941, there was still no over-all labor shortage, information from the State Employment Service and the Federal Security Agency tended to show that such a shortage was not far off. On March 15, the Division of Placement and Unemployment Insurance of the Department of Labor began a labor recruiting drive. The ninety-three public employment offices of the division were used as centers for registering those who were either still employed or who were not using skills useful in defense work. The Governor urged, in a newspaper release of March 26, that everything possible should be done "to ascertain labor shortages and to prevent useless migration of workers." Three days later, in a move to force greater utilization of the State's labor supply, the Governor appointed a special committee "to consider ways and means for dealing with the problem of discrimination in employment on defense contracts." Miss Frieda S. Miller, the Industrial Commissioner, was chairman of the committee which included representatives of industry, of labor, and of civic, religious, and racial groups. In his letter to the prospective members, the Governor said:

It is at least an equally serious challenge to the sincerity of our desire to defend and strengthen our democratic way of life, when trained, experienced, willing workers, who need jobs and who know the need for workers, are refused on grounds that are obviously un-American.

Within seven months the chairman could report that opportunities in defense work for racial and religious minorities had greatly increased.

While an ultimate shortage of labor was generally anticipated even as early as 1940 and consequently the State Employment Service had little difficulty in obtaining from industry and the municipalities cooperation in measures to alleviate it, another group of problems coming under the collective designation of "civilian protection" were completely new and required the building up of an altogether distinct organization to take care of them. In the spring of 1941, the task of protecting persons and property from the effects of anticipated aerial bombing loomed as the third most important problem of defense in New York State.

For some time prior to the Defense Council meeting of February 28, at which this topic was first broached, the Governor had been in correspondence with various individuals, notably the President of the United States. The experience of the British during the winter of 1940-1941 could not fail to arouse Americans to the possibility that similar things might happen to them in the near future. The Governor finally brought the matter before the Council by reading a letter from the President to the effect that purely passive defense measures involving air-raid shelters, gas masks, and blackouts were properly the responsibility of local communities in contrast to active defense measures which were the responsibility of the Army and Navy. On the other hand, it was recognized by the Council that until the Federal government could offer the states some guidance in these matters there was very little that they could do. Accordingly, no action was taken, and it was decided to await the appearance of manuals promised by the War Department. Two weeks later, the situation had progressed sufficiently so that the Governor was given the power to appoint a Director of Civilian Protection. On May 8, he designated Major General John F. O'Ryan, former Commander of the 27th Division and Police Commissioner for New York City, as Director of Civilian Protection, and charged him with the

responsibility for preparing and executing a plan for the protection of civilians.

Numerous other problems were taken up in the first four months of 1941, one of them being the integration with local defense council activities of the work of the county agricultural defense committees in preparation for the summer's planting and harvesting. However, probably the most important development relates to the local defense councils. Within two weeks after the passage of Chapter 22, creating the State Defense Council and authorizing creation of the local defense council organization, Defense Coordinator Poletti initiated the policy of channeling all sorts of directions and suggestions to the local councils. From that time on, these local organizations were rapidly incorporated into the State-wide pattern of defense. That this was a conscious effort on the part of the State leaders was shown by a letter to all councils (signed by the Governor) directing them to act as coordinating agencies for all defense activities in their communities. The result was that to an increasing degree the year 1941 witnessed the coordination of most of the Statewide programs and activities, not only on the State level but on the local level as well, through the instrumentality of these councils. Hardly a day went by without a letter or some suggestion from the Governor. The theory of decentralization was applied with a vengeance and appeared to be working.

4. May 8, 1941 — December 31, 1941. The appointment of General John F. O'Ryan to head the State Office of Civilian Protection marked the beginning of the delegation of major portions of the defense program in New York to especially selected individuals who were members neither of the defense councils nor of the established State departments. To be sure, there had been one or two appointments prior to this, but in the case of the Committee on Discrimination in Employment, Miss Miller was also the

Industrial Commissioner, and in that of the Defense Information Committee, Mrs. Helen Nolan, although not a department official, was operating in the field of publicity and was without responsibility for the work of committees in the local communities. It was General O'Ryan's appointment that paved the way for the subsequent appointment of Mrs. Winthrop Pennock, on July 18, to head the Division of Volunteer Participation, later called the Office of Civilian Mobilization, of Mr. Murray Willard, on December 19, to head the State Salvage Committee,[1] and the borrowing of Dr. Maurice F. Neufeld from the Division of Commerce, on December 22, to organize and direct the short-lived New York State Bureau of Rationing. Each of these leaders of necessity was forced to work through the local defense councils, with the result that the stream of communications which began to descend upon the local councils early in March grew, by the end of the year, into a torrent. Fortunately, the programs began at different times, and none maintained its peak intensity throughout the year.

As program after program developed and the State Defense Council sent out directive after directive in connection with civilian protection, defense production, conservation of metals, petroleum, and waste paper, and finally the rationing of rubber goods and tires, it became imperative that, by some means, closer contact be established between the State Council and the local councils. For a time, two field men were attached to the headquarters office of the Defense Council. Later they were transferred to the Office of Civilian Mobilization and three additional field men were recruited. This force maintained liaison between Albany and the communities throughout the war emergency. Exception in this respect was the Civilian Protection program: it had an organization which from top to bottom was virtually independent.

Not only did the State send representatives to the localities, but occasionally it called representatives of the localities to Albany. Systematic efforts were made to keep the mayors and chairmen of the boards of supervisors abreast of developments. On June 10, the Governor addressed a three-day conference of mayors in Albany, a conference devoting one entire day to the defense program. His speech outlined the work already done and pointedly stated that the local defense councils could anticipate greater and greater demands as the year progressed. This time, however, he did not confine himself to the problems of production and civilian protection, but emphasized the need for coordinating and mobilizing the health resources of the State. Quick action, he declared, was necessary in connection with the problem of housing in defense production areas, as was the need for close cooperation between the local councils and the county agricultural defense committees. The Governor took care to praise the popular morale and spirit which were undoubtedly extremely high in spite of the many demands being made at this time upon the communities. Increasingly, from then until December 7 and Pearl Harbor, despite the rapidly increasing number of programs and organizations, there was a growing coordination and focusing of the State's defense program. The pattern came to consist of direction from Albany, compliance on the local level, and a gradually developed grouping of related activities under the specific jurisdictions of a small number of leaders: General O'Ryan for Civilian Protection, Mrs. Winthrop Pennock for Civilian Community Services, Dr. M. P. Catherwood for the production program, and Dr. Lewis A. Wilson for the training activities of the Department of Education.

Considerable effort was spent in establishing the Office of Civilian Protection

---

[1] The original name of the committee was The New York State Committee on Conservation of Waste Materials.

under General O'Ryan. Several organizations previously independent were temporarily placed under his supervision. At first the New York State Committee on Fire Defense, appointed on April 4 from among the leaders of the State firemen's organizations, pursued an independent course. Its personnel was well established and fire fighting was an important and highly specialized activity. With the co-operation of the defense councils, indexes of all fire-fighting personnel and equipment were prepared and made available to both State and Federal civilian protection authorities. A grant of $25,000, by the Defense Council made possible, on June 13, the initiation of a State-wide Fire Defense Training Program under the auspices of the Bureau of Public Service Training. Similarly the New York State Health Preparedness Commission, designated, June 17, as the Health and Medical Section of the State Defense Council, had a prior existence and a record of well-planned activity. Both these programs were ultimately placed under the general supervision of the State Director of Civilian Protection.

It was mid-July, however, before General O'Ryan initiated his plan for a State civilian protection organization. On July 14, *Civilian Protection Bulletin No. 1,* outlining the component parts of the civilian protection organization, was sent to all the local defense councils. This was soon followed by *Bulletin No. 2,* outlining procedures for the enrollment and control of air-raid wardens. Three days later, *Bulletin No. 3* followed with additional information and a chart showing the internal organization of the local civilian protection forces. *Emergency Medical Service Bulletin No. 1* which came from Washington and outlined procedure for creating an emergency medical organization within each local council of defense, reached the defense councils September 2. The integration of the Emergency Medical Service was rendered relatively simple by the previous

work of the State and local Health Preparedness committees. A fourth bulletin on the duties and training of air raid wardens appeared September 12.

Other related activities were brought under General O'Ryan's supervision in the latter half of 1941. British plans for the evacuation of London had impressed American observers. Since it was then considered likely that New York City would ultimately be bombed, the appointment of a committee to prepare plans for the evacuation of the metropolitan area was believed to be essential. General O'Ryan was asked to head the committee. The supervision and operation of the air-raid observation posts, requested June 18 by the First Interceptor Command, was the responsibility of the Federal government; it should be noted, however, that the organization and manning of these posts by seventy-five local defense councils were accomplished with the help of the American Legion and under the direct supervision of the State Director of Civilian Protection.

Similarly, $5000 was appropriated in November for a Plant Protection Institute to be conducted by the Bureau of Public Service Training of the State Department of Education under Civilian Protection auspices. The Statewide fire defense training program inaugurated June 13, and which was giving instructions to 200,000 members of volunteer fire departments all over the State, was likewise placed under the supervision of General O'Ryan. Special training in gas defense, introduced as a result of a discovery that the Japanese were in the possession of gas at the battle of Midway, was also placed within the Civilian Protection framework. Since it was anticipated that extensive bombing might develop shortages of water, widespread fires, and formidable obstructions to highway traffic, and to prepare for such emergencies which might demand facilities beyond those available in any one community, three "mutual-aid" plans

Governor Herbert H. Lehman

Governor Lehman was New York State's Chief Executive during the first two years of preparation for national defense and the first year our Nation was at war.

were developed to make possible, when necessary, the pooling of the resources of extensive areas. These plans were all to operate under the local directors of Civilian Protection.

The rapid multiplication of programs on the local level, combined with the eagerness of individuals to find specific tasks and help in winning the war, led to the decision to create what was at first called a Division of Women's Activities, known for a time as the Division of Volunteer Participation, and finally designated the Office of Civilian Mobilization. To head this new agency, the Defense Coordinator selected, on July 18, Mrs. Winthrop Pennock who had been prominent at Syracuse in community activities and Junior League work. To publicize adequately the functions assigned this office, a meeting of representatives and executive secretaries of all councils of social agencies and other community welfare organizations was held at the Executive Mansion August 5. Delegates met with Mrs. Pennock to discuss plans for coordinating the efforts of volunteers all over the State. The program was favorably received and a week later Governor Lehman urged all defense councils to set up a division to handle the registration of volunteers, volunteers ready to carry on not only regular community services then expanding, but also to aid with additional programs expected to come from the State and Federal governments.

In a letter to the local defense councils of August 14, Mrs. Pennock pointed out that a woman of unusual ability was needed to head this division. She described her qualifications thus:

1. The woman must be thoroughly conversant with the total possibilities of volunteer service in your community, both of a short-range nature immediately connected with defense, and a long-range nature connected with the reinforcement of your existing community service.
2. She must be a woman of wide interests, willing to submerge her own personality and enthusiasm in the common cause of the community. She should not be the promoter of any one particular organization of volunteers.
3. She must be a woman of sufficient age, experience, and prestige to command the respect of all groups.

A meeting of over thirty Statewide women's organizations held on September 8 in Albany achieved the coordination of their local programs with that of the local defense councils. Subsequently, 175 representatives of the local counties met in Albany for a two-day training institute at which the need was emphasized for coordinating under the Defense Council the miscellaneous defense activities of the community. Various specific tasks which could be achieved by volunteers were outlined, particular emphasis being placed upon Civilian Protection programs and the necessity for upholding and maintaining, as a contribution to the defense program, existing community services.

Gradually the Volunteer Office, as it was known, became the local headquarters for innumerable volunteer activities. It provided for preinduction training, training for the day care of children, the administration of nursery schools, civic education for adults, aliens, and out-of-school youth, recreation programs, the sale of defense bonds, local information committees, and speakers' bureaus. In November the Governor ruled that these volunteers were responsible to the State office under Mrs. Pennock. The importance of the volunteer offices was so clearly recognized that the day after Pearl Harbor a telegram was addressed to each defense council chairman directing that if he had not previously done so, he should at once create a volunteer office.

Although the Japanese attack on Pearl Harbor came as a complete surprise to the average American, the event found New York State well prepared. Not only had the program for Civilian Protection reached a stage where all activities were centralized in Albany, but also, under the Bureau of Public Service Training, the personnel recruited for Civilian Protection had received considerable training. Mutual-aid programs had been worked out in cooperation with the localities. The defense production plan had been brought safely over the subcontracting hurdle. The State Division of Housing was working in close cooperation with the Federal Security Agency to alleviate housing problems in the principal centers of defense production. A concerted attack upon the problem of labor shortages had been developed by joint action of the State Education Department, the State Department of Labor, and the Regional Office of the War Manpower Commission. At least fifteen different community service programs were well launched and operating with workers provided by the local volunteer offices. The State had shown its readiness to cooperate with the Federal government in all campaigns to conserve critical materials, to induce citizens to buy coal in summer, and to promote the sale of defense bonds and stamps. A Defense Information Committee, created in April and consisting of prominent representatives of the newspapers, the radio, and the newsreels, was working energetically to publicize the various defense activities of the State departments and Defense Council agencies, and in September and October had assisted with the New York State Defense Council exhibit for the Civilian and National Exposition held at Grand Central Palace in New York City. This committee had worked also with the Department of Commerce in the two-day defense-production clinic in New York City, and was doing everything possible to acquaint the citizens of the State not only with what was being done but also with the reasons for the measures being taken, and with the part that each individual could play in the total defense effort of the State.

The extent and importance of the preparations dating before December 7 is made clear by enumerating the steps taken immediately after that crucial date. On December 8, the local councils were directed to enroll all volunteers as quickly as possible through the local volunteer offices. That same day they were also instructed by telegram to intensify the training program for all Civilian Protection personnel. The following day Governor Lehman announced the reorganization of the State Fire Defense Committee under the chairmanship of Joseph N. Sullivan, Fire Chief and Commissioner of Public Safety of Utica. On December 10, local councils were instructed to cooperate with the Treasury in the sale of defense bonds and stamps. A meeting of the State Defense Council held this same day resolved to appropriate $80,000 for the creation and maintenance of farm-machinery repair clinics during the winter, anticipating still greater demands for farm produce in 1942. A week later, the mutual-aid plan for highway repair and debris clearance already referred to was put into operation under the supervision of the Director of Civilian Protection. A State Bureau of Rationing was established in accordance with instructions received from the Office of Price Administration on December 22, the Deputy Commissioner of the Division of Commerce being placed in charge with less than two weeks in which to perfect a Statewide organization. Without the local councils, previously organized and accustomed to function at short notice, these rapid moves would have been impossible. Finally, before the end of the year, a State Advisory Committee on Conservation of Waste Materials, the future State Salvage Committee, was created with authority to appoint local committees in each city and county for coordinating all efforts to collect waste materials for purposes of salvage.

The United States, as Governor Lehman stated in his 1942 Message to the Legislature, was "no longer in the grandstand." The Nazis had been building a war machine for years, and America would have to match her achievement in months. It would be a fight to the finish, a battle of an unlimited number of rounds. Upon New York State, with one-tenth of the nation's population and with the foremost industrial structure in the country, rested tremendous responsibilities. New York State was not caught unprepared.

CHAPTER TWO

State Aid to Federal Programs

IN GOVERNING an area as large as the United States, administrative decentralization is a necessity. For central offices, such as the War Department, the Treasury, the War Production Board, or the Office of Price Administration to deal directly with thousands of individual and widely scattered communities is virtually impossible. The sheer numbers of local units of government, combined with the expanse of territory to be covered, forced the Federal government to depend upon the states for the establishment and operation of intermediate administrative bodies to serve the numerous branches of the wartime program.

The Selective Service administration was the first to be set up, taking form directly after the signing of the Burke-Wadsworth Bill on September 16, 1940. As already mentioned, in New York State this event had been anticipated. A standard Selective Service plan, based upon the recommendations of the Joint Army and Navy Selective Service Committee, was promulgated September 8 by Governor Lehman. By the time of the Japanese attack, draft boards had come to function smoothly and the state had already furnished 111,006 men to the Federal forces.

Immediately following Pearl Harbor, the Treasury Department requested the states to secure the aid of the local defense councils in the sale of defense bonds and stamps. Governor Lehman promptly communicated with them, giving the names and addresses of the Treasury's district representatives for upstate New York.

On December 8, furthermore, an order was issued by the Office of Price Administration freezing all new rubber tires and tubes. Ten days later, in compliance with instructions he had received from Washington to notify the local defense councils that rationing of tires and tubes would begin about January 4, Governor Lehman urged them to make immediate preparations to set up the machinery necessary to handle rationing in the communities.

The following day he announced that he had appointed a State Advisory Committee on Conservation of Waste Materials to carry on a "continuing salvage program" in New York State under the direction of the Defense Council. The function of this committee would be to cooperate in a national program to salvage all waste materials needed for the war effort, and return them to those industries where they would be most useful.

These four programs — Selective Service, Bond Sales, Rationing, and Salvage — are excellent examples of the dependence of the Federal government upon cooperation by the state. Without the local defense council, New York would never have been able to carry out, so soon after Pearl Harbor, its assignments from Washington. These councils effected the necessary coordination of effort in the individual communities. Leadership was necessary, from top to bottom, in administering, interpreting, and selling each of the programs. The existence of a national emergency, imperfectly realized by many Americans prior to December 7,

1941, never could be questioned after that date, and despite the appearance of black markets, sporadic violations of Office of Price Administration regulations, and periodic slackenings in bond purchases, popular support remained firm until after the defeat of Germany.

SUPPORT OF THE ARMED FORCES

Selective Service was the first Federal program to which the State of New York gave full support. As early as July 29, 1940, Governor Lehman sent a telegram to the Senate Military Affairs Committee endorsing a selective compulsory military service law on the basis that New York State's efforts to stimulate recruiting had failed to produce the number of enlistments necessary to build up an adequate military defense. That being so, a compulsory system which called "for sacrifice and service from men of every race, of every national origin, and of every religious faith" was the only possible way of producing the desired result.

On September 8, the details of the Selective Service plan for the State of New York were made public. Under the provisions of the Burke-Wadsworth Bill, the Governor was charged with the administration of the system. In anticipation of this responsibility, he had been working for some time with the Adjutant General and the Lieutenant Governor on plans which followed closely the recommendations of the Joint Army and Navy Selective Service Committee. The Adjutant General was designated the State Executive Director, and headquarters were established both in Albany and New York City. The entire machinery which went into operation in the State on September 16, 1940, by presidential proclamation, consisted of:

1. Local draft boards of three members designated by the Governor and appointed by the President for areas containing not more than 30,000 population.

2. Advisory boards of three members to be attached to each local board for the purpose of assisting and advising registrants in preparing questionnaires, claims, and other papers.

3. One or more examining physicians who were to be attached to each local board for the purpose of examining registrants called for the service.

4. One advisory board, consisting of specialists, for approximately every ten local boards to render expert professional opinions on doubtful cases. (Fifty-three medical boards for 540 Selective Service boards.)

5. A government appeal agent attached to each local board to represent the interests of the government, the registrant, and the employer by filing appeals with appeal boards in cases where the local boards appeared to have erred in granting deferred classifications to registrants, or a disqualification on account of physical deficiencies.

6. Boards of appeal, of which there were twenty-four for the state, and which would have power to review appeals from rulings of any local board with respect to classifications, and to affirm, modify, or revise the same if circumstances required.

The Governor was faced immediately with the problem of recommending to the President the appointment of several thousand persons for local boards, for boards of appeal, as government appeal agents, and as examining physicians. Responsibility for these appointments was personally delegated to leaders of the local communities on the theory that they knew their own people more intimately than did the Executive, and that there was a better chance of getting acceptable boards than if all the appointments were made from Albany. The mayors were asked to recommend members for the local boards in the municipalities and the county judges members for boards outside the municipalities. Recommendations for appointment as government appeal agents were made to the Governor by the State Bar Association, and recommendations for examining physicians and dentists by the State medical and dental societies. The Governor made his selections from such recommendations.

The President's proclamation called for the registration on October 16, 1940, of all persons born on or between two specific dates—October 17, 1904 and October 16, 1919. On October 9, the Governor issued a proclamation calling attention to the registration, and directing all registrants in New York State to appear

. . . at such polling places as may be designated by the respective boards of election having jurisdiction in the election district in which (they) reside, or in which (they) may appear to be on that day, and thereafter to comply promptly with whatever may be required of (them) and pursuant to the provisions of said Act.

The State boards of election were further directed to carry out "the registration in the manner provided by law and the regulations issued thereunder." All persons were warned of the penalties provided in the law for neglecting or refusing to comply with the act, or making any attempt to prevent or obstruct its execution. Employers were called upon to release workers to register. All public officers of the State, counties, and municipalities were directed, and residents of the State requested, to aid and facilitate registration. Similar procedure was followed at subsequent registrations.

The work of election boards at the first registration was invaluable. Without their cooperation, registration would have been delayed until after the formation of the local Selective Service boards. The election boards, accustomed to handling large groups of citizens, with assistance from the New York State Police carried out the registration of over 1,700,000 men. The State Police facilitated registration by establishing centers that stocked supplies of registration cards and, when need arose, by making rapid

deliveries to boards of election that had been unable to anticipate the size of their registration. This cooperation was repeated at subsequent registrations, and throughout the entire war period the State Police were especially helpful to State headquarters with short-form reports.

The medical examination and screening of selectees drew heavily upon personnel and facilities of the State Departments of Health and Mental Hygiene. A comprehensive program of X-ray examinations of registrants was worked out at the suggestion of Dr. Robert E. Plunkett, General Superintendent of Tuberculosis Hospitals, and voluntarily placed in operation in New York State by the Department of Health in cooperation with the United States Army. This program, which was likewise put into effect in New York City by the New York City Department of Health, took advantage of the opportunity furnished by Selective Service examinations to screen for tuberculosis, and every selectee in New York State had the benefit of this service. X-ray equipment was furnished by the State and by some local tuberculosis agencies and partly by the Army. State and local agencies also furnished personnel and read all films.

The success of the program in preventing the induction into the armed forces of active cases to the number of approximately 1 per cent of all inductees examined was such that the Army, in view of the cost to it of tuberculosis cases from the last war,[1] decided to place the program in operation in the rest of the Second Corps Area. Certain other sections of the country initiated X-raying in the

---

[1] Tuberculosis during and after the First World War among those who were in the United States armed forces during that war, cost $960,000,000 in hospitalization, vocational training, compensation, and insurance. This represented an average cost of about $10,000 for every case.—Dr. Ramsay Spillman in October 19, 1940, issue of the *Journal of the American Medical Association.*

early stages of the Selective Service program, and finally it was adopted by the Army on a national scale. Under no other circumstances would it have been possible to examine such a wide segment of the population for traces of this human scourge with such beneficial results in reducing its long-range prevalence in the State.

The State Department of Mental Hygiene likewise performed valuable service. War put a tremendous strain upon a person's psychological make-up, and those who were mentally unstable were most likely to go to pieces. In situations where quick thinking was necessary, a mentally defective or mentally unstable enlisted man or officer might make a strategic or tactical mistake that would be costly to the outfit and conceivably result in its being wiped out. Screening to eliminate poor mental risks started late in the previous war. When the proportion of relatively unstable recruits shipped to France during the war became sufficiently large to cause serious trouble, General Pershing finally cabled to the United States urging that from then on every division be screened before it left for Europe.

In this war, screening was adopted very early, enabling Selective Service to do a more thorough job. In New York this work was performed by the State Department of Mental Hygiene. To prevent induction of individuals likely to be unfit mentally for military service, preinduction psychiatric examinations were made by members of the medical staffs of the Department's mental institutions. Originally the work was done at a few of the local draft boards but, after January, 1942, most of the psychiatric examinations were shifted to the Army induction stations, and State hospital psychiatrists were made available to the surgeon of the Second Corps Area for service at regional induction stations in Buffalo, Rochester, Syracuse, Binghamton, and Albany. As an aid to more accurate classification of selectees, the Mental Hygiene Department with the assistance of War Council funds, made available to the Selective Service System its central index of patients for the purpose of identifying registrants who had been treated at one time or another in institutions under the jurisdiction of the department. Previous hospitalization for a mental condition was regarded by the induction boards as presumptive evidence of mental instability. Abstracts of medical records were made available upon request to examining physicians of local boards, or other authorized representatives of the Selective Service System. The department furnished approximately 40 per cent of the total psychiatric personnel in all induction stations, and the greater majority of such personnel to upstate centers. Approximately 450,000 names were checked by the department during the war, of which 0.0073 per cent were identified as "probable" cases. State hospital psychiatrists also assisted in New York City, where one central station was set up for the entire metropolitan area.

As a further aid to more effective screening, the practice was begun of having social workers take personal histories of registrants before examination. This system aided in securing a more efficient selection of inductees. Under this procedure, the abstract of the social history of the registrant was submitted to the local board, which either classified the selectee or forwarded the information to the induction center for use by the Army physicians in their final classification.

To the Department of Mental Hygiene also fell certain aspects of the problem of educating the public to meet the mental strain incident to the war. In carrying out public education in mental health and morale, lectures and radio talks were given to air-raid wardens and other defense groups. Professional and popular literature covering anxiety and morale, prevention and control of panic, psychological effects of war upon the civilian population, mental problems of children in wartime, psychological warfare, military and Selective Service psychology, and utilization of the mentally handicapped in war services was published and distributed by the department. Especially noteworthy was the series of pamphlets on *Anxiety and Its Control, Morale and Its Control,* and *Fatigue and Its Control* issued by the Military Mobilization Committee of the American Psychiatric Association, in the planning and editing of which members of the department staff assisted. A popular edition of 10,000 copies was published by the department and distributed throughout New York State. Under the authority of Section 36 of the War Emergency Act, the Department of Mental Hygiene transferred to the United States Army for use as general hospitals, three institutions with a total of 5000 beds. War manpower demands upon the Department resulted in a total reduction in institutional staffs of approximately 3000 persons.

The State Department of Education assisted local boards by furnishing the scholastic records of registrants before induction. This work was actually performed by secondary schools under the direction of the department, and information on physical health, aptitudes, and character proved distinctly valuable to the boards in making difficult selections. The Division of Military and Naval Affairs of the Executive Department served as host to the induction teams of the armed forces. Armories were made available where necessary to serve as offices for handling large numbers of persons.

Following registration, it became the task of the local Selective Service boards to place all registrants in one of four classes: Class 1, those available for service immediately; Class 2, those deferred because of the importance of their services to the country; Class 3, those deferred because of dependents; Class 4, those deferred because induction would be undesirable to the government.

The classification of individuals was a difficult task, and the entire matter of deferment was one with which local groups throughout the State were closely concerned. Very close to one-fifth of all registrants in the country were deferred for reasons of physical unfitness. Decision in that field, however, was a technical matter as indicated above and was competently handled by the machinery originally set up in 1940.

On the other hand, deferment of men because of the importance of their services in industry and agriculture involved a process of fact finding more difficult than that required of the physician. In New York State an advisory committee on both State and local levels assisted in determining the essential character of men in agriculture. These war boards were composed of four or five men representing the Agricultural Adjustment Administration and other Federal and State agricultural organizations, with the County Agricultural Agent usually acting as secretary. When an individual farmer was classified 1-A, his board would call for a farm survey to be made by the Agricultural War Board. Blanks for these surveys were worked out by the Agricultural Conference Board,[1] and provided for an exhaustive description of the farm on which the individual in question was located. On the basis of this information, the County War Board recommended to the local board either deferment or induction, in accordance with the provisions of the Tydings Amendment providing deferment for essential agricultural workers. If it decided that the individual should be deferred as an essential worker, its decision was usually accepted. If for any reason the decision was questioned, the War Board had the power to appeal the case.

Deferment of industrial workers was

---

[1] See Chap. VI.

usually in the interests of the company with whom the registrant was employed. If the man was essential, his employer requested deferment. A decision in the matter was then made by the local board on the basis of the evidence presented and with the usual possibility for appeal. By December 31, 1942, out of a total of over 835,000 men in the armed forces from the State, inductions under Selective Service numbered approximately 490,000.

By the end of the war, the total figure for all members of the armed forces from New York State, including women, members of the National Guard, volunteers, inductees, and others from outside the State, was 1,638,044.

The responsibility of the State in the military field did not end with the local operation of the Selective Service machinery. It became more and more necessary, as the war continued, to secure an adequate number of volunteers, both men and women, for the auxiliary branches of the armed forces — the WACS, WAVES, SPARS, Marines, and Air Cadets.

To assist in an advisory capacity with this special problem of recruiting, the Second Service Command created a Civilian Advisory Committee for mobilizing all available recruiting resources throughout the State. The principal drives were for the Women's Army Corps. Fourteen WAC recruiting offices were established in cities all over the State and extensive use was made of the local war councils, especially the volunteer offices. One of the chief campaigns for members of the WAC was held during the period September 27 — December 7, 1943, at the request of the Chief of Staff, United States Army, and the Commanding General of the Second Service Command.

In New York, Governor Dewey, who had assumed office January 1, 1943, adopted a number of measures to ensure the success of this campaign. On October 2, 1943, he called upon all citizens eligible to join the WAC to do so and enlist in the service of their country. He also requested the executive of each municipality to take an active part in the drive, and recommended the appointment of a voluntary WAC Recruiting Committee for each municipality. Practically all municipalities acted upon the Governor's request. Furthermore, the facilities of the New York State War Council were used as information centers, and in many cases the block plan[1] was brought into operation in addition to the volunteer offices of the local war councils. The first company of WACS recruited under this program was sworn in before Governor Dewey on the steps of the State Capitol, October 18, 1943. As a result of these efforts, a total of 1037 women were enlisted.

Other drives for WAVES, SPARS, and Marines took place in 1944 and 1945 and were supported by the same type of organization, with the addition of Veterans' organizations, the American Red Cross, Girl Scouts, and the Minute Men of the Agricultural Extension Service. To each of these drives, Governor Dewey lent his efforts, making available all facilities of the State.

Preinduction training was operated by the State Department of Education with the assistance of the Military Training Division, Second Service Command. The chief of the Preinduction Branch, Military Training Division, visited high schools, talked to principals, advisors, and students, and in general helped to coordinate this program. Preinduction training was designed particularly to prepare prospective inductees for adjustment to life in the armed forces by providing information that would assist them in meeting personal problems created by their new status. While not generally carried on throughout the State, it was extremely successful in certain areas where it seemed to meet the definite needs of the prospective inductees and

---

[1] Described on p. 136

their families. Support for this program was provided by the Offices of Civilian Mobilization and War Training of the State War Council in cooperation with local volunteer offices, with the American Red Cross, and with the armed services of the United States.

The public school system of the State likewise made available its equipment and staff for the conduct of training centers for the Signal Corps, and especially for Preflight Training in 1942 and 1943. In both years, the State Legislature passed appropriations to cover equipment and, in public secondary schools, part of the cost of organizing and teaching Preflight Training and other courses of instruction in Junior Aviation. The Civilian Pilot Training Program, under the direction of the Civil Aeronautics Administration, also gave flight training to individuals unable to meet the physical standards required in the Army Air Force.

In a number of ways, the citizens of New York State found it possible to maintain contact with friends and relations after their induction in the service. In addition to the work of such national organizations as the American Red Cross and the United Service Organization, whose chapters and clubs were largely staffed by local people, many war councils developed their own programs for keeping in touch with their own boys and girls.

An outstanding local program was that of the Ithaca Camera Club which made it a point to photograph the families of servicemen from Ithaca and to send each a set of the pictures. Some of the letters received from service personnel indicated how much these pictures did to maintain morale. A number of war councils edited and sent out news letters on local happenings. Many local newspapers mailed free copies of each issue. Schools sent periodic letters describing school activities, and many sent the school paper. The countless letters, gifts, and photographs that went abroad daily need hardly be

mentioned, for practically every family knew what correspondence of that sort meant. They could, however, do much more than that for those who were temporarily stationed inside the State. Volunteers manned United Service Organization Centers, Red Cross, and Daughters of the American Revolution canteens, and put in countless hours entertaining and feeding the servicemen. Servicemen were entertained at dinner in private homes, were given free tickets to movies, stage shows, and athletic events, and in many cities were provided with free transportation on trolleys and buses. Every conceivable method was employed to make the individual serviceman feel that those for whom he was fighting were interested in him as a person and wanted to repay him as much as possible for the sacrifices he was making in the defense of his homeland.

The vast majority of the activities of this nature carried on by volunteers in New York and elsewhere were organized under the sponsorship of the American Red Cross, founded in 1880, and of the United Service Organizations (USO), established February 4, 1941. By direction of the War Department and concurrence of the Navy, the services rendered the armed forces by these two organizations were clearly outlined to prevent overlapping of effort. A Joint Statement of March 2, 1943, covered their activities in Army and Navy stations and outside both within the continental limits of the United States and abroad.

The Statement is in part as follows: "The American Red Cross, under its Congressional Charter and Army and Navy Regulations *furnishes volunteer aid to the sick and wounded of armies in time of war and acts in matters of voluntary relief and in accord with the military and naval authorities as a medium of communication between the people of the United States of America and their Army and Navy. The Red Cross is responsible for service of this type* to organizations and units of the armed forces in garrison or wherever serving on active duty in the field or proceeding in transit as members of an organized body under orders, and for social service and recreational programs in hospitals and for convalescents.

"The United Service Organizations, Inc., is a corporation organized under the laws of the State of New York with the approval of the President and the Secretaries of War and the Navy representing the joint efforts of The Young Men's Christian Associations, the National Catholic Community Service, the Salvation Army, the Young Women's Christian Associations, The Jewish Welfare Board, and The National Travelers Aid Association, to provide services of a religious, social, and recreational character for members of the armed forces. *The primary responsibility of the USO in its present program is to serve members of the armed forces outside of military reservations when off duty or on leave.* With minor exceptions principally a few long established Army and Navy YMCA buildings, *the USO does not conduct club operations inside camps. The major USO activity in camps is that of USO-Camp Shows, Inc.,* which provides theatrical productions and concerts, with appearances and schedules determined by the military authorities.

"The activities of the American Red Cross and the USO are carried on in close cooperation and consultation and with the objective of insuring the most effective use of the resources of both organizations in the interest of the men of the armed forces and their families. . . ." *

The Red Cross was thus recognized as the "sole non-military agency to operate with an expeditionary force." USO Clubs were therefore not established during hostilities in Africa, Europe, China, Japan and other war theaters. USO-Camp Shows, however, went everywhere,

as the sole channel through which the entire amusement industry made its special contribution to the entertainment and morale of the armed forces.

Except for its work in connection with disaster relief, indicated briefly in Chapter IV, the Red Cross devoted most of its organization to support of the armed forces. In its 112 New York chapters, the overwhelming majority of Red Cross workers were volunteers. Each chapter was obligated, in accordance with the Congressional charter, to render Home Service to service- and ex-servicemen and their families and to organize for disaster preparedness and relief. Other authorized activities could be undertaken where local conditions warranted. The following list of the Red Cross services and units reveals the extensive character of their activities in the State during the war:

Home Service
Camp and Hospital Council Service
Nursing Activities
Volunteer Special Services
Blood Donor Service
Nutrition Service
Junior Red Cross
Hospital Service
Ship Service
First Aid, Water Safety, and Accident Prevention
Prisoner of War Packaging Centers
Service in Veterans' Hospitals
Disaster Preparedness and Relief and Civilian War Aid
Camp Service
Claims Service

A brief description of some of the more important Red Cross services follows.

Upon the Home Service lay the dual responsibility of helping to maintain morale in the servicemen's homes and of supplying necessary information about home conditions to commanding officers. Especially valuable was documentary evidence furnished by the Service that enabled service personnel and their fam-

---

* Italics by the author.

ilies to receive every advantage from the allotment and allowance legislation.

Home Service workers were experienced in social service and trained in Red Cross welfare policies. They secured social and family histories for hospitals and military authorities which were used as a basis for determining proper medical treatment and for granting emergency furloughs. Advice was often given the serviceman's family on business difficulties or assistance provided from Red Cross relief funds. Medical or dental care, eye glasses, special diets, or clothing were frequently furnished for children of servicemen. From July 1, 1941, to July 1, 1945, Home Service in the chapters of the State assisted over 1,800,000 service cases, 260,000 ex-service cases, and 250,000 civilian cases. Since several types of assistance rendered to families required referral to an appropriate local agency, and since the volume and kinds of requests received by the Red Cross were staggering, the Home Service maintained close cooperative relations with the State Departments of Health and of Social Welfare. This was especially true when the Emergency Maternity and Infants' Care Program was first introduced into the State to take care of the wives and infant children of servicemen.[1]

Another Red Cross unit was the Camp and Hospital Council Service which provided emergency and supplementary equipment, supplies, and services by channeling the resources of a community through Red Cross field directors to the various Army and Navy installations in the United States. During the peak of the war period, the Camp and Hospital Councils operated in 211 Army and Navy installations and veterans' hospitals in the State of New York. In the majority of these, the councils furnished day rooms and provided additional recreational and entertainment

equipment in the form of small musical instruments, grand and movable pianos, public-address systems, etc. Complete landscaping was provided for some of the installations, while garden equipment and furniture were provided for many. Occasionally, swimming pools and golf courses were added where the need for such was imperative in rehabilitation treatment. Extra comfort items and subscriptions to magazines were always provided. Especially noteworthy was the work of the councils in providing service personnel with interesting entertainment, including Broadway shows, concert artists, and amateurs.

Among the Red Cross Nursing Services were (1) recruiting professional nurses for the Army and Navy, and for Red Cross Emergency Service; (2) disaster nursing; (3) classes in home nursing; (4) public health nursing; (5) cooperation with Volunteer Special Services in the preparation and supervision of Volunteer Nurses' Aides. Red Cross representation was maintained on all nursing service committees of the State Nursing Council for War Services and on other State nursing associations on the State level. From March, 1944, to April 30, 1945, the Red Cross paid the salaries of two secretaries of the Nursing Council for War Service, and the Area Director of Nursing Service served as a committee member on the New York State Nursing Council for War Service in 1944 and 1945. The recruitment of 9,328 nurses for the armed forces from December 1, 1942, through September, 1945, was an outstanding achievement. To teach homemakers and potential homemakers to give simple nursing care to the family under a doctor's guidance and to promote better community and family health, four Red Cross home-nursing courses were offered. Over 140,000 certificates were issued for completion of one or more of these courses.

Similarly, during the war a total of

---

[1] See Chapter VIII. p. 242

nearly thirty thousand volunteer nurses' aides were recruited and trained. These nurses' aides were given an eighty-hour training course to prepare them to assist nurses, thereby freeing registered nurses for those services that only graduate nurses could perform. Nurses' aides worked in hospital wards and clinics, official and volunteer public-health nursing agencies, visiting nurses associations, school health services, industrial health clinics, and, at the request of commanding officers, in Army general and station hospitals, veterans' administration hospitals, and Marine hospitals. During the war they assisted at blood-donor centers and worked with the Mobile Blood Donor Units. They were present when ships arrived and sailed, assisting troops, repatriates, and war brides.

Other volunteer special services, in addition to the Volunteer Nurses' Aide Corps, included the Canteen Corps and its aides. This corps was organized and its personnel trained by the Red Cross Nutrition Service for mass feeding in emergencies. During the war canteen members served refreshments to troops on hospital trains, to embarking and debarking troops at the Port of New York, to personnel on planes of the Air Transport Command, to service personnel at numerous veterans' information centers, and to inductees at Selective Service boards.

The Production Corps, another auxiliary service of the Red Cross, in which New York's citizens played their part, had three divisions. The first made surgical dressings in vast quantities for the Army in time of war (with materials provided by the War Department) and at all times for local hospitals. The second, knitted sweaters, caps, socks, and other articles to be distributed on request of commanding officers to meet emergency needs of servicemen. The third sewed garments and comfort articles for men in Army and Navy hospitals, filled kit bags for service-men going overseas, and made clothes for local needs and foreign war relief.

The now famous Blood Donor Service was established at the request of the Surgeons General of the Army and Navy and was a cooperative undertaking with the National Research Council, whose Division of Medical Sciences was responsible for technical supervision. Technical requirements limited this service to thirty-one Blood Donor Centers in large population areas located near the laboratories which had contracts with the War and Navy Departments to process blood for the armed forces. Plasma and whole blood were provided in large amounts through mobile units which visited nearby Red Cross chapters to procure blood from donors they had previously enrolled. During the war, residents of New York State volunteered over 2.3 million bleedings.

The Field Service of the Red Cross covered every United States military and naval installation in the country and overseas. All personnel at such locations were entitled to the services of a resident or itinerant Red Cross director. Service was likewise extended to civilian pilots of the Air Transport Command, members of the Merchant Marine, and personnel of the armed forces of the United Nations when on duty in the United States or its possessions. Personal and family problems referred to the field director varied as widely as human nature. In general, the director provided individual counsel and guidance to personnel in the armed forces and made contacts where necessary between servicemen and their families. Under certain circumstances he provided financial assistance and certain social, economic, and health information needed in considering welfare questions or disciplinary matters. Information was also furnished on Federal and State legislation on veterans' affairs, and individual counseling service and assistance was given to men being

separated from service. At certain Army
and Navy installations, psychiatric so-
cial-work programs were also conducted.
As of December, 1945, there were twenty-
one camps in New York State staffed
with twenty-one field directors, seventy-
two assistant field directors, and fifty-
seven field assistants.

The Red Cross Hospital Service was
essential as the needs of the sick and
wounded presented problems more pressing than those of the able-bodied. Nearly
two hundred Red Cross directors and
other personnel were involved in the
eight station and eleven general hospitals in New York State. A special feature
of the Hospital Service was the assignment of workers to hospital trains transporting wounded from ports of debarkation to Army hospitals near the men's
places of residence. Since New York was
one of the principal ports of debarkation,
this became an important and tremen-
dously active service during the period
when casualties were being returned in
large numbers. The numerous details
handled by this Service correspond generally to services, already mentioned as
performed by the Field Service for able-
bodied members of the armed forces.

Field directors and assistant field directors in the Red Cross Claims Service handled all phases of veterans' problems associated with pensions, hospitalization,
and medical treatment, insurance, death
pension, and other benefits of the Veterans' Administration offices and hospitals.
In these institutions, Red Cross field directors had access to all records of any
veteran who designated the American
Red Cross as his representative. As of
December 31, 1945, of 207,000 World
War II cases filed with the Veterans' Administration in the State of New York,
156,000 claims had been processed and
completed. Of these, 40 per cent were
handled by the Red Cross. In September,
1945, a full-time Red Cross field director
was appointed to coordinate the Volunteer Red Cross Services in each hospital.

During the summer of 1942, the commanding general of the New York Port
of Embarkation secured from the War
Department permission for the American
Red Cross to operate on the piers and
furnish service to returning troops. In
April, 1943, this Ship Service had been
so successful that further permission was
secured for the Red Cross to serve embarking troops as well. Thereafter, Red
Cross volunteers served all embarkation
and debarkation operations in the port
area.

While the Red Cross was furnishing
these emergency services to personnel in
the armed forces it was also carrying on
many services that applied more specifically to the needs of civilians. When the
multiplicity of Red Cross activities and
the number of persons who benefited
from its services are considered, the debt
that the American people owe the organization becomes apparent. New Yorkers
may well feel proud that the first local
chapter of the American Red Cross was
founded by Clara Barton in 1881 in the
Livingston County village of Dansville.

During the early days of the United
Service Organizations, the second major
wartime service unit, an agreement was
made with the New York State War
Council, for purposes of administrative
clearance, regarding selection of communities in which the organization would
work. Contacts between the USO and the
local war councils were usually through
the latter's section on recreation. Local
USO Clubs were able to secure exhibit
materials, lantern slides, and films from
the State departments. Virtually all the
leading State officials supported the work
of this organization, and Thomas Dewey,
before becoming governor, acted as chairman of the first national USO campaign.

In New York State and elsewhere
throughout the country peak USO operations in March, 1944, included 3,055
USO Clubs, Traveler's Aid Service units,
Troops-in-Transit Lounges at transportation terminals and junctions and Clubs-

on-Wheels to serve troops on maneuvers, isolated garrisons and outposts, the Coast Guard and American guards at prisoner-of-war locations. In big cities the problem was how to keep a lonesome service man from getting lost among the crowds of local citizenry. In smaller places the question was often how to keep the town from getting lost among the service men. Coffee, doughnuts, cigarettes and an easy chair, were the first demands of Troops-in-Transit, as they passed through USO lounges on their way home, on pass, or waiting to catch a bus back to camp.

All sorts of emergencies arose, such as the S.O.S. "Wanted at once: 100 Japanese-American Hostesses", sent out by the Nyack, New York, USO-Club when a contingent of Nisei troops stopped in for their final leave before shipping out. Nyack wanted to give them a farewell party. Within a few hours, one hundred and twelve girls were on their way from New York City and the party was a big success. Wrote Private George Inai, one of the soldiers, "A grand time and some swell memories. We're on our way now and hope to return soon."

USO Clubs were one of the main centers for service women and service wives. During the war years, many women who wished to keep their families together followed their husbands to camp towns and ports of embarkation. Some settled there temporarily some permanently, waiting and hoping for their husband's return. Others joined their men at posts where they were scheduled for lengthy duty. In all these cases, wives were able to look to USO for the only recreation and companionship they could receive in a strange town. Help with trouble, planning, information on housing, playpens for children, arts and crafts classes, discussion groups, layette clubs, and the development of other social groups, proved a very tangible contribution to the happiness of wives of men in service.

During the war, USO services helped maintain the morale of men and women working in war plants and living in dangerously over-crowded boom-towns. Recreation at USO cooking classes and teas, community sports programs, arts and crafts work and "state night" parties helped to offset the fatigue and loneliness of newcomers in war plant communities. Actual program costs were largely assumed by the war workers themselves. At the end of the war USO rapidly transferred its industrial work to local responsibility and withdrew in February 1946.

In addition to the professional entertainers of USO-Camp Shows, and the clerical and maintenance staff, the backbone of all USO service was the relatively small nucleus of 3,000 professional workers. These were kept in continuous touch with the needs of the organization through Training Conferences and Staff Institutes. With the end of the war and the return of thousands of service men to civilian life, greater stress was placed upon rehabilitation. Information was made available to service men on all topics currently in their thinking-schools, vocations, trade and business opportunities, the G. I. Bill of Rights — most of the work being carried on through clinics conducted by community experts. In support of these projects, the USO and its six member agencies published or distributed more than 200 different booklets and pamphlets on educational and religious subjects. Religious programs were an especially important part of all USO activities.

One of the most rewarding jobs for USO was with the war casualties. There were over 500 USO Clubs located near the 168 military and naval hospitals. These clubs, which originally provided a link between home and military service, were frequently the convalescent veteran's first contact with normal civilian life. Since needs vary according to the type of disability and returning servicemen required more personalized service, the program was adapted to fit a changed and varied situation. More and more time was devoted to individual talks, conferences and suggestions. More serious opportunities were offered, such as classes of arts and crafts; "quiet" rooms for men who enjoyed classical music recordings; group discussions on such topics as current events, veterans rights, and business opportunities.

Young and old participated in volunteer service. Boys emptied ashtrays, helped in check-rooms or ran errands; girls made cookies and candy, washed dishes, and helped in many other ways to relieve older sisters and mothers. Older people served on committees, as senior hosts and hostesses, as snack bar workers and office aids. They sewed on buttons or chevrons, managed check rooms, planned entertainment, gave out information. Others conducted arts and crafts classes, dramatic performances, forums, music discussions and athletic activities.

Much as servicemen appreciated the work of the USO volunteers, the volunteers themselves were glad of an opportunity to be of service. There is the example of a mother in an upstate New York community whose son was killed. She went to a USO Club and offered to do something behind the scenes like washing dishes because she did not wish to meet people, although she wanted to do something for the boys and girls in service. Wash dishes she did — for a whole year — until suddenly she found she was no longer alone. She was with people and she was talking with other women. Through service she had been able to leave the world of loneliness behind her.

The story of the USO and Red Cross volunteers is one of the thrilling chapters in the wartime history of cooperation between American races, creeds, groups, and individuals.

RATIONING

Conservation Efforts Prior to the Outbreak of War. Rationing and conservation had one common purpose, to restrict the use of commodities in short supply, and thereby to make such quantities as were available go as far as possible. Rationing, however, was compulsory while conservation was not, and represented a detailed effort to distribute supplies fairly among all consumers. Regulation of distribution was not involved in the various conservation programs, and before the inauguration of compulsory rationing in January, 1942, several Federal organizations attempted to persuade Americans to conserve supplies of needed raw materials through programs of voluntary restriction.

The first of these conservation drives concerned gasoline. In the spring of 1941, British losses from the operations of Nazi submarines resulted in the diversion of over 50 tankers from an Atlantic fleet of approximately 260 to the British shuttle service. Others were taken from the private oil companies for use by the American Navy. The result during the summer of 1941 was a considerable deficiency in monthly deliveries of petroleum products along the Atlantic seaboard.

In view of this situation, Petroleum Coordinator Ickes requested the governors of the eastern states to cooperate in bringing about a 20 per cent voluntary conservation of petroleum products. In line with this request, Governor Lehman appointed the Commissioner of Motor Vehicles to act as State Conservator of Petroleum Products. On July 23, a pamphlet, accompanied by a covering letter from the Governor, explaining the situation and outlining ten ways to save gas, was sent to the chairman of each defense council. It bore the slogan, "Make four gallons do what five did before and save gas for Uncle Sam." The Defense Information Committee, a Statewide service agency of the Defense Council, through newspapers and the radio inaugurated a publicity campaign on gas saving. On August 12, the Governor wrote to the various State departments urging that their personnel try to cut gas consump-

Officer Candidates

A group of officer candidates leaving class at the United States Naval Schools of Indoctrination and Training at Cornell University, Ithaca, New York.

PLATE NO. III

tion by one-third. He also relayed to the people of the State a prediction from Washington that enforced rationing of motor fuel would be the only alternative if this voluntary campaign were unsuccessful. Voluntary conservation methods rapidly became insufficient after the attack on Pearl Harbor and, on the eastern seaboard, gasoline rationing began May 15, 1942.

The 1941 campaign to conserve gasoline was begun in the final week of the nation-wide drive for scrap aluminum, a program staged by the Director of Civilian Defense. The two campaigns initiated the drives which did much to conserve and salvage strategic, critical, or essential materials. At the suggestion of Washington, the policy of urging the use of substitutes was suggested to the local defense councils in a letter of July 9, 1941. Again, on November 27, ten days before Pearl Harbor, the Governor forwarded to the defense councils an appeal — this time for the salvage of waste paper. These various appeals found the people of New York not only willing to cooperate but also geared to function through their State and local defense council organizations.

The Japanese attack on the East Indies cut off 98 per cent of America's supply of rubber.[1] The country was left with enough rubber on hand to cover civilian consumption for one year, but in view of the tremendous demand for rubber by the various branches of the armed forces extreme care was imperative in order to ensure that the supply should last as long as possible. It was anticipated that eventually production of synthetic rubber would become adequate to meet all needs. Accordingly, the day after the attack, the Office of Price Administration froze all sales of new rubber tires and

tubes and prepared a plan for rationing these two commodities, basing quotas upon an 80 per cent cut in civilian supply. After January 5, eighteen classes of individuals were to receive purchase certificates. Governor Lehman directed the local war councils to appoint local rationing boards of three members each and also county rationing administrators.

To organize rationing in New York and to coordinate the efforts of over 220 local boards, the New York State Bureau of Rationing was established December 22, 1941. This new organization was placed under the direction of Dr. Maurice F. Neufeld, Deputy Commissioner of the Division of Commerce. Personnel was hastily borrowed from various State departments and a plan worked out whereby the bureau would act as the liaison agent between the Federal government and the local rationing boards. The following operations were undertaken:

1. To give aid and advice to the local war councils in setting up their rationing boards and coping with their initial problems of securing equipment and personnel.

2. To send out to the local war councils (*a*) thousands of pamphlets issued by the Washington office and containing detailed instructions regarding the rationing of new rubber tires and tubes; (*b*) the necessary application blanks, certificates, inventory forms, and printed regulations.

3. To distribute quotas and maintain records in accordance with the regulations.

4. To interpret the entire rationing program to the citizens of the State, a process which involved answering frantic inquiries and interpreting as satisfactorily as possible the maze of Washington regulations. (In those days, he who could read and understand legal phraseology was king.)

5. To set up a logical division of labor within the central bureau itself.

---

[1] Report of Dr. Maurice F. Neufeld on the New York State Bureau of Rationing; see also his address before Empire State Town Meeting February 1, 1942.

The entire period between the establishment of the State Bureau of Rationing and the inauguration of rationing on a national scale was less than two weeks, and the bureau and the local war councils had to move rapidly. Rationing was new. Prominent and respected citizens of the communities, who were not connected with politics, were requested to serve on the rationing panels without salary and to take charge of administering the various programs. As one chairman put it, "I forgot all about politics and religion and tried to get men for the job. We had a good board." Usually a paid chief clerk was provided, and one or two stenographers. All nonpaid members upon taking oath of office became Federal agents, and later the stenographic force was put under civil service.

The authority and responsibilities of the local boards were:

1. To receive and pass upon applications for rationing commodities. (The rationing of tires and tubes began December 30, of automobiles February 12, of typewriters April 12, of sugar for industrial and institutional users April 27, and for consumers May 4, and of gasoline May 15.)

2. To be responsible for the maintenance of records of all applications received, of certificates issued for the purchase of rationed articles, and of applications denied.

3. To prepare periodic reports for the local and **county administrators** as well as for the State Bureau in Albany.

The problem of working space and equipment was solved in many different ways. Offices were secured in school buildings, purchased outright, or located in war council offices, in courthouses, in chambers of commerce, or in almost any place where space was available. Early in March, the Federal government appropriated funds for the operation of the rationing program. These funds were allocated by the State Bureau for the maintenance of minimum staffs in the local

boards, but until the middle of 1943 such funds were inadequate.

In the last analysis it was the people of New York State who made possible the early success of the rationing program. Without volunteer help successful functioning of the local boards would have been out of the question. These volunteers, many of them supplied from the Volunteer Office of the War Council, helped with the organization of the board rooms. Others assisted in interpreting to the people of their communities the regulations on gasoline, tires, fuel oil, canned foods, sugar, and other rationed commodities, and in taking the responsibility for those interpretations in the light of known local conditions. Volunteers also took care of the interminable processing of the applications. Board members and volunteers neglected their personal affairs, worked days, nights, and holidays, and took upon their own shoulders every responsibility that came to them from the State office. The chairman of one board, an English mining engineer, did a splendid job of organization, but worked so hard to get equipment and personnel for the office that shortly afterward he nearly died from a heart attack.

The central bureau in Albany did its best to help solve problems of personnel, space, and equipment, but its field staff could not do the job single-handed.[1] The availability of volunteer help for the rationing program through the local offices of volunteer participation saved the day. Fortunately, the liaison between the State War Council and the State Bureau of Rationing was excellent throughout. Certain difficulties, however, originated

---

[1] The county administrators mentioned above were at first responsible for the proper administration of the rationing program in their respective counties and the allocation to each board and the allocation of those tires and tubes available under quotas determined by Washington and Albany. Those functions, however, were gradually absorbed by the district offices, and after some two years the office of County Administrator was discontinued.

in Washington and neither the State nor the localities could do much about them. Perhaps the worst was delay. Rarely was it possible for the State Bureau and the local board to secure amendments and new rulings sufficiently in advance of the date on which they were to become effective. Hence, time essential for studying them and for interpreting their significance to the public was often lacking. Sometimes the public learned of changes through the newspapers as the result of press releases from Washington days or weeks before the State Bureau and local boards were informed. Delay was also exasperating when letters requesting interpretations, letters addressed from Albany or later on from the district offices, went long unanswered. Since within the Office of Price Administration itself responsibility for public announcements was not centralized, matters of interpretation created confusion, and tremendous pressures developed when, as not infrequently happened, subordinate officials gave out interpretations based on inadequate consideration. Occasionally, an insufficient number of forms would be sent out, or forms would be received days or even weeks after a program was scheduled to go into effect. It took money, time, and patience to rectify these errors. While nobody on the local level understood why these things had to be, each cheerfully "passed the buck" to "the government" and did the best he could under the circumstances. When, in May, 1942, at the end of four months of operation, the Office of Price Administration decided that rationing should become strictly a national program, in New York State procedures had been successfully established and popular support was good. On May 15, the State Bureau was discontinued, its functions transferred to the regional Office of Price Administration in New York City, and its personnel and records split between that office and the subordinate office of the Albany District.

During the first phase of rationing, while it was still a State program, State authorities cooperated completely. State and municipal police helped to maintain civilian morale by enforcing rules and investigating complaints of violations. They also assisted by facilitating emergency deliveries of rationing forms and blanks. The freezing of all new cars, January 2, 1942, led the Governor to launch a campaign to persuade drivers to share the use of their cars. With war workers and shoppers alike, "doubling up" and "car pools" became the custom. As part of the general attack on the problem of conserving gasoline and rubber, a bill was passed by the State Legislature, in April, 1942, providing for a forty-mile speed limit. Exactly five months later, in line with Federal recommendations based upon the Jeffers report, the War Council lowered the limit to thirty-five miles an hour.

The State government also did its best to conserve its own rubber and gasoline by inaugurating in 1942, under the direction of its Automotive Rationing Committee, a pool first of tires, then of chauffeurs, and finally of cars. In June, shortly after his appointment as State Mileage Administrator, the Commissioner of Motor Vehicles called a conference of State and Federal officials for the purpose of discussing proposed methods for reducing governmental vehicular mileage. The conservation program then placed in operation included vehicles owned and operated by the State of New York, vehicles owned and operated by the counties, cities, and villages of the State, and privately owned vehicles used in the service of these government units. Over 181 local mileage administrators were appointed, and each government unit, following the principle of home rule, determined its own program for mileage reduction. Substantial savings were achieved by suggestions on ways in which conservation could be practiced submitted by the State to the local administrators.

Mileage administrators were also appointed by the heads of all State departments, and in some of the larger departments even for single divisions. Procedure was worked out involving the use of State-owned cars, privately owned cars used in the service of the State, and privately owned vehicles used by State employees for driving to and from work. Since quarterly reports had to be filed by the State Administrator with Washington, quarterly reports were required from local mileage administrators. At the height of the program, reports were received from more than seventy agencies. These reports indicated a drop, in 1943 and 1944, over 1941 of more than 20 million miles driven in the service of the State, or a reduction of approximately 35 per cent. If to the State figures are added those from the local government units, a reduction of more than 40 million miles over 1941 figures was achieved in 1943 and 1944. This represents savings of approximately 3 million gallons of motor fuel, thousands of tires, and a money saving of over 2 million dollars each year.

Conservation of heating fuels also became an important aspect of the State's program. A Statewide campaign to get people to buy coal in the summer, first launched in 1941, was repeated with still greater success the following year under the direction of the Division of Commerce, and with the active cooperation of the New York State Retail Solid Fuel Merchants Association, Inc. In August, 1942, an appeal was made to all who could conveniently do so to convert their oil burners to the use of coal, or to insulate their houses and prepare for a one-third cut in their supply of fuel oil.

In 1942 as the rationing program developed, the State War Council gave the assistance of three of its major agencies. Beginning in the summer of 1942, for the benefit of the local councils, war council agencies, and State departments, all rationing news was carried in the *Official Bulletin,* edited by the Office of War Information. Two other agencies which worked closely with the local boards were the Office of Civilian Mobilization, already mentioned in connection with the services of its local volunteer offices, and the War Transportation Committee, whose regional representatives worked through the transportation members of the local war council to conserve gasoline and tires on school buses and private cars used for transportation between homes and factories.

Although the State's duty in the active administration and enforcement of the rationing program ended in May, 1942, on a number of subsequent occasions the force of its authority was placed squarely behind the purposes and policies of the Office of Price Administration. Active and continuous support of Federal war policies was inaugurated early in the spring of 1943 by Governor Dewey and firmly adhered to until the summer of 1946. This course was chosen deliberately despite the fact that as time went on popular dissatisfaction with certain Office of Price Administration restrictions and with the inability of Federal authorities to enforce them more adequately became increasingly vocal.

Although rationing was no longer a concern of the State government during 1943, Governor Dewey became the recipient of an increasing volume of protests. The ban on pleasure driving, begun January 7, 1943, proved especially unpopular, but increased demands from the armed forces, which threatened seriously the gasoline reserves on the eastern seaboard, made it imperative. Restrictions on the use of fuel oil also created irritations and many who converted their furnaces to coal suffered when coal was scarce, however, it was the ban on pleasure driving that remained the chief point at issue. The Governor stood firmly behind the ban and issued a proclamation, on January 7, 1943, directing law enforcement agencies of the State, and requesting those of the municipalities, "to lend their aid and effort to the execution" of the ban by reporting violations to the nearest War Price and Rationing Board. The order was lifted for a time in March and April, 1943, but was reimposed in May.

Even the regional distribution of gasoline came in for criticism. During the spring of 1943 many citizens of the State were chafing at the differential in the value of "A" gasoline rationing cards between the eastern seaboard and Middle Western states. Since gasoline rationing began on the eastern seaboard and slowly proceeded westward, the initial stages of necessity bore more heavily on New York and the other eastern seaboard states than on the states in the Middle or Far West. The Governor was besieged by letters complaining of the unfairness to easterners of existing regulations for gas rationing. Correspondents demanded that he secure for the State a reasonable share of the nation's gasoline and hinted, without justification, that New York was being penalized for having elected a Republican Governor.

On June 18, 1943, Governor Dewey addressed a strong letter to Mr. Ickes, outlining the difficulties imposed by the new ban, stressing the problem of transportation for war workers, and the necessity of gasoline for the production and distribution of food. Exploring the situation thoroughly, he suggested (1) greater use of the Barge Canal as promised by the Federal government in March, and (2) the diversion of some of the surplus petroleum products in Middle Western tanks to the east by means of tank cars. These two measures should, he felt, tide the State over a critical sixty-day period until extension of the "Big Inch" pipeline to the east could be completed. Action by the Petroleum Coordinator was requested, and soon afterward an order was issued by the Petroleum

Coordinator that no unloaded canal boats should proceed in an easterly direction.

Meanwhile, the State Administrator had begun cooperating with the War Production Board's Rubber Director to conserve rubber. William M. Jeffers, Rubber Director of the War Production Board, requested that race tracks located at some distance from metropolitan centers, and reached by most patrons by automobiles, be closed for the duration of the war. Opposition to the proposal was substantial. Throughout 1942 racing had been allowed to continue in the face of the rubber rationing program and of the growing shortage of rubber. The Governor detailed his Executive Assistant to investigate the New York racing situation in relation to the necessities of war. On March 12, 1945, Governor Dewey released the report. It was based upon consultation with racing officials, and others concerned with the racing business, and recommended compliance with the Jeffers report. Racing at Saratoga was discontinued for the duration, and the August meeting at Saratoga was accordingly transferred to one of the four metropolitant tracks for which rail transportation facilities were easily available.

Gasoline and tire rationing were not the only vexing questions. Vegetable growers of the State protested price ceilings on vegetables while hundreds of New York City dwellers signed petitions to secure enforcement of price ceilings on food of every kind. To make matters worse, there developed in New York City during the fall and winter of 1942-1943 a large black market in meat. These food problems were acute, and Governor Dewey, who occupied middle ground between producers and consumers, was faced with a difficult decision. As Office of Price Administration regulations were Federal law, ceilings were enforceable only in Federal courts. At the War Council meeting of April 28, 1943, a letter was read from Mayor LaGuardia to the Governor requesting the War Council to adopt an order for the enforcement of Federal rationing, freezing, and price-fixing regulations. After considerable debate, the Council passed Resolution 294, which read as follows:

RESOLVED, that

1. Solely for the purpose of enforcement, all regulations and orders established by the Price Administrator, pursuant to the Emergency Price Control Act of 1942, as amended by Public Law 729 — 77th Congress, and Public Law 151 — 78th Congress, are hereby adopted and promulgated in the State of New York;

2. Every violation of any such regulations or orders shall constitute and be an infraction of this order, triable and punishable pursuant to the provisions of the New York State War Emergency Act, as amended.

This action, placing the enforcement resources of New York behind Office of Price Administration regulations on a State-wide basis was illustrative of Governor Dewey's policy of throwing full State support to the wartime programs of the Federal government. Unfortunately Governor Dewey's subsequent bid for the cooperation of neighboring states in the suppression of black market operations received scant support.

In New York, however, all violations of Office of Price Administration regulations were henceforth triable in State courts. This was the wisest move possible for curbing what the New York War Council termed the "widespread violations of price ceilings," which were "endangering the equitable distribution of food supplies to the people of the State of New York," and tending to "break down all measures designed to prevent inflation." The resolution was inevitably attacked as being unconstitutional but its legality, defended by Attorney-General Goldstein, stood the test in the courts, and under its provisions, by the middle of April, 1944, the sheriff's office of New York City alone had brought in

to the magistrate's court over 1600 cases.[1] This substantial support to Office of Price Administration officials undoubtedly helped to curtail the black market in New York State. The War Council consistently readopted the resolution in 1944 and 1945.

On February 1, 1945, the War Production Board issued Utilities Order U-9, commonly referred to as the brown-out, the purpose of which was to save fuels used in the generation of electricity by prohibiting certain unnecessary uses of electricity. At the request of Chairman Krug of the War Production Board, the New York State War Council adopted Order No. 21 to provide for State enforcement of this Federal regulation. The promptness of the War Council's action in carrying out this recommendation evoked from the Federal authorities several appreciative telegrams.

In his 1946 message to the Legislature, when speaking of temporary war emergency statutes, Governor Dewey declared, "Some, such as legislation implementing federal price control, should be continued." He likewise emphasized the need for continuing the rent controls on commercial properties in New York City, which had been provided at the 1945 session of the Legislature upon recommendation of a Joint Legislative Committee. Furthermore, should the Office of Price Administration withdraw its supervision in the field of residential rents, he recommended that the State be prepared in advance to place in effect its own regulations.

The Governor's recommendations were acted upon by the Legislature. Three clearly related laws were enacted, of which Chapter 274 proved to be the

---

[1] Testimony of Mayor LaGuardia given on April 17, 1944, before the Senate Banking and Currency Committee, considering extension of the Emergency Price Control Act. (Hearings before the Senate Committee on Banking and Currency on S. 1764, 78th Cong., 2nd sess., pp. 658-659.)

most significant. Chapter 274 enacted March 30, 1946, set up a temporary State Housing Rent Commission. The commission was to consist of a single commissioner, with power to promulgate regulations and orders to stabilize or reduce rents, by setting maximum rents for housing accommodations within specially designated rent-control areas where such action appeared necessary. The law, however, was to take effect only upon the withdrawal of Federal rent-control provisions. Its purpose was expressly stated to be "to prevent exactions of unjust, unreasonable and oppressive rents and rental agreements, and to forestall profiteering, speculation, and other disruptive practices tending to produce threats to the public health. . . ."

The subsequent failure of Congress to continue the Office of Price Administration or to provide an acceptable substitute amply justified the wisdom and foresight of the Legislature in enacting this measure. Three hours before the death of the Office of Price Administration at midnight on June 30, 1946, Governor Dewey appointed the former New York City Comptroller, Joseph D. McGoldrick, to act as commissioner under the law. All rents in Office of Price Administration rent-control areas were frozen under the New York law at the existing Federal ceilings, and the commission went into operation that night with a million-dollar appropriation. There is no question but that during the war the government of New York State acted wisely to protect its own citizens from the dangers of rising prices, and that it was unusually provident in continuing to do so during the period of reconversion.

SALVAGE

Statement of the Problem. When a country arms and goes to war the strain on the raw materials of industry becomes terrific. Civilian consumption must be reduced by rationing, and also articles used and worn out, but composed of critical materials, must be retained or reclaimed, collected, and returned to the factories for reprocessing. Especially critical in the early days of World War II was rubber, since we were cut off from our customary supplies. However, America was fortunate in that, as one of the by-products of her high standard of living, she had accumulated over the years scrap metals, rags, paper, and a large quantity of reclaimable rubber. The problem was to ferret out these materials and return them to the proper industrial channels.

The salvage problem is easily stated: Salvage was interpreted to cover all materials needed for war production, and whatever materials the nation needed at a given moment would be called for by Washington. State and local salvage committees would then get busy and bring these materials in. In the summer and fall of 1941, before any national salvage machinery had been organized, shortages in aluminum, gasoline, and waste paper appeared. As early as September, the Governor was informed by an official of the Conservation Bureau of the Office of Production Management that an over-all plan for the "continuing salvage of waste materials" was in preparation. In December, just before Pearl Harbor, this same bureau requested the assistance of the Office of Civilian Defense, headed by Mayor LaGuardia, in expediting the "inauguration of a continuing national salvage program." By then it was pretty well known what materials the country must retrieve. These included scrap metals of all kinds, rags, used rubber, waste paper, and fats. A detailed plan for the operation of a campaign was drawn up November 29 by the Chief of the General Salvage Section, Bureau of Industrial Conservation, Office of Production Management. On December 19, in response to a request from this bureau, the Governor appointed a State Advisory Committee on Conservation of Waste Materials[1] to conduct "a continuing salvage program." The committee was to be part of the New York State Defense Council with an office in Albany. Washington, it was agreed, would issue general directions and pay the expenses of the office, but the program would operate under the sovereignty of the State, and the executive secretary of the committee and his staff would be considered as State officials. The membership of the committee, selected partially on a geographical basis, included the following:

> R. Murray Willard, chairman
> Delos Walker
> Alfred Rheinstein
> Herbert L. Carpenter
> Daniel H. Roblin
> Dean Alfange
> Mrs. Guy W. Cheney
> Jacob Ark
> William L. Lentz
> Herman Symansky

Early in January, 1942, at a time when there was little salvage organization on the Federal level, William Arnoldy, the executive secretary of the committee, went to Washington to receive instructions. He was the first of the State executives to be sworn in, and after a number of pleasant interviews returned to Albany with instructions to use his own judgment. Within a month local salvage committees consisting of representatives from a wide range of community organizations had been appointed by the chairman of each of the city and county defense councils. Local salvage chairmen were checked and rechecked for efficiency by the State office, and those who were interested primarily in the honor were weeded out gradually and replaced by individuals who would work. In view of special conditions existing there, New York City was allowed its own committee and chairman.

Within the counties, the township plan of operation, suggested by J. Franklin

Bonner of the Monroe County Planning Board, was adopted. According to this plan, each township had its own chairman and committee, and these in turn were responsible to the county chairman. In a few counties consolidation of the county committee with the committee of the dominant city occurred, notably between Syracuse and Onondaga County, Utica and Oneida County, Glens Falls and Warren County, and Binghamton and Broome County. As soon as the local committees were set up, nine regional meetings of county and city chairmen were held throughout the State to discuss methods and to help in the solution of mutual problems. The State War Council supported the plans of the State committee throughout and recommended the inclusion of the salvage chairman as a member of the local war council. The State committee issued no directives, and while the local committees were kept informed of objectives through releases sent from Albany, their methods of delivering the goods were of their own devising. Between 25 and 40 per cent of the ideas for getting in salvage proved effective, and efforts were made to pool the most successful ideas from each section of the State.

Salvage was one of the most difficult of all the programs to get under way, for it possessed no glamour. It was a routine job that could not compare with civilian protection. Gradually, however, as the danger of bombing receded and shortages of materials increased, its importance became clear. It developed finally into one of the most successful of all war council activities. One reason perhaps for this success was that goals were tangible, and workers could see what they were doing. Furthermore, money could be made in salvage drives, money which for the most part was pledged to charity, for publicity for future salvage drives, or for specific community projects. These varied widely but included such things as the rehabilitation of the fighting men at the end of

---

[1] The name was later changed to "The New York State Salvage Committee."

the war or payments to their dependents, the purchase of library books and of an X-ray machine, support for Boy Scouts and Girl Scouts, paying off mortgages, and painting public buildings. Paper, scrap metals, rubber, and fats were especially remunerative. Another of the secrets of success was the excellent publicity in the local press. Merchants contributed magnificently in advertising the salvage drives. The general interest remained high until V-E Day, waned considerably between then and V-J Day, and dropped off sharply thereafter. In New York State the program was officially discontinued on September 30, and in the nation on October 31, 1945.

Outside of the five boroughs of New York City, some 280,000 salvage workers participated, without receiving compensation for their labor. In diverse areas, people reacted differently to the salvage program. In the rural districts, a straightforward story as to what was needed and why it was needed was sufficient. Farmers and their families would work after hours to get in the scrap as a single matter of duty. In the larger cities, distractions were many and neighborly relationships at a minimum; here it was important to have systematic and extensive publicity to induce cooperation. An illustration or two of patriotism and willingness to work displayed in the salvage drives may be of interest.

In and around Wellsville there was much abandoned oil-well equipment. The local salvage committee made a contract with a junk dealer to handle whatever they could collect. They asked him where to put the scrap and he showed them a middle-sized storeroom located in his yard. The next day he was absent, observing a religious holiday. Upon his return the following day not only was his storeroom filled but the entire yard as well. He could not get into the yard himself, nor could he extricate his car left there the day before. The dealer had been in the business twenty years, yet he

had completely underestimated possibilities.

In the small town of Granville, in the northern part of the State, the men of the fire department wished to pay off the mortgage on their fire house and equipment, both recently purchased following a disastrous fire. When approached about the scrap metal program the treasurer of the fire company saw a chance to do something for his country and at the same time to pay for the fire house and trucks. He and his men organized into shifts and on alternating Sundays, with blow torches and a couple of cases of beer, proceeded to some abandoned quarries nearby. There they dragged out the scrap metal, cut it to specifications, and shipped it off by carload lots to the steel mills. The news spread, and the Sunday excursions for scrap were filmed by a local photographer. Later on, William Arnoldy was invited to the burning of the mortgage on the fire house, a community celebration which included a turkey dinner and the showing of the motion pictures.

Paper was the item in which the best work was done by youngsters. Boy Scouts, Girl Scouts, Grange Juniors, and 4-H Club members searched for waste paper both in and out of the schools. In Elmira a competition was set up among the grades with results published in the newspapers. One little fellow bought $1,200 worth of war bonds with money received for the waste paper he had collected, and was promptly invited to talk over the radio. In the Elmira-Chemung County Ranger programs, a girl collected 56,000 pounds and two boys 81,000 and 101,000 pounds respectively. In Brooklyn, children began to collect paper in wagons and baby carriages. They ran out of wheels and besieged the borough Director of Salvage for wheels. He appealed to the newspapers who promptly put on a campaign to collect wheels for the transporters of waste paper.

In October, 1942, a scrap metal drive

was put on in the schools of the State. All the students involved had the privilege of naming a Liberty ship. The name eventually chosen was "Lou Gehrig." In this competition the school receiving the greatest amount per capita could select a representative to send to the launching of the ship at Portland, Maine. A little school at Speculator won first place, a school in a small town near Oneonta won second place, and a tiny town in Orange County placed third. Three youngsters, each with a chaperon, came to Albany and were entertained before being put on the night sleeper for Portland. The boy from Speculator had never before seen a train nor a trolley car, and merchants had to outfit him with clothing to enable him to make the trip. He was spotlessly dressed, but perhaps the most uncomfortable boy in the world. On going to the Capitol to see the Governor, he came to a revolving door and stopped abruptly, saying he was "not going to get caught in that trap."

An unusual organization was developed at the very start among the professional scrap metal dealers. As the principal connecting link between civilian collectors and the consuming steel mills, they were the only people who knew how to sort and process the scrap. Since, for example, an automobile contains seventy-eight different kinds of metal, experience is required in sorting. Early in 1942, a meeting of scrap dealers was called at Albany by the Secretary of the State Committee and an agreement was reached whereby the dealers would cooperate as a group with the salvage program. Every two months William Arnoldy appointed a new Grievance Committee from among the men themselves. Any complaints received were to be referred to the five men on that committee. If they could not settle the matter, it would be passed on to him. Never once did the dealers prove unable to settle a matter among themselves. The arrangement worked so well that toward the end

of the war the executive secretary did not bother even to appoint a new Grievance Committee. The same plan was used for the waste paper dealers, who likewise worked together for a common objective. Unfortunately, at the end of the war, the cooperative plan was abandoned and the situation deteriorated to the *status quo ante*. A brief resume of salvage operations for the period 1942-1945 follows.

Summary of Operations, 1942-1945. The story of salvage operations in New York State lacks any definite pattern or continuity, as the main programs were fixed nationally and the special drives were linked to national shortages, some of which were chronic, others of sudden occurrence and frequently unanticipated. Salvage was a constant series of drives first for one item, then for another, with an undercurrent of routine pick-ups for items in chronic short supply such as fats, paper, and tin. Like a general directing his forces in battle, the War Production Board directed the salvage armies toward first one objective, then another, only in this instance orders were accompanied by explanatory publicity to help people understand why collections were necessary in the amounts called for.

In January and February, 1942, the main outlines of the campaign were blocked out. Folders printed in Washington listed the principal articles and the places where they were usually to be found, such as attics, cellars, and garages. Paper bailers were made available for purchase by collecting organizations, such as churches, Red Cross units, Boy Scouts, and schools, because paper dealers were reluctant to accept crumpled waste paper. Main emphasis, it was announced, would be placed upon the following materials: paper, rags, rubber, iron, steel, brass, copper, aluminum, zinc, lead, and tin foil. A continuing flow of publicity was planned from Washington and from Albany. Window cards were introduced in some places to indicate, when displayed, that scrap was ready.

On the back were printed full instructions as to what to save, how to save it, and where to dispose of it. Unusual cases of civic or individual salvage efforts were given wide circulation, such as the purchase by the city of Syracuse of forty miles of single trolley tracks for the sum of $1.00, or the work of Cayuga County in raising through three feet of ice a side-wheeler — the *Frontenac* — built about Civil War times. People were not allowed to forget for a moment the need for salvage.

By March, 1942, Washington began to call for more rubber and tin. In June the shortage of rubber became acute and on the 15th the President inaugurated "the President's Campaign for Rubber." The drive was sponsored by the petroleum industry through the local salvage committees. Careful explanations were given as to why rubber was short, and the fact pointed out that prewar consumption of rubber in the United States was 50 per cent of the world's entire output. At the end of the drive, the quantities of rubber salvaged exceeded the handling capacity of transportation companies and reclaimers of rubber. It took many weeks before the accumulations were finally cleared up and sent to government stock piles.

Late in June, in addition to the rubber and metal programs, a National Household Fat Salvage Campaign was inaugurated and carried on for the duration of the war. Publicity was handled directly through the butchers by certain glycerine interests. Later on, this campaign had to be taken over and pushed by the salvage committees of the State.

The scarcity of metals began to make itself felt early in the fall of 1942, and in September the War Production Board requested the American Legion to assist in collecting memorial trophies, field pieces, and statues. Had it not been for a natural reluctance to request the donation of historical and sentimental relics, these articles would have been asked for earlier. Even cemetery superintendents were approached for scrap metal. At about the same time, owing to an increase in the country's detinning capacity, the collection of prepared tin cans was extended from the larger cities to the rest of the State and continued until the fall of 1945. A drive for both torn silk and nylon hosiery was also added in 1942, and after a year's campaign, the national total of over 2 million pounds was consigned to a warehouse in Green Island, New York for sorting and shipping to the reclaiming mills.

In the fall of 1942, Washington inaugurated a "National Salvage Program," which called for a number of different kinds of publicity designed to reach various groups of the population and aimed primarily at scrap metals. The campaign was supported by national advertising furnished by the American Industries Salvage Committee. The newspapers campaigned vigorously on behalf of a part of this program — the "National Scrap Harvest." Piles of scrap were accumulated at designated centers, inventoried, and shipped to the mills as needed. The national goal was one hundred pounds per capita. The drive proved to be one of the most successful for the reason that excellent publicity aroused the public to a high pitch of enthusiasm and made every one salvage-conscious.

On October 2, 1942, the national School Salvage Program was inaugurated in New York State by Governor Lehman and Dr. George T. Stoddard, State Commissioner of Education. Two hundred and twenty-two schools collected over 25 million pounds of scrap metal and were given the privilege of naming one of the new Liberty ships. At this time the efforts of the scrap committees were in many places coordinated with the Block Leader Plan of the Office of Civilian Mobilization, and house-to-house canvassing was undertaken to get 100 per cent cooperation from individuals.

Among other devices to get people to collect scrap metal were the plan to have every citizen bring in ten pounds on the first anniversary of Pearl Harbor, and the so-called Jalopy Round-up carried out by local American Legion Posts. In justification for this intensive concentration upon metals, it was pointed out that whereas in 1917 each soldier, sailor and marine required about 90 pounds of steel, in World War II mechanized warfare had raised the ratio to 4900 pounds per man.

By the end of 1942, salvage had been accepted by the people of the State as a major program for which there was continuing need. The collection of practically all items had been started including, paper, rags, rubber, iron, steel, brass, copper, aluminum, zinc, lead, and tin. On some of these the War Production Board set periodic quotas such as the 910,000 tons of scrap iron and steel set for the first half of 1942, of which an estimated 99 per cent was filled, and the 1,208,000 tons of scrap metal assigned to New York in the second half of 1942. Figures on salvage collections for 1942, or for any other year, however, give no accurate picture because it was too difficult to keep records in the rural areas, or, because of the artificial character of State boundary lines, to keep them in the towns bordering other states.

One legal question came up in 1942 in connection with the use by municipalities of the funds secured from the sale of salvage. In answer to an inquiry from a community as to what it might legitimately do with the proceeds, the State War Council, on November 5, passed the following resolution:

RESOLVED, that the New York State War Council recommends that all local war councils, municipalities, and agencies utilize proceeds received from the sale of salvage and scrap contribution to the war effort by the people, in the securing of additional salvage and scrap for the war effort, and that any surplus may be contributed to war charities.

In general, this policy was followed, although local communities frequently spent funds for some appropriate project needing support at the time.

The salvage work was harder in 1943 than in 1942. Transportation facilities were much more critical and the nation-wide gas rationing was a difficult obstacle for many local committees. Besides, the more obvious sources had been cleaned up and great ingenuity was required to find materials. By 1943, however, the State organization of 106 Salvage for Victory Committees, composed of leading representatives of business, civic, labor, youth, farm, industrial and welfare groups, and 973 subcommittees operating under them, was experienced and resourceful. It was in 1943 that the scrap rubber drive and the silk and nylon hosiery campaign were brought to successful conclusions.

In April, May, and June of 1943, an intensive advertising campaign was conducted to double the collection of waste fats. Waste paper, which had been pretty well taken care of early in 1942, was brought back into the picture because of its many uses in connection with food, clothing, ammunition, shell containers, bomb bands, wing tips, practice bombs, temporary camp buildings, water pipes, and many other war activities. New items asked for included cotton rags, old rope, and burlap bags. All during the fall, the emphasis remained on metals and paper, with Governor Dewey issuing a proclamation on waste paper salvage late in December, 1943, to prevent paper plants in the western part of the State from having to shut down. When, at the end of 1943, the War Production Board awarded pennants for excellence in salvage collections, twenty-two New York cities and forty-one of the fifty-seven counties were credited with having exceeded the quota of one hundred pounds of scrap per capita.

The year 1944 witnessed a tightening up of the entire State organization through the increased integration of the activities of the State salvage committees with those of mayors, war councils, highway superintendents, the Office of Defense Transportation, and the Office of Price Administration. This produced greater results and a quicker shipping of the materials collected in any given area. An intensified educational campaign was put on to make the need of salvage as clear to the average individual as possible. Special displays of salvage and war materials were arranged at thirteen county fairs and war fairs and at the State War Council exhibits. The results were good. In the first six months of 1944, over 800,000 gross tons of scrap iron and steel were collected — over 98 per cent of the quota. Included in the educational campaign was an especially detailed statement of the 700,000 military uses for paper and paper products. Waste-paper stock piles were especially low on January 1, 1944, and it was only by the fine cooperation of the schools, the Boy and Girl Scouts, the service clubs, the American Legion, and representatives of war industries including newspapers, magazines, and private concerns, that the country's reserves were kept abreast of current needs. In 1944, New York furnished 634,000 gross tons, slightly less than one month's requirements for the national program. In spite of that, however, paper continued to be the number one critical war material from June, 1944, until the summer of 1945.

Two other important items were rags and the ubiquitous tin. In April, 1944, with the inventories of the dealers 25 per cent below normal, and the Army and Navy as well as war industry demanding more wiping cloths than were available, the collection of rags was temporarily pushed hard. The revolution in Bolivia, from which most of the country's tin was coming, pointed up the continuing need for that metal. New York's record in the salvage of tin cans was good. New Yorkers collected and released more than 35 million pounds of prepared tin cans in the first six months of 1944. Tin salvage, however, was a continuing program, and lasted on into 1945 along with paper.

Salvaging was strictly a war activity, and since many materials were no longer required in great quantities once fighting stopped, organized salvage efforts came to an end September 30, 1945, six weeks after V-J Day. The executive secretary, however, was directed by the War Council to give whatever aid was still required in support of the fat salvage campaign. Shortages of waste paper, tin, and used fats, continued with the prospect that these materials would not be plentiful until prewar sources were again available, but thenceforth commercial agencies were to carry on the work of salvaging. In spite of the many difficulties that had to be surmounted, the record of the State throughout the period of three years and nine months of salvage operations was consistently good, and one in which the thousands of men, women, and children who helped to make it so can take a just pride.

WAR BONDS

The sale of war bonds and stamps remained throughout the war under direct supervision and control of the United States Treasury. Organized May 1, 1941, as the Defense Savings Staff, the name of this special branch of the Treasury Department was ultimately changed to the War Finance Committee.[1] This division was organized administratively on a state, bank district, county, and town basis, and administrative personnel were appointed as direct representatives of the Treasury Department. Quotas for each drive were fixed by states, subdivided by counties, and then by towns. The New York State organization, of which both governors

---

[1] The four successive titles of this committee with dates of changes were: May 1, 1941, Defense Savings Staff; Apr. 17, 1942, War Savings Staff; June 30, 1943, War Finance Committee; Jan. 1, 1946, United States Savings Bonds Division.

acted as honorary chairman, was completed by October 1, 1941.

During the course of the war, over 500,000 men and women assisted the local War Finance committees as volunteer salesmen of bonds and stamps, the largest participation of any state in the Union. Approximately 3 million New York employees bought "E" Bonds under the payroll savings plan. Plants having the payroll deduction plan were entitled to qualify for the Treasury "T" flag by enrolling 90 per cent of all employees with an average deduction of 10 per cent of their pay. Upon such performance they were awarded the flag, which corresponded somewhat to the Army and Navy "E" award. In all, nearly 10 million New York men, women, and children were at some time during the war years owners of war bonds.

New York State was able to help put the successive war bond drives across in three ways. On December 29, 1941, Governor Lehman put into effect for all employees of the State a voluntary payroll deduction plan, continued under Governor Dewey, whereby deductions in the amounts authorized by each employee were used for the purchase of war bonds. The original appeal was based partly

upon the security of the investment, partly upon the need of the country for dollars, and partly upon the disaster which failure to support the fighting front might conceivably entail. As a result of this appeal, and of the systematic coverage secured in New York State on sales of "E" Bonds, through May 31, 1946, approximately 21,500 State employees purchased bonds whose maturity value totaled $17,931,600. As of July 1, 1946, this plan was being continued to combat inflation despite the fact that the war was over.

Under both Governor Lehman and Governor Dewey, the State cooperated with the Treasury Department in a second way by making available its Statewide War Council organization of volunteers to support the eight Federal war loan drives (Table 1).

In October, 1942, by way of assistance to the Treasury in the First War Loan Drive, a memorandum issued by the State Office of Civilian Mobilization, one of the agencies of the State War Council, set forth an agreement between that office and the New York State War Savings Staff of the United States Treasury. The agreement included an invitation to the chairmen of the local War Savings

Table 1. Federal War Loan Drives

Loan	Official sales period	Interest date	Period during which sales of nonmarketable securities (war savings bonds and notes) were included in loan
First	Nov. 30, 1942 — Dec. 23, 1942	Dec. 1, 1942	Dec. 1, 1942 — Dec. 31, 1942
Second	April 12, 1943 — May 1, 1943	Apr. 15, 1943	April 1, 1943 — May 8, 1943
Third	Sept. 9, 1943 — Oct. 2, 1943	Sept. 15, 1943	Sept. 1, 1943 — Oct. 16, 1943
Fourth	Jan. 18, 1944 — Feb. 15, 1944	Feb. 1, 1944	Jan. 1, 1944 — Feb. 29, 1944
Fifth	June 12, 1944 — July 8, 1944	June 26, 1944	June 1, 1944 — July 31, 1944
Sixth	Nov. 20, 1944 — Dec. 16, 1944	Dec. 1, 1944	Nov. 1, 1944 — Dec. 31, 1944
Seventh	May 14, 1945 — June 30, 1945 (Individuals) June 18, 1945 — June 30, 1945 (Corporations)	June 1, 1945	April 9, 1945 — July 7, 1945
Victory	Oct. 29, 1945 — Dec. 8, 1945 (Individuals) Dec. 3, 1945 — Dec. 8, 1945 (Corporations)	Nov. 15, 1945	Oct. 29, 1945 — Dec. 31, 1945

committees to serve as members on the local war councils, and placed at the service of these chairmen the volunteers registered in the local volunteer offices. Subsequently, in March, 1943, a memorandum was sent to the chairmen of the local war councils, volunteer offices, and Civilian War Services by Mrs. McNab, the State Director of Civilian Mobilization, urging full assistance to the local War Savings Staff of the Treasury Department in the Second War Loan Drive scheduled for April, 1942. The memorandum stated that it was the task of the volunteer offices to furnish volunteers under the technical direction of the local Treasury representatives.

In providing manpower for the war bond campaigns, the Division of Civilian War Services of the State Office of Civilian Mobilization willingly played a part subordinated to that of the local War Finance committees, cooperating only where necessary to ensure the success of the drives. On some occasions, however, the local war councils were forced to take over complete charge of bond sales to meet the quota for their municipality in a particular campaign. In such cases the local chairmen of Civilian War Services and of the volunteer offices were in a position to render vital assistance. The availability and eagerness to help of such organizations as the Boy Scouts, the Girl Scouts, the Campfire Girls, and 4-H Club members, all of whom had pledged full cooperation for such purposes to the State Office of Civilian Mobilization, assisted greatly in boosting community totals. Public-spirited citizens from all walks of life, whether connected directly with war councils or not, gave willingly of their time and energy. Every sales device known to human ingenuity was employed to get people to buy bonds. Every luncheon club in town — racial, civic, or fraternal — got behind the campaigns with prizes, contests, bingo parties, scholarships, and what not. Millions of dollars

of newspaper space was donated periodically by local merchants to help their community meet its quota. In fact, to no other Federal program was it possible for so many citizens of the State to afford such consistent and wholehearted support.

Another similar example of State support was the War Savings Program in the schools and colleges under the direction of Dr. A. K. Getman of the Education Department. Asked to serve as a member of the Defense Savings Committee in October, 1941, he was given charge of its education section. The function of his committee was to encourage systematic thrift instruction and savings through the purchase of stamps and bonds in the public and private educational institutions of the State. As a result of its work in the schools, bonds and stamps were used as object lessons in the value of thrift in classes devoted to civics, history, and economics, while total purchases by school children between November 1, 1941 and September 1, 1945 totaled 321 million dollars.

School children played an important part in the war loan campaigns, not only through their own purchases of bonds, but by interesting their families in buying them. Many school children were bond salesmen. The work of the schools was recognized by the award of the Minute Man flag. This was allowed to be flown by schools having 90 per cent of the students enrolled in the stamp-bond program. Participation was the sole factor in this award. The amount of money did not make any difference. Thus, some youngsters might buy only a ten-cent stamp each month and still be counted.

The State government was able to assist the United States Treasury in a third way through the investment of the State's surplus funds in government bonds. The First War Loan Drive was the only one of the eight drives conducted prior to January 1, 1943. To this drive, the State of New York made a subscription out of the surplus in the State treasury. In the second and all subsequent drives, since the surplus in the State treasury actually belonged to all the people in the State, instead of making the State's subscription through a few banks in a single city, the Comptroller allocated portions of the State surplus to the fifty-seven upstate counties and to New York City in amounts approximating 10 per cent of their war loan drive quotas. The percentage of the municipal quotas supplied by the State varied from drive to drive, but continued to be allocated in proportion as among the counties and New York City.

In the Fifth War Loan Drive, by agreement with the United States Treasury, the State's subscription of 100 million dollars for the purchase of United States Treasury Savings Notes, Series C, made possible the payment of the cost of an aircraft carrier. In accordance with naval tradition of naming aircraft carriers after famous battles, the carrier was christened the *U.S.S. Lake Champlain,* and carried a plaque reading as follows: *"The U.S.S. Lake Champlain,* sponsored and made possible through the purchase of war bonds by the people of the State of New York."* This subscription was allocated to the various localities: 65 million dollars to the fifty-seven upstate counties and 35 million dollars to New York City. The amount allocated to each upstate county of the 100-million-dollar subscription approximated 10 per cent of its war loan drive quota. Total State subscriptions in all drives came to $452,-373,000. These funds represented surpluses from many of the State's accounts including (1) the Sinking Fund, (2) Trust Funds, (3) the Postwar Reconstruction Fund, and (4) the State Employees' Retirement System. Out of this total, $300,996,000 were allocated to the fifty-seven upstate counties and $151,-377,000 to New York City. In this way the counties as well as New York City received credit for the State's investment

of funds belonging to the people of the State as a whole.

As a result of State support and the patriotic efforts of the people generally, New York State purchased in the eight war loans a total of $44,449,000,000 worth of bonds. This figure represented 30.3 per cent of all war bonds sold in the country between May 1, 1941, and December 31, 1945. At least 70 per cent of the $20,000,000,000 worth of "E" bonds purchased by the country at large were purchased under the payroll savings plan. In New York, out of $2,278,000,000 worth of "E" bonds purchased during the war, about $1,594,600,000 were purchased by payroll deductions.

The fact that New York's total purchases of bonds were out of line with the relative size of her population was partly due to the presence of many large corporations with headquarters in New York City. These corporations invested funds for individuals all over the country in the purchase of bonds which were usually credited within the limits of New York State. For example, insurance companies in New York State purchased a total of 9.458 billion dollars worth of bonds representing 42.8 per cent of all bonds purchased by the insurance companies of the country. Similarly, New York corporations purchased approximately 16 billion dollars worth of bonds representing 30.5 per cent of all bonds purchased by corporations in the United States.

Nevertheless, the record of sales of bonds to individuals for the eight war loans shows that New Yorkers did not rely upon the big corporations alone. Individuals bought 7.395 billion dollars worth of bonds representing 17.1 per cent of all bonds purchased by the individuals of the country. Approximately 3.155 billion dollars of this total represented purchases of savings bonds and notes of which, as already indicated, 2.278 billion dollars represented purchases of "E" bonds, — 11.4 per cent of all "E" bonds purchased in the country.

War Bond Rally

Throughout New York State, in communities small and large, groups gathered together to promote the sale of war bonds. This picture is the scene of a war bond rally held in front of the U. S. Sub-Treasury Building in Wall Street at the celebration ceremonies of the 150th anniversary of the New York Stock Exchange.

At the peak, 2,800,000 New York employees were enrolled in the payroll savings plan.

Statistics of bond purchases by organized labor in New York State are likewise impressive. Of the national total of 5 billion dollars in war bonds, estimated by the United States Treasury to have been purchased by the CIO from May, 1941 through December, 1945, the New York State CIO contributed approximately one-fifth, or about 1 billion dollars. Purchases by the New York State A.F.L. are estimated to have approached 1.2 billion dollars. A safe estimate of total purchases of all types of war bonds by organized labor in the State, both by individuals and by union treasuries, would run well over 2.2 billion dollars.

The total war bond record of the State is one of which New York may be particularly proud, especially because of the reliance placed upon them throughout the war by the United States Treasury to furnish a very substantial portion of the nation's war bond sales. In the Victory Loan, looked upon as the most difficult of all campaigns, individual New Yorkers oversubscribed their quota by 81.2 per cent, and in so doing purchased 19 per cent of all bonds purchased by the individuals in the country. New York's quota for "E" bonds was actually oversubscribed by 16.2 per cent. Thus the expectations of the Treasury proved to be well founded. The results are a tribute to the excellent work of the 500,000 men and women associated with the New York State War Finance Committee.

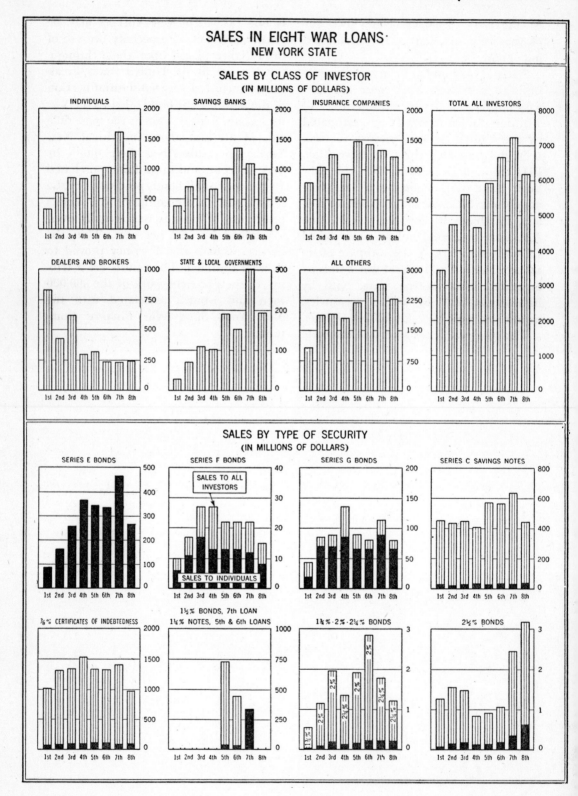

SALES IN EIGHT WAR LOANS·
NEW YORK STATE

SALES BY CLASS OF INVESTOR
(IN MILLIONS OF DOLLARS)

SALES BY TYPE OF SECURITY
(IN MILLIONS OF DOLLARS)

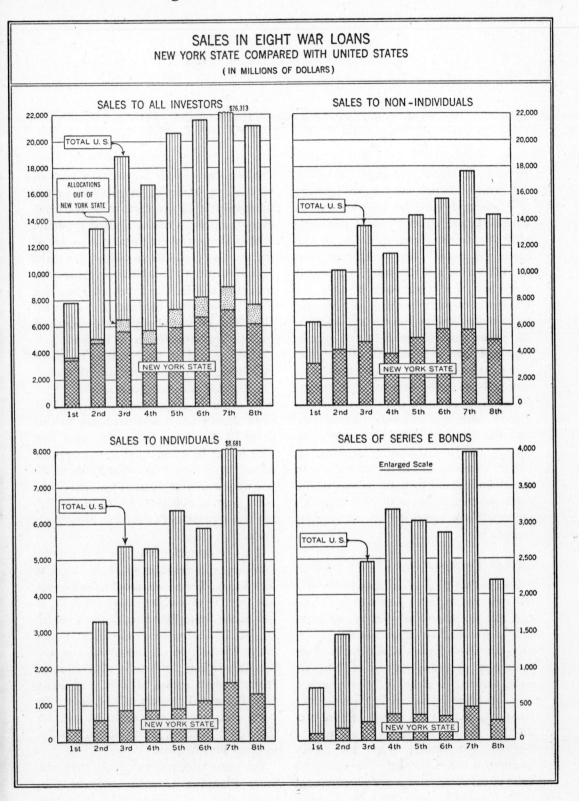

SALES IN EIGHT WAR LOANS
NEW YORK STATE COMPARED WITH UNITED STATES
(IN MILLIONS OF DOLLARS)

CHAPTER THREE

Production for War

THE extraordinary capacity of the United States for producing weapons and material of war was the decisive factor, although by no means the only one, in the ultimate defeat of Germany and Japan. Next in importance to the recruiting and training of a superb army was the equipment of that and other armies with weapons and supplies superior to those of the enemy. This was the prime task of the men and women who remained at home. All other home-front activities were aimed directly or indirectly at facilitating its performance. Other types of work were frequently essential, such as the production of food and the necessary industrial raw materials or the provision of transportation, but they were means to the ultimate end: armament second to none. It was in this field, production for war, that the State of New York compiled an outstanding record.

ANALYSIS OF THE PROBLEM

The fall of France in May, 1940, with the subsequent call of President Roosevelt for fifty thousand planes and capacity to produce an equal number annually, effectively launched the national rearmament program. As one of the principal industrial states of the country, New York was immediately plunged into what was at the time called defense production. Since initial demands of the Federal government were for heavy weapons it was natural that the first contacts of the Army and Navy procurement officers would be with those large industrial concerns with whom they had always done business. In relation to the total volume of contracts to be let, however, these firms had a limited capacity. Unless the entire productive capacity of the country could be employed, it would be impossible to handle the rearmament program within the limits of the time that Washington believed to be available. This seems to have been understood in New York State from the beginning.

How would it be possible to effect quickly such a gigantic mobilization with the slightest possible dislocation?

In order to understand what the first steps should be, it was necessary to discover in detail just what the State had with which to work. That is, to ascertain what plants were idle, what kinds of labor were available in what localities, and what types of machines useful in producing war equipment existed in New York State.

This information was not available in 1940 and the problem was how to get it in a hurry. To whom should the Governor turn in this emergency? Initially, it was to the State Planning Council under Dr. M. P. Catherwood, the Joint Legislative Committee on Industrial and Labor Conditions under the direction of Assemblyman Irving M. Ives, and many able industrial leaders of the State. In particular, one private organization, Associated Industries, Incorporated, was interested and helpful.

For some time prior to June, 1940, the State Planning Council and the Ives Committee had been working together.

The Council had undergone extensive reorganization the year before and was in an excellent position to undertake the tasks which the Governor decided to give it. At a meeting in the Executive Office attended by representatives of both the Ives Committee and the State Planning Council, the Council received definite instructions to devote its efforts primarily to the defense program. In particular, it was authorized to discover what might be made available to the Federal government in the way of production facilities and labor. Two surveys were begun in July, one of idle plants, the other of labor trends in one hundred of the State's principal industries. Likewise projected was a directory listing manufacturing firms with five or more employees and selected nonmanufacturing establishments. In October, a trial of a survey method for measuring productive capacity was conducted in the Buffalo area by the Council, aided by officers of the Advisory Council for National Defense and Associated Industries, Incorporated. This survey yielded valuable information for the later machine-tool inventory conducted in the spring of 1941. In organizing these surveys, the State Planning Council received advice and assistance from some of the nation's foremost manufacturing concerns.

While the Council's studies were in progress, on August 1, 1940, Governor Lehman appointed the New York State Council of National Defense[1] to advise him in all matters connected with the State's defense program. On this Council were a number of prominent manufacturers and businessmen personally famil-iar with the problems of securing increased industrial production.[2] Their contributions to discussions at Defense Council meetings influenced the formulation of major defense production policies which were subsequently carried out by the State Planning Council and its successor, the Division of Commerce.[3]

It became clear to the members of the Defense Council that many manufacturers engaged in civilian production must ultimately convert to war production; that eventually the government might have to apply pressure and force the change, but until that time came everything possible should be done to encourage New York manufacturers to accept government contracts. It was also obvious that if the national rearmament program were to remain on schedule, the efforts already made in the fall of 1940 by a few large concerns to subcontract part of their work must be expanded enormously. Not for patriotic reasons alone was the Defense Council interested in aiding this expansion in every way possible; it realized also that subcontracting would help to reduce most quickly the residue of unemployment still persisting inside the State's borders even in 1940. Complete utilization of existing plant facilities was therefore an aim proper for both State and Federal governments. Once taken, this position was maintained vigorously.[4] Not only would the building of new plants require time and valuable materials otherwise more directly available for war production; but also by dislocating the existing supply of labor and necessitating the establishment of additional community services such as

---

[1] The name was immediately shortened to *Defense Council* through usage. After Pearl Harbor it was changed by the War Emergency Act to *New York State War Council*.

[2] Mr. John Hancock had been a Naval Officer during World War I in charge of Naval Purchasing. Mr. Thomas A. Morgan, president of the Sperry Corporation, and Mr. Charles E. Wilson, president of the General Electric Company, were both letting subcontracts by the end of 1940.

[3] The Division of Commerce was created April, 1941. One of its three bureaus was the Bureau of Planning.

[4] A proposal by the Army to concentrate on building a large number of plants back of a line 250 miles from the coast would have hurt New York industry and prevented the use of much available equipment. It was accordingly opposed by the Council and exceptions were allowed in some instances.

schools, roads, public utilities, and housing it would create a vast number of secondary social problems.

ROLE OF THE DEPARTMENT OF COMMERCE

The ideas just outlined were carried to Washington early in January, 1941, by the Governor and members of the Defense Council and placed before the heads of the Office of Production Management. It was from one of the resulting conferences, after effective use of the information then available from the surveys of the State Planning Council, that there came General Knudsen's request for the State to embark upon a survey of facilities for metal working. This survey was assigned to the new Division of Commerce which in completing the task made use of the services of the local defense councils.[1] The results of this survey were successfully used by the Division to furnish prime contractors with information on the location of the machine tools they so badly needed for the manufacture of parts. This referral service, however, was at the time too slow to take care of the mounting volume of contracts being let in the State.

This bottleneck was eliminated after the Division of Commerce developed the idea of production clinics. These clinics consisted of meetings of prime contractors with potential subcontractors. The former listed the parts and products they needed to have made, and the latter stated which they were in a position to produce. The first such clinic was held early in April in Binghamton on an experimental scale. Its success seemed to warrant wide extension and the Governor gave the Division permission to try one in Buffalo. This one also was successful. Others followed in Rochester, in Syracuse, and in Albany. The numbers of manufacturers in attendance grew steadily until a climax was reached in

New York on August 13 and 14. At the first meeting in Manhattan, 42 prime contractors, 24 government agencies, and 836 potential subcontractors were present; in Brooklyn on the following day 36 prime contractors, 24 government agencies, and 600 potential subcontractors participated. Officials of the Office of Production Management who attended the New York City clinics were so impressed with these "marriage bureaus" that they started using the idea on a national scale. The importance of the clinics resulted primarily from their timing. Later they lost their value, for once contact had been made between a prime contractor and a number of subcontractors adequate for his needs, his interest in further clinics disappeared.

The net effect of the work of the Defense Council and its primary agent in the field of industry, the Division of Commerce, was to put New York State at the forefront of defense production, both in its initial rate of expansion and in dollar volume of contracts let. In many respects the early role of the Division of Commerce was nothing more nor less than that of a State agency, through which New York manufacturers found employment with Uncle Sam. Its services to the businessmen in New York State expanded continuously in 1941 and thereafter, and its facilities increased correspondingly.

In January, 1942, with financial assistance from the Defense Council, the Division of Commerce opened a Washington office[2] for the purpose of following more closely the Army and Navy production requirements and helping government procurement officers and New York businessmen arrange mutually satisfactory contracts. A New York City office was opened in August of the same year to consider the unemployment problem and work out measures to help bring

---

[1] Established Sept. 22, 1940.

[2] The Division of Commerce became the Department of Commerce April 1, 1944.

that city's share of defense contracts into line with the national average. Operations increased so rapidly in both offices that in 1943 expansion of facilities became imperative.

The activities of the Division of Commerce in the field of production may be broken down into four principal types:

Furnishing information and acting as a liaison agency between the Federal government and the private manufacturer in the letting of war contracts.

Acting as consultant to individual firms beset by war-related, industry-wide problems and faced with the necessity for making major adjustments.

Investigating the social and economic needs of industrial areas and formulating practical programs for the development and maintenance of essential social services in individual communities.

Promotional and research activities resulting in miscellaneous publications.

In 1943, with the production program in high gear, the Division added a fifth function when it began to lay the groundwork for its attack upon the problem of reconversion to a peacetime economy.

All functions of the Division of Commerce drew heavily upon its files of current information and upon the abilities of the members of its research staff. Reference has been made to several inventories of production activities prepared in 1940 and 1941. To these in subsequent years were added a cumulative list of defense contracts awarded to New York State firms, and a cumulative list of all new defense plants. The Washington office constantly furnished information to the business agencies and private concerns of the State on government procurement procedures and on production policies and needs. Manufacturers were informed whenever advantageous opportunities became available. In turn, the State office supplied government officials with information on prospective sources of supply for all sorts of war materials.

While this liaison work was for a short time conducted entirely by means of mimeographed releases, after the defense clinics had served their purpose there developed a growing amount of work with individual companies. The division was especially helpful to individuals in securing government contracts at times when curtailment of materials needed for their civilian production threatened to force them out of business. It helped with new financing, with the discovery of substitute materials to permit continued civilian production, or with conversion to the manufacture of related products for war. Carpet manufacturers were guided into the making of canvas, duck, and blankets; jewelry manufacturers into jewel bearings for instruments; precious-stone cutters into slit-quartz for oscillators; a watch firm into electrical precision parts; and a number of firms into the making of surgical instruments. In many instances, before reliable conclusions could be reached it was necessary to make a brief analysis of the chief characteristics of an industry and of the probable effects upon it of Federal orders. Industries thus surveyed included boots and shoes, leather gloves, canning, rubber, textiles and clothing, and wire and steel.

Some areas of the State presented problems which were broader than those of a single industry. The Niagara frontier was the only critical labor shortage area according to the standards of the War Manpower Commission. Its labor shortage had developed in 1941 and continued to trouble State and Federal officials until 1944. New York City, on the other hand, remained until late in 1943 the primary labor pool of the State, with unemployment rolls increasing during 1941 and the first half of 1942. This problem reached such proportions that the Governor presented a detailed report on war contracts and unemployment in the city to the President of the United States, and on the basis of this report a commit-

tee of top Federal officials was appointed
to cooperate with the Defense Council in
an effort to alleviate conditions. Marked
results were shown toward the third
quarter of 1942 by a drop of eighty thousand in registered unemployed. It was
not, however, until 1943, after Governor
Dewey had ordered a detailed survey of
1000 distressed plants in the metropolitan
area, and the results of the survey had
been presented to the smaller War Plants
Division of the War Production Board,
that a wider distribution of war work
and of essential civilian production requirements began to affect a rapid reduction in the abnormal number of registered unemployed.

Wartime unemployment in New York
City, as a matter of fact, had been one
of the issues of the 1942 gubernatorial
campaign. One of Mr. Dewey's campaign
speeches had been devoted entirely to the
need for vigorous action to put the unused manpower and equipment of the
city and State fully into the war. He cited
the fact that while other parts of the
country were looking for workers, New
York City alone had four hundred thousand unemployed, and pledged prompt
remedial steps if he were elected. Within
a week after his election as Governor, Mr.
Dewey appointed a special committee
headed by John W. Hanes, formerly
Under Secretary of the Treasury, to study
business and employment opportunities
in New York City. Other members were
David Dubinsky, president of the International Ladies Garment Workers Union; Delos Walker, Vice-President of R.
H. Macy, and Elliott V. Bell, later State
Superintendent of Banks.

The committee's report was a masterly
analysis of the New York situation. It
pointed out the worsening competitive
position of the city and declared that "a
concerted effort" would be required to
reverse a declining economic trend. Into
that effort would have to go the intelligence and energies of the best minds
among the city's leaders in industry, com-

merce, and labor. Effective aid would also
have to come from the State.

In its conclusions, the committee recommended that the Division of Commerce become a full-fledged department
with greatly expanded functions. It ad-
vocated strengthening the Washington
office into a veritable "ministry to Washington from the Empire State." Along
the same line, in view of the importance
to the State of the economy of New York
City, it strongly suggested the establishment of a branch office in the city to
specialize in the problems of the metropolis. A number of other specific recommendations pointed the way toward a
more intensive effort by the State to secure the cooperation of industry, labor,
commerce, and the civic authorities to remove the handicaps holding back business and employment in the City of New
York, and to develop a program for encouraging the future expansion of its
economic life.

The increase in the tempo of State action following the change in administration was felt in every branch of government. The vigorous handling of farm
problems is outlined in Chapter VI. In
the sphere of industrial war production
the incident of the heat exchanger shells
is typical. On January 29, the Governor
received a telegram from the president
of the Foster Wheeler Corporation of
New York City revealing that one of its
subcontractors in Syracuse had fifteen of
these shells, which act as condensers to
cool gasoline. In the process of welding
they had lost their shapes, and they required rerolling before being shipped.
The shells were badly needed for a new
oil refinery in Port Arthur, Texas, scheduled to turn out 336,000 gallons a day of
100-octane aviation gasoline. For lack of
the shells, completion of the refinery was
already two weeks behind. The telegram
requested the use of the facilities of the
Barge Canal Terminal in Syracuse which
had the only available pyramid roller in
the area. Under the War Emergency Act,

however, State-owned equipment could not be placed at the disposal of private industry, no matter how urgent the need.

The Governor and his advisors met immediately with the leaders of the Legislature. All agreed that the State should act to speed the final completion of the shells. An amendment to the War Emergency Act was drafted conferring upon the Governor power to make State-owned equipment available, for compensation, to private corporations engaged in war production. Passage of the bill was pledged in advance. That evening representatives of the Foster Wheeler Corporation and its subcontractor, the Butler Corporation, went to Albany. Agreement was reached covering rental of the State's facilities and the payment of workmen's compensation insurance charges. All that was on a Friday. On Saturday morning the condensers were moved into the Barge Canal Terminal and the work was started. The following Monday the necessary legislation was unanimously passed by the Legislature and became law. The work was finished in the Syracuse shop within five days, and the condensers were installed in the Texas refinery within ten days after the emergency had come to the attention of the Governor.

The detailed representations in the interest of one thousand distressed plants in New York City, made by the Governor to the Smaller War Plants Division of the War Production Board, have already been mentioned (see page 56). In this matter, the Division of Commerce had acted as the fact-finding agency. Additional burdens were soon placed on this division, whose Commissioner, Dr. M. P. Catherwood, was retained in the new administration as one of the Governor's principal advisers on industrial development. Early in the 1943 session, legislation was passed granting to the Division special funds to institute a State-wide program in the interest of business expansion. Approval was also secured for the establishment of an office in New York City as recommended by the Hanes Report.

For the second time the 1943 Legislature gave unanimous approval to a constitutional amendment for the creation of a Department of Commerce in the State government. This proposal, originating in 1942 with the Joint Legislative Committee on Industrial and Labor Conditions, was passed by the people in November, 1943, and enacted into law by the 1944 Legislature. The new department was the first to be created since 1927.

Early in September, 1943, Commissioner Catherwood reported to the Governor a marked improvement in business conditions and employment in New York City. Not only had there been a substantial increase in the value of war contracts awarded the State, but this improvement had been shared by the city. Not only were its average monthly employment figures and weekly pay rolls higher, but between the first six months of 1942 and the first six months of 1943 unemployment, as measured by the average number of claimants per month receiving unemployment insurance benefits, had declined 62.7 per cent. Compared with June, 1942, home relief cases for June, 1943, had dropped 51 per cent. Business failures for the first six months of 1943 had dropped 47.1 per cent from the corresponding period in 1942, New York City, and with it the State, was finally approaching 100 per cent participation in the war.

Studies of numerous communities which had expanded rapidly as a result of war contracts were begun in 1943 and continued in 1944, anticipating the appearance of postwar problems. Here again the problems were broader than a single industry, broader even than any single aspect either of civilian or war production. The Department of Commerce went into such matters as industrial sites, resources, transportation, power, labor supply, and other factors which would have an important bearing upon the ability of those communities to handle successfully the tasks of economic reconversion, and of the reemployment of returning soldiers and war workers. Among the communities studied were Port Henry, Watertown, Elmira, Lockport, Rome, Schenectady, Buffalo, and Syracuse.

These studies marked a definite transition from the original task of expanding war production for the Federal government to a second task, that of postwar industrial maintenance and development which, it was anticipated, would devolve upon the Department toward the close of the war.

The spirit of this new departure was indicated by the title of a booklet, *A Man Can't Live on Glory,* published in 1944 and distributed to over 100,000 New York firms. Full employment, nearly 6 million jobs in private employment alone, it said, would make possible the successful integration of approximately 1 million returning servicemen and 2 million war workers. To make sure that New York would be able to maintain its competitive position in the nation's peacetime economy, the department began to investigate opportunities in foreign trade, new processes, new products, and new materials. In March, 1944, tenday surveys were made in Warren, Ulster, and Dutchess counties to learn the principal industry, the chief characteristics of the population, the type of labor supply, purchasing power, transportation facilities, and other resources. As the war neared its close, this type of study was continued in other areas and became standard procedure. Increased emphasis was placed upon manufacturing and retailing trends, upon possible future markets, and upon opportunities for business expansion. Unused plants were visited and new firms interrogated to discover why they had located in particular communities.

To encourage the maintenance of full

production, to expand facilities within the State, and to attract new business from outside, the department inaugurated a many-sided industrial development program. It presented the innumerable opportunities for business in New York through a well-illustrated graphic brochure, *New York Means Business,* which, along with the services of the department, was featured in a program of national advertising.

The relatively sudden ending of the war with Japan, August 14, 1945, immediately posed in its acute stage the problem of reconversion[1] which the Department of Commerce had been anticipating for at least two years. A conference with the Governor, shortly after V-J Day, led to his appointment, on August 20, of a State Reconversion Service Agency composed of Dr. M. P. Catherwood, chairman, Charles H. Sells, Superintendent of Public Works, and Edward Corsi, Industrial Commissioner. On September 20, in order to speed the program, the War Council, at the suggestion of Governor Dewey, allocated $50,000 to the Division of Commerce.

The purpose of the Reconversion Service Agency was to help business convert speedily and soundly to civilian production. At the first meeting of the agency, August 20, it was decided that the Labor Department should take a census of the amount and the effects of layoffs in employment in the major industrial centers of the State. This would afford precise information on available manpower. It was also decided to offer New York State industry all possible assistance in procuring materials and machinery needed for civilian manufacturing. An announcement was made of the start of a five-year 840-million-dollar public-works program; at the same time, thirty new unemployment insurance offices were set up at different points in the State to

---

[1] For a fuller discussion of this subject, see Chapter IX.

cushion the shock of unemployment due to unavoidable temporary layoffs.

Two weeks later, on September 6, Governor Dewey began a series of moves to hasten reconversion to civilian use of forty-one large government war plants built in New York State during the war at a cost of 150 million dollars. These plants, containing 16 million square feet of floor space had, at peak production, employed over two hundred thousand workers.

Another move on the part of the Reconversion Agency was the appointment of a Woman's Council under Miss Jane Todd, Deputy State Commerce Commissioner, to secure through government planning "better job visibility for women." The Council was to coordinate in some central spot by means of panel surveys and a series of clinics information about New York's women and their business and job opportunities. Studies were also undertaken on job possibilities in the fields of housing, transportation, science, food, and domestic service.

Still another step in the Reconversion Program was an invitation from the Governor to manufacturers in other states, setting forth the advantages of the State as a location for business. Among the inducements listed were moderate taxes, New York's excellent record of labor stability, its unexcelled transportation facilities, and its proximity to the largest retail market in the country. The full support of one of the best equipped departments of commerce was promised in providing full and concrete information on available sites. Resulting inquiries were followed up by special representatives of the department.

As a final step in the Reconversion Program, Governor Dewey announced, November 8, 1945, the New York State Plan for Small Business Expansion. The war had closed 100,000 small businesses in New York alone, and their replacement was essential to the general prosperity. Since small businesses comprised 90 per cent of the concerns of the State, and since small businessmen and women were natural leaders in their communities, it was essential either that they re-enter business themselves, or that their places be taken by others.

The purpose of the plan was to create new job opportunities through the reestablishment and expansion of the basic structure of the State's private economy. Sound and experienced counsel was to be made available to veterans and all others wishing to start their own enterprises, as well as to owners of existing establishments desirous of improving their positions. In cooperation with the regional offices of the Department of Commerce, a field staff was made available to the communities. With the assistance of ten attractively designed booklets available for free distribution in the amount of 1 million copies, these men were able to supply information on such important factors in business success as methods of cost accounting, modern advertising and display methods, market conditions, and technical information as to new products, new processes, and new materials.

In addition to its regular information and liaison services, and its special assistance to individual businesses and communities, the department engaged in research and as a result produced a number of miscellaneous publications. As an aid to State and local officials and private business, a *War Agency Handbook* was brought out in 1942 and revised in 1943, which described State and Federal agencies engaged in the prosecution of the war. In cooperation with the Office of Price Administration, several bulletins were prepared on rent-control regulations and circulated among chambers of commerce and local war councils. A broad survey of aviation and its postwar possibilities was undertaken, out of which evolved a Statewide pattern for subsequent development. Investigations of mineral deposits in New York State led to the resumption of operations in a number of abandoned workings and the opening of other deposits in connection with national defense requirements. At a number of points the Department was able to facilitate these proceedings.

In short, the war period presented a unique opportunity for usefulness of which the leadership of the department took full advantage, thereby deserving completely the confidence reposed in it by two successive State administrations.

THE PROBLEM OF INDUSTRIAL MANPOWER

No matter how well the War Council and the Department of Commerce might have functioned to bring government procurement agents, prime contractors, and subcontractors together, it would have made little difference in the long-run development of the war production program if the labor force available for war production had been insufficient in numbers, ineffectively trained, poorly housed, undernourished, or antagonistic to its employers. The contract between the government and the manufacturers was but the beginning of the production process. It was the point of departure — an industrial looking-glass through which the employer lightly stepped — only to be confronted with another world of secondary problems in the fields of labor management, industrial relations, housing, health, and morale. Any discussion of New York State's war production effort must accordingly include consideration of the manner in which these related problems were met and solved.

New York State with 10.2 per cent of the country's total population comprised the second of the War Manpower Commission Regions. In addition to Regional Headquarters in New York City, there were six area offices located respectively in Albany, Utica, Syracuse, Rochester, Buffalo, and Elmira. Scattered throughout the State and also under authority of the War Manpower Commission were nearly seventy-five United States Employment Service offices, with over twenty-five additional branches. It was the responsibility of these two agencies, and up to December, 1941, of the New York State Employment Service, to see that war production in the State of New York was not impeded for lack of adequate supplies of labor. According to the 1940 census, the State had a labor force of over 6 million persons, of which 3.52 million men and 1.45 million women were employed, and 1 million or slightly more than 16.3 per cent were unemployed or employed on public emergency work. With the inauguration of the rearmament program, however, everything changed.

The principal labor problem in 1940 was to discover from among the ranks of those still unemployed the right men for the essential jobs. In that year, the State's unemployed labor pool was still of considerable magnitude. In June, home relief rolls still numbered approximately 265,000 individuals, and in the same month the number of job seekers registered with the State Employment Service topped 675,000. This picture, however, began to change rapidly in the last half of the year. Between June and November, New York State manufacturers received over a billion dollars worth of war contracts. In this respect the State was third in the nation, although not primarily a heavy industry area. It is little wonder that relief rolls began to drop, that by the end of 1940 the number of registered job seekers was down to 505,000, and that women were actively seeking work through the State Employment Service. Total 1940 placements in all industry were reported by the Employment Service to have reached 318,000, a 58 per cent gain over the preceding year. Correspondingly, it also reported a 52 per cent drop in placements on public projects for the same period, and in November, for the first time since 1929, the

Labor Department's index of factory employment topped the 1929 level at 100.

To take care of the problem of finding the proper number of workers for defense production were the usual number and types of employment agencies actively in operation in New York State. Every manufacturing concern had its own private employment office, which drew prospects from a fairly limited area. Independent private agencies were numerous. The State Employment Service, functioning up to December 19, 1941, under the direction of the Industrial Commissioner of the Department of Labor, had over ninety branch offices throughout the State. On file in these offices were registrations for all workers covered by unemployment insurance as well as those on Works Progress Administration. All registrations were broken down into skilled, semiskilled, and unskilled categories and likewise typed according to the newly adopted standard classifications for jobs comprising nearly thirty thousand titles. The files were constantly checked and rechecked, and recruiting was consistently maintained through radio and magazine advertising and in cooperation with unions and nonprofit employment agencies. Primary emphasis was placed upon skilled labor, especially machine designers, skilled machinists, tool and die makers, molders, sheet metal workers, loftsmen, coppersmiths, and ship fitters. Secondary skills needed by the defense industries were discovered in many registrants who had primarily wished to do something else. In addition, employers and the schools were helping in the recruitment of men for training.

The Federal government was also taking an active part in the employment field through the Works Progress Administration, the National Youth Administration, and the United States Employment Service. These agencies all cooperated in supplying to factories the necessary skilled, semiskilled, and unskilled workers. Shortly after Pearl Harbor, on December 19, the New York State Employment Service was taken over by the United States Employment Service, which was itself under the War Manpower Commission. It was a fortunate coincidence that the War Manpower Commission Director for Region II, Mrs. Anna M. Rosenberg, was already a member of the New York State War Council, and was thus able to bring to the Council an over-all picture of the manpower situation. In return she was able to keep in touch with the methods employed by the Council to ease the labor shortages created by the war emergency.

The task of the War Manpower Commission was fourfold:

1. To recruit people not already working
2. To transfer workers from less to more essential jobs
3. To keep people on essential jobs
4. To get out the greatest possible production with the number and types of workers available

To accomplish its purpose the Commission set up a series of manpower controls within the framework of which all labor movements henceforth took place. These controls were as follows:

1. Imposition of employment ceilings on all firms in a given area.

Three kinds of ceilings were used: (*a*) a ceiling which permitted expansion of the labor force; (*b*) one which allowed maintenance of the existing level; (*c*) one which required a reduction in the number of workers. New York City was the only area without these ceilings. Buffalo, Rochester, and Albany had ceilings for both males and females, while Elmira, Syracuse, and Utica had them for males only.

2. The granting by Area Manpower Priority Committees of priority referrals to companies manufacturing vital war materials. This would require that the United States Employment Service re-

cruit intensively for openings to which priorities were given.

3. Manpower Priorities Committees, composed of representatives of the armed services, government agencies, and one or two state agencies, were in a position to advise the War Manpower Commission Area Director on a plant-by-plant basis. Action on priorities and ceilings was usually taken upon their recommendations.

4. The imposition of a forty-eight-hour minimum work week for the purpose of releasing for essential war work those no longer needed under the system of longer hours in less essential work. This was not too successful.

5. The classification of areas into four groups according to the extent of the labor shortage in each. This served as a guide to procurement agencies which would place contracts where labor was most plentiful. Of the twenty-one classified labor market areas in Region II as of January, 1944, two were classified in Group 1 as areas of either actual or anticipated acute labor shortages; five in Group 2 as areas of slight shortages or of anticipated balance between supply and demand; ten in Group 3 as areas of balanced supply and demand or slight surplus; and four in Group 4 as areas of considerable labor surplus.

Controls were operated by War Manpower Commission officials, although decisions were made by them only with the advice of the Labor-Management Advisory Committees, of which there were one for each of the seven major areas, one for the region as a whole, and one for farming. Controls alone, however, would never have been sufficient to provide an adequate supply of labor. By June 30, 1943, the approximate peak of the war effort, not only had nine hundred thousand of the 1 million persons unemployed on April 1, 1940, been absorbed, but in various ways the labor force had been expanded. Instead of the 5 million persons at work on April 1, 1940, by June 30, 1943, there were 6 million persons at work in the State, and in addition approximately 1 million other persons in the armed services. Where these extra people came from and by what methods they were added to the labor force is discussed in the following sections.

HOW WAS THE LABOR FORCE EXPANDED?

New Yorkers can well be proud that by virtue of constant application to specific problems as they arose and by the use of ingenuity and the capacity for improvisation that Americans inherently seem to possess, the State avoided the permanent development of a drastic labor shortage. This does not mean that there were no shortages at all, but rather that the problems presented were not allowed to remain permanently unsolved. How was it possible that at no time during the period of the war was essential production seriously curtailed for want of the right kinds of labor?

It goes without saying that private industry did the best it could to help itself by taking measures to expand production through the complete utilization both of its labor force and its plant facilities. In many cases it became the rule to have three shifts, thereby providing twenty-four-hour operation of available equipment and obviating the necessity for an increase in plant capacity. Overtime was practically universal. Late in 1940 and early in 1941 industry also became conscious of the need for training workers on the job to perform more difficult operations. This "on-the-job" training, or "training within industry," was encouraged by the State Employment Service and the War Manpower Commission, and was actively aided by the State Education Department as a logical responsibility of private corporations. The result of this training was in many cases the upgrading or promotion of the employees as soon as they had demonstrated the capacity to handle their new jobs.

In a number of skilled trades the training period required was so long as to make it virtually impossible to expand the number of workers in a sufficiently short time. The only way this difficulty could be met was by breaking down the job into a number of steps which could be performed by semiskilled workers under the supervision of a skilled man. A typical example of this was the occupation of lens grinder. This subdivision of jobs was a process which in many cases successfully broke bottlenecks arising from skilled labor shortages.

Employers were also forced to change their attitude with regard to certain types of labor, and the war consequently resulted in an influx of certain classes of workers hitherto regarded either as undesirable or inefficient.[1] The labor force was further expanded after December 7, 1941, by the relaxation of employment age limits, both statutory[2] and self-imposed. The forty-year-age deadline on the hiring of new employees was dropped and employers subsequently discovered it to have been largely an imaginary difficulty. In fact, the entire depression-born concept of a labor buyer's market had to be scrapped. The 1940 census showed 1,453,000 women employed in New York State. By April 1, 1945, this figure had risen to more than 2 million, over 34 per cent of the State's entire labor force. By 1943 and 1944, the demand for women in industry was so strong that in order to speed war production to the utmost, Governor Dewey and the State War Council embarked upon a 2-million-dollar Child Care Program[3] to allow women with children to remain in war production.

Not only were women drawn into war production, but also a number of persons from occupations formerly completely dissociated from the world of business

[1] Discussed more extensively on pp. 67-69.
[2] Discussed more extensively on pp. 65-66.
[3] See Chapter VIII.

found employment in war plants. Students and teachers in high schools and colleges, attracted by higher salaries and stimulated by a desire to do something tangible to help win the war, gave up summer vacations and entered defense plants. After the first few weeks of muscular adjustment had passed, they proved to be intelligent and satisfactory workers. High salaries also attracted farm laborers in large numbers. This group was particularly welcome as they were in many respects semiskilled in the use of their hands, and used to hard work and long hours.

A number of racial groups were not at first accorded equal opportunities for participating in war production work. The problem was recognized early in 1941, and it was largely due to the work of the State War Council and its Committee on Discrimination in Employment that these cases were taken in hand early and the integration of such special groups into the labor force brought about through persuasion and education. In fact, through the leadership of the War Council, the State government was able in many ways to help with the expansion of the labor force.

STATE AID IN EXPANDING THE LABOR FORCE

Measures taken by the State to aid private employers through an expansion of the labor force were numerous and varied. Especially noteworthy were (1) vocational training for war production workers, (2) the appointment by the State War Council of a Committee on Discrimination in Employment to integrate minority groups into the war production program, (3) the authorization of the Industrial Commissioner to grant dispensations from the labor laws where maximum war production was being hindered, and (4) certain miscellaneous activities of various State departments in the fields of accident prevention, industrial hygiene, health, and nutrition.[1]

It was apparent at the very beginning of the nation's program of rearmament that the demand for skilled and semiskilled labor would greatly exceed the initial supply, which during the depression years had undergone drastic reduction. Under the circumstances, to the recruiting and placing of workers the State hastened to add training. On July 1, 1940, the State Education Department with financial assistance from the State and Federal Government inaugurated a training program for industrial war production workers under the direction of Oakley Furney, Assistant Commissioner for Vocational Education. During the five-year period of operation, under this program approximately 1 million men and women received training for industrial employment at the public high schools and technical schools of the State. The engineering colleges of the State also conducted with Federal funds an Engineering, Science, Management, War Training Program.

Full advantage was taken of the excellent mechanical equipment available in the public high schools for training in the more important trades and industrial occupations, as well as of their large number of trained teachers. The program was built around the staff of the Bureau of Industrial and Technical Education which was expanded to supervise training programs in over 150 communities. Funds in excess of 3.5 million dollars were allocated to New York State by the United States Office of Education for the purchase of shop equipment. Of this amount, 60 per cent was used by local boards of education to extend their vocational-school equipment for war training. While a majority of the schools were operated by local boards of education, thirty-six were under the direct supervision of the Bureau of Industrial and

Technical Education. Eight of the latter were at universities and technical schools.

The program of Vocational Training for War Production Workers was divided into preemployment and supplementary courses. Preemployment and "refresher" training prepared individuals to enter essential industries for the first time, or after a period of considerable inactivity; supplementary training was given to persons already employed to enable them to take on work of a more advanced nature in connection with their regular job, or to shift to approximately similar work in industries manufacturing essential materials. Until 1942, supplementary training was much more important than preemployment training. Then for about a year, from the middle of 1942 to the middle of 1943, the emphasis was placed upon preemployment training. With employment at its peak, the tables were again reversed owing to increased emphasis upon inplant and paid-trainee training.

In-plant training consisted of special courses given in shops rather than in schools, where workers developed skills directly needed in the performance of their immediate tasks. Paid-trainee courses were developed for workers already employed, who were sent to schools for additional training and paid for the period of their training. Junior training courses were conducted for young persons still in high school to enable them to accept employment during vacations and upon graduation. Boys were thus prepared for employment in essential industries unless called into the armed services, while most girls were free to continue working for the duration of the war. With the help of representatives of management and organized labor, special courses were prepared for small groups of employees with specific training needs. Examples of such were courses in welding for plumbers, elements of electronics for union electricians, and the care and maintenance of certain types of indus-

---

[1] For nutrition see Chapter VI.

trial electronic equipment and stoker operation for railroad fireman. Fifty-nine training manuals were developed by the Bureau of Industrial and Technical Education with a total circulation of over two hundred thousand copies. Distribution of these monographs included the forty-eight states and ten foreign countries.

In many plants the shortage of supervisory personnel made the expansion of production difficult. The preemployment courses prepared large numbers of men and women to perform specialized phases of skilled occupations, but the influx of large numbers of these semiskilled workers made necessary a larger increase in supervisors. The Bureau of Industrial Service developed courses in industries for supervisors, foremen, and personnel managers, in which during the period of the war approximately sixty thousand men were trained.

The increasing number of women who received training and employment as a result of these courses is significant. They revealed superior adaptability and their performance of essential work in such fields as light assembly, aircraft, inspection, tracing, radio, machine shop, and welding demonstrated unusual skill in work requiring finger dexterity. Women thus took full advantage of the opportunity to prepare themselves for war work and made a remarkable contribution to winning the war. Vocational training was thus an absolutely essential instrument for producing quickly an adequate supply of skilled and semiskilled workers for those industries whose needs for special personnel could have been met in no other way.

WAR EMERGENCY DISPENSATIONS

Another measure which had the effect of expanding the labor force was the granting of dispensations from existing labor laws. No sooner had the nation been plunged into war than the War and Navy Departments urged employers to ensure maximum production of essential war materials by full utilization of labor and machinery on a twenty-four-hour day and seven-day week basis. On December 11, 1941, the Secretaries of War and of the Navy sent Governor Lehman a telegram, urging him

To use your authority to prevent . . . peacetime restrictions from interfering in any way with maximum possible production in the war industries in your state.

The following day, the Governor called a conference to set up machinery for relaxing, pending the convening of the Legislature, the peacetime restrictions of the Labor Laws. The Lieutenant-Governor, the Industrial Commissioner, the legislative leaders of both political parties, the president of the New York State Federation of Labor, and the president of the New York State Industrial Council (CIO) were all present at this meeting.

It was agreed that although temporary relaxation of the Labor Laws was imperative in order to meet immediate production demands, nevertheless basic labor standards must be maintained if maximum war production was to be reached. British industrial experience had shown that when work weeks were lengthened excessively in the dark days following Dunkerque, after the initial patriotic spurt output was considerably lowered through fatigue, industrial accidents, and work stoppage. It was to avoid such adverse effects on production in New York State that the Industrial Commissioner was empowered to grant dispensations upon application from individual employers, only when it could be shown that the restrictions imposed by the Labor Laws interfered with maximum production. This emergency procedure was approved by the Legislature on January 28, 1942, to apply retroactively to cover all such decisions of the Industrial Commissioner prior to the enactment of the law.

Specifically, Chapter 4 of the Laws of 1942, known as the War Emergency Dispensation Act, gave the New York State Industrial Commissioner the right to suspend the operation of the Labor Laws for a six-month period in all industries manufacturing war materials, and to permit both men and women over eighteen to work longer hours, on night shifts, or as much as seven days per week. As subsequently amended by Chapter 315 of the Laws of 1943, these provisions were extended to include essential civilian industries as well. Because of public realization of the importance of maintaining child labor standards, no variations were at first authorized for minors under eighteen. However, in view of the mounting pressure of a critical labor market and the increasing number of minors employed, an amendment was enacted in 1943 which gave the New York State War Council power to authorize the Industrial Commissioner to grant dispensations for sixteen- and seventeen-year-old minors.

Throughout, the act was administered on behalf of the Industrial Commissioner by the War Emergency Dispensation Committee. Well over 40,000 decisions involving over 7,800 plants and more than 650,000 workers were rendered with but 19 appeals. The reason for the small number of appeals lay in the closeness of the relations maintained with the Army and Navy Procurement Divisions, the care with which each claim was investigated, and to labor-management conferences prior to granting dispensations.

The provision as to minors under eighteen was very carefully administered by a special committee of the State War Council under Assemblyman Irving M. Ives, composed of representatives of both labor and industry working with the War Emergency Committee. Dispensations were granted to individual employers only, never to entire industries. Furthermore, they were granted only after careful investigation by representatives of the State Department of Labor, and only upon approval of the two labor leaders who were members of the War Council. Of all plants receiving dispensations, three-fourths were engaged in manufacturing. Of all workers covered by dispensations, 96 per cent were factory workers with the greatest number in the metals and machinery group. Two-thirds of all workers covered were employed by up-state firms. Complete harmony prevailed within the committee on fundamental principles. All were men of practical common sense, who realized that while the emergency required deviation from the letter of the law, under no circumstances should it be used to effect permanent changes in the labor code, which had been developed in the State after so many years of struggle.

As a protection against the possible effects of long hours and night work on the physical well-being of boys and girls, it was decided to limit working hours to a maximum ten-hour day and a maximum fifty-hour week. At least a thirty-minute lunch period was required, and no seven-day weeks or night work beyond midnight were permitted. These restrictions and the care with which each case was considered were highly necessary since it was found subsequently that the jobs largely held by minors were without a future, that few promotions were granted them, and that for many reasons most employers were opposed to hiring minors except as a last resort. On September 1, 1945, shortly after the close of hostilities with Japan, by common consent all dispensations affecting sixteen- and seventeen-year-olds were terminated, and the War Council Committee abolished on October 31, 1945. All other dispensations, affecting persons over eighteen years of age, were subjected to review, and if without justification were canceled.

STATE OPPOSITION TO DISCRIMINATION IN EMPLOYMENT

The dictum that "justice is efficiency" was never more clearly illustrated than in connection with the employment of minority groups in war production. For some time prior to March, 1941, evidence had been accumulating that various minority groups were encountering difficulty in making their skills available for defense. On March 29, 1941, Governor Lehman appointed a Committee on Discrimination in Employment as part of the New York State Council of Defense, for the purpose of encouraging complete utilization in defense work of all patriotic individuals without consideration of race, color, creed, or national origin. The committee, of which the Industrial Commissioner was chairman, consisted of twenty-seven members representing industrial, labor, civic, and racial organizations.

Although the war emergency had turned the spotlight on the undesirable effects upon the National Defense Program of discrimination in employment, the committee decided to attack the problem of discrimination as a whole and to center attention both on the solution of immediate problems raised by the war and upon a more extensive program to alleviate those forms of discrimination deeply rooted in the social fabric. The cooperation of Federal officials and of the State Employment Service was secured and a public relations campaign undertaken to secure expressions of support from leaders of the State. Individual replies were incorporated in news releases for trade papers and house organs in many fields to bring home to the communities the weight of leadership in support of democratic employment practices. Individual complaints were referred to responsible agencies for investigation, and Sections 42 and 43 of the Civil Rights Law and Section 220-E of the Labor Laws no longer remained inoperative. As a means of focusing public attention upon the necessity for efficient use of minority groups, the committee actively sponsored a three-day State-wide observance of "National Defense Through Democratic Employment Practice," beginning December 5, 1941. New Jersey and Michigan joined New York under the slogan, "Make Democracy Work at Home," and statements for this three-day observance by Wendell L. Willkie, Pearl S. Buck, Bishop William T. Manning, Rabbi Wise, and Alfred E. Smith were widely circulated.

In March, 1942, the first field force in the country to deal with matters of discrimination in employment was established and trained to approach employers and community agencies with reason and persuasion. The work of the committee was likewise extended in 1942 to investigations of public and private defense-training schools, employment agencies, and labor unions to determine whether they pursued discriminatory labor policies, and to take appropriate action to eliminate undesirable practices. In 1943, the committee took up the problem of housing, which was proving to be a bottleneck in the employment of minority workers. It was also found that mere acceptance of a minority group was not sufficient — that acceptance in the highest skill was another matter, for many firms employed members of minority groups only in menial capacity. Upgrading was thus given special attention by field investigators. Other practices common in many plants were the use of quotas based upon race, color, religion, or national origin in hiring or discharging personnel; the segregation of racial groups within the plant; and inequalities in terms and conditions of work which had their origin in the same attitude. The employment of women, especially women of minority groups, was at first resisted by many firms, and a number of cases involving both employers and unions were referred to district attorneys for prosecution under the law.

On August 4, 1943, Governor Dewey reorganized the committee for more effective action, with Dr. Alvin Johnson, Director of the New School for Social Research in New York City, as chairman. The Governor stated that the committee "would undertake intensive and continuous work in the elimination of economic and social discrimination in the development of ever greater unity in the war effort." In 1944, the committee proposed legislation to establish a permanent commission "for the declaration and enforcement of the right of employment, regardless of race, creed, color, national origin or ancestry, and for investigation of the various problems of discrimination." The proposal was made late in the session, and carried with it severe penalties. The Governor believed more study was required by the Legislature and postponed action that session.

However, in June, 1944, "In order to insure careful and unhurried consideration of the conditions of discrimination and the potential effectiveness of the proposed statutory remedies," Governor Dewey created a temporary bipartisan legislative commission of twenty-three members, under the chairmanship of Assemblyman Irving M. Ives. After seven months of hard work including extensive hearings throughout the State, this commission, in turn, brought in a bill to create a permanent State Commission against Discrimination.

Under the terms of the bill complaints regarding discrimination in employment were to be filed with the five-man commission which was to attempt to adjust matters through conciliation. Failing this the commission would issue "cease and desist" orders which were subject to speedy judicial review and enforcement. Violation of one of these orders was to be a misdemeanor punishable by a fine not to exceed five hundred dollars or imprisonment up to one year, or both. The bill took cognizance only of the field of employment and placed heavy emphasis upon a long-range program of education. Its basic philosophy was expressed in one statement incorporated in the text: "The opportunity to obtain employment without discrimination because of race, creed, color or national origin is hereby recognized as and declared to be a civil right." There was no doubt about the position of the administration.

In his 1945 message to the Legislature the Governor declared, "the need for action in this field of human relations is imperative." In introducing the bill into the Assembly, Mr. Ives made the statement, "I mean business on this thing." As matters turned out, before the bill was finally passed both the Governor and the majority leader of the Republican Assembly were required to stand shoulder to shoulder against formidable opposition from employer groups, chambers of commerce, boards of trade, merchants' associations, some trade-union brotherhoods, and other organizations. These were able to command active support from a number of upstate legislators. Arguments ran all the way from fear of one-sided enforcement by a blackmailing, racketeering commission to general statements that the law would create greater racial tension instead of less and that discrimination was an abstract right, older than any law or constitution. Discrimination was held to be in effect simply the right of choice, and toleration could not be brought about by coercive legislation. Eventually by dint of hard fighting behind the scenes and in public hearings the supporters of the bill were overwhelmingly victorious. The bill passed the Assembly by a more than three-to-one majority and became Chapter 118 of the Laws of 1945.

The experience of the commission in carrying out its assignment under the Ives-Quinn law did not bear out the dire predictions and dismal forecasts of the opposition. Disruption of plant morale, mass withdrawals of employees, or retirement of industry from the State, so freely predicted by the bill's opponents, did not materialize. There was actual evidence of cooperation from employees and management. Some of its original left-wing supporters, however, disappointed at the essentially moderate administration of the provisions of the law, referred to it as "perfectly harmless." The inference, however, that the law was innocuous was certainly not warranted.

Quietly and without fanfare the commission proceeded to build up a State-wide organization with offices in New York City, Albany, Syracuse, Buffalo, and Binghamton. Conciliation councils, provided for in the legislation, were established in New York City, Buffalo, Syracuse, Albany, Broome County (Binghamton), and Westchester County. During the course of the commission's first year of operations approximately five hundred complaints were considered, of which not one failed of settlement in the stage of conference and conciliation. The commission was able to make rapid strides in the elimination of discriminatory job-application blanks and want ads. Cooperation from newspaper publishers, publishers' associations, advertising managers, and agencies was willing and effective. Without waiting for complaints the commission investigated certain utility companies, shipping corporations, and labor organizations. It inaugurated a series of conferences on discrimination in education with school and college administrators. Members of the commission also appeared before legislative committees in other states to make available the experience of New York in the administration and enforcement of its law. Massachusetts recently passed an antidiscrimination law largely modeled on New York precedents.

The commission's Bureau of Education, Public Relations, and Research was extremely active through press releases, radio broadcasts, magazine articles, pamphlets, and posters. Studies were undertaken of the changing incidence of discrimination in employment, of the economic cost of discrimination, and of the public's reception of observable changes in employment patterns.

Without claiming that discriminatory employment practices have now been eliminated in New York State or that the number of complaints received indicate the extent of such discrimination, the commission regards the evidence as indicating a distinct movement on the part of employers away from their former discriminatory practices. Although the law has teeth, these have not been required. This fact would appear to demonstrate that New York's legislation was both wise and workable, and that it contained effective equipment for carrying out the purposes in view.

INDUSTRIAL RELATIONS

The success of the war production efforts of the State depended in no small measure upon the willingness of both workers and employers to compose their differences (in time of war) without the necessity of work stoppages through the calling of strikes or the institution of lockouts. Disputes, though bound to arise even in time of war, could not, in the common interest, be permitted to interfere with production. An analysis of industrial disputes during the period 1937-1944 indicated that New York State had one of the best records of constant employment among eleven of the leading industrial states of the country. The following summary is based upon figures supplied by the Bureau of Labor Statistics, the United States Conciliation Service, the New York State Department of Commerce, and the New York State Board of Mediation.

The general strike pattern of the United States showed a decline in labor unrest from 1937 to 1940. In 1941, however, the rapid rise in production activity, coupled with an increased cost of living, stimulated industrial controversy throughout the nation to such an extent that the number of strikes called was exceeded only by the 1917 and 1937 totals. The attack on Pearl Harbor caused an abrupt decline in strike activity which was reflected in the 1942 figures. Thereafter, the nation relaxed its restraint and the number and duration of strikes increased in 1943 and 1944.

In the prewar period, New York followed the general downward pattern of the rest of the country, but during the war period its record of labor stability diverged sharply from those of the other manufacturing states. It will be seen from Table 2 that of the eleven leading industrial states of the country, New York was the only state in which time lost as the result of strikes declined each year since 1941. Compared to a 42 per cent decline in man-hours idle due to work stoppage or strikes in New York State from 1942 to 1944, the number more than doubled in the ten other states combined. According to Table 3, which places all states on a comparable basis in regard to time lost, New York had the best record of any of the eleven states in 1944, having lost only fifteen man-days per 100,000 of available working time compared to an average of 106 for the ten other states combined. Regarding the number of workers involved in strikes (Table 4) the State's record is likewise commendable. By 1944, the number of such workers had dropped 75 per cent from the 1941 peak while the total for the ten other states had actually increased. Even in the number of strikes, the least important of the strikes data, New York's war record is exceptional. Although the number of strikes in the United States as a whole, as well as the total for the ten states other than New York, showed a definite increase after 1942, the number of strikes in New York continued to decline each successive year following 1941 (Table 5).

These figures, however, do not mean that there were relatively few disputes between labor and management. On the contrary, New York, with its large labor force and its high dollar volume of contracts, had a large number of situations arising during the war whose settlement required assistance from the United States Conciliation Service and the State Mediation Board. The extent to which these situations were disposed of without work stoppages throws light on relations among the leaders of labor, of management, and of the State. In Table 6, it will be noted that of the seven most populous states in the country, all of whom as the work progressed made increasing use of the United States Conciliation Service, New York with 6305 had the third largest five-year total of situations disposed of by the United States Conciliation Service. That she should rank high in this respect was to be expected. What is important, however, is that she should be fifth out of the seven in the total number of strikes, and that, in the fiscal year 1944-1945, with the exception of California, she should have the lowest percentage of strikes to total controversies of any of the seven. An excellent job was apparently done in composing differences before they could result in work stoppages.

A similar picture is provided by figures on the work of the New York State Board of Mediation, created by the 1940 Legislature on recommendation of the Ives Joint Legislative Committee on Industrial and Labor Relations. This State Board of Mediation was the only state agency of its kind in the country having an agreement with the Federal government allowing it, as well as the United States Conciliation Service, to certify cases in New York State directly to the National War Labor Board. In the four years, 1942-1945, the State Mediation Board handled a total of 1958 mediation cases and was instrumental in avoiding an interruption of work in most of them. Furthermore, the total of 4452 disputes submitted for arbitration during these four years indicates that the board played

Table 2. Man-days Idle as a Result of Strikes, United States, New York State, and Ten Other Industrial States, 1937-1944

	1937	1938	1939	1940	1941	1942	1943	1944
United States	28,424,857	9,148,273	17,812,219	6,700,872	23,047,556	4,182,557	13,500,529	8,721,079
New York	3,180,741	1,789,181	1,236,547	1,247,401	2,171,937	376,451	307,323	218,609
California	1,940,979	966,712	1,038,109	457,559	1,798,907	224,131	83,479	126,856
Connecticut	268,160	94,902	92,534	69,838	272,903	22,984	23,194	76,458
Illinois	1,434,863	399,630	606,953	462,227	1,590,783	291,346	772,229	745,319
Indiana	967,851	239,783	381,290	278,756	657,154	221,067	433,780	354,468
Massachusetts	602,037	184,914	346,417	256,025	529,830	407,809	254,005	406,034
Michigan	3,924,752	349,553	2,499,115	195,297	1,897,649	258,623	592,270	1,836,903
New Jersey	935,054	384,506	539,476	381,732	1,058,308	197,550	169,490	332,714
North Carolina	85,524	56,875	101,624	93,164	105,085	24,254	103,368	68,057
Ohio	3,938,424	322,222	768,961	322,922	1,312,970	317,085	1,019,039	705,065
Pennsylvania	3,695,671	1,410,615	3,043,306	904,939	4,136,788	763,567	4,265,225	1,379,781
Ten States	17,793,315	4,409,712	9,417,785	3,422,459	13,355,327	2,728,416	7,716,079	6,031,655
United States excluding New York State	25,244,116	7,359,092	16,575,672	5,453,471	20,875,619	3,806,106	13,193,206	8,502,470
Rest of United States (37 states)	7,450,801	2,949,380	7,157,887	2,031,012	7,520,292	1,077,690	5,477,127	2,470,815

SOURCE: United States Department of Labor, Bureau of Labor Statistics.

Table 3. Man-days Idle per 100,000 man-days of Available Working Time of Non-agricultural Employees, United States, New York State, and Ten Other Industrial States, 1937-1944*

	1937†	1938	1939	1940	1941	1942	1943	1944
United States	307	108	194	70	217	36	112	75
New York	255	154	98	97	159	24	21	15
California	350	188	188	79	274	29	9	16
Connecticut	151	60	54	38	125	9	10	34
Illinois	204	63	88	64	200	35	90	87
Indiana	388	113	158	109	218	69	130	108
Massachusetts	146	49	82	58	110	80	48	81
Michigan	880	95	61	44	381	49	105	336
New Jersey	264	117	144	96	236	41	35	70
North Carolina	47	33	52	47	48	11	45	31
Ohio	161	64	141	56	201	45	136	97
Pennsylvania	425	184	378	105	436	75	419	140
Ten States	393	109	214	74	256	48	132	106
United States excluding New York State....	315	101	209	66	225	38	126	84
Rest of United States (37 states)	214	91	202	56	186	25	118	55

* Agricultural strikes which are few in number and of small magnitude, especially in industrial states, are included.
† The number of nonagricultural employees for this year is based on an average of the last six months.
SOURCE: Bureau of Labor Statistics.

Table 4. Workers Involved in Strikes, United States, New York State, and Ten Other Industrial States, 1937-1944

	1937	1938	1939	1940	1941	1942	1943	1944
United States	1,860,621	688,376	1,170,962	576,988	2,362,620	839,961	1,981,279	2,115,637
New York	221,391	122,032	135,984	104,446	204,284	57,824	91,272	50,999
California	79,314	45,791	83,679	32,735	114,134	26,309	29,602	26,599
Connecticut	18,491	7,765	10,609	6,184	33,616	7,881	9,099	24,665
Illinois	99,355	27,394	74,017	27,548	110,946	66,772	132,059	152,015
Indiana	56,430	14,518	30,838	16,605	80,311	32,164	80,058	93,516
Massachusetts	55,360	14,941	34,832	21,911	57,415	74,580	37,269	48,440
Michigan	354,499	76,968	130,410	25,773	333,571	114,723	274,531	568,738
New Jersey	65,783	49,289	29,550	34,415	91,292	39,286	57,283	93,298
North Carolina	7,436	6,999	7,936	4,921	18,731	4,828	18,511	11,056
Ohio	207,428	46,846	50,458	29,752	164,294	64,031	297,145	216,360
Pennsylvania	323,432	114,568	179,320	105,064	488,498	162,803	414,012	328,220
Ten States	1,267,528	405,079	631,649	304,908	1,492,808	593,377	1,349,569	1,562,907
United States excluding New York State....	1,639,230	566,344	1,034,978	472,542	2,158,336	782,137	1,890,007	2,064,638
Rest of United States (37 states)	371,702	161,265	403,329	167,634	665,528	188,760	540,438	501,731

SOURCE: Bureau of Labor Statistics

Table 5. Number of Strikes in United States, New York State, and Ten Other Industrial States, 1937-1944

	1937	1938	1939	1940	1941	1942	1943	1944
United States	4,740	2,772	2,613	2,508	4,288	2,968	3,752	4,956
New York	897	764	726	553	763	372	296	265
California	259	168	215	219	384	147	109	103
Connecticut	93	45	38	84	84	93	86	44
Illinois	272	138	151	133	226	279	343	492
Indiana	188	67	79	67	161	93	130	195
Massachusetts	277	123	116	104	175	151	127	196
Michigan	306	95	89	73	252	261	413	562
New Jersey	309	198	190	179	264	174	177	202
North Carolina	29	18	15	23	34	26	57	45
Ohio	298	116	96	149	341	238	467	549
Pennsylvania	641	352	315	301	545	410	571	821
Ten States	2,622	1,320	1,304	1,282	2,466	1,812	2,430	3,209
United States excluding New York State	3,843	2,008	1,887	1,955	3,525	2,596	3,456	4,691
Rest of United States (37 states)	1,221	688	583	673	1,059	784	1,026	1,482

SOURCE: Bureau of Labor Statistics

Table 6. *Situations Disposed of by United States Conciliation Service for Fiscal Years*

State	1940-1941		1941-1942		1942-1943		1943-1944		1944-1945	
	Number	Workers involved	Number	Workers involved	Number	Workers involved	Number	Workers involved	Number	Workers involved
New York	409	258	656	588	1,540	2,112	1,845	1,355	1,855	1,021
Pennsylvania	478	379	677	424	1,410	1,149	1,857	1,626	1,797	939
Illinois	272	129	544	321	1,447	672	2,651	936	2,068	786
Ohio	475	156	758	578	1,641	846	2,227	906	2,355	989
California	388	233	616	494	1,387	770	1,617	969	2,153	2,882
Texas	109	24	152	59	313	152	376	236	500	266
Michigan	379	680	599	780	1,416	1,038	1,835	1,355	2,336	1,973

SOURCE: U. S. Conciliation Service

Table 7. Duration of Strikes in Nation during War Period

Year	Average strike duration, days
1940	20.9
1941	18.3
1942	11.7
1943	5.0
1944	5.6

Table 8. Percentage of Strikes to Total Situations Disposed of, Fiscal Year 1944-45. First Seven Most Populous States

State	Strikes	Total situations	Per cent strikes to total situations
California	99	2,153	4.6
Illinois	252	2,068	12.1
Michigan	497	2,336	21.2
New York	156	1,855	8.4
Ohio	389	2,355	16.5
Pennsylvania	395	1,797	21.9
Texas	63	500	12.6

SOURCE: United States Conciliation Service

an important role in encouraging disputed matters to be resolved through arbitration rather than through economic warfare. This is especially true if one compares the 531 cases settled by arbitration in 1939 as against an annual average from 1941-1945 of over 1000 cases.

The work of the board in handling disputes submitted to it for mediation was outstanding, and in five years, 1941-1945, the number of strikes terminated through voluntary mediation was 963. This involved a drop of over 81 per cent from the 1941 total of 469 strikes terminated to the 1943 and 1944 totals of 97 for each year. Those disputes submitted to mediation before strike action had taken place and in which such action was averted by the efforts of the board reached the five-year total of 1612.

The confidence that the board inspired as a result of its work was illustrated by the fact that in 1945, of the 159 mediations handled in the upstate area over 25 per cent were initiated by employers, 52 per cent by unions, 8.8 per cent by both employer and union, and only 14.2 per cent by initiative of the board itself. In not a single case was it necessary to issue a fact-finding report for which the 1941 legislation provided. The work of the various individual mediators saved labor, management, and the public many millions of dollars during the war and helped materially to speed the war effort in the State of New York.

If one were to attempt an explanation of New York's enviable wartime record in the field of industrial relations, a considerable variety of factors would have to be taken into account. One of the most important was the voluntary "no strike" pledge taken by most labor unions shortly after the outbreak of war.

This was observed with commendable fidelity until after V-J Day. The work of the State and Federal agencies, such as the Board of Mediation and other subdivisions of the New York State Department of Labor, the War Manpower Commission, and the United States Conciliation Service did a remarkable job of reducing disputes to questions of fact and eliminating work stoppages. Labor and management worked together on advisory committees for the area directors of the War Manpower Commission, on the State War Council itself, and on a number of its subcommittees. The labor officers for the Army, the Navy, and the Air Forces were extremely active in smoothing out difficulties in the plants under their jurisdiction. These men negotiated constantly with both labor and management in an effort to maintain production at top speed in those plants having vital contracts with the armed services. Labor leaders on the labor-management committees likewise put forth strenuous efforts to influence union members against stoppages. Individual employers were willing to make concessions to fill their contracts on time. Winning the war was the prime consideration and patriotic motives prevailed practically universally.

This was especially true for New York City which, during the war, although it had the highest proportion of foreign-born of any of the major cities of the country, did not experience a single strike of any significance. Foreign-born first- and second-generation Americans understood the war aims of the allies as clearly as the average American. Many of them had left Europe to escape the very same treatment accorded opponents of the Nazis and Fascists. For the first time in their lives they had discovered what it meant to live in a democracy of free men. Their patriotism, reinforced as it was by personal experience, was in many respects more deeply emotional than that of those who had in the literal sense inherited the land. For these reasons, New York City experienced little sabotage. Aliens carried on the war effort in the best American tradition, thereby demonstrating that fear of their loyalty and the consequent necessity for carefully controlling their actions were without foundation.

THE USE OF PRISON INDUSTRIES

Highly important contributions to war production for Federal agencies and the armed forces were made by the prison industries of the State under the direction of Thomas B. Bergan, First Assistant Commissioner in Charge of Industries. The use of prison labor was still another example of the expansion of the labor force, to say nothing of the conversion of plant facilities. Under the supervision of a War Council Committee, composed of the majority leader of the State Senate, a representative of industry, and the presidents of the two major labor unions of New York State, contracts totaling nearly a million dollars of essential materials were filled between July 17, 1942, and November 28, 1945. The principal products included virtually all of the Osnaburg or camouflage cloth used by the armed services, aluminum and other metal ware, Navy work shirts, Coast Guard and Merchant Marine blankets, United States Army carpenter chests, tool handles, and many other articles produced in small quantities. In all cases the interests of private industry and labor were safeguarded by the close scrutiny given each proposed contract by the Prison Industries Committee of the War Council. No contract was accepted that could be handled by private industry under government specifications. Contracts for paint brushes, blankets, and flags were rejected, but nineteen different types of contracts were completed by the Division of Prison Industries of the State Department of Correction in the seven institutions of Attica, Auburn, Clinton, Great Meadow, Sing Sing, Napanoch, and the Westfield State Farm. At Clinton a regular second shift was operated for three complete years. Extra hours, in addition to the normal working day, were likewise put in at all of the other institutions.

Contracts were signed with the United States Navy, United States Quartermaster-Engineers, the United States Treasury, Quartermaster Corps, Coast Guard, Maritime Commission, United States Naval Training Center at Sampson, Army Service Forces, Detroit Ordnance Depot, and the Defense Supplies Corporation. For Civilian Defense units the merchandise produced consisted of blankets, stretchers, night sticks, furniture, steel lockers, and shoe repairs. As a by-product of the participation of Prison Industries in war production, the inmates of the prisons benefited by serving their country. It was evident that the opportunity to redeem, in some measure, their self-respect had the effect of greatly heightening morale, thereby immeasurably reducing the danger of prison disturbances.

MAINTENANCE OF INDUSTRIAL SAFETY, HEALTH, AND SANITATION

Loss of working time through the absence of workers from their jobs was a common concern of management, and the State Departments of Health and Labor. If absenteeism could be cut, or its increase prevented, the net result would be equivalent to an expansion in the labor force. It was, therefore, important that wartime problems of industrial health and sanitation be met and solved quickly.

During the war, the Division of Industrial Safety Service of the State Department of Labor maintained full inspection in all the industrial plants of the State. Since inspection in New York had been constant for some sixty years, it was not necessary during the war to develop new services. The division did, however,

cooperate in the various safety campaigns conducted in specific industries by the United States Department of Labor. Such specific drives included those relating to the prefabricated-metal industry, the meat-packing industry, the wood-working industry, and the paper and pulp industry. Although the number of industrial accidents reported under the Workmen's Compensation Law for the years 1940 to 1945 showed a 36 per cent increase from the 1940 figure to the peak figure for 1944, this record was better than that of many of the other industrial states. Furthermore, it must be considered in the light of certain wartime changes in the labor force. As indicated on page 62, the New York labor force underwent an expansion of approximately 22 per cent between 1940 and the fall of 1943. Second, there was a marked influx of new, inexperienced workers, many of them women who had gone direct from their homes and who possessed no previous factory training. The incidence of accidents among this group was naturally considerably higher than among male workers of long experience. Furthermore, during the war new legislation tightened considerably the reporting of accidents to the Workmen's Compensation Board. These three factors taken together should modify considerably any conclusion likely to be drawn from a hasty glance at the accident figures themselves, given in Table 9.

Table 9. Number of Industrial Accidents Reported under the Workmen's Compensation Law for the Years 1940-1945 Inclusive

1940	528,467
1941	635,983
1942	713,731
1943	710,707
1944	717,029
1945	664,830

Health problems peculiar to war industries arose from exceptional circumstances, such as:

1. The use of new and unfamiliar toxic substances some of which were required by War Department specifications.

2. The introduction of unexpected health hazards resulting from the sudden use of unusually large amounts of toxic chemical substances, which in small amounts previously presented no problem.

3. A reduction in air space per worker due to the increase in number of machines and workers without any corresponding increase in the size of workrooms.

4. The introduction of new machinery and new manufacturing processes.

5. The construction of new buildings.

6. The location of plants in remote areas, far from eating facilities, hospitals, or other medical services.

7. The speed with which all these changes took place.

In the early years of the war, speed was all-important: speed in the completion of plans for new building; speed in the hiring and training of large numbers of workers; speed in the installation of new machinery and equipment; speed in setting into motion new processes involving the use of new materials.

Under such circumstances, workers in war plants were exposed to an ever-increasing number of poisonous substances provided by the ingenuity of American manufacturers in meeting the requirements of modern mechanized warfare. This rapid multiplication of health hazards required the development of adequate safeguards to maintain productivity at a high level through the prevention of accidents and the protection of health. Without adequate attention to this group of new problems, large numbers of man hours might have been lost through absenteeism.

To meet this obvious need, the Division of Industrial Hygiene of the Department of Labor organized a special program. To all plants in New York State receiving government contracts it sent a letter outlining the technical services rendered by the division — medical, chemical, and engineering plant surveys, dust counts, air analyses, and physical examinations of workers. It also distributed check lists of articles on the toxicity of specific industrial chemicals, check lists of toxic substances requiring safeguards, engineering drawings of ventilating systems for typical operations, and articles and drawings particularly adapted to the plant in question. Each letter was followed up by visits to the plant, consultations with plant physicians on medical problems raised by war contracts, and special field studies of particular cases such as the aircraft plants, or of the use of industrial chemicals such as the poisonous solvents. To go into detail with regard to studies made by this Division of substances such as bensol, chlorinated naphthalene, and the diphenyls, trichlorethylene, radium, lead, X-rays, talc, carborundum, and so on, would be impossible. Suffice it to say that the work of the division in this field expanded greatly as a result of the war.

In the field of engineering, the functions of the Division divided into three main categories:

1. Examination of plans and specifications of industrial exhaust systems submitted by industry to the Department of Labor for approval

2. Plant investigations, especially foundries and stone-cutting operations

3. Special studies and research on engineering aspects of industrial hygiene

The safety program of the division involved visits to plants in connection with accident prevention and the investigation of specific accidents. Trade schools were likewise inspected to ensure safe practices and the use of proper machine guards. Supporting this work at all times was an education program consisting of publications, special articles in the *Industrial Bulletin,* and lectures of both technical and popular nature delivered to labor unions, groups of factory workers, industrialists, consumers' league, and other interested lay groups.

The reception by industry of the program of the Division was excellent. Medical, chemical, and engineering services were warmly received by men who were too busy pushing production at a dizzy pace to give time to the consideration of health hazards. The tendency was to turn these over to plant physicians, who found themselves hard-pressed to provide adequate routine medical care for a suddenly increased number of workers. Something had to be neglected, and in many cases physicians had relatively little opportunity to study the toxic properties of the new substances being used. Assistance from the Division of Industrial Hygiene was consequently accepted gladly through both visits to the plants and by correspondence. Requests for technical assistance received by the department indicate a wide variety of problems raised by war production. Some of these requests are listed below:

1. Industrial plants desired help in eliminating health hazards.

2. Labor unions desired protection for groups of workers in special industries or processes where illnesses had occurred.

3. Insurance companies were interested in reducing their incidence of compensation cases in a given plant.

4. Practicing physicians wanted information on the toxicological properties of substances which they suspected were responsible for the illness of some of their patients, or desired guidance in the treatment of occupational diseases.

5. Plant physicians wished assistance in techniques for the early recognition of injury to health resulting from exposure to toxic chemicals in their plants, as well as advice as to the type of medical supervision necessary to keep their workers healthy, efficient, and productive.

6. Industrial chemists desired suggestions with reference to the use of safe substitutes for toxic materials, or information as to techniques for the evaluation of toxic exposure by the use of air analysis.

7. Industrial engineers wished advice and assistance in engineering techniques for the control of noxious dusts, gases, fumes, and mists by means of ventilation and other safe-practice procedures.

8. Labor and health departments throughout the country were interested in the experience of New York State in industrial hygiene administration and techniques.

9. The United States Employment Service consulted the medical staff of the division with reference to placement of handicapped workers, soldiers given medical discharges from the army, and so on.

The second department whose normal work was in many respects greatly augmented, and which had to perform its functions with greatly curtailed personnel, was the State Department of Health. Tremendous shifts in population such as coincided with the rapid expansion of industrial operations in 1941-1942, tended in numerous instances to create potential health hazards. Large numbers of workers and their families descended upon communities in which housing, water supplies, sewage disposal, and other facilities were inadequate to handle increased demand. Some individuals from rural areas, lacking previous exposure to the common communicable diseases and hence having developed no immunity to them, were susceptible to these diseases. Others, from out of State, where smallpox was more prevalent than in New York, were possible sources of infection to New York residents. Many workers working long hours "burned the candle at both ends," providing fertile soil for the development of tuberculosis. It was necessary also to take action to prevent the spread of venereal diseases. Preventive work of this sort devolved upon the Department of Health.

New York was fortunate in avoiding widespread epidemics which often accom-

The Army-Navy "E"

The personnel of manufacturing and industrial plants throughout New York State exerted their efforts to earn the coveted pennant as a symbol of patriotism.

pany wars. Only two diseases approached epidemic proportions, meningococcal meningitis, a disease frequently accompanying war, and poliomyelitis, or infantile paralysis, which usually attacks children and consequently has little effect upon war production.

From the beginning, the department concentrated heavily upon maintaining the health of war workers. It expanded a previously adopted program of X-raying selected groups of the population by undertaking mass chest X-ray surveys among industrial workers. Much of the X-raying was done by contract with a commercial company, but thousands of films were read in the central office of the Department, and by members of the staff of tuberculosis hospitals. Additional clinics were scheduled in war plants and attempts made to persuade managers to protect the health of their workers through vaccination.

The Division of Sanitation likewise found its duties rapidly expanded. Assistance was extended by the Division's engineers to many war industries in connection with investigations of sites for industrial plants. Special attention was devoted to obtaining satisfactory sources of water supply and to developing sanitary methods for disposal of sewage and waste. Special concern was shown for the protection of workers and military personnel around important military establishments and war industries. This general program of assistance to military authorities and contractors consisted of supervision over water and sanitary facilities furnished to workmen in trailer and other camps, over private water supplies within such areas as were available to war workers or soldiers, and over sanitary control of restaurants and public eating places. To handle this work, loans of two to three sanitary engineers at a time were secured from the United States Public Health Service. Similar assistance was also provided in connection with the sanitary problems of the various housing projects.

EXPANSION OF THE LABOR FORCE

The cumulative effect of efforts put forth to secure a labor supply adequate for purposes of war production are reflected in the employment figures for the period 1940-1945. These indicate both the rate and extent of wartime expansion. Active job registrants on file in the United States Employment Service declined from a high point of 676,505 in June, 1940, to a low of 83,269 at the end of December, 1943, after which regular active file counts were discontinued. On the other hand, six-month totals of placements rose steadily from 110,723 at the end of June, 1941, to 1,177,540 at the end of December, 1945. Semiannual totals for nonagricultural placements followed the same trend from 107,679 at the end of June, 1939, to 690,457 at the end of December, 1945. Generally speaking, the most rapid expansion took place in the employment of men in the metalworking branches of manufacturing industries. Geographically, this occurred upstate in the period prior to May, 1942.

The placement of women in nonagricultural occupations rose steadily from 48,734 at the end of June, 1939 to a high of 234,147 at the end of June, 1943, after which there were slight declines to a low of 207,966 at the end of December, 1945. From 1940 to November, 1944 the number of employed women rose 37 per cent to a total of 1,988,800. In the same period the number of women in manufacturing plants doubled. In 1944, the apparel industry had the greatest number, 245,000, followed by metals and machinery with 192,000. However, the most striking increase in the employment of women occurred in metals and machinery, which included the major war industries. From 28,000 in June, 1940, to 192,000 in November, 1944, was a rise of 580 per cent.

Nonwhite placements in nonagricultural employment, at first largely as domestic workers in private households, showed a similar trend from a year total in 1939 of 23,793 to a high six-months total at the end of December, 1944, of 185,573. The figures for 1945 were very nearly comparable, but placements as domestic servants dropped to little more than half the total figures. It is interesting to note that approximately 87 per cent of the nonwhite placements and 77 per cent of women placements were made in New York City, whereas more than 50 per cent of placements in manufacturing were made in the upstate area. On the basis of the July, 1943, figures, the upstate employment rolls for all industries were slightly under 65 per cent of those of New York City.

Of the 2 million women workers finally mobilized during the war period, it has been estimated that at least 80 per cent would like to continue working after the war — practically all of them for reasons of economic necessity. This trend, which has been in effect since the previous war, will undoubtedly continue. The same will also be true, but to an increased extent, of nonwhites. With them it was a case of breaking down the barriers to employment and, once accomplished, this integration into the labor force should proceed as rapidly after World War II as did that of women after World War I.

WAR HOUSING PROGRAM

Shelter is a fundamental human need. Nevertheless, the inauguration of the war production program in 1940 caught the State, after ten years of depression and no housebuilding to speak of, with a dangerously low supply of private housing units. The additional dislocation caused in numerous communities by the sudden influx of large numbers of war workers was therefore bound to present a serious problem. While the period of acute shortages may be said to have lasted from 1941 to the spring of 1944, at

no time during the war was the need for housing ever adequately met.

As early as September, 1940, at a conference of mayors of upstate cities, the need for adequate housing for war workers was discussed by the State Commissioner of Housing. It was agreed then that the immediate need was for an inventory by regions of available housing in the several rental ranges. The State Division of Housing proceeded with plans for these surveys and in March, 1941, the State Defense Council made funds available for additional field personnel to assist with community surveys and with the organization of local housing authorities to prepare plans for the building of State and federally financed housing units. The same month, in a letter to thirty-five city and six county defense councils in war-impact areas, the Governor pointed out that housing could very well become one of the bottlenecks of the war production program. Decent homes at appropriate rents had to be available for men and women working in war plants. Already it had been reported that because of lack of accommodations workers in a certain plant had quit their jobs.

Homeless in-migrant workers were converging daily on the thirty-three war producing centers in the State. At Sampson, where a great naval training station was being built, about twenty thousand construction workers flooded the area. Many of them arrived penniless, looking for jobs. They slept on park benches, at police stations, in jails, wherever they could. In one instance, contractors rented an old, unused loft building for temporary shelter. At Romulus in Seneca County, eight thousand in-migrant workers made their beds in trucks, trailers, automobiles, and old barns along the countryside. Here the lack of adequate water supply and sanitary facilities led to the outbreak of a few typhoid cases, and for a short time the area was threatened with a typhoid epidemic. Prompt action of the Division of Housing, which called on the State Department of Health, succeeded in checking the disease in time. These are merely typical examples. Such conditions to greater or lesser degree prevailed in many of the war production centers in the State.

Under these circumstances a thorough survey of existing community vacancies and of the physical condition of the dwellings available was imperative. The State Commissioner of Housing was charged with general responsibility for housing matters under the State Council of Defense. Soon afterward, at the request of the Defense Housing Coordinator in Washington, the State Division of Housing assisted in setting up Homes Registration Bureaus in twenty-two localities, whose functions would be to keep current the vacancy data secured through the surveys and assist incoming families to find quarters.

Working closely with Washington and with the communities, the State Division of Housing assisted in solving the two major types of problems. In small communities, where no problem had previously existed, but where the location of war plants had caused a sudden influx of workers beyond the capacity of the existing facilities, it was decided that Federal funds should be made available for temporary housing since existing shortages were directly traceable to defense activity. On the other hand, problems arising from imposing a substantial additional demand upon an already existing housing shortage were considered the proper concern of the State. Here, additional dwellings would meet not only the immediate needs of war workers but at the end of the war would be open to the use of low- and moderate-income families in accordance with the law, thus constituting a permanent addition to the housing facilities of the community.

During the 1941 legislative session, the Public Housing Law was amended to permit localities to obtain State funds for projects where the shortage of safe and sanitary dwellings was impeding the National Defense Program. At the end of the emergency these facilities would be available for low-income families under arrangements similar to those applicable to other State housing projects. Five projects were built with State funds in Niagara Falls, North Tonawanda, Tonawanda, Schenectady, and Elmira, respectively, and opened for occupancy in 1943. A sixth was constructed in New York City near the Brooklyn Navy Yard, and a seventh a year later in a downtown area in Utica. Special housing arrangements were made in cooperation with the Federal government in the vicinity of the Sampson Naval Station, the Army Air Depot at Rome, the Army Hospital at Utica, Pine Camp, Camp Shanks, and the Seneca Ordnance Depot. In many cases, the permanent housing projects financed by loans from the State were located on vacant land, and slum clearance — one of the principal purposes of the State program — instead of being carried out immediately was provided for at the end of the war. The State's subsidy to local communities or authorities at the end of the war would take the form of annual grants to keep rentals low and make it possible for low-income families to obtain occupancy.

One advantage derived from the war was the great volume of renovation and reconversion which took place. This had the net effect of improving conditions. As might be expected, however, the units were smaller and posed a problem after the war from a livability standpoint. One other advantage was that the experience of communities with wartime housing problems rendered them much more conscious of their over-all housing needs. Yet despite all efforts, the housing situation was never really met at any time during the war, and with the return of servicemen, demand for dwellings far outstripped supply. The postwar housing crisis is described in Chapter IX.

Under the stimulus of the temporary emergency in housing Governor Dewey also took steps to speed up the long-range program for permanent housing and rehabilitation of urban areas. Under Article 18 of the New York State Constitution, adopted in 1938, the Legislature had been empowered to authorize the borrowing of 300 million dollars by the State to be used for loans to municipalities or their housing authorities to finance housing projects for families of low income. The amendment also empowered the Legislature to authorize contracts for payment by the State of subsidies totaling 5 million dollars. The purpose of these State loans and subsidies for housing was, as indicated above, to produce accommodations at rents within the means of low-income families who would otherwise be living in substandard dwellings.

The authorization in 1938 of loan funds in the amount of 300 million dollars had for numerous excellent reasons not been fully utilized during the war. In 1945 and 1946, at the Governor's suggestion, the Legislature twice raised the amount of the annual subsidies for low-income housing, thereby enabling the Commissioner of Housing to pay out as much as 9 million dollars a year. In 1946, the Legislature made available for public housing loans the remaining 80 million dollars of the 300 million dollars authorized by the Constitution.

As of April 1, 1947, the State Division of Housing had outstanding loan contracts totaling slightly more than 228 million dollars for thirty-four low-rent permanent housing projects. Applications for three additional upstate projects had been approved. Thus progress was being made on public housing projects in New York City, Yonkers, Portchester, New Rochelle, Mount Vernon, Hempstead, Schenectady, Utica, and Elmira.

Further steps in the expansion of the program for State-supported low-rent housing were sponsored by Governor Dewey and approved by the 1947 Legislature. As a result, proposals to amend the State Constitution in the matter of housing will come before the people at the next general election.* These propositions, which have been opposed by some real-estate interests, call for (1) the creation of a new 135-million dollar slum clearance and public housing fund to be added to the 300 million dollars now nearly committed; (2) the increase of the maximum amount of State subsidies outstanding in any one year to help maintain the low-rent character of State-aided public housing from 9 to 13 million dollars; and (3) the increase in the permissible amount of public housing subsidies contracted for by the State in any one year from the present maximum of 1 million dollars to 1.5 million dollars. In view of the continued shortage of materials and labor and of the high cost of both, and the consequent dearth of low-rent private building, these moves on the part of the State seem eminently justified.

One advance in the field of permanent housing and community development can be attributed to the influence of Governor Dewey. The old practice of placing a public housing project in the middle of a slum area, without any thought of the surrounding neighborhood, was abandoned. Such hit and miss practices frequently exposed new housing to contamination by the surrounding slums and did little to halt the spread of urban decay. The new State-aided housing projects were located so as to encourage individual builders to join in the reclaiming of larger areas. By providing park, recreational, and other facilities and by coordinating public improvements such as schools, streets, and highways, with housing in integrated neighborhood patterns, the State encouraged individual builders to join in improving entire neighbor-

---

* These proposals were approved in November, 1947.

hoods. Planning in which the State, the municipality, and private capital cooperated in the construction of good housing for all income groups thus achieved better community relationships as a logical result of the solution of permanent housing problems. In this program the State acted as the instigator of social and economic rehabilitation in urban areas, thereby making it easier for communities to help themselves.

NEW YORK'S ACHIEVEMENT IN WAR PRODUCTION

New York's record in war production was outstanding. With a relatively moderate expansion of her plant facilities, she turned out the highest dollar volume of war supplies of any state in the country. Such an achievement was possible primarily because of the energy and devotion of the workers and the willingness and ability of employers to turn out war equipment. However, had not all phases of the war production problem been well handled, the efforts of management and labor would have been seriously handicapped. Had the Department of Commerce, or the Department of Labor, or the Division of Housing, or the State War Council, with its various committees, each failed to perform its duties effectively, the final results would have been far less gratifying.

The wartime expansion of New York State's manufacturing plant and equipment did not keep pace with the rate of expansion of the country as a whole. From July, 1940, to May, 1944, the value of industrial facility projects authorized in the United States totaled 27.17 billion dollars. This compared favorably with the country's total prewar plant estimated in terms of gross tangible assets at 39.6 billion dollars. While the expansion in the country's manufacturing capacity was thus enormous, especially when crowded into less than six years, New York's share in this enlargement of plant was 1.549 billion dollars, or 5.7 per cent

of the national total. If this percentage is compared to the State's 10.2 per cent of the total population, its 12.1 per cent of total factory wage earners, and its 12.6 per cent of all manufactured products produced in the country, it is evident that the State had a relatively small share of facility projects. In this respect it was surpassed by California and Texas and equaled by Pennsylvania. One advantage, however, was that New York's industrial pattern was changed less than that of the country as a whole by wartime increases in plant and equipment. Postwar reconversion problems would for this reason be less acute, and the problem of migrant labor more easily handled.

Of the total increase in plants in the State, more than 25 per cent was for the production of aircraft, 18 per cent for ships, 15 per cent for ordnance, and about 8 per cent for electrical equipment. The geographical distribution of these new facilities corresponded roughly to the total of war supply contracts let in each of the major war production areas of the State. The New York metropolitan area, embracing New York City, Nassau, and Westchester, received 35 per cent of the facilities of the State, and the Buffalo area, comprising Erie and Niagara counties, received 29 per cent. The two areas together accounted for 64 per cent of the facilities and 67 per cent of the contracts. One exception was Syracuse which, although ranking third among the areas in plant expansion, was exceeded by both the Capital District and the Rochester area in the volume of contracts for supplies. For the State as a whole, the manufacturing plant was expanded by approximately $1500 for each factory wage earner employed in 1939. In three areas, however, this ratio was extremely high, viz., Buffalo with $4574, Elmira with $4022, and Syracuse with $3508. The significance of these figures lies in the fact that to operate facilities of such an expanded character large

numbers of additional workers were required. As a result, labor shortages appeared, especially in Buffalo, and at the
same time housing facilities for so many
additional workers presented an immediate problem. In Erie, Nassau, and
Broome counties, aircraft facilities pre-
dominated, ships in Kings and Richmond, while ordnance was widely distributed. Also well scattered over the
State were facilities for the production of
machinery, food, and miscellaneous
manufactures. Nearly all of the facilities
in St. Lawrence county, and a considerable part in Queens, were set up for the
production of nonferrous metals.

With the end of the war, the conversion of this new plant to peacetime operations became a problem.[1] It was estimated that over 75 per cent of the new
plants, consisting largely of aircraft manufacturing facilities, were easily convertible — far more so than was expected at
the beginning of the war. Other factors
affecting the convertibility of war plants
were the 24.1 per cent of privately financed facilities, most of which were not
likely to constitute a conversion problem,
the 47 per cent of the total cost which
was spent upon expansions and conver-
sions rather than entirely new building,
and the 59.7 per cent of the total cost
which went into equipment. It would appear from the foregoing that instead of
being mostly white elephants, the plants
built in New York State during the war
were assets rather than liabilities.

In contrast to her rather meager share
of the war facility contracts, the contribution of New York State to war production exceeded that of any other state.
War supply contracts in New York State
from June, 1940, to June, 1945, totaled
approximately 21.5 billion dollars, 11.3
per cent of all contracts in the United
States, and 23 million dollars greater
than the total awarded in Michigan with
its vast automotive production. Produc-

tion was more heavily concentrated in
the aircraft, communication equipment,
and miscellaneous categories than it was
in the nation as a whole. Of the State's
total, 35.2 per cent was for aircraft, 22.9
per cent for ordnance, 6.1 per cent for
ships (exclusive of orders to New York
Navy Yards), 9.6 per cent for communication equipment, and 28.2 per cent for
miscellaneous products. The State's importance in the miscellaneous group was
due to its large clothing industry and a
host of similar industries normally producing nondurable consumer goods. In
certain categories the State made an outstanding record. It produced 21.9 per
cent of all communication equipment in
the country, 12.9 per cent of all aircraft,
and 10.2 per cent of all ordnance. These
achievements were the result of the full
utilization of its existing manufacturing
establishments. As in the case of facility
contracts, the New York metropolitan
area was first in the dollar volume of
supply contracts. Of the State total, it
received 43.6 per cent, the Buffalo area,
23.3 per cent, and the Albany-Schenec-
tady-Troy area, 11.8 per cent. With the
exception of the metropolitan area
which, in 1939, contributed 60.5 per cent
of all manufactures, for all the State's
other industrial areas the percentage of
war contracts was higher than the 1939
percentage of manufactures. The areas
of large relative wartime expansion were
the same ones already mentioned in connection with facility contracts, viz., Elmira, the Capital District, Buffalo, and
Syracuse.

One index of excellence in the fulfillment of contracts for the Army and Navy
was the Army-Navy E award. Out of a
total of 4283 plants receiving the award
in the United States, 483 of these were
in New York State. These organizations
were honored for meeting stringent eligibility requirements based upon excellence in quality and quantity of production, a low rate of absenteeism, avoidance
of work stoppages, maintenance of fair

---

[1] See Chapter IX.

labor standards, training, record on accidents, health, and cooperation between management and labor. Plants which maintained an outstanding record for six months after receiving the original E award were granted the star award. Seventy plants in New York received one star. Additional stars could be won by continued outstanding performance for succeeding six-month periods until the flag carried four stars, after which the interval was increased to one year. In the State, sixty-nine plants flew two stars, eighty-four three stars, ninety-seven four stars, twenty-five five stars, and two won the extraordinary distinction of six stars. Only eight plants in the entire country achieved six stars.

In reviewing the record compiled by the 13 million inhabitants of New York State, it is impossible to avoid the conclusion that in war production a great deal of their success may be attributed to four factors: (1) the high level of intelligence, the common sense, and the special skills of the working population; (2) the initiative, intelligence, and good judgment of management; (3) an alert political leadership which aided without dominating the industrial life of the State; all three of which are in turn the product of (4) generations of unhampered development under a system of general education in a free society. Since such factors cannot be created overnight in any part of the world, it is up to the government and the people to make sure through the exercise of constant vigilance that they continue unaltered.

Table 10. Distribution of Major War Supply Contracts, Industrial Area, and Major Object, Cumulative June, 1940 — June, 1945

Area	Total	Aircraft	Ships	Ordnance	All others
			(Millions of Dollars)		
United States	189,741	58,665	29,474	48,271	53,331
New York State	21,499	7,561	1,305	4,924	7,709
Albany — Schenectady — Troy	2,536	206	101	970	1,260
Binghamton	445	196	1	77	171
Buffalo	5,008	3,930	118	274	687
Elmira	302	2	26	213	61
New York Metropolitan Area	9,366	3,060	847	1,928	3,531
Rochester	1,215	20	28	560	607
Syracuse	902	57	70	320	455
Utica	637	5	7	360	265
Rest of State	1,088	85	107	222	672
Percent of Total					
United States	100.0	30.9	15.5	25.4	28.1
New York State	100.0	35.2	6.1	22.9	35.9
Albany — Schenectady — Troy	100.0	8.1	4.0	38.2	49.7
Binghamton	100.0	44.0	0.2	17.3	38.4
Buffalo	100.0	78.5	2.4	5.5	13.7
Elmira	100.0	0.7	8.6	70.5	20.2
New York Metropolitan Area	100.0	32.7	9.0	20.6	37.7
Rochester	100.0	1.6	2.3	46.1	50.0
Syracuse	100.0	6.3	7.8	35.5	50.4
Utica	100.0	0.8	1.1	56.5	41.6
Rest of State	100.0	7.8	9.8	20.4	61.8

SOURCE: War Production Board, *War Supply and Facility Contracts by State and Industrial Area Cumulative through June 1945.*

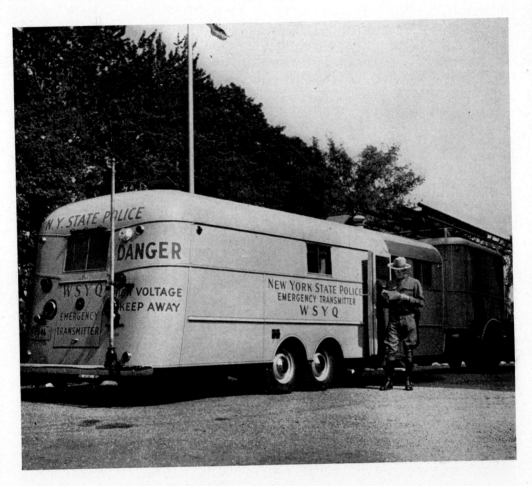

State Troopers

The New York State Police maintained a mobile radio sub-station with transmitting and receiving apparatus ready to operate from any point in the State.

State Guardsmen on Parade

Part of the 14,000 members of the New York State Guard march in review past
Governor Dewey at special military ceremonies in New York City's Central Park.

Table 11. War Supply and Facility Contracts, United States and Leading States (Millions of Dollars)

Area	Supply contracts through June, 1945						Facilities through May, 1945		
	Total	Aircraft	Ships	Ordnance	Com. equipment	Other	Total	Industrial	Military
United States	189,741	58,665	29,474	48,271	9,929	43,402	27,172	16,998	10,174
New York	21,499	7,561	1,305	4,924	2,070	5,638	1,549	1,114	435
Michigan	21,476	6,936	1,268	11,447	100	1,724	1,314	1,234	80
California	17,127	9,272	5,156	561	120	2,020	2,525	1,014	1,511
Ohio	16,553	5,624	1,456	4,704	274	4,495	1,385	1,219	166
New Jersey	13,250	3,972	2,575	1,454	2,172	3,078	747	453	294
Illinois	12,994	2,586	443	4,379	2,108	3,478	1,498	1,289	208
Pennsylvania	12,967	976	1,780	4,652	558	5,001	1,542	1,277	265
Indiana	8,739	3,461	463	3,268	319	1,228	1,147	961	186
Connecticut	8,117	4,163	297	2,347	148	1,162	281	256	25
Massachusetts	6,757	844	1,749	1,177	789	2,699	568	369	199
Texas	7,160	1,795	1,568	643	1,126	2,028	2,004	1,167	838
Maryland	5,030	2,116	1,016	394	914	590	515	238	277
Wisconsin	4,623	727	832	1,794	21	1,249	455	400	55
Washington	4,568	1,974	2,105	130	2	357	669	341	328
Missouri	3,512	1,110	151	1,495	42	714	681	538	144
Kansas	2,924	2,524	44	209	45	102	577	370	208
Oregon	1,802	1	1,593	30	...	178	264	101	164
Georgia	1,764	547	416	223	1	576	396	110	286
Minnesota	1,632	144	117	802	13	556	338	330	8
Virginia	1,625	12	982	286	1	344	842	278	564
Oklahoma	1,524	1,147	6	96	1	274	498	225	273
Alabama	1,506	77	566	491	...	373	633	446	187
Louisiana	1,439	245	567	201	u	427	642	388	254
North Carolina	1,358	63	479	105	...	709	482	102	380

u: Under $500,000

SOURCE: War Production Board, *War Supply and Facility Contracts by State, Industrial Area, and County Cumulative through June, 1945.*

CHAPTER FOUR

Defense of the Home Front

DURING the Second World War the defense of the home front in New York State against all forms of enemy action short of actual invasion became the joint responsibility of four State agencies: (1) the State Police, with a numerical strength of 1000 men, (2) the State Guard, with 16,000 men, (3) the New York Wing of the Civil Air Patrol, with 4800 men, and (4) the State Office of Civilian Protection, with a State-wide organization of between 600,000 and 700,000 civilian defense volunteers.

To its normal peacetime functions, the State Police added the prevention of sabotage, cooperating with the Federal Bureau of Investigation in apprehending individuals known to be aiding the enemy, and extensive assistance to the Army and Navy in connection with movements of troops and materials of war. The State Guard was created to take the place of the federalized National Guard and to afford a reserve force which could be brought to the aid of civilian authorities in case of internal emergency. The Civil Air Patrol engaged in all sorts of observation and rescue work, transportation of key men and materials, and until 1943, the spotting and occasional bombing of submarines along the Atlantic seaboard.

The establishment of a State Office of Civilian Protection was deemed necessary in 1941 to coordinate all volunteer services likely to be required in communities under attack from the air. During that year, and in 1942, pursuant to the newly enacted War Emergency Act, a large number of protective agencies were brought under the authority of the Director of Civilian Protection.

Among these agencies were the Air Raid Warning, Control, and Report Centers, all training activities in connection with civilian protection, the State Gas Officer, the Forest Fire Fighters Service, the State Property Officer, the Emergency Medical and Emergency Welfare Services, the State Fire Administrator, the Office of Highway Repair and Debris Clearance, various mutual-aid plans involving the State Police, Fire Mobilization, Water Supply and Emergency Milk Supply, and the Civil Air Patrol. It was the duty of the Director of Civilian Protection to coordinate the activities of these agencies, and in time of attack to direct their operations.

The chances of invasion were considered to be remote, and even had it occurred, invasion would have been a Federal problem. The possibility of aerial bombing, on the other hand, was seriously considered, and in such an event America would have needed defenses of the type whose value had been proved in England during the German blitz. Actually, however, no enemy bombing occurred on the east coast. Furthermore, there was practically no sabotage, far less than the experience of World War I had led us to anticipate. Except for the work of the Civil Air Patrol, certain activities of the State Police and the handling of occasional emergencies of an accidental or natural nature, protective action on the home front remained at a minimum. That this was so does not detract from the essential character of the four agencies, nor must it obscure the fact that while Americans were fortunate to avoid air attack, unlike so many people whom attack and invasion found unprepared, they were prepared even though attack and invasion did not materialize.

THE NEW YORK STATE GUARD

The creation of the New York State Guard was undertaken to provide the State with some military force in case of emergency. In July, 1940, General William N. Haskell, in command of the New York National Guard, organized an office force for the purpose of drawing up plans for the creation of the New York Guard, if and when the 25,000 National Guardsmen were inducted into the Federal service. A restriction in Section 61 of the National Defense Act, which forbade the states in time of peace to organize military forces other than the National Guard, was removed October 21, 1940, largely through the personal efforts of Governor Lehman. By October 15, a plan of mobilization and tables of organization on a basis of 50 per cent of the National Guard personnel had been prepared and published in a pamphlet entitled *Information Circular for Personnel of the New York Guard of the State of New York*. The age limits for officers were twenty-one to sixty-three inclusive, and of enlisted men eighteen, subsequently seventeen, to fifty-five. Regimental commands were designated by General Haskell before his departure for Federal service.

On October 25, 1940, the New York Guard was organized pursuant to General Orders No. 40 and Major-General William Ottman was placed in command. At least one unit of the Guard was assigned to each of the seventy-four National Guard Armories in the State. By December 30, 1940, nearly ten thousand officers and men had been enrolled,

a very creditable showing in view of the fact that service in the Guard carried no remuneration and exacted a sacrifice of appreciable time and energy.

The duty of the Guard was to aid civilian authority in time of crisis. Initially, it was considered possible that sabotage of military installations, factories, or of the labor force might be attempted. As it turned out, that danger was overestimated. From the beginning the War Council took the position that the protection of private property was the responsibility of the possessor, and that the State Guard was to be used only for tasks that were really vital. Accordingly, with the help of the Army, the State Police, and the Office of Civilian Protection, factories organized and trained their own protection personnel. No situations developed to proportions warranting the calling out of any part of the New York Guard in 1940 or 1941. The only two occasions during the entire war period for the use of a portion of the Guard came in July, 1942, when a company was called out for full-time duty during a flood in the vicinity of Olean, and in February of 1945 at the height of the traffic tie-up due to heavy snow and high winds, when a number of regiments were mobilized by the Adjutant General along the Hudson and Mohawk Valleys and as far west as Buffalo. These units were placed at the disposal of the Governor's Emergency Committee, whose operations were under the direction of Commissioner Sells of the Department of Public Works. Their chief function was to keep the railroad tracks clear, and thus permit shipments of grains and foodstuffs to reach their destinations.

In 1943, an agreement was reached between the Second Service Command and the New York State Guard, which provided for joint operations against any threat of invasion. The New York State Guard Emergency Plan, Field Order No. 1, was completed May 15, 1944, providing for close cooperation with Federal forces, State and local police, and offices of civilian protection to preserve the sovereignty of the State in all domestic emergencies and to cope with disasters.

Equipping the State Guard was delayed somewhat as the need for weapons and equipment for the United States Army had first priority, but the delay in securing equipment had no serious consequences, for by 1943 the turn in the tide of the war made it highly unlikely that Germany would be able to attack the east coast. Furthermore, the remarkable unanimity brought about in this country by the Japanese attack on Pearl Harbor and the efficient work of the Federal Bureau of Investigation in rounding up suspicious aliens together produced a remarkably calm internal situation compared to that of the previous war.

In the beginning, there was some difficulty in maintaining membership at a satisfactory level. For a number of reasons the average turnover in the personnel of the Guard was high, reaching an average in 1943 of 81 per cent and in some units going over 100 per cent. Many members entered the armed forces, or finding it impossible for personal or business reasons to maintain regular attendance, dropped out altogether. In October, 1943, Lieutenant-General Hugh A. Drum was placed in command, and in May, 1944, with the backing of Governor Dewey, a recruiting campaign was launched which successfully maintained the strength of the Guard at around 16,700. In 1943 and 1944 attendance averaged approximately 85 per cent.

THE STATE POLICE

The New York State Police took an active part in State and Federal defense preparation programs, and, after the declaration of war, in matters closely associated with internal security. The wartime activities of the thousand members were closely related to military movements, the protection of war plants,

investigations of the Federal Bureau of Investigation, and the work of the State Traffic Commission, the State War Transportation Committee, and the State Office of Civilian Protection. Owing to the war its activities were greatly enlarged and were carried on with a depleted staff, whose devotion to duty deserves commendation.

Early in the summer of 1940, the Governor called a series of conferences to formulate a plan for the speedy mobilization in event of an emergency of the thirty thousand members of the numerous police units of the State. The State Defense Coordinator, representatives of the State Police, the New York Association of Police Chiefs, the Sheriffs' Association, and the mayors of large cities participated in these conferences and created the New York State Police Mobilization Plan, announced July 23, 1940. Under this plan, the State was divided into eight mobilization districts, seven of them coextensive with the territories of the seven troops of the State Police. The eighth included New York City. Within each of the seven mobilization districts, the troop captain of the State Police was designated as mobilization coordinator, and, in the case of New York City, the Police Commissioner.

As in almost every other branch of State service, the Police Mobilization Plan necessitated taking an inventory of personnel and equipment, and of the possibilities for their assemblage and utilization outside of their own municipal areas. This was completed in September, 1940, and revised in January, 1942. The operation of the plan provided for the assumption of command by any Chief of Police of any city within whose limits an emergency occurred. Outside the city limits, the Governor would designate a commander to serve during a mobilization period. To set the plan in operation, in the event of an emergency, the authority within the district where the emergency occurred would communicate with the district mobilization coordinator and inform him of the extent and nature of the situation and the probable number of men required. The district mobilization coordinator would then inform the Governor who would order a police mobilization and, with the exception of New York City and Nassau county, would designate the officer to take charge of a disaster or emergency situation. Chapter 422, Laws of 1941 gave legislative sanction to the police mobilization plan almost without change. The 1942 session of the Legislature passed Chapter 544 of the Laws of 1942, subsequently signed by the Governor, which transferred the 1941 provision for police mobilization from the General Municipal Law to the New York State War Emergency Act. It was believed at the time that New York was the first State to have a plan for police mobilization. Certainly the plan itself, either in whole or in part, was followed by many other states, and personnel from the New York organizations were called to other states to inaugurate similar procedures.

Communication was by means of the State Police teletype system, supplemented by State and municipal radio transmitters, and by two-way radio equipment in all mobile units. The plan of mobilization was carefully explained to all municipal police officials and to leaders of the city and county war councils. Close liaison was maintained between the Division of State Police and the Office of Civilian Protection. A control room somewhat similar to the Civilian Protection control centers was established at each State Police barracks to regulate and record the distribution of police resources. This gave instantaneous visual evidence of personnel and equipment mobilized and in reserve. To provide coordination with all civilian protection plans for the use of fire, medical, and other emergency personnel and equipment, the troop control room was kept in close touch with the local Office of Civilian Protection.

The New York State Police cooperated closely with the Federal government in a number of ways. As early as 1940, the Federal Bureau of Investigation requested assistance from the State Police on inquiries relating to subversive activities by suspected persons and organizations within the rural areas of the State. Extensive reports were prepared and forwarded to Washington, and close cooperation was likewise maintained with Army and Navy Intelligence, as well as other branches of the Federal government engaged in the prosecution of the war. For example, at an early period the State Police were instrumental in training Military Police for the Army. Whether due to the systematic character of these early efforts, or to the relatively small number of enemy saboteurs in action during World War II, there was an exceedingly small amount of sabotage — far less than was generally supposed.

The State Police had other important responsibilities. The Army conducted frequent military movements and dispatched trucks carrying live explosives along main highways of the State. It was the task of the State Police to provide escorts for both of these activities and the superintendent served as liaison officer between the armed forces and civilian police authorities in all such cases. In many instances, members of the State Police also acted as consultants to public utilities and industrial plants in preparing precautionary measures to guard their properties. In this case it was closely associated with the Second Corps Area of the United States Army in outlining a comprehensive policy to safeguard utilities and industries.

The State Police rendered valuable assistance to a number of State agencies. Two of its officers were members of the Defense Committee of the New York State Association of Chiefs of Police, which worked closely with the State Defense Council and the Director of Civilian Protection in the training of auxiliary police. In 1941 and 1942, members of the police took part in the discussions of committees working on the problems of evacuation, the reduction of traffic accidents, and the organization of State-wide blackouts. Many served as official observers for air-raid drills and practice blackouts, submitting reports on their observations to the Director of Civilian Protection. They also conducted investigations for the State War Council to determine the necessity for closing streets or restricting traffic in the vicinity of war production plants and military installations.

Instructors were provided for two driver-training programs, carried on by the Office of War Training, i.e., the driver-training program for civilian volunteers for the emergency driving of motor vehicles during air raids, and the School Bus Driver Training Program organized to train four thousand drivers in the operation and conservation of school buses. The emergency truck control stations, established by the State War Council through the Metropolitan Defense Transport Committee, though commanded by civilian personnel were supervised by the State Police.

During 1941, a housing shortage developed at Kendaia in connection with the construction by the Army of a 12,000-acre ammunition storage plant. Housing for the nine thousand employees presented a problem as well as a serious health menace, as construction workers lived in tents, automobile trucks, and other makeshift shelters without facilities for sanitation or water supply. The War Plans Coordinator assigned a detail of State Police to work with the Division of Housing in checking all available rooms and lodgings in the area. The survey was completed within forty-eight hours and remedial steps immediately undertaken. Similarly, in the summer of 1941, a test survey of available housing facilities for evacuees was made in Sullivan county. The State Commissioner of Housing and the Chairman of the Health Preparedness Commission jointly undertook this survey with the cooperation of the local War Council and the State Police.

The supervision of highway traffic conditions was another activity in which the State Police worked closely with such State agencies as the Traffic Commission and the War Transportation Committee. The rising curve of highway accidents was naturally a subject of concern, and the Division put forth its best efforts to keep the rate as low as possible. New York's increase during the war years was well below that of the national average.

CIVIL AIR PATROL

Perhaps the most active of all the national civilian protection agencies and certainly the most versatile was the Civil Air Patrol established on a national basis in November, 1941, by the national Office of Civilian Defense. The basic purpose was to set up a civilian air force to assist both the armed and civilian defense agencies of the country. Ten days before Pearl Harbor, Governor Lehman received notification of the impending formation of such a force, which ultimately developed within New York State into an organization of approximately 4,800 men and women pilots, observers, ground crews, and specialists. Headquarters for this New York Wing were established in New York City, Albany, Schenectady, Syracuse, Buffalo, and Jamestown. The personnel was composed of private citizens ineligible for service in the armed forces, who owned their own planes, bought their own uniforms, and paid their personal expenses. Much of their flying was done at night in all kinds of weather conditions, without parachutes, and over areas where icing and engine trouble inevitably meant a crash.

At the outset, all enrollments were thoroughly checked by the Federal Bureau of Investigation and an individual's application included fingerprints, photographs, and detailed statements of previous training and experience. This system effectively guaranteed the loyalty and trustworthiness of the members of the Patrol, and in not a single instance was confidence misplaced. Early in 1942, an extensive program of military and technical training was undertaken to perfect the discipline and skill which were to characterize the operations of the New York Wing. A year later, in April, 1943, the Civil Air Patrol was made an auxiliary of the Army Air Forces, and in June the New York Wing became an agency of the Civilian Protection Division of the State War Council.

Its most spectacular and least publicized function was the antisubmarine patrol maintained until August 31, 1943, along the Atlantic seaboard. Early in 1942 the menace of German submarines along the Atlantic coast reached such proportions that the then available Army and Navy facilities were unable to cope with it, due to the necessity of deploying their slender resources in other theaters of war. In March, an experimental Civil Air Patrol base was established at Atlantic City, known as Coastal Patrol Base No. 1, from which pilots, observers, mechanics, and so on, using their own light planes, undertook to patrol the coastal waters from New York Harbor to below Cape May. The unqualified success of this seemingly unorthodox operation quickly led to the establishment of other bases, so that within a few months all shipping along the entire coastline of the United States was protected by the Civil Air Patrol. Coastal Air Patrol Base No. 17 was established July 1, 1942, at Suffolk Airport, near West Hampton, Long Island, and staffed by personnel from the New York and Pennsylvania Wings of the Civil Air Patrol. That same month approval was given to arm the planes with bombs. This step, plus a perfected communications system, accounted for the destruc-

tion of a number of enemy submarines by bombing, and the sinking of many more by naval vessels directed to the quarry by radio reports from patrolling Civil Air Patrol planes. Many hundreds of seamen while adrift were spotted and saved by surface facilities summoned to their assistance. In the history of the war, there was no finer example of self-sacrifice, devotion to duty, and ability to hang on under adverse and discouraging circumstances than that set by the men of the antisubmarine patrol. Over thirty lost their lives, and many more were seriously injured. In this work it is safe to say that New York's contribution in pilots, observers, mechanics, and technicians was as great as, or greater than that of any other state. Deactivation came in August, 1943, when the Navy took over the antisubmarine defense work from the Army Air Forces.

The New York Wing of the Civil Air Patrol was the first to organize an industrial courier service known in the State as the First Courier Command for the flying of key men and vitally needed materials between war production plants, their branches, and subcontractors. Pilots and planes were on duty from dawn until dusk, and the Command had flights under way on ten minutes notice from its bases in Albany, Schenectady, Syracuse, Buffalo, and Jamestown. At a time when the commercial airlines were greatly overburdened, these facilities were of positive assistance in keeping the production lines of our factories moving, and practically every major war industry in the State availed itself of this emergency service.

Late in 1943, Army authorities requested the national Civil Air Patrol to organize a number of bases throughout the country for the purpose of towing the sleeve targets at which Army Air Forces pilots and gunners in service aircraft could fire under conditions more closely approximating those in actual combat, and also to fly at stipulated heights over antiaircraft artillery units for the purpose of training them in accuracy in picking up moving targets with searchlights and radar. The base established at the Flushing, Long Island, Airport made an outstanding record of day and night flights in this connection.

The first official forest patrol in New York State was flown October 3, 1943 in cooperation with the Conservation Department. Its aim was to assist forest rangers in discovering and reporting a forest fire from the air before it could do much damage. The test plane was in continuous radio-phone communication with the fire-tower observers along the route and the success of this test led to an enlarged patrol, which cooperated effectively for the balance of the season both with the Commission and the Bureau of Forest Fire Control.

Innumerable miscellaneous missions were flown at one time or another by the Civil Air Patrol. On short notice, "Search Service" was instituted for missing aircraft and boats, and assistance rendered in other emergencies and disasters. One search mission in August, 1945, covered the entire Adirondack area and discovered a large Army transport missing since the previous year. Many flights were carried out at the request of United States engineers, who were inspecting from the air the camouflage on various factories, plants, and military installations in and around New York City. The flights to test camouflage, carried out frequently under adverse weather conditions, were often flown successfully by women flyers.

In 1944, the commanding general of the Army Air Forces requested the national Civil Air Patrol to undertake an intensive campaign to recruit young men for the Army Air Forces. Since all available Air Corps personnel were badly needed overseas, the use of members and facilities of the Civil Air Patrol for recruiting duty was essential and proved highly satisfactory. In May, 1944, the administration of the aviation cadet qualifying examinations was entrusted to the Civil Air Patrol. At the same time, it was requested to undertake on a national basis the recruiting of applicants for the Women's Army Corps. This was set up as a separate operation in New York State under the Civil Air Patrol Director of WAC recruiting.

In connection with civilian protection blackouts and the Airplane Spotter Service, over eight hundred hours were flown in observation. Special emergency measures, such as those in connection with boats caught in the ice in Lake Erie without food, the flying of food and medical supplies to isolated farms and communities when snowbound, the flying of plasma to scenes of disaster as in the case of the Wayland train wreck, and searches for escaped German prisoners were all included in the regular line of duty. Air shows and free rides to bond purchasers helped to stimulate public interest in the sale of war bonds. Cooperation was likewise extended to units of the New York State Guard on field maneuvers through the use of plane-to-ground communications.

One of the least understood but probably most important contributions of the Civil Air Patrol lay in the training provided its own personnel. Courses of study were provided for all members on a large number of subjects allied to military and civilian aviation. Attendance at classes in these courses was compulsory for those desiring to maintain membership in the organization. This helped to ensure that the improvement of skills and the acquisition of new ones would be a continuous process. On October 1, 1942, the grade of Civil Air Patrol Cadets was authorized embracing boys and girls from the ages of fifteen to eighteen. The number of cadets attracted by this provision justified an extensive training program designed to supply the Army Air Forces with a constant backlog of desirable young men ready to enlist when they reached eighteen. The *Preflight Student's Manual*

Air Raid Spotting Center

An air defense information center, acclaimed as best equipped in the world, was set up in New York City. As part of the Army's Air Defense of the Eastern Seaboard, civilian volunteers received reports from civilian observers.

which was used covered all phases of preflight training, military, physical, and technical. Within the New York City area this work was carried on by the Greater New York Cadet Training Group. Each summer, with the cooperation of the Army Air Forces, a considerable number of cadets were sent to Mitchel Field and the Rome Army Air Base to receive a week's preview of Army life and to inspect the facilities and installations there available.

As may be judged from these incidents, the exploits of the New York Wing of the Civil Air Patrol constitute one of the most romantic chapters of the entire war. Not only were the activities of its 4800 members thrilling and dramatic, but they were frequently of very real and immediate assistance at some crucial point in the State's war effort. If gratitude for services rendered can ever be commensurate with the risk involved, these men and women of the Civil Air Patrol are entitled to full measure from the hearts of their fellow citizens.

OFFICE OF CIVILIAN PROTECTION

Had the Germans succeeded in bombing the east coast of the United States, the most important of all the War Council agencies would have been the Office of Civilian Protection. Under its direct supervision from the time of the passage of the War Emergency Act came all training, organization, and direction of the volunteer and paid services likely to be required in the event of bombing from the air. Fortunately, the detailed preparations made by this office during 1941 and 1942 were never called into combat. There were many instances, however, where civilian protection forces rendered invaluable service in the field of fire protection and in disaster relief. Even were this latter fact to be ignored, the time and effort put into the New York Civilian Protection Program were undoubtedly a good form of insurance.

As mentioned in Chapter I, the first discussions of the protection of civilians, war plants, and utilities took place in the State Defense Council in February, 1941. At that time, however, the plans of the Federal government were also in the discussion stage. While it was clearly recognized that matters of active defense were the responsibility of the armed forces, and conversely that duties lying within the sphere of passive defense belonged to the State and its communities, until the Federal government had worked out the national program in sufficient detail there was little that New York or any other state could do to prepare for the program in advance. In April, an officer from the Second Corps Area in charge of the civilian defense problem was interrogated by the members of the State Defense Council, but no decision was reached other than that the State should await a go-ahead signal from the Federal government.

Nevertheless, despite this "wait and see" attitude, the entire matter of civilian protection seemed to the Council sufficiently urgent to warrant the appointment of a Director of Civilian Protection, and the Governor was accordingly authorized to secure a suitable person. The decision of the Defense Council to set up an Office of Civilian Defense and to appoint a director sprang from the knowledge of England's bitter experience and the fear that, should England be defeated, America's chances of avoiding a similar fate would be slight. Under the circumstances, it seemed foolhardy not to prepare for all eventualities.

Accordingly, on May 8, 1941, Governor Lehman appointed Major-General John F. O'Ryan (Retired) as Director of Civilian Defense for the State of New York. This preceded by nearly two weeks the President's appointment, May 20, of Mayor LaGuardia of New York City to head the national Office of Civilian Defense. Shortly thereafter it was arranged with Mayor LaGuardia that in New York

State civilian defense activities would be handled through the existing State Defense Council organization. Accordingly, the chairman of each local defense council was asked to appoint a director of Civilian Defense for the city or county, and to stand by for further instructions from the State.

The chief tasks confronting the State Director of Civilian Defense were (1) the creation of a paid Statewide organization (to supervise and direct the organization and training of all local units), (2) the creation and training of a local volunteer civilian defense organization as a division of the local defense councils, and (3) the coordination of all existing municipal and private services with the Statewide civilian protection plans, since civilian defense was regarded as a local problem and all organizations were designed to function in the communities.

On June 12, 1941, the Governor wrote chairmen of all local defense councils urging the formation, training, and instruction of auxiliary fire and police corps, as well as corps of "street wardens" for cities and heavily populated communities. A week later, following a request from the Federal government, he also wrote the local defense councils asking them to organize air observation posts and to use in that connection the services of the American Legion. This marked the beginning of the aircraft warning system, of which the setting up of forty-six warning centers was the second stage. These two principal tasks were carried on simultaneously all during 1941 and the early part of 1942.

The Organization of the Civilian Air Raid Warning System. The principal problem of the Army Air Forces, in the solution of which the State played a part, related to the spotting of enemy aircraft. The Air Corps desired accurate information indicating the number, type, speed, altitude, and direction of possible enemy aircraft. It decided that in New York

such information could be supplied best by a grid of over 1400 observation posts. On the basis of their reports, a warning signal would be given to the Interceptor Air Squadron commanders for the purpose of enabling them to intercept the enemy air forces at the desired point. That was the first phase of the operation of the Army's Warning System. The second phase was reached as soon as the objective area of the enemy aircraft had been sufficiently determined. A second warning order would then be given to the civilian defense forces, on the ground in that area, to prepare for the coming attack. In order to accomplish this, a network of forty-six District Warning Centers was established.

The initial work in setting up this system was completed in 1941, when approximately 1330 air-raid observation posts were organized by the State Office of Civilian Defense with the assistance of local defense councils and the various posts of the American Legion, and turned over to the United States Army for supervision. Late in 1941 and early in 1942, the United States Army Air Forces organized and placed in operation information and filter centers at New York City, Albany, and Buffalo, and a filter center in Syracuse. Upon receipt of sufficient information from the observation posts, the centers would send out over special Army telephones the necessary air raid warnings to those of the forty-six district warning centers whose particular area appeared to be threatened. At the same time 108 county and city control centers and approximately 1500 report centers in villages and townships were organized by the State Office of Civilian Defense on a twenty-four-hour basis to which air raid warning signals were relayed by civilian protection personnel from the forty-six district warning centers. In all of the district warning centers and control centers unlisted telephones were installed to assure satisfactory communication signals in the conduct of practice blackouts and air raid drills. This system operated until December 15, 1943, at which time the United States Army issued instructions to consolidate the forty-six district warning centers to twenty-five. This was done by reducing twenty-one centers to sub-district warning centers receiving their signals from another warning center instead of the Army Information Center. On June 10, 1944, the United States Army discontinued the operation of all Army Information Centers and the dissemination of air raid warning signals henceforth became the responsibility of the State.

Building the Civilian Protection Organization. The entire concept of civilian protection was colored by the experience of England in the blitz, and the expectation of air bombing along the east coast. Observers were sent across the Atlantic to study the organization of the British defense, and Englishmen in this country were consulted frequently. The task of building up a State organization among civilians which would operate under a unified command, and still be capable of action in a limited emergency, was not easy. Fortunately, many of the normal private and public services such as police, fire, medical, highway, public welfare, and the Red Cross which would be needed in a crisis were already being organized for emergency functions by their existing leadership. The functions of these separate organizations were finally coordinated under the Director of Civilian Protection and their activities integrated with those of the local civilian protection organizations built upon the decentralized war council system in each city and county. Thus, the civilian protection leadership had three functions: (1) the training of civilian volunteer forces, (2) the coordinating of those forces with existing public services on a Statewide basis, and (3) cooperation with headquarters of the Second Service Command in all matters of defense.

From the start, the organization of civilian protection in New York State proceeded simultaneously on both State and local levels. On the State level, in addition to the director and assistant director at headquarters in Albany, there were set up on June 23, 1941, three districts, Northern, Southern, and Eastern, each under a deputy director. Field representatives and additional personnel were subsequently added. In February, the three districts were subdivided into five, Northern, Metropolitan, Central, Niagara Frontier, and Southern Tier, with headquarters for the deputies in charge located respectively in Albany, New York City, Rochester, Buffalo, and Binghamton. This represented the greatest extent of the State organization. In June, 1943, at the end of the North African Campaign, the Southern Tier District was eliminated. In March, 1944, a further consolidation eliminated the Central District, and in July the Metropolitan District also, leaving the State divided into Eastern and Western districts. Finally, on June 30, 1945, civilian protection was placed on a reserve basis.

All during the summer of 1941, the State staff was engaged in supervising the establishment of local civilian protection organizations under city and county directors. Subsequently the entire organization was given legal status in the War Emergency Act passed by the 1942 Legislature. In the cities, although the mayor could be Director of Civilian Protection, generally speaking it was considered wise for this busy official to appoint a special Director for Civilian Protection, who, by virtue of his office, became a member of the city war council. Approximately half of these officials were paid. County directors were appointed by chairmen of the Boards of Supervisors and by virtue of their office became members of the County War Council. The mayors of each village and the supervisors of each town became Deputy County Directors. Occasionally, city and county organizations were consolidated. All offices were kept open twenty-four hours a day, seven days a week, with the cost of maintenance defrayed by the municipality.

As outlined by the War Emergency Act, the duties of the local directors were numerous and complex. Not only did they have to enforce all laws, rules, and regulations of the State War Council, of the local war council, and of the State Director of Civilian Protection, but they were also permitted to adopt and promulgate their own regulations and issue orders, which were not inconsistent with those issued by the State Director of Civilian Protection or those issued by the State Council.

1. In connection with the guarding and protection of water supply, railroads, public utility services, bridges, docks, highways, airports, public buildings, factories, plants, vital and strategic materials and other focal points of attack, the loss or destruction of which might menace or endanger the security and safety of the civilian population, impede the military forces, or impede the war effort.

2. With respect to (a) practice blackouts and air raid drills, (b) warnings and signals for drills or attacks and the mechanical devices to be used in connection therewith, (c) the effective screening or extinguishment of all lights and lighting devices and appliances, (d) the shutting off of water mains, gas mains, electric power connections and the suspension of all other public utility services, (e) the conduct of civilians and the movement and cessation of pedestrian and vehicular traffic prior, during and subsequent to drills or attack, (f) the integrating of municipal and volunteer agencies.

Their cooperation with local councils was required in the recruiting, assignment, training, and organization of volunteers for the Civilian Protection forces, in the preparation of plans for evacuation, and whenever necessary in assisting Federal, State, and local officials and agencies. All control centers and report centers came under their jurisdiction, as well as the usual municipal officers and agencies whose functions in time of emer-

gency had to be coordinated with Civilian Protection forces. Their cooperation was required in the administration of all practice blackouts and air raid drills. In short, upon them fell the ultimate responsibility for the successful operation of the entire civilian defense machinery, a responsibility of no mean proportions.

Once the civilian defense organization had been systematized, it was then in condition to be activated by the Eastern Defense Command, which, on December 13, 1941, in a statement entitled "Army and Navy Policy on Civil Air Raid Warnings" declared that the commanding general of the First Interceptor Command would be the sole authority in the Second Corps Area for originating civilian defense air raid warnings. Responsibility for their execution, however, would continue to rest with the State Office of Civilian Defense. The Army would send the air raid warnings direct to the Civilian Defense District Warning Centers. Directors of Civilian Defense Air Raid Control Centers would alone be responsible for sounding the sirens and alerting the civilian defense districts. All night alerts were to be "blackouts" and both general blackouts and practice blackouts would be ordered only by the commanding general of the First Interceptor Command. As a matter of fact, until April, 1943, all practice blackouts were conducted by the New York State Office of Civilian Protection with the approval of the Army over unlisted telephones in District Warning Centers. After April, 1943, the Army instruments were used.

The forty-six District Warning Centers in New York were set up between December 15, 1941, and January 15, 1942, by the First Interceptor Command of the Army Air Force. By the end of 1941, nearly two hundred thousand volunteers had been recorded and assigned to special duties. By June, 1942, the number had reached five hundred thousand. Once the major outline of the organization had been filled in, details received greater attention. Regulations having the force of law were issued from time to time by the State Office of Civilian Protection covering such subjects as the control of lighting in the coastal zone of the State, the control of lighting during blackouts, the conduct of railroads during air raid alarms, the moving of vehicular and pedestrian traffic during blackouts, and the employment of different warning signals, all of which were finally standardized on a Statewide basis. All air raid protection regulations were finally systematized in Bulletin No. 1, issued January 27, 1943, pursuant to an order of Lieutenant General Hugh A. Drum, commanding the Eastern Defense Command and First Army. The New York Civilian Protection regulations were brought into line with the Army regulations April 23, 1943.

Meanwhile, early in 1942, Congress appropriated funds for supplies and facilities for civilian defense. On May 15, 1942, General O'Ryan was succeeded by Lieutenant General William N. Haskell, who in turn resigned at the end of the year and was succeeded on April 8, 1943, by Colonel Edward C. O. Thomas, who remained in charge of the State Office until June 30, 1945. Upon his resignation, Deputy Director John J. Farrell, who had been with the organization continuously since June 23, 1941 became Acting Director and remained in charge until October 1, during the period of gradual liquidation.

Civilian Defense Training Programs. Although in time of emergency much would depend upon the intelligence and common sense of the individual citizen, British experience had supplied a sufficient number of object lessons as to skills required in the event of air attack to justify efforts on a Statewide basis to train volunteers in the performance of special functions. A list of those performing special defense functions on the British model included: air raid wardens, auxiliary police, auxiliary firemen, bomb reconnaissance agents, staff units, road repair squads, demolition and clearance squads, decontamination squads, utility repair units, emergency medical services, rescue squads, nurses' aides, fire watchers, emergency food and housing units, messengers, and drivers. The United States Office of Civilian Defense adopted these classifications and prepared handbooks on the duties of each for distribution to the Civilian Defense forces of the entire country.

England's experience with the "blitz" naturally called attention to the dire need of a systematically organized defense against the principal agent of destruction—fire. In a single month the loss of firemen in some of England's large cities, including London, equaled their total paid staffs, and estimates were that for every regular member of an English fire department five auxiliaries were required to cope with conditions created by modern warfare. Proper selection and training of such forces was an important task. With this thought in mind, the Governor on April 14, 1941, appointed a Committee on Fire Defense composed of representatives of the fire chiefs, volunteer firemen and the paid firemen of the State. Its first task was the preparation with the aid of local defense councils of a Statewide inventory of fire-fighting equipment and personnel to show the extent and character of the existing defenses against fire and the possibilities for mutual aid among the municipalities of the State. A Fire Defense Training Program, designed to train the State's volunteer fire forces in wartime fire-fighting methods, was begun June 13, 1941, at the request of the Governor, the State Defense Council, and the State Fire Defense Committee. This was the first of the Civilian Defense Training programs and was subsquently expanded to include paid firemen and the auxiliary firemen of the Civilian Protection organization.

The preparation of the training materials was placed in the hands of the Bureau of Public Service Training of the Education Department. Sections on the handling of war gases, explosives, and incendiary bombs were included along with fundamentals of fire fighting. Advice was secured from outstanding fire chiefs, from Americans who had observed British fire-fighting methods at first hand, and from Englishmen available at the time in this country. The Fire Chiefs' Advisory Committee approved the course July 7, whereupon six fire instructors were engaged, sent to the Edgewood Arsenal School of the United States Chemical Warfare Service for special training, and their services then offered to local war councils, fire chiefs, and school officials. Classes were inaugurated in twenty-two counties in September, 1941, and in eighteen additional counties in January, 1942. Pamphlets on the organization and training of civilian auxiliary fire-fighting forces and on industrial fire prevention and protection were prepared and placed in the hands of the State fire chiefs. During the first year of the program, training in basic firefighting tactics was provided for 21,000 volunteer and paid firemen in sixty-one county fire schools. In turn, these were assisted in the training of thousands of auxiliary firemen as part of the civilian protection forces of their own communities. In New York City special teacher-training courses were given to the 1700 officers of the fire department to enable them in turn to instruct fire auxiliaries. Similar preparation designed especially to cope with the unusual fire-protection problems of the Niagara Frontier Zone was provided for 600 fire instructors in a locally financed fire college in that area.

A Statewide program for the training of all home owners in incendiary bomb control and extinguishment was undertaken December 9, 1941, at the direction of the Governor. Sixty police and fire department graduates of the Edgewood Arsenal School were deputized as instructors, in addition to the enlarged nine-man instructional staff of the Fire Training Program. Through their efforts 2500 fire-department instructors were trained, who then carried up-to-date information through demonstrations and lectures to the local communities. In addition, two films, "Stop That Fire" and "Fighting the Fire Bomb," depicting the control and extinguishment of incendiary bombs, were shown in December to approximately ten million persons through the medium of commercial theaters and the training classes. These films inaugurated an instructional film service which subsequently developed into the Film Division of the Office of War Training. In this Statewide program of mass education supplementary media were also employed, such as the radio, bus and trolley cards, and billboard advertising.

By June, 1942, the problem of civilian defense training was regarded by the State War Council as something more extensive than simply the training of volunteer and auxiliary firemen in fire defense. The various branches of Civilian Protection personnel had become clearly differentiated and to them had been added by action of the War Council specially trained technicians in charge of the operation of the Mutual Aid Water Supply System, of the Plant Protection Schools, and techniques for protection against war gases. Under these circumstances, it appeared logical that some central training agency should be set up to handle all civilian defense training programs, and a plan of the Director of the Bureau of Public Service Training for the establishment of a State Office of War Training was approved by the State War Council. The office was established June 15, 1942, as a cooperative service agency with an ample budget. Its responsibility was to plan Statewide civilian war training courses, to prepare and publish instructional materials, and to acquire or produce instructional films. It was to develop and maintain standards for civilian war instruction and to assist in coordinating and supervising all war training programs. Thus was established what was at that time one of the most advanced, centralized, professional training agencies anywhere in the United States. New York City followed suit by authorizing its own Division of War Training, January 1, 1943.

Between June 15, 1942, and the discontinuance of the State Office of War Training on May 1, 1944, the following training programs were developed by the Office of War Training at the request of State agencies: Fire Defense, Plant Protection, Air Raid Wardens, Block Leader, Civilian Defense Driver, Preinduction Driver, School Bus Driver, Emergency Sanitation and Water Service, Child Care, Gas Reconnaissance Officers and Instructors, War Gas Protection, Instructor-Training, Milk Pasteurization Plant Superintendent, Food and Drug Officials.

Perhaps the most important of the training programs were those devoted to plant protection, air raid wardens, war gas protection, and emergency sanitation and water service supply. Plant protection training developed in close touch with the Fire Defense Training Program. In addition to the development of over twenty-five plant fire brigades, starting in October, 1942, plant protection schools for more than a thousand industrial executives were held in Schenectady, Rochester, New York City, and elsewhere. Training in the protection of war industries from enemy attack, sabotage, and normal hazards was given by officers of the United States Army, officials of the United States Office of Civilian Defense, and other specialists.[1] The Chief State Fire Instructor served as a member of the instructional staff of the Plant Protection School, conducted at New York University for more than 450 persons. Upon request, he also made surveys of over 125 plants and presented recommendations to improve plant protection organization and facilities.

The War Gas Protection Training Program was begun in the spring of 1943 in collaboration with the State Gas Officer and experts of the United States Chemical Warfare Service, the Office of Civilian Defense, and other Federal and State war agencies. Under the Office of Civilian Defense Operations Letter No. 104, the appointment of Senior Gas Officers was undertaken by a number of the local war councils. All responsibility for the training of these men was placed in the hands of the State Gas Consultant by the Director of Civilian Protection. Early in 1943, with the help of the Office of War Training, he proceeded to hold five training schools in Buffalo, Syracuse, Albany, Garden City, and Mount Vernon. In each case the Second Service Command furnished physical demonstrations of gas attacks and the proper methods of handling them. Local war councils, including those of Westchester and Erie Counties and the cities of Buffalo, Utica, Niagara Falls, and Syracuse, trained their own qualified gas reconnaissance officers. In New York City the Chief of the Gas Defense Unit conducted ten schools for over four hundred gas reconnaissance officers. In all cases instruction emphasized primarily detection of gases and protection against their harmful effects.

---

[1] Wartime precautions taken by large, critical plants, included such steps as the establishment of a central control room, the training of personnel in plant protection methods, enlarging the system of plant guards, the identification of employees by fingerprints and photographs, the instruction of employees on general procedures, the institution of blackout precautions, and occasionally the adoption of camouflage.

To provide instruction concerning the protection of food from contamination by war gas or by other enemy action, as well as decontamination methods, a four-day War Training Laboratory was attended by thirty-one food control chemists of the northeastern states. This laboratory and a previous training institute attended by 121 officials were organized at the joint request of the Emergency Council of Food and Drug Officials in the northeastern states, the State Department of Agriculture and Markets, the State Department of Health, and the State Gas Officer.

Since the Office of War Training was directed to place special emphasis on all training in the protection of life and property, the training of air-raid wardens assumed prime importance. A standard course was developed and launched during October, 1942, at a series of twelve regional training institutes for instructors and officials of the Air-raid Warden Service. The total number of instructors prepared at these institutes for the training of local wardens was over 1500. A manual, including home-study outlines, was made available to all instructors attending the schools.

Likewise, at the request of the State Coordinator of Water Supply and the State Department of Health, the Office of War Training organized five three-day regional training institutes to familiarize all Water Superintendents with standard instructional materials which they, in turn, were to present to local water works auxiliaries. Approximately forty local schools, attended by over six hundred water officials, were conducted and an Emergency Sanitation and Water Works Manual, including lessons in the operation of the emergency water service, was published. Technical details were of course prepared by the State Coordinator of Water Supply. The soundness of the training program and of the whole Mutual Aid Water Supply Plan was dramatically demonstrated August, 1942,

by the speed and effectiveness with which local officials handled the emergency created by the flood at Olean.

Generally speaking, the Office of War Training provided funds for the publication of manuals of instruction on subjects where instruction was deemed necessary. Its staff cooperated closely with the officials of the State Departments, the State War Council agencies, and in many instances with local war councils themselves, in making arrangements for the training schools. The procedure followed by the office was dictated by the size of the State and was twofold — a small group of leaders in any particular sphere of activity were selected on a geographical basis and brought together for a thorough course of instruction, both in subject matter and in teaching methods. These would then serve as instructors in local communities. This decentralization of the instructional process was on the whole surprisingly effective in covering the State. In many instances the manuals, developed cooperatively between the Office of War Training and the particular State agency involved, received wide distribution throughout the United States. This was especially true of the *Emergency Sanitation and Water Works Manual,* the local *War Training Committee Handbook,* and the *School Bus Drivers' Manual.* It was not the function of the Office of War Training to provide technical material itself, but rather to arrange the material attractively, develop methods for its circulation and use within the State, and arrange for the holding of classes. The quality of instruction depended to a large extent upon the interest and previous training and experience of the local instructors and consequently varied somewhat. Cooperation with State agencies, likewise dependent upon the personal equation, varied also.

The Gas Defense Program. Shortly after Pearl Harbor, the New York State Health Preparedness Commission was requested by the State War Plans Coordinator to study chemical warfare and its probable effect upon the civilian population. In conferences with the Medical Division of the United States Office of Civilian Defense and the State Director of Civilian Protection it was decided that since the physicians of the Emergency Medical Service had direct responsibilities for protecting the public health against the effects of air raids, they should be given instruction in this technical phase of chemical warfare. Accordingly the Office of Civilian Defense sponsored an intensive five-day course in the Medical Aspects of Chemical Warfare at the University of Cincinnati College of Medicine. This course, the first of its kind, began February 23, 1942, and was attended by four physicians from New York State representing the Health Preparedness Commission, the State Department of Health, and Cornell and Columbia Medical Schools.

Shortly afterward Dr. David D. Rutstein, of the Department of Health, was appointed by the Commission on a part-time basis as its Medical Officer for Gas Protection. The State Medical Society and the nine medical schools of the State were soon brought into a program of instruction for the physicians in the Emergency Medical Service of the State. A standard six-hour course was prepared using as a model that given in an intensive five-day postgraduate course in the Medical Aspects of Chemical Warfare, April 20-25, at the University of Cincinnati. This had been taken by twenty of the leading physicians of the State, two from each medical school and representatives of the Department of Health and of the State Medical Society, who were to form the nucleus of instructors for the entire State.

A report on the problem of gas defense and the training program being developed was called for by the State War Council in May, and approved for the Council by the Director of Civilian Protection. In June, details were arranged between the Director of Civilian Protection and the Director of the Office of War Training Programs for carrying out a Statewide program of instruction. Priority was at first to be given to the local chiefs of Emergency Medical Service of the local war councils, to physicians serving in the emergency medical field units and designated casualty hospitals, to State district health officers, and to municipal health officers. The general development of the New York State program attracted the attention of the Medical Division of the Office of Civilian Defense, which in June, 1942, requested the full services of the Commission's Medical Officer for Gas Protection, to set up a similar program for physicians in other target areas of the country.

Likewise in May, 1942, the Federal Office of Civilian Defense urged each State Director of Civilian Protection in a seaboard area to appoint from personnel of the Department of Health a State Gas Officer to be responsible for the development of its defense against gas. Shortly afterward, at the battle of Midway, June 4-6, 1942, the United States Navy captured a Japanese cruiser loaded with poison gas. That focused the attention of the military forces of this country on the possibility of gas attack. Accordingly the State War Council followed the suggestion of the Office of Civilian Defense promptly and in July selected for the position of State Gas Consultant the chief chemist of the Department of Health, Dr. Wellington T. Gilcreas. This official was appointed subject to the supervision of the State Director of Civilian Protection, who sent him to training courses conducted by the Bureau of Chemical Warfare for senior gas officers at Amherst College, at the University of Cincinnati, and at Boston.

In August, 1942, the New York State Gas Consultant drew up a scheme for a State-wide gas defense organization, which was temporarily withheld from operation pending word from Washington. By a coincidence, his plan was subsequently submitted to the first Medical Gas Officer of the United States Office of Civilian Defense, and became the basis for its Operations Letter No. 104, dated January 11, 1943, relative to the appointment of Senior Gas Officers and the organization of Gas Defense Units. Action in New York State followed the appearance of this letter. The new Civilian Protection Director, Colonel Edward C. O. Thomas, issued a memorandum calling for the appointment by each local War Council of a gas officer to organize defense against chemical warfare in those areas susceptible to attack. Approximately half of the war councils took action.

In 1943, training schools for Senior Gas Officers and for staffs were held in cooperation with the Office of War Training in Buffalo, Syracuse, Garden City, Mt. Vernon, and Utica. The program covered methods for the field identification of chemical warfare agents, and instructions relative to the organization and training of Gas Defense Units. Special emphasis was placed on drills in the handling of gas incidents and attention was called to the possibility of industrial accidents and sabotage which would produce conditions comparable to conditions resulting from actual warfare. Nearly 500 persons were trained in upState schools and approximately 450 were trained in schools conducted in New York City. The larger cities had a very definite advantage in the way of trained personnel since they had industries and universities from which they could draw instructors. Courses on the medical aspects of chemical warfare defense were given to nurses, physicians, and other medical personnel. On the whole, these training courses provided a minimum of trained gas personnel throughout the critical sections of the State.

The development of military operations in Europe and Asia induced the need for an emphasis upon problems of civilian protection, including defense against gas. As a result, during 1944, the interest of the gas defense personnel was maintained largely in case local emergencies should arise requiring their services. One or two of these accidents did occur. At Highland a train loaded with gas went off the tracks. Fortunately, no damage was done. In Brooklyn, a worker dropped a chlorine cylinder in a sewer. Fifty or sixty people had to be hospitalized. Preparation for this type of accident rather than for enemy bombing was stressed until the end of the war. However, with the increase in submarine warfare and the introduction of the rocket bomb, the possibility of attack still remained, and a new type of gas discovered in the possession of Rommel's Afrika Corps kept chemical warfare in the public eye. During the latter part of 1944, the gas officers were virtually inactive and their positions were abolished in May, 1945.

Cooperation on the Gas Defense Program was unusually close between the State and New York City, the Federal Office of Civilian Defense and the State Office of Civilian Protection, one of the reasons being that, in a highly specialized field like the chemistry of gases, the chief personnel were well-acquainted, and were men of high caliber who understood what had to be done. Furthermore, the Gas Program was more than just insurance. It helped impress upon the minds of the people that a war was being fought, and in this respect helped sell war bonds. Interest in the Gas Program varied greatly among communities, and was especially strong in Niagara Falls, Rochester, and a few other cities which themselves manufactured gases of various sorts.

Emergency Medical Service. In view of the high level of civilian casualties resulting from German bombing in England, the formation of an effective Emergency Medical Service as part of the

State's Civilian Protection organization was a logical, precautionary move. In this respect, New York State was especially fortunate in that the leadership for this particular job had already been developed through legislative action over a period of several years prior to the outbreak of the war. The story goes back to 1940, and concerns the personnel and plans of the New York State Commission to Formulate a Long-Range Health Program, under the chairmanship of Assemblyman Lee B. Mailler. The diversion of the work of this committee to the medical aspects of Civilian Defense came about as the result of a series of conferences in June and July of 1940. The commission had offered its services to the Governor in connection with the defense program in the middle of June, and on July 17 it was commissioned by the War Plans Coordinator to assemble and analyze data relative to the health resources of the State and to ascertain their probable effectiveness in the case of a national emergency.

The commission lost no time in assuming its new responsibilities. In addition to its task of inventorying the health resources of the State, county by county, it faced a number of specific problems all of which required a systematic joint attack on the State and local levels by various health groups. Among these problems were:

The establishment of a means whereby communities would not be depleted of their health resources in the event of a crisis.

The formation of mobile emergency squads of physicians, surgeons and nurses capable of being immediately transported to any area experiencing a catastrophe.

The physical rehabilitation, wherever possible, of men rejected under the Selective Service Act.

A program of medical care to guard the physical fitness of workers in the productive war industries.

The commissioning of certain leaders in the medical profession as instructors in military surgery.

A coordinated plan of health instruction for the civilian population in preventive medicine, sanitation, and emergency first aid.

A ready supply of drugs, surgical supplies, and serums for all communities.

A speedy physical examination and classification of industrial workers and the rehabilitation of those with physical defects.

Cautions to safeguard the water supplies and sewage disposal systems, and the creation of auxiliary water supplies.

The maintenance of a balanced diet for the public and the use of adequate substitutes in the event of a food shortage.

The rapid immunization of the public against such diseases as typhoid, small-pox, tetanus, and diphtheria.

In the event of invasion, diseases not now prominent in the country might appear and would have to be efficiently dealt with. These diseases might include epidemic typhus, cholera, yellow fever and malaria.

The mobilization of resources to combat an extensive epidemic of influenza.

The maintenance of control methods for venereal diseases.

Accomplishing an orderly evacuation of the civilian population with due regard for essential health services, and in a manner that would not interfere with the military forces.

The prevention of panic among the civilian population and the utilization of all necessary safeguards against the hazards of enemy attack.

Ensuring adequate public health nursing services for each community.

The maintenance of schools for the training of nurses in their expanded duties.

Plans should be made in agreement with the military organization concerning which hospitals might be commandeered by the military.[1]

To find and evaluate this knowledge most thoroughly, it was essential that much of the work be undertaken at the local level. A health mobilization conference was accordingly held at the Academy of Medicine in New York City on July 30, 1940, and was attended by representatives of sixteen Federal, State, and

---

[1] Leg. (1941) 64, p. 10

private health organizations[1]. The general problem of civilian health in time of war was thoroughly discussed. An Advisory Subcommittee on Health Preparedness was appointed, and in August it recommended that each county create an Advisory Health Preparedness Committee, consisting of representatives of the principal county organizations concerned with public health, to handle all problems of a medical nature anticipated in connection with air attacks. This recommendation was approved by the newly formed State Council of Defense and, at its request, county committees, usually headed by the chairman of the Medical Preparedness Committee of the local County Medical Society, were created during the latter part of 1940 and throughout 1941. On March 6, 1941, a Statewide Health Preparedness Conference sponsored by the State Defense Council and the commission was held for representatives of local Health Preparedness committees. The State organizations represented on the Advisory Subcommittee of the State were given the opportunity to outline desirable health preparedness programs for the local committees. The meeting was followed by personal visits of Mr. Mailler and Dr. John J. Bourke to each of the fifty-seven counties and the establishment of active committees in each.

Under Chapter 483 of the Laws of 1941 continuing the Mailler Commission, its new responsibilities in connection with civilian defense were outlined as follows:

... the Commission hereby continued shall have the power, and it shall be its duty, on its own motion or upon the request of the Governor, or of the New York State Council of Defense, to undertake, supervise or direct (a) the making of studies, surveys and analyses of the nature, extent, location, and availability for use of the health facilities and resources of the state, and (b) the formulation, and execution of plans for organization, coordination, and mobilization of all services and skills pertaining to health for state and national defense purposes, and for the coordination of all activities affecting health or related thereto.

In view of this new assignment, the commission's name was shortened June 17, 1941, to the New York State Health Preparedness Commission, and shortly afterward it was designated as the Health and Medical Section of the State Council of Defense.

Thus by the middle of 1941, the State Defense Council had placed a statutory commission in charge of the medical aspects of civilian defense, and with its sanction that commission had already built up a Statewide organization of local Health Preparedness committees in the counties. With the aid of these county committees and in cooperation with the Medical Society of the State of New York, the Hospital Association of New York State, the State Nursing Association, medical schools and public and voluntary health agencies, surveys were made of all health facilities, hospital beds, of the principal needs for additional nurses, for doctors, and for additional facilities, together with approximate costs. Studies were undertaken in connection with the problem of evacuating civilians from New York City, and investigations conducted into many other local health problems. This early action at the local level laid a firm foundation for the Emergency Medical Service of Civilian Protection.

---

[1] Association of American Medical Colleges, Hospital Association of Greater New York, Hospital Association of New York State, Medical Society of New York County, Medical Society of the State of New York, American Federation of Nurses, American Public Health Association, American Red Cross, National Association of Public Health Nurses, New York City Health Department, New York State Association of Approved Laboratories, New York State Department of Health, New York State Journal of Medicine, New York State Nurses Association, United States Public Health Service, Westchester County Department of Health. Leg. Doc. (1942) 64, p. 12

In June, 1941, Dr. George Baehr, a member of the New York Health Preparedness Commission, who was thoroughly familiar with its work on the medical side of Civilian Defense, was appointed Chief Medical Officer of the United States Office of Civilian Defense. It immediately became his task to develop a national Emergency Medical Service. On July 7, a conference took place between General John F. O'Ryan, then State Director of Civilian Protection, Dr. George Baehr, Chief Medical Officer of the Office of Civilian Defense, Assemblyman Lee B. Mailler, former Senator Leon A. Fischel, and Dr. John J. Bourke, the three latter being respectively chairman, counsel, and research director of the commission. The work of the commission was integrated with the Civilian Protection Division of the State War Council through the appointment of Dr. Bourke as Consultant to the State Office of Civilian Protection. In September, the Medical Division of the United States Office of Civilian Defense published Bulletin No. 1, outlining the organization of a national Emergency Medical Service. In New York, conversion of the existing County Health Preparedness committees into the Advisory Committees to the Chiefs of local Emergency Medical Services called for in Bulletin No. 1 was easily accomplished.

At its peak strength, the New York State Emergency Medical Service consisted of 2454 mobile emergency medical teams, whose personnel included 2454 doctors, 4808 registered nurses, and 7812 medical auxiliaries. Casualty stations numbering 1489 were established, over 17,000 stretcher teams were formed, and regular or converted ambulances with a capacity of over 8400 persons were made available. Adequate equipment, consisting of stretchers, cots, first-aid pouches, blankets, morphine ampules, and blood plasma banks, was on hand.

Especially important was the development for New York State of a satisfactory supply of blood plasma through the joint efforts of the Health Preparedness Commission, the Medical Division of the United States Office of Civilian Defense with the assistance of the United States Public Health Service, the American Red Cross, and the Army. In April, 1942, the commission's Statewide inventory of the blood plasma supplies on hand in the hospitals of the State showed only 3264 units, 755 of them in New York City. The value of plasma was so clearly demonstrated at Pearl Harbor that there was no escaping the conclusion that the State should greatly expand its own reserves for civilian defense purposes. Public reaction was favorable, and in different ways, partly with Federal funds, partly from the Red Cross, a total of 23,000 units was collected at base hospitals and in the custody of chiefs of the Emergency Medical Services in counties having small but vital war plants. The increased recognition of the value of plasma in the treatment of trauma and shock in time of war should carry over and make possible the development of local blood banks for use when accidents occur in homes and on farms.

All general hospitals in the State were part of the Emergency Medical Service. The hospital care of casualties was planned upon the basis of local self-sufficiency, and for this reason all hospitals were linked with the local civilian protection control centers and with certain casualty stations in the area. However, to provide for the possibility that hospitals in a given area might become overcrowded, a Statewide system of casualty receiving and emergency base hospitals was established. The largest single source of facilities for base hospital uses throughout the State was the twenty-six institutions of the State Department of Mental Hygiene. Plans were perfected for keeping close check on the ability of each institution to provide emergency base hospital bed space. In the area surrounding each of the larger cities of the

State emergency bed space was maintained constantly, and equipment for 10,500 beds was supplied the State of New York by the Medical Division of the United States Office of Civilian Defense. Agreements were worked out with the United States Public Health Service and the Red Cross delimiting mutual spheres of activity.

To provide medical staffs for the twenty-five base hospitals established in New York State, affiliated base hospital units were developed according to a plan outlined by the Surgeon General of the United States Public Health Service. These affiliated units were each composed of fifteen physicians chosen for their qualifications in surgery, internal medicine, laboratory, and X-ray work. Two nurse executives and a dentist were also assigned to each unit. Supervision lay with a director assisted by division heads for the Surgical and Medical Services. Those eligible for this staff, which would take care of the peak casualty loads from air attack in their area, were physicians over forty-five and younger physicians physically disqualified for Army service. Those appointed were commissioned in the reserve of the United States Public Health Service, and if called to active duty they were to receive the pay and allowances of their equivalent military rank. Technical preparation was provided in the form of a full week af active duty at Halloran Hospital for training in war surgery and war medicine.

It was the duty of the local Chief of Emergency Medical Service, who was a Civilian Protection official, to direct all medical resources in his community in the event of catastrophe. To carry on these functions, he was assisted by medical and nurse deputies, and advised and aided by the local Health Preparedness Committee. The resources of official and voluntary organizations, the medical and nursing professions, hospitals, health departments, Red Cross, and other agencies in his area were all available to him, and to him fell the responsibility for the plans, organization, and training to ensure satisfactory field casualty service.

The mobile emergency medical team, consisting of one physician, one nurse, and two or more auxiliaries, was the focal point of local organization. Behind this team, in hospitals, schools, or other public buildings, were casualty stations for treating the slightly injured, or victims of shock and hysteria not requiring hospitalization. Plans for the rapid admission and evacuation of patients, including the expansion, if necessary, of facilities to care for more patients than usual, were prepared under the guidance of the State Commission and its field staff of five full-time medical officers. These officers kept a constant record of the emergency medical strength of every locality in the State, and all such information was made available to the surgeons of the Second Service Command, the State Guard, the Chief Medical Officer of the Coast Guard of the Third Naval District, and the commanding officer of each of the five Army Districts of the State.

Once the initial job of organization had been completed, the work of supervision was maintained with a skeleton staff and, as the danger of bombing receded with the progress of the war in Europe, greater attention was paid to the possibilities for usefulness in connection with normal civilian disasters. In a number of such cases, the Emergency Medical Service proved its value under difficult circumstances. Its excellent organization and the training of its medical teams were responsible for prompt treatment and hospitalization of many who otherwise might have perished. A number of incidents may be cited, such as railroad wrecks, an explosion in an electric plant, a food poisoning epidemic, the crash of a pilotless plane into an aircraft factory, a chlorine gas poisoning accident, and others, all unpredictable, in all of which Emergency Medical Service showed what it could do when confronted with necessity for action. A citation of merit and certificates and letters of commendation have been awarded to about twenty local units and individuals engaged in its activities. As a typical example of the way in which this Service operated, the report on the railroad wreck which occurred August, 1943, at Wayland, Steuben County, is here given in full. This serious wreck resulted in scores of dead and injured. The Emergency Medical Services of Wayland, Steuben County, Livingston County, and Rochester acted promptly and efficiently to reduce the loss of life. The manner in which the emergency was handled is outlined below.

REPORT ON WAYLAND, NEW YORK RAILROAD WRECK[1]

The Lackawanna Limited, carrying approximately 500 passengers, collided at 5:32 P.M., on August 30, 1943, with a freight engine which had overrun a switch about 50 yards east of the station at Wayland, New York. The engine of the Limited sheared off the front end of the switch engine, and smashed the driving cylinder. Both engines left the track, the freight engine coming to rest against the side of the third coach of the Limited, pouring live steam from its broken cylinder through the shattered windows of the coach. The passengers jammed the aisles, many dropping, unconscious, as they breathed steam. Some passengers threw themselves to the floor and covered their heads with coats. In spite of hot water on the floor, the majority of those who took this action were saved. Windows on the side of the car opposite the freight engine were broken by persons inside and outside of the car, allowing some of the steam to escape. Uninjured passengers on the train, including several members of the armed forces, quickly removed all persons from the car. Twenty of the passengers in the ill-fated cars were found dead; seven died shortly after removal. Twenty-two of the dead were young women; two, young girls, and three, men. The passengers of the coach

[1] Leg. Doc. No. 75 (1942-1943).

had included seventeen young women of the Women's Land Army, en route from the New York area to Silver Creek, New York. In addition to those injured by steam in the stricken coach, a railroad superintendent who was thought to have been riding in the cab of the locomotive of the Limited, was crushed to death.

Wayland, New York, is a town of approximately 2,000 population in an essentially rural area in southwestern New York State. It lies just south, in Steuben County, of the Steuben-Livingston County line. It is approximately 50 miles south of Rochester; 80 miles southeast of Buffalo; and 6 miles east of Dansville, New York, a town of about 5,000 population.

The Emergency Medical Service of Wayland, Steuben County, Livingston County, and Rochester acted promptly and efficiently to minimize the loss of life. The manner in which the emergency was handled is outlined below.

Notifications of Accident

A deputy sheriff witnessed the accident and reported it immediately to his superior by two-way radio. The Buffalo office of the Delaware, Lackawanna & Western Railroad immediately notified the Chief of Emergency Medical Service of Livingston County. The Chief of Emergency Medical Service of Steuben County was also notified.

General Mobilization

The Control Center of Wayland was activated immediately by Mr. Tembrook, the Local Commander. Mr. Campbell, the County Commander, reported at the local Control Center promptly. Air-raid wardens and auxiliary police assisted in handling spectators. Few orders were issued from the Control Center, because, it is reported, "everyone knew his job and did it without being told, and when that was done he turned to another task."

Mobilization of the Emergency Medical Service

Mobile medical teams, each composed of one doctor, one registered nurse, and one or more nurses aides, responded as follows:

Cohocton .... 1 Team
Wayland .... 1 Team
Dansville .... 1 Team
Bath
    Hospital .... 1 Team
    Veterans' Facility ..... 1 Team

Each of these teams was transported to the site of the accident by ambulance, either an undertaker's ambulance or an improvised ambulance. Other doctors and nurses in Wayland and the surrounding area reported to the Wayland Hospital and the Wayland Casualty Station. A public health nursing squad composed of 10 public health nurses specially trained for duty with the Emergency Medical Service was dispatched to Wayland from Bath, New York.

Transportation

Serious casualties were taken immediately from the site of the accident to Wayland Hospital in two ambulances provided by Wayland, one provided by Naples, New York, and the five ambulances which carried the mobile medical teams to Wayland.

Hospitalization

Fifty-six casualties were taken to the Wayland Hospital, which is a private hospital with a capacity of 17 beds. Thirty-three of these were discharged during the evening, following treatment. Seven were admitted to the Wayland Hospital, 11 transferred to the Bath Hospital, 3 to the Dansville Hospital, and 2 to the Corning Hospital. One of those admitted to the Wayland Hospital died the following morning. One patient was transferred to the Strong Memorial Hospital at Rochester, New York, from the Bath Hospital the day following the accident. Seven of the persons injured were considered in serious condition 48 hours following the accident.

Casualty Stations

The casualty station, established by the Emergency Medical Service at the Masonic Temple in Wayland, New York, was activated. Approximately 40 persons with minor injuries were treated at this casualty station. It had been equipped locally with two medical field team kits.

Supplies and Equipment

To supplement the supplies and equipment available at the hospital and at the Casualty Station it was necessary to draw heavily upon the emergency medical supplies from the local drug store. The local Chapter of the Red Cross quickly furnished the required number of blankets and cots. It also supplied canteen service. Oxygen tanks were dispatched to Wayland from Bath, Corning and Dansville.

Plasma

Approximately 16 units of plasma were used during the first 24 hours. The following quotations from a report made by Dr. Arthur M. Johnson, Chief of Emergency Medical Service of Rochester, describes the way in which plasma was made available.

"At 7:25 P.M., on August 30, 1943, I was notified by the chief operator of Dansville, New York, that a serious railway accident involving over 100 people had occurred at Wayland, New York, and that Dr. Gerald E. Murphy, Mt. Morris, New York, Chief of EMS of Livingston County, requested immediately 20 units of plasma for the seriously burned cases. I immediately contacted Mr. William A. Lang, Deputy Director of Civilian Protection, and requested him to engage a plane. I proceeded to the Strong Memorial Blood Bank and withdrew 20 units of dried plasma and then proceeded to the Municipal Airport. The plane was ready and immediately took off for Dansville as the Wayland Field was unlighted. Mr. Lang arranged by telephone to have the sheriff's car pick up the plasma at Dansville and take it to Wayland, about five miles away."

The following day, Dr. Ward Oliver, District Medical Officer of the Office of Civilian Protection of the State of New York, delivered 30 additional units of OCD plasma to Dr. Schafer, Chief of EMS of Steuben County.

Care of the Dead

The dead were taken immediately from the site of the incident to undertaking parlors of the village of Wayland. None were burned beyond recognition.

Records and Identification

The local Chapter of the Red Cross assumed responsibility for the maintenance of records concerning the injured, and the identification of the dead and living. Four persons remained unidentified 24 hours following the accident.

Post-mortem Examinations

Dr. James J. Sanford, Coroner of Steuben County, ordered an autopsy on one of the victims. The findings in this case were considered to be applicable to all the dead. The post-mortem examination revealed extensive second degree burns of the body, ulcerations of the mouth, trachea and bronchial tubes. The lungs were dry and indurated.

Supplementary Emergency Medical Service Resources

Certain Emergency Medical Service resources were available but not required. The Mount Morris Tuberculosis Sanitarium, which is approximately 20 miles from Wayland, had complete plans for the evacuation of the 450 beds of that institution. It was, however, not necessary to use these beds. Dr. Johnson, Chief of EMS for Rochester, after a quick survey, ascertained that accommodations could be arranged in Rochester for 100 patients. He also ordered ambulances of the Rochester Emergency Medical Service and the personnel of the Red Cross Motor Corps to stand by. He notified Dr. Murphy, Chief of EMS of Livingston County, of these arrangements. At 10:10 P.M., Dr. Murphy notified him by telephone that neither the ambulances nor beds would be needed and that he would need no more plasma that night.

In May, 1945, when Civilian Protection forces were placed on a reserve basis, Lee B. Mailler, Chief of the Emergency Medical Service, sent a letter to each local chief of the service, in which he said:—

Although we were very fortunate to escape enemy attack, the value and utility of the Emergency Medical Service training were graphically illustrated by the excellent work it performed at various civilian disasters in the state. This was possible only because of unselfish, personal sacrifice in time and energy, regular drills, often during night blackouts and even under bad weather conditions, as well as long hours of voluntary effort freely given. Functioning through Emergency Medical Service, your community thus prepared itself to aid its citizens in any contingency. All of this was done in spite of increasing work placed on doctors and nurses due to the fact that many medical personnel had joined the armed forces. The Emergency Medical Service fills a glowing page in the history of community cooperation on the home front in wartime. We are happy and proud to have served with you.

Emergency Evacuation and Welfare Services. One of the possibilities that had to be faced in connection with air bombing was the necessity for evacuating large groups of the population of the State from target areas. The successful evacuation from London in six days of 1,500,000 people, including 700,000 children, had required the preparation of plans not only for actual evacuation but also for the preparation of places for their reception. In line with the current belief of the State War Council that all possible eventualities should be prepared for, test surveys were made in September, 1941, of available housing in Sullivan and Orange Counties. Later in the same month, the Governor announced that invitations had been extended to certain State department heads, New York City officials, and chairmen of approximately twenty city and county defense councils to attend a conference on evacuation. A committee to study the entire question was suggested by the conferees and was appointed by the Governor, October 22, with the Director of Civilian Protection as chairman. At its first meeting in November, four subcommittees on Population, Housing, Transportation, and Health were set up and weekly meetings held to consider their reports. Contacts were made with the states of Connecticut, Pennsylvania, New Jersey, and Vermont, and on one occasion the President of the London County Council appeared before the committee and gave the benefit of his experience during the first part of the war, when the partial evacuation of the city of London was carried out. Research was carried on with the help of all available information, both American and British. A long report was issued by the committee in April, 1942, covering five major aspects of the problem: (1) the number of evacuees in the contemplated evacuation area, (2) transportation, (3) the reception areas in which evacuees were to be housed, (4) the care of the evacuees in reception areas, and (5) cost.

Special attention was given by the State Education Department to the evacuation of school children from "target areas," of which New York City with more than 1 million school children was by far the largest. Detailed planning for housing, feeding, recreation, and continued schooling was undertaken in cooperation with other State departments, and the experience of the British who, in September, 1939, had moved six hundred thousand children away from London in four days was carefully studied. Subsequently, plans were brought to completion even though it had been decided earlier that the intensity and duration of bombing likely to be received did not "justify the emotional, psychological and economic readjustments of evacuation."[1]

Since the entire matter of evacuation was without precedent in this country, no guiding principles or policies were imposed upon the committee. Unlike most civilian protection activities, instead of being remedial in character, evacuation lay in the field of prevention. The committee assumed that in an emergency, while individuals would largely decide as to their own evacuation, they could be considerably influenced by public authorities. Consequently, advanced planning of a detailed character was highly desirable. Evacuation from all target

areas in the State was considered, and although surveys were made even of possible reception areas, no organization was contemplated until further developments occurred. The surveys indicated a lack of available housing in counties adjacent to the New York Metropolitan District, and in upstate target areas very little indication was found of a desire on the part of persons to evacuate these centers. Medical problems were closely considered and the need for additional medical care and hospital facilities was clearly indicated in the event of an emergency.

As a result of the participation in the discussions of the State Department of Social Welfare, a brief memorandum was prepared by that Department in April, 1942, entitled "Social Welfare Services in Evacuation." Subsequently, on May 1, 1942, the State War Council appointed the Social Welfare Commissioner to the post of State Director of Emergency Welfare Services and Evacuation. Under Article 5 of the War Emergency Act, his task was to render assistance to families and individuals who might be deprived of their livelihood, or homes, or otherwise be affected by enemy action. Likewise under the law, these services were made a branch of the State Office of Civilian Protection, and a plan prepared for the development of local emergency welfare services. Assistance in the establishment of these local organizations was rendered by the State Director to permit State and local welfare districts to benefit from Federal reimbursement. Plans were developed in all evacuation areas by May 15, 1942, and by direction of the State War Council an agreement was negotiated on July 6, with the American National Red Cross covering participation of local Red Cross Chapters in the emergency welfare services of the State.

The State plan for Emergency Evacuation and Welfare Services provided assistance to families and individuals affected by enemy action through the creation of emergency welfare centers oper-

---

[1] From information supplied by Commissioner E. R. Van Kleeck in charge of evacuation planning for school children.

ated by the Red Cross in zones laid out by the localities. The welfare centers were to provide information and referral services, registrations and interviewing, cash or vendors' orders with which individuals could purchase food, shelter, clothing, furniture, moving facilities, and any other necessities temporarily unavailable to them. While the great majority of the local war councils developed plans for the operation of Emergency Welfare Services, State and local officials gave special attention to war production centers and target areas. Close liaison was also developed with other protective services, especially the Emergency Medical.

Mutual-aid Plans. The basic idea behind each of the six mutual-aid plans was simple. When it came, disaster in this war would be on such an extensive scale that no matter how well organized they might be, the forces of any one community would be overwhelmed. Because this possibility existed, there would have to be substituted for the tradition of community independence the fact of community interdependence, and the consequent necessity for organizing all available State and municipal public services on a regional basis.

Except for sabotage, which was regarded primarily as the concern of the Federal Bureau of Investigation, of the police, and of private guards protecting manufacturing plants, disaster was thought of in terms of air bombing. The possibility was sufficiently real to induce the State War Council at one time to authorize taking out insurance on public buildings and upon the State system of canals. Accordingly, between the summer of 1940 and the spring of 1942, as a means of organizing a State-wide defense against anticipated disaster from the air, six different mutual-aid plans were drafted and approved either by the State War Council, or by the Governor. In each case, inventories were taken of equipment and personnel available for operations in case of emergencies. Prior

to Pearl Harbor, these plans had no statutory authority. With the declaration of war, however, the situation changed. Four of the plans were adopted by the 1942 Legislature as part of the War Emergency Act and a fifth reenacted from the previous year. The sixth plan, that for snow removal, was authorized December 29, 1942, by the State War Council, but never became part of the War Emergency Act.

Police Mobilization. The first of the mutual-aid plans has already been covered in the section on the State Police. It is sufficient to indicate here that while it was prepared in 1940, it was first incorporated in the General Municipal Law by Chapter 422 of the Laws of 1941. In 1942 it was transferred to the War Emergency Act. This law empowered the Governor at his discretion, whenever the public interest required it, to authorize all police officials of the State to make available for duty wherever assistance was requested all or any part of the forces and equipment under their control.

State Fire Mobilization and Mutual Aid Plan. The plan to mobilize all firefighting equipment on a State-wide basis was prepared in 1941 by the State Committee on Fire Defense. Following its appointment, in April, it undertook an inventory of all fire apparatus and equipment in the State, paying particular attention to the date of manufacture and operating condition, the location and size of each fire department, the number of apparatus available, and the amount of additional equipment which could be accommodated. This inventory was the basis of the mutual-aid plan which was developed pursuant to Section 32 of the War Emergency Act providing for the formulation of a Fire Mobilization and Mutual-Aid Plan by a State Fire Administrator, who was to have full control over its execution once approval had been secured from the State War Council.

The aim of the plan was to render

State-wide mutual aid in the event of actual bombing, sabotage, fires, or any other war emergency where local or county mutual aid plans proved ineffective. It did not contemplate interference with local mutual aid plans, which had in some instances been worked out in advance of this State plan. Appeal for assistance under the plan could be made to the local Director of Civilian Protection, who would contact the State Office in Albany. That office in turn would dispatch assistance from other areas through the medium of the State Fire Administrator. Under no circumstances would a fire department be deprived of all its apparatus, and only those departments with sufficient pumpers would be detailed to points where help was needed. Although possibly required to travel considerable distances, pumpers would be drawn only from areas that had escaped bombing or areas where there was no need for such apparatus. Assignments were to be made only when (1) the assisting departments were outside of the county requiring aid, (2) the hose thread was the same or if adaptors were available, (3) the water supply was adequate, (4) sufficient apparatus remained at home to care for possible emergencies with the help of the local county mutual aid plan. In all cases, the fire chief normally in charge in the vicinity of the fire would remain in charge of all outside forces.

The operation of the plan was under the immediate supervision of the State Fire Administrator who, in turn, was subject to the general jurisdiction of the Director of Civilian Protection. The division of the State into the five regular civilian protection zones, each under a Deputy Fire Administrator, coincided with the outlines of the parent organization. Each of the five zones was divided into city and county organizations under a local fire administrator, and plans were worked out jointly for mutual aid on a local scale. Outstanding among these

plans were those prepared by Monroe, Westchester, Suffolk, Nassau, Putnam, Dutchess, Ulster, Erie, Niagara, Chautauqua, and Columbia Counties. The organization and training of more than sixty thousand auxiliary firemen were completed, and in a number of large fires, railroad wrecks, and other emergencies these assisted the regular fire departments with good results.

Mutual Aid Plan for Water Service. No defense against urban fires is possible without an adequate water supply, nor can public health be maintained satisfactorily if it is contaminated or cut off. In fact, water supply was considered as critical to war production by the Army, the United States Public Health Service, and the Office of Civilian Defense. Consequently, for the War Council to authorize the formulating and placing in operation of a comprehensive Mutual-aid Plan for Water Service in the event of emergency was a logical procedure. Like other mutual-aid plans this one was part of the Civilian Defense Program, was under the control of the Director of Civilian Protection, and involved cooperation between local waterworks officials and local defense councils. It followed the specific recommendation of a special committee of water-works experts appointed at the request of the Governor by the Mayors' Conference and the State Department of Health. In substance, the plan was similar to one in operation throughout England which had proved highly successful in maintaining and protecting water service in English communities under the most severe conditions of *blitzkrieg* warfare.

Constituting as it did one of the first lines of civilian defense, water service was of vital importance to all groups in the State. Because of its importance to public health, the New York plan had the unanimous endorsement of the members of the State Health Preparedness Commission. Under its provisions New York State municipalities were prepared to maintain water service in emergencies, including extraordinary demands in the event of disasters, fires, floods, drouths, hurricanes, or other catastrophes. In certain areas of the State, particularly the areas supporting large and important national defense industries, it was essential to interconnect adjoining public water supplies so as to maintain water services in the event of failure of any one supply. So that accidents to mains did not have the effect of disrupting the entire water service until repairs could be effected, distributing systems in some communities needed reinforcement in order, at given points, to supply water from more than one direction. Provision was likewise made for the rapid assembly of materials and personnel for repair purposes.

For purposes of administration and control, the State was divided into twenty-two water service zones, nineteen of which were coextensive with existing State Health Districts. Three others included Nassau, Suffolk, and Westchester Counties. The administration of the plan was placed in the hands of the State Water Supply Coordinator, who was assisted by zone and assistant zone water-supply coordinators in each of the twenty-two subdivisions. These officials were all experienced in the water-works field, the assistant coordinators being the District Sanitary Engineers of the State Department of Health, and the County Sanitary Engineers of Nassau, Suffolk, and Westchester Counties. All of the work was in the hands of practical water-works men with the machinery of the assisting Health Departments added to ensure proper consideration of health interests. Administratively, the plan fitted into the Civilian Protection organization as the Division of Water Main Emergency Repairs in the State Office of Civilian Protection, according to which the State Water Supply Coordinator acted as technical advisor to the State Director of Civilian Protection. A similar relationship was maintained on the local level

between the subordinates of both organizations.

As approved by the Defense Council, October 14, 1941, and subsequently enacted by Chapter 574 of the Laws of 1942, the State Mutual-aid Plan for Water Service had a number of specific objectives, divided into two distinct fields:

A. General preparation for emergencies not directly connected with Civilian Protection plans for the mobilization and direction of civilian protection services.

B. Preparations in connection with Civilian Protection, especially integration of local water departments with the Civilian Protection Plan of each community, and the organization and training of water main emergency repair crews and other auxiliaries needed in the event of an actual emergency.

Under Subdivision A belonged the following specialized functions:

1. The interconnection of public water-supply systems, and approved industrial or other water supply systems.

2. The preparation and maintenance of accurate maps of distributing systems, or the up-to-date revision of existing maps including accurate records of the location of valves and other vital parts of the systems.

3. The frequent testing of valves and fire hydrants to assure that these are in proper working condition at all times.

4. Collaboration wtih local fire officials in regard to:

    a. Surveys and preparation for use of all possible emergency sources of water supply.

    b. The characteristics of valves and fire hydrants and the needs for hydrant adaptors.

    c. Surveys of distribution systems for defects and weaknesses and development of plans for their correction.

5. Collaboration with local power and other utility officials in regard to conditions that may affect operation of the water supply, and the measures to be taken to assure its functioning in an emergency.

6. Collaboration with local fire and war industry officials to correct deficiencies in

water service and fire protection furnished to war industries.

7. The adoption of such measures as are reasonable and consistent with the needs of each particular community to protect against possible water works sabotage or fifth column attacks.

8. The preparation of a detailed inventory of water works personnel, equipment, materials and supplies and the submission of such data to the Zone Water Supply Coordinator.

Under Subdivision B there were these functions:

1. Collaboration with chairmen of local war councils for the purpose of integrating the civilian protection features of the Mutual Aid Plan with the plans of local councils.

2. Technical advisory assistance on all matters related to water supply to the State Director of Civilian Protection, his deputy directors and assistants, and the local war councils.

3. The organization, training, equipment and operation of water main emergency repair crews and other auxiliary or reserve water works personnel, to function through the local water superintendent under the local council.

The entire plan reached a point of stabilization during 1944 by which time approximately 240 municipal water supply systems had been interconnected for the mutual benefit of their respective communities. An inventory of water works personnel and equipment was likewise compiled as a necessary part of the total plan for securing auxiliary and regular water works men trained through the Office of War Training and with the help of the New York Section of the Water Works Association to carry out all necessary functions. A comprehensive manual on procedures and methods was prepared and placed in the hands of water works authorities and of the local war councils.

Once again, under the stimulus of war and the example of a hard-pressed ally, New York took precautions which proved their value even in time of peace.

A number of serious emergencies occurred between 1942 and 1945 in which the Mutual-aid Program for Water Supply Services made possible prompt and successful remedial action.

Two major emergencies occurred in 1942 and 1944 in widely separated parts of the State. In August, 1942, the Alleghany River flooded three thousand cellars out of a total of five thousand buildings in the city of Olean, and disrupted an important water supply main of the city, thus draining the system of water. Damage also occurred at Salamanca, Portville, Randolph, Little Valley, Belmont, and Angelica. The Department of Water of the city of Buffalo dispatched fire engines, pumps, and repair crews to Olean and greatly assisted municipal and health officials in restoring conditions to normal. On the Atlantic seaboard, the hurricane of September, 1944, interrupted telephone, electrical, and water supply services in many communities in Nassau and Westchester Counties. During this emergency, water was supplied through interconnections from adjacent systems not using electrical power. The well-organized mutual aid program of the two counties functioned smoothly in rendering aid and in providing for the exchange of personnel and equipment.

Several other emergencies of a somewhat more limited type occurred in 1945. The principal water supply conduit of the village of Fonda was disrupted in March, 1945. Repairs were made by employees of the city of Johnstown with Johnstown supplies and equipment. In July, a local cloudburst at Springwater, Livingston County, resulted in the complete filling of a small impounding reservoir with sand and gravel and the clogging of the supply main leading from this reservoir to the village. The small water company was unable to meet this emergency and very extensive assistance was rendered by personnel from the Water Department of the City of Rochester, including the distribution of potable water in a tank wagon during the emergency. In September, difficulties at the pumping station of the Greenport Water District, Columbia County, were relieved by the use of water from the distribution system of the city of Hudson through an interconnection installed as a result of the Mutual-aid Program. Likewise in October, 1945, a serious shortage of water in the Lathams Water District, Albany County, was relieved by the cities of Schenectady and Watervliet furnishing water through interconnections with the systems of that water district. Had not preparations been made in advance to handle such situations as these, serious inconvenience and impairment of public health would very likely have occurred.

Mutual-Aid Plan for Highway Repair and Debris Clearance. Another part of the State's civilian defense program, approved by the Governor December 16, 1941, was the Mutual Aid Plan for Highway Repair and Debris Clearance. Modeled on the plans already established for Police and Fire Mobilization and Water Service, it followed the specific recommendations of a special committee of State and municipal engineers appointed by the State Department of Public Works and the State Conference of Mayors to outline a practical plan for cooperation and assistance between the State and its municipalities. In this case, also, arrangements were based on the experience of the British and applied to New York State in anticipation of bombing.

The main feature of the plan was a central pool of equipment and personnel available on short notice for work in any stricken area. This pool consisted of State highway forces centrally located at their district headquarters, with garages, repair shops, and personnel. As a second line of reserve, except in the areas where emergency existed, were county, town, city and village forces. Exact disposition and use of State, county, municipal, and private equipment and personnel depended upon the circumstances of the

emergency and the resources of the district. Orderly and quick procedure was outlined for the full utilization in any district of whatever units of the extensive highway maintenance facilities were needed. Urgent peacetime needs in the event of natural disasters, such as fires, floods, and hurricanes, could also be met.

The State was divided into eleven zones, ten to be coextensive with the State Highway Districts, the other to comprise New York City. In charge of the operation of the plan, as State Coordinator, was the Assistant Commissioner of Highways of the State Department of Public Works. The ten State Highway District Engineers were Zone Coordinators. In New York City the Coordinator was designated by the Mayor. County Superintendents of Highways, and officials responsible for street construction and maintenance in the cities, as designated by the mayors, would be Assistant Coordinators in each zone. Such plans required a State-wide inventory of highway and maintenance personnel, equipment, and supplies which was immediately begun and pushed to completion. The resulting information was made available through all public works and highway officials within each zone. Personnel were provided with identification cards and, wherever possible, were fingerprinted. Upon requests for aid by a governmental unit, the Zone Coordinator was empowered to put the plan into operation to the extent required and to make needed items available. Interzone requests for aid were to go to the State Coordinator, who had authority to use any or all local equipment and personnel to repair damages to bridges and highways and to remove debris anywhere in the State. In 1942, the Legislature incorporated this plan in the War Emergency Act.

Mutual-Aid Plan for Emergency Milk Supply. In view of the heroic efforts made to maintain milk deliveries to consumers during the bombing of London, and of the possible consequences to public health from a failure in pasteurization, as evidenced by an outbreak of five thousand cases of typhoid fever and five hundred deaths in Montreal, a mutual-aid program for maintaining the safety and continuity of public milk supplies appeared highly desirable. On May 4, 1942, the Governor inaugurated such a plan by the appointment of a Director of Emergency Milk Supply from the staff of the Department of Health. A staff was quickly assembled consisting of an associate director, twenty-two district directors, and sixty-one local directors. A survey was made of the facilities, capacities, and equipment of some 1,400 milk pasteurizing plants in the State and agreements were made with certain key plants, particularly those with independent water and electrical facilities, to pasteurize milk for other plants in the event of damage either to individual plants or to public water systems resulting from bombing or sabotage. A temporary amendment to the Public Health Law, Chapter 500 of the Laws of 1942, was sponsored by the State War Council, giving the State Commissioner of Health authority to embargo milk supplies in the event of possible contamination resulting from sabotage and to order the transfer of milk supplies from one community to another in the event of local shortages resulting from war damage. Furthermore, key pasteurizing plants were encouraged to make provision for blacking out their plants in the event that twenty-four-hour operations were necessary in helping other plants during an emergency. All milk plants were advised to investigate the antecedents of their employees and to lock refrigerators against possible attempts by saboteurs to spread destruction through contamination of the milk.

No incidents arose during the war requiring a real test of the efficacy of this plan. However, one case of suspected sabotage, through the addition of a chem-

ical substance in a can of milk delivered by a farmer in an isolated section of the State, was quickly reported through County Headquarters of Civilian Protection to the District Director of Emergency Milk Supply. The milk was embargoed and a prompt investigation showed the substance to be rock salt. In another instance, a severe sleet storm completely crippled the power system of a city. With the cooperation of the County Highway Department milk supplies were taken to a neighboring city where they were pasteurized, bottled, returned, and delivered on time. Damage due to flood in another part of the State occasioned a further demonstration that uninterrupted supplies of pasteurized milk could be maintained under the plan.

Mutual-Aid Plan for Snow Removal. The maintenance of essential highway transportation in the wintertime is dependent to a large extent upon the efficiency of snow-removal equipment. It so happens that in New York State such equipment is largely in the hands of the cities and counties. Although the State does have a certain amount of its own, under State law it does not do any snow removal on State highways. During the summer of 1942, the counties and towns of New York State were confronted with the problem of securing replacements for worn-out snow-removal equipment. The problem was acute because of the order of the War Production Board freezing all truck equipment in the hands of manufacturers and dealers.

In view of the situation, a committee of the County Highway Superintendents' Association meeting with the State Commissioner at Albany decided upon a survey of the age, number, size, and condition of all snow-removal units. Questionnaires were sent out and a representative set of answers received from thirty-three counties. Indications were that during the winter of 1941-1942, snow had been removed from a total of 9632 miles of county highways and from a total of 35,110 miles of town highways. The work was done by approximately 470 county snow-removal truck units and 1540 town units. Approximately 375 tractors and graders also were used. Of this total nearly half of the truck units were under four-ton capacity. More than a quarter were over six years old, and of these nearly 300 were over nine years old.

The situation appeared so serious that it was estimated that should prolonged storms occur in the ensuing winter, 75 per cent of the mileage then under snow removal would have to be abandoned. This would handicap plants manufacturing war materials, since many workers could not report to work until roads were opened. Food stuffs might be seriously delayed in transit between rural areas and cities. School buses would likewise be brought to a standstill and health facilities, dependent upon the mobility of doctors and nurses, would be seriously curtailed. The previous winter, planes occasionally had been used to drop food.

As a result of these gloomy forebodings, the New York State War Council on December 29, 1942, authorized a Mutual-aid Plan for Snow Removal, which provided for the pooling of equipment on a county basis. In essence the plan, which was never given legislative authorization, called for the establishment in each county of an agency to be known as the County Office of Snow Removal, headed by the County Superintendent of Highways. Whenever a municipality should request this official for aid in removing snow and ice from its streets and highways, he was authorized to furnish it by providing whatever equipment and personnel he deemed necessary from the county, or any municipality within the county. All personnel and equipment, as a matter of general principle, were to be under the supervision of the official in charge of snow removal in the receiving municipality. No municipal equipment, however, could be loaned without the permission of its owner. County Superintendents of Highways were authorized to present mutual-aid plans to County Boards of Supervisors, and, if desired, cooperative plans could be worked out by two or more counties. The municipality requesting and receiving aid was to pay all expenditures.

Although this plan necessarily applied only on a local basis, it was worked out in conjunction with the State Division of Highways, which subsequently in a number of instances aided large cities such as Buffalo and Rochester with what equipment it had available. Generally speaking, it may be said that with the exception of the severe storms of late January and early February, 1945, which created a temporary State-wide transportation crisis, snow-removal equipment proved adequate during the war.

Miscellaneous Civilian Protection Activities. Defense of the home front took a number of forms which were necessary, but which in themselves involved less than the usual amount of organization, personnel, or expenditure. In this category may be placed the Forest Fire Fighters Service, the fingerprinting activities of the Correction Department, and the closing of roads and posting of property by the Attorney General.

The Forest Fire Fighters Service. The Forest Fire Fighters Service was established within the national Office of Civilian Defense, July 11, 1942, in accordance with the policy of the Facility Security Program of the Office of Civilian Defense "to safeguard forest lands, and other timber facilities and resources, to prevent and control fires which might endanger such facilities and resources, and to minimize the effect of any such fires." The function of the Service was to cooperate with the Forest Fire Protection Agencies of the Departments of the Interior and of Agriculture, with the State Forestry officials, and with private forest fire protective organizations. The National Coordinator appointed as State Coordinator for New York the Director of the Division of Lands and Forests of the State Conservation Department. To conform with State statutes and procedure, this appointment was confirmed by the State War Council September 22, 1942. A plan of organization was drawn up and approved October 19, 1942, by the Director of Civilian Protection, who had supervisory jurisdiction.

The principal objectives of the Forest Fire Fighters Service in New York State were:

1. To promote forest fire control throughout the forest regions of the State through publicity and educational channels provided in the Office of Civilian Defense, in the State War Council, and in the Conservation Department.

2. To increase the number of potential participants in forest fire suppression forces.

3. To provide a training plan which would meet conditions prevailing in the forest regions of New York State.

Under the State plan as outlined in Memorandum No. 1, the twelve District Forest Rangers in charge of the fire towns and fire districts of the State Conservation Department, and the eight District Foresters in charge of the so-called forest districts were appointed District Forest Fire Fighters Service Coordinators. Under them in Districts 1 to 12 the Forest Rangers were to act as local coordinators and in Districts 13 to 20 inclusive the town supervisors would act in a similar capacity. Enrollment of Forest Fire Fighters through the District and local Coordinators was carried out intensively in 1943, and the total enrollment reached 19,834. In addition to being provided with an identification card issued by the County Office of Civilian Protection, each enrollee was provided with an arm band and insignia, and a training manual issued by the State War Council. Training classes were organized for all Forest Rangers, and instructional material was provided through the United

States Forest Service for the approximately six thousand fire wardens of the State. Forest fire suppression was also included in the State War Council training program for volunteer firemen. Since the Forest Fire Fighters Service functioned largely on a county basis, the strength of its organization varied directly with the importance of the forests in each county. The Service was concluded in New York State by the disbandment of the Office of Civilian Defense on July 1, 1945.

One of the principal results of the operations of the Service, partly because of the intense effort put forth in the enrollment drive, was an increased popular appreciation of the problems of fire control. In the fall of 1942, the United States Forest Service inaugurated an intensive forest fire prevention campaign which was conducted in New York State through the Office of the State Coordinator and supplemented by the normal activities of the State Forest Fire Control Agency. Furthermore, people were approached by the Rangers for recruitment purposes at a time when they were willing to listen to a discussion of forest fire control.

Considering the extent of New York's forests, there was a surprisingly small need for extra personnel for the control of fires. According to the Director, in no case did a fire occur that could be directly attributed to sabotage with the intention of destroying a particular supply of timber needed in the war effort, or diverting from their duties a large number of soldiers located in a particular section. This can be said with a fair degree of certainty as the Service was looking for saboteurs and was prepared for them. The size of the enrollment was a good indication of the cooperation which the people of the State were willing to give in this particular activity.

Statutes for Protection of Defense Industries. Two statutes were enacted at the 1941 session of the Legislature to safeguard plants manufacturing vital munitions. Chapter 869 empowered the State Council of Defense, upon petition, to issue orders authorizing such industries to post signs on and about their properties reading, "No Entry Without Permission." Unauthorized entry was to constitute a misdemeanor. Chapter 870 empowered the Council, upon petition of any industry engaged in war work, to authorize local authorities to close adjacent streets, or to restrict traffic, if such action appeared necessary for adequate protection. The Attorney General, a member of the Council, was appointed by it as a committee of one to report on all petitions filed under the provisions of these two chapters. Upon receipt of a petition, an investigation was conducted and a report made for the purpose of showing whether (1) the industry came within the provisions of the statute, and (2) the labor relations between the industry and its employees were such that the granting of the petition, either to close streets, or to post property, could not in any way be used to prevent the rights of workers to organize or enforce their just demands as provided for in the statute. Actually, investigations were handled through the nine regional offices of the Department of Law without increase in personnel or funds.

For a somewhat similar protective purpose, the 1941 Legislature adopted Chapter 452 requiring all manufacturers, dealers, and individuals intending to keep or possess explosives to take out an annual license, which required certification of compliance with the safety provisions of the Labor Law, to be obtained for every type of storage magazine. The effect of the law was to make the Labor Department, through its Bureau of Mines, Tunnels, Quarries, and Explosives, a clearinghouse for the name and address of every user, purchaser, or possessor of explosives. In this way, control of the distribution of explosives was made possible and the public was thus protected against potential saboteurs.

Fingerprinting. One of the measures taken in connection with the State-wide program of civilian protection was the fingerprinting of volunteer Civilian Protection personnel. Two main purposes underlay this project. First, it was recognized that such fingerprints could be cleared through the Division of Criminal Investigation of the Correction Department, and in that way, if prospective air raid wardens, fire wardens, and the like happened to have criminal records, that fact could be made available to the proper Civilian Protection personnel. In this way, undesirable personnel would be excluded from activities which by their very nature would have brought them into close personal contact with people in their immediate neighborhood. In the second place, the Fingerprint Program was intended to ensure positive identification in the event of a catastrophe.

The Fingerprint Program was begun within the Division of Criminal Identification of the Correction Department in conformity with a directive issued February 1, 1942, by the State Office of Civilian Protection. Funds provided by the War Council augmented the staff which, after a training course, was put to work classifying and searching the fingerprints of Civilian Protection personnel received from the local war councils. By March 31, 1943, when the program was discontinued, a total of approximately 120,000 sets of fingerprints had been received and filed.

The following day, however, April 1, 1943, at the request of the Second Service Command and Third Naval District, the Division took over the task of receiving, classifying, searching, and reporting on the fingerprints and miscellaneous inquiries originating from the various Army and Navy Depots and related agencies under their jurisdiction. By March 31, 1945, when this program began to slacken, 120,000 fingerprints and 41,000 miscellaneous inquiries had been handled. From July 1, 1945, through August

31, 1945, the War Council again assigned employees to the Division to carry on a second Civilian Defense Identification Program. On September 10, 1945, all contributing agencies were notified that the Division would no longer accept fingerprints or inquiries of a civilian defense nature, since, following the cessation of hostilities in August, such requests had dropped off 90 per cent.

The value of the Identification Program in connection with civilian defense matters, particularly as regards taking fingerprints of employees of Army and Navy Depots and Arsenals, was obvious. It was thereby possible to exclude all questionable individuals entirely, or at least exclude them from work of a confidential nature. Approximately 8 per cent of the hundreds of thousands of fingerprints and miscellaneous inquiries received in connection with the Civilian Protection and National Civilian Defense Program were identified. There is no question but that the combined efforts of the War Council employees and the permanent employees of the Division contributed greatly to the internal security, especially as regards activities in the northeastern part of the United States.

State Property Officer. The Office of the State Property Officer was established May 1, 1942, for the purpose of effecting the allocation and delivery of protective equipment for the United States Office of Civilian Defense to the State of New York, and to nearly 350 of its communities. Each community receiving Office of Civilian Defense equipment had a local property officer responsible to the Federal government for the equipment allocated to his community. Under its two property officers, Daniel J. Langan and his successor after August 1, 1943, Gardner LeRoy, both of whom were accountable for all property delivered by the Office of Civilian Defense to the custody of the State, records were kept of all Office of Civilian Defense properties delivered to local property officers within the State. Technical assistance was also furnished by the State to local property officers in the discharge of their duties.

The division of protective equipment and insignia among the State and its localities generally followed certain major classifications. Gas protective and detective equipment and certain kinds of medical equipment, such as hospital and folding beds, were allocated to the State and stored by it in institutions of the Department of Mental Hygiene strategically located for purposes of quick distribution. On the other hand, certain identification insignia, helmets, firefighting equipment, and in the case of some of the larger urban centers medical equipment and gas masks were allocated to the communities. All medical supplies allocated to the State were subject to the disposition of Lee B. Mailler, Chief of the Emergency Medical Service, and similarly all gas equipment allocated to the State was under the disposition of F. Wellington Gilcreas, State Gas Consultant.

Although the State Office was established in May of 1942, most of the equipment was not available in quantity until the following December. As much of it consisted of types utilized by the Army, toward the end of the war New York State was used as a warehouse for the purpose of storing surplus Army equipment. Much of this property was never used, so a Federal Disposal Program was begun August 1, 1945, under the War Assets Administration. Under this program, purchases of supplies on hand were made by the State of New York and its communities directly from the Federal government. In the sale of all equipment, the State Property Officer worked closely with representatives of the Federal agency, and the program was completed by October, 1946.

Communications. The State-wide "Civilian Protection Warning System,"[1] was based upon a network of commercial telephone facilities manned, with the exception of a few key posts at Army locations, entirely by civilians. Since direct personal warning and subsequent communications were accomplished best through voice messages, the commercial telephone system primarily was relied upon for communications. However, because of the widespread damage possible from aerial attack, the basic telephone system was to be supplemented, in an emergency, by the available facilities of the State Police Teletype System, the telegraph facilities of the telegraph and railroad companies, and by radio for intracommunity messages, in the order named. Since the telephone was basic, at the request of the State, the State Communications Officer was provided by the New York Telephone Company. While this was the largest company, for complete State-wide coverage the warning system utilized the central offices, lines, and personnel of 169 separate telephone companies operating within the State of New York.

Telephone messages from the 1,400 observation posts went direct to the four Filter Centers and three Information Centers, thence to the 46 District Warning Centers, the 109 Control Centers, and the approximately 500 Report Centers. Special telephone company-designed equipment and operating procedures assured not only speedy handling of the "Army Flash" calls from the observation posts, but also safeguarded against unauthorized reports. The Army's Air Raid Precaution Officers located at each of the three Information Centers alerted the Civilian Protection personnel through the special lamp-equipped telephone installed at the request of the Army Air Force in the District Warning Centers. Blue, yellow, red, or white signals, there received, were telephoned to the Control and Report Centers and from there fanned out to schools, hospitals, police, fire stations, utilities, industrial concerns,

and thousands of individuals. Arrangements in New York City[1] were specially designed by the New York Telephone Company. Through the use by the telephone companies of emergency operating procedures — priority handling of calls and a standard prearranged routine — warnings were disseminated with maximum speed and accuracy.

In addition to warning the District Warning Center, the Army also notified the State Control Center. This State Control Center was established to provide a coordinating point from which the State Director under the authority of the provisions of the New York State War Emergency Act might order the dispatch of the necessary assistance from any point within the State. An essential part of the State Control Center's functions was to decide the relative importance of the request for help on the basis of the greatest values to the welfare of the State and the nation as a whole. In addition to the Director of Civilian Protection, the State Control Center was manned by Chiefs of the following divisions:

Emergency Medical Service
Mutual Aid Water Supply
Emergency Milk Supply
Police Coordinator
Office of War Training
State Coordinator — Forest Fire
   Fighter Service
State Gas Consultant
Highway Repair and Debris Clearance
State Property Officer
State Fire Administrator
Communications Officer

This State Control Center was fully equipped to permit communication by the division chiefs with their organizations.

Experience gained from the war indicated that an efficient communication system could be developed, utilizing in the main existing facilities, provided that

[1] See pp. 334-335.

adequate operating procedures were instituted and that personnel were adequately trained.

Pride of achievement is one of the greatest of human satisfactions and in no other wartime program was this so widespread as in Civilian Protection. Civilian Protection was largely a man's world; men did the planning, men called the signals, and men ran the plays. In many of the smaller communities it was one big stag party thoroughly enjoyed despite the time and effort required. In the larger cities, however, women played an important part in many of the protective services, membership running as high as 20 per cent of the total force. In no other program could the results of months of organization and training be seen at a glance from the roof of an office building, or from a city street intersection, or from the crossroads of some country village. The director of the Civilian Protection forces of a large upstate city was not exaggerating when he referred to the personal thrill it gave him to watch the lights go out, one by one, as far as he could see and realize that in that demonstration was represented the fruits of months of work, late nights, long conferences, and the successful cooperation of thousands of human beings.

The Civilian Protection organization was the pet program of the men of the community. To it they brought all their pent-up desires for an active part in the war. In that organization they saw their chance to do their bit for their country and thus in some way make up for their absence from the front. Business executives delighted to exercise their gift for organization and their skill with details. In one city after another men came out of retirement to head the Civilian Protection organization. Many of them accepted no pay whatsoever, satisfied merely with the sense of a patriotic duty well performed. One might almost say that civilian protection became a hobby were it not for the fact that it was also

taken seriously. The care that went into the preparation of the control boards, the efficiency with which the different levels of telephone notifications were worked out, and the satisfaction in maintaining an unbroken twenty-four-hour watch at the warning, or the report center, can only be understood by those who participated. The feeling that if it came to a showdown over here, the outfit was ready to do everything possible to minimize casualties and protect its home and community was a real compensation for the sense of being out of things and at a great distance from the war.

There was another by-product of membership in Civilian Protection, which was just as real. Men derive a certain solid satisfaction from getting together. Civilian Protection drill nights and training nights had a welcome air of informality along with their seriousness of purpose that made for new acquaintances which under no other circumstances would have been possible. A common danger and a common purpose brought people together wholesale and made the stranger feel he was really becoming a part of the community. The small-town atmosphere of friendliness was imported into the larger cities so characteristically vast and impersonal. To many men who had never had a feeling of being in authority and who never would again, the position of air-raid warden or auxiliary policeman or auxiliary fireman gave a sense of importance and usefulness — a relationship to the people of the community that would never be forgotten. Those midnight discussions with other members of the force as to whether a particular light was really out or not, as to how long the blackout would last, as to why they did not get the warning signal systematized so that a fellow could know what was going on; or as to when the war would be over, or the kind of war job he would be forced to take when his business folded up, seem now to be out of another world. Yet at the time they were all very real and completely absorbing. In the dark, the only index to a man is the tone of his voice and the tenor of his thoughts.

It was not to be expected, however, that interest would remain high and enthusiasm keep fresh after the invasion of North Africa in November, 1942, and the invasion of Italy in the summer of 1943 had reduced the likelihood of danger from across the Atlantic. In the middle of 1943, the State Director had to combat personally all sorts of rumors regarding the winding up of the program, and it is a credit to the State organization and the local directors that from a sheer sense of duty and because of the slim possibility of trouble, they kept things going despite a decline in enthusiasm until the end of the war in Europe.

One change in emphasis was possible and this was made officially. The potential usefulness of the Civilian Protection forces in the event of peacetime disasters was carefully pointed out and the occurrence of various incidents in which they rendered valuable service reinforced this position. Over twenty different citations, or certificates, of merit were issued to local Civilian Protection organizations for services in connection with floods, train wrecks, food poisoning incidents, and other disasters. Already, at a distance of but a year, some have been inclined to belittle the value of Civilian Protection. It cannot be emphasized too strongly, however, that in New York State, as doubtless everywhere else, its success was a demonstration that the civilian population could be organized to cope with disaster from the air and that though Americans, unlike the British and the population of the Continent, fortunately never had to experience actual bombing, they had prepared themselves as best they could in advance of the event.

CHAPTER FIVE

The Mobilization and Direction
of Volunteers

JUST as the protection of life and property on the home front was in the hands of the men of the communities, so the mobilization and direction of volunteers in support of the numerous community services required during the war was, at the beginning, largely participated in by women. The division of these wartime functions was a natural one. Men understood, and it was natural that they should perform, the functions of protection; women understood and could best provide answers to the social needs of the community.[1] As Governor Lehman expressed it in August, 1941, "There can be no disarmament of our social services in time of war." The total strength of the population definitely depended upon their continuing to function.

The creation of what was first known as the Women's Division of the Defense Council, subsequently changed to the Division of Volunteer Participation, September 30, 1941,[2] was the answer to what had grown to be a very pressing problem by the summer of 1941, viz., how could the individual energies of the population, both men and women, be employed to the best advantage in the furtherance of the war effort? Individuals all over the State, whether organized or not, were willing and eager to take some part. They wanted to help with the preparations for defense, and after Pearl Harbor, in the prosecution of the war. Without some form of direction, however, whether on a State or local level, confusion, overlapping, and perhaps an ultimate sense of frustration and futility would have been inevitable. The appointment by the State Defense Council of a Director of Volunteer Participation was in recognition of the need for State leadership in this field.

From this beginning there developed a network of over six hundred city, county, town, and village volunteer offices as a division of each local war council. Their importance grew steadily from 1942 to 1945. Their initial task of procuring volunteer personnel for the innumerable drives and campaigns was expanded later on as the actual planning and direction of these projects came to rest to an ever-increasing extent in the hands of their

---

[1] There were, however, groups of women in the protective services, and men who contributed splendidly as chairmen of many of the Civilian War Service divisions of the local war councils. The early emphasis upon women volunteers as distinct from men was an implied refusal to recognize their equality. Actually the state was extremely fortunate in the continuing leadership of a large number of its early women chairmen of the volunteer offices. For various reasons, men were not able to render continuing service to any comparable extent. Furthermore, by the end of the four years of war the sharpness of the early line between the women's sphere of war activity and that of the men had been definitely and extensively blurred.

[2] March 27, 1942, in accordance with a change in policy on the part of the National OCD, the name was fixed permanently as the New York State Office of Civilian Mobilization.

chairmen. By 1945 the field representatives of the State Office of Civilian Mobilization had so functioned, that they had in fact, though not officially, become representatives of the War Council Headquarters in addition to their own office.

Without this State-wide organization of volunteers, numbering approximately 10 per cent of the population, headed on the local level by the volunteer office and guided where necessary by representatives of the State office, the vast resources latent in the population would undoubtedly have been dissipated in much useless activity with consequent impairment of popular morale. By sifting the programs that came out of Washington and intervening to prevent the State from going off on occasional tangents it saved the energies of New York citizens for those programs that per man-hour would yield the greatest returns to the war effort. In spite of inevitable organizational difficulties — conflicts of jurisdiction and clashes of personality — the mobilization and direction of more than one million volunteers in New York State were successful on a hitherto unprecedented scale. This applied both to those who took part in civilian protection and to those who devoted their time and energy to community war services. It is no exaggeration to say that twenty years of experience in community organization were telescoped into the four hectic years of the war. New Yorkers, along with their fellow Americans, proved willing and above all capable of adapting themselves to the organizational requirements of a total war.

CREATION OF A WOMEN'S DIVISION WITHIN THE STATE DEFENSE COUNCIL

Circumstances surrounding the appointment of a person to undertake the organization of a Women's Division of the State Defense Council are well known. Until June, 1941, the Council had concentrated primarily upon the fields of war production, civilian protection, and the emergency aspects of public health services, such as Emergency Housing, Emergency Medical Services, and Emergency Welfare Services. Up to that point there had been little place given to women in the defense program, and various women's organizations in the State felt that women could play an important part, and that the situation should be remedied. The task of finding a competent woman who would be capable of developing plans for using women's energies in support of the war effort fell to the Lieutenant Governor as Coordinator of War Plans. After canvassing the field of those experienced in the organization of community services, he entrusted the task to Mrs. Clarice Leavell Pennock of Syracuse, a former teacher of sociology and history, and a long-time worker in community projects.

From the outset the new director had the understanding and wholehearted backing of the Governor and War Plans Coordinator in putting into operation the three main aspects of the volunteer program. First of all, a plan for the use of these volunteers had to be worked out and some very careful, straightforward thinking done as to just where these volunteers could fit into the defense program. The Governor was convinced they could play an important part. The problem was to systematize their efforts. It was decided that a central coordinating unit to integrate the expanding program of volunteer service with existing community service was the best solution. The second problem was thus to induce local defense councils to appoint as a member a representative woman to set up such an office for recruiting, classifying, and placing volunteers. The local volunteer offices were to be the backbone of the entire program. It was essential then, in the third place, to secure for a State-wide program of this sort whole-hearted support from the welfare agencies and women's organizations of the State. They would have to be convinced of the importance of working through the local volunteer offices.

To secure support for the new State program and thus assure harmonious public relations from the beginning, three meetings were called by the new director in as many months. At a luncheon meeting at the Executive Mansion, August 5, 1941, Governor Lehman addressed the executives of New York State's welfare agencies on the needs of the time and the part which they could play in mobilizing their own communities.

. . . As I see it, the task which faces you today is to relate yourselves to community efforts which must be made to maintain and sustain the general morale. Mrs. Pennock's work appears to have three major divisions. In the first place, she will stimulate the development of those activities which are by nature emergency in their character. I know that some people feel that since there is no immediate crisis we should postpone our preparation for such work. It does not seem to me that such a suggestion can be entertained by any well-informed citizen. Of course, I hope we will never have occasion to use the emergency measures; but to be forewarned is to be forearmed. We would be guilty of the grossest kind of negligence if we did not prepare now for the dangers that may materialize.

In the second place, there is a need to develop some process by which we keep our people informed of the changing world scene and relate those changes to fundamental principles which underlie this government. It has become increasingly apparent that these values which are cherished by all of us and which express our individual and collective freedom were not easily acquired, but that they can be lost to all of us and the generations which follow us by a simple process of neglect and forgetfulness.

The third phase of our work and it is the one to which you are asked specifically to give thought — is that which bears on the continuing social services, both public and private, and which underlies the individual and collective life of the people of this and every other state. After all, the aged do not become young nor do the sick suddenly become well, nor do the multiplicity of social problems faced by the youth suddenly evaporate because we are directing our attention towards defense. Rather, it is the experience of other countries as well as our own that these problems steadily become intensified and more complicated in their nature because of our complex industrial and social development. It is apparent then that there can be no disarmament of our social services. . . .

Finally, I want to stress with you the fact that a Democracy must present the opportunity to its citizens to function intelligently, and that the element of participation by the individual citizen in his community and his government is vital in regard to the health and well-being of our national life. It is inconceivable to separate the citizen from his government or his community. This means that we must then proceed to develop our community efforts, to see to it that training facilities exist, and to work out opportunities for volunteer skill to be used in the day-by-day life of the individual or the group.

This fourfold emphasis upon (1) the support of emergency defense activities, (2) education in the fundamental questions then at issue between the dictatorships and the democracies, (3) the maintenance of essential social services as a fundamental line of defense in time of war, and (4) the morale value of providing every citizen with an opportunity to participate in the defense of his own community, was to be a permanent characteristic of the New York State Civilian Mobilization program. In the discussions that followed the Governor's talk, the directors of the social welfare agencies agreed to support the State program by encouraging their local defense councils to establish volunteer offices and centralize all volunteer activities in them. In all cases, existing groups were to be used as far as possible to induce participation on the part of women volunteers. Once again attention was called to the experience of England which underlined the importance of having a strong organization of women.

This first meeting was followed up by a letter from the Governor, August 14, to the chairmen of the local defense councils, urging the appointment of "an outstanding woman in your community who would serve as liaison between the Division of Women's Activities and your council." In this letter, jointly drafted by the Governor and the new director, the following points were made for the consideration of the councils:

1. The woman must be thoroughly conversant with the total possibilities of volunteer service in your community, both of a short-range nature immediately connected with defense, and a long-range nature connected with the reinforcement of your existing community services.

2. She must be a woman of wide interests, willing to submerge her own personality and enthusiasm in the common cause of the community. She should not be the promoter of any one particular organization of volunteers.

3. She must be a woman of sufficient age, experience and prestige to command the respect of all groups.

Immediately upon the appointment of this woman to the defense council, she was to make contact with Mrs. Pennock who would help her with problems of organization. At no time was there a doubt in the mind of the Governor but that women could, if given the chance, play an important role in the defense program of the State and nation.

On September 8, a second meeting of representatives of over thirty women's organizations was held in the Executive Chamber at the Capitol. First came a full-length introduction to the work of the Defense Council from the Governor. In discussing the State's preparations for defense, he laid stress upon the importance of women's organizations. He urged that they get behind the local defense councils to maintain public morale in support of defense measures. They were likewise to press for the inclusion of a woman on the local defense councils

and to help mobilize the woman power of the community to maintain those permanent social services more essential in wartime than ever.

By the end of September, the task of mobilizing volunteers had been broadened in the minds of the State's leaders sufficiently to warrant the change of the name from the Division of Women's Activities to the Division of Volunteer Participation. Men as well as women could, and would, be volunteers. It was perhaps unfortunate that the entire volunteer program which came to embrace all activities of the community was with difficulty disassociated in the minds of many men from the fact that originally it had belonged to the Division of Women's Activities and therefore, as so many of them thought, was of secondary importance compared to Civilian Protection.

A third meeting, this time an institute for women members of local defense councils, was held in Albany, October 16. Once again the Governor reviewed the defense program and emphasized the importance of securing the cooperation of all citizens in performing the functions of a democracy. He laid great stress upon "strengthening the unity of our people," and "increasing the efficiency of our community organization." He cited at first hand information on the English experience in the evacuation of the children from London, saying,

In England, the volunteer tradition in welfare work and community service has been longer established than it has here in America. With the Nazi menace so much closer to her shores, with the lesson that was brought home to her in the last war, in the months between Munich and the declaration of the war she had organized volunteer services to an extent undreamed of here. It was a volunteer navy of small boats, manned by amateurs and fishermen, that saved England's army at Dunkirk. Evacuation of children from London was rapidly accomplished through combined volunteer and government efforts.

He refuted the Nazi charge that democracies were not efficient and claimed that our entire history and experience disproved it.

These three meetings were successful in achieving their principal objectives, that of obtaining the support of the women for the local defense councils and the program of organizing volunteers as well as the participation of men in volunteer activities other than those of Civilian Protection. While the support of women's organizations was being secured for the State program of volunteer participation, the State Office under Mrs. Pennock was being organized in Albany and relations were established with those State and Federal departments and war council agencies principally concerned with the defense program. Plans were developed for getting in touch with the mayors and the chairmen of the county boards of supervisors to induce them to appoint women heads of volunteer offices. A small office force was acquired, much of it loaned from other departments. With the help of specialists, different types of material were prepared for circulation, including a manual on procedure for volunteer offices. Field activities were begun and thenceforth required constant direction. Regular weekly staff meetings were inaugurated and attended by State and Federal officials, who brought their programs which required citizen understanding and participation before the Office for consideration. Particularly close relations were maintained with the regional representatives of the Office of Civilian Defense, who frequently worked with members of the staff in the office. In accordance with an understanding arrived at with the Office of Civilian Defense, Federal communications were directed to the Albany Office and were there screened, simplified, and passed on to the local councils. The masses of printed material emanating from Washington in quantities as high as ten tons at a time were sorted and distributed throughout the State. Bulletins and newsletters were also prepared by the State Office in which methods that proved successful in carrying out a program in one locality were indicated for possible adoption elsewhere.

It was not easy in the beginning to reach a clear understanding with the State departments and war council agencies, either on matters of general policy or on methods of procedure to be followed in approaching the local councils. Conflicting instructions from the various agencies were one of the principal sources of confusion during the early years. Agreements, both oral and written, were slowly arrived at with most of the State agencies operating in the fields of civilian protection, public health, and community services. Similar difficulties were encountered with some of the Federal agencies, who did not at first realize the necessity for "clearance" with the State Office before approaching local war councils for assistance. Federal-State relations became standardized only after it became clear that in New York State there was no administrative vacuum into which the Federal government could advantageously move.

To help with the establishment of local volunteer offices, and to assist in the process of keeping administrative lines in order, the two field men, who had been working out of War Council Headquarters on the establishment and direction of the local war councils, were made available in November, 1941, to the Office of Volunteer Participation. This marked the beginning of that organization's field staff which grew to seven, covering the State in a manner similar to that established under the Office of Civilian Protection.

The establishment of local offices took time. Although many of the larger councils were perfectly willing to establish volunteer offices and pay for their equipment and services, to the smaller communities the matter of costs was an important item and the lack of direct connection with the war effort of many of the tasks to be performed by the office made it difficult to convince city councils or county boards of supervisors that the expense was justified. Only after the attack on Pearl Harbor and the sending out of a telegram by the Governor ordering the creation of a volunteer office did coverage of the State become 100 per cent. Even under those circumstances, extreme tact had to be used to avoid the accusation of State dictation in local affairs.

Although at the time the fact that they were dealing with volunteer offices and were without authority to command acceptance of their suggestions weakened the position of the field staff, it was probably a blessing in disguise. It was perfectly true that the field representatives of the Office of Civilian Protection, the only other organization dealing directly with the local councils, were paid considerably more than those of the Office of Volunteer Participation, and that they had deputies to assist them. This distinction was also perpetuated on the local level by the fact that directors of Civilian Protection, if not officeholders, were in many instances paid, while the heads of the volunteer offices were themselves volunteers. It was also a fact that under the War Emergency Act the local directors of Civilian Protection could in time of emergency direct the operations of the local organizations and enforce compliance. That was necessary to secure maximum efficiency in time of crisis. Furthermore, there was no doubt but that the war councils tended to pay very little attention to the representatives of a women's organization in 1941 and 1942, when the accent was on civilian protection. Under the circumstances, this was to be expected. What was not realized at the time was that in dealing with volunteers, especially those heading the local volunteer offices, the only possible way of accomplishing results was through

persuasion, and by means of an organization that would admit of variation in the acceptance of a given program. Variety of approach was inevitable in different communities, and no rigid, semimilitary arrangement could have succeeded for a moment. The field men from the State Office of Civilian Mobilization were appreciated precisely because they had no absolute authority to command and for that reason were willing to be of assistance within the framework of the local situation. In the hectic days following Pearl Harbor, these State representatives were of great practical value in helping green organizations set up their files and develop a system for handling the masses of volunteers who wanted to do something. Their usefulness, however, would have ceased abruptly had they insisted upon applying universally a rigid plan of operations.

ADDITION OF A SECTION ON CITIZEN MORALE

The Japanese attack on Pearl Harbor effected a remarkable change in the country's attitude. In the summer of 1941, the morale of the defense councils occasioned considerable concern. Many people were far from convinced that America was in danger of bombing or invasion. Publicity had placed too much emphasis upon physical dangers, too great a reliance upon inspiring fear and terror as a means of awakening popular support of the defense program. Many thoughtful people felt "that only by the slow, patient up-building of a morale based on understanding of the value of democracy and its spirit"[1] would our active participation in the world struggle on the side of the democracies become a matter of ultimate certainty. How long in the face of a world crisis would America's lethargy last? Would it take an actual attack to rouse us?

[1] Memorandum to the State War Council by the late Dr. Dixon Ryan Fox.

This preoccupation with what was called citizen morale, while understandable at that time, seems at this distance somewhat unreal. The fact is that Pearl Harbor satisfactorily took care of the matter of morale, although not in the way prescribed by educators and publicists. There was no question after December 7 as to whether we should, or should not, enter the war. We were in it. That had been settled, and settled for the overwhelming majority of the country. Witness what happened to the "America First" group.

Nevertheless, toward the end of December, 1941, at the suggestion of the late Dr. Dixon Ryan Fox, president of Union College and chairman of the Conference on Democratic Processes, the State Defense Council appropriated funds for a Section on Citizen Morale to be placed within the Office of Volunteer Participation. The relationship between the policies of the Office of Volunteer Participation and those of the Section on Citizen Morale was never particularly close, and supervision by the parent organization was purely nominal.

The new section operated from the beginning under three handicaps. Since the country was at war, the original need for awakening people to the danger of indifference to the issues being fought out in Europe no longer existed. Furthermore, once we had entered the war a large group, composed especially of the male members of the population, preferred to prosecute it vigorously and forget about the issues, whether of the war or of the peace to come. The program pursued by the Section likewise suffered from the inability of its leaders to phrase clearly enough for the comprehension of the average man and woman just what it was they were driving at. Lack of understanding on the part of many people promoted not only impatience with those who in a crisis seemed to be merely talking instead of acting, but in some cases even a conviction that such activities,

whatever they were, were dangerous. Because these could lead to radical social changes or be misdirected it was thought they should be discontinued.

This shows that any program which deals with the minds of men must apparently resign itself to an inability to produce tangible results. Concrete justification, therefore, is difficult when specifically called for by opponents who do not comprehend either its nature or its purpose. Furthermore, for most people morale is a by-product of successful action rather than of discussion — the achievement of goals not necessarily thought out in advance, but goals that are easily visible in the form of planes, ships, and guns, or comprehensible in the form of ton miles or billions of dollars. Even had the Citizen Morale Program been perfectly conceived and diplomatically executed, it would have been an extremely difficult program for which to secure popular acceptance. As circumstances turned out, on December 1, 1943, it was the first of the War Council programs to be abolished.

ESTABLISHMENT OF THE DIVISION OF CIVILIAN WAR SERVICES

In accordance with an outline in the manual for local defense councils, published in the summer of 1941, there had been appointed in various communities of the State a number of defense council committees in the fields of housing, nutrition, child care, consumer interests, youth problems, and recreation. As the war progressed, some of these activities received increased emphasis and their growing importance appeared to warrant some form of coordination. Accordingly, in a letter to the local defense councils, dated February 25, 1942, Lieutenant Governor Poletti recommended that "were it not already in existence as an integral part of its defense organization, each county and city defense council set up a section to be known as the Community Service Section."[1] The purpose of the Section was to review individual programs in the light of over-all community needs, thereby eliminating functional duplication or gaps and assuring priority to problems of major importance. Direction of individual programs remained untouched, but coordination was achieved by a Chairman of Civilian War Services. In many instances, this person was a man who gave his services and time to the War Council.

The task of establishing the divisions of Civilian War Services was entrusted by the State Coordinator to the Division of Volunteer Participation, whose volunteer offices were pretty well organized by the end of February, 1942. Members of the field staff of the Department of Social Welfare were made available for the purpose, partly to save money and partly because that department had long been in the field of community services. Administratively, the arrangement did not prove satisfactory, and as the field staff of the State Office of Volunteer Participation became adequate for the task, it gradually took over liaison with the Civilian War Services Section as well as with the volunteer offices. By the end of the year there were ninety-one Civilian War Services divisions wholly or partially organized and operating, and seven regional conferences of the chairmen of these divisions had been held on the needs of youth in wartime.

The change in the name of the State Division of Volunteer Participation to that of the State Office of Civilian Mobilization, a change brought about March 27 in accordance with a change in Federal policy, was not immediately followed by any pronounced alteration in functions. These remained the same, viz., to assist in the establishment of local volunteer offices, of Community Service sections, and of Citizen Morale programs. As we shall see, however, the word "mo-

---

[1] Changed in August, 1942, to Civilian War Services.

bilization," implying as it did active responsibility for the implementation and in some cases initiation of war programs by civilians, opened the door wide to the evolution of the State and local offices along new lines.

PROGRAMS OF 1942

Quite apart from the problem of setting up a Statewide organization was the problem of acting as a servicing agency in connection with programs whose success was desired by Federal and State departments. Support of such programs became the major function of the Office of Civilian Mobilization. Throughout the war, wherever the assistance of volunteers was necessary, the local offices did their best to furnish them. In 1942, the activities of the volunteer offices reflected the pervading emphasis upon preparations for disaster from the air. Programs for which it furnished volunteers were training for first aid and home nursing, for the aircraft warning service, and the forces of Civilian Protection. In the fall, it sponsored a program for the average householder known as Fighting the War at Home, which was partly a discussion course, partly a preparation for self-reliance in the event of emergency. Emphasis was placed upon preserving material things such as furniture and other household articles from damage. All through 1942, the accent was upon fear and self-preservation, as in time of disaster people would in a large measure have to help themselves.

The North African campaign turned the tide and helped to lessen the tension. This event occurred at the same time as the election of the first Republican governor in twenty years. Mr. Dewey had pledged his new administration to a vigorous prosecution of the war in all its phases. As a result of this promise, and of the policies which implemented it, from the beginning of 1943 the greater number of the programs centered less upon protection of persons and property

than upon support of (1) Federal programs, (2) war production, (3) production and preservation of food, and (4)
maintaining the working efficiency of the
individual through child care, recreation
and physical fitness programs, and improved health services. Under the stress
of war the strength of a community was
finally seen to be in proportion to its
capacity to produce goods and services.
One more step, however, was to be taken
in 1942 before it was to be possible in
some localities to bring to the support of
the war programs the full strength of
the community.

THE BLOCK PLAN

The Block Plan was sponsored by the
Federal Office of Civilian Defense as the
best answer available to the problem of
organizing communities intensively. Actually the block plan in all but name had
been put into operation in Syracuse in
December, 1941. A women's organization
consisting of what were called personnel
officers was set up parallel to that of
Civilian Protection. This counterpart of
the air-raid wardens was used for the
civilian protection survey of families for
evacuation purposes and later on for
work of other kinds. It developed an independent existence and in 1942 experience gained through its operations
proved influential in establishing the national block plan. This plan, as it came
from Washington, was the last of the
major structural innovations incorporated into the New York State pattern
for the organization of volunteers. In a
number of ways it paralleled the Civilian
Protection organization of zone and sector wardens created in 1941. The block
leaders, however, were concerned with
the mobilization of popular support behind civilian war services, such as salvage, transportation, war savings, services
for servicemen, recreation, consumer interest, nutrition, health and medical care,
welfare and child care, housing, education, agriculture, labor supply and train-

ing, and plant protection. Incidentally,
the organization afforded a means of getting vital war information into every
home rapidly and accurately, and conversely of collecting information from
the home when needed by local war
councils for purposes of community planning. Essentially, it was a means of getting things done in a hurry on a community basis, and, since the war, it is
being continued in some places without
the name for purposes similar to those
for which it was originally designed.

The Block Leader Program was first
introduced into New York State under
the sponsorship of the Office of Civilian
Mobilization in October, 1942. Its acceptance by the local war councils was relatively slow in spite of the support given
it by the State War Council in a resolution of March 30, 1943. This resolution
called for the appointment of a Chief of
Block Leader Service as a member of
each local war council, who would have
complete charge of all block leaders in
his community. As a rule the block plan
was set up as a subdivision of the volunteer office under the direct control of its
director, although in some localities its
chief was an independent person. At the
same time the War Council made it clear
that use of this service would require
prior approval by the local council.
Councils, however, were, when practicable, to give precedence to campaigns
scheduled by the State Office of Civilian
Mobilization. Since the possibilities for
political manipulation inherent in the
block plan were clearly recognized, the
War Council expressly stated "that under
no circumstances were the Block Leaders to be used for policing, or to obtain
information pertinent to policing, or for
the solicitation of money for private
agencies, or for the dissemination of
propaganda for the benefit of any class
or group." To avoid confusion and duplication of effort, all State or Federal
programs were to be cleared first through
the State Civilian Mobilization Office in

Albany. This, however, was sometimes difficult to enforce, as many Federal agencies never did get very clearly in mind the need for obtaining "clearance" for a program on the State level.

By July, 1943, approximately 80 per cent of the war councils had established a block leader service or its equivalent, and in many instances results were highly satisfactory. An unusual record for the selling of war bonds and stamps was made by the block leaders in Syracuse who, as the result of a carefully prepared two weeks' publicity campaign, sold 30 million dollars worth in three hours. In a similar campaign to secure additional personnel for hospitals, an estimated 2,200 inactive registered nurses were discovered and urged to reenter service, and approximately 1,100 practical nurses, not previously listed, were registered. In connection with recruiting for branches of the armed services, in a report dated August 3, 1943, the Director of the Office of Civilian Mobilization reported the recruitment of 1,715 WACS, 607 aviation cadets, and 44 for other branches.

Projects carried out by means of the block plan included meat-sharing and car-sharing campaigns, household salvage, surveys of the number of children requiring day care, the sale of war bonds and stamps, survey of registered nurses, a campaign to interest girls in nursing, food preservation and canning instructions, the distribution of a pamphlet entitled, *A Personal Message to the Mothers, Wives, Fathers, Brothers, Sisters and Friends of Servicemen from General Marshall and Admiral King,* urging them not to talk about military movements, and the location of candidates for interviews by WAC and Aviation cadets. These programs were undertaken in cooperation with six State departments or War Council agencies, four Federal agencies, and in one case the survey of the number of children requiring day care, at the request of Governor Dewey. In the latter case, however, the request was not made originally to the block plan or Office of Civilian Mobilization leaders. In addition, many local campaigns were undertaken at the discretion of individual war councils, such as the explanation of point rationings as an aid to local ration boards, and the promotion of victory gardens. The total number of volunteers enrolled in block plans was approximately twenty thousand.

If the block plan is considered on the basis of the State as a whole, it can scarcely be regarded as an unqualified success. In some respects the term was a misnomer, since in rural communities where it frequently worked satisfactorily, the organization was by social groups or on an activity basis and not geographical. By subsequent agreement the Minute Men of the Extension Service took over the functions of the block plan in rural communities where they were active. Speaking generally, the success of the plan depended primarily upon how it was used and for what purposes. Where purposes were regarded as unimportant, such as distributing throwaways, or relaying messages, individuals lost interest. Where the organization was reserved for campaigns of real importance, such as securing specific information, supporting campaigns for war savings bonds and stamps, salvage operations, etc., it proved successful and morale remained good. In a number of instances, it attained outstanding success, but these were not sufficiently numerous throughout the State to justify the conclusion that its overall operations were successful.

CONTINUED EXPANSION — 1942

All during 1942, the principal effort of the field staff of the State Office of Civilian Mobilization lay in the field of structure. By the end of the year volunteer offices had been established in 106 of the 108 local war councils. The campaign to induce the formation of a section on Civilian War Services had, by December, reached approximately 80 per cent coverage. Considering the fact that a number of the county war councils located in rural areas had little prior experience in community organization and suffered from relatively few dislocations, this percentage was extremely good. The final task of organization, that of setting up within each war council the block leader system, was proceeding rapidly by the end of the year, and by February, 1943, had reached approximately 75 per cent coverage.

The creation of a State-wide organization, including volunteer offices, divisions of Civilian War Services, and the block leader system, for intensive coverage of urban communities required not only the efforts of a field staff but the holding of regional conferences throughout the State to permit closer contact among war council officials. The opening conference was held in Syracuse in 1942, and following that conferences were held in Watertown and Albany, at which instruction in the training of block leaders was provided. During the month of January, 1943, others were held at Canandaigua, Buffalo, Utica, Binghamton, New York City, and Lake Placid. These proved helpful to both the field staff of the State Office of Civilian Mobilization and the executives of the city and county war councils. With the work of organization largely behind it, the State Office of Civilian Mobilization turned its energies to increasing the effectiveness of the volunteer offices and securing better community planning by the Divisions of Civilian War Services.

One of the means of increasing the effectiveness of the Volunteer Offices and preventing duplication of effort on the local level was the negotiation of State-wide agreements with a number of agencies having extensive organizations of their own. As early as April, 1942, an arrangement was worked out with the Office of Civilian Protection for a system of "clearance" through one especially designated individual in each office.

Later on, in June, arrangements were made for the centralization of Civilian Protection enrollment and records in the Volunteer Offices. Similar arrangements with the Department of Social Welfare involved biweekly meetings between two representatives primarily to keep in touch with the formation of community service sections within the local defense councils. Careful attention was given to the need for precise understandings between the two field staffs to avoid any overlapping or confusion. Similar plans were developed with the Director of the State Nutrition Committee and with the State Liaison Officer with the American Red Cross. A Federal agreement, reached March 25, between the Office of Civilian Defense and the National Red Cross on registration of volunteers from the Red Cross special services promised to improve relationships between the local chapters of Red Cross and the local Volunteer Offices.

From August 29, 1942, to August 28, 1943, at least eight such agreements are recorded in the Official Bulletin of the State War Council. Memorandum No. 4 gave correspondence between the Director of the Extension Service and the Deputy Director of the State Office of Civilian Mobilization to the effect that coordination between the county chairmen of Civilian Mobilization and the County Extension Committee would be designed to eliminate duplication of either organization or service. "Clearance" on the State level would precede development of any program in the rural areas. Registration in Volunteer Offices, while not required of the County Committee as a whole would be urged on all members as individuals who found it possible to act as volunteers. This agreement pertained to towns of 2500 population but did not extend into the larger cities. Memorandum No. 50, likewise with the Extension Service, prevented duplication of functions between block leaders and the Minute Men of the

Extension Service. Where Minute Men organizations existed, they were to take over the functions of the block plan, and a prior consultation was required before the block plan was put in operation in all villages under 2500. Agreements were likewise reached in September with the regional office of the Boy Scouts of America, in October with the State War Savings Committee, and in December with the State Salvage Committee. The latter provided for the integration of the local salvage organizations into the block plan, and likewise for full use of the block plan in salvage operations, thereby preventing duplication of effort between the two organizations. Similar agreements were reached in January, 1943, with the First Fighter Command, in February with the Girl Scouts, and in August with the War Manpower Commission.

In order to effect greater coordination among the thirty-five different State War Council programs, and enable the State War Plans Coordinator to keep in touch with them more easily, on June 9 the State War Council divided its programs into three major divisions, of which Civilian Mobilization was one. The chairmanship of the division was entrusted to the director of the Office of Civilian Mobilization and involved the coordination of nine programs in the fields of education, war training, physical fitness, nutrition, health, and social welfare. Regular meetings were held at which representatives of the State departments and War Council agencies compared notes and reported on the activities of their respective organizations.

PROGRAMS, 1943-1945

The number of separate campaigns sponsored in four years through the State Office of Civilian Mobilization, or upon the initiative of local volunteer offices, ran well over a hundred. As already indicated, emphasis upon protection of life and property from disaster gave place to the support of permanent Federal programs, and such State activities as war production, food production, conservation of transportation equipment, and the maintenance of the health and welfare of the population. Throughout, Civilian Mobilization served as a supporting agency for every program that promised aid to the war effort.

As outlined in Chapter II, the principal Federal programs operating in New York State were Selective Service, with all the accompanying recruiting drives for WACS, WAVES, SPARS, Marines, and Aviation Cadets, the war bond drives, sponsored by the Treasury Department, the salvage drives, under the direction of the War Production Board, and the operation of War Price and Ration Boards by the Office of Price Administration. Volunteers were used in the rationing program, not only for processing fuel oil and gasoline applications in 1942, but in 1943 in connection with the distribution of ration books Two and Four. Although in the cities local salvage committees used volunteers for house-to-house canvassing, in many instances rural communities, instead of making use of volunteers registered with the Office of Civilian Mobilization, relied upon special groups such as churches, lodges, women's groups, fire companies, and company employees. Extensive help was furnished War Finance Committees in connection with the Third, Fourth, Fifth, and Sixth War Loans. In the case of the Syracuse Liberty Belles, it took the form of house-to-house canvassing. Elsewhere, volunteers were used to man booths and arrange publicity.

An outstanding example of the use of volunteers and of volunteer offices occurred in 1943 and 1944 in connection with the recruiting of WACS, WAVES, SPARS and Marines. In many instances, volunteer offices were loaned as recruiting headquarters and became centers of community-wide publicity. All support possible was given to the armed services.

Another group of activities centered

upon the maintenance of the morale of all servicemen at home and abroad. Campaigns were conducted on local initiative to secure for the servicemen of the community gifts, books, scrapbooks, and even photographs of their wives and children. Volunteers manned United Service Organization centers and Red Cross Canteens, and helped with publicity on campaigns for the security of military information. Such activities were a permanent part of the support furnished by the home front to the armed forces of the Federal government.

One of the earliest forms of assistance rendered the war production program by volunteers was the taking, in 1942, of a survey of housing facilities in a considerable number of the war impact areas. In fact, surveys of all kinds were largely dependent upon the work of volunteers. As examples may be cited the child care, evacuation, housing, and machine-tool surveys. In Rochester an outstanding job was done in supplying volunteers for the ration board and the rent registration program. Another extremely important volunteer activity was the recruitment of paid as well as volunteer workers for industrial plants. This work was especially valuable in 1943 and 1944 at a time when employment was at its peak and labor reserves were practically exhausted. An outstanding example of the value of such efforts was the Volunteer Center in Syracuse, which by recruiting both paid and volunteer workers for industry succeeded in preventing Syracuse from being declared a number one labor shortage area. For its achievement, the city of Syracuse was presented in 1943 with the War Manpower Commission flag, the first flag to be given to a city for the recruitment of war workers, and the second awarded in the country. Likewise in support of war production, volunteer offices aided in giving publicity to the campaign to conserve critical resources; assisted with the home accident survey in 1943, and in 1944 took part in the collection of milkweed pods to supplement kapok for use in life-preserver jackets.

The use of volunteers was especially noteworthy in connection with the production of food. As we shall see, a shortage of farm labor was one of the principal problems faced by the State during the war, and the Farm Manpower Director welcomed the efforts of the local volunteer offices to secure part-time volunteers from nearby communities for harvesting crops, such as hay, fruits, and vegetables, and for work in canning plants. As early as 1942, volunteers were used in the farm and home safety campaign, and in 1945 to help with the farm machinery survey. The volunteer offices also took part in publicizing the victory garden programs of 1943-1945, and in furnishing assistance for the "Share the Meat" program and the food preservation activities of the Emergency Food Commission. The importance of volunteer efforts in connection with food and nutrition increased with each year of the war as the food problem became progressively more complex.

Volunteer offices were of assistance to the War Transportation Committee in the formation of car-sharing groups in 1943. Publicity was also given, in 1944, to the "Don't Travel" campaign sponsored by the Office of Defense Transportation.

With the prolongation of the war and the appearance of shortages of materials and manpower, more and more came to depend upon the efficiency of the working individual. It was at this point that the social services of the communities became inextricably bound up with the prosecution of the war. Primarily, the child care, recreation, physical fitness, health, nursing, welfare, and Red Cross programs all operated in the field of prevention. Because of that fact and because prevention is essentially a defense against future possibilities, individuals who do not live at least partly in the future may be slow to comprehend the importance of work in these fields. Comprehension does require imagination at this point. However, as their connection with absenteeism and the working efficiency of the individual grew clearer, the importance of these services became recognized.

Social services could not have been carried on during the war without volunteers. They were widely used in connection with the surveys of child care needs and of prospective foster homes in 1943. An inventory of recreational facilities for members of the armed forces, sponsored by the United Service Organizations, was conducted with the aid of volunteers. However, the greatest number of surveys were those in connection with the two fields of health and nursing. In 1943, a survey was made of potential male volunteers for hospitals. Several inventories of both registered and practical nurses were conducted for the War Nursing Council. Volunteer instructors for nursing classes were enrolled in 1943, and the same year an inventory was conducted of prospective nursing students. Volunteers were used in connection with surveys by the Health Department of smallpox and diphtheria immunization and in connection with a survey of preschool clinics. The Red Cross blood banks likewise depended heavily upon the recruitment of volunteer blood donors.

The above enumeration of instances in which volunteers were useful, which undoubtedly could be tripled if space permitted, gives a good indication of the extent to which the essential work performed by citizens of the State on the home front depended upon volunteer activities. By the end of 1943, the State Office of Civilian Mobilization reported over a million volunteers enrolled in Civilian Protection and Civilian War Services combined. This number approximately equaled the number of men and women from the State who entered the armed forces.

ADMINISTRATIVE EVOLUTION OF THE STATE OFFICE OF CIVILIAN MOBILIZATION

Although the administrative evolution of the State Office of Civilian Mobilization has been included with the general historical narrative, it seems wise at the risk of some repetition to recapitulate briefly at this point the principal steps in the development of the State Office and indicate their significance. It has already been pointed out that the chief function of the Division of Women's Activities was the creation of the local volunteer offices and that the public relations problem of securing support from social agencies and women's organizations was successfully surmounted. It has been noted that the original emphasis upon women volunteers was soon broadened to include men, and that the phrase "Volunteer Participation" was substituted for "Women's Activities." The problem of securing 100 per cent coverage of the State was finally settled by the attack on Pearl Harbor which made the establishment of the remaining offices relatively easy. Guidance was continually furnished by the State Office which drew upon specialists on its own rapidly growing staff to help the local offices get under way in an efficient manner. The obligations of the local offices, as originally conceived, were limited to furnishing volunteers for both civilian protection activities and civilian war services. No responsibility existed either for the guidance, or the operation, of local programs.

In practice, however, it proved impossible to maintain such self-restraint. The need for coordinating civilian war services on a local level in the face of the indifference of many war councils to all but civilian protection activities resulted in the assignment to the Office of Volunteer Participation of the task of establishing divisions of Civilian War Services within the local councils. The establishment of these divisions, and their subsequent supervision, required from the

State Office far more in the way of community planning than had been anticipated. Consequently a borrowed field staff of two was augmented by members from the State Department of Social Welfare. Since it was necessary, however, to determine broad policies, and since the field staff of an established department were accustomed to certain procedures, it soon became evident that if the responsibility was to belong to the Office of Volunteer Participation it would have to have its own staff. The arrangement was thus shortly dissolved and the field staff subsequently increased to seven.

A further administrative development took place in June, 1942, as a result of the need for better integration of all war council programs on the State level. The formation of three main divisions of which the Division of Civilian Mobilization was one, gave to its chairman, the Director of the Office of Civilian Mobilization, the position of coordinator of the programs in the field of community services. While this conferred no real power, it did offer an opportunity for learning at first hand what policies were being formulated on the State level, and thus made possible the instruction of the Office of Civilian Mobilization field men as to the situation they would be likely to encounter in the communities.

The establishment of the block plan in the fall of 1942 provided a further means of reaching the majority of individuals in a community, but it involved the local civilian mobilization offices more deeply than ever in the planning and direction of programs calling for its use. As additional responsibility for the operation of State-wide programs was also thrust upon the State Office of Civilian Mobilization, relations with Federal, State, and local agencies became more complicated. Early difficulties about keeping Federal agencies out of local communities until they had first cleared with the State Office gave way to complex relations with various State departments and agencies. The

Civilian Mobilization organization, however, was strong enough and sufficiently experienced by the fall of 1943 to handle effectively the larger and more pressing problems that appeared in 1944 and 1945, once the State began to feel the real effect of the war-caused shortages.

On September 1, 1943, the exact halfway mark in the official life of the Office of Civilian Mobilization, Mrs. Pennock resigned as director, and on October 7, Governor Dewey appointed as her successor Mrs. Walter Scott McNab of Schenectady. Two of the most important problems facing the new director were those of public relations with the other agencies of the State and the maintenance of morale among the members of her staff. Closer working relations were established with the Departments of Education, Health, and Social Welfare, with the State Nursing Council, with the State Committee on Child Care, and with the College of Agriculture and the School of Nutrition at Cornell. One administrative change introduced by the new director was the entrusting of special programs to individual field men, who were thus in a position to follow up on all developments. In the final eighteen months of the war three of the major programs, farm labor, hospital personnel, and recreation were concentrated in the hands of individual members of the staff. The latter program, upon which, for the last year and a half, nearly 50 per cent of the time of the Office was spent, will be discussed in Chapter VIII.

The concentration in individual hands of responsibility for programs was not the only means employed to maintain morale. After more than two years of war, some of the staff were tired. Others left to take paid positions elsewhere or to go into the services. As a result, replacements had to be found that would fit into the existing group. This was important as the office force was closely knit and shared all interests and efforts in common. The new appointments turned out to be excellent, and the Director possessed the happy faculty of evoking cooperation and generating good will in an organization which was now thoroughly established and needed but to get its second wind to function smoothly for the duration of the war. Attention also had to be given to the local offices. Some of the chairmen were not so busy in the latter part of 1943 as they had previously been and wished the State Office to provide further programs. Decisions as to what was necessary for these people to do in their own communities and what would merely have been "busywork" were by no means easy. A general stimulus to continue the job at full speed was supplied in January, 1944, by a State-wide meeting of all local Civilian Mobilization people held in Albany. Regional meetings followed in Garden City, Bronxville, Newburgh, Buffalo, Rochester, Binghamton, Utica, Albany, and Plattsburg, which tightened up the entire organization and gave it renewed vigor.

These steps, together with the previous change of name to Civilian Mobilization, a title indicating very general and quite extensive functions, plunged the State Office into the field of community planning and program making.

The conduct of the Civilian War Services programs on both State and local levels can perhaps be made clearer if described in business terminology, for what the Office of Civilian Mobilization really did was to sell to the communities as a wartime need local, State, and national programs in support of the war effort. The Deputy Director in charge of these programs held a position corresponding to that of sales manager for the New York territory. The chairman of the Office of Civilian Mobilization corresponded roughly to the president of the firm. As might be expected, occasional differences arose as to aims and methods, especially with regard to the big question — to expand or not to expand the operations of the company. The sales manager, however, could point to a steady expanson of the operations of the firm and the development of a State-wide market for many of the products available through the efforts of the sales organization. Some of these products were made in the company's own workshops. Others were nationally advertised brands, for which his firm was the New York distributor. Carrying the business analogy still futher, the local communities — whether city or county — may be regarded as sales territories in charge of dealers represented by the local chairmen of Civilian Mobilization, of Civilian War Services, or of the volunteer offices. Naturally, where there was more than one dealer to a territory, competition might ensue, especially in the case of conflicting claims to exclusive selling rights. These disputes had to be resolved by the field men of the Office of Civilian Mobilization, who performed the work of district sales managers.

In fact, much depended upon the persistence and finesse with which these district managers sold the programs prepared by the State Office. They had to perform two main functions. First, they had to analyze their territories in terms of the marketing possibilities for the products of their firm, or to employ the parallel phrase in terms of war time community needs — for additional housing, recreation, health, and child care facilities. Report after report was sent to company headquarters outlining the sales opportunities in the different communities, the amount of sales resistance likely to be encountered, the capacities of their dealers, and the popular response to their wares. Reports of this sort had to be prepared on the ground, as the capacity of local war councils and of the chairmen of the local offices of Civilian Mobilization to report accurately on the needs of their communities varied widely.

Second, once the needs of a territory had been ascertained, the most appropriate methods for selling the products at that time "on the market" had to be devised.[1] It was unfortunate that the sales force, both district and local, had gone with the company without much prior sales experience in this particular line. In fact, it was a relatively new field anyway, this field of Community War Services, and the technique of selling in it had to be acquired gradually. Besides, maximum consumption of the product frequently depended upon the organization of the community, as ultimate consumers were in many instances groups rather than individuals. In practically all such cases, the field representatives or sales force were of definite assistance to the local representatives.

By the end of the war, it is hardly surprising that a very respectable sales organization had been built up, based upon good relations between the district and local representatives and a fund of experience in selling a special line of products. The sales force had learned that the market for individual products varied widely with communities. Rural areas had less need for certain items than did urban. The importance of advance advertising, of knowing the right people, and of having the right local sponsorship was revealed in countless instances. Similarly, the value of tact and diplomacy had become evident, compared with bluntness and dogmatism. And then, just as these lessons were being thoroughly assimilated, the war ended, the bottom dropped out of the market, production ceased, and the sales force was disbanded. Yet, during the war, markets had been developed in certain communities for such items as additional recreational facilities, child care centers, provisions for wider participation of young people in community life, and other improved so-

cial services. Furthermore, it was a good omen that of the Office of Civilian Mobilization sales force, four of the six remained in State service, three in one department, and that a fifth went with the Federal government; all of them in positions where their wartime sales experience should prove valuable, and in the same area where they could deal with those people with whom they had made contacts during the war.

In a number of respects, the administrative lot of Civilian Mobilization personnel was a difficult one. The field men, especially, were dealing with volunteers who had to be persuaded. Although local war councils were required by law to "cooperate with and assist the State Council" and to "perform such duties and services as it may direct," the Office of Civilian Mobilization was not expressly mentioned in the War Emergency Act. On the other hand, Civilian Protection representatives although likewise dealing with volunteers were in a legal position to command virtual military obedience from subordinates all along the line. While the reason for this is obvious, the disparity of position was irksome to men who toward the end of the war were supervising most of the emergency programs conducted in the communities of the State. This supervisory work was done in the name of the State War Council, its headquarters having no field staff, although actually the men were not themselves working out of headquarters.

During the period 1944-1945 occurred the nearest return to the original administrative method of 1941, whereby contact was made with the local war councils through field men directly responsible to headquarters. The permanent interruption of this direct line of communication, which occurred in November, 1941, was perhaps the biggest administrative mistake of the entire war period. Thenceforth, the field staff of the Office of Civilian Mobilization found it-

---

[1] A discussion of these "products" has already been given under the sections on "Programs, 1942," and "Programs, 1943-1945."

self interpreting to local volunteer offices and even directly to local war councils most of the programs officially sanctioned by the State War Council, without having the authority and prestige which would have accrued had they come straight from headquarters. Where these men were best known and where they inspired the most confidence they were called upon to interpret the War Emergency Act, as few local chairmen would write to headquarters on a matter involving Community War Services when they had confidence in the State Civilian Mobilization representative. This situation proved to be a constant source of embarrassment and frustration to men who took the work seriously and believed in its importance. Consequently, the increasing use made toward the end of the war of the Office of Civilian Mobilization field staff, was a welcome return to the substance of the original plan of organization.

THE EVOLUTION OF THE LOCAL VOLUNTEER ORGANIZATION

The process by which the Division of Community War Services developed to its final position as a general information center for all local war council programs, and as the chief ally of those who would provide public and private services to the community, resembled in some respects the evolution of the State Office of Civilian Mobilization. The suggestion from Washington for the creation within local war councils of a section of Civilian War Services was readily accepted in New York State as a means of coordinating related programs. Unfortunately, in some cases instead of establishing this group of nonprotective community services under new chairmen independent of the Director of the Volunteer Office (and consequently on a par with the Director of Civilian Protection), in smaller places the chairman of the local volunteer office either assumed the chairmanship of the Section on Community War Services or retained supervisory control over the new director. Perhaps this was because the responsibility for the creation of the office had been placed with the State Director of the Office of Civilian Mobilization.

Imperceptibly, such a procedure added community planning to the functions of the original volunteer offices, because without it no well-integrated Civilian War Services program could be carried out. A month later, March 27, 1942, when the name Civilian Mobilization was adopted with the added implication of direction, many volunteer chairmen considered the stage had been set for an unlimited expansion of functions whenever necessary. This was a mistake. As it turned out, in some communities there was a distinct vacuum in the area of community planning and volunteer mobilization into which the new Office of Civilian Mobilization promptly moved. On numerous occasions, however, where no such vacuum existed, well-meant efforts of the Office of Civilian Mobilization chairmen conflicted with the activities and interests of other local committees. These were often bewildered by the appearance of another boss on the local level, in addition to the State department or War Council agency from whom they had hitherto been receiving help and guidance.

The relationship between the volunteer office, the Division of Civilian War Services, and the Office of Civilian Mobilization was often dependent upon the relative balance of vigorous personalities. No set pattern was characteristic of the entire State. The first two were frequently both under the third. Sometimes all three were separate. Occasionally the terms "volunteer office" and "OCM office" were interchangeable. Relations varied from personal friendship and harmony of the closest sort to rivalry among equals and the dominance of all by one vigorous leader. Only those offices, however, where a broad-based organization with a board of interested advisors had been created, or where a single individual in the confidence of the local political leaders was willing to continue in a voluntary capacity, were able to survive the coming of peace.

During the first two years of the war, when the principal emphasis was upon civilian protection, the local volunteer office and the Division of Civilian War Services were in many localities considered of little importance. This was true partly because men who were picked originally for the part they could play in protecting the community dominated the War Council, and found it difficult to understand why community services required emphasis in time of war. Not being trained to think along these latter lines, there was no particular reason why police and fire chiefs should understand. It was also partly true because only in 1943, as personnel shortages in the service occupations became drastic, was the importance of these services brought home forcefully to the community at large. The administrative mistake was to load up the War Councils heavily with protection-minded individuals to the later exclusion of representatives of other community services.

With the successful prosecution of the North African campaign, however, the chances of the Civilian Protection organization ever being called upon to function as originally intended faded rapidly. At approximately the same time, the home front began to feel the impact of shortages. Gradually, it became clear even to the most protection-minded individuals that the maintenance of the efficiency of the individual was after all at the bottom of the successful functioning of the home front. The open support of the child care program by the State administration, an increasing emphasis upon the necessity for maximum food production, the struggle to maintain intact all available transportation equipment, the desperate need for the raw materials of industry, all

merged as main lines of endeavor, and with them the importance of the volunteer office as a resource for badly needed personnel. Then again, people learned by doing, and the functioning of the community as a group brought about by dire necessity possessed in itself an educational value. It constituted a demonstration of what could be done in the way of community action if the urge were great enough, and made clear the potential value of a community-wide organization at any time — whether in war or in peace. Just as the war period accelerated the development of aviation and research in electronics so in the same way it advanced the techniques of community organization. It is our misfortune, however, that in the field of human relationships knowledge is acquired at far greater cost and retained with far more difficulty than it is in the field of the exact or applied sciences.

EFFECTS OF THE WAR PERIOD ON COMMUNITY ORGANIZATION AND PARTICIPATION IN COMMUNITY LIFE

The war brought to the communities of the State new forms of organization and new leaders. Not only were those organizations existing prior to 1941 stimulated to greater endeavor, but new organizations, of necessity created to meet wartime problems, appeared and made their way into the community. Of these, the volunteer offices and divisions of Community War Services, by affecting the life of the inhabitants at innumerable points, exerted the greatest influence.

War also brought with it the discovery of new talents as a result of the creation of an unprecedented pool of volunteers, many of whom were totally unknown to community leaders prior to the war. Once these men and women had received a part in the life of their community, no matter how small, their interest in maintaining its welfare was permanently aroused. Large numbers of them, especially in the more efficiently organized centers, were desirous of keeping on with volunteer work after the cessation of hostilities. Playing a part in the life of the community is one of the surest ways to develop a spirit of intelligent citizenship. For the first time these people became vitally interested in the government and problems of their community. It is interest of this sort that produces better and more effective citizens. A typical example is that of a lady who volunteered to work in a dispensary, was soon placed in charge of all volunteers, and was finally asked to become a member of the governing board of the institution. As wartime pressures tended to force greater cooperation, there resulted greater mutual understanding and respect among members of the community with the inevitable discovery of unsuspected reserves of leadership.

Unfortunately, with the cessation of hostilities, it was apparent in many places that organizations which had depended upon the personality and leadership of one individual, no matter how efficiently they had operated during the war, had not developed a sufficiently broad basis of support to continue once that leadership was withdrawn. One of the best examples of a volunteer office, which is now rendering the same active service to its community that it did in time of war, is the Volunteer Center, Inc., of Syracuse. The leaders of this organization frankly ascribe their continuing successful operation to the policy adopted during the war of setting up a strong advisory board whose help was sought constantly, and whose support was invaluable in tying together all groups of the city. The result has been that purely on the basis of indispensability, the Center has become an accepted social institution, constantly used for all sorts of community purposes. The organization is fortunate in having not one but a number of outstanding leaders to cooperate with each other on a basis of personal friendship and close agreement on aims and methods.

Without exaggeration it may be said that the war experience added greatly to the self-consciousness of New York communities. Those whose organization pattern survived the war have gained a permanent instrument for social betterment. Those who have lost the wartime agencies are vaguely conscious of something lacking in the community picture. It is possible, if not altogether probable, that out of this dissatisfaction will come in time a revival in one form or another of a community agency, devoted to over-all planning in the interests of the general welfare.

CHAPTER SIX

Agricultural Production and Nutrition

WHEN a country goes to war one of the principal tasks confronting those who are not called into the armed forces is the production of an increased supply of food. The slogan "food will win the war" contains more truth than many nations (to their cost) have realized until too late. In our highly complex modern society the social class which performs the function of raising food has a tremendous responsibility to the rest of the nation, one which is increased immeasurably in wartime. In New York State this heavy burden fell upon 5 per cent of its population of 13 million, but fortunately for all concerned the farmers proved to be one of the most energetic, intelligent, and well-organized groups in the entire State.

FARMERS OF NEW YORK

Human ingenuity develops best under difficulties, and the farmers of New York State have had their share of obstacles to surmount. The story of the development of the present characteristics of New York agriculture is briefly told. During the course of the nineteenth century the farmers of the State were forced to meet increased competition from two directions. The opening up of the West with its extensive methods of farming and the development of the water and rail network in the north-central zone flooded the northeastern states with grain and meat products of a quality and quantity and at a price such as to tax to the utmost the competitive powers of New York farmers. Under his pressure they gradually shifted their emphasis from meat and grains to the production of more bulky products, such as milk, butter, cheese, eggs, fresh fruits, and vegetables. In these lines their proximity to a rapidly increasing urban population gave them an advantage over their more distant rivals. Transportation costs were heavily in their favor, as was also the time factor in the marketing of perishable commodities.

However, as manufacturing centers developed on all sides, they found themselves faced by a second form of competition. Industry paid higher wages than farmers could afford, and cities offered attractions that the countryside found it difficult to equal. Consequently, the trend of intrastate migration from rural areas to the cities steadily increased. Financial competition, however, forced New York farmers to make a further adjustment. In order to match the wages paid in industry, only those lands which were found by experience to be most productive were retained in cultivation, and only those methods which proved to be most efficient in the use of labor and most rewarding in terms of higher yields per acre were employed permanently. This trend is illustrated by the increase in production, the decline in the total number of workers, and the decline in the number of acres in cultivation since 1910.

Table 12. Trends in New York State Agriculture, 1910-1940

Year	Acres of land in farms	Number of persons engaged in agriculture	Index of crop and livestock production (1895-1904-100)
1900	22,648,000	375,990	100*
1910	22,030,000	378,657	103*
1920	20,633,000	314,774	101*
1930	17,980,000	267,373	101*
1940	17,170,000	210,434	110*

* Averages of the 10-year periods centered on the census years indicated.

The results of this period of 150 years of constant struggle for survival illustrate what men can do if they must. Immediately prior to the outbreak of World War II, New York ranked seventh in the country as a food-producing state. Agricultural wages were decidedly above the national average and the standard of living of New York farmers compared favorably with that enjoyed by farmers in any of the leading agricultural states in the country. To survive, however, New York farmers had to develop qualities of initiative, foresight, and leadership which were to prove invaluable during the war. In very few other states before the war did there exist the same number of active farm organizations and the same spirit of willing cooperation in the solution of mutual problems. If "the Lord helps those who help themselves," New York farmers had established an excellent claim to assistance from the Almighty. They were going to need it.

THE PROBLEM OF FOOD IN WARTIME

It is a well-known fact that war increases the demand for food, but the reasons for this are not so thoroughly understood. From time immemorial, war has been an easy way by which to solve the unemployment problem. The production of weapons and equipment under contract with the government resembles closely a highly specialized public

works project with the government paying the bill. As a result, for three or four years during World War II more civilians had more money in their pockets than they had ever had in their lives, and they spent a good share of it for more and better foods than they had ever enjoyed before. War workers and soldiers burn up more energy than they do in ordinary peacetime occupations, and consequently have to take in more food to maintain a balance. Soldiers especially require highly concentrated proteins and vitamins. In the spring of 1941 Congress passed the Lend-Lease Act. Thereafter, the stream of shipments to our allies included food. As the quantity of supplies increased so did the amount of food required for foreign shipment. Four per cent of our national production went to lend-lease countries in 1941, 10 per cent in 1942, and 11 per cent in 1943. Despite the cessation of lend-lease shipments, the demand has remained high ever since the liberation of the war-torn areas.

In view of these demands for food it was necessary for the Federal government to get the farmers of the country to raise their production sights as high as possible. This was done in regional, state, and county meetings in which the entire national picture was presented; after general discussion of local conditions, a decision was reached by the farmers themselves as to how much above the production of the previous year the goals should be set. All organizations concerned with the food-production problem cooperated in reaching these decisions, and the published goals were those that had been previously agreed upon among these groups. Until shortage of manpower evident even before Pearl Harbor began to make itself seriously felt in the fall of 1942, New York farmers did remarkably well. Nineteen hundred and forty-two proved the best production year in New York agriculture, as well as being probably the best crop year in history for the entire country.

The general wartime food program for New York State was designed to achieve three specific objectives:

1. To provide the kinds and quantities of foods that would maintain adequate nutrition for the greatest number of American civilians and soldiers, for our allies, and for those countries freed from Axis control.

2. To get the food which had been produced to the consumer in a wholesome condition with a minimum of waste and with as little loss of nutritional value as possible.

3. To persuade the people of the State to shift their diet substantially in order to make it possible to expand the number of individuals that could be fed from the same acreage.

The first two objectives are, of course, obvious, but the third requires some explanation. Why shift diet in wartime? The answer is that for a period prior to the outbreak of war the United States had ceased to be a net food exporting country — food imports had begun to exceed food exports. Consequently, since we had no surplus, the only way to feed civilians and soldiers and yet have food left for lend-lease and the liberated countries was to change diet. It is possible to feed directly with grain six or seven times as many people as can be fed indirectly with the meat of the cattle and hogs raised on the same amount of grain. It does become necessary to supply vegetable substitutes for some of the nutritional essentials otherwise supplied through meat. Since New York agriculture had already made its own shift to the production of just such substitutes what shifting remained fell to the lot of the average consumer, and became strictly a matter for his intelligence, his conscience, and his nutritionist. As we shall see below, the latter did his best.

War creates strange circumstances, and one is an increased demand for food at just the time food becomes more and more difficult to supply. New York farmers were caught in a giant squeeze between an increasing demand for food and a steadily deteriorating set of working conditions that under normal circumstances would have curtailed their ability to produce. There was little to be gained by expanding acreage, since the use of poorer land would require more manpower to operate. The exodus of men from the farms was accelerated by both the pull of high wages in war industries and the calls of Selective Service. In peacetime, lack of manpower might have been counterbalanced by increased use of machinery, but machinery production was cut to the bone and only by extensive repairs were the available machines kept in operation. Normal supplies of feed for dairy herds and poultry failed to move from Middle-Western production centers because ceilings on corn were low, and farmers found it more profitable to feed hogs, and so to market the grain as meat. There was thus a chronic feed shortage. Seed and fertilizer were at times scarce, and transportation by rail and water for feed and crops was short because of increased demand for the movement of munitions, coupled with a rapid deterioration in equipment. The railroads were in the same squeeze as the farmer. Supplies and containers ran short and costs, especially costs of feed and labor, went up. Fortunately through 1944 agricultural prices rose slightly faster than agricultural costs, otherwise there would have been no incentive but patriotism to keep the farmer at his task from dawn to dusk. His lot was not made easier by news from the industrial world of demands for the retention of the forty-hour week, and wages of $.80 to $1.00 and $1.25 an hour. Yet under conditions such as these combined with the normal uncertainties and oddities of "old man weather," the farmers of New York consistently bettered the 1935-1939 average of food production.[1]

FORMATION OF THE NEW YORK STATE AGRICULTURAL DEFENSE COMMITTEE

Perhaps initially the most important reason for New York's outstanding success on the food front lay in the fact that her farmers anticipated the difficulties in store for them and organized early to meet the emergency. The foresight and resourcefulness developed by 150 years of competitive farming counted in the hour of trial. Many farmers, remembering trends during the previous war, wisely concluded that a second war would bring a recurrence and intensification of similar circumstances. For such recurrence they began to prepare shortly after the fall of France. With the farsighted guidance and influence of the late Dean C. E. Ladd and Extension Director L. R. Simons of the State College of Agriculture, two men who had played vital food-production roles in World War I, steps were taken to mobilize the agricultural resources of the State for wartime conditions. As Edward S. Foster, Secretary of the Conference Board of Farm Organizations, put it: "We are hoping for the best, but at the same time we are preparing for the worst."

With characteristic independence and without consulting State officials, the New York State Conference Board of

Farm Organizations[2] took the first definite move to put New York State agriculture in a position to aid the National Defense Program. On June 22, 1940, it passed a resolution creating a New York State (Emergency) Agricultural Defense Committee:

To cooperate with the National Defense Council, the Extension Service, the Colleges of Agriculture and Home Economics, the State and Federal Departments of Agriculture, and any other national or state agencies dealing with defense measures in making available insofar as possible the agricultural resources of New York State and to assist farm people in the various farm groups in the State of New York to study and appraise their agricultural resources and agricultural needs in the light of national and international conditions.

The Conference Board also invited the following State and Federal organizations to designate representatives to serve on the new committee: New York State Agricultural Conservation Committee, New York State Agricultural Land Use Planning Committee, State Farm Security Advisory Committee, Production Credit Associations, State Soil Conservation Committee, and the New York State 4-H Extension Federation.

County units of the member organizations were requested to designate in turn representatives to form county agricultural defense committees with "like intent and purpose." It should be remembered that there were at this time no State or local defense councils. Apart from possible surveys of the agricultural resources of the various counties, no prediction as to the scope of the work or service of these committees was pos-

---

[1] See table on p. 162.

[2] Comprised of the New York State Grange, Dairymen's League Cooperative Association, New York State Farm Bureau Federation, New York State Federation of Home Bureaus, New York State Horticultural Society, New York State Vegetable Growers Association, Cooperative G.L.F. Exchange, and the New York State Poultry Council.

sible. The memory of the First World War was still fresh, and these men knew that with a war in Europe shortages of all kinds were likely. In fact, the minutes of the first meeting show that there was general concern about a shortage of farm labor which was even then beginning to manifest itself near the major centers of war production. Farm supplies, dairy feed, fertilizers, seeds, and farm machinery were discussed, and future possibilities thoroughly canvassed in each case. Thus it was the independent farm organizations which first took the lead in New York and provided a "correlating agency of farm men and women" to act whenever necessary in furtherance of the National Defense Program. Governor Lehman was notified of the action and thereafter was kept informed.

The establishment of Selective Service in September, 1940, presented New York farmers, already conscious of the migration of farm labor to war industries, with their first major war problem. After submitting, at the Governor's request, the names of representative farmers for appointment to the appeal boards, the Agricultural Defense Committee took counsel as to how best it could cope with the inevitable threat of the draft to farm manpower. Characteristically, the decision made was to "take the bull by the horns" and discuss the entire farm labor problem with the State headquarters of Selective Service. At a meeting held in Ithaca representatives of the Agricultural Defense Committee and the Extension Service of the College of Agriculture met with Major Harry Lemp to consider methods of clarifying the status of essential farm workers. The farm group presented their problem and the Major presented his. How were the draft boards to decide when an agricultural worker was essential? It was pointed out to the Major that the farm deferment blank then in use was inadequate, and that the farmer seeking deferment should supply additional information on the produc-

tive capacity of his farm. At the request of Major Lemp the group agreed to prepare for local draft boards a so-called yardstick for measuring such capacity. With the help of the College of Agriculture this was done, and, though subsequently modified, the principles involved were eventually adopted by the National Selective Service headquarters. A supplemental farm deferment blank was also prepared by the Agricultural Defense Committee and made available to the number of 377,000 without cost to local draft boards.

Late in the fall of 1940, the county agricultural committees offered their services to the draft boards to assist farm youth in the proper handling of questionnaires. Most of this work fell on the county agricultural agents who acted as secretaries for the County Agricultural Defense Committees and the USDA war boards. These war boards included one representative of each of the Federal "action" agencies in the county, such as the Agricultural Adjustment Agency, the Soil Conservation Service, the Farm Security Administration, the Farm Credit Administration, and the Extension Service. Under Selective Service regulations, USDA boards were designated as the official body responsible for submitting information and making recommendations on agricultural deferments. Members of the County Agricultural Defense Committees and farmers designated by them aided the county agricultural agent in making investigations and in obtaining factual information for war boards and Selective Service boards. Deferments were requested only when they were really necessary, and the confidence of the local boards was thereby secured and retained for the duration of the war. By April, 1941, the work of these farmer committees had become so important that the Governor wrote to both city and county defense councils urging them to appoint the chairman of the County Agricultural Committee as a member of the council. Thus within a year of the establishment of the New York State Agricultural Defense Committee the farmers of the State had received unmistakable recognition both from Selective Service and from the State Defense Council. They had won the right not only to speak out for themselves, but also to be consulted on all measures affecting their interests.

New York farmers, however, were not satisfied merely by steps taken to protect their essential help from induction into the armed forces. As harvest time approached in 1941, it became all too apparent that more workers would be needed than were available. The largest group of potential farm laborers not subject to induction were the high-school students. Accordingly, on August 12, the State Agricultural Defense Committee telegraphed Governor Lehman and the legislative leaders as follows:

Farmers are facing critical labor shortage. Shortage of seasonal workers by September 1 expected to exceed 30,000. Education law should be amended to protect districts against loss of State aid when excusing students for harvest work. Strongly urge Certificate of Intent protecting districts pending legislative action. Both Education and Labor laws legalize excusing students fourteen years and over for harvesting perishable crops. Will not conflict with adult workers for they are not available in sufficient numbers. Hope Defense Council will take favorable action next meeting.

(*Signed*) E. S. FOSTER, *Secretary*

This request was approved the same day at a meeting of the State Defense Council, and a resolution adopted recommending that the Governor and the leaders of the New York State Legislature sign a Certificate of Intent that at the next legislature a law would be adopted:

Authorizing the Commisioner of Education, under rules and regulations prescribed by the Board of Regents, to release from school for not more than ten school days,

for harvest work during the emergency, pupils fourteen years of age or over in school districts outside of cities.

When the bill was finally passed at the 1942 session, it applied both to cities and to counties and permitted the release of students of fourteen years of age and over for a total of twenty days. Later, the period was extended to thirty days. The County Agricultural Defense Committee and the County Defense Council as well had to certify to the local school authorities that the assistance of these pupils was necessary. The local school districts were to suffer no loss in State aid for these absences.

The point of the next attack on the food front was farm-machinery repair, and here again the Agricultural Defense Committee was the spearhead. In the fall of 1941, they took the matter up with Dean Ladd of the College of Agriculture. Through him, on December 10, a plan was represented to the Defense Council for assistance to farmers during the winter in the repair of their equipment. The idea was similar to one which had operated in 1917. Farmers could bring their machinery to local garages where clinics would be held to advise on the best methods of repair. Fifteen trained mechanics, each covering four counties and supplied with a half-ton panel truck, would be able to cover most of the farms of the State. The trucks would be equipped with tools, serving as portable machine shops. The Defense Council, impressed with the growing shortage of farm machinery and the necessity for maintaining in repair every serviceable unit, voted $80,000 to the College of Agriculture for organizing "clinics for the inspection, repair, reconditioning, and maintenance of farm machinery, and for employing a staff of trained instructor-mechanics, and for purchasing necessary trucks and other equipment." This program proved its worth immediately, and was continued substantially unchanged through 1945, and placed on a permanent basis by act of the 1946 Legislature.

Three months after Pearl Harbor, in February, 1942, at the annual meeting of the Association of Towns, the New York State Council of Defense presented seven speakers who described in some detail "New York's War Preparedness Program." The second talk, "War and the Farmer," was given by Chester DuMond, then chairman of the State Agricultural Defense Committee. Speaking for the farmers, he laid down a six-point program for the maintenance of agricultural production in New York State, summarized below:

1. To guarantee to farmers prices sufficient to provide them with the incentive to produce in greater volume, and to work longer hours to do it.

2. To arrange for the operation of labor camps in sections where large forces were needed for seasonal farm work. (This was actually in process of negotiation with Federal agencies, where it was designed to use itinerant labor too little skilled for machine-shop work.)

3. To plan with the Department of Vocational Education for the use of selected boys, and possibly girls, from the larger cities in harvesting crops.

4. To recruit some force similar to the Women's Land Army of World War I for light work on fruit and vegetable farms.

5. To help farmers to readjust their operations so as to produce the foods which were needed most. This was to be pushed to avoid plowing up unsuitable, marginal land, and the introduction of inept, untrained individuals as managers.

6. To cooperate with all State and Federal agencies, including the Department of Vocational Education, the State and Federal Employment Service, the United States Department of Agriculture, and the Civilian Defense authorities in each county.

The policies here outlined resulted from shrewd collective intelligence applied to remembered experience, and presaged the program fully developed during 1943.

Spurred by increasingly critical difficulties, New York farmers gave more and more attention to their problem of farm labor. Hitherto, labor shortages had been met by increased hours of family labor, but by September, 1942, critical shortages both in year-round and in seasonal labor were appearing, and the State Agricultural Defense Committee concentrated on the problem. Reports began to come in of farmers forced to curtail operations or even to liquidate part of their stock. It was alarming as a preview of what would be in store for many farmers in 1943 unless a general attack on the problem developed during the winter months.

In November, 1942, the farmers once more took the initiative by inviting three specialists from the faculty of the State College of Agriculture to investigate the entire matter and recommend a program. Aided by a technical advisory committee, they conducted a survey of growers, canners, and others, and on the basis of information received they drew up in December a twelve-point Farm Labor Program for submission to the State War Council. The program was approved by the Regional Farm Labor Advisory Committee of the War Manpower Commission, and on December 1, 1942, without waiting for State or Federal backing, the New York State Conference Board of Farm Organizations employed Dr. T. N. Hurd of the College of Agriculture and made his services available full time for the sole purpose of placing in immediate operation the Farm Labor Program for which he had been in part responsible.

Substantial cooperation was immediately forthcoming from the State War Council for an organization that knew not only what it wanted, but also was doing everything it could to work out its own salvation. On December 1, 1942, the Council agreed to the continuation of the Farm Machinery Repair Program, and at the same meeting passed a resolution requesting "All groups planning statewide programs to help meet the farm labor shortage, to obtain clearance with the New York State Agricultural Defense Committee of the State War Council, to promote correlation of effort, and to avoid duplication and over-lapping." In effect, this designated the farmers' committee as the semiofficial agricultural subcommittee of the State War Council. Later the War Council took the next logical step by resolving that in matters of agriculture the County Agricultural Defense Committees should be the official subcommittees of the county war councils. Before continuing the story further a brief statement is necessary regarding the assistance which other organizations in the State were attempting to furnish New York's embattled farmers.

The State-supported program for teaching, research, and extension in the field of agriculture which centers at Cornell University made available to the farmers and homemakers of each county personnel of scientific and specialized administrative competence: the county agricultural agents, the home demonstration agents, and the 4-H Club leaders, as well as numerous members of the college faculty who served in various consultative capacities. Funds were supplied to the extension program in part by the Federal, State, and county governments, and in part by membership fees of individual farmers. In 1942, the state leader of the 4-H Clubs, whose offices are located at Ithaca, was placed in charge of the Victory Garden Program. Although 4-H Clubs were designed to train young people, primarily, in good methods of agriculture and homemaking, the Victory Garden Program was extended to adults as well, and in the first year was extremely successful. Although no vic-

tory garden figures are available for 1942, the 1942 enrollment of rural boys and girls in the 4-H Clubs was 85 per cent above that of the previous year. Food preservation and storage was an important factor in the Victory Garden Program, but here again no figures are available. Interest was keen, however, and expectations were high for an expanded program in 1943.

The State Department of Agriculture and Markets, located at Albany, performed regulative and statistical functions necessary in connection with marketing agricultural products, and with estimating the acreage needed for future plantings. That its personnel was following the farm situation closely is evidenced by a 1942 report of the Director of the Bureau of Statistics, from which the following quotation is taken:

There is reason to believe that if food production in New York is to be continued at or about 1942 levels, there must be unusually careful planning as to all operations, including equipment, fertilizer, seed, and labor supplies. The tremendous pull of the armed services and industry, and the economic limits to wages that can be paid farm help under prevailing price and wage relations will make the manpower situation especially acute . . . There is very acute unrest and dissatisfaction among farmers at the prospect of even greater pressure on farm women, children, and aged men, and the use of part time, inexperienced, and frequently inefficient and untrainable help, in agriculture, particularly during a period when public policy appears to support the forty-hour week, and with industrial wage levels substantially out of line with the prices of many farm products.

In the fall of 1942 everyone agreed that manpower was agricultural problem number one.

The State Education Department, through its Bureau of Agricultural Education, under the direction of Dr. A. K. Getman, had charge of a number of programs connected with agricultural education. Early in June, 1940, Congress passed an act, subsequently renewed each year until 1945, providing funds for establishing in the schools a war training program in food production. In New York State over 65,000 individuals, in the schools of some 350 communities, were enrolled in classes devoted to training in farm machinery and repair, in farm production, and in management of the various fields of dairying, poultry raising, crop growing, vegetable gardening, fruit growing, and food preservation. Agricultural shops in the high schools were provided with needed equipment, and specialized courses in repairing machinery were offered which assisted thousands of farmers to keep in a maximum state of repair their automotive, electrical, and field machinery. When on June 30, 1945, Federal funds were withdrawn, the State War Council kept the program alive for the remainder of the fiscal year.

Even before the development of the Federal Victory Farm Volunteer Program, New York City schools in conjunction with the Bureau of Agricultural Education of the State Education Department started in 1942 what was called the Farm Cadet Victory Corps, composed of boys who, after training, were placed on farms in regions adjacent to the city. The youngsters worked for varying periods of time, some in camps, others on individual farms. The program proved a success and was subsequently continued through 1945 under the supervision of the Director of Farm Manpower.

Three Federal agencies may likewise be counted among the active allies of New York State's farmers. The United States Employment Service, through its State-wide network of branch offices, handled under contract with the Extension Service the recruitment, placement, and transportation of intrastate workers. As will be remembered, this service had taken over all placement work in the State upon the federalization of the State

Employment Service in January, 1942. An Advisory Committee was appointed by Mrs. Anna M. Rosenberg, Regional Director for New York State of the War Manpower Commission, with the function of considering and approving policies and programs dealing with agriculture. Mr. Hurd and also Mr. L. R. Simons, Director of the Extension Service, were members. The Farm Security Administration was assigned by the War Food Administration responsibility for housing and transporting imported farm help, such as those from Kentucky, the Bahamas, and Jamaica. These three Federal organizations worked closely with representatives of both the private and public agricultural groups of the State, and furnished proof of a fact sometimes disputed: that where private individuals and groups show a disposition to take the initiative in working out their own problems, State and Federal officials are usually glad indeed to have them assume the leadership.

Obviously, however, one essential ingredient for continued success was still missing. There was lacking in the farm program up to this time the official backing of the State government. The need was for State funds adequate for handling the farm manpower problem, and for a State organization at a sufficiently high level to be capable of speaking for the State as a unit in its relations with other states and with the Federal government as well, regarding matters of farm labor, farm machinery, transportation, and feed. It was at this point, just when many ideas looking toward such organization were in the air, and when the farmers of the State had definitely gone as far as they could without official aid, that Thomas E. Dewey became Governor of the State of New York. He placed the authority and resources of the State government squarely behind the men who had so signally shown themselves deserving of official support.

In the gubernatorial campaign of 1942,

the Republican platform contained a plank on agricultural policies stating that the party "would continue to take the lead in promoting the economic interests of the farmers." It pledged "continued support of scientific research in agricultural production" and "assistance in meeting the problem of labor shortages." After the election there was naturally some questioning as to how well the new Governor understood farm problems. It was perhaps fortunate that at this juncture a man should be elected to the highest office whose interest in agriculture dated from his boyhood in a rural community, and that recently this should have been revived with his purchase and operation of a four hundred-acre dairy farm. Such circumstances, therefore, actually proved a guarantee not only of interest in farm problems, but also of an understanding somewhat unusual in the chief executive of a populous eastern state.

When Governor Dewey arrived in Albany he was immediately deluged with requests for action on the food problem. For the moment it was his number one problem, and his first three public addresses reflected his preoccupation with the needs of farmers particularly and of consumers generally. Within five weeks he had determined that there was need for State action. Early in February he dispatched Mr. Hickman Powell, his personal representative, to Ithaca to discover what was being done about the 1943 farm program, and to obtain suggestions as to the proper responsibility of the State government in the solution of the farm labor problem. The Governor was very much impressed by the manner in which the farm organizations had taken the initiative even to financing a full-time executive to expedite their program. However, they lacked funds for large-scale action, and could not afford to wait longer for Washington to decide how the farm labor problem

of 1943 was to be handled. It was up to the State to act and act fast.

On February 6 and 7, Mr. Powell met with the Technical Advisory Committee of the Agricultural Defense Committee in Ithaca. The next day the session was transferred to Albany where Governor Dewey himself participated. It was decided that the primary need was for formal State recognition of, and participation in, the Manpower Program, that this program should be continued exactly as planned, and that the State should support the program officially and with adequate funds until Federal assistance should be forthcoming. The following day, the Governor appointed Dr. T. Norman Hurd as Director of Farm Manpower to coordinate all existing agencies, private, State, and Federal, in accordance with the plan that he and others had worked out the previous fall for the Agricultural Defense Committee. The sum of $50,000 was immediately secured from the War Council to push the program which was ultimately (although not until April 29) put on a firm basis by the allocation through the Extension Service of $420,000 of Federal funds. Prompt action with $50,000 early in February was worth as much to farmers as delayed action with $420,000 late in April.

It was soon evident, however, that more than financial aid was needed, and once again Powell was requested to review the situation and present recommendations. This time, his report covered every phase of the farm problem, from labor, which was currently being taken care of, through feed, machinery, transportation, and supplies to nutrition. His conclusions were these:[1]

Many of the difficulties are special to this part of the country, many are special to a single section of our State. Yet every part of our food production, supply and distribution

[1] *Public Papers of Governor Thomas E. Dewey,* 1943, p. 384.

machinery must function to capacity or the present crisis, which you forecast long ago, will become worse. These problems are not being solved by the national government and apparently they cannot be.

In short, there is a vacuum. Just as you moved to provide State direction of the farm labor problem, I recommend similar action with regard to the whole food production problem.

The following day, March 23, at a meeting of the Governor with the legislative leaders, it was agreed that an Emergency Food Commission should be created. The members of the State War Council were polled and their consent obtained, and at its next meeting that body allocated funds for the program of the commission. Allocations to the commission for 1943-1944 ultimately totaled over $500,000.

In announcing the creation of this commission, the Governor stated that in various specialized fields individual members would be assigned responsibility for helping food producers in New York State meet the obstacles which were constantly arising under wartime conditions. Its functions, he said, would lie in three general fields. The commission was to:

1. Help New York farmers attain maximum production, partly through alleviating such shortages as those in labor and machinery.

2. Assure continued shipment into the State of feed and other necessary supplies.

3. Guide "with foresight and common sense" the adaptation of New York citizens to necessary changes of diet.

The membership of the Emergency Food Commission was divided evenly between practical farm leaders engaged in the business of producing and distributing food and the research and administrative experts in the field from the faculty of the New York State College of Agriculture. Collectively it was as able a group as could have been found anywhere in the State. The commissioners,

their affiliations and assignments, were as follows:

H. E. Babcock, Grange-League-Federation; Chairman, Board of Trustees, Cornell University (Chairman)[1]

Austin W. Carpenter, President, Eastern Federation of Feed Merchants (Feed, Seed and Fertilizer)

Chester C. DuMond, Commissioner, Department of Agriculture and Markets (Executive Director, succeeding Dean Ladd)

T. Norman Hurd, Farm Manpower Director

Carl E. Ladd,[2] Dean, N. Y. S. College of Agriculture (Farm production phases of food-supply problems)

Joseph McAllaster, feed merchant (Community Facilities)

L. A. Maynard, Director, School of Nutrition (Nutrition)

Henry W. Rathbun, Vice-President of Dairymen's League (Transportation and Gasoline)

L. R. Simons, State Director of Extension, College of Agriculture (Farm Labor and Victory Gardens)

Harold M. Stanley, Secretary, N.Y.S. Grange (Farm Supplies)[3]

Mrs. Roger W. Straus, civic leader (Director, New York City Nutrition Program)

Dr. W. I. Myers,[4] Dean, N.Y.S. College of Agriculture (Farm production phases of food-supply problems)

Warren Hawley,[5] President, N.Y.S. Farm Bureau Federation (Farm Supplies)

Earl C. Foster, Executive Secretary, former County Agricultural Agent of Allegany and Oneida Counties

Essentially, the work of the commission was to coordinate the efforts of agencies already existing, but subsequently it became necessary through War Council appropriations to bring the State

---

[1] Resigned Dec. 16, 1943.
[2] Deceased August, 1943.
[3] Succeeded H. E. Babcock as Chairman.
[4] Succeeded Dean Ladd, fall of 1943.
[5] Appointed Dec. 16, 1943.

squarely behind several other groups: the Farm Cadet Victory Corps Program ($100,000); the Farm-machinery Repair Program ($60,500); the nutrition work of the Colleges of Agriculture and Home Economics, both upstate ($149,225) and in New York City ($100,000); and the Victory Garden Council ($30,515). Formal State recognition of the work of existing agricultural organizations was thereby combined with direct financial participation in a State-wide program under the guidance of a group of able and representative leaders. It now became possible for the New York State Emergency Food Commission to speak for the entire State in any crisis and to be assured of the Governor's willing cooperation whenever required. With the possible exception of California, no other state attained the same combination of flexibility of operation with centralization of leadership.

The creation of the Emergency Food Commission was a remarkably shrewd piece of human engineering. It was no easy task to persuade the former head of the largest farm-purchasing organization in the country to take on the responsibility for New York's food-production program, or to secure one of his keenest competitors for a strategic post on the same commission. Yet these men were big enough to comprehend their common interest in the solution of the State's food problems, and also to take a hand in easing the situation for neighboring states. The commission spoke not only for New York but frequently for the entire northeast.

In the fall of 1943, a Northeastern Governors' Feed Committee was formed with Dean W. I. Myers, of the College of Agriculture, as chairman. This body functioned successfully and often during the series of emergencies arising as a result of chronic feed shortages from 1943 to 1946. In this connection it was felt necessary early in 1944 to have closer relations with the War Food Adminis-

tration. Mr. Austin W. Carpenter, a member of the commission, became its representative in Washington, with headquarters in the Washington office of the State Department of Commerce.

There are indications that the commission refrained from extending its nutrition program to New York City until its chairman was requested by city officials to do so. The invitation was accepted, and on June 12 Governor Dewey appointed Mrs. Roger W. Straus of New York City to head a nutrition program for the metropolitan area.

From its inception the Emergency Food Commission under the very able leadership of H. E. Babcock of Ithaca, attacked its problems vigorously. Week after week it met in all-day sessions. To each member, in line with his interest and abilities, it delegated a special phase of the farm problem and, in turn, most commissioners appointed individual advisory committees to assist in determining facts and policies. Lacking as it did both regulatory and compulsory powers, nevertheless, because of the ability and representative character of its membership, the commission successfully correlated all agencies of the State of New York in a full-scale attack on the problems of food production. As its chairman put it, the task of the commission was to make New York State "conscious of fundamentals." To do this it was necessary to anticipate trouble and be sufficiently farsighted to deal with crises before they became acute.

Constant touch was maintained, therefore, with the food situation not only in the State but in the country at large, and all possible methods employed to facilitate New York's production of agricultural commodities. The commission made frequent recommendations to the Governor and took direct action itself in assisting producers, processors, and consumers to make the best use of facilities and available food. It was thus a commission for action, and not simply a planning or advisory group; its forte was leadership. It neither duplicated nor overlapped the work of any Federal or State agency, but drew from such groups assistance of all kinds. Fortunately for the commission, New York State agriculture was already well organized so that the decisions of the commission could in most instances be based upon accurate, up-to-date statistical information. It was, therefore, possible for the appropriate subcommittee to report to the commission on a new problem without first having to collect for itself the necessary statistics.

Throughout the life of the commission unanimity of opinion prevailed both on fundamental aims and on the proper methods of attaining them. Such agreement made possible speedy and efficient functioning to remove obstacles in the path of maximum production and utilization of food. This agreement on fundamentals is well illustrated by the publication of a Wartime Food Program for New York State which provided a long-range plan into which all activities of the commission and of all cooperating agencies could logically be fitted. It is reproduced here in full:

New York State Emergency Food Commission
Albany

A Wartime Food Program for New York

Production

1. Encourage the production of every possible pound of milk on New York farms. Fluid milk is the most important animal product for providing satisfactory diets for our large city population under wartime conditions.

 a. Utilize as much as possible of the pasture, hay and silage for the production of milk and the maintenance of dairy herds.

 b. Concentrates are scarce and getting scarcer. Procure 500,000 tons of high protein feeds, and 1,500,000 tons of grain from outside the State as the minimum necessary to maintain milk production for the next year.

 c. Maintain the supply of skilled farm labor.

 d. Improve hay and pasture crops by proven practices.

 e. Raise heifers to maintain dairy herds.

 f. Use for beef cattle and sheep only pasture and forage that cannot be utilized by dairy herds.

 g. Convert milk used for butter and fluid cream into fluid use if necessary to meet city demands without rationing.

2. Produce ample acreages of crops to be used directly for human foods that are adapted to the State, such as potatoes, vegetables, and dry beans. In addition to increasing the number of people that can be fed from New York farms, transportation can be saved by producing these perishable bulky foods near cities.

3. Use remaining crop acreage for the maximum production of silage, hay and feed grains for dairy cattle.

4. Use available supplies of poultry feed primarily for egg production.

5. Maintain fruit production in areas well adapted to these crops.

6. Push the New York farm labor program vigorously so as to provide the amount of skilled year-round and seasonal labor necessary for maximum food production.

7. Maintain the New York Farm Machinery Repair Program so as to keep available farm machines in good working condition.

8. Procure necessary quantities of new farm machinery, fertilizers, spray materials, and other essential farm supplies for maximum food production.

9. Continue the New York Victory Garden Program in order to increase supplies of vegetables for city consumers.

Nutrition

1. Tell people why changes in their diets are necessary. Help them make changes so as to get the best possible nutrition from the kinds of food available.

2. Help people get the food necessary to meet their nutritional needs.

3. Do everything possible to insure that all food produced in the State is used by preserving all foods not currently consumed and

Emergency Food Commission

Appointed by Governor Thomas E. Dewey with H. E. Babcock as Chairman, to help attain maximum food production and aid in civilian nutrition problems.

minimizing wastage of nutrients from the farm to the table.

The first report of the commission, presented to the Governor June 7, 1943, was a commentary on the above program. It consisted of an analytical statement of the general food problem under 1943 conditions; a discussion of the adjustments necessary in production and consumption, and of the relation between supplies and price ceilings, with a presentation of the urgent need for a surplus sufficient to feed foreign peoples. The second report on nutrition was presented to the Governor two days later and from then on, at intervals, appeared reports on all the important phases of the State's wartime agricultural program.

What New York's farmers faced has nowhere been better stated than by the commission's able and farsighted chairman, Howard E. Babcock, of Ithaca, when at the Food Forum of the Dairymen's League June 16, 1943, he said bluntly:

We have reached the point in the prosecution of the war where there isn't a chance in the world of our producing adequate quantities of the kinds of food to which this country's civilian population has been accustomed.

He went on to outline the necessity for shifting the diet of New York citizens to direct use of the grains which were formerly used indirectly in producing hogs, poultry for meat, and in the fattening of mutton and beef. A week later he sent to Governor Dewey a telegram which is here reproduced in full, as it reflects the anxiety at that time felt by the farmers over the lack of concern shown by the administration in Washington regarding the problems in the northeastern states:

Even with the best of producing weather from now until fall, the country is irretrievably headed for badly balanced food production. Too little milk in relation to pork. Not enough cereals and soybeans. This would be serious at any time. It is tragic today.

Due entirely to mismanagement by the Federal government, pigs are eating not only their normal share of the corn crop, but the shares which normally go to the dairy cow, the hen, and industry. Following the largest corn crop in history, the corn available per animal unit April 1, 1943 was less than a year ago.

The structure on which New York farmers have built the production of the enormous quantities of fresh eggs and fresh milk which are vitally needed to protect the health of urban residents is collapsing like a house of cards. No corn is coming into the State. Corn industry plants are closing daily. They are prevented by price ceilings from competing for the corn they need. As these plants close, the State's supply of gluten feed, a byproduct of the corn industry, and one of the principal high protein feeds on which the State's milk production is based, is shut off.

Many feed stores in the State are already entirely out of livestock and poultry feed. All feed stores are rapidly depleting their inventories. Many report that for every thirty bags of feed they hand out, they can only replace twenty. The production of poultry for meat is drying up. In some sections pullets and laying hens are being sent to market. At the present rate of disappearance, the necessary concentrated feeds for dairy cows, already voluntarily rationed to stretch them as far as possible, will soon be insufficient. When this happens the State's milk production will decline rapidly. The whole situation boils down to a fight in which every consumer has a stake; a fight to secure the feed necessary to keep up the State's production of fresh milk and eggs. New York urban residents can and will have to adjust their diet. They will have to eat more of the soybeans and cereals which are now being fed directly to animals. Even with expert guidance, they cannot safely make this shift in diet without the protection of minimum requirements of fresh milk, especially for the young, the sick, the infirm, and the old.

Considerations other than that of securing an adequate food supply for ourselves, our allies, and the people of countries freed from Axis domination dictate a half dozen different food policies. The result is a hodgepodge of plans — not a program — a hangover of the food surplus complex of the thirties, seasoned with political expediency.

It was this situation, so clearly summed up by its chairman, with which the Emergency Food Commission wrestled until the end of the war. The degree of its success may be measured by the fact that in 1943, 1944, and 1945 the production of food in New York State continued, under extremely adverse circumstances, the record set in 1940, 1941, and 1942 of surpassing the 1935-1939 averages. Evidence of the farmers' efforts is shown in the following figures on the combined tonnage of milk, eggs, fruits, and vegetables produced in the war years, as compared with the prewar averages. Had it not been for the unseasonable weather in the spring of 1945 which destroyed two-thirds of the fruit crop, the production of that year would have been the highest on record.

Table 13. *Food Production, New York State*

Year	Tons
1935-39 average	6,107,532
1940	6,365,638
1941	6,657,875
1942	7,085,802
1943	6,368,100
1944	6,599,411
1945 (estimated)	6,966,483

SOURCE: Report of Director of Farm Manpower Service for 1945.

Brief discussions of the programs carried on by the divisions of the Emergency Food Commission merit description.

THE FARM LABOR PROGRAM

The appointment of T. N. Hurd as Director of Farm Manpower was made at the War Council's meeting of February 9, 1943, upon recommendation of the Governor. The need for a single responsible head to coordinate the entire program was clear and the resolution stated that Mr. Hurd was:

To coordinate the work of all existing agencies dealing with the farm emergency, Federal, State and local, in addition to all farm organizations and to individuals and groups interested in the farm program to the end that there be an adequate coordination of the efforts to provide manpower for the farms of New York State.

The outlook for manpower in February, 1943, was by no means a cheerful one. Lend-lease demands for food were up 100 per cent over 1942. Feed was less plentiful than a year before and in addition to a shortage of 10,000 to 15,000 year-round workers, it was estimated that 100,000 seasonal workers would have to be secured somewhere by harvest time. Yet no program, nor even the funds with which to develop one, had been provided by the Federal government. Backed by funds from the State War Council, the Farm Manpower Service threw into gear the program which had been developed in cooperation with the farm organizations, and within a month was able to report significant progress.

For the next three years, as a result of the effective coordination of all State and Federal agencies, the New York Farm Labor Program maintained an adequate supply of "regular" or year-round help on farms and recruited a total of more than 375,000 volunteer seasonal workers to harvest and process large crops of fruit and vegetables. Although farm labor was but one problem, it was by far the most vital and in its ramifications the most complex. An inadequate Farm Labor Program would have been immediately reflected by a decline in the annual harvest of fruits and vegetables. The methods which sustained the supply of farm labor are worth enumeration.

The secret of the success of the Farm Labor Program lay in the unity and cooperation promoted among Federal, State, and local agencies and the farm organizations. The successful functioning of the agencies and groups as a single unit during the entire three years demonstrates the logic and clarity of the program and is a credit to the character of the leadership operating in New York agriculture. The staff members of the various agencies, including county agricultural agents, farm placement representatives, Farm Cadet Supervisors, farm labor camp staffs, and other employees, worked tirelessly to achieve the goals set by the Farm Manpower Service and deserve the highest praise for their efforts in organization and administration. These agencies are as follows: The Extension Service of N.Y.S. College of Agriculture, the United States Employment Office of War Manpower Commission, the Office of Labor of the War Food Administration, the War Department, the Association of New York State Canners, the State Department of Education, the State Department of Health, the State Department of Labor, the State Department of Conservation, the State Department of Agriculture and Markets, the Office of Civilian Mobilization, the State Child Care Committee, the Home Missions Council, the Farm Manpower Service, and numerous other agencies and volunteer groups.

In his final report to the Emergency Food Commission, Mr. Hurd summarized the tasks performed by these various groups:

The Extension Service assumed the primary responsibility largely with Federal funds, but assigned to the Employment Service the responsibility for the recruitment and placement of all farm help. The Office of Labor provided Jamaican and Bahamian workers and furnished transportation and medical care for them. The War Department made available Italian and German prisoners of war, who were used in farm and food processing work. The Association of New York State Canners participated actively in local mobilization drives and in the organizing of farmer-processor associations to operate prisoner of war camps. The State Health Department provided camp inspection service, issued camp permits, and provided public health nursing, clinic and health educa-

tion services in all camps except those for Jamaicans, Bahamians, and prisoners of war. The Office of Civilian Mobilization of the State War Council, through its local volunteer offices, aided significantly in local recruitment drives. The State Child Care Committee and the Home Missions Council operated child care centers in migrant camps. The Farm Manpower Service aided in coordinating and expediting the farm labor activities of all these agencies and assumed the responsibility for the Farm Cadet Victory Corps, money for which was appropriated by the State War Council. This program, itself, however, was administered by the State Department of Education and the local schools.

Farm labor problems consisted first, of getting and keeping sufficient regular or year-round farm help to do farm work which required considerable skill and physical ability; and secondly, recruiting, transporting, placing, and housing necessary seasonal workers for the harvesting and processing of food, primarily fruits and vegetables.

The farm manpower problem was twofold: to find and retain permanently on the farms sufficient skilled labor to do the regular year-in year-out work that varies little from season to season, and in addition to supply seasonal workers sufficient to care for fitting the soil and planting and harvesting the crops. Naturally, losses of regular workers to war industries and the armed forces were high. To compensate for this, the Office of Farm Manpower through the Extension Service did its best to familiarize farmers with the Selective Service regulations and to assist those interested and qualified to obtain deferments. Selective Service questionnaires were reviewed to discover workers with farm experience. Over the three-year period more than 19,200 year-round placements were made by the United States Employment Service. To a limited extent use was made of conscientious objectors and inmates of institutions. Additional labor was attracted from the less productive areas of the State, and five hundred Newfoundlanders together with laborers from Kentucky and West Virginia were imported. Women were trained for work on dairy and poultry farms, and wherever possible the use of laborsaving devices was encouraged.

Seasonal workers were more easily secured, but vast numbers were needed. The widely varying sources for this type of worker necessitated pooling the facilities of many organizations to provide recruiting, housing, training, transportation, insurance, and health protection. To meet the needs of farmers and food processors for seasonal labor between 1943 and 1945, the farm labor program mobilized approximately 167,000 adults from city, village, and rural areas. School youth, including 15,000 high-school and college youth recruited from the metropolitan area, reached the total of 150,000. Also aiding the program were: New York City adult vacationists (9,000), Jamaicans and Bahamians (10,800), Italian and German prisoners of war (10,800), soldiers and sailors from military camps and training centers (5,600), and regular Army troops assigned by the War Department in 1943 (1400). Over 30,000 migrant workers were housed and fed in public camps operated primarily by the Extension Service with funds allotted for that special purpose. All of these played their part in harvesting New York's annual 2.5 million-ton crop of fresh fruits and vegetables.

No program of this magnitude can be operated without having other matters of a collateral nature appear which require attention. A practical device to increase the flexibility of the labor force was the cooperative association formed to finance and contract for large numbers of seasonal workers, and for erecting the needed facilities to care for them. Over thirty farmers' associations and thirteen membership associations of farmers and processors were originated to make possible county-wide use of manpower. This device is one example of the development

of local responsibility in the solving of the Farm Labor Problem.

In the case of the migratory workers, despite shortages of material, equipment, and labor, considerable improvement was effected as a result of the State's efforts in the housing facilities supplied by large farm operators. Early in 1945, the War Council appointed a special committee on Migrant Farm Labor Camps. This group made several tours of inspection over the State and recommended improvements in sanitation, housing, and supervision. Thus they supplemented and implemented the work of the Inter-Departmental Committee which in 1944 recommended revisions in the Sanitary Code and made other specific provisions for "improving living and working conditions."

Inasmuch as the large majority of seasonal farm labor was unskilled, efforts were made to provide at least a minimum of training prior to employment on farms. Training was provided partly by the Extension Service through the use of leaflets, charts, moving pictures, lectures, and demonstrations, and partly by the Education Department through the courses for Farm Cadet Victory Corps workers in the State institutes of agriculture and at a selected number of high schools. In the Institute of Agriculture at Farmingdale, a training program was likewise provided from 1943 to 1945 for members of the Women's Land Army who were preparing for full-time farm work.

Not only was seasonal labor secured, housed, and trained, but insurance was also developed at low rates to protect both farmers and workers. Prior to February, 1943, there were no statistics available to indicate the number of workers needed, or where and when they would be in demand. One of the first notable accomplishments of the Farm Manpower Service was securing personnel for this work and developing a method of obtaining from about eight hundred farms monthly reports to form the basis for a periodical publication on *Employment and Wages of Farm Labor in New York.*

"The best laid plans of mice and men" cannot, however, anticipate the vagaries of the weather. In 1943, because of an unusually late spring, the vegetable harvest was delayed until it overlapped the apple-picking season in western New York and in the Hudson Valley. Consequently, a number of workers larger than was originally anticipated had to be provided. Despite the cooperation of school boards in postponing the opening of schools, running on half-day schedules, or excusing some students for as long as three weeks; despite the willingness of city and village employers to arrange vacations and permit the taking of accumulated leave, or of temporary leave; or even despite the enthusiasm of college professors for working on farms and in canning factories, the situation grew steadily worse. From August 30 to November 15, canneries were exempted by the Director of Civilian Protection from compliance with blackout regulations. Finally, on September 8, Mr. Hurd appealed to the Governor for help. Six hundred men were needed immediately for canning factory work in western New York, one hundred for farm work in the same area, and four hundred for apple picking in the Hudson Valley.

The following day Governor Dewey sent this telegram to General Marshall:

Desperate shortages of farm and canning factory help is endangering vital harvesting and processing of million tons of fruits and vegetables in New York State. Despite widespread success of State farm recruitment program, volunteer labor is not sufficient to meet temporary peak needs resulting from unseasonable weather. Western New York farms and canning factories need at least seven hundred men within next four days. Hudson Valley farms need additional five hundred men if crops are to be saved. I am reluctant to add to your great burdens but war effort makes additional help imperative. Surrender

of Italy would seem to make use of Italian prisoners of war possible in previously prohibited seaboard area where need is desperate. I urgently hope you can approve use of at least twelve hundred Italian war prisoners in New York State for this work. Immediate action is necessary to save the food produced and processed in this State.

Within five days, having first received certification from the War Manpower Commission, General Marshall made available 1,300 troops for "agricultural purposes in New York State." These were later replaced by prisoners of war. The courteous manner in which the War Department cooperated and the willingness of the soldiers to work were greatly appreciated both by the farmers and by the administration.

Early in January, Mr. Hurd sent to the Governor a memorandum on the farm labor outlook for 1944. While the anticipated volume of production would be greater than in 1943, and thus the demand for manpower to harvest would be larger than ever, the supply of labor would actually be lower. This serious situation was aggravated by ration-point reductions and removals which had produced an unfortunate complacency on the part of farm workers with regard to the food situation, a complacency which was being increased by victories abroad. To this communication the Governor sent a characteristic reply:

January 21, 1944

Memorandum to Mr. T. N. Hurd
I have your letter of January 18th. It's a tough job. Go to it.

T. E. D.

Later that spring the situation seemed unchanged. Acreage increases planned in New York for canning crops were much above the national average, and estimates were that a total of 140,000 seasonal workers, 15,000 more than in 1943, must be recruited. Where could they be found? Mr. Hurd was forced to ask the

Governor's aid in convincing the War Department that the State needed prisoners of war in numbers increasing from 2,500 in June to 6,000 in September. Five different attempts, all unsuccessful, were made to boost the inadequate allocations made to New York State. For a time it looked like discrimination. Eventually, however, New York was allotted 4,000 German prisoners, and during the summer conditions became somewhat more favorable. In fact, so well had the 1944 plans been laid that more workers were mobilized in that year than ever before or since, and total production was substantially above that of 1943.

The coming of both V-E and V-J Days somewhat before harvest time eased the 1945 situation. Numbers of veterans began to return to the farms, and the total number of acres planted in 1945 showed no increase over the previous year. Actually, the number of workers recruited for all categories was slightly less than in the preceding year. Methods had been pretty well worked out for taking care of migrants and out-of-state workers. Had it not been for the loss of two-thirds of the fruit crop owing to frost and a cold, wet spring, total food production in 1945 would have exceeded any previous year's output.

THE PROGRAM ON FARM MACHINERY

The farm problem most closely linked with manpower was that of farm machinery. In many ways the two were supplementary, both being created by the same need for power. As we have seen, the commission inherited the Farm-Machinery Repair Program which had been inaugurated late in 1941 under stimulus of the Agricultural Defense Committee. This had proved its worth immediately, and was supported from its inception by War Council funds. Since after 1941 no adequate supply of new farm machinery was available, and since in most communities local repair services

were inadequate, the maintenance of this program was vital. Through the mobile repair units over 100,000 contacts were made, and more than 17,000 machines repaired or adjusted for efficient operation. Particular attention was paid to the protection of electrical equipment which was virtually irreplaceable, and to the development of home-made laborsaving devices such as the buck rake.

The Emergency Food Commission's advisory committee on farm machinery was not, however, primarily concerned with this program except when it became necessary to expedite the delivery of spare parts. Its chief problem was to secure for New York's farmers the full quota of farm machines to which they were entitled and, if possible, to see that that quota was increased or varied in accordance with the individual needs of the farmers. The appointment of the Food Commission came too late in the season to allow the subcommittee on farm machinery to exercise much influence upon the 1943 Farm-Machinery Program. According to Commissioner DuMond, about all that was possible was "to smoke out" the machinery not yet released to the State, to work out rental fees for sharing existing machinery, and to look ahead to 1944 with the idea of obtaining as much steel as possible for repair parts.

In August, 1943, a cooperative survey was undertaken to establish the quantity and types of machinery which, if available, the farmers would like to buy for the 1944 season. The figures were based upon requests filed with the County Farm Machinery Ration Boards, upon the total numbers of each kind of farm machine sold in 1941, and upon surveys made by the Wartime Minute Men of the Extension Service and the crop reporters of the Department of Agriculture and Markets. At the time the study was made, neither the method of rationing nor the amount of machinery that would be allotted to New York in 1944 could be known. Under the plan governing the transportation and distribution of farm machinery then in effect, there was no guarantee that New York State would receive for 1944 either the quantity required nor the kind and types of machines specified. The results of the survey were ready early in October, and the report based upon them threw some important light on the Farm Machinery Problem.

Two-thirds of the 26,188 applications for purchase made to the Farm Machinery Ration Boards were for new machines rather than for replacements, with the emphasis overwhelmingly (77 per cent) on tractor-drawn equipment. The outstanding example was the demand for plows, 97 per cent of which were to be pulled by power. There was little doubt but that the war was stimulating the mechanization of agriculture, especially in a region such as New York where the type of farming pursued required a large amount of labor per acre. Unfortunately, the increased demand was coming at the very time when the 1943 quota of machines for New York State was set at only 20 per cent of 1940-1941 sales. Furthermore, the amount of equipment actually sold that year was about 25 per cent less than the quota and represented 58 per cent of the applications accepted. The inability of farmers to supply their wants in 1942 and 1943 served greatly to increase the pressure for machinery in 1944. An example was cited by the Governor at one of the War Council meetings of one hundred bids at the ceiling for one grain binder from farmers of thirteen counties. The auctioneer finally put the bids in a hat and let the bidders draw for it.

Another fact revealed was that prior to the war the large farms purchased from four to five times as much machinery per farm per year as did the small farms, the amount increasing with the size of the farm. The needs expressed for 1944, however, varied sharply from that pattern as the large farms requested little machinery beyond their purchases of 1941-1943, while the small farms were requesting two to three times as much as before. Two conclusions could be drawn from this information. First, was the fact that under the stimulus of war the process of mechanization, which had been proceeding slowly on the smaller farms, was being rapidly brought about. Second, it was clear that increase in food production would be possible from the smaller farms which had not yet approached as closely as the larger farms to maximum production.

With the pressure on the 1944 quotas mounting steadily, the commission presented its findings to the State Agricultural Adjustment Agency which supported a request from New York State that the War Food Administration grant substantial increases in the farm-machinery allotments. The rationing program, however, was taken off early in the summer of 1944 and subsequently the distribution of machines was left up to the manufacturers, who were forced to make allocations since at that time they were in no position to fill the quotas allotted to the various states. The commission wrote every New York Congressman pointing out the shortage of skilled manpower in the farm machinery field, and urging that everything possible be done to alleviate the deficiency. Despite efforts, many machines arrived too late in the fall of 1944 to be of any use that season, and by January, 1945, the lag in production was 25 per cent. Increased pressure was put upon the farmers through the press and radio to have their machinery repaired and in shape early, while representations were made to both the War Production Board and the War Food Administration on the importance of granting farmers "blanket priorities for the purchase of farm equipment repairs and parts and equipment needed in the production of food." Throughout the summer and fall of 1945, conditions remained unchanged. Labor and steel for the manufacture of farm machinery were scarce, and the lag in filling quotas continued. The work of the commission was consequently centered upon expediting the shipment to New York farmers of badly needed repair parts. This service was performed willingly and effectively by the Albany office, which traced orders back to the manufacturers and speeded delivery in every possible way. During 1947 the procurement of adequate amounts of farm machinery was still a major bottleneck in New York State's food production program.

FEED, SEED, FERTILIZER, AND ANIMAL NUTRITION

Next to farm labor the most difficult and persistent problem to tax the ingenuity of the Food Commission was the shortage of feed. It was but partially a war problem as New York State and the entire northeast had long since become a feed deficit area. At the time the commission was created conditions in the State were critical. A subcommittee on animal nutrition to consider feed and nutrition problems was immediately established composed of animal and poultry specialists from the College of Agriculture, and representatives of the large and the small feed manufacturers and retailers. Its functions were twofold: (1) through research to discover substitutes for products in short supply, and (2) to keep track of the actual feed situation, both nationally and within the State, for the purpose of keeping the Emergency Food Commission constantly informed. The commission in turn would then act by creating special operating committees to handle specific situations. In this way the constant flow of feed was maintained from the grower through the mixer and distributor to the farmer. It was this life line for the dairy cow and the hen which after 1942 was continually breaking down at one point or another and re-

quiring the constant attention of the commission.

When the commission's subcommittee on animal feed was first formed, it faced a number of minor shortages which, in 1943, were cleared up permanently. Oyster shells, an important source of calcium for hens, were no longer being crushed because for the crushing process the ceiling on wages was set so low that employers could not compete for labor. When nothing was done to remedy the situation, the research personnel on the animal nutrition committee went to work and discovered a blue limestone in New York State which could be crushed with the same beneficial results to the "rigidity of the New York egg." Shortages of animal and milk by-products called for switches to other sources of proteins, minerals, and vitamins.

Fertilizer was running low as another result of low wage ceilings and of the unwillingness of manufacturers to ship their product long distances. The commission organized among the fertilizer dealers a campaign which galvanized the manufacturers into action and prevented a fertilizer famine at the start of the season. Nitrogen, one of the most important plant foods, was so short that early orders of the government had prohibited its use in fertilizers. At the commission's request this policy was reversed, and complete fertilizer once more became available. A shortage of grass, legume, and some vegetable seeds was threatened by low ceilings. As a result of representations made in Washington, the commission was able to have these ceilings removed.

The principal concern in the spring of of 1943, however, was the serious shortage of feed grains. Before it could move to remedy the situation, it was essential that the commission secure immediate first-hand knowledge of the stocks which New York distributors had on hand. A telegraphic survey of 150 feed dealers quickly revealed fifteen to be completely out of either corn or wheat and, with the exception of oats, no grain to be in more than fifteen days supply. Protein feeds were especially short and crushed oyster shell virtually nonexistent. New York dealers were getting close to the bottom of the barrel, and like the sands of an hour glass the supply of feed was running out. Thereafter, constant touch with the situation was maintained by checking weekly with fifty selected dealers throughout the State.

To meet the situation as promptly as possible a campaign was immediately begun in cooperation with the Extension Service and pushed throughout the summer to get farmers to produce more and better home-grown feeds, especially roughages, and to adopt feeding practices resulting in maximum production and minimum waste of feed. As a result of research on emergency feed problems, the committee was able to supply the feed industry and farmers generally with pertinent information not only on available supplies and less well-known substitutes, but on general problems of animal nutrition raised by changing types and quantities of feed. Reports issued directly to the feed industry through the medium of the Cornell feed service were supplemented by others from the commission and personal contacts with the feed industry and government agencies. Throughout the war period cooperation between the members of the Food Commission and representatives of the feed industry, feed agencies, and farm organizations was excellent.

Early in May, 1943, owing to a drop of 50 million bushels in the spring oat crop, New York feed stocks reached the lowest point on record. Despite all the efforts of the commission the outlook grew steadily worse. A special feed-supply report early in June revealed alarming shortages of corn and wheat feeds. Yet in the midst of their difficulties the farmers were not without a certain grim humor. In answer to the commission's inquiry on the state of their inventories, one wrote in, "Have tried for the past three weeks to buy corn. No dice." Another replied, "All trade has increased production on account of the government asking for more meat, eggs and milk. The government should see to it that America in order to produce should have the grains to do same. There is no bull attached."

Unless, however, the Commodity Credit Corporation were to dispose of some of its 30 million bushels of wheat, or the OPA were to raise the ceiling price of Midwestern corn sufficiently to move some of it to the East, the only hope of the commission seemed to lie in discovering other sources of grain. Without waiting for the first two eventualities, the commission appointed a subcommittee to investigate the possibility of importing Canadian grain. Through regular channels, and on a delivered basis in Buffalo, commitments for the shipment of 2.5 million tons of Canadian barley were secured. This amount, which nearly compensated for the loss of the oats, was given top priority by the WFA. After several months had been spent by the committee in securing an adequate number of boats for its transportation by water to Buffalo, delivery by November 15 of 2.5 million tons of Canadian and Northwestern grain, and rail shipment of 400,000 tons more from the northwestern part of the United States could definitely be counted upon. Would these supplies be sufficient? They would not.

At the same time that the commission's subcommittee was working on the importation of grains, the commission itself was working out an eight-point program to relieve the feed situation. It was outlined by the chairman as follows:

1. Urge the War Food Administration to withdraw their floor prices on heavy hogs.
2. That the commission support the allocations of corn to the corn manufacturing industries called by the trade the "wet corn industries."

3. That the commission ask the cooperation of the ore industry and allied interests to support its request for bottoms for shipping grains through the Great Lakes.

4. Suggest that the Governor and the Commissioner of Agriculture state that as far as New York State is concerned the "line has not been held" since barley was $13.80 a ton higher than the ceiling price of corn.

5. The commission should enlist New York City's support for more feed corn to supply the milk it needs for a proper diet for its people.

6. To enlist the efforts of industry through its employees to recognize the seriousness of the feed situation in the northeast.

7. Start negotiations on importation of feed grains from Argentina and Australia.

8. Urge the War Food Administration to reprice vegetable proteins used in dairy feed to enable these proteins to move from their source of supply to the northeastern feed deficit area.

In a letter on August 9, 1943, to War Food Administrator Marvin Jones, H. E. Babcock, chairman of the commission, stated that even after full allowance had been made for the greatest economies in the feeding of poultry and livestock, for the maximum use of home-grown feed, and for the shipments of feed from Canada and the Northwest, the northeastern states still faced a deficit of 1,755,000 tons of low-protein feed for the period from November 15, 1943 to July 1, 1944. Normally, this grain would be brought in by rail and boat from the Midwest, but wartime price ceilings had prevented this and effectively placed the entire feed deficit problem beyond the power of the commission to solve alone. All it could do was to bring the matter to the attention of the War Food Administration and ask for help. The gravity of the situation was confirmed when the October crop reports showed farm stocks of oats, corn, and wheat in New York State to be 58 per cent lower than at the same time the previous year. Action of some sort was necessary and the commission finally asked the Governor to send some of its members to look for surplus corn. The telegram cited the situation as "desperate," and blamed the ineffectiveness of the War Food Administration for the plight which threatened the milk and egg production of the entire northeast.

Three days later the Governor appointed a seven-man committee and dispatched it into the surplus corn-producing areas in the Midwest to discover whether or not, under existing regulations, the northeastern states could expect shipments of corn. If the grain were not to become available, plans would have to be made for the liquidation of poultry flocks and dairy cattle. With one hog in the country for every human being, the problem was to push the hog away from the Midwestern feed trough so that the northeastern dairy cow and hen could get their share.

The result of the ten-day survey was extremely discouraging. An expanded livestock population in the Midwest, with such low ceiling prices on corn that it was cheaper to feed it to hogs than ship it east, plus an increased industrial demand for grains would exhaust the surplus at the source. The report to the Governor called upon the War Food Administration for a specific program to maintain the milk and egg supplies of the 30 million inhabitants of the northeastern states. Realizing the seriousness of the situation, Governor Dewey took the lead in the formation of a Northeastern Governors' Feed Committee to study the feed problem and develop a concerted program for alleviating the shortage.

It was fortunate indeed that an unforeseen combination of favorable factors postponed the crisis sufficiently to give the War Food Administration time to act. The 1943 crop of hay and silage had been especially large, and in combination with the feed conservation program and purchases of Canadian barley had compensated for the 69 per cent drop in the spring grain crop. Contrary to expectations, considerable quantities of Midwestern corn were forced east before cold weather owing to their high moisture content. The Office of Price Administration finally raised the ceiling price on corn which decreased considerably the crop of spring pigs. Although livestock numbers were at a record high level, and stocks of feed grains on farms January 1 were approximately 13 per cent smaller than at the same time the previous year, the commission was able through repeated promptings to induce the War Food Administration to provide through importation large quantities of Canadian wheat, oats, and barley, and some corn from Argentina. In June, thanks to excellent growing weather, pastures were lush and the hay crop was generally good. Temporarily the crisis had eased.

The winter of 1944-1945 presented a slightly different problem. The balance between feed and livestock was more nearly normal, and in New York the 1944 grain crop was larger than usual. Feed wheat was available in good supply through the Commodity Credit Corporation and a large tonnage of this grain was used in dairy and poultry feeds. Storms and subzero temperatures in January and February, along with labor shortages in feed mills, resulted in freight bottlenecks which tied up rail movement of feed to country plants. The emergency ultimately required the appointment by the Governor of a special committee whose work will be described under the section on transportation.

With the clearing of the transportation problem, the feed situation again became tight. The great increase in the number of growing chicks and the higher feeding rates for dairy cattle under the stimulus of the subsidy on milk made heavy inroads on the available feed supply. Corn failed to move through from the corn belt and the last quarter of the 1945 feeding season was again a period of critical shortage. By October 1, the government subsidy on milk and dairy products had influenced farmers to the point where they were feeding herds at a level 13 per cent above that of the previous year. The feed problem was apparently perennial.

In its final report to the commission, the subcommittee on animal nutrition outlined its operations during 1945:

1. Accurate monthly appraisals of the livestock population and available feed supplies with the publicizing of these appraisals to livestock and poultry farmers in the State by bulletins, news releases and radio.

2. Close work with the feed management branch of War Food Administration, the Department of Agriculture and the War Production Board on the securing of a molasses supply for use in livestock feeds for the farmers of the State.

3. Frequent spot checking on available feed ingredients and the advising of feed manufacturers and retail suppliers whenever available feed ingredients were located.

4. Work with feed manufacturers and mixers, particularly the smaller operators at country points, on feed formulas with emphasis on supplying information as to how substitute feed ingredients could be used most effectively from a nutritional standpoint in dairy and poultry rations.

5. Consistent contact with national policymakers looking toward the importation of flax from South America for processing in the United States through which linseed oil meal, a valuable feed ingredient, would be made available for livestock feeds; and the like importation of animal proteins greatly needed for poultry rations.

TRANSPORTATION

In wartime, with rapid increase in the volume of goods to be moved and steady deterioration of the equipment available, transportation problems assume major proportions. Here again is encountered the familiar wartime squeeze — more to be done, and less with which to do it. The function of the Food Commission's subcommittee on transportation was to expedite the shipment of farm supplies and products, stepping in whenever a breakdown threatened. Specifically, its task was threefold: it had to ensure under all conditions regular delivery to farmers from sources of manufacture essential feed grains, fertilizer, machinery, and supplies; it had to accelerate the reverse flow to the urban centers of farm products, meat, milk, vegetables, and eggs; on the farms themselves, it was responsible for providing supplies of gasoline adequate to maintain in operation the trucks and tractors so essential under wartime conditions of labor scarcity. Practically every aspect of the food-production problem had an angle involving transportation.

In the spring of 1943 when the subcommittee on transportation was created, a shortage of fertilizer already threatened. This was reported as being caused by a scarcity of boxcars. Fortunately, investigation revealed to the committee that the bottleneck was not transportation but a labor shortage in the process of loading at the plants. When this difficulty was once clearly recognized, it was easily remedied, and that first problem solved.

Not so easily disposed of was the chronic shortage of gasoline for farm use. In normal times New York State receives a large percentage of its gasoline and fuel oil by tankers coming up the Atlantic coast from the Gulf. Such deliveries were sharply curtailed by the war, and supplies were of necessity rerouted to ports on the Great Lakes, shipped eastward by tankers and rail cars to Buffalo, and thence by rail or by barge through the Erie Canal. The spring of 1943 was marked by heavy rains, and when at last they ceased, delayed plowing and planting were rushed simultaneously in many regions of the State. The unusually heavy demand for farm gasoline came at a time when prevailing west winds had packed the eastern end of Lake Erie with ice, preventing the early and scheduled movement of supplies stored in the Buffalo harbor area. With all available tank cars engaged in furnishing fuel oil and gaso-

line for the armed services, and fuel and heating oils to industry and householders in the northeastern states, the Petroleum Administration for War was averse to diverting cars for the movement of gasoline. As the necessity for gasoline on the farms became increasingly acute, the commission was able to force the diversion to central New York points of limited supplies intended for other destinations. It was not until a telegraphic survey of the situation was made by the fifty-five county agricultural agents, however, that the commission was able to confront the Petroleum Administration for War with "irrefutable evidence of idle tractors and indications of worse to come." This specific information regarding farmers, suppliers, and distributors unable to secure badly needed nonhighway gasoline brought complete cooperation. From then on the Petroleum Administration for War relied with confidence upon the commission's reports and requests for additional gasoline. All through the summer the meager supply had to be distributed with care, but the system based upon up-to-the-minute information functioned successfully.

There were likewise innumerable local problems which arose from time to time to confront the commission's committee on transportation. Emergency supplies of gasoline were frequently required for school buses transporting war workers to and from factories or volunteer workers during planting or harvest. Emergency supplies were occasionally in demand for trucks hauling milk and other agricultural products to market. Aid was also furnished to truckers in meeting Office of Defense Transportation requirements, or in securing special permission to operate. In these and many other ways the committee was able to be of service in maintaining farm transportation.

One of the more extensive single operations was negotiating for a larger allotment of boats used for transporting grain to Buffalo in the fall of 1943. This deal involved competition for bottoms with the iron mines and the steel companies. The commission also cooperated in maintaining flexibility in regulations limiting loading in mixed cars, and thus prevented an artificial bottleneck which threatened to retard the movement of grain.

The worst situation encountered by the committee came in January and February of 1945. A combination of snowstorms, winds, and subzero weather slowed the flow of feed and fuel, milk and food. A gradual paralysis of transportation set in threatening disastrous consequences. On January 18, the Food Commission appointed an Emergency Committee which, aided by the county agricultural agents, investigated conditions. They reported that of 1,037 feed dealers, 14 per cent were entirely out of dairy feed and 12 per cent out of poultry feed. The Emergency Committee maintained daily contact with Buffalo and to speed delivery began tracing cars for individual dealers. A survey of country feed dealers revealed that of 74 reached, 52 had a supply of dairy feeds good for two days or less, and 38 had the same supply of poultry mash. A spot check of 1,000 farmers in 144 selected communities on January 27 revealed that 30 per cent had three days' supply or less.

Two days later, Governor Dewey declared a Statewide emergency and alerted the New York State Guard. He named an Emergency Committee with Charles Sells, Superintendent of Public Works, as Emergency Director of Transportation and Supplies. Dr. Harold H. Schaff, Executive Secretary of the State War Council, and a member of the committee, assumed the task of obtaining reports from all local war councils on the fuel, feed, and food needs of their particular localities. He also obtained from the major railroads of the State detailed information on their most pressing operating requirements. In certain areas of

the State, storm and high winds on February 1 and 2 blocked every secondary road and brought the movement of fuel and feed, milk and food perilously close to a standstill. Anxious watch was kept day by day on the milk supply in large cities, on the fruit, vegetable, meat, egg, and poultry supplies of the large markets, and on the ability of farmers located on secondary roads to reach the main highways with their produce.

In view of the extent of the tie-up and the necessity for handling essential shipments of war equipment, the Office of Defense Transportation was forced to declare a general embargo on rail shipments from February 3 to February 7. Exemptions were declared only for items whose transportation was deemed essential to the war effort. Provision was made for loading feed under special permit, but the time required for securing a permit promised to be larger than the duration of the four-day embargo. Yet somehow stock had to be fed. With the State Police reporting increasing numbers of livestock suffering from lack of feed and with calls coming in from county agents citing critical cases, the Emergency Committee acted. At the instance of Commissioner Sells, Dr. Schaff and Earl Foster arranged for a State-wide truck pool to move feed from manufacturers to country dealers during the four-day period of the embargo. Privately owned trucks and vehicles of the State Department of Public Works were placed in trucking pools and made available where their services were most needed. In all, 1,384 truckloads totaling 10,278 tons of dairy and poultry feed were transported during the four-day period and the crisis was met. For the rest of the spring the situation remained tight, but fortunately supplies continued adequate and transportation gradually improved.

VICTORY GARDENS

The Victory Garden Program was developed at a National Victory Garden

Conference, held December 19 and 20, 1941, at Washington, D. C., at the joint invitation of the Office of Defense Health and Welfare and the United States Department of Agriculture. Because the Extension Service of the Department of Agriculture was declared a war emergency agency to handle the production of feed, food, and fiber under the national "Food for Freedom Program," the Service was also asked to assume the program for victory gardens. Consequently, in New York State, the State Victory Garden Program was under the direction of L. R. Simons, Director of Extension at the State College of Agriculture. This garden program was necessary to help (1) ensure an adequate supply and ample reserves of food for the armed forces; (2) release large amounts of protein and vitamin-rich food for the allies; (3) build up stock piles of food with which to meet emergencies and to provide food for famished Europe and Asia at the end of the war; (4) relieve transportation and (5) contribute to the home food supply and to individual family health. The net effect of the program in New York State was to add nearly a quarter of a million acres to the land in use for farming, and to increase significantly the production of home-grown vegetables.

Following the recommendations of the National Victory Garden Conference, the New York State Director of Extension appointed an Extension Service Wartime Committee on Victory Gardens with Professor H. C. Thompson as chairman to formulate a plan for the organization and preparation of a State-wide Victory Garden Program. On January 20, 1942, representatives of forty-four State agencies, organizations, departments, clubs, and institutions came together at Albany and constituted themselves the New York State Victory Garden Council. They adopted a State Victory Garden Program as proposed by the Extension Service Victory Garden Committee, and

elected L. R. Simons, Director of Extension Service, chairman, and Albert Hoefer, 4-H Club Leader, executive secretary. The county 4-H Club agents were requested to act as county victory garden coordinators.

Immediately following the January meeting, the executive secretary proceeded with the organization of county victory garden councils patterned after the State Council. By the first week in March, the organization of county victory garden councils in fifty-five counties was completed. Throughout 1942, although the chairman of the State Victory Garden Council was appointed on the Division of Labor, Industry, and Agriculture of the New York State War Council, victory gardens as such were not represented directly on the State War Council. This program, which was distinctly an emergency war activity to encourage the production of home food supplies, received no formal recognition by the State or local war councils until the spring of 1943. The Council did, however, make appropriations for the printing of leaflets and for other minor expenditures.

In January, 1943, at the second annual meeting of the State Victory Garden Council, it was decided to extend the organization to include cities, towns, and suburban areas with provision for separate victory garden councils to function under the established county organizations. Staff members of the Departments of Vegetable Crops and Floriculture of the New York State College of Agriculture were released in the spring of 1943 for organizational and leader-training assignments in the Victory Garden Program.

At the first meeting of the newly created Emergency Food Commission, March 31, 1943, the recommendation of the State Victory Garden Council that formal recognition be given to it and the county victory garden councils by the State War Council was approved. At the request of Governor Dewey, the recommendation of the Commission was mailed to all members of the Council, and approval was secured by separate ballot. According to the resolution, the War Council designated the State Victory Garden Council as its official Committee on Victory Gardens, and recommended to the local war councils similar action with regard to county and city victory garden councils. The allocation of local funds to these councils was expressly authorized. By the same resolution, the Victory Garden Program in the State was placed under the general supervision of the Emergency Food Commission. Director L. R. Simons was a member of the Commission.

In the larger cities, special problems were encountered in securing for the use of victory gardeners vacant lots suitable for growing crops. The Greater New York Victory Garden Committee definitely recognized that in many sections of the city gardens were an impossibility and no encouragement was offered to roof gardens, water-culture gardens, or gardens in any situation where success was unlikely. Important possibilities, however, were recognized in the boroughs of Brooklyn, Queens, Richmond, and, to a lesser extent, in the Bronx. The greatest emphasis was placed upon the garden in which the home owner would take full responsibility. Allotment gardens, however, in which persons were assigned land that they did not own, presented a special problem since there was little suitable city-owned land properly located for use as allotment gardens, and no organization existed equipped to handle the complicated problems involved. School gardens in New York City had been a part of the city's school program for many years, and were extended in 1943. Industrial gardens offered some possibilities which industrial concerns developed on their own responsibility. Promotional publicity, informational bulletins, and lectures were utilized to develop interest, both in the metropolitan area and throughout the State. Especially valuable was the *Victory Garden Bulletin,* published in 1944 and distributed through the county coordinators.

In three years, victory gardens contributed greatly to the total food production of the State. It was estimated that 1.5 million gardens were planted each year on approximately 200,000 acres. Vegetables produced were valued at more than 20 million dollars.

HUMAN NUTRITION

Populations involved in war must accept extensive alteration of their food habits. Far removed as she was from the physical combat, New York State could not avoid the dietary repercussions. The war invaded every farm and every factory; it also invaded every kitchen. Change in eating habits was one inevitable result of total war.

To make the change intelligently and with a minimum of loss to health and energy required a wise and effective nutrition program. Wisdom could come only from research; effectiveness depended upon the systematic organization of a State-wide campaign of education and publicity, coupled with practical demonstrations of approved methods for preparing and preserving those foods which should be included in the properly balanced diet. As might have been expected, the scope and intensity of nutrition work gradually increased with developing shortages in the food supply.

Prior to the appointment of the Emergency Food Commission, the nutrition activities in the State were widespread but lacking in coordination. Many were convinced that nutrition would be an important subject, but plans were more numerous than effective. The State Nutrition Committee, composed since 1938 of representatives of a number of State departments and of the Cornell College of Home Economics, had been given its name by the Dean of the College of Agriculture, and in May, 1941, had become the official representative of the State War Council in matters of nutrition. In most counties and cities local and independent committees had been set up, and at the request of the State Committee, and directly in line with the then current interest in the problem of evacuating urban areas, these local committees conducted a State-wide survey of possibilities for mass feeding. In 1941, the New York State College of Home Economics trained 130 persons to teach canteen courses in their communities. The head of the Department of Institution Management at Cornell also revised the *Red Cross Manual* for teaching canteen courses. This manual was in turn used throughout the United States and in many foreign countries. In January, 1942, the School of Nutrition was given funds by the university and by the State War Council for research on war-connected problems. The College of Home Economics proceeded to give intensive school training to 147 extension agents and county leaders in food preservation, covering the latest principles and techniques. Canning schools were conducted under the direction of the Extension Service in over half the counties of the State as part of the Food Conservation Program.

Late in the spring of 1942, these efforts being still somewhat disjointed and lacking in focus, the State War Council decided that State-wide coordination of all nutrition programs was desirable and necessary. On June 17, it created an Office of War Nutrition Services "to coordinate the nutritional activities of all State War Council committees and State agencies in this field, and to effect optimum nutrition for war workers." Dr. Edward S. Rogers of the Department of Health, who was appointed director without curtailment of his other duties, relied heavily upon the personnel and equipment of the New York State College of Home Economics, the Cornell School of Nutrition, and the New York State Nutrition Committee. Special emphasis was placed upon improving the nutrition of war workers through wider use of brewers' yeast and other vitamin-bearing substances in lunches, and through the extensive introduction of nutritious snacks between meals. The mobile kitchen, a reconditioned truck, was developed at the college for use in feeding large groups of persons. This truck became a teaching device in demonstrating emergency feeding procedures. However, difficulty was experienced in developing a systematic program that clearly defined the spheres of activity for the different organizations and also in securing general acceptance of the lines of authority from the Office of War Nutrition Services to the localities. Nor as yet had any attempt been made to integrate the nutrition program with New York's parallel program of food production.

Preservation and efficient preparation for every bit of food produced were generally and correctly regarded as being extremely important, but the fact that it would be necessary, ultimately, to shift the diet of all the 13 million inhabitants of the State was, in 1942, neither clearly appreciated nor publicly emphasized. As with the Farm Labor Program, so also in the field of nutrition, 1942 was a year of experimentation in many directions by different groups using a diversity of methods to push a variety of programs. However, the first mile of any general educational program is always the hardest, and the experience gained proved to be of great value when the major crisis arose in 1943.

When in March, 1943, Governor Dewey created the Emergency Food Commission, responsibility for the State program both for human nutrition and for animal nutrition was assigned to Commissioner L. A. Maynard, Director of the School of Nutrition at Cornell Uni-

Food Problems During World War 2

Mrs. Roger W. Straus, member of the Emergency Food Commission of the New York State War Council, checks a list of food items recommended in one of many demonstrations during the food rationing period of the war.

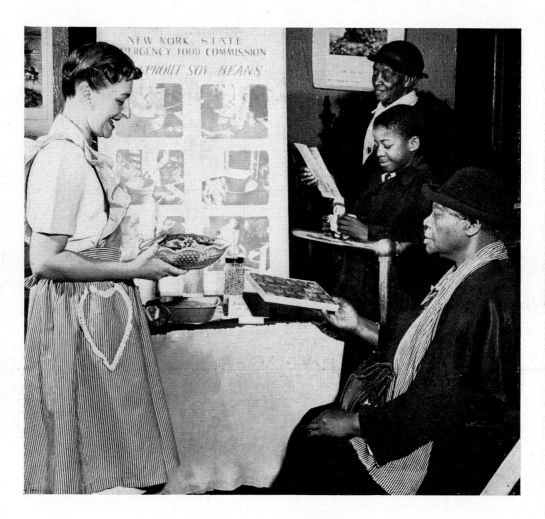

Instructions in Nutrition

How to keep families well nourished amid wartime shortages is demonstrated to Harlem homemakers by a State Emergency Food Commission nutritionist.

versity. Dean Sarah G. Blanding[1] of the College of Home Economics was appointed director of the human nutrition activities, with the State Nutrition Committee, headed by Dr. Elizabeth Gardiner, as the commission's principal advisory body on problems affecting human nutrition. The commission assumed responsibility for the activities previously carried out by the Office of War Nutrition Services. Early in June, following a conference with Mayor LaGuardia, the commission with the aid of War Council funds established a nutrition program for the metropolitan area, with Mrs. Roger W. Straus in charge with the status of a member of the commission.

The first concern of the Nutrition Division of the Food Commission was the creation of a unified and responsible administrative organization based not upon volunteer committees, but upon paid professionals trained in the field of nutrition. The direct line of communication from the commission to the people of the State lay henceforth through the home demonstration agents, and the twenty-six newly created emergency nutrition agents of the extension service of the College of Home Economics. Complete coverage in all counties and cities was made possible by additional War Council funds, and the extension personnel, as agents for the Emergency Food Commission, was for the first time given the authority and backing of the State War Council. They, in turn, worked closely with over seventy-five county and city nutrition committees, comprising representatives of local groups interested in the problem of nutrition. Through this organization, it became possible to cover the entire State with a single, coordinated program stemming directly from the Nutrition Division of the Emergency Food Commission.

In 1943 it appeared unlikely that sufficient food to feed both the human and

animal population of the country would continue to be available. Any considerable liquidation of the livestock would ultimately entail the loss of animal products needed in human diet. This assumption, while in general true, proved needlessly pessimistic. It was, however, felt that as soon as people failed to secure the usual amount of animal products (milk, eggs, meat, butter, and lard) in their diet, they would need help in securing adequate nutrition. The division reasoned that a diet low in animal products need not necessarily be inadequate. With proper guidance the people in the State could learn to shift to direct consumption of grains, of grain products, of legumes such as soybeans, and could maintain with these both health and energy. The shift necessitated, however, supplies adequate to meet certain minimum requirements with such foods as fresh eggs and fresh milk. These supplies had to be protected and made available.

Desiring that the inevitable shift should be as painless as possible, the Nutrition Committee set forth a seven-point Wartime Food Program, and in the ensuing three years it managed to unite all agencies both public and private in active support of one or more of those seven principles. The seven points of the program follow:

1. Tell people why it is necessary to make changes in their diets. Point out that although we shall have to make some changes in the kinds of food we eat, there will be enough food for everyone in this country.

2. Through an active educational program, eliminate waste and help people adjust their diets to available food supplies in such a way as to maintain health, vigor, and morale.

   a. Expand the nutrition extension program to provide adequate coverage for every city and community in the State.

   b. Maintain up-to-the-minute information on available and prospective food supplies throughout the State, particularly in the larger cities. By regular use of the press and radio, tell the housewife what is available and what is likely to be scarce. Give

---

[1] Now president of Vassar College.

her the necessary information so she can plan ahead.

c. Act as a clearing house for ideas on planning meals and different ways of preparing foods to make them both palatable and nutritious. Help the housewife make the best possible use of available food supplies.

d. Publicize the importance of eliminating waste of food nutrients either in preparing food or by way of the garbage can.

3. Do everything possible to maintain an adequate supply for New York consumers of critical foods, such as milk.

4. Anticipate food problems arising from changing supplies and shortages, and develop new food products and methods of preparing food.

5. Undertake an active food-preservation program. Everything produced from New York farms and victory gardens not eaten this summer should be preserved or stored for next winter.

6. Provide an advisory service on nutrition for industrial plants engaged in feeding war workers. This will become increasingly important as the food situation becomes more acute and some form of differential rationing becomes necessary.

7. Provide an advisory service on the handling, processing, and storage of food for processors, transportation companies, wholesalers, and retailers. Publicize the importance of proper handling to avoid waste of nutrients between the farm and the table.

Of the seven points enumerated above, number 3 was the only one which was not actively administered by the Nutrition Division. As we have seen, the commission made it a cardinal policy to maintain undiminished New York State's supplies of milk and eggs, and the problem thus became one for the subcommittee on feed whose work has already been outlined. It was this emphasis upon the production of milk and eggs that revealed the basic unity between the program of the commission for food production and its program for nutrition. The broad outlines of the food-production program were based upon the fundamental principles of both human and animal nutrition.

Immediately upon its formation, the Nutrition Division concentrated upon point 5 by promoting a very large program for food preservation and thereby making sure that the excess production of the summer of 1943 was preserved or stored for winter use. This program became the major activity of the Division until after the harvest, and at appropriate seasons was maintained in full force for the duration of the war. Special attention was paid to the operation of the pressure cooker and it was estimated that through the use of thousands of leaflets, weekly radio programs, weekly newspaper columns, and twenty-six copies of a color film on canning prepared by the College of Home Economics and duplicated with special funds from the War Council, home preservation of foods was increased over previous years by 55 per cent. Fruits and vegetables, jams, jellies, and marmalades were processed and nearly 5 million pounds of food were preserved in farm freezers. Over 90,000 pounds of vegetables were dehydrated, more than 10 million pounds stored in bulk, and a large amount preserved by brining and salting.

In January, 1944, the commission set forth, under item 2 of the Wartime Food Program, the following nine nutrition goals as the basis for its education campaign to eliminate waste and help people adjust their diets properly.

1. Eat more beans, soybeans, and soybean products.
2. Use more grain foods, better breads, good spreads for bread, more cereal dishes.
3. Use more vegetables, and cook them to save minerals and vitamins.
4. Make meat supplies stretch farther.
5. Serve hearty breakfasts for everyone every day.
6. Prepare good lunches, especially those carried by school children and war workers.
7. Make full use of home-preserved foods.

8. Eliminate waste caused by spoilage, poor selection, and poor preparation and cooking of foods.

9. Interpret the "basic seven" nutrition recommendations of the United States Nutrition Program, according to the food supplies and habits of the people of New York State. Make these so adaptable that in spite of shortages of rationing, and varied incomes, homemakers can ably guard the good nutrition of their families.

About ten thousand copies of the "Goals" were distributed to nutrition workers in every county of the State. County and city nutrition committees used them as a guide in a program designed both to fit their local needs and also to tie into the State-wide program. To give the local committees help in developing these goals, the commission edited and published leaflets and small bulletins on each subject, and supplied information for use in radio and news print publicity.

Subhead 2a of the seven-point Wartime Food Program had already been achieved through extra War Council funds, and the main emphasis was henceforth placed upon 2b and 2c. In 1944, food-information centers and consultant services were found to be more effective than the earlier method of public demonstrations before interested groups. These new agencies depended for their effectiveness upon the interest of the average housewife in seeking specific answers to problems with which she was confronted.

Point 4 of the Wartime Food Program called for active research in the development of new foods. This was developed along three lines, (1) soybean products, (2) more nutritious bread, and (3) new fruit and vegetable spreads for use on bread. Of these three, experiments with soybean products received major emphasis. A small research committee started work in the fall of 1942 and developed methods long known to the Chinese for sprouting the soybean both in the home and commercially. Sprouting added vita-

min C and cut down by 80 per cent the time required in cooking. In anticipation of a critical failure in the food supply, plans were developed for converting into sprouting establishments existing canning factories. These during the winter could deliver sprouted soybeans in carload lots. Success with the other programs of the Emergency Food Commission made unnecessary resort to this expedient, but in case of need it could have been used.

The campaign to popularize the use of soybeans was undertaken with energy and enthusiasm. Newspaper and radio men were introduced to the idea of the "mighty bean" at a highly publicized luncheon held at the Governor's Mansion, and subsequently written up in the July 15, 1943 number of *Life* magazine, with illustrations showing the various steps in sprouting and cooking soybeans. In September an article in *Reader's Digest* carried the subject to an even wider public, and as a result of the nearly twenty-five thousand inquiries received by the commission during the year a leaflet giving answers for the more frequent questions was finally prepared. The seven regional nutrition conferences of that winter continued the campaign by featuring the use of soybeans as the first of the goals for 1944. A bulletin, *Soy Beans,* giving the results of many studies as well as recipes developed by the commission, was published in 1945.

The more nutritious bread developed consisted of soybean flour and some other ingredients along with the usual wheat-flour mixture. The formula was sponsored by the commission and published, and bread made in accordance with it was sold experimentally in Ithaca. The research on new spreads for use on bread developed such bases as pumpkin, carrots, berries, and citrus fruits.

One effective way of helping women with their food problems was to show them how to use advantageously available foods, providing for this purpose recipes and practical suggestions. These were developed in the test kitchen maintained at the College of Home Economics for preparing and testing all recipes publicized through leaflets, newspaper articles, and radio releases. This kitchen was also used in developing methods for packing appetizing, nutritious lunch boxes, for utilizing the bumper crop of peaches, and for making cold drinks that would contain food values and yet be palatable and popular. Experiments with the use of brewers' yeast (a food extremely rich in B vitamins), in baked products, and in entrée dishes were continued and the test kitchen used in proving the recipes.

Perhaps the one most important change in nutrition customs to come from war experience was the rapid expansion of "in-plant" or "on-the-job" feeding. This largely resulted from the industrial nutrition program begun tentatively in the fall of 1942 and greatly expanded in 1943 by the Food Commission. This sixth item of the Wartime Food Program proved surprisingly popular, once employers had had a chance to gauge its results. It was based on the belief that industrial plants with lunchrooms offered fertile ground for nutritional education, if workers could obtain quickly and inexpensively attractive and tasty food. In December, 1943, Emergency Food Commission funds were made available to employ an industrial nutritionist to work with the Division of Industrial Hygiene of the State Department of Labor. Later, the program was expanded on a regional basis and full-time industrial nutritionists were assigned to each of the six upstate areas in which the Department of Labor had an assistant labor commissioner. These areas were Buffalo, Rochester, Syracuse, Albany, Utica, and Binghamton. A commission nutritionist also worked in the metropolitan New York area. By November, 1945, these workers had assisted approximately 130 plants with in-plant

feeding problems. The goals of their work included (1) promoting good nutrition through serving simple, well-balanced, satisfying meals; (2) employing safe practices in sanitation; (3) planning efficient working arrangements with available equipment; (4) organizing work to save time, effort, and food. Counsel on large-scale feeding problems was not confined to war plants. The commission's nutritionists helped to set up kitchens in fifty farm labor camps which housed a total of six thousand temporary workers.

Although with regard to aims and general direction the human nutrition program was a unit, New York City with its 2.5 million families of diverse origins and food habits was a unique problem. Its 7 million people constituted the largest retail food market in the country, and the extraordinary density of the population necessitated the use of an unusually large staff of nutritionists and the complete mobilization of the press and radio service of the city. So successful was the New York City program that the purchase and preparation of food became front-page news.

It was fortunate that the Governor was able to find as commissioner for the metropolitan area a woman of the prominence and ability of Mrs. Roger W. Straus. To her was entrusted the task of setting up the nutrition program of the Food Commission in the five boroughs of New York City proper and the counties of Suffolk, Nassau, Westchester, and Richmond. The success of the program was in no small measure due to her interest in the work, to her untiring energy, to her wide aquaintance with the leaders of the city, and to her ability to present the situation forcefully to the general public. Branch offices were finally established in each borough and each county, and the work inaugurated under a separate allocation from the State War Council. Liaison between the metropolitan and upstate Nutrition Programs was furnished by Dean Blanding of the Cornell College of Home Economics.

The work in New York City included many different kinds of nutrition services and was made available to all groups and races. In the summer and winter of 1943, with the cooperation of the churches, nutrition demonstrations were carried on in Harlem, and from then on the services of the commission were taxed to capacity. Nutritionists were sent into factories, and exhibits were staged in connection with the *Herald Tribune* Forums, department stores, the Civilian Defense Volunteer Office in Pershing Square, and innumerable large gatherings and conventions. The largest public project undertaken by the commission in Manhattan was the Wartime School for Housewives. This was opened in the spring of 1944, and attended by over one thousand women. The purpose of the school was "to give practical and immediately useful information on the purchase, selection, preparation, care, and conservation of food consistent with modern nutrition standards and in conformity with the State War Program."

Outside the city, a variety of methods was used to reach the individual housewife. One function of the Commission was to train Civilian Defense volunteer office workers and Red Cross nutrition instructors. Nutrition talks to workers in industrial plants reached the housewife through the husband. A nutrition trailer carried nutrition goals and instructions on proper wartime feeding to women in all sections of Suffolk county. The county nutritionists carried on a number of weekly columns in the local press, and the large metropolitan dailies consistently gave generous space to the program. The radio networks and local stations used spot announcements and scripts, and commentators included nutrition information on their programs.

In two years of operation, from July 15, 1943, to June 1, 1945, the metropolitan branch of the New York State Emergency Food Commission gave nearly 2,200 demonstrations and held more than 12,500 meetings. Classes established for the training of lay workers numbered 84, and a total of over 360 exhibits were prepared and displayed at strategic points throughout the area. In addition to hundreds of hours and columns of free publicity, the staff itself delivered 84 specially prepared radio talks, and released over 1,350 news stories. As a result, it was possible for the staff operating in the field as well as the offices of the commission to make a grand total of over 600,000 personal contacts. It is estimated that through the medium of meetings and personal contacts, a total of nearly 2.5 million persons were reached, either directly or through some member of their family. It was of course impossible to estimate how many families were influenced through the press, through exhibits, and through the radio. Of all the programs of the Emergency Food Commission, not only in New York City but likewise upstate, only that on human nutrition reached directly or indirectly the major portion of the State's population.

Conclusion

The striking success achieved by the New York State Emergency Commission is reflected not only in the totals showing farm production for the years 1943-1945, but also in the fact that despite persistently unfavorable conditions, both local and national, New York farmers were able to maintain production of milk and eggs unimpaired. At no time was substantial liquidation of dairy herds or poultry flocks forced upon New York's farmers, a fact which demonstrates the success of the Feed Program. Somewhat less directly, it also shows the effectiveness of the programs concerned with farm labor and farm machinery. The maintenance of the flow of feed to farmers and of bulk milk to the plants attests the success of the Transportation Committee. The impact of the Nutrition Program is reflected in the extent to which housewives and the public generally became conscious of the dietary values of foods, and of the necessity for a correct combination of proteins, minerals, and vitamins. Widespread increases both in small-scale private gardening and in summer canning attest the skill of the Victory Garden Council and of the Nutrition Division as well as the necessity of the times. Facts such as these are patent and amply demonstrate that the wartime food production and nutrition programs of the State were skillfully handled.

There were many reasons for these splendid achievements. Most fundamental of all was the basic soundness of New York's prewar agriculture. Her individual farmer was an intelligent operator of superior efficiency. The farm organizations during the years had built up a leadership which was competent and respected. The program of research and the State-wide agricultural extension service, which were developed at Cornell University and were designed to encourage the application to agricultural practice of the latest methods and discoveries, reflected the wisdom and foresight of the people of the State. Especially important was the close cooperation, existing before the war and needing but further development, between the farmers and the extension service of the State Colleges of Agriculture and Home Economics. Taken together these factors supplied a firm foundation upon which to build a wartime program for food production.

It is questionable, however, whether the farmers, even with such capable leadership, would have been entirely able, alone and unaided, to cope with the tough problems of 1943, 1944, and 1945. Had it not been for the genius and finesse displayed by Governor Dewey in gathering into an Emergency Food Commission the outstanding leaders of the numerous and diverse groups present in New York agriculture, the people of the State might have had far more difficulty with their wartime diet. The Governor's instant perception of the necessity for placing the authority and resources of the State squarely behind the farmers, and the need for an over-all policy-making committee with sufficient authority to coordinate all phases of agricultural production, and to represent the State as a whole in its dealings with the Federal government, stamped him an outstanding executive. In this commission, however, it was again the combination of leadership of the practical farmers aided by specialists trained in the field of agriculture that enabled the commission to fulfill its task successfully. To the effectiveness of this combination, to the complete confidence which the Governor accorded it, and to his willingness to assist it whenever his cooperation was desired, the people of New York State owe what was probably the best agricultural production and nutrition program in the nation.

Perhaps the most important and enduring result of the State's wartime agricultural experience has been the development and publication by the commission of a long-term agricultural program for the State. This program first appeared late in 1944, and is based squarely upon belief in the "interdependence of various segments of New York State's economy — the dependence of New York consumers upon New York farmers for adequate supplies of food; the dependence of farmers on consumers for a market for their products; and the dependence of both upon business and industry to provide jobs at good wages for the large non-farm population." With the purpose of setting up certain "long-time objectives" and of indicating the means to be employed in attaining them, the commission set forth the following program designed to provide a good diet for every citizen, and to place on an economically sound basis those industries engaged in producing, processing, transporting, and distributing foods:

1. Bring all the resources of the State to bear upon the basic problem of maintaining employment and income for the people of the State.

2. Increase efficiency and reduce production costs on New York farms by continuing to support actively research, extension and other programs to assist farmers in reaching these objectives.

3. Get top-quality foods to the consumer more cheaply and conveniently.

4. Continue to recognize the place of farmer-owned and controlled cooperatives in New York agriculture.

5. Continue on a permanent basis the State's wartime program to provide consumers, both urban and rural, with better information on how to use available foods to obtain a good diet and provide for research and the training of workers in human nutrition.

6. Assure the availability, especially for children, of the amounts of milk and other protective foods needed to provide good growth and health.

7. Provide the advantages of modern health, educational and recreational facilities, good roads and electric service in areas suited to farming and rural residential use. Resume State purchase and reforestation of land not suited to either of these uses.

8. Give strong support to the recently established program of advising and helping ex-service men and war workers who desire to locate in the rural areas of New York State.

This program furnishes a set of goals sufficiently attractive to call forth in time of peace the energy and devotion which accomplished so much in time of war.

CHAPTER SEVEN

War Transportation

IN NEW YORK, as in every other state of the Union, there developed a race between the end of the war and the end of transportation equipment. At the time of Pearl Harbor, the existing supply of motor vehicles and tires was known; their normal rate of loss and depreciation was known, but the length of the war could not be ascertained and, consequently, it was impossible to measure the extent of conservation that was essential. The only safe and logical position was to assume that the war would last forever and that, therefore, maximum conservation would be necessary at all times.

HIGHWAY TRAFFIC

The entire war effort depended upon transportation. America was literally a nation on wheels. At the time of Pearl Harbor over 75 per cent of its labor force relied upon automobiles for transportation to and from work. A shift to mass transportation was vitally needed, but not possible to any large extent. Americans were too widely scattered in rural and suburban areas to permit public transportation facilities to carry any large proportion of those workers who customarily used private automobiles. Acute housing shortages developing in the vicinity of war plants made it impractical for large numbers of workers to move to locations where walking to work could be possible. Since new automobiles, trucks, buses, and tires would not be forthcoming, it was up to the people of New York State to see the war

through to its end with the equipment on hand in January, 1942. The fact that New York did this successfully and that a transportation breakdown, such as would have impaired seriously the State's war effort, was avoided was largely the result of the foresight and intelligence of those State officials concerned with problems of highway transportation and of the loyal cooperation which they received from individual citizens. Lacking either intelligent direction or general compliance with regulations, New York State could never have achieved its extraordinary record in highway transportation.

Highway traffic was but one aspect, although by far the most complex, of the State's wartime transportation problem. Bordering upon both the Great Lakes and the Atlantic Ocean, New York's wartime transportation problems involved not two, but three primary divisions: highways, railways, and waterways. The first and last developed on a definite State pattern but the railways, interstate in operation, were only indirectly local facilities. Since wartime regulation of the railways was under control of the Office of Defense Transportation and since water traffic was relatively minor, highway transportation was the State's major wartime transportation problem.

Defense Highway Traffic Committee. Regulation of New York's highway traffic has been to a large extent since 1936 in the hands of the State Traffic Commission. The acceleration of war production in this country after the middle of

1940, combined with the work of the War Department in building up a new army, were bound to create traffic problems of a semimilitary character, problems which the commission sooner or later would be called upon to consider. At the request of the Secretary of War, in February, 1941, the Governor appointed the members of the existing State Traffic Commission as a Highway Traffic Advisory Committee to the War Department. This group consisted of the Commissioner of Motor Vehicles, the Commissioner of Highways, the Superintendent of State Police, and an Associate Commissioner of Education. In their new capacity they became the Defense Highway Traffic Committee. By Chapter 792 of the Laws of 1941, in matters having to do with highway traffic as affected by national defense, the Traffic Commission was empowered to:

1. Cooperate with the agencies of this and other states and of the Federal government which are connected with national defense, in the formulation and execution of plans for the rapid and safe movement over the highways of troops, vehicles of a military nature and materials affecting the national defense.

2. Coordinate the activities of the departments or agencies of the State government from which commission members are named in a manner which will best serve to effectuate any plan for the rapid and safe movement of troops, vehicles, and materials.

3. Solicit the cooperation of officials of the various political subdivisions of the State in the proper execution of plans.

4. Take an inventory, by counties, of the trucks and buses in the State, publicly and privately owned, which would be available in case of emergency affecting the national defense.

5. Conduct, in conjunction with any interested public or private agencies, a highway safety and driver training program as an aid to the national defense.

From the time of its appointment until it was superseded by the War Transportation Committee, the Defense Highway Traffic Committee's activities were divided into the work of its member agencies: the Traffic Commission, the Bureau of Motor Vehicles, the Division of Highways of the State Department of Public Works, the State Police, the Department of Education, and of its principal subcommittee, the Metropolitan Defense Transport Committee. In May, 1941, this Metropolitan Defense Transport Committee was organized on an interstate and interdepartmental basis. It was concerned primarily with the control of motor-truck routing in and around New York City, the laying and marking of a network of secondary highways, the control and routing of civilian food supply traffic and of emergency petroleum distribution, and with preparations for the emergency transportation of civilian evacuees from the metropolitan area — in short, with all problems of emergency transportation of goods and passengers.

Of the four major subdivisions of the Defense Highway Traffic Committee, the Traffic Commission was concerned chiefly with the investigation of highway conditions in the State, and with the solution of those transportation problems arising in the larger cities and in the immediate vicinity of manufacturing plants. Its object was to prevent the development in these areas of transportation bottlenecks, especially at rush hours. Until the end of 1941, it operated principally in New York City, along the Niagara Frontier, and in the vicinity of war plants.

The Bureau of Motor Vehicles was engaged chiefly during 1941 in preparing for emergency use by the War Department an inventory of trucks and buses. This was handled as a Works Progress Administration project with the local war councils assisting. More than three hundred thousand vehicles were covered in the period between September 15, 1941, and March, 1942. A request for a second inventory came from the War Department late in the year and was complied with as part of the 1943 registration procedure. The records of drivers were checked repeatedly for the Army, and similarly confidential information was furnished for the Federal Bureau of Investigation.

The Division of Highways, in turn, was occupied in 1941 and 1942 with the construction of additions to the State system of military highways, construction centering largely on roads giving access to war plants and Army camps. A rapid increase in troop movements, starting in 1941, continued during 1942, and the State Police, whose Superintendent had been appointed by the Defense Highway Traffic Committee as liaison officer with the Army, were used to escort these movements and guard against accidents. They likewise supplemented the work of the Traffic Commission by maintaining a continuous survey of highway traffic conditions. But the pattern of activities concerned with troop movements, war plant traffic, and movements to and from large urban centers was abruptly and radically altered in December, 1941. The attack on Pearl Harbor and the loss of the East Indies made imperative immediate and systematic conservation of all motor vehicle equipment.

Creation of the War Transportation Committee. For the country as a whole, entry into war with Japan meant the loss of 92 per cent of its supply of crude rubber. It ended the manufacture for civilian purposes of tires from natural rubber, and the inauguration of tire rationing four weeks after Pearl Harbor was the first and logical consequence of the loss of our rubber supply. On January 2, 1942, all sales of new automobiles were frozen. Automobile rationing began January 15, and on January 31 the War Production Board ended the manufacture of automobiles. Bulk deliveries of gasoline were cut by the War Production Board toward the end of April, and in July, on the east coast, gasoline rationing went

into effect. These measures placed the country's highway transportation in a straitjacket, and New York State, one of the most highly mechanized states, was no exception, losing completely its normal income of cars and tires and receiving a severe cut in its gasoline. In view of the uncertainty as to the length of the war, drastic conservation was the only possible course that would for any length of time (1) guarantee essential transportation for military movements and production, (2) ensure facilities adequate for essential business, and (3) at the same time permit limited mileage for necessary personal errands.

When a person who has been living on a large annual income discovers that he must live on far less, he will, if he is wise, alter his mode of life and proceed to make available personal equipment and savings last as long as possible. This was exactly New York's position. The coming of the war changed everything. Prior to Pearl Harbor the State had received over 200,000 new passenger cars annually. From February 2, 1942, to June 30, 1945, it received through rationing fewer than 30,000. The normal annual prewar replacement of school buses was around 600. None were available for 1942 and 1943. Instead of being able to buy its prewar annual purchase of approximately 2 million tires of all sizes, under rationing New York had to be satisfied in 1942 with approximately 400,000, a cut of 80 per cent. The consumption of taxable gasoline, which in 1941 ran close to 1.9 billion gallons, was cut to 1.42 billions in 1942 and to a low of 1.08 billions in 1943. It was fortunate in view of these cuts that equipment on hand at the end of 1941 consisted of approximately 2.52 million registered passenger cars, 347,000 trucks, 31,000 buses, and over 15 million tires. In addition, inventories of passenger cars in dealers' hands as of January 2, 1942, totaled over 50,000, and tire inventories as of December 31, 1941, came to approximately 800,000. For the duration of the war, New York's transportation system was to depend upon this new and used equipment on hand at the beginning of 1942, and upon what little additional equipment would be available under rationing.

Since the rate of tire consumption was 3 per cent per month and since the normal life of cars and buses was also calculable, there was an obvious threat of a breakdown of motor transportation. The equipment on hand must be made to last. Somehow, without interference with war production, the life of tires and vehicles had to be extended. A high per capita ratio of motor vehicles, although undoubtedly an index of prosperity, was also an index of dependence, and in time of war this dependence could prove extremely embarrassing for in New York 2883 communities were without rail transportation. Not only was industry partially dependent upon trucks for the shipment of both raw materials and finished goods, but it was even more dependent for its labor supply upon the bus and the private automobile. In some of the large plants only 6 per cent of the workers used mass transportation.

Indications of the altered pattern that New York's highway transportation was to assume for the duration of the war were already appearing early in 1942. As compared with the corresponding period in 1941, there were for the two months of January and February a 6.6 per cent decrease in traffic on State highways outside city limits, and a 3.4 per cent decrease in gasoline sales. In rural areas generally, for the first three months of 1942 as compared with the same period in 1941, the State Police reported a decrease in pleasure driving, a reduction in speed (except for cars of war workers), and an increase in commercial traffic. Passenger car traffic between cities and their adjacent industrial areas was on the rise. Late in April, 1942, R. C.

Georger, Secretary of the Defense Highway Traffic Committee, had occasion to utter a surprisingly accurate prophecy:

Our forecast for the future, therefore (he said), is considerably lessened traffic on a State-wide basis, but increased congestion and accidents in specific localities, which will require special treatment. At a later period, this congestion will begin to disappear, due to the wearing out of existing cars and tires, and gasoline rationing. The emphasis will then shift to the necessity for mass transportation, and the pooling of rides to enable workers to reach their places of employment.

It was this picture, clearly visible by April, 1942, that suggested to the committee the possibility of lessening the ultimate severity of the situation by immediate measures to (1) provide necessary mass transportation, (2) encourage the pooling of rides, (3) eliminate unnecessary driving, and (4) reduce speed.

Early in 1942, in order to provide the machinery and authority necessary to cope with increasingly complex traffic problems, the State Traffic Commission had devised a carefully thought out State-wide plan to conserve motor vehicles, gasoline, and tires, and to protect business, industry, and essential transportation from the effects of the inevitable shortages to come. The plan was approved by the State War Council on May 12, 1942, and with two major exceptions was in substance the program outlined shortly afterward by the National Director of the Office of Defense Transportation. The Federal program, however, did not include the valuable State-wide War Council organization already established in New York, nor did it provide in connection with bus operations the authority that proved to be an indispensable part of the New York Conservation Plan. Designed primarily to maintain transportation services intact in the face of wartime conditions, the New York War Traffic Conservation Plan called for the conservation of vital materials and manpower, and outlined five main objectives:

1. The conservation of tires, gasoline, and vehicles

2. The staggering of working hours

3. The improvement of mass transportation, and the provision of additional mass transportation to replace worn-out private vehicles

4. The correction of traffic bottlenecks and the improvement of traffic conditions

5. The training of drivers for emergencies

The methods outlined to accomplish each of the five major objectives of the plan were detailed and comprehensive. In order to conserve tires, gasoline and vehicles, it was proposed to (1) reduce the speed limit, (2) promote group rides through a car-sharing program, (3) pool retail deliveries, (4) budget private driving, (5) emphasize the importance of vehicle and road maintenance, and (6) encourage walking and the greater use of bicycles, trolleys, and buses. Traffic studies at some of the larger war production plants showed that, with tires good for only fifteen months on the average, the number of workers per vehicle was under two. By doubling the number of workers per vehicle, this inefficient use of tires and gasoline could be eliminated, and the life of both tires and vehicles doubled.

The proposal to stagger hours of work in war industries, as well as large department stores, commercial concerns, retail stores, office buildings, and schools was aimed at eliminating the customary morning and afternoon peaks of traffic movement In this way the overcrowding of trolleys and buses, also critically short in numbers, could be partially overcome. It was pointed out that in the fall of 1941 staggered working hours in Washington, D. C., cut peak traffic loads 50 per cent, and by the better load distribution thus obtained made possible transporting a greatly increased number of passengers with no corresponding increase in the number of vehicles.

To compensate for the restricted use of private passenger cars, it was planned to increase the capacity of mass transportation by operating existing buses and trolleys at top efficiency. Innovations included the elimination of duplicate runs, the introduction of skip stops, the shortening of routes, the provision of additional feeder routes and express service, greater emphasis upon preventive maintenance of vehicles, improved methods for fare collection, and extension of the use of school buses. It was pointed out that on certain lines it had been customary for buses to pick up passengers at any point, with stops frequently as close as every hundred feet. To reduce time and wear and tear, official stops were designated at approximately every six hundred feet.

One of the traditional functions of the Traffic Commission had been the study and elimination of traffic bottlenecks. War inevitably made traffic conditions worse, and areas of congestion became fruitful sources of accidents. Congested spots produced by parking in business districts, around war production industries, or by the convergence of a number of heavily used traffic arteries tended to slow traffic. Changes were required not only to speed traffic at these spots but also to lower the number of accidents that such conditions invited. Methods of treatment outlined in the War Traffic Conservation Plan included the improved use of traffic devices, the designation of preferred routes, the improvement of parking areas, a reduction in the speed of vehicles, a selective enforcement of regulations, certain physical improvements, and radical engineering changes. It was determined that adjustment of the setting on traffic signals to reduce the cycle from sixty to forty seconds and to alter the time to meet the shift in loads on the major and minor streets could in many instances result in a marked acceleration of the general movement of vehicles.

In view of an anticipated need for expert drivers capable of operating vehicles under the most adverse conditions, a plan was proposed to train a large number of persons for emergency driving. Instruction was to be available to old as well as new drivers, and the latest methods were to be taught in order to conserve men and materials. Training was to be made available to members of the Civilian Defense Drivers Corps, the Motor Transport Corps, the Motorcycle Corps, and also to high-school students, new adult drivers, and bicyclists.

To put the above War Transportation Plan into operation, on May 12, 1942, the State War Council replaced the Defense Highway Traffic Committee with a State War Transportation Committee consisting of the members of the Traffic Commission plus representatives of the Public Service Commission, and of the bus industry. As defined by the War Council, the duties of the new committee were "to promote the conservation of vehicles, gasoline and tires, and the conservation and improvement of transportation, including mass transportation, throughout the State." To accomplish these ends it was given the "authority to request and obtain" cooperation and assistance from all State and municipal agencies and officials, including local War Councils.

The War Transportation Committee had no intention of sitting in Albany and making decisions at long range. The New York State War Council organization already blanketed the State with its 108 local war councils, and the committee wisely made use of existing machinery by requiring each local council to appoint an Administrator of War Transportation, who would represent in that area the authority of both the appointing council and the State War Transportation Committee. Each local administrator was required to organize a War Transportation Committee of representatives from official and unofficial groups in the community, a committee which would single out and grapple with the transportation problems of the vicinity. Through these the Conservation Program ultimately reached individual car owners, business establishments, industrial plants, and transportation companies. The determination of the extent of their own transportation problems and, under the guidance of the State Committee, the coordination and direction of all efforts to deal with them, became the primary responsibility of these 105 administrators and their committees. Care was taken by the War Transportation Committee in Albany to build up the prestige of the administrators in their communities by acting only after their recommendations had been received. By arrangement with the State Office of Price Administration and War Manpower Commission offices, they were placed in close touch with the local rationing boards and with United States Employment Offices. To instruct the administrators and to standardize local procedure, a War Transportation Manual, explaining in detail all phases of their work, was prepared and issued by the State Committee.

The guidance of local committees was in the hands of five field agents stationed in Albany, Utica, Syracuse, Rochester, and Buffalo. In the New York metropolitan area this work was at first handled on a voluntary basis by a former director of the New York City Regional Plan Association. Later it was taken over by the Director of Port Development of the Port of New York Authority. These men kept in touch with the local committees in their territories, made special investigations where necessary, and lent the assistance and backing of the State Committee whenever situations proved difficult. Through the War Transportation Committee the field staff could draw at all times upon the ten traffic engineers of the Highway Department as well as upon the seven traffic supervisors of the

State Police. At Albany, the technical staff of the State Committee, partly recruited from the personnel of the departments represented upon the Traffic Commission, was paid in part from funds of the State War Council. R. C. Georger, Secretary of the State Traffic Commission, became the Director of the War Transportation Committee, thereby assuring a certain continuity of experience in the direction of the program.

New York's efforts to conserve its highway transportation resources and at the same time to provide adequate transportation service where necessary thus took the form of a wartime operation in which the State War Council, the Department of Public Works, the Department of Education, the Bureau of Motor Vehicles, the Division of the State Police, and the State Traffic Commission cooperated, with aid extended from time to time by the Public Service Commission. Being a temporary War Commission, the War Transportation Committee was bound neither by long-standing precedents nor by the fear of creating precedents, and in the field of highway transportation the powers, granted to it by the State War Council, were broader than those of any existing State department. The results accomplished under the program came from unusually close cooperation between State and Federal authorities and from the strength of the New York State and local War Council organizations. These last supplied as administrators of war transportation men of ability and good standing, capable of coping successfully with the transportation problems of their communities. The majority of situations where important traffic problems developed were successfully overcome by the local administrators and their committees. Yet organization without the understanding and willing compliance of the great majority of the population would not have been enough. That popular cooperation was forthcoming in spite of inconvenience is

a tribute to the intelligence and patriotism of the average citizen. He proved himself willing to do his bit once he understood what was necessary.

The Operation of the War Transportation Conservation Plan. It took the War Transportation Committee approximately four weeks, from May 12 to June 15, 1942, to complete its organization and to put into running order the major phases of the War Transportation Conservation Plan. These phases were three in number: (1) the maintenance of transportation adequate for all essential purposes as long as the war should last, (2) the conservation of transportation equipment, and (3) the maintenance of the free flow of traffic throughout the State. The basic over-all task of the committee was to provide adequate transportation, but this would have been impossible without conservation. Fortunately, Federal restrictions on the use of gasoline and tires and on the manufacture of cars, trucks, and buses — restrictions which could have been imposed successfully only on a nation-wide basis — laid the foundations of the Conservation Program in every state. In 1942, accordingly, the most pressing problem facing the War Transportation Committee was the conservation of all available transportation equipment. The State simply had to give up the feast to avoid the famine.

Certain positive functions in connection with the provision of additional highway transportation could be performed best by a State agency. At no time during the period of conservation could essential transportation be allowed to suffer. Consequently, toward the end of 1943, as equipment began to wear out and the Conservation Program became accepted and its operation more nearly automatic, the committee found a greater proportion of its time occupied with the problem of providing transportation at vital points throughout the State. This positive function was not performed by the Office of Defense Transportation, which was primarily a restrictive organization, nor was it a function of the Federal agency to ensure that adequate transportation facilities, on hand in the right place at the right time, be able to operate with the utmost efficiency. Instead, it became the task of the State War Transportation Committee, especially those of its members from the Traffic Commission, to facilitate the smooth flow of traffic.

Thus the three functions of the committee were interrelated. Adequate transportation depended upon successful conservation of equipment and favorable operating conditions. Conservation of equipment had to be accomplished by facilitating the free flow of vehicles in traffic and by eliminating traffic problems. Traffic problems could best be handled on the spot, each as a separate case; hence, the need for local administrators in the role of trouble shooters. The administrators, together with their committees, also became vital cogs in the State-wide publicity campaign designed to secure public acceptance and cooperation for the entire program.

The Provision of Essential Transportation. To furnish adequate transportation facilities whenever necessary, it became imperative that within the boundaries of the State the War Transportation Committee should have powers commensurate with its responsibilities. Although for legal and other reasons the early request of the War Transportation Committee for power to issue orders on its own responsibility was denied, the War Council passed promptly practically every order dealing with major policies requested by the committee. The committee was thereafter free to issue its own administrative rules and regulations within the framework laid down by these orders. This power was increased when it became obvious that an agreement on policy and administrative functions should be reached between the Federal Office of Defense Transportation and the State War Transportation Committee. In July, 1942, after several conferences, such an agreement was reached and was approved by the War Council. It allowed the New York Committee to rewrite Office of Defense Transportation orders regulating motor vehicles to make such orders conform to New York State conditions and, following Office of Defense Transportation approval, to recommend these orders to the State War Council for adoption. Interpretations and enforcement of these orders fell to the State Committee, and the Office of Defense Transportation would voluntarily withdraw from active control of bus operations in New York State. This arrangement between the Office of Defense Transportation and the State of New York was unique and worked out extremely well. It took the administrative burden from the Federal agency and replaced it with a remarkably effective State enforcement agency.

The advantages of State administration were considerable. Wherever possible, the War Transportation Committee simplified the language of the Office of Defense Transportation orders, but the principal benefits accrued from the greater flexibility of interpretation possible to the State agency. Time lag and red tape were cut to the bone. Not only were decisions rendered quickly, but cases were also examined thoroughly both by the local administrators and by the field agents of the State Committee, all of whom were in constant touch with each other and with headquarters by telephone. Working at a distance and without adequate staff, the Federal government would have been in no position to judge the merits of individual cases. The State Committee, through its network of transportation administrators, had the interest and the facilities to consider local needs and to advise with industry and communities on the best possible methods for meeting their transportation problems.

One striking example of the value of local administrators in dealing with emergency situations comes from Broome County. In June, 1943, a strike of bus drivers appeared imminent in the Binghamton area, the result of changes in schedules required by the Office of Defense Transportation Order for 20 per cent curtailment of service. It so happened that the local administrator was a well-known, public-spirited citizen. He acted promptly. On his own initiative, he addressed a meeting of the bus drivers in the small hours of the morning and succeeded in presenting the reasons for the Office of Defense Transportation Order so clearly and convincingly that the strike was called off. After the incident, the attorney for the bus company wrote the War Transportation Committee as follows:

Let me say also that I feel that this incident is a striking vindication of the policy which has been followed in this State of decentralizing emergency supervision of war transportation. It was the presence locally of a high-minded citizen with the authority and the imagination to act that saved the situation.

A subsequent report of this administrator revealed the number and quantity of essential war munitions being prepared in his area and indicated that had the bus strike taken place, production on such articles as Link Trainers, many Ansco photographic supplies, twenty-millimeter aircraft cannon, and other important items for the Army, Navy, Marine Corps, and Coast Guard would have been seriously impaired.

Office of Defense Transportation was not the only agency to secure administrative assistance from the War Transportation Committee. At the request of the committee and with the approval of the Public Service Commission, the War Council on July 7, 1942, issued Order No. 3 which empowered the War Transportation Committee to issue temporary certificates of necessity permitting the inauguration of new bus lines or the extension of existing bus lines pending final determination by the Public Service Commission. This order cut the time consumed in the consideration of petitions from four weeks or more to forty-eight hours. Its purpose was in line with the declared policy of the Legislature "that during the present war emergency necessary additional passenger transportation should be promptly provided and that to carry out this policy temporary certificates of convenience and necessity, and temporary amendments to outstanding certificates should be granted without the procedure necessary and desirable in normal times." On July 21, 1942, the War Transportation Committee received additional power from War Council Order No. 5 to regulate charter bus operations and to limit such service to military and naval personnel, the armed forces of the State, war workers, selectees, and to certain other classes. To provide additional bus service where expanded transportation facilities were found to be necessary, both franchise and charter operations were authorized.

In addition to the buses operated by common carriers, there were in New York about three thousand school buses which in themselves constituted an important source of transportation. The first order issued by the War Council, May 12, 1942, empowered the War Transportation Committee to authorize the use of school-owned buses for the transportation of defense and agricultural workers, the armed forces of the State and Federal government, and participants in War Training classes, as well as to authorize the lease of such school-owned buses to any common carrier which operated buses.

Delegation to the War Transportation Committee by the Office of Defense Transportation and the State War Council of power to authorize and regulate the use of mass transportation facilities

Pedal-Power Progress

When strict rationing of gasoline and rubber limited motor transportation, many
of New York State travelers and commuters made wide use of journeys by bicycle.

PLATE No. XII

for war-connected purposes was one of the chief factors in the success of the New York program. Knowing local conditions in a way not possible for the Office of Defense Transportation, the New York Committee was empowered to and did make exceptions within the framework of War Council orders that the Office of Defense Transportation, bound by more rigid rules, could not make. The New York Committee never forgot that its functions were not exclusively restrictive; where transportation was needed it felt bound to provide it. Its ability to provide transportation with a clear conscience, in the face of a national program of conservation, resulted from its unusually active supervision and enforcement of existing orders in New York State. Unessential transportation was almost completely eliminated, thereby helping not only the war effort but saving vital equipment for a later period when it would be badly needed.

To administer its orders, the committee had to evolve a system of informal priorities. Regarding the establishment of new or additional bus service, it is recorded in the minutes that "Unless extenuating circumstances are shown, the Committee will not approve of the establishment of new or additional bus service wherein no relation to the war effort is shown," and that "on considering the authorization of additional bus service, consideration shall be given to the net savings of rubber and gasoline, and the net increase in the war effort before such additional service is authorized." Top priority among persons went to members of the armed forces of the State and Federal government. Second in order came war production workers and farm laborers, and a close third, business and professional travel. School children had first claim on school buses where no other transportation was available, and for distances considered too

great for walking. Members of authorized War Training classes were allowed the use of charter buses, as were groups recruited for the purpose of entertaining wounded veterans.

The use of transportation equipment itself was never rationed, but through publicity campaigns a definite attempt was made to promote popular realization of how the committee preferred to have equipment used. Walking was advised under all practical circumstances. Where distances were prohibitive and trolleys or trains were available, those facilities were to be used in preference to motor vehicles. Where neither trains nor trolleys were available, the ordinary franchise bus was preferable to the individual's personal car. Similarly, school children could fall back upon school buses if no other form of mass transportation were available. Lacking buses, however, the final alternative was the private automobile, which was estimated to be the only possibility for approximately 70 per cent of the war workers of the State.

While this series of preferences held true generally, it was by no means possible for the War Transportation Committee to lay down a fixed policy applicable under all circumstances for the duration of the war. Transportation conditions were bound to change and policies were changed to meet them. While the emphasis was originally upon the conservation of private passenger cars, the shortage of bus tires at one point in 1944 became so acute that for a time no new lines were authorized, and in certain localities individuals were urged once more to make use of their own cars. On the other hand, in certain rural areas of the State where, in 1942, many passenger cars were old and traveling conditions unusually difficult, it became necessary before the end of the war to inaugurate new bus lines because of the disappearance from the roads of privately owned cars. As the war continued, increased dependence upon charter buses was reflected in an upward curve in the number of permits granted by the committee.

Many problems connected with mass transportation were miscellaneous and not of a regulatory nature. The committee had to consider draft deferments for bus drivers and mechanics and to provide special transportation for agricultural workers. Adjusting the supply and demand for new buses and securing priority ratings for the acquisition of parts required that the committee provide constant liaison between individual operators and the Federal government. In most cases operators with Office of Defense Transportation problems were given individual attention by the committee. In fact its excellent relations with Federal officials, which enabled it to secure prompt and favorable action in cases of hardship or necessity, were the subject of favorable nation-wide radio comment as being so distinctly at variance from the pattern of futile controversy with Federal agencies frequently pursued by State governments.

In order that its activities with relation to mass transportation might meet, to the extent possible under wartime conditions, the best interests of the bus industry, the committee established a Motor Bus Advisory Committee to advise and assist it in its work. The members of the Advisory Committee were appointed upon recommendation of the various associations of bus operators, and their selection formed a fairly representative cross section both of the industry and geographically. This committee was of great assistance to the War Transportation Committee.

The figures in Table 14 illustrate action taken by the War Transportation Committee with regard to the operation of buses:

Table 14. Bus Permits and Certificates

Permits for Charter Bus Operation

Year	Issued	Denied	Revoked
1942	112	123	0
1943	504	74	39
1944	774	59	41
1945	728	35	3
TOTALS	2,118	291	83

Permits for Use of School-owned Buses

Year	Issued	Denied	Revoked
1942	16	1	3
1943	40	5	0
1944	48	2	5
1945	15	3	5
TOTALS	119	11	13

Certificates for Operation of Bus Routes

Year	Issued	Denied	Revoked
1942	80	33	0
1943	61	11	3
1944	23	6	1
1945	26	2	1
TOTALS	190	52	5

The Conservation of Transportation Facilities. Although the provision of adequate transportation was the most important task of the War Transportation Committee, it could never have been accomplished without a full-scale Conservation Program. The conservation of tires, gasoline, and vehicles was a joint project of Federal, State, and local authorities. The Office of Price Administration rationed tires and gasoline, the Office of Defense Transportation regulated sales of new automobiles, and the State of New York limited the speed of motor vehicles, prohibited the racing of motor vehicles, took steps to conserve tires and cars operated by the State Departments, and established a special agency, the War Transportation Committee, to handle its major transportation problems. The top speed limit for all motor vehicles was reduced to forty miles per hour by the State Legislature on April 21, 1942. On September 22, this was cut to thirty-five miles per hour by Order No. 12 of the State War Council, and this latter limit remained in force with one or two amendments until the spring of 1946 when the State Legislature reestablished the prewar limit of fifty miles per hour.

As applied to mass transportation, the Conservation Program affected school transportation, trucks, and in many cases passenger cars. On July 22, 1942, the State War Transportation Committee was given power by War Council Order No. 6 to enforce upon intercity common carriers of passengers by bus the elimination of wasteful operations, the observance of certain operating standards, and the execution of measures to conserve tires and equipment of every sort. Order No. 9, applying to motor carriers of property (trucks), was issued by the War Council August 13, 1942, and gave regulative authority to the War Transportation Committee for similar purposes; in addition it forbade call backs and special deliveries, reduced the frequency of deliveries, and required a 25 per cent reduction of total mileage from 1941 figures. This order also included certain loading and operating requirements. It was supplemented at the same time by Order No. 10 relating to the conservation of motor equipment of certain common carriers. Order No. 10, which provided for joint operations among carriers, was designed to ensure full loads on all trips. A number of war transportation administrators in milk-producing areas carried out the spirit of these last two orders by actively furthering cooperative trucking arrangements between producers, thus eliminating wasteful mileage and effecting full utilization of producers' trucks. To avoid duplication on numerous rural pickup routes, loads were exchanged and milk routes jointly operated.

Orders No. 6, 9, and 10 were reissues of Office of Defense Transportation orders, and although they stood on the books as State regulations most of the administration in connection with them remained in the hands of the Federal authorities. No Office of Defense Transportation order or corresponding State War Council order was ever issued regarding intracity common carriers of passengers by bus. There was, however, a well-publicized twelve-point policy issued by the Director of the Office of Defense Transportation outlining the chief methods by which bus companies could render the most efficient service. As a result of the heavy passenger traffic handled by bus companies all during the war, loadings approximately doubled. This increase, combined with the elimination of 85 per cent of the unnecessary and less profitable service, meant that compliance with the Federal policy was not alone in the interest of the war effort, but contributed as well to the financial welfare of the bus operators themselves.

In the War Transportation Manual, issued by the State Committee in July, 1942, the twelve points of the Federal Bus Conservation Program, together with seven others added by the War Transportation Committee, were outlined and briefly discussed. Several of the more important of these should be mentioned here. Perhaps the greatest opportunity for increasing the carrying capacity of existing urban buses lay in the plan for staggering working, store, and office hours, and the opening and closing hours of schools. To secure the full use of all street railway lines, a number of devices could be employed such as the discontinuance of bus and trolley coach service in competition with existing street railway lines, the spreading of stops to intervals of from 660 to 1200 feet, and a reduction in the number of runs made during slack hours and to suburban points. Charter buses were to be employed solely for carrying defense workers to and from employment. The same restriction was placed on the emergency use of school buses. In some instances restoration of old vehicles to service became necessary, and a reduction was made in spare equipment requirements. Interiors of available vehicles were rearranged to increase seating and standing capacity. Street traffic control regulations were altered so that the movement of mass transit vehicles received precedence and the timing of traffic control devices was adjusted to secure maximum efficiency of traffic flow. Wherever necessary, these and other methods of conservation were put into operation by the committee and its staff throughout the State. Studies of war transportation conditions were continued, and, upon request of the War Manpower Commission, advice and assistance were furnished regarding numerous transportation problems bearing on the labor supply market.

In several cases involving transportation for large numbers of war workers, the committee was able to secure additional railroad service as a means of supplementing overburdened bus lines or rapidly deteriorating private cars. The Long Island Railroad provided additional service between Riverhead and Greenport for Suffolk County workers in the Long Island war plants. Railroad commuter service from Cadosia to Sidney was inaugurated on June 7, 1943. In a period of two years this line carried a total of 251,877 passengers between Cadosia and Sidney, while another line between Norwich and Sidney carried 396,913. To have provided equivalent service by buses originating in Norwich and Cadosia would have required approximately 1.6 million bus miles.

In the latter part of 1944, as a special conservation measure, the War Transportation Committee sponsored a training program designed specifically for operators of trucks and buses. The bulk of the course was devoted to the art of maintaining vehicles in good running order. Instruction was modeled on courses already being given for Civilian Defense drivers and for drivers of school buses by the Office of War Training and the State Department of Education. The need for training drivers of transit buses

and freight-carrying trucks in maintenance became evident with the growing deterioration of equipment and an increasing shortage of truck and bus tires. The course was given first to fleet supervisors and carried by them in turn to their drivers. Instructional materials were developed with the aid of motor-fleet men, training experts, and manufacturers. These materials were recognized as most effective for the purpose intended. Using Federal funds, fleet supervisory training schools were started in Albany and Buffalo, in May, 1945, for supervisors representing over ten thousand drivers. Other schools were held in Syracuse and New York City. Men prominent in the motor transportation industry became interested in the program, and operators of some of the largest fleets in the State, both transit and truck, sent their key men to these schools for training. The end of the war in Europe caused the withdrawal of Federal funds and the program was discontinued before it had reached completion.

The maintenance of New York's fleet of 3,200 school buses upon the most efficient and economical basis possible was likewise part of the program for conservation of mass transportation. The normal replacement of school buses was approximately six hundred per year. Actually, replacements during the war were as follows:

	Year	New school buses
	1942	0
	1943	0
	1944	153
(January 1 to	1945	240
September 22)		

From these figures it is apparent that school transportation had to be maintained almost entirely with buses already in operation in 1941. The use of these buses for other than school purposes as authorized in Orders No. 1 and 14 increased deterioration. To make these vehicles last for the duration of the war, all possible methods of conservation had to be employed.

In the fall of 1942, the Office of Defense Transportation issued regulations on transportation of children to school which eliminated all but the most essential service. At the request of the Office of Defense Transportation and in agreement with the State Education Department, the committee drafted an order regulating school transportation in New York State. Local school authorities and associations, representing public and private schools of different levels, were consulted in the preparation of this draft. Approved by the War Council and issued as Order No. 14, effective February 9, 1943, it followed, in general, Office of Defense Transportation regulations but adapted them to conditions peculiar to New York State and designated the War Transportation Committee as administrator. Henceforth, the committee maintained a continuous review of all school transportation in the State, both to improve efficiency and to eliminate that which did not conform with the provisions of the order. Gasoline was allocated by the Office of Defense Transportation only following certification by the committee.

Although few definite figures are recorded, sample studies from locations where statistics are available indicate that in the operation of school buses during the war several million miles were saved. This naturally meant a substantial reduction in cost to the communities. Instances of such savings from the reduction in the use of school buses were innumerable, but the lack of sufficient data on school bus operations prior to the war makes figures unreliable. However, a few typical cases are worth citing. One school district consolidated its bus routes and eliminated the need for three school buses. In another, the use of two school buses and five seven-passenger cars was eliminated. In a number of cases, buses thus released were utilized in the relief of heavily overburdened franchise bus lines. For example, a school-owned bus which was freed by the revision of a school transportation schedule was subsequently operated for the transportation of aircraft workers between Hicksville and the Grumman Airplane Factory.

Order No. 14 included the requirement that each driver of a school bus, usually a person employed only part time, obtain a Regents Public Service Certificate for the completion of a course of bus-driver instruction. This course in driver training, prepared in 1943 by the State Education Department, emphasized methods of preventive maintenance which should yield benefits to the majority of schools long after the war is over. Measures were taken by the committee through State-wide meetings of school officials to ensure that the provisions of Order No. 14 were fully understood. Every possible assistance was given to those responsible for school transportation in the reorganization of bus routes in accordance with the order. Maximum operating efficiency consistent with the furnishing of adequate transportation for the children of the State was thereby obtained.

Realizing that the transportation of pupils involved problems peculiar to schools, the committee created a School Transportation Advisory Committee to advise in the formulation of policies and to assist in the administration of Order No. 14. This committee was extremely useful as the constant support of its members secured splendid acceptance of the regulations by individual school superintendents. The membership of the committee, composed of representative parents, boards of education, and practically all types and classes of schools, was so strongly convinced of the necessity for the work of the War Transportation Committee that at no time did it favor relaxing the wartime limitations embodied in Order No. 14. At its final meeting, August 24, 1945, the Advisory

Committee adopted the following resolution with the request that it be forwarded to the Commissioner of Education:

WHEREAS the School Transportation Advisory Committee believes that in many school districts the transportation provided for school children prior to February 9, 1943, the date on which State War Council Order No. 14 became effective, was beyond the real needs of the situation, and

WHEREAS it believes that school transportation was originally intended to enable pupils, residing beyond a reasonable walking distance from the schools which they attend, to reach school regularly and obtain their education without undue hardship, and

WHEREAS the Advisory Committee believes that transportation should be provided only for children to whom the foregoing statement applies, and

WHEREAS the Committee further believes that school buses should not be used on trips to points at remote distances from the school, such as sightseeing trips to Washington, now therefore be it

RESOLVED: that the School Transportation Advisory Committee believes that certain advantages obtained through the operation of War Council Order No. 14 should be retained and therefore recommends to the State Departent of Education that a definite policy be established by said Department to limit the excessive use of school transportation; such policy to provide, among other things, that transportation be furnished only for pupils living beyond a reasonable walking distance; and that transportation along short spur routes not be permitted, except in cases involving hazard or hardship to pupils, in order that the time between the departure of all of the pupils from the school and their arrival home not be extended unduly by the time required to transport a few pupils over short spur routes.

The conservation of private passenger cars involved many aspects of control that deeply affected the average citizen of the State and his private automobile. Since car owners could not be forced either to maintain their vehicles in good condition or to drive so as to economize on gasoline and tires, supervision of 2 million operators was out of the question. The entire campaign for preventive maintenance, conducted with the aid of the State Office of War Information, had to be put on the basis of education and persuasion. Publicity material was issued in the form of car stickers, bus, subway, and trolley cards, posters, billboard signs, cartoon strips, and kits of material for local newspaper releases and for radio stations. To make clear the need for conservation, War Transportation administrators, whose job it was to get the basic facts across to the public, were supplied with current data on the State and national supply of tires, gasoline, and vehicles. In the *War Transportation Manual,* already referred to, the contrast was emphasized between the extent of the rubber shortage and the State's current rate of tire consumption. The factors affecting tire wear, inflation, speed of operation, quick stops and starts, brake adjustment, and wheel alignment were considered one by one. Factors affecting gasoline consumption, speed, engine efficiency, quick stops, and dragging of brakes were carefully explained. Other factors affecting vehicle wear, such as the lack of maintenance, speed, road surface, and weather conditions, were also enumerated. Throughout the war period it was assumed by the State Committee that if the public understood the conditions under which the nation was prosecuting the war, and if people were told what to do to avert a breakdown in local transportation, there would be no difficulty about cooperation. This expectation proved correct and public acceptance of regulations and adaptation to wartime conditions were in general very satisfactory.

The principal methods of conserving passenger cars, apart from rationing gasoline and regulating speed on State highways, were of three kinds: (1) preventive maintenance of equipment, tire-life inspections and proper inflation, adequate greasing, and voluntary engine inspection, (2) elimination of unnecessary use, and (3) the fullest possible utilization of the car during operation. The purpose of Federal restrictions on the sale of gasoline and tires was primarily to ensure that persons, to whom transportation by passenger car was essential, should obtain from reserves not allocated in advance to the armed forces the supplies necessary to enable them to perform essential driving. A valuable by-product, however, was the conservation of the vehicle itself accomplished by the limitations placed upon nonessential driving. However, restrictions in themselves were not sufficient to accomplish the end sought, nor, likewise, were the various voluntary methods for preventive maintenance. In addition means had to be provided to enable passengers and drivers to get together for the purpose of filling to capacity those cars permitted to operate.

As the situation became more acute, the development of the group-ride program provided many citizens of the State with a means of transportation, transportation otherwise not to be had. Group-riding or car-sharing programs were conducted by approximately 90 per cent of the local transportation administrators; those who were inactive in this respect were so, usually, because no problem was involved. Working with the local ration boards, the administrators established employee-management transportation committees to sponsor car-sharing clubs in 1,044 of the 1,131 plants in the State employing over 100 workers.

An unusual group-riding plan was placed in operation by the War Transportation Administrator for Broome County. The special feature distinguishing this from other plans was the use of parking space at the junction of main roads, space where partially filled cars could be parked while their occupants rode to work in full cars. Twenty of these self-dispatching stations were located at stores, gasoline stations, and garages in various villages and hamlets through which workers in Binghamton normally drove on their way to and from work. Apparently, the plan operated smoothly and solved the local problem by filling cars at the place of convergence.

At first, manufacturers were slow to accept partial responsibility for securing transportation for their workers. They were much more concerned to provide transportation for raw materials; transportation of personnel had always been taken for granted. Only when the need for labor became critical did many companies show a willingness to organize car-sharing clubs among their employees. A number of far-sighted organizations anticipated their needs, and by successfully transporting their workers these showed the way to others. On the whole, passenger car loadings in New York State, which increased from 1.7 to 3.7 persons per car, were higher than the national average, and loadings among industrial workers were especially high as compared to shoppers and churchgoers. During 1942 and 1943, and until it became an established part of the general labor-transportation pattern, stimulation of car-sharing or club-rides required a major share of attention from the administrators. Later it became a matter of necessity and operated with little difficulty. Individuals transporting themselves and other workers for pay did not come under the restrictions imposed by the Public Service Commission upon common carriers. Car-sharing among shoppers and among parents taking children to and from school, while pushed by the State Committee, was by no means so universally adopted; it lacked the essential elements of regular hours and economic necessity. These two programs were dependent largely upon acquaintance among individuals in a neighborhood and were subject to constant interruptions.

Maintaining a Free Flow of Traffic. The third function of the War Transportation Committee, over and above providing and conserving transportation, was the maintenance of as free a flow of all vehicular traffic as circumstances would permit. There were two phases to this work of the committee. The first consisted of routine measures, surveys, and studies of traffic conditions undertaken by the Traffic Commission, the Department of Public Works, and the State Police. Work of this sort was greatly increased by the war, and the assistance of the local transportation administrators was of great value. For example: a bad condition on the Niagara Falls Boulevard in the vicinity of the Bell Aircraft Plant was eliminated by the installation of a semivehicle activated signal and the widening of a side road. Changes in parking regulations and traffic signals on Genesee Street in the city of Buffalo materially improved the flow of traffic to the Curtiss-Wright Plant and by reducing travel time was equivalent to the addition of several buses in the transportation of workers to the plant. New construction, additional signals, and revisions of parking regulations in the vicinity of an aircraft plant on Long Island also greatly improved conditions. By July, 1943, the committee could report the removal of 426 traffic signals and the changing of 3258 stop and go signals to flashing or part-time operation.

The second phase of the work of the committee consisted in the elimination of traffic bottlenecks in the vicinity of war plants, whose appearance was definitely a war-caused phenomenon. Here the work of the local administrators was invaluable. Not only were they able to discover these bottlenecks as they developed, but their familiarity with the local situation made it possible for them to analyze the causes and with the help of

their committees to take appropriate action to remedy the situation.

One of the principal methods employed by the transportation administrators to ease traffic tie-ups during rush hours was the inauguration of a program of staggered hours for the opening and closing of stores and offices, and the changing of shifts in the larger manufacturing plants. One outstanding example of the advantages of the staggered-hours program was the city of Buffalo. In the fall of 1942, the load on the 825 street cars and buses operated by the International Railway Company in the city of Buffalo had reached the saturation point during hours of peak traffic. No more equipment was available, congestion and delay were serious, and the transit load of 480,000 passengers a day was increasing at the rate of approximately 6 per cent per month. A comprehensive survey of the situation led to an order issued by the Buffalo War Council directing the staggering of hours of industry in certain zones, of different types of business in downtown areas, and of the schools. Ultimately this was followed by action of the Erie County War Council and was approved by the State War Transportation Committee. The reduction in the number of passengers carried during peak periods by transporting these passengers during hours in which street cars and buses had been previously operating at a fraction of their capacity enabled mass transportation in the city to meet the strain imposed upon it by wartime conditions.

Another outstanding achievement by one Administrator of War Transportation was the staggering of hours in industries, stores and offices along more than twenty of the thirty bus routes in the city of Syracuse, and in Onondaga county. The program was placed in effect after a detailed study covering several months and including many conferences with industrial heads, public officials, and civic leaders. Since cooperation among the interested parties was voluntary and little or no opposition was encountered on the part of the public, no compulsory action on the part of the War Council was necessary. The capacity of existing vehicles in the Syracuse area was thereby vastly increased. Similar staggering of hours was affected in Schenectady, Utica, Rome, and other smaller communities. In these instances also the staggering of hours was effected by voluntary agreements obtained by the local administrators, and War Council orders were not issued.

Since bottlenecks not only affected transportation adversely by causing excessive tire wear and gasoline consumption, but also greatly increased the number of traffic fatalities and injuries in New York State, it was to the interest of the community, as well as of the State, that they be promptly eliminated. Blind intersections, improperly marked hazards and routes, poorly timed traffic signals, unmarked obstructions in the road, signs and signals hidden by foliage, poorly maintained pavement markers and stop signs, and poorly maintained road surfaces all contributed in peace as well as wartime to the toll of motor vehicle accidents. The addition of increased wartime traffic to these normal factors greatly accentuated the rate of motor vehicle accidents. While from 1940 to 1944 there was a definite decline in the total number of traffic fatalities and injuries involving pedestrians in New York State, accidents other than those involving pedestrians continued at a normal peacetime level until 1943, when they dropped 33 per cent to a wartime low. Perhaps the most important index was the fact that, excluding New York City and rural areas, the percentage of total accidents in the State rose approximately 10 per cent from 1940 to 1944. This reflected traffic congestion in and around war plants in the war impact areas of the State. In general, however, traffic condi-

tions through the State were good during the war emergency, and all possible action was taken to facilitate its flow.

Summarizing the major shifts in the activities of the War Transportation Committee, it may be said that the initial emphasis, apart from the completion of its State-wide organization and the establishment of definite relations with Federal agencies, was placed in 1942 and 1943 upon the conservation of equipment through the development of the group-rides program, and the provision of additional transportation through the granting of petitions to operate charter buses. Once the group-rides program became stabilized and staggered hours had been worked out for those of the larger cities in need of them, the committee gave greater attention to the problems being raised by a shortage of mass transportation facilities. By October, 1942, rural traffic was approximately 50 per cent below normal, but in spite of increased city traffic, bus companies were forced by the Office of Defense Transportation in May, 1943, to cut service 20 per cent. This required considerable adjustment by individual companies which were glad to avail themselves of assistance from the committee. By October of 1943, the crisis in transportation was at hand. There was a manpower shortage of mechanics, parts men, and operating personnel, and a materials shortage of truck and bus tires and recapping rubber. By February, 1944, employment was at its peak and the committee confined its work almost entirely to maintaining existing services. In April, 1944, came the first case in which bus service had to replace private cars in transporting war workers. In May, 1944, an acute shortage of heavy-duty truck and bus tires developed. This continued throughout 1944, because synthetic rubber could not yet be successfully employed in their manufacture. Throughout the latter part of 1944 and the spring of 1945, provision of adequate transportation proved an increasingly complex problem, and in 1945, despite the approaching termination of the war in Europe, the committee found itself busier than ever. As an example, the number of charter bus permits reached its peak in the spring of 1945. Late in 1945, the situation began to improve with the decline in employment, the ending of both wars, and the consequent lessening of military needs. On September 15, 1945, it was announced that the War Transportation Committee would cease to exist October 31, 1945, and such functions as were proved to be of continuing necessity were at that time transferred to the Traffic Commission.

RAILROAD TRANSPORTATION

No account of transportation can omit the war record of the railroads. However, railroads are the most difficult of all agencies to consider on a purely state basis, since the activities of the major systems have always cut across state lines. It is possible, however, from information on the railways of the country as a whole, on the total operations of the six major systems serving the State, and from available figures applicable solely within New York State, to give an approximate picture of the prodigious feats of wartime transportation accomplished within the State by the roads which served it.

The peak year for wartime traffic for the country as a whole was 1944. In that year, 70 per cent of the country's commercial freight traffic was transported by rail. Of the more than 100 million tons of Army freight goods moved that year, the railroads carried 89 per cent. The comparison with 1918, the peak year of World War I, is striking. The 737.6 billion revenue ton miles handled in 1944 were almost twice the number carried in 1918, while the 95.57 billion revenue passenger miles were 2.2 times those of 1918.

Although in no other country were the railroads able to function during the war with less inconvenience to the traveling and shipping public, or to transport the same volume of military traffic at the same speed and for the same distances, these achievements were accomplished under severe handicaps. The railroads, as in the case of all other services, public or private, were caught in the usual wartime squeeze — scarcity of equipment, of materials, and of manpower, with which to perform more work than ever. Had there not taken place during the preceding twenty-five years a remarkable increase in efficiency, the necessary miracle would not have occurred. Actually, however, the efficiency in the handling of freight and passengers, developed since 1918, had been so extraordinary that in 1944 the record load of 738 billion revenue ton miles and 96 billion passenger miles was handled with one-third fewer locomotives, one-fourth fewer freight cars, and three-tenths fewer passenger cars than were used in 1918 to carry 405 billion revenue ton miles and 43 billion passenger miles. The number of employees in 1944 had likewise been reduced from the 1918 figure by nearly 25 per cent.

In some ways, the picture of railroad traffic in New York State during the war differed considerably from that just described for the country as a whole. The railroads of New York State had to handle an immense amount of traffic originating in the State and an even greater amount originating outside the State but passing through it to the Port of New York and to New England and Canada. To portray a valid picture of this traffic it becomes necessary to examine (1) the amount of revenue freight hauled, (2) the amount of passenger-miles hauled, (3) amounts of freight originating and terminating in the State, and (4) traffic density. The problem is complicated by the fact that railroads cross state lines and statistics for a single state are available only for freight originating and terminating. It is best presented by considering certain statistics of the six major railroads serving the State of New York, which together operated 78 per cent of all main track roadbed. These were, in order of the amount of road, second track, and all other main track operated in New York State, the New York Central (5006 miles), the Erie (1455 miles), the Delaware and Hudson (990 miles), the Lehigh Valley (833 miles), the Delaware, Lackawanna and Western (734 miles), and the Pennsylvania (618 miles). Of these roads, the Delaware and Hudson had the largest percentage of its track in New York State — approximately 80 per cent — while the Pennsylvania with only 4 per cent had the lowest. However, the New York Central with approximately 30 per cent of its entire system in New York State operated more track than the other five put together and figures for its operations were correspondingly significant.

The peak year for revenue freight hauled by these six roads was 1943. Between the years 1940 and 1943 the revenue freight hauled by them clearly paralleled the national increases for it rose 86.2 per cent (from the 1940 total of 87.46 billions of ton miles to the 1943 peak of 162.86 billions). Of these totals, the New York Central carried 29.30 and 54.94 billion ton-miles in 1940 and 1943 respectively, an increase of 87.5 per cent. These two figures — 86.2 per cent and 87.5 per cent — were approximately 10 per cent under the national increase of 94.8 per cent for the same period.

The percentage increase in the number of passengers carried by the same roads from 1940 to the peak year of 1944 was far greater. The 1944 figure of 24.21 billion passenger miles represented a 228 per cent increase over that of 1940. The increase on the New York Central lines for the same period was approximately 200 per cent. These two figures — 228 per cent and 200 per cent do not compare with the national increase, however, which was over 300 per cent. These figures on freight and passenger traffic

show the tremendous increase in railroad traffic caused by the war. Yet they do not indicate a true picture of traffic density. Nor, since they are based on figures for six interstate systems, do they show the situation within New York State itself. Yet they do indicate the differentials in the rate of expansion of freight and passenger traffic between roads operating in a relatively highly developed industrial area and roads operating throughout the rest of the country.

Although it is possible to get from certain figures a rough approximation of the amount of business done by each road in New York State, the method assumes a constant traffic density over the entire system, which would be only approximately valid. By using the number of miles of road operated in the State in relation to the total mileage of the system, and applying that percentage to the freight and passenger statistics available for the entire system, the results give a fair estimate of the business hauled in New York alone. Furthermore, assuming a constant traffic density on these systems, the percentage increases for freight and passenger movements, referred to above — 87.5 per cent and 228 per cent respectively — would also apply to rail transportation within New York State.

There is, however, a more accurate check on revenue freight hauled by the major roads to be secured from Schedule 541A of the Annual Reports of each road to the Interstate Commerce Commission. This schedule shows number of tons of revenue freight (carload traffic) originated and terminated annually by geographic areas. Figures applying to New York State alone are available and are broken down into five categories: (1) the products of agriculture, (2) animals and products, (3) products of mines, (4) products of forests, and (5) manufactures and miscellaneous. According to figures from this schedule, total freight originating in New York State on the six major railroads increased 51 per cent

(25.57 millions of tons, in 1940 as against 38.48 millions for the peak year of 1944). The increase for the New York Central for the same period was 42.8 per cent.

Total freight terminated in New York State on the same lines during the same period increased 39.1 per cent (from 52.91 million tons in 1940 to 73.66 million in 1944). The increase for the New York Central was 38.2 per cent. The percentage of increase from 1940-1944 for six major railroads in freight originated was 12 per cent greater than in freight terminated. However, during the same period, the volume of freight terminated in 1944 was 91 per cent larger than the volume of freight originated that year. Furthermore, whereas the absolute increase for the four years 1940-1944 in freight originated was approximately 13 million tons, the tonnage of freight terminated rose by 21 millions. This would indicate that normally, and to a similar extent even in time of war, owing to its large consumption of industrial raw materials, and to the proximity of the Port of New York, New York State received nearly twice as much freight as it originated.

Although, as indicated, not only was New York State with its great port a freight importing area, but the traffic density — the number of passengers and the amount of freight hauled per mile of road — on the six major roads serving the State, was greater than for the rest of the country. It is common knowledge that passenger traffic during the war expanded to enormous proportions. The 1944 peak of 95.57 billion passenger miles carried by the Class I railroads of the country represented a 302 per cent increase over 1940 figures. Although the increase in this category for the six major roads serving New York State was, as had been pointed out, only 228 per cent for the same period, their 1944 density was 117 per cent higher than the national average (916,177 passengers hauled per mile by the six roads, 421,407 per mile for the rest of the country).

Not only was passenger density thus more than twice as great in the area served by these roads as in the nation at large, but the same was also true for freight density. In 1944 Class I railroads of the country with an estimated total of 226,800 miles of road hauled a record total of 737.6 billion ton-miles of revenue freight, or 3.25 million tons of revenue freight per mile of road. In contrast, the six major roads of New York State, which in 1940 operated 78 per cent of all road lying within the borders of the State, and which in 1944 operated a total for their six systems of approximately 26,425 miles of road, hauled that same year a total of 159.46 billion ton-miles of revenue freight or 6.03 million tons of revenue freight per mile of road — a figure indicating a freight traffic density roughly 82 per cent higher than the national average.

While it would thus appear that in the peak year of the war passenger traffic was more than twice as heavy and freight traffic more than four-fifths again as great as in the rest of the country, this density was for the six systems as a whole, not for the part of each lying in New York State. Furthermore, the freight figures included both freight originated and freight terminated in all states touched by these systems, not simply New York State. Since, however, the figures for freight originated are available both for the entire country and for New York, a comparison is possible in this category.

In 1944, the national average for revenue freight originated for all Class I railroads amounted to 6,576 tons per mile of road. This was only 2.6 per cent more than the 6,401 tons of revenue freight per mile of road originated in New York State on the lines of the six major roads. Since New York, in 1944, originated only 2.6 per cent less revenue freight tonnage per mile of road than the average for all the roads of the country, that part of the 82 per cent greater freight density already indicated for the six roads as a whole, which could reasonably be ascribed to New York, could only be accounted for by freight terminated within its borders. It is reasonable to infer that within these borders not only was freight traffic heavier than the national average but that this fact was largely due to the great volume of freight pouring into the State from the Middle and Far West and from Canada.

The outstanding divisions of revenue freight originated and terminated which illustrated this situation, were (1) Animals and Products, (2) Products of Forests, and especially (3) Products of Mines. The ratio of freight originated to freight terminated varied by road and by year in these divisions from a ratio of 1 to 2 up to as high as 1 to 7. In the division of Manufactures and Miscellaneous, which included the entire war production tonnage hauled by rail, out of a total of 242 million tons hauled, there was less than a 16-million-ton difference in tonnage between the originated and terminated freight. The Lehigh Valley, Delaware, Lackawanna and Western, and Pennsylvania Railroads, which served the western and southern part of the State, picked up approximately 4 million more tons of Agricultural Products inside the State than they brought in from the outside, but the other three roads carried enough more to swing the balance in the other direction by 8.5 million tons out of a total of 74 million.

In the light of the above evidence it is no exaggeration to say that the railroads of the State of New York, represented in this discussion by the six roads considered, performed a remarkable feat during the war. Although they had to handle freight increases up to 85 per cent and passenger increases up to 225 per cent, the fact that the density of freight and passenger traffic on their lines was over 80 per cent and 115 per cent respectively higher than the national average meant that they were under far greater pressure. Because of their strategic position in relation to the Port of New York and to the principal manufacturing centers of the State it was absolutely essential that they carry on steadily at peak efficiency. The record of New York as the nation's number one state in the total of supply contracts let, and of the Port as the dispatching point for more than 25 per cent of the country's export tonnage, depended absolutely upon the performance of the railroads. No matter how difficult it is to assess, there is no question but that the contribution of the men and women who operated the roads during the war was a magnificent one.

WATER TRANSPORTATION

New York happens to be the only state to border both the Great Lakes and the Atlantic Ocean. Under these circumstances, it was fortunate that the terrain was such as to make it possible to link the bodies of water by a canal. Clinton's Ditch, as the original 355-mile Erie Canal was once called, together with its three modern branches, was in a strategic position to assume some of the burden placed by the war upon the railroads and the highways. It is somewhat surprising, therefore, to note that traffic on the New York system of barge canals declined during the war from 4.7 million net tons in 1940 to a low of 2.5 million in 1944. This showing was especially disappointing in view of the appropriation of funds by the 1943 Legislature to finance installation of control signals and dredging of the western section of the canal. Startling also is the fact that with the entrance of the United States into war, the direction of traffic changed suddenly from a westward flow of 58 per cent in 1941 to a westward flow of only 22 per cent in 1942.

The character of cargoes also changed during the war. For the six years, 1940 to 1945 inclusive, the ten principal commodities in order of tonnage shipped were:

1. Petroleum and its products
2. Grains
3. Miscellaneous ores (primarily bauxite)
4. Sulphur
5. Scrap iron
6. Pig iron and billets
7. Sand, stone, and gravel
8. Chemicals and drugs
9. Fertilizers
10. Pulpwood

The tonnage of all these items declined markedly with the exception of bauxite, sulphur, and pulpwood. Scrap iron and fertilizers held up fairly well and one smaller item, paper and paper products, actually showed considerable increase. The 50 per cent drop in tonnage carried on the canals from 1940 to 1944 was largely caused by reductions in available supplies of civilian commodities, primarily petroleum and grains, and lack of imports. A large percentage of petroleum and its products was reserved for the armed forces and the remainder rationed for civilian use.

Another factor in diminishing volume was the extraordinary reversal of traffic, a trend which reduced the cargoes available for westbound boats. Petroleum, sulphur, and molasses, which customarily came up the Atlantic coast by tanker, thence proceeding westward on the canal, were diverted from their usual routes by the activity of submarines and also by the shift of available tankers to the transatlantic shuttle. Due to wartime conditions, these products, normally shipped from Texas ports on the Gulf of Mexico to the key points on the eastern seaboard, were rerouted. Much of the petroleum was pumped through the "Big Inch" and "Little Big Inch" pipe lines from Texas to New York and Philadelphia; some moved in tank cars to the same destinations. Of receipts from these

"rush" movements, civilians received only a small proportion. The balance was transported by water up the Mississippi River, to Chicago and across the Lakes to Toledo and Buffalo.

Rerouting caused a number of other alterations in the methods of shipment. Many canal vessels carrying petroleum products proceeded to Toledo for their cargoes and this extra five hundred miles (Buffalo to Toledo and return) consumed more time en route as compared with cargoes loaded at Buffalo, causing a loss of at least two loaded trips per season for each vessel so engaged. Sulphur in prewar days moved along the same channels as petroleum products. With the reversed movement, it arrived by steamer at Buffalo, where part of it was transferred to canal vessels and the balance was stored on the dock, and ultimately shipped by rail. Other items which normally moved west, notably sugar and fertilizers, practically disappeared from the list. Of the larger items, scrap iron and bauxite, because of their origin within the State, alone clung to the westward route.

To this lack of westbound cargo, and the decline in total tonnage requiring shipment by water, must be added a third factor — a shortage of bottoms. From 1940 to 1944 the fleet of cargo-carrying boats operating on the canals declined from 578 to 226. Some of these were requisitioned by the government, and sent all over the world; some were sold to other interests and removed completely from canal service, while still others were operated in and around New York harbor, where the demand for boats was greater.

Thus, instead of expanding along with traffic on the railroads and highways, critical conditions on the Atlantic seaboard and the decline in the volume of civilian commodities normally carried by barge prevented shipping on the canal system from bearing its share of the steadily mounting burden of wartime

Table 15. Tonnage and Directional Flow on New York State's Canal System of Ten Most Important Wartime Commodities Listed in Order of 1940-1945 Tonnage (000 omitted)

Commodities	1940			1941			1942			1943			1944			1945			Grand Totals
	Total tonnage	East	West	Total tonnage	East	West	Total tonnage	East	West	Total tonnage	East	West	Total tonnage	East	West	Total tonnage	East	West	
Petroleum and its products	2,102	313	1,788	2,177	446	1,730	1,818	1,642	175	1,570	1,427	143	1,308	1,065	243	1,583	764	818	10,558
Grain	662	656	6	605	591	14	208	205	3	88	67	22	72	48	24	605	604	1	2,240
Misc. ores, primarily bauxite	.6	0	.6	85	0	85	311	0	311	524	0	524	437	0	437	236	0	236	1,599
Sulphur	179	0	179	42	8	34	251	251	0	185	185	0	221	221	0	144	144	0	1,022
Scrap iron	137	8	129	163	2	160	177	1	176	79	.2	79	115	0	115	63	0	63	734
Pig iron and billets	287	284	2	182	176	6	82	79	3	56	56	0	26	26	0	24	24	0	657
Chemicals and drugs	114	113	0	196	195	0	88	88	0	50	50	0	70	70	0	73	73	0	591
Sand, stone, and gravel	104	51	53	174	128	46	222	178	44	31	17	14	4	2	1	10	1	8	545
Fertilizers	274	15	259	112	17	95	20	2	18	16	3	13	7	3	4	8	3	5	437
Pulpwood	33	33	.3	8	8	0	0	0	0	65	65	0	72	72	0	104	104	0	282
Total	3,898	1,473	2,425	3,744	1,571	2,170	3,177	2,446	730	2,664	1,872	795	2,332	1,507	824	2,850	1,717	1,131	
Total all commodities	4,768	1,924	2,843	4,503	1,884	2,618	3,539	2,737	802	2,824	1,989	834	2,506	1,651	855	2,968	1,812	1,156	

traffic. The importance of the latter factor is clearly shown by the failure of canal traffic to increase in volume with the decline in the danger from submarines, but rather to increase in tonnage at a later date because of the return of petroleum and other products to the civilian market. The facilities of the canal, as well as of the Port of Albany with its 13 million bushel grain elevator and its access to ocean navigation by way of the twenty-seven-foot depth of the Hudson River, were available, but in World War II circumstances over which New York had no control prevented their being used to capacity.

Table 16. Billions of Passenger Miles Operated by the Six Principal Railroads of New York State, 1940-1945; Total Track Operated by these Roads in New York State, and the Percentage of New York State Track to the Total Track System of Each Road

Railroads	Percentages of N.Y.S. track to total track	Total N.Y.S. track* in 1940	Billions of Passenger Miles					
			1940	1941	1942	1943	1944	1945
New York Central......	30.5	(5,006)	3.04	3.50	5.45	8.50	9.29	8.78
Erie	38.0	(1,455)	.31	.32	.42	.59	.70	.69
Delaware & Hudson....	79.6	(990)	.04	.04	.07	.09	.11	.10
Lehigh Valley..........	42.5	(833)	.11	.11	.19	.39	.45	.41
Delaware, Lackawanna, and Western.........	44.0	(734)	.43	.43	.53	.62	.62	.63
Pennsylvania	4.0	(618)	3.44	4.32	7.82	12.16	13.04	12.79
TOTALS			7.37	8.72	14.48	22.35	24.21	23.40

Table 17. Billions of Ton Miles Operated by the Six Principal Railroads of New York State, 1940-1945; Total Track Operated by these Roads in New York State, and the Percentage of New York State Track to the Total Track System of Each Road

Railroads	Percentages of N.Y.S. track to total track	Total N.Y.S. track* in 1940	Billions of Ton Miles					
			1940	1941	1942	1943	1944	1945
New York Central......	30.5	(5,006)	29.30	36.37	49.51	54.94	51.92	44.36
Erie	38.0	(1,455)	8.05	10.05	12.64	15.96	15.00	13.05
Delaware & Hudson....	79.6	(990)	2.89	3.94	5.45	5.81	6.10	5.54
Lehigh Valley..........	42.5	(833)	4.12	5.20	7.28	8.49	9.38	6.88
Delaware, Lackawanna and Western.........	44.0	(734)	3.36	4.26	5.23	6.42	5.82	5.26
Pennsylvania	4.0	(618)	39.74	52.08	67.01	71.24	71.24	63.67
TOTALS			87.46	111.90	147.12	162.86	159.46	138.76

* This figure includes miles of road; miles of second track; miles of all other main tracks.

Table 18. New York State Gasoline Consumption, Annual Totals (Gallons)

Year	Taxable	Nontaxable	Total
1937	1,702,620,974	113,151,750	1,815,772,724
1938	1,684,671,746	117,543.905	1,802,215,651
1939	1,768,288,521	132,426,998	1,900,715,519
1940	1,836,976,683	133,567,895	1,970,544,578
1941	1,898,480,705	159,590,068	2,058,070,773
1942	1,426,298,861	168,795,432	1,595,094,293
1943	1,085,170,674	213,442,760	1,298,613,434
1944	1,147,989,807	255,435,396	1,403,425,203
1945	1,305,919,643	193,997,390	1,499,917,033

SOURCE: New York State Department of Taxation and Finance.

Table 19. New York State Annual Gasoline Sales to Federal, State and Municipal Governments (Gallons)

Year	State and Municipal	U. S. Gov't.
1940	57,514,254	13,589,469
1941	59,409,104	17,408,408
1942	49,895,787	35,781,211
1943	44,801,162	82,765,082
1944	45,624,450	110,376,680
1945	50,465,577	57,429,083

SOURCE: New York State Department of Taxation and Finance.

Table 20. Nonhighway Usage of Gasoline: Agriculture, Industry and Commerce, and Construction (Thousands of Gallons)

Usage, nonhighway	1940	1941	1942	1943	1944	1945
Agriculture	23,866	23,913	22,658	29,122	28,820	33,000 (Est.)
Industry ⎱ .... Commerce ⎰	16,854	25,274	30,352	43,359	52,410	
Construction	14,095	13,077	12,808	9,682	7,011	

SOURCE: Public Roads Administration, based on refunds.

CHAPTER EIGHT

Maintaining the Efficiency of the Individual

WHETHER in peace or war, the producing human being is dependent for the maintenance of his personal efficiency upon food, shelter, clothing, sleep, recreation, medical care and other more specialized goods and services. In times past, society has been indifferent to inequalities in the extent to which all individuals have shared in these goods and services. Distribution with a capital "D" is still a problem. However, some little time before the advent of World War II, American thinkers had begun to consider an inefficient individual as a wasted natural resource. The concept that social justice spelled economic efficiency had already appeared here and there above the intellectual horizon.

It took the depression of the 'thirties and the second World War, with its total involvement of the civilian population, to drive home the importance of using all the capacities of all the people all the working week. The need for adhering to this principle became increasingly obvious as the war progressed and shortages of all kinds made themselves felt. The efficiency of the producing unit on the home front became, therefore, a prime consideration, and the extent to which war could interfere with that efficiency became more and more evident as 1942 gave place to 1943, 1944 and 1945.

To maintain the strength and morale of individuals and their continued presence in the labor force or in the ranks of volunteers, various programs were set on foot through the medium of the State and local war council organization as well as by existing State departments. These included care for children of working mothers, the recruiting of nurses, additional efforts to maintain and improve the health of all citizens, a statewide program of physical fitness, increased attention to recreational opportunities and welfare problems, and a special interdepartmental program in the interests of youth.

THE CHILD CARE PROGRAM

During the war the State of New York developed a program of care for the children of working mothers which was unique in the nation. In no other state were funds appropriated for the direct operation of child care centers, and probably in no other state was the supervision and assistance to individual child care projects carried to such a high degree of competency. The New York State program had two phases, one for the preschool child and one for the school-age child. At its height, 266 centers for the care of children of working mothers were established in communities all over the state and kept open for the convenience of the mothers from nine to twelve hours a day. Overall direction lay with a State committee whose chairman had executive responsibilities and was referred to as director. At a later date, for purposes of policy determination the State War Council formed a subcommittee of its own on child care whose chairman was Speaker Oswald D. Heck.

Designed primarily to encourage women to enter war production, Federal and State appropriations for child care centers developed as a by-product an entirely new service for children of working mothers, a service which brought health, safety, and happiness to thousands of children while freeing mothers to make their contribution to the war effort. The gradual conversion of the Governor and War Council from hard-headed sponsors of strictly wartime measures, adopted solely to increase the labor force in areas of shortage, into increasingly sympathetic and understanding supporters of measures designed to alleviate one of the worst social problems of the machine age was a real romance of World War II. The New York State Child Care Program illustrated the fact that by forcing emergency relief measures the accentuated social problems of wartime could sometimes induce government to accept responsibility in a new field.

At its peak in July, 1945, the New York State Child Care Program reached 10,821 children enrolled in 161 nurseries and 105 play centers in the State, and included 12 per cent of the national total of children in child care centers. Approximately 40 per cent of these centers were located in New York City, and 60 per cent in 37 upstate communities and 12 migrant labor camps. Actually, since April, 1943, there were two programs: one, the upstate program, in receipt until February 28, 1946, of both Federal and State funds, while the other operated on State funds in such communities as were not eligible for Federal aid, i.e., New York City and a very few up-

State municipalities. Federal allocations for child care in New York State for the three-year period, 1943-1946, totaled $2,-957,398.74. State appropriations for the same period approximated $2,000,000.

For a number of reasons, at least a year was required to develop a smoothly running program in New York, since Federal policy could hardly be considered to have been stable until the spring of 1944. From the beginning two fundamental weaknesses plagued the Federal program under the Lanham Act, and for some time delayed full-scale operations. The first weakness was uncertain administration. Changes of Federal policy were frequent, and each change necessitated quick adjustments by sponsors of local child care projects. Also annoying was the length of time taken to process Federal applications. These frequently remained in Washington for months while the patience of communities slowly became exhausted. That a successful program was ever developed in the face of the complex Federal requirements is a tribute to the zeal of Federal, State, and local agency representatives determined to make the program work in the interest of the war effort and that of the mothers and children involved.

A second difficulty was that Federal aid for child care under the Lanham Act was given in the form of direct grants to local sponsors instead of as Federal grants-in-aid to the State. Although customary Federal procedure in other states tended to ignore the state authorities, such action was completely unsuited to New York with its highly developed wartime pattern of State and local relationships, and was consequently not permitted. In the field of child care the New York State War Council Committee on Child Care had been working since 1942 with the child care committees of the local war councils on community organization, while the State Departments of Education and Social Welfare had begun even earlier to perform valuable services in developing proper standards of care for children. Furthermore, the War Council was supporting its own child care program in New York City without Federal aid, and in 1943, to facilitate the smooth operation of the upstate program, voted to supplement Federal grants to communities in that area.

It was New York's activity in the field of child care that made it impossible for the Federal government to follow the methods used in other states, forcing instead the development of a coordinated plan, under which both Federal and state governments worked with the local sponsoring agencies. There were periods when this process did not run very smoothly, but on the whole the relationships between the Federal and state agencies were satisfactory. At the time when the state granted aid to projects then in receipt of Federal funds, state aid was essential to the operation of these projects. Two months later, however, the Federal government changed its financial policy and the projects could then have operated without state aid. The Federal government appreciated the fact that the state continued its contribution to the projects. It was distinctly fortunate when, in the summer of 1945, Federal support for child care projects was in some cases withdrawn that the New York State program, instead of disintegrating as did the child care programs in so many other states, actually proved flexible enough not only to carry the Federal burden whenever necessary, but even to continue its own expansion in New York City. In these respects New York's program was indeed unique.

The story of the creation of the New York State Child Care Program, like the stories of other war agencies, begins in the prewar era. Even in peacetime, society has its sore spots, and private and public welfare organizations in New York had struggled for over twenty-five years to cope with innumerable problems created by poor living conditions, broken homes,

and resulting neglect of dependent children. With the coming of the war, the situation deteriorated still further through disruption of the normal economy and widespread migration of families to war production centers — trends inevitably accompanied by dislocations of normal family life. Fathers left for the cities attracted by the high wages available in war industries; mothers were tempted, or forced, into industry. When every adult is either in the armed forces or away in a war plant, teen-age children suddenly inherit great freedom of operation with but slight restraint from their own immature personal judgment. Teachers and playground directors who would normally supply services of an educational and character-building nature are no longer at hand. War brings a lowering of standards, of safeguards, and of supervision and eliminates many wholesome features of normal family life and stable community atmosphere.

Since the First World War, the State Departments of Education and Social Welfare have maintained bureaus concerned with the operation of nursery schools, day nurseries, and foster homes for children whose home life has been dislocated or destroyed. For twenty-five years churches and private and public welfare agencies have shown concern over the employment in industry of mothers with young children; in community planning they have opposed such employment practices. Similar opposition was expressed as early as 1941 by the War Manpower Commission, when it declared that the employment of women with small children should be encouraged only in such war production centers as had exploited and exhausted all other sources of labor. As late as 1942, the opposition to the employment of women with young children was so strong that communities tended to shut their eyes to the fact that mothers actually were entering industry and that children actually were being neglected. However, in the latter part of 1942, in the face of evidence which could no longer be ignored, this ostrichlike attitude gradually broke down and communities which previously had taken the wishful position that since women with children should not work, therefore there was no child care problem, began to face the fact that an emergency existed and that care must be provided for the children of working mothers.

The evidence was undeniable. In the State of New York during the first six months of 1942 the Board of Social Welfare recorded that in thirteen upstate counties marked by concentrations of war industries, delinquency increased by 22 per cent, child neglect increased by 39 per cent, and first admission of children to foster care increased by 33 per cent. Bare figures should not be relied upon too heavily, but these did indicate a developing wartime problem which at first only the professional private and public welfare agencies were able to recognize.

The reasons for this wartime increase in the need for child care were numerous. Women were urgently needed in industry and in various essential civilian services. In 1942 the War Manpower Commission estimated that within a year a quarter of a million women would be needed for new positions in the State's war industries. Already in those counties affected by war production between four and five hundred thousand women were working outside their homes at war jobs and at essential civilian industries. The war industries could use women, and women in turn needed money. In 1942 mothers as well as fathers were taking advantage of high wages in war industries to increase family earnings and build future economic security. One result of this situation, the figures of the Commission indicated, would be at least 57,000 children between the ages of five and fourteen years whose mothers were working in war industries. In quite another category, however, from the standpoint of these government agencies interested solely in manpower problems, were numbers of children whose need for out-of-school care arose not because their mothers were working, but because war had brought disruption to their families and communities. The programs of the Federal Works Progress Administration and of the Federal Works Agency were designed to provide additional manpower rather than child welfare. Only later, when mothers became "wives of servicemen," and they, or the guardians of their children, became incapacitated or were otherwise unable to care for them, did State rules permit the entry of children of servicemen into the centers. Private and State organizations in New York, however, groups such as the local Welfare Societies and the Bureau of Child Care, Development and Protection of the Department of Education and the Bureau of Child Welfare of the Department of Social Welfare, were interested in the care of children generally.

Organizations in the Field of Child Care Prior to October, 1942. The first attempt to meet the State's wartime problem of child care was made in September, 1941, three months before Pearl Harbor, when the representatives of the State Departments of Education, Health, and Social Welfare approached Mrs. Pennock, State Director of Civilian Mobilization, with the suggestion that her office sponsor an informal State Child Care, Development, and Protection Committee. Such an interdepartmental committee was formed and subsequently enlarged to include also representatives from the Departments of Mental Hygiene and Labor, and from the College of Home Economics at Cornell. At first the connection between this committee and the State War Council was only through its informal liaison with Mrs. Pennock's organization, but by a memorandum of June 23, 1942, it was placed under her direction formally and made immediately responsible to the Council.

The principal functions of this committee were to supply encouragement to local war councils in the creation of local child care committees, and to aid them in the development of community programs for handling child care problems.[1] Nursery schools, day nurseries, housekeeping services, foster day care, aid-to-dependent-children programs, and the recreational and leisure-time programs of the community were all to be utilized. When in May, 1942, through interpretations of the Lanham Act Federal funds became available in defense areas to provide day care facilities for the children of working mothers, the State committee issued a memorandum setting forth the kinds of projects eligible, the methods for determining needs, and the procedure to be followed in applying for funds. Field consultants for this expansion, and in fact the supervising force for the entire State program of child care, were supplied by drafting into service the field staffs of special bureaus within the Departments of Education and of Social Welfare, or, in the case of the former's Bureau of Child Development, payment by the State War Council during the summer of 1942 of extra staff.

As preliminary moves, between January and October of 1942, the State Child Care Committee effected the training of approximately three thousand volunteer child care aides and also prepared and circulated widely eight bulletins dealing with various aspects of the program. By September, 1947, almost half of the local war councils had appointed committees on child care. These were composed largely of representatives of such groups in the community as were interested either in children or in manpower problems, the boards of education, the official

and private welfare and health agencies, and the churches, as well as industries, labor organizations, the United States Employment Service, and the War Manpower Commission. This early recognition of the need in time of war for community agencies to protect children, especially the children of working mothers, was supported by publicity and promotion carried on through the Department of Education, the Department of Social Welfare, and the Office of Civilian Mobilization. The way was thus paved for the subsequent development of a successful program for child care in New York State.

While New York State on its own initiative was thus moving into the child care field, the WPA Nursery School Program and the Child Care Program announced under the Lanham Act were developing uncertainties. The officials in charge of these showed little enthusiasm for the unfolding state programs. Lack of harmony between Federal and state programs and inadequate coordination between the Federal organizations themselves created a confused situation in which for six months little was accomplished. The WPA Nursery School Program, originally conceived in 1933 primarily as a project to provide employment for needy teachers, worked largely with the children of relief clients. As war reduced the relief load, by autumn of 1942 many nurseries were closed. Congress accordingly expanded the scope of the remaining projects and in 1942 earmarked 6 million dollars of WPA funds for the employment of nonrelief personnel to provide facilities for children of working mothers. Such personnel not being available in New York State for work with WPA projects, the program proved unworkable. Furthermore, in 1941, WPA was absorbed by the Federal Works Agency. In spite of the previously mentioned Congressional expansion of the WPA program, the FWA began itself, through the expanded interpretation of

---

[1] The War Emergency Act was amended by Chap. 196 of the Laws of 1943 to authorize local war councils to appropriate funds for child care.

the Lanham Act, to offer grants for the establishment of child care centers for children of working mothers. This was done because the WPA, despite Congressional support, could not develop an expanded program because of the prejudices which had grown up against it during the depression. However, the conditions of deficit financing under which these new Lanham Act grants were first offered were not acceptable to the municipalities of New York State. Consequently, until late December, 1942, when the Federal Works Agency changed its policy, the over-all result was a general stalemate achieving complete frustration.

The Creation of the Official State Committee on Child Care, Development, and Protection. Unfortunately, difficulties were by no means a Federal monopoly. During 1942 differences within the State Committee on Child Care had been aired in the public press. Disagreement concerned the relative emphasis to be placed upon nursery schools and day nurseries. By the end of the summer, it was felt that the Committee did not sufficiently represent the private charities interested in child care problems. Furthermore, administrative difficulties arose in coordinating the efforts of organizations unable to agree either on aims or on methods. Accordingly, after several discussions, the War Council decided to abolish the Committee on Child Care, Development, and Protection, and to create in its place under the name of "The State Committee on Child Care, Development, and Protection" an advisory committee whose members should be appointed by the Governor, and whose chairman should be a paid employee of the War Council. Miss Elsie M. Bond, an assistant secretary of the State Charities Aid Association, was appointed chairman, with direct authority over all departments and agencies involved.

Miss Bond brought to her task valuable experience, having aided in the organization of child care facilities in various parts of Europe after the First World War and having been connected with the Charities Aid Association in dealing with legislative matters in Albany. The new committee included representatives of the State agencies on the former committee, and in addition others from organized labor and from private charitable groups. While carefully refraining from direct operation of centers, it assumed responsibility for developing the child care committees of the local war councils, and for assisting them both to make such surveys as were necessary to determine the need for child care facilities, and to formulate community plans for providing the equipment and services needed. Aid was also supplied in making out applications for Federal funds under the Lanham Act and later on, as will be seen, for State funds. An independent office was established with field and clerical staff of its own.

In first reporting to the War Council, December 15, 1942, Miss Bond took note of the current situation. Industries were becoming impatient at the failure of communities to provide child care centers; existing child care facilities were being fully utilized, but certain women were still being forced to leave the labor force, or to lose time from work, because they could find no way to provide for the care of their children; because married women, though anxious to work, could not arrange for care of their children, defense training schools were experiencing increasing difficulty in securing women to fill their classes; large numbers of children were being left to shift for themselves with door keys tied around their necks, or with lunches tied to the front doors of their homes, or under the purely nominal supervision of neighbors. Nevertheless, widespread recruiting of women for industry was at that very time under way, and within the next few months the drive promised to become even more intensive. In short, there was an immediate need for additional facilities and for a continuing extension of the Child Care Program. Federal aid under the Lanham Act was to be secured neither easily nor quickly — it had taken six months for the city of Lockport to receive the only Federal funds to be granted in New York State up to December 15 — and it appeared doubtful whether under these circumstances Federal aid could ever be made readily available.

Short of financial assistance from the State, which the Council was not yet willing to consider, the only thing possible was to increase the staff of the State Child Care Committee sufficiently to allow it to provide direct service to the child care committees of the local war councils. If these were to establish active centers, they would need aid and guidance from the State in order to meet the requirements of the Federal government. Although it was willing to provide assistance of this sort to those child care committees located in war impact areas, the War Council was not willing that Miss Bond's committee should cover the entire State regardless of the degree of urgency for its services. The Council did, however, authorize all possible efforts to get the Federal government to make grants under the Lanham Act direct to New York State for allocation by the War Council to individual child care projects. Unfortunately, these efforts failed completely.

The War Council Undertakes the Financing of Child Care Projects. On December 30, 1942, the Federal Works Agency, recognizing the difficulties attendant upon its program of deficit financing, changed its policy and announced Lanham Act grants for nursery schools and other child care facilities in war impact areas on a basis of 100 per cent Federal contribution for all costs not met by fees and local contributions. The WPA was to continue to finance and expand its nursery schools upstate provided the local sponsoring agency applied for Lan-

ham Act funds. Once such funds were made available, WPA was to withdraw. Since, however, New York City was classified as an area of labor surplus, Lanham Act funds were not available for the continuation of WPA nurseries or for new child care centers for that area. On the basis of the new dispensation, a large majority of the upstate communities having WPA nursery schools applied for grants, filling out elaborate application forms with the help of the State Department of Education and of the State Child Care Committee.

Suddenly, on February 13, 1943, the Federal Works Agency again changed its policy. Instead of a Federal grant of 100 per cent for the costs of operation, other than those met by fees and contributions, the local sponsor was itself required to meet 50 per cent of these costs from fees and local contributions, although rent, equipment, and renovation of buildings still remained a 100 per cent charge on Federal funds. The status of the New York State applications for Lanham Act funds and months of work by public-spirited citizens were thus endangered. At the request of the Federal Works Agency, applications from New York State were nevertheless filed without change, but action on them was delayed, with no satisfactory explanations, until April. Although in April Federal funds were finally forthcoming, the result of the new policy was to give all child care centers outside New York City a distinctly precarious financial structure. In order to cover 50 per cent of the operating costs, local committees frequently set fees so high that mothers could not afford to send their children to the centers. Consequently, these centers were often only partially filled and some, in spite of Federal grants received, did not open at all.

It was the shift in Federal Works Agency policy on Lanham Act grants that brought about New York State's direct participation in the child care program. Ever since his assumption of office on January 1, Governor Dewey had been receiving complaints regarding the lack of facilities for children of working mothers in war impact areas. Owing to possible discontinuance of the WPA program in New York City, pressure upon the State for action to improve the situation in the metropolitan area increased steadily. On February 5, the War Plans Coordinator, Lieutenant Governor Wallace, requested the local war councils to make a survey of the number of mothers employed in war work, and of the precise nature of the emergency in their respective regions. A few days later, in a memorandum to the Governor, the chairman of the State Child Care Committee called attention to the fact that probably Federal funds under the Lanham Act would not be available for the thirty-five communities whose applications were already on file in Washington, and that consequently in the absence of Federal support and in order to avoid criticism, the State itself might have to provide care. She suggested that an appropriation of 5 million dollars for the administration of child care centers be divided equally between New York City and the upstate area.

The change in the Federal Works Agency policy on Lanham Act funds and the uncertainty as to whether the localities which had applied for Federal grants for 100 per cent of their operating costs would be able to begin operations if only 50 per cent of the costs were provided, together with the prospect that WPA nursery schools would be closed by the first of May, convinced the Governor that State action was necessary to provide a consistent and stable plan. On March 10, he recommended to the State War Council a detailed program to meet the emergency and declared that New York could no longer afford to wait upon Washington's indecision, but must join with the localities and with the parents of the children in assuming responsibility for a wartime program of child care. The

Governor's recommendations, as approved by the Council, were introduced in the Legislature by Abbott Low Moffat and passed as Chapter 196 of the Laws of 1943. The law provided for an appropriation to the War Council of 2.5 million dollars and for a State-wide program of day care for the children of mothers engaged in war work as defined by Section 79 of the War Emergency Act. This definition was extremely broad and included:

the manufacture, production and distribution of articles, materials, and supplies for war on or for contracts for the United States Army or Navy, and for any other agency of the United States, or for any associated power of the United States . . . or services performed in connection with any other occupation, activity or employment essential to the effective prosecution of the war or necessary to promote and protect the public health and welfare, and the safety and security of the people of the state.

In line with the then current thinking of the Council, responsibility for financing this program was recommended to be divided equally among the State, the municipalities, and the parents. On March 30, 1943, the War Council allocated the sum of 1 million dollars to meet the State's one-third share of the cost of operating child care centers. Local war councils, municipalities, and school districts were authorized by Chapter 196 to administer child care and the latter two were authorized to appropriate funds for the purpose. Subsequently on May 4, 1944, by Order 16 of the War Council it also became permissible for school districts to charge fees for the maintenance of child care facilities.

The operation of the program was divided as a matter of actual practice between New York City and the upstate areas which the War Manpower Commission had certified as war-impacted, or areas of manpower shortage. Originally, however, by War Council Resolution 282, the financial responsibility of the

State was carefully limited. State aid was to go only to communities not eligible under the Lanham Act for Federal funds, and every eligible project was required by the War Council to "qualify and apply." Since Federal funds were subsequently granted to all upstate communities which qualified and applied, actually, prior to October 1, 1943, State aid was made available only to New York City.

It was under these arrangements that local agencies acted either as sponsors or operators, or as both sponsors and operators, of child care projects. Counties, cities, towns, villages, local war councils, and school districts were eligible for both Federal and State aid. Private corporations were eligible for Federal aid but not for State aid because under the State constitution State funds cannot be granted to private corporations. In some instances municipalities and war councils acted as sponsors of a project and delegated responsibility for operation to a child care committee of a local war council or a private social welfare corporation. The State Education Department, under an order of the War Council, sponsored and operated projects in two upstate communities. In New York City the Mayor's Committee on Wartime Care of Children acted as the sponsor (or applicant for State aid) with responsibility for operation delegated to various agencies.

Administrative Evolution. The administration of the program was entrusted to the Executive Secretary of the War Council, and in early days innumerable terms and conditions were attached to grants of State funds. Under the first child care rules, dated April 28, 1943, upon approval of municipal authorities applications were to be filed with the Executive Secretary by local war councils, which were required to certify that there was need for the centers. The municipalities were to certify that two-thirds of the costs would be borne locally. All projects

had to qualify under the Lanham Act if they could do so. Plans for such centers as were to be conducted in public schools were to be approved by the State Education Department, while all others were to be approved by the State Department of Social Welfare. Centers were to be supervised by the State agency responsible for approval.

The original program was intended not to place the War Council in the role of Santa Claus, but was carefully predicated upon the assumption that State aid ought to be necessary only in communities where Federal aid was not available. The War Council had been careful to place upon its own grants every reasonable restriction, and obviously was entering the Child Care Program with caution. The story of the expansion of this program in the State of New York is the story of an increasing appreciation by the Council of the extensive character of the State's responsibility under wartime conditions for the care of children of working mothers. That this evolution was not planned or foreseen, but took place under the logic of circumstances, does not detract from the credit due the War Council for seeing the problem through even into the period of reconversion.

Having once embarked upon a program of child care, the War Council became immediately concerned with the administrative details incident to its successful operation. The public had to be informed, and the Executive Secretary was soon involved in extended interpretations of the Moffat Act and in patient explanations of the rules laid down in April by the War Council. Question after question arose for determination with regard to matters of eligibility for child care, details of methods of financing the projects, and restrictions placed upon the grants. Gradually, almost imperceptibly, the process of interpretation led to liberalization of the rules in the interest of easier and quicker administration. Signs appeared early that several of the original provisions might be too severe. Where wages were low, parents were frequently not able to pay one-third of the cost of a project, so it was agreed to waive that requirement and to recommend simply that two-thirds of the cost come from the total of local contributions and parent's fees. Furthermore, the two-thirds guarantee of costs could not always be enforced since certain cities claimed they could not constitutionally underwrite deficits in a fashion that would amount to pledging their credit.

The location of child care projects became a matter of considerable importance shortly after the passage of the Moffat Bill. Many of the WPA nursery projects had been situated in school buildings, but the question arose as to whether the maintenance of a child care project in a religious school, even though operating outside school hours, would be a violation of Section 4 of Article 2 of the New York State Constitution. On May 12 the Attorney General addressed to the State War Council an opinion as to the application of Chapter 196 of the Laws of 1943, stating that there was "no prohibition against the granting of funds for child care aid in conformity with Chapter 196 of the Laws of 1943, to any organization, public or private, social or charitable, *providing* the child care project was not conducted or maintained in the same structure, building or edifice as any school or institution of learning wholly or in part under the control of or direction of any religious denomination." This decision was not clearly understood, and subsequently a clarification statement for the press, phrased in more affirmative style, proved satisfactory.

In July, 1943, attention was called by the Commissioner of Education to the fact that the defeat of the Thomas Bill in Congress had left unchanged the curious situation upstate, an arrangement under which the State of New York was involved in the Child Care Program

merely as a minor consultant with Federal control over the projects steadily increasing as a result of local financial difficulties. This was partially remedied in September by the decision of the War Council to supplement Federal grants up to 15 per cent of the costs of operation. The result was that from that time forward the upstate projects were in a position to meet their expenses, and the State had a voice in the program of each center.

In the spring of 1944 it was again found essential to liberalize the child care regulations. Since State aid was now so generally available, the requirement that to receive State grants applicants must be declared ineligible for Lanham Act funds had become obsolete and was abolished. Certification of need by the local war council was henceforth considered unnecessary. The matter of Federal control, however, still plagued the Council, and to prevent the Federal Works Agency from continuing to ignore the State Child Care Committee, the War Council amended Order 16 on May 4, so that no agency in the State could operate child care centers without first securing approval from the State Committee on Child Care and from either the Education Department or the Department of Social Welfare. This order effectively strengthened the State's authority.

It was likewise at the May 4th meeting that certain financial arrangements were radically altered. Instead of paying only on the basis of a percentage of the total expenditures of the up-State project, as had been agreed in September of 1943, henceforth payment might, in the alternative, be made on a per diem basis. This latter alternative greatly reduced the amount of bookkeeping involved and increased the speed at which payment could be made. Per diem rates that the state would pay for nursery-school children were set between twenty-three cents and twenty-five cents, and for school-age children between fifteen cents and seventeen cents. Until the fall of 1945, when Speaker Heck, as chairman, was authorized to approve applications, all per diem or 15 per cent grants were handled by the subcommittee of the War Council. Attendance records were, in the interest of speed, kept and submitted for monthly audits to the staff of the State Child Care Committee, which was thus able to do without the services of a bookkeeper. Furthermore, if desired by the project, State reimbursement was to be payable monthly, and, pending applications for Federal funds, State grants were to be made available in order to avoid delay in opening new centers.

From 1943 until the end of 1944, by which time regulations had been pretty well worked out, the process of evolution was essentially one of cutting unnecessary red tape without at the same time losing control of operations. That this was substantially accomplished within two years' time is a credit to the wisdom and industry of the big three in the Child Care Program — the Executive Secretary of the War Council, the Chairman of the War Council Subcommittee on Child Care, and the Director of Child Care.

Expansion of the State's Responsibility for Child Care. Sheer administration, however, was perhaps the least of the worries of the War Council. Underlying every discussion of the Child Care Program was the question of the legitimate extent of the State's responsibility. The fundamental purpose of the program was obvious. There was a war to be won. A direct way to help with the war effort, and the fundamental purpose which throughout the emergency underlay the New York State Child Care Program, was to supply additional manpower for the war industries of the State. The social implications of child care, though obvious, were secondary. As one of the Council members so clearly phrased it during one of the discussions, "Is this a war woman-power problem, or is this a State conscience problem for its children? Which department should it be in? Is it essentially a war man-power or woman-power problem?" To which the Governor replied in part, "It is a real woman-power business. I think that was the unanimous opinion when we launched it and there has been no change from that."

Actually, before the end of the war, it became both, as the question of providing necessary social services to enable breadwinners to work and at the same time to make adequate provision for the care of their children had arisen for serious consideration. Women with children were not encouraged at any time to enter industry except in areas where there was a manpower shortage. At first, in these critical areas it was also believed fair to expect one-third of the costs to be paid by working parents who had children in child care centers. Nor was it considered to be the State's responsibility to extend financial aid to those projects which in 1943 were in receipt of Lanham Act funds. Only when the War Council learned from its Child Care Committee that the federally supported projects were not being completely utilized did the conviction begin to develop that the State had a general over-all responsibility for the successful operation of all projects within its borders, and that through the War Council's Child Care Committee methods should be devised to expand the program where it was needed to fulfill the basic responsibility of the State for furnishing manpower to its war industries.

This assumption on the part of the State War Council of responsibility for the successful operation of all projects was induced in part by a report prepared in July, 1943, by the State Child Care Committee and submitted to the War Council for consideration, together with comments by Commissioner Stoddard of the Education Department. According to this report, all but a few of the twenty-two centers in upstate New York were incurring deficits, the average deficit being 10 per cent. Fear of such deficits was having a paralyzing effect upon the expansion of the program. In an attempt to collect the 50 per cent of the costs not provided by the Federal government, the communities had based their fees upon consideration of the average deficit rather than upon what parents could reasonably bear under prevailing wages. The result was fees much too high for the majority of working mothers. To avoid possible deficits, many of the centers for which Federal funds had already been granted were not being opened, and those that were opened provided care for considerably less than half the number of members originally anticipated. With the exception of Rochester, Norwich, and a few other places, efforts to raise locally funds needed to supplement fees had proved a failure. Feeling that, if needed, State funds already appropriated for child care should be used to supplement Federal funds, industrialists were loath to raise funds to finance deficits. There was no doubt in their minds as to where the responsibility of the State lay.

Furthermore, criticism of the use of State funds solely in New York City, which was not strictly a war impact area, was increasing as grants were denied to war impact areas financially hard pressed to provide other emergency services needed. Community Chests were either unable or unwilling to supplement projects operated by governmental agencies, and municipalities and boards of education, whether financially able or not, felt that the costs of these emergency services should be borne by the Federal and State governments, the more especially since in the case of New York the Legislature specifically appropriated funds for child care. Commissioner Stoddard further stated that since the War Council ruling prevented the utilization of State funds on projects already in receipt of Federal grants, cities could not make up their deficits by calling for State appro-

priations. The result was that in a program whose total cost was approaching 2 million dollars, the State's share up to this time had been negligible. Consequently, in order to remove the difficulties in financing which were preventing effective operation of the Federal Child Care Program, the State Child Care Committee recommended:

1. That the rules governing state grants for child care be amended so as to permit state grants for such part of the local share of costs of child care projects receiving federal funds as cannot be met by revenue from fees paid by parents and local contributions and appropriations, but not exceeding 20 per cent of the operating costs of any project

2. That the Executive Secretary of the War Council be authorized to allocate state funds to meet such deficits upon receipt of an application from the Board of Education, or the governing board of county, city, town or village in which a welfare child care project is operating, providing the agency operating the project is eligible to receive state funds

3. That state grants to meet deficits be made with the understanding that if in subsequent quarter or quarters, the revenue from fees exceeds the costs of the project, refunds shall be made to the state up to the amount previously granted by the state to meet the deficit of the project.

Should the State's financial responsibility be extended? If fees were to be lowered sufficiently to fill the projects to capacity, the State must underwrite deficits. The War Council felt this decision was too great to be made without further study on its own part. Where did the matter of responsibility lie? Did it belong to the Federal government, to the State, to the community, to industrial plants, to the mothers, or to some combination of these? What fees were fair? Those which would meet the deficits, or those the mothers could afford to pay? What share could the comunity legitimately be expected to provide? What were the average costs of an efficiently run program? Should they be the same everywhere, or was it natural that they should vary? Faced by a prediction that **three** hundred thousand more women would be added to the employment rolls of the State within the next seven months, to prepare the matter for the consideration of the Council the Governor appointed a subcommittee with Speaker Heck as chairman, and as members Mrs. Gannett, Messrs. Hollander, Morgan, Riordan, and Schoellkopf. The first report of this subcommittee on Child Care was considered in September, 1943. The meeting was a crucial point in the entire New York Child Care Program, and the chairman of the committee was somewhat reluctant to introduce the subject.

"Governor," he said, "may I report that in the vernacular a wonderful apple was handed to me when I was made chairman of this committee? We have had the time of our lives. We have been besieged by people, particularly in the western part of the state, who want aid and assistance."

Aided by a statistician, the committee had visited a number of the projects and gathered information as to costs, fees, wages of working mothers, the average number of children per mother attending the centers. The labor turnover and the percentage of employees of different companies who used child care centers were checked. The entire investigation was for the purpose of answering but one question: Should the State pay one-sixth of the operating costs of projects where 50 per cent was paid by the government?

At the end of the report, which was jammed with statistics but carried no recommendations, discussion became general. Beyond doubt, the Council felt the urgency of the occasion. A statement by Major General Philip Fleming, Federal Works Administrator in charge of child care projects under the Lanham Act, was quoted to the effect that the Federal government would have to tighten up on its grants unless the projects were used to capacity. Apparently, however, capacity attendance would not be possible until fees could be brought low enough to

allow more mothers to take advantage of the centers. If this were not done, possibly Federal funds might be withdrawn. Speaking for the War Manpower Commission, Mrs. Rosenberg informed the Council at this point that, with peak employment approaching, the commission had now reversed its position and was encouraging women with small children to go into employment in places where, as in Lockport, Niagara, Buffalo, and Tonawanda, the labor supply was especially tight. Furthermore, she pointed out that in some companies the labor turnover for women with children was as high as 100 per cent. The reasons? Women workers thought that they were neglecting their children, and that neglect was resulting in impaired health and welfare. When questioned as to why they did not avail themselves of the day care centers, mothers pointed out that transportation facilities were difficult and the centers located far from their homes; some were afraid their children would catch diseases; others were earning such low salaries that they could not afford to pay the fees, and when they did work the additional expense of marketing at bad hours was such as to render employment hardly renumerative. Despite all this, with labor shortages widespread in the State and peak employment anticipated within three to six months, there seemed to be only one answer: a wider distribution of child care centers and lower costs to mothers.

Because of the variation in costs from project to project, the decision to underwrite deficits up to 15 per cent of the operating expenses of all projects in receipt of Lanham Act funds would make necessary close investigation by the State Child Care Committee of each upstate center. The administration of the grants would likewise involve a terrific amount of detailed supervision. A single formula simply was not adequate to cover the situation. Nevertheless, despite this fact, under the leadership of the Governor the

War Council took the fatal step and adopted Resolution 333 authorizing 15 per cent State aid to projects in receipt of Federal funds. The chairman of the Sub-committee on Child Care promised to draw up a feasible plan for administering the grants and to set up certain standards and regulations as guides for the executive secretary in making allocations. No change took place, at this time, in the rules of April 28, 1943.

If the State had a responsibility to spend its own money in the interests of child care centers, it likewise had an equal responsibility to see that the funds were carefully managed. Good financial management was related to the question of fees, to that of costs, and to the extent and manner of State grants. As circumstances were to prove, those fees were fair which mothers could afford to pay. Capacity to pay depended upon wages. Unfortunately again for the peace of mind of the Council, wages varied widely from community to community and from industry to industry. Here also as in the case of the State's contribution to each child care project, the fees charged by each center had to be determined in relation to local conditions. There just did not seem to be any general rule which could be applied outside of the old principle of charging what the traffic would bear. Since the purpose was to fill the centers, whatever fees proved acceptable would have to be maintained, and those fees which by experience proved too high would have to be lowered. The average fee was finally fixed at between $2.50 and $4.00 per week.

The matter of costs was one of the most difficult of all problems to get at, as here again there was a wide variation from community to.community. In the beginning, both the State Child Care Committee and the Federal government were without experience in estimating costs, and original figures were consequently entirely theoretical. In New York City where State aid alone was furnished,

there was a maximum of $30 per month per child in the estimated budgets for the first year of operation. This was an unwritten policy adopted by the War Council. In the upstate Federal program, where the projects were considered part of the local economic and social pattern, the local scale of salaries prevailed and contributions varied widely. Variation was thus the rule, and a process of experimentation and mutual agreement became a permanent feature of the program. With rising prices and a tightening labor market, the cost of supplies and the scale of salaries went up. When in the fall of 1943 the attitude of the Federal government on budgetary items became extremely liberal, it proved virtually impossible for the State Child Care Committee to carry through its policy of inducing the localities to meet as large a share of the cost as possible themselves. Generally speaking, depending upon the community's standard of living, the extent of local contributions toward the expenses of operation, and the scale of fixed costs maintained by the authorities in charge of the buildings and equipment, per capita costs varied from $30 to over $50 per month.

Because costs varied so widely and because the War Council contemplated the support of Lanham Act projects, the State Child Care Committee was called upon constantly to furnish facts and figures. Long and exhausting were the discussions on costs. No general principle proved acceptable, with the result that it was finally agreed that the State Child Care Committee should scrutinize carefully each individual budget, and reach a decision as to the State's proper share of the expenses based upon local conditions. By January, 1944, all applications in which 15 per cent of State aid was involved had been individually approved. The chairman of the Child Care Committee had gone over these budgets and proved to the satisfaction of the members of the War Council subcommittee "that she knew what she was doing," and that the State's blanket percentage guarantee of the costs did not mean the underwriting of bad management. One member of the subcommittee in particular, who had begun by being quite skeptical of this new expansion of the State's responsibility, became enthusiastic enough to approve heartily a raise in salary for the chairman of the State Child Care Committee, who, on the same occasion, was given credit by another member for having straightened out "the most difficult program in the War Council."

Financial arrangements, however, did not have a chance to crystallize at this point, as the induction of large numbers of fathers, which began late in 1943, brought additional applications for child care centers. By the spring of 1944, new difficulties confronted the executive secretary of the Council and once more extension of State support seemed to be necessary. In certain upstate areas, not designated by the War Manpower Commission as areas of labor shortage, the Federal Works Agency had refused to grant Lanham Act funds. There were some communities, however, in which child care centers were badly needed, that for this reason were unable to establish them even though the centers had received the specific approval of the War Manpower Commission. To correct this situation, and to enable the State to make grants to projects pending receipt of Federal funds, the Council on May 4, 1944, approved a resolution granting State funds in excess of one-third of the cost of operations to projects not in receipt of Lanham Act funds. These cases were extraordinary and were individually considered by the subcommittee.

Until the fall of 1944 all New York City projects were lumped together and their costs considered in the aggregate. In exceptional cases, to permit the expansion of the New York City program where necessary, or the establishment of

essential projects upstate, a second resolution granted $100,000 to be used for rent, repairs, and equipment. The reason for this step, which extended State support to a field other than operating costs, lay principally in the exhaustion of the supply of buildings, equipment, and funds, with which New York's social agencies contributed to the operation of centers, thereby supplementing payments by parents. Over thirty neighborhoods, which were not in a position to open centers without grants for rent, equipment, and repairs, had applied to the War Council for assistance. Factors in this decision were information and recommendations from the State Child Care Committee and the recommendations of the chairman of the subcommittee and of the Regional Director of the War Manpower Commission.

At the same time, expenditures were also authorized for a third category. We have mentioned (1) operating costs, and (2) rent, equipment, and repairs. In anticipation of the drafting of a large number of fathers, an appropriation of $50,000 was approved to be used for exploratory research and practical experiments in several centers of the State in connection with the development of foster day care primarily for children under two years of age. The policy of extensive drafting of fathers was not pursued, however, and the anticipated need for the program was less than expected. It was discovered, however, that it was easier to find foster homes than had been anticipated. The program eventually operated six projects, of which three remained in operation until March 31, 1946.

From this point on, the State took the initiative in providing child care facilities wherever they seemed necessary. There were localities needing centers for which, however, no local sponsor could be found. To meet this situation the War Council, by a ruling of the Attorney General, was allowed to make the State

Department of Education its operating representative and by one of its special orders to make it possible for that department to receive Federal funds through the creation of a separate child care fund "in the custody of the Commissioner of Taxation and Finance, to which shall be paid all grants to and fees received by such projects."

In November, 1944, because original estimates of costs had proved too low, the War Council extended the highest per diem rates, previously applicable only in the larger nursery schools and day nurseries, to all centers regardless of size. It furthermore decided that retroactive to July 1, 1944, when the War Food Administration had withdrawn its grants to New York City projects, the State and New York City were each to provide one-third of the total operating costs of these projects and that, in addition, the State would pay the difference between the revenue from parents' fees and agency contributions and the remaining one-third of the costs. Since parents' fees and local contributions did not quite amount to one-third of the total, the agreement had the effect of raising the State's contribution to New York City projects slightly above the customary one-third.

Expansion of a different order was involved when, in the summer of 1944, child care centers were opened in some of the migrant farm labor camps. In May of that year a field representative of the State Child Care Committee was detailed to handle child care centers in migrant labor camps. These centers were operated with Federal funds by the Home Missions Council and with private funds by the Catholic Charities of Buffalo. The program reached its peak in the summer of 1945 with the operation of nurseries and play centers in forty migrant labor camps.

Strangely enough it was the servicing of these centers by the State Committee which led to an investigation of condi-

tions in the camps by a committee of the War Council. In December, 1944, the duties of staff members of the State Child Care Committee assigned to these camps were brought up in a War Council meeting. Owing to widespread violations of the labor laws, the State Committee, being itself a representative of the State's authority, was much disturbed as to whether it should continue to function in the camps. If it did, it could either remain silent on the state of affairs or make reports to the Labor Department which would embarrass the Home Mission Council, which was by no means responsible for the conditions. After a long discussion in the Council, which revealed a deplorable situation of long standing, the Governor appointed a special War Council Committee on Migrant Camps, headed by Dean W. I. Myers of the Cornell College of Agriculture. It was generally agreed that the problem confronting the committee was more than a war question — a peace question as well — divided into housing, health, and child care, and that it was clearly tied in with the general problem of farm labor in New York State. Thus it was that out of one aspect of the Child Care Program there developed in 1945 a full-scale investigation of conditions in the migrant labor camps.[1] In her final report in February, 1946, the Director of the State Child Care Committee recommended the continuation of the centers with State funds, under the responsibility of a State agency.

Services Rendered by the Child Care Centers. In view of the fact that final approval of the State Child Care Program became overwhelming, it is important to indicate briefly the nature of the services that were rendered by the centers, and the extent and character of the local problems which had to be met by the field staff of the State Committee

---

[1] The work of this committee is described on pp. 244-246; 298.

on Child Care. One of the most important was the easing of tension within the family circle by taking from the working mother for part of the day the responsibility for care of her children. Such relief for the mother who works acted as a stabilizing factor in family relations. In New York City where the combined income of 97 per cent of the fathers and mothers using the centers did not exceed $65 a week, care for the children was the only means of guaranteeing for the family anything approaching a satisfactory standard of living.

The services rendered by the centers to children can be grouped roughly under nutrition, health, recreation, education, and personality development. One of the primary results of children's association with the child care centers was an increase in weight. Particular attention was given the program of feeding, which consisted of a hot midday meal, midmorning and midafternoon snacks for preschool children, and a midafternoon snack for children of school age. In some centers, when necessary, both breakfast and supper were served. Gains of five to twenty-five pounds were recorded within periods of from two to three months.

Closely associated with the nutrition program was the health program. Many children were for the first time subjected to regular medical examinations with the usual vaccinations and inoculations and daily health inspections. Systematic records of weight and other health data were kept. Consultations with mothers as to diet and health habits were frequent, and periodic examinations by physicians were made when indicated. Cod-liver oil, or an equivalent, was given to preschool children.

To those of us who have been accustomed to adequate nutrition and medical care, the urgent need for these things in certain areas of the State can hardly be realized. A migrant labor camp installed a child care center in the summer of 1944. A two-year-old made his first appearance one morning bringing his own breakfast—a cold cob of corn, a tomato, three dried prunes, and a bottle of beer. At another center, a fourteen-year old girl refused to go into the doctor's office until she had finished her cigarette. In reply to his mother, another child said, "Don't holler at me. They don't talk that way to me in the center."

At one of the centers in the western part of the State, a three-year-old girl came to a nursery school in October. While she seemed to be normal in all respects, she exhibited a peculiar rolling gait, and handled herself quite awkwardly. The mother said she had been under the care of a pediatrician since birth and that he had repeatedly assured her it was something that would be outgrown. However, when the doctor connected with the center examined the girl, the diagnosis was quite different. At the time of her birth the hip bones had been pulled from their sockets and the girl had learned to walk with both hip bones dislocated. With the doctor's help the family located a competent orthopedic surgeon who took X rays and confirmed the diagnosis. The girl was placed in a hospital encased in a cast and her treatment, which took about a year, resulted in her being able to walk like a normal healthy person. Her father and mother were overjoyed and, as may be imagined, exceedingly grateful to the child care center. The mother of another little girl, also a child in the same hospital for the very same treatment, heard about the case and about the child care center. She entered her daughter there likewise, not only because the father was in the service and she had to work, but also because she had heard how wonderful the teachers were to the first little girl, and how splendid the equipment was for exercising unused muscles.

The recreational facilities of the centers were extremely important and consisted of indoor and outdoor play equipment, as well as cots, blankets, etc. Special emphasis was placed upon athletics, dramatics, handicrafts, and other special interests. The social adjustments that the children made in learning to live with each other and the sense of security afforded by having a regular place to go for fun with other children were valuable factors in the development of their personalities. The program and staff of most of the centers were formulated and trained on the job. In New York City programs for school-age children were under the general supervision of the Play School Association which had had long experience in this particular field. The centers in New York were located in parish houses, in buildings operated by social agencies, in housing projects, in many kinds of buildings especially rented for the purpose, and after 1945 in a few school buildings. Up-State, the great majority of centers were located in school buildings. The hours of operation averaged between eight and twelve a day, six days a week, for children under five, and for school-age children the centers were opened before school, during the lunch hour, after school closed, all day Saturdays, holidays, and during vacations. In view of what is now known regarding the importance to children of care and affection and the emphasis that must be placed in the formative years of life upon good nutrition and careful medical checking, there is no question but that on the basis purely of social need the wartime Child Care Program completely justified itself. Since this was not the primary purpose, however, justification should be sought principally along the lines indicated by the Chairman of the War Council Subcommittee on Child Care in a broadcast he made in 1944:

When I talk about women in war jobs and the need of child care centers and their cost,

I think of a certain quiet village in upstate New York. Before the war it had a population of 2500. Since the war began, its population has increased threefold or more and many residents from surrounding districts come in to work. It is the site of a factory which manufactures a small mechanical device which is an essential part of all war planes and tanks. Without it a plane will not fly and a tank will not rumble across the battlefield. Now there is a State child care center in this village. Let us say that this center makes it possible for fifty women to work in that war industry so that bombers in even larger numbers may unload their deadly freight on enemy countries, and so that tanks in even larger numbers may rumble on to victory over the battlefields of Europe and Asia. Then, by this contribution alone our child care program is eminently worthwhile. Now multiply that result more than two hundred times and you have a truly significant contribution to the war effort on the home front in New York State. Multiply that result by three thousand and you will be convinced of the importance of child care centers in the production program of the nation.

The Role of the State Child Care Committee. The importance of State leadership in the development of the New York Child Care Program cannot be overemphasized. There would have been far fewer child care projects in operation, and far less organization to the program, had there been no State Child Care Committee with a staff of field workers trained to community organization. Active direction and leadership devolved upon the chairman, who served as director, and upon the competent staff of field representatives. Detailed negotiations among various community groups and frequent representation of private agencies in their dealings with the governing bodies of municipalities called for tact and perseverance. Staff members gave advice on State policies and through their chairman acted as liaison between the localities and the War Council. For over a year it was necessary for all groups interested in child care to concentrate upon educating the mothers for whose use the centers were designed. This process of education included a campaign which made use of posters, leaflets, radio announcements, lectures, meetings and moving pictures, especially the film showing the nursery school program developed by the Department of Education and the Office of War Training, and the short trailer with an introductory statement by Governor Dewey showing both the preschool and the school-age programs. Thanks to the cooperation of the motion-picture theaters, the latter was shown all over the State. By the summer of 1944, this campaign began to bring results in terms of improved community understanding and appreciation of the value of the services provided for the children. The engineering of this campaign was primarily the work of the State Child Care Committee.

When the War Council undertook direct financial support of child care centers in New York City, and later upstate, administrative duties fell to the lot of the State Committee. Although by resolution of the War Council in the summer of 1943 the special subcommittee, under the chairmanship of Speaker Heck, was given the power to determine policy and make grants, nevertheless, the State Committee continued to possess primary administrative responsibility with regard to the local child care centers. It alone was in constant touch with each center and only the State Child Care Office could make available on call basic information regarding the program. Furthermore, the recommendations of its chairman served as the basis for allocations of War Council funds, and her advice and judgment continued to influence decisively not only the administration, but the long-range policies of the entire State program. It was the initiative of the Committee, based upon first-hand contacts with local administrative problems, which carried to completion the process of simplifying War Council regulations. It was likewise the assistance of the committee in preparation of applications both for Federal and State grants which frequently made the difference between establishment and nonestablishment of child care centers. The careful scrutiny of individual budgets and the close track which was kept of local expenditures won for the Committee and the State program the confidence and respect of those members of the Council who associated social services with loose financial arrangements. The willingness of members of the subcommittee to accept figures and recommendations of the chairman of the State Committee is proof of the confidence that they ultimately came to place in her judgment.

The principal difficulties which faced the State Child Care Committee lay in the fact of the direct Federal grants to local communities, which in other states were accompanied by Federal advice and supervision of the local centers. In New York State, with its own administrative agency, it was necessary for the field staff of the Child Care Committee to trail the Federal men around to find out what they wanted in a community, so as to avoid giving different advice. Furthermore, the creation by the War Council of an emergency agency at once presented a possibility of duplication of the work of the two permanent agencies concerned, viz., the State Departments of Education and of Social Welfare. Since both these departments had supervisory powers over the child care centers, the State Committee in working out cooperative relationships avoided as far as practicable duplication of effort. Although the Federal program gave some slight recognition to the place of the two permanent State agencies in that applications for Federal aid to projects in their respective fields were to be referred to them for an expression of opinion, there was no recognized place in the

Federal administrative program for the State War Council agency. All three State agencies, however, had regulations applicable to child care centers which it was their duty to place in force. It was fortunate, therefore, under these circumstances, that it was possible for the State Committee to establish good working relationships with the Federal Works Agency.

Another difficulty, however, lay in the slowness with which the Federal machinery operated. In this connection, decisions obtained from the State within forty-eight hours on centers in the New York City program may be contrasted with periods of anywhere from three to six months required for Federal approval of upstate projects. In spite of the fact that the local operating agencies in an upstate project had to deal successively with the Federal Works Agency, the Child Care Committee of the State War Council, the Department of Education or Social Welfare, and the child care committees of the local war councils, the system worked better on the whole than would have been expected considering the presence of so many organizations with conflicting ideas and jurisdictions. Perhaps the secret lay in the catalytic action of the children, whose interests all groups really had at heart.

The War Council's Acceptance of the Child Care Program. The strong appeal that the Child Care Program made to those who were closely associated with it is demonstrated by the subtle change in the attitude of the War Council itself. Apart from the satisfaction that the council took in the efficient administration of a difficult program, or the settlement of perplexing questions of policy, most problems generated little real enthusiasm among the members. There was something about the Child Care Program, however, that distinguished it from the others, although in the beginning this difference was not anticipated. The appointment of the Subcommittee

on Child Care was a routine timesaving procedure whereby a smaller group took over the task of thrashing out questions of policy and presented its findings to the next full meeting of the council. The Speaker's reference in September, 1943, shortly after his appointment as chairman, to the fact that the Governor had thereby handed him "a wonderful apple," was certainly lacking in enthusiasm. In the spring of 1944 he was saddled with additional administrative responsibilities by the liberalization of the child care rules, responsibilities that he undertook somewhat reluctantly. The program was still a "headache" and he undoubtedly expressed the feeling of the majority of the council when he raised the question as to whether the State intended to provide child care facilities after the war was over.

With the entrance of the Child Care Program upon a period of relatively smooth administrative sailing, and after visits paid to a number of the centers by members of the subcommittee, the outlook of that committee began to change. This was reflected in the remarks of its chairman at the July meeting.

You will recall [he said], that when we liberalized the Child Care Program generally, you authorized the subcommittee to allocate and expend certain funds for equipment, repairs, rents, etc. I can assure you that if any of you ever take the time to go through these child care projects, you will be convinced that we did a wise thing. In some of these projects the people are so enthusiastic about taking care of the children while the mothers are working in war industry, they used to send some of the children out to bring in orange crates. The kids took them, sandpapered and painted them to provide some of the furniture, some of the equipment with which to make these centers more pleasant. As I say, after a while I will really begin to like my job as Chairman of the Child Care Committee.

With the attainment in the summer of 1944 of administrative stability and an operational scope commensurate with the responsibilities of the emergency, the administration of the Child Care Program ceased to be a "headache." The subcommittee accordingly felt justified in pointing to its handiwork with pride. In September, its chairman spoke over the radio on a phase of "war activity that had escaped the attention that it deserves in our nation," and declared roundly that "it was no easy task to organize and set up child care units. It required tact, understanding and administrative ability." After reviewing the development of the program in 1943 and 1944, he continued, "The Child Care Center, outside the bright light of publicity that attends many other war activities, has demonstrated its value as an important factor in American war production."

While the principal object of the Child Care Program was still to aid in war production, other considerations had by this time made an impression upon the subcommittee. In setting forth the temporary nature of State child care activities, the Speaker emphasized the importance of family influences in the life of the child.

Once the war has been finally won [he said], the activities of child care will gradually diminish, particularly as an emergency measure. The Child Care Program is in no sense meant to take the place of the home but merely to supplement it during the war. Once the emergency has passed, we hope that it will be no longer necessary for child care centers to function, but rather, that our children again may grow up under the priceless and sacred influence of home and family.

In such a hope everyone concurred, but the use of the word "hope" betrayed the realization that there was a possibility of the need for child care facilities continuing on after the period of the war in the same areas of the State where before the war a similar need had gone unrecognized. In short, the social values of the program had been discovered by the organization which had undertaken its operation originally solely as an aid in the expansion of the labor force. It had likewise been recognized that the disruption of normal family life occurred under certain conditions of economic maladjustment, which although greatly accentuated by war not only had had a prior existence but threatened to persist with irritating stubbornness into, and beyond, the period of reconversion. It was this understanding of the extent and character of the need, and the satisfaction which was derived from being able in some measure to take care of it, that by the winter of 1944 had generated genuine enthusiasm in the subcommittee. The spirit of the local committees and of the State Child Care Committee undoubtedly had helped to spread this contagion.

In December, 1944, the subcommittee reported to the War Council on the New York City program, recommending that the Council assume additional financial responsibilities. Its chairman prefaced the report with these words:

"Frankly, though I was not very enthusiastic when I first got this job of child care, they are really doing a good job. I am really getting a little bit enthusiastic. I may really be one of the protagonists of this thing."

He pointed out that his committee had had no complaints at all and recommended that the War Council accept the recommendations. He went into detail in describing the state of repair in which he had found some of the centers — located in cellars, unpainted, without furniture, and forced to use orange crates as closets for clothes and rubbers.

"I feel good," he said, "when I am able to go away from some of these centers and make recommendations to help some of these people out. New York City is the place where they need help."

Another member, referring to Buffalo, remarked, "They have done a magnificent job. They have been closed for the third time (due to infantile paralysis) but have kept their people intact and increased their enrollment. The centers are in good shape."

The Governor's comment at the end of the committee's report was, "I take it the Child Care Committee is getting a great deal of gratification out of this work."

To which the chairman replied, "That is right. We like it."

From this verdict there was no change.

New York Takes Over the Entire Federal Program. In January, 1945, in upstate New York 39 projects in receipt of Federal aid were operating 151 nurseries and play centers with 5250 children enrolled. When the federally aided program reached its peak in July, there were 42 projects with 102 nurseries with 3540 children, and 74 play centers with 2931 children enrolled. Of these projects 38 were also in receipt of State aid.

As the Federal program was subject to many uncertainties in 1945, it was fortunate that the State program was sufficiently flexible to act as a stabilizing factor. During the early part of the year, there was a long delay in the appropriation of additional funds by the Congress. No application of the Federal Works Agency for additional funds seemed likely to secure from Congress the amount necessary to continue full operation of the Federal program. During this period of uncertainty the State faced the dilemma of either extending its responsibiltiy to cover the Federal commitment, or of acquiescing in the closing of the entire upstate program. This program was at its peak with enrollments steadily increasing. Under the provisions of Chapter 412 of the Laws of 1944, an increased proportion of the women whose children were using the centers were wives of servicemen and disabled veterans, widows of servicemen, and other women who were the sole support of their children. Nevertheless, with war production employment on the decline

after V-E Day, the Federal Works Agency refused all new applications for grants and adopted a stricter policy as to eligibility for care in child care centers receiving Federal funds. No grants were to be made for buildings, repairs, or equipment; all grants were to be on a quarterly basis only; breakfast and supper were to be extra, and the maximum daily fee was to be raised from $.50 to $.75. Projects where less than 50 per cent of the mothers were employed in war production or essential work were threatened with closure, and here and there support was withdrawn entirely. In short, all the signs of contraction in the Federal program became visible.

In June, 1945, the War Council once more faced the question of extending the State's responsibility. It was then decided that since the continuation of upstate projects on the reimbursement basis customarily followed by the State would not be possible without Federal assistance, and since the New York City program was already operating without Federal funds on a different basis, to avoid the appearance of discrimination against the upstate projects the State would undertake to operate all upstate centers from which the Federal government decided to withdraw on the basis of the yardstick already in use with the New York City centers. In strict accord with this decision of the War Council, the State stepped in wherever the Federal government stepped out and in July, after careful review of the facts, an additional $110,000 was made available for child care in preparation for any future emergency.

Shortly after V-J Day (August 14), it was announced that Federal aid would be discontinued September 30 for twelve of the New York State projects, and on October 31 for the other thirty. This announcement reflected the current national policy of the Federal Works Agency. At the time it was made, twenty-seven of the forty-two up-State projects had already worked out, or were working on plans to continue with State aid. The withdrawal of Federal aid[1] created anxiety, not only upstate but in New York City also, for fear the State would adopt a similar policy there. To ease the tension and remove all doubt as to the immediate future of the child care projects in New York State, Governor Dewey announced, August 31, that the State would maintain the child care program intact until the end of March, 1946, and that projects from which Federal aid had been withdrawn would be eligible for State aid on the same basis as New York City.

In making his announcement, the Governor cited the report of the chairman of the War Council's Child Care subcommittee as follows:

Moreover, the child care centers have aroused genuine community interest and cooperation wherever they are established throughout the State of New York. Not only the mothers concerned, and their families, but the neighbors really appreciate this service. I might add that this is in sharp contrast to conditions in other states where almost complete indifference prevails.

The War Council was proud of its Child Care Program and intended to see it through to the end of the reconversion period. The need for day care of children in many communities was as great as ever. Over 50 per cent of the children covered by a sample survey of the up-State centers had fathers in the armed forces, or mothers who were the sole support of the family. Many of the other children had mothers who needed to work because the earnings of their husbands were insufficient to support their families during the period of high taxes

and increased cost of living. The report ended on a new note:

I suggest that the continuance of the Child Care Program on a limited scale is an essential part of the state government's contribution to reconversion. During this transition period, it is essential that women who have to work may have adequate care for their children, and the community interest which the centers have created is clear evidence that the communities will be grateful if the state continues to help as long as will be necessary. I urge, therefore, that a policy be adopted of continuing this child care on a limited scale during the reconversion period.

Thus the basis for the State's support of child care had been broadened by force of circumstances from the relatively narrow purpose of supplementing the labor supply in war impact areas to include the welfare of children of mothers engaged in essential occupations, of wives and widows of servicemen, and of women who were the sole support of their families. There was as yet no acceptance of the all-embracing goal of adequate care for all children. That was still the social worker's dream of the future, but it is worth noting that New York State had been the first to announce its intention, upon the withdrawal of Federal aid, to provide support for all child care projects. It is also significant that upon the original announcement of the intended withdrawal of Federal aid in the fall of 1945, in the shower of letters from all over the country which caused Washington soon to reverse itself and continue child care, the proportion of communications from New York State was noticeably small. New York State mothers turned to Albany rather than to Washington and were not disappointed.

The appropriation for child care was continued by the 1946 Legislature for the 1946-1947 fiscal year. The field staff of the State Child Care Committee was taken over by the Youth Commission, and the chairman of the committee stayed to effect transfer and then, under

---

[1] Owing to pressure brought upon the President and upon Congress, Federal aid was subsequently continued until February 28, 1946. In March, 1946, twenty-six projects were continued with War Council funds until the entire program was transferred to the Youth Commission.

doctor's orders, was forced to leave for a much-needed rest. While by no means indicating the acceptance of permanent State responsibility for child care programs, nevertheless, the placing of the Child Care Program under the Youth Commission guaranteed that in New York State extent of need for services to children of working mothers would be carefully scrutinized during 1946. This was an enlightened policy of social experimentation of which the people of the State could well be proud.

Following its transfer to the State Youth Commission April 1, 1946, the Child Care Program underwent close scrutiny. A report of the Commission transmitted to the Legislature by Governor Dewey March 4, 1947, presented interesting findings.

The emergency needs of the depression and World War II which were met by child care centers were "made work" for unemployed teachers and "woman power" for war industries. In 1946 these needs no longer existed. Furthermore, the average monthly child care attendance figures for 1946 (5500-5600) indicated that the State program benefited but a limited number of children. The reasons for this were the high per capita cost (approximately $62.50 per month), of which the State paid, on the average 40 per cent, and, despite increases in enrollment in New York City, the lack of widespread acceptance elsewhere of the program by local communities as a social responsibility or financial obligation.

The commission pointed out, however, that the Child Care Program should no longer be maintained as a separate administrative entity, but now that the emergency was over should once more be integrated with the permanent structure of State government. This it felt could be done by leaving up to the localities the decision as to whether their child care centers should be continued (1) as nursery schools under the supervision of the Department of Education, (2) as day nurseries under the supervision of the Department of Social Welfare, or (3) as part of a general recreation or delinquency prevention project under the State Youth Commission.

Under the Education Law, private groups and public-school districts were permitted to operate nursery schools, but without financial support from the State. Day nurseries, on the other hand, were eligible for State aid through the Department of Social Welfare. In certain communities the commission recognized a potential need for daytime facilities and training as an experimental measure for the protection of children from unwholesome community conditions. Only in such cases, as part of a community-wide program for the prevention of juvenile delinquency, did the report suggest that continued support might be forthcoming from the State Youth Commission.

On the basis of these and other findings the Commission recommended:

1. That the general day care program be discontinued, except that State aid should be extended, where needed, until October 1, 1947, so that the localities affected might ascertain their needs and make arrangements necessary to meet these needs.

2. That local communities determine whether they wish to retain the existing day care centers, either as (a) nursery schools, under education auspices, or (b) day nurseries, under voluntary or public welfare agencies.

3. That local communities, in working out plans for continuing nursery schools, should consult representatives of the State Youth Commission if they believe their projects might qualify for State aid under the State Youth Commission Act.

4. That local groups, in planning to continue day nurseries, should work with local welfare authorities if they wish to make these services available to children in needy families, thus providing the

opportunity to meet family needs through State-aided public-assistance grants.

The recommendations of the commission were acted upon by the Legislature. It continued the Youth Commission until 1950; continued until April 1, 1948 the day care program for children in migrant labor camps under the supervision and financial aid of the Youth Commission; and continued the rest of the Child Care Program only until October 1, 1947.

The principal development since the close of the 1947 legislative session has been the creation in New York City of a City Youth Bureau under Chapter 556 of the Laws of 1945, and the plan announced August 19 for the operation of seventy-four of the city's ninety-six child care centers for three months from October 1 to December 31, 1947. This program will constitute part of a city-wide effort for the prevention of juvenile delinquency. Thirty-five hundred children will be taken care of in the centers located in neighborhoods with high rates of delinquency. During the three-month period, a program of research and fact-finding will be conducted to determine the permanent disposition of the project.

Similar delinquency programs are being considered in several of the upstate urban centers. Elsewhere, however, child care is being permanently incorporated with other public and private activities under the supervision of the Departments of Education and Social Welfare.

THE WAR NURSING PROGRAM

One profession upon which the war placed a terrific strain was that of nursing. War produced casualties, and casualties required hospitals and nursing services. This extra demand for nursing services had to be met without curtailing seriously civilian requirements at home. The problem demanded the most effi-

cient use of all available nurses and the training of replacements for those entering service with the armed forces.

In the country at large the need for a national organization in the field of nursing was recognized in 1941. With the hope of avoiding confusion and duplication of effort, a National Nursing Council for War was formed at that time by several national nursing organizations to initiate and direct a unified war nursing program. This Council represented all national nursing organizations[1] and allied organizations directly concerned with nursing. A program was developed which included the formation of State and local Nursing Councils for War Service modeled on the national pattern.

In New York State, as far back as 1939, two years before the formation of the National Nursing Council for War Service, the New York State Nurses Association tried to anticipate the effect of a long war upon nursing service. It was impossible to foresee the extent of Army and Navy requirements. No one knew accurately the number of nurses in New York State, nor even how many of the approximately 56,000 registered with the Education Department were active. The 19,000 members of the State Nurses Association represented but a fraction of those available in the State. To get a clear picture of the situation, an inventory was obviously essential.

In 1940, as part of an initial survey under the direction of the United States

---

[1] American Nurses Association, National League of Nursing Education, National Organization for Public Health Nursing, Association of Collegiate Schools of Nursing, National Association of Colored Graduate Nurses, American Red Cross Nursing Service, Council of Federal Nursing Service, International Council of Nurses, Division of Nurse Education of the United States Public Health Service, Nursing Division, Physical and Athletic Service, War Manpower Commission, Subcommittee on Nursing, Health and Medical Commission, Federal Security Agency, American Hospital Association, American Medical Association, Members-at-Large.

Public Health Service, the State Nurses Association conducted a State-wide inventory of nurses. This voluntary survey was completed in fifteen months at a cost to the Association of approximately $21,000, and furnished information on 40,852 nurses, of whom 26,707 were of military age.

Simultaneously, a program was undertaken by the New York State Nursing Association to recruit students for schools of nursing as shortages were already being felt, and greater shortages were believed imminent. By 1941, local student recruitment committees in the sixteen districts of the State Association were functioning. Likewise, the State League of Nursing Education, concerned with the education of student and graduate nurses, compiled and published requirements for admission to schools of nursing in New York State. In 1941, the New York State Emergency Medical Program, functioning under the State Health Preparedness Commission and its county units as part of the State Office of Civilian Protection, was successful in bringing nurses from hospital staffs and many formerly inactive nurses into Emergency Medical Squads, prepared to function in time of disaster.[1]

The New York State Nurses Association finally took the leadership in the formation of a State Nursing Council for War Service since it recognized that the problem of supplying nurses for military and civilian needs would require the assistance of all State nursing organizations and allied groups, as well as of the consumer public. Accordingly, in August, 1942, in line with national recommendations, it converted its Inventory Committee into the nucleus of the State Nursing Council for War Service, which, henceforth, served as the coordinating body for New York State nursing programs. A constitution and by-laws were

set up, and representation secured from all organizations in the State interested in the problem.

The principal objectives of the Council were:

1. To study nursing needs and resources in New York State and keep an up-to-date roster of licensed and auxiliary nursing personnel

2. To plan for and assist in enlistment and distribution of nursing services in the fields of (a) military service, (b) civilian population including professional nursing and auxiliary services, and (c) Emergency Medical Service

3. To act as a clearinghouse for war nursing programs on State and local levels, and for the collection and dissemination of information on war nursing

4. To cooperate with other agencies having related functions and to assist in recruiting well-qualified students for schools of nursing.

The work of the Nursing Council was supported by the State Nurses Association until August 1, 1943. Local nursing councils having been organized in 1942 in many communities, especially in New York City, field visits were undertaken to enlist their cooperation in the national program. As wide representation as possible was secured among community groups interested in hospitals, schools of nursing, public health agencies, school nursing, and industry. By March, 1943, forty-eight of the fifty-five councils were organized and working on recruitment of students for schools of nursing and on a better distribution of nursing service. Rosters were maintained locally and additional surveys conducted. As the pinch of nursing shortage became more keenly felt in 1943, councils endeavored to meet this need for nurses by reactivating nurses who had retired and by stepping up programs to recruit more students for schools of nursing. Refresher courses helped to return many nurses to the profession, and these nurses were used to give care to patients and as teachers and

---

[1] Compare Emergency Medical Program, Chap. IV.

supervisors in connection with these courses and with the very successful Red Cross program for the training of nurses' aides and the teaching of home nursing classes. The program grew rapidly and soon was far beyond the ability of the small headquarters staff to carry it. This situation was brought to the attention of the New York State Health Preparedness Commission, and through its interest, financial support for the duration of the war was secured from the New York State War Council.

Two federally sponsored war programs were initiated in 1943 at the suggestion of the National Nursing Council. Under the Bolton Act, the United States Public Health Service was authorized to provide all-expense scholarships in schools of nursing for qualified candidates. Students enrolling under the plan became members of the United States Cadet Nursing Corps, and in return were required to pledge their services upon graduation for either military or essential civilian nursing until the end of the war. Through its state and local recruitment committees already at work on Nursing Council programs, the National Nursing Council acted as the recruiting medium for the Cadet Nursing Corps. In New York State, under the Bolton Act, fourteen in-service courses were sponsored by the League of Nursing Education leading to the positions of supervisor and head nurse.

A second program was set up under the direction of the central office of Procurement and Assignment of the War Manpower Commission, whereby the supply and distribution committees of the local Nursing Councils became Procurement and Assignment Committees for the War Manpower Commission. To them fell the task of classifying 47,000 registered nurses as of essential need at home or availability for military service. In addition, they handled appeals and subsequent reclassification of more than 15,000 nurses and carried out special projects, such as the classification of senior nursing students and of the selected number of nurses for postgraduate study. The Procurement and Assignment Committees also assisted Selective Service in a review of male nurses with occupational deferments, and certified as to the need for continuing deferment of those in essential nursing positions. During the poliomyelitis epidemic, they referred available nurses for work in that emergency. At all times they followed up nurses classified as available for military service or available for relocation, in a continuous effort to fit every nurse into the position where she was most needed and best qualified to serve.

The President's surprise message of January, 1945, requesting registration which would in effect draft nurses, focused the attention of the entire country upon the need for nurses in military service. The Army and Navy had by this time begun to procure nurses on their own behalf (at first this responsibility was delegated entirely to the Red Cross). The Red Cross redoubled its efforts; many meetings were held with procurement and assignment prepared to function under any Selective Service legislation that might be enacted. As a result of these combined efforts, during the first six months of 1945, 2200 nurses were recruited for the Army and Navy from New York State alone. The grand total of 17,199, who were assigned from the country as a whole, satisfied fully the military requirements and made further consideration of a "draft" unnecessary.

During the latter years of the war, before overworked civilian agencies could spare nurses for military assignment, it was essential that others be available to step in and fill their positions. The appeal to inactive nurses was carried on by every known method. Meetings, personal visits, and publicity were all employed and successfully prevented the collapse of civilian nursing service. Reports compiled by the American Medical Association show that during the war approximately 14.6 per cent of the regular nursing care in the general hospitals of New York State was given by part-time nurses. It was these who made possible the State's remarkable record of nurses assigned to service with the armed forces. From the beginning of the war to September 30, 1945, the total number of nurses assigned to service from New York State was 9328, or approximately 12 per cent of all nurses assigned in the United States, and 26 per cent of those nurses active in New York State.

The most successful feature of the replacement program was the recruitment of students for schools of nursing. As part of this program, a series of twenty-nine meetings attended by representatives from thirty-two counties was held throughout the State in the early part of 1945. Local recruitment committees, school-nurse teachers, guidance counselors, and others in a position to offer the greatest help to prospective students were given information regarding the pressing need for nurses. As a result, during the school year 1944-1945, New York State admitted 6114 students to schools of nursing, an increase of 2321 over enrollments in 1939-1940.

The end of the war did not mean the end of coordinated thinking, planning, and action under the leadership of a State-wide nursing organization. Owing to a growing shortage of nurses at home, a number of projects directly related to the war continued in operation after V-J Day. These included (1) efforts to staff civilian hospitals and health agencies more adequately; (2) a continued program of student nurse recruitment, both for schools of nursing and for colleges and universities offering postgraduate courses; (3) the upkeep of a roster of nurses to furnish statistical information basic to postwar planning; (4) the absorption of WACS, WAVES and Medical Corpsmen with experience in nursing, and of nurses aides, into the field of nursing where they were best qualified to serve; (5) the provision of courses to provide nurses with preparation for teaching, head nurse, and supervisory positions, and for special fields of psychiatry and orthopedics; and (6) the establishment of standards for approval by the Department of Education in connection with clinical courses given in hospitals and graduate nursing courses leading to a degree in colleges and universities.

To coordinate these programs it seemed logical that some kind of machinery be maintained, and that continued support be sought for projects now under way. The benefits gained from the development of local leadership and the participation in mutual problems by citizens and nurses alike should not be lost. Good nursing service to the public could be attained only through a program providing for continuing study of community nursing requirements and resources, one that assures community participation in planning and support from organized nursing groups, doctors, hospital administrators, and public and private health agencies. Accordingly, the State Nursing Council for War Service voted on November 16, 1945, to function as a coordinating body after the war program ends. This vote was endorsed by the State Nurses Association, the State League of Nursing Education, and other wartime members of the Council.

HEALTH

In wartime, the health of 13 million people was no small matter. Upon its maintenance at a high level depended top-speed war production. The national effort, however, placed an unusual tax upon the health of every man, woman, and child in the country. Changes in diet, changes in occupation, and a reduction in the personnel and facilities available for the maintenance of medical care in the communities presented problems not found in time of peace. Ordinarily, a community can by virtue of the amount of money it spends on community health services largely determine its own death rate. Within limits public health is purchasable. This, however, became less true during the war, as medical and nursing personnel were drawn into the armed forces, and the consumption of protective foods was to some extent curtailed by rationing.

Work of the Health Preparedness Commission. While health is basically an individual matter largely determined by good judgment and inherited physical characteristics, certain fundamental public health services are essential for the maintenance of proper living conditions. These services are especially needed in time of war, and upon the community, the state, and private professional organizations falls the responsibility for adequate provision. In the State of New York during the war over-all planning in the field of health was in the hands of the Health Preparedness Commission, ably counseled by its Advisory Subcommittee on Health Preparedness. This subcommittee was composed of representatives of Federal and State Agencies, and of private professional organizations in the field of Health and Medicine.[1]

The subcommittee effectively correlated the work of these organizations, and although trained personnel was scarce, the wartime Health Preparedness Program successfully maintained medical protection for the individual and the community.[2] Early in February, 1941, the Advisory Subcommittee recommended a number of programs designed to provide essential information regarding health

resources in the State. Since adequate preparation for the handling of wartime health problems required the collection of accurate data on existing health facilities and available trained personnel, a number of organizations, with the advice and assistance of the Health Preparedness Commission, undertook surveys for that purpose. Such surveys were:

1. A survey of laboratory facilities by the Department of Health and the Association of Public Health Laboratories.

2. A survey of hospitals and possibilities for hospital expansion by the New York State Hospital Association and the Health Preparedness Commission (referred to in Chapter IV).

3. An analysis, county by county, of the list of medical reserve officers furnished by the Corps Areas Commander to county Health Preparedness Committees that they might review the names of the physicians and specify those considered essential to the maintenance of adequate civilian health services in the local communities.

4. A survey of the nurses of the State by the New York State Nurses Association.

5. An inquiry into the hospital care of the mentally ill, with special reference to the problems surrounding the proposed demolition of Manhattan State Hospital, New York City.

The policy of the commission was to follow closely the activities of the various State and Federal departments having wartime health responsibilities and to guide its own enterprises so as to avoid interference with activities already in progress. Especially close relations were maintained with the Health and Medical Committee of the National Defense Council and with the regional Defense Coordinator of Health, Welfare, Recreation and other related activities. In furtherance of its wartime health program on March 6, 1941, an all-day Statewide Health Preparedness Conference, spon-

---

[1] For a list of the members of the Advisory Subcommittee see p. 108, note 1.

[2] In the section on Emergency Medical Services, p. 106, reference has already been made to the work of the Health Preparedness Commission, to the establishment by the Health Preparedness Commission of County Advisory Health Preparedness Committees, and to the special Emergency Medical Organizations built up within the framework, and under the direction, of the State Office of Civilian Protection.

sored by the New York State Defense Council and the Commission, was held in Chancellor's Hall, Albany. Members of the local Health Preparedness Committees and others in the State interested in the field of health generally were addressed by twenty-three experts in various health fields. The conference served as an invaluable stimulus to action in the localities, as a result of which the foundation was laid for the later institution of the Emergency Medical Service.

By the end of 1943, when the Emergency Medical Services had reached a maintenance level, the commission returned to its original responsibilities and took up once more its work with the local Health Preparedness Committees on a long-range health program for the State. Detailed studies, field trips, and inspections by staff members of the commission had made clear the degree to which local community relations affected the distribution of medical care and health services. It was also recognized that although plans could be drawn at the national and state levels, the doctors distributing medical care and the public they served would eventually have to solve their own problems at the local level. Voluntary cooperation between professional groups and the lay public was therefore essential to permanent accomplishment in the field of community health. Accordingly, it was decided to appoint an Advisory Committee on local Health Preparedness Committees to include within its membership health officers from small, medium, and large upstate cities, and to publish health, medical, dental, and social welfare reports.

In October, 1943, suggestions emanating from a meeting in New York City led to setting up in three typical areas of the State sample studies on health and medical care facilities, services, problems and needs. The areas studied were the following:

1. Washington County, because of its agricultural nature, general rural aspects, and relatively stable condition despite the war.

2. Seneca and Ontario Counties, because of the development of the Sampson Naval Training Station and the Seneca Ordnance Depot in Seneca County, and the problems created by the influx of attendant personnel into Ontario County.

3. Niagara County, because of its current problem of industrial war production and concurrent influx of population.

The studies were planned by the commission staff in cooperation with the State Departments of Health and Social Welfare, and with Dr. Oliver W. H. Mitchell of the State Medical Society, and Dr. Arthur M. Johnson, Chairman of the Advisory Committee on Health Preparedness Committees. These county studies had a twofold purpose:

1. To indicate the health and medical care facilities and services available, to evaluate their effectiveness, and on the basis of the information, make suggestions for the improvement of the services.

2. To provide the commission with information enabling it to interpret the local viewpoint and problems, and to estimate the effect that any governmental proposal might have upon these areas.

The Medical Society of the State of New York was likewise alive to problems which would confront its membership with the entrance of the country into World War II. Accordingly, it established a State Committee on Medical Preparedness, and at its suggestion each County Medical Society established a County Medical Preparedness Committee. The functions of these county committees were the blueprinting of medical resources in the counties and cooperation with the state society in the completion of questionnaires and surveys of approximately 25,000 physicians in New York State.

The New York State Nurses Association likewise appointed a Health Preparedness Committee, whose aims were:

1. To increase the first reserve of the Red Cross

2. To retain sufficient teachers and directors of nursing in the local communities

3. To increase the number of qualified public health nurses

4. To complete an inventory questionnaire regarding nurses in New York State.

Wartime Activities of the State Department of Health. The wartime activities of the New York State Department of Health were carried on in close cooperation with the New York State Health Preparedness Commission. Members of the department played roles on the Commission's Advisory Subcommittee by providing technical knowledge in the field of health and statistical information on health conditions throughout the State of New York. The twenty district offices of the department supervised and served the communities of the State, as in time of peace, through the prevention and control of disease, the prevention of accidents, the provision of services to mothers and children, and provided technical advice to communities in connection with public health nursing, sanitation, and diagnostic problems.

As early as the summer of 1940, when military maneuvers were held in St. Lawrence County, the Department of Health began to feel the impact of the coming war. Like most other public services it was caught in a gigantic squeeze characteristic of all military conflicts. While faced with a rapidly diminishing staff, especially of medical, sanitation, engineering, and nursing personnel, with which to maintain its normal peacetime services, it was confronted with additional work incident to problems raised by war. As a result, the department established a system of priorities affecting not only all public health projects but also departmental work along other lines. This administrative policy was followed more and more closely as the nation progressed from a neutral to an actively belligerent status. Intensification of efforts was in this way permitted on projects having the greatest bearing upon the health of civilians and of military personnel while absent from military reservations. The success of the policy was especially evident from the absence of serious epidemics among war workers which, had they occurred, might seriously have affected production. Although it was necessary to curtail certain less significant efforts, during the war years no public health project was abandoned.[1]

Certain activities of the Health Department were definitely affected by the war. In the case of communicable diseases, New York State was fortunate in not experiencing any of the widespread epidemics which frequently accompany war. Precautionary measures against smallpox and diphtheria were taken early through an intensive campaign to increase the number of vaccinations against these diseases. Additional clinics were scheduled and attempts made to persuade managers of industrial plants that they should protect their employees in every way possible. In some instances, arrangements were made for members of the staff to go into industrial plants to vaccinate workers. Careful check was maintained on the prevalence of all communicable diseases. Fortunately, the State escaped a major epidemic during World War II and apparently, if the experience of the men in the armed forces is an accurate indication, the increased mobility of the population in the last two decades has resulted in wider immunity to certain childhood diseases, such as measles and mumps.

In 1942, members of the staff of the Health Department were called in consultation on an outbreak involving a con-

---

[1] The work of the Health Department has already been discussed briefly in Chaps. II and III in connection with the support of the armed forces and the maintenance of industrial health and sanitation.

siderable number of cases of epidemic keratoconjunctivitis (a disease of the eye) in a large war plant in Schenectady, which had begun to interfere with production. The infection apparently reached the east coast following a spread across the country from the west coast. After the institution of extremely rigid aseptic techniques in the eye dispensary, the epidemic dropped to negligible proportions and after a few months no more cases appeared.

Meningitis, due to the meningococcus, is another disease that commonly appears during wartime. In fact, medical textbooks refer to it as a disease of children and soldiers. The present war was no exception. England, in 1940, was the first to notice an increase in incidence. There the epidemic reached its peak in 1941. In this country a rise was first noticed early in 1942, and except for the usual lull that this disease shows during the summer months, its incidence grew steadily. The number of reported cases for upstate New York, exclusive of military reservations, was 101 in 1941, 172 in 1942, 708 in 1943, and 707 in 1944. By November, 1944, the number of new cases was on the decline and continued to fall in 1945. Thanks to the sulpha drugs and to penicillin, the fatalities from this disease were sharply reduced. Fortunately, also, these drugs were effective against the secondary pneumonia which followed severe cases of influenza, and which in 1918 caused most of the deaths during that epidemic. As a result, the relatively mild form that spread throughout the country in December, 1943, caused few fatalities.

The only other disease attaining epidemic proportions during the war was poliomyelitis, of which 4179 cases and 234 deaths were reported in upstate New York in 1944. The two principal foci and those in which the disease first made its appearance were (1) Erie County, and (2) Chemung and Steuben Counties combined. Cases numbering 1069 were reported from Erie County, of which 637 were in the city of Buffalo, 304 from Steuben County, and 231 from Chemung. The counties particularly affected later in the 1944 season were Nassau, Monroe, Broome, and Westchester. During the peak of the epidemic in the late summer, major emphasis had to be placed upon control of the disease. Many requests for diagnostic assistance were answered by State Health Department authorities. Assistance was given in making arrangements to provide adequate therepeutic facilities and nurses trained in physical therapy were recruited and assigned where needed. Orthopedic nurses were also shifted to the epidemic areas. Arrangements were made for hospitalization when indicated, and cooperation sought from appropriate official and nonofficial agencies for underwriting emergency medical and hospital services. Even after the acute phase of the epidemic had passed, the departmental load remained great because of the necessity for providing adequate aftercare for a period of many months. In 1945, there was a marked falling off of cases compared with 1944, but the 636 cases reported for upstate New York in the first eight months was still high. Cases were distributed generally throughout the State, with only six counties having none to report. Major concentration was again in Erie, Monroe, Westchester, and Broome with the addition of Suffolk and Montgomery Counties.

Tuberculosis (see discussion in Chapter II) also had to be combatted under wartime conditions. For more than fifty years prior to 1942, New York State had experienced an almost continuous decline in the tuberculosis death rate. In that year, the downward trend in the resident tuberculosis death rate was not only interrupted but reversed. Also, through the use of new methods of mass X-raying, as in the Selective Service, industrial, and other case-finding projects, many hidden cases were discovered. This reverse trend continued into 1943, and since the disease was primarily one of persons ordinarily found in lower income brackets, active assistance of welfare commissioners and medical social workers was enlisted. Greater emphasis was placed upon the need for public health education for the purpose of impressing upon the man in the street the value of early diagnosis, prompt treatment, and segregation of infectious cases. The rise in the tuberculosis rate in the United States and in New York State was, however, relatively slight and largely accounted for by the increased strain upon individuals brought about by the heightened tempo of war.

On July 1, 1943, the New York State Emergency Maternity and Infant Care Program administered by the New York State Department of Health was set up under regulations of the Children's Bureau of the United States Department of Labor. The object of the plan was to provide payment for maternity care for wives and medical care for infants under one year of age of servicemen in the "four lowest pay grades in the armed forces." Grants of Federal funds were made to the State for this purpose and allocated on its behalf by the State Department of Health for payment of services rendered by private physicians. These payments were considered as added compensation to men serving in the military forces receiving such low pay that they could not readily provide care for their families. Women had the privilege of selecting any licensed physician they wished, provided the physician was willing to accept them for care under the terms of the plan. They could also select any hospital approved by the American College of Surgeons, or any other hospital meeting the minimum standards of the Children's Bureau, or any maternity home licensed by the State Department of Health, provided such hospital or maternity home was willing to accept them as patients.

No discussion of wartime health problems would be complete without mention of the control of venereal diseases since they were transmitted more frequently in times of war as a consequence of the manner in which the life of the average citizen was altered. In 1942, the number of new cases of syphilis in the State began to increase, a change which became more rapid in 1943. In the early years of the war, the increase was spotty as in many smaller communities the impact was slight. This experience was not unique as Scotland recorded a 100 per cent increase in venereal disease admissions to its government operated clinics, and England and Wales underwent percentage increases more than twice the size of ours. Elsewhere in the United States, data indicated that the increase was at least as great as and in the southeast greater than the increase in New York State.

The problem of the control and elimination of venereal disease received considerable attention from the State Department of Health, despite loss to the armed forces of members of the staff of the Division of Syphilis Control. In cooperation with the Second Service Command, efforts were made to suppress prostitution and to locate sources of infection to troops. Unknown cases were located by intensive contact investigations, with special attention to cases reported in areas adjacent to military reservations. Cases discovered at induction centers were referred by arrangement with military authorities to district health officers for follow-up. Serological tests and second tests for positive reactions were performed by the Department of Health and a plan for rechecking positive cases was formulated by the Division of Syphilis Control. From November, 1940, to September, 1945, the State Laboratory and the branch laboratories in New York City examined 733,812 blood specimens of selectees. After February 1, 1944, the Division of Laboratories and

Research was relieved of the program of blood examinations of all selectees for evidence of syphilis and, except for selectees processed through the Albany Induction Center, that work was carried on by local, private laboratories under contract with the Army.

The School Lunch Program. The health of children must be carefully watched in time of war. The State Education Department was able, with Federal assistance, to make an important contribution to the health of school children by maintaining throughout the war a program of hot lunches and midmorning milk in the schools. The School Lunch Program was originally begun during the depression when the Federal government was doing its best to support farm prices and use agricultural surpluses. The United States Department of Agriculture was at that time making available to the schools of the country surplus commodities of all sorts, and on the basis of these receipts many schools started feeding programs. The outbreak of war in Europe and the entrance into it of this country in 1941 resulted in the gradual disappearance of these surpluses. Because many schools found themselves unable to finance their programs without assistance, either in cash or surplus commodities, and since the nutritional needs of children, highlighted by the number of rejectees who were obviously undernourished, would increase during wartime as a result of food shortages and the employment of more women outside the homes, the Department of Agriculture secured in 1943 a Congressional appropriation of 50 million dollars for the support of school lunches. From this fund, reimbursement was to be given the schools for three types of lunches — the complete lunch, a supplemental lunch, and milk only. A school was reimbursed for all lunches served which met the requirements, provided it operated on a nonprofit basis and gave meals free to those who could not afford to pay.

New York State received a financial subsidy in 1943, and Dr. E. R. Van Kleeck, Assistant Commissioner for Instructional Supervision, was appointed director. Supervision of the program was placed in the hands of the Bureau of Home Economics Education under its then chief, Miss Marion S. Van Liew, and her successor, the acting chief, Miss Treva E. Kauffman. Applications for the use of Federal funds were processed and approved by the Bureau. Interest in the program grew rapidly in New York to the point where allocations from the Federal government were completely exhausted. Funds for the supervision of the program by the Education Department were received from the New York State War Council until March 31, 1946, and supplemented by legislative appropriation for the period through June 30, 1946. By that time nearly 2500 schools had been approved for the use of Federal funds. Exactly a year later the total was 7375 schools with an average of 525,468 daily lunches served.

In the administration of the program, it was recognized that success depended not alone upon the reimbursement of funds for school lunches. In-service and pre-service training of personnel for the supervision and management of the school lunch were also essential. This was effected in cooperation with the Home Economics Departments of the colleges and universities of the State. The need for additional personnel to serve as cook-managers was partly met by the institution of training in the State technical institutes. Seventeen one-day training schools were attended by 750 school lunch cooks and managers. In the summer of 1946, three one-week schools were conducted for these women. The program was expanded.

Advice and assistance were secured from all groups in the State interested in the operation of the schools. On June 7, 1945, a State School Lunch Advisory Committee consisting of representatives of parents, school administrators, and other organizations familiar with the program was organized to assist the director in adapting the State program as fully as possible to the needs of the schools. Regional conferences were held in 1944 and 1945, and attended by nearly 2000 school superintendents, principals, school-board members, home economics teachers, school lunch directors and managers, school nurses, P.T.A. representatives, extension leaders, and others. All phases of school lunch operation and management were considered. Opportunity was given for general discussion of such topics as the use of rationed foods, management problems, keeping adequate records and accounts, noon hour schedules, and the use of student help. Departmental supervisors were also in attendance at numerous meetings of organizations and agencies concerned with the problems of school administration. The School Lunch Program was also described and explained to the staffs and students of the teacher training institutions of the State. Close cooperation was maintained with the Joint Legislative Committee on Agriculture.

The experience of school personnel with the wartime program of school lunches has undoubtedly convinced most of them of the close connection between adequate nutrition, improvement in health, and increased attendance and improved scholarship. If spent at school, the noon hour becomes part of the educational program in such matters as health, good food habits, improved social behavior, and good citizenship practices. Although the value of the program was generally recognized, the need for trained personnel, additional equipment, and professional advice on its most efficient utilization still remains.

Supervision of Migrant Labor Camps. The problem of housing large numbers of migratory workers, although present prior to the war, was accentuated

after 1941 by the use of out-of-state seasonal laborers forced upon growers and canners by the induction of their usual labor supply into the armed forces. Problems of housing, sanitation, food supply and preparation, child care, and adequate living conditions became acute with the introduction of large numbers of workers accustomed to a lower scale of living. From 1942 to 1945, various reports and investigations were made by State authorities concerned with the supervision and operation of these camps. Remedial legislation was proposed and adopted in 1944, 1945 and 1946, and by the end of 1946, a vast improvement had been effected in available facilities and methods of operation in the migrant labor camps.

In the decade of 1910 to 1920, there were numerous farm and labor camps about which little is now known. Labor was hauled by wagon from nearby cities to camps where the laborers lived. From 1920 to 1930 many of these camps were unoccupied as laborers commuted in large numbers by automobile from their homes in the city. Supervision of the few existing farm labor camps was supplied by local health officers under the general provision of the public health law regarding nuisances and communicable diseases. From 1930 to 1940, there were perhaps between 100 and 150 farm labor camps in operation each year of which, roughly, 100 were in Erie County. Although these camps usually fell under the definition of a "camp" as defined by the Sanitary Code, enforcement of this provision by local health officers was neglected, and in 1940, responsibility was transferred to the State Department of Health. In 1941, there were approximately 100 labor camps of all kinds on record of which those for farm labor were only one portion. No figures on farm labor camps, however, were available until 1943. The extensive use of this type of camp in the last three years of the war — 1943 — 287, 1944 — 285, 1945 —

273 — reflected the altered character of the farm labor problem.

The production of food depended during the war primarily upon four classes of farm labor: (1) all-year-round, (2) local seasonal, (3) day-haul, and (4) migrant. In New York State, until 1941, there was no need for migrant labor from other areas of the country, but as the demands of Selective Service reduced the available number of all-year-round, seasonal, and day-haul workers, it became necessary for growers and canners to supplement their labor force by importing large numbers of Negroes, Jamaicans, Barbadians, Kentucky and Pennsylvania mountaineers, and prisoners of war. Not only were some of the farm operators and labor contractors little interested in providing adequate living quarters and sanitary facilities for their people, but the migrants were themselves accustomed to a lower standard of living than that of the workers they had replaced, and it was difficult to get them to change their habits overnight. The war had to be won and there was always the possibility that by forcing them to conform too radically to changes required, they might take offense and New York might suffer from an inadequate supply of farm labor.

In July, 1942, as a result of complaints regarding farm labor camps, Governor Lehman requested information about them from the State Departments of Labor and Health. The report of October, 1942, which was based upon inspection and conferences, pointed out the welfare problems involved, suggested that the Department of Social Welfare be added to the group, and stated that there was a need for the following services in connection with the camps:

1. Fixing responsibility for establishment, layout, sanitary facilities, maintenance, and continuous supervision

2. Providing medical and nursing services, especially for the discovery and treatment of tuberculosis and syphilis

3. Adequate decent housing

4. Adequate decent cooking and eating facilities

5. Facilities for the care of small children

6. Control of the hiring and paying of labor

7. Fixing responsibility for the importation of labor

8. Control of the conditions under which labor is transported, both intra- and interstate.

It was pointed out in the report that the problems arose almost entirely in connection with industrialized agriculture, and that the recruitment of labor from great distances resulted in race prejudice, differing standards of living, and a high incidence of syphilis. In the fall and winter of 1942 further conferences took place, but the change of administration and the death of one commissioner and the resignation of another delayed until March the submission of a final report to Governor Dewey. This report was turned over to Mr. T. N. Hurd, who besides being appointed Director of Farm Manpower was likewise made chairman by the Governor of a committee consisting of representatives of the Departments of Health, Labor, Welfare, Agriculture and Markets, and the Division of State Police to study the problem of increased food production and the related question of the housing and maintenance of imported labor.

As a result of the combined suggestions and studies of all the Departments, in 1944 changes were introduced in the Sanitary Code to provide a higher quality of housing. Proceeding from an interdepartmental conference March 8, 1944, and upon express direction of Governor Dewey an interdepartmental committee was established to consider all phases of the farm labor problem under the continuing chairmanship of Mr. Hurd. It was also agreed that the Health Department was to assume responsibility for the twin problems of housing and sanitation.

This Interdepartmental Committee on Migrant Labor at present consisting of representatives of the State Departments of Health, Social Welfare, Agriculture and Markets, Labor, and Education, the Division of State Police, the Extension Service, the Youth Commission and its Division of Child Care, and the Commission on Interstate Cooperation continued to meet regularly. The work of the committee resulted in consistent improvement in the general situation.

Since the new Sanitary Code governing Farm Labor Camps did not become effective until July 1, 1944, in the middle of a growing season, the Health Department accepted temporary expedients made necessary by shortages of materials so as not to interfere with food production. All camps, however, were required to have satisfactory and safe water supplies and a satisfactory sewage disposal system, or sanitary privies, before permits were issued in 1944. Difficulties with enforcement, however, led to a series of State-wide meetings of growers and processors in the fall and winter of 1944-1945 for the purpose of discussing and interpreting the requirements of the State Sanitary Code governing farm labor camps.

In February, 1945, the State War Council appointed a Committee on Migrant Camps, under the chairmanship of Dean W. I. Myers of the State College of Agriculture, to study conditions and recommend legislation for other programs designed to improve the working and living conditions of migrant laborers. The first report of June, 1945, recommended strict enforcement of the Sanitary Code, provision of an adequate Child Care Program, and urged further study of problems of medical and hospital care, child labor, labor contracting, and Workman's Compensation Insurance. In August, 1945, an interim report to the Governor from the Commissioner of Health indicated marked improvement in housing, sanitation, medical and nursing care,

and facilities for child care and transportation. The 1945 Legislature amended the Vehicle and Traffic Law to require additional safeguards for labor being transported by truck.

In February, 1946, appeared the final report of the War Council's Committee on Migrant Camps which, in addition to citing 1945 improvements, listed a number of problems remaining to be solved. It recommended registration with the State Industrial Commissioner of certain labor agents for the purpose of protecting farm workers in the matter of hours and wages. It also recommended that workman's compensation insurance be recommended to farmers and that premium rates, if possible, be lowered. A third recommendation called for an amendment to the health law enabling district State health officers to close migrant camps upon failure to comply with the Public Health Law or the Sanitary Code after warning had been duly given the violator. The 1946 Legislature enacted this provision as Chapter 502 of the Laws of 1946, and in Chapter 501 enacted the recommendation for the registration of labor agents. The other recommendations involving programs of Health and Child Care were likewise carried out to a large extent with the guidance and advice of the Interdepartmental Committee and under the supervision of the Youth Commission.

THE STATE PHYSICAL FITNESS PROGRAM

The Physical Fitness Program of the State of New York was the joint product of two organizations with overlapping personnel, the Division of Health and Physical Education of the State Education Department and the State Office of Physical Fitness, an agency of the State War Council. For many years in New York State, health and physical education had been a local school responsibility. The experiences of World War I stimulated legislative action which, at intervals between 1916 and 1936, increased the supervisory staff of the Division of Health and Physical Education. As a result of legislation in 1916, the State set minimum standards for health and physical fitness in a syllabus first published in 1917. In 1937, regulations were adopted by the Board of Regents outlining specifications for definite types of physical and health education to be administered by local school boards. The coming of the Second World War focused attention sharply on developments in this field, and accented the need for a more intensive program — wider in its coverage than that being provided for the schools. As men entered the armed services and more women entered business and industrial life, there came increased recognition of the necessity for developing and maintaining individual physical and social fitness.

The term physical fitness is generally used to describe the organic power, strength, agility, endurance, health, and vitality needed for everyday living and for emergencies. The term social fitness is used to include qualities of personal character such as courage, initiative, loyalty, sportsmanship, fair play, and capacity for cooperation and teamwork likewise essential for the same purposes and under the same conditions. These qualities can to a considerable extent be developed in young people through the media of sports and physical education. Those who have participated in athletics themselves know from personal experience that qualities developed in athletic competition can be retained in later life, and frequently have proved of extreme value in totally different fields of activity.

After the inauguration of Selective Service in September, 1940, attention was drawn to certain physical deficiencies in American youth revealed by the unexpected number of rejections for medical reasons. Impressed by items appearing even earlier in the public press, which indicated that many applicants for enlistment in the armed forces were physically unfit,[1] Governor Lehman requested the Commissioner of Education to furnish him with information as to the physical education program in the schools and information as to the physical education program in the schools and information as to what could "be done by the Department of Education to improve the physical fitness of the young men and women of our State." The commissioner replied in January that while there was practically unanimous agreement in the department that the present program of health and physical education was sound, the chief necessity was "a vigorous enforcement of the law and of the regulations adopted by the Regents in 1937." These regulations had called for instruction in physical training and kindred subjects for all pupils above the age of eight years. To carry this program into effect, regulations of the Commissioner of Education provided for (a) health education, comprising health services and health teaching, and (b) physical education and recreation. Trustees and boards of education were required to provide "approved and adequate personnel and facilities" and to "maintain for each child cumulative records" covering essential features of the program.

Throughout 1941, the Division of Health and Physical Education of the State Education Department under the direction of Dr. Hiram A. Jones was active in pushing this program in the schools. The data on the condition of American youth, which was constantly accumulating from the physical examinations incident to the building up of the American Army, induced various organizations interested in physical fitness to bring considerable pressure upon the State War Council for the creation of

[1] For six months prior to August, 1940, 29 per cent of those examined for enlistment in the Southern New York Recruiting District were rejected for physical unfitness.

some Statewide authority capable of developing a Statewide physical fitness program outside, as well as inside, the schools. A number of conferences were held that year between representatives of Selective Service, of the Army, of the State Association for Health, Physical Education, and Recreation, of the Division of Health and Physical Education, and of many other private and public organizations interested in the subject.

Meanwhile in Washington a unit was created within the Office of Civilian Defense devoted to improving the physical fitness of the people of the country generally. It requested the Governor to appoint a State Director of Health and Physical Education whose duties would be to promote the physical fitness of the people in New York State, particularly men of military age, by making available to them classes in gymnastics and other forms of physical education.

At a meeting of the State War Council, January 29, 1942, the entire subject was discussed and a plan for the appointment of a Director of Health and Physical Education for New York State was approved. On March 13, Dr. Hiram A. Jones, Director of the Division of Health and Physical Education of the State Education Department, was appointed Director of a Division of Physical Fitness within the State War Council. Dr. Jones was given a staff, a small budget, and a State Advisory Committee on Physical Fitness. He was also directed to use existing personnel and facilities whenever possible and to work out his program in cooperation with the local war councils. Six months later at a meeting of the State War Council, October 6, 1942, the Advisory Committee on Physical Fitness was superseded by a new Committee on Physical Fitness created as an official agency of the State War Council. This Committee on Physical Fitness, consisting of representatives of public and private schools, colleges, industries, labor, and other interested groups, functioned

as an operating committee within the Office of Physical Fitness, of which Dr. Hiram A. Jones was made director.

By October, 1942, the State Office of Physical Fitness had a well-developed plan of operation. Physical Fitness Committees had been created in approximately 80 per cent of the State war councils outside of New York City. A field staff assigned to regional districts organized, directed, and supervised the War Council's program of activities for speeding up development and maintenance of motor skills, strength, stamina, courage, endurance, and morale. These individuals were professionally qualified in physical training and capable of actively directing the work of over 4000 physical training instructors employed in the public schools by the local boards of education, of over 600 physical training instructors and coaches employed by private schools, colleges, and universities, as well as of physical training instructors and coaches employed by industrial plants, park departments, Y.M.C.A., Y.W.C.A., Y.M.H.A., C.Y.O., American Turners, athletic clubs, and others.

Under the direction of the staff of the Office of Physical Fitness local programs were developed, training centers established, and games and other physical activities promoted among men of military age not yet in the service. Youth outside the schools, workers in defense industries, and members of civilian protection forces were also included. Furthermore, although the work of the State Office was devoted primarily to groups outside the schools and in that respect represented a pioneer effort, nevertheless, because its director was also director of the Division of Health and Physical Education of the State Education Department, it intensified in a number of ways the regular physical education program of the public schools.

In the matter of facilities, upon which the War Council's Physical Fitness Program largely depended, New York was reasonably well supplied, although its equipment was still far from the standard desired by the Education Department. There were in the State over 3,200 gymnasiums, 800 athletic fields, 2,000 playgrounds, scores of swimming pools, and numerous outdoor courts for tennis, hand ball, and volley ball available through the public schools and institutions. Similar equipment was in use among private schools and colleges in the amount of 300 gymnasiums, 75 athletic fields, and 200 playgrounds. An undetermined number of facilities were also maintained by religious organizations, athletic clubs, and industrial plants. Vast numbers of municipal parks included outdoor courts, athletic fields, skating rinks, and swimming pools. For camping, hiking, skiing, tobogganing, and snow-shoeing, use could be made of over seventy-two state parks and preserves in the Catskill and Adirondack mountains, and elsewhere.

In order to place the school program in line with the out-of-school program, Commissioner George D. Stoddard, on September 8, 1942, wrote superintendents and principals of schools urging them to put into effect the recommendations of the Regents that school authorities adjust their schedules in order to reserve sufficient time for giving physical education and instruction to all children. Part of his letter follows:

Whether our youth and adults are engaged in the production of war materials going to the armed forces, or protection of our civilian population, they must be *FIT* — that is strong and able to endure. The Physical Training Program conducted in the schools for the coming year should be properly adapted to include events and emphases set forth in the War Council Physical Fitness Program. If the youth and adults in our state are to be served adequately in this emergency, the schools must make an all-out effort to see that facilities are used to full capacity in carrying out the War Council's program.

The scope of the State Physical Fitness Program was expanded in the fall of 1942 to include guidance in healthful living, competitive programs for boys and young men, and combative and team sports. The latter were emphasized because of their special contribution in developing physical and emotional training needed by men in the armed forces. Physical Fitness Clubs were organized for girls and young men and participants engaged in active team sports. A program for maintenance rather than development of physical capacities was provided for people engaged in civilian protection and war industry. Field services included physical fitness training clinics, institutes, conferences, demonstrations, and meetings for instructors and leaders. These were conducted on a regional basis by school personnel and officials of clubs, industrial establishments, and other agencies both private and public. Many schools arranged additional time for physical education activities, which in addition to developing physical strength, endurance, coordination, and skill included time and training in badly needed preinduction work, such as rope climbing and swimming. Both men and women physical education teachers volunteered to conduct classes for out-of-school youth and adults.

Apparently, the need was great. The fact that nearly 50 per cent of the first 2 million young men called under the Selective Service Act were rejected as unfit to serve their country was a challenge. Early experience in invasion and combat showed that American soldiers had not been adequately developed physically to perform on land, nor did they have endurance to sustain themselves in the water during landing operations. In the early stages of the war, it was estimated that only 10 per cent of the men of the armed forces were able to handle themselves expertly in the water. By January 20, 1943, more men had been drowned than had been killed in action.

As a result, military and naval authorities had released the statement that in the short time available in basic training it was impossible to train men entering the armed forces for action in the water, unless they had fundamental training in essential swimming and water safety skills prior to entrance into the armed forces. As a result, to the War Council swimming program were added achievement standards indicative of those skills basic to the ability to handle oneself in the water.

To condition and harden men physically and to aid in the development of the skills, competitive spirit, and determination necessary to overcome physical obstacles on land, the armed forces developed a Military Obstacle Course. Accordingly, there was developed within the War Council's Physical Fitness Program a 100-Yard Obstacle Course, generally referred to as Commando Training. The obstacles selected stressed the development of the fundamental skills of running, jumping, hurdling, vaulting, climbing, balancing, dodging, and tumbling.

Printed materials developed by personnel from the Office of Physical Fitness and from the Division of Health and Physical Education of the State Education Department were widely used in the schools and outside. These manuals and handbooks for use in the promotion of the War Council program were prepared after intensive study of reports submitted by those charged with the enforcement of the Selective Service Act. In addition to handbooks on swimming and the 100-Yard Obstacle Course, the Office of Physical Fitness prepared nine pamphlets covering such subjects as *Combative Activities and Sports, Track and Field Activities, Gymnastic Apparatus and Tumbling Activities, Team Sports,* and *Fitness First, a Manual for Young Women.*

Reports indicate that over 5 million persons received training through the War Council program. The materials developed were in wide demand not only in the State but elsewhere in the country and were sought on several occasions for training programs in the armed forces. For example, two sixteen-millimeter sound motion-picture films were produced in 1943 through the combined efforts of the Office of Physical Fitness and the Education Department, and shown widely. *Fit to Fight on all Fronts* covered the general program of activities for both boys and girls, and *Can You Take It?* depicted preinduction physical fitness training for older boys. These films were developed in cooperation with Selective Service Headquarters and the War and Navy Departments, and they were produced with the cooperation of the film units of the State Departments of Conservation and Health. The second film was described by the Chief of the Observation Division of Headquarters, Army Service Forces, as "the best film of its kind we have seen."

A parallel program conducted by the Division of Health and Physical Education of the State Education Department, also under Dr. Jones's direction, sought to ensure full utilization of existing facilities. In line with the War Council program, it organized special courses for physical fitness, first aid, home nursing, and other activities to meet community needs. Local authorities were urged to use to capacity, after five o'clock, their gymnasiums, playgrounds, and athletic fields for physical fitness and recreation programs, especially in the areas with large numbers of defense industries. This side of the Division's activities showed a steady increase all during the war.

On the other hand, the health protection and guidance services were streamlined in order to make more efficient use of the smaller number of professionally trained personnel available under wartime conditions. Pupils under school supervision were instructed to use part of their earnings for dental and medical care. Increased attention was given to adequate lighting, eye-testing techniques, and medical and educational follow-ups for pupils with impaired vision. The Tuberculosis Control Service Program was extended to include ninth- and twelfth-grade pupils.

Increased interest and concern for effective health teaching were noted among school administrators, parents, and medical and dental organizations. Many schools initiated specific courses in health teaching at the junior and senior high-school level. In spite of the shortage of qualified physical education teachers, many of whom entered military service, an increased number of high schools required daily periods of physical education as well as a certain number of credits in the subject for graduation. In all these courses, increased use was made of the Physical Fitness achievement standards, Physical Fitness certificates, and other materials prepared by the State Office of Physical Fitness.

The result was an improvement in the quality of physical education programs and in the preinduction training for boys and young men. Constant check was kept upon the physical fitness activity standards and in June, 1944, a State Technical Committee on Physical Fitness Standards, appointed by the State Director of Physical Fitness, revised the original manuals to review existing provisions and programs for competition in athletic sports, and to secure recommendations for the extension of competition in the six competitive areas of the program. A State Technical Committee on Athletic Competitions was also appointed.

Accomplishments and Response. Among the organized groups that gave early approval and support to the Physical Fitness Program were the New York State Congress of Parents and Teachers, the American Legion, Department of New York, and the New York State Association for Health, Physical Education, and Recreation. At the end of six months, the program had been commended by officials of the Selective Serv-

ice System and cited for "its directness of attack in building physical strength and skill." Henry Stimson, Secretary of War, in writing of elements advantageous to recruits, confirmed the soundness of the New York program when he stated, on June 16, 1943, "A good physical condition is extremely important, and a knowledge of basic military drill relatively unimportant. The War Department does not recommend that military drill take the place of physical education in the schools and colleges during this war period."

The Chief of the Medical Division of the Selective Service System, Colonel Leonard G. Rowntree, in an address before the New York City Association for Health and Physical Education Teachers on January 20, 1945, said,

New York State under the direction of Dr. Hiram A. Jones, with the guidance and support of the State War Council and the State Office of Education has really done a splendid job. In fact, New York State in my opinion, has developed a model which should be used nationally. I particularly wish to emphasize the appreciation of the Joint Committee on Physical Fitness of your graded activity standards, your certification procedure, your step in the direction of credits and the need for credits, and the importance of starting at the elementary school level, fourth grade and up. Likewise your emphasis on accumulated records both in health and physical fitness, which activities are steps that are essential and in the right direction.

During the last three years I have been in very close touch with your physical education program. The health teaching syllabus should be adopted not only in New York State but throughout the nation and there should be a syllabus for the elementary as well as for the junior and high schools.

Similar approval of the New York program was expressed by Colonel Theodore E. Bank, Chief of Physical Education Direction for the United States Army,

One of the most outstanding, if not the most outstanding examples of state initiative in the preparation of physically fit candidates for Selective Service was furnished by the State of New York under the leadership of the late Dr. Hiram A. Jones.

His program of physical fitness through six competitive areas[1] which emphasized competitive activities for all and which set up a program of graded physical fitness standards, not only brought about a more efficient manpower in the State of New York, but also set a pattern for other states to follow.

Evidence from all sides attested to the fact that the program was successful in meeting the most critical physical needs of the time. The New York program was openly admired by other states, and exerted considerable influence outside the State. Credit for its achievements belongs to Dr. Jones and to the State War Council under the leadership of both its war-time Governors, for without the Council's support the initiation of the program would have been impossible.

Early in July, 1945, to permit an orderly transition to a peacetime program, Dr. Hiram A. Jones undertook by consultations with teachers and physical education administrators to revise the wartime Physical Fitness programs and standards to serve long-range peacetime needs. Unfortunately, in August, 1945, Dr. Jones was fatally injured in an automobile accident. This tragedy was followed shortly by the untimely death of Dr. Harold H. Schaff, Executive Secretary of the New York State War Council, whose keen interest in the development of the Physical Education Program had been frequently demonstrated.

While coming too late to effect a change in the fall program for physical education in the schools, the sudden ending of the war and the double loss of leadership and influential support resulted in the closing, October 31, of the Office of Physical Fitness. This left many of the schools without a clear understanding of the revision in the activities and standards of the Physical Fitness Program drawn up during the summer, and many others without manuals, printed forms, or award certificates that they had anticipated obtaining from the Office of Physical Fitness in the usual way during the year.

Following negotiations between the War Council and the Education Department, the Office of Physical Fitness was revived from December 20, 1945, to March 31, 1946, under Ellis H. Champlin, Acting Director of the Division of Health and Physical Education of the Education Department. The Division of Health and Physical Education undertook to carry out as fully as possible the field services scheduled under the Office of Physical Fitness. Demonstrations and conferences were held in various parts of the State, and confusion incident to the temporary closing of the Office was eliminated. Publication of material was continued and more than five hundred thousand copies of forty-two items were distributed on request to well over three hundred schools in the first quarter of 1946. The sound motion pictures produced by the Office of Physical Fitness, *Fit to Fight on all Fronts* and *Can You Take It?*, continued in wide demand, not only in New York State, but in all parts of the country, principally because they contained much material of a lasting physical education value.

The return to the Education Department of the direction of all physical fitness activities ended the wartime Physical Fitness Program as a separate War Council agency. In all probability, the schools of the State constitute the principal existing agency best suited to carry on and promote popular education in the value of physical development. It is

---

[1] 1. Team sports, especially football, basketball, baseball, soccer, hockey, lacrosse, and volley ball.
2. Swimming and water safety.
3. Individual, dual, and combative sports.
4. Track and field activities.
5. One-hundred yard obstacle course.
6. Gymnastic apparatus and tumbling activities.

expected that shortages of personnel will be eliminated with the return of servicemen to the State, and that use, during the war, of school facilities for adult recreation programs will continue as a permanent program in many communities. Furthermore, the accelerated program of physical education for boys and girls of school age, established in accordance with standards of physical ability set by the Office of Physical Fitness, will remain as a major contribution to the development of physical education in the schools.

RECREATION

Recreation as a partial remedy for nervous and physical exhaustion due to overwork in war plants, and for certain social strains and stresses clearly revealed by the war, was fostered in New York State by five agencies. The work of the State Office of Physical Fitness and of the Division of Health, Physical Education, and Recreation of the State Education Department has been discussed above. This section deals briefly with the Recreation Committees of the Office of Civilian Mobilization, the program of the Department of Commerce to publicize the vacation attractions of the State, and the creation by the Governor of the Temporary State Youth Commission to coordinate the work of State departments in an all-out attack on the problems of delinquency. The use of leisure time is a problem confronting every individual and every community. Its solution requires intelligent planning in relation to the amount of disposable time, to the character of available facilities, and to the momentary inclination or moods of the individual. One of the best answers to this problem is adequate recreation.

In its broadest sense, "recreation" is far more than the development of individual physical fitness. The word carries with it the idea of relaxation, mental recuperation, and personal enjoyment. While these satisfactions may all be derived from strenuous physical exercise, not all individuals enjoy the same forms of recreation or even benefit from them. The human battery can be recharged in many ways. In fact, were a definite form of recreation to become a compulsory community activity, its therapeutic value would largely be lost. In time of war especially it is important that young people and adults under unusual mental and physical strains have ready access in their communities to adequate recreation facilities.

In the early years of the war, the Federal Security Agency Office of Defense Health and Welfare Services undertook in cooperation with the national Office of Civilian Defense to organize and supervise local recreation committees. The aim of these committees was to establish recreational activities, to help maintain high-level industrial production, to support individual morale, and to contribute to the general community welfare so vital to the prosecution of the war.

During 1942, the Office of Civilian Mobilization concluded that in the field of recreation there were disadvantages in the current practice of having Federal directives and Federal supervision operating immediately upon the communities of the State. This became particularly true with the passage of the War Emergency Act which made specific reference to State War Council powers in relation to health, welfare, and recreation. Accordingly, in December, 1942, an operating agreement was signed between the Federal Security Agency, the Second Regional Office of Civilian Defense, and the Office of Civilian Mobilization of the New York State War Council. From then on the Office of Civilian Mobilization assumed responsibility for encouraging recreation programs through the appointment of special committees on recreation by local war councils. Exceptions were made only where a particular Federal responsibility existed because of the heavy impact upon a community resulting from the establishment of such war plants as the aircraft factories near Buffalo and the Rome Air Depot.

From the beginning of this program attention of both the State Office of Civilian Mobilization and the local recreation committees was centered primarily upon the broad sociological aspects of recreation, rather than upon its purely physical benefits. The provision of adequate facilities was regarded as the responsibility of industry, local government, public and private institutions, and the community generally. In recreation as a community-sponsored project was seen a partial answer to the problem of the correct use of leisure time by young and old alike. It was likewise regarded as an important answer to juvenile delinquency then, in 1942, on its usual wartime increase. This broad interest in the problem of community recreation was distinct from the emphasis placed by the State Office of Physical Fitness primarily upon personal physical development. Furthermore, it also included more elements of the population than did the program of recreation in the schools conducted by the Division of Health, Physical Education, and Recreation of the State Education Department.

On July 7, 1943, the Office of Civilian Mobilization called a regional meeting at Syracuse to consider the questions of juvenile delinquency and to inquire into a remedy. This followed publication of the reports of hearings on the subject held by the State Department of Social Welfare. The meeting in Syracuse was followed by six others across the State, attended by local war council officials, school superintendents and principals, clergy, police chiefs, children's court judges, private agency workers in the field of youth welfare, welfare officials, women's organizations, men's service clubs, and others. From evidence presented at these meetings it was clear that the lack of recreational facilities and programs was an important contributing

factor in the deterioration of juvenile morale and that its absence also tended to increase adult absenteeism and to aggravate forms of family difficulties. It was also obvious that juvenile delinquency could hardly be treated as a specific disease, but rather as a symptom of a community's failure to meet its responsibilities to youth and to the parent through existing organizations such as schools, churches, public playgrounds, and private youth service organizations such as the Y.M.C.A., Y.W.C.A., C.Y.O., Boys Clubs, or Y.M.H.A.

In line with powers granted the New York State War Council under the War Emergency Act to mobilize and utilize the resources of the State for war, the Office of Civilian Mobilization felt justified in putting special emphasis upon human resources as factors of the utmost value in its prosecution of the war. Since young people were especially influenced by the removal of the authority of a father or older brother from the household, by the absence of mothers in defense plants, or the sudden uprooting of the home by its removal to the location of a war industry, the Office of Civilian Mobilization regarded protection of youth as a vital part of the program for conserving human resources. In this connection it was found in the recreational field, as in some others, that certain local agencies were actively engaged in plans and programs having little reference to what others were doing. Little coordination of these efforts existed. An overlap and waste of energies occurred at some points, while at others unfilled gaps were clearly apparent. There was a considerable gap, for example, between public and private agencies, and in some cases actual rivalry.

To bring about more efficient local operation and to create a better community pattern, an Advisory Recreational Committee was formed by the Office of Civilian Mobilization representing on the State level the principal agencies, both public and private, concerned with the field. This committee held its first meeting in New York City May 15, 1944, and thereafter continued to meet monthly.[1] The committee's work resulted in agreement among its members on basic principles and reports were sent to all local recreation committees. Suggestions were also passed on to the communities in the fields of planning, finance and operation. The State Committee was ready at all times to consider problems and to operate as a service agency for the local committees. A monthly bulletin appeared incorporating suggestions by the State Committee, and citing successful examples of significant cooperation in the field of community recreation.

At a meeting in New York City on September 6, 1944, the following series of recommendations was approved and sent to the local committees:

1. That wider use be made of school facilities

2. That communities be aware of the relation of recreation to war production

and later to conditions resulting from reconversion

3. That the citizens who have returned from service should be integrated into the general community program as early as possible, and not segregated and set apart

4. That family recreation should be given special study

5. That every city should have its own statement of resources, existing programs, etc., as a basis for further plans

6. That the problem of the needs of youth in the field of recreation should be studied

7. The rural and village problems should be studied throughout the counties

At the same time that the State organization was strengthening individual local recreation committees, it was negotiating operating arrangements with national and State organizations. One example of such an agreement was the result of a conference with the State Housing Commissioner. It was agreed that a cooperative attempt should be made to see that new housing developments and housing units provided adequate space and facilities for recreation. Inasmuch as the problem of recreation in the rural counties was a matter of some difficulty owing to transportation problems, an agreement was reached with the Recreation Committee of the Extension Service of the College of Agriculture to prevent overlapping or gaps in service. Conferences were held with the national offices of the American Federation of Labor and the Congress of Industrial Organizations resulting in a common understanding on plans for support by these organizations of local community recreation committees. Similar working arrangements were made with the State Federation of Women's Clubs and the State Congress of Parents and Teachers. The aid of the American Legion and the Veterans of Foreign Wars in support of recreational efforts in certain com-

---

[1] Membership of Committee: Peter J. Mayers, President, N.Y.S. Recreation Executive's Association; Mrs. Ruth C. Osborn, Liaison Executive for War Services, Girl Scouts, Inc., Liaison Executive for Association of Youth Serving Organizations, Inc., including Boys' Clubs of America, Inc., Camp Fire Girls, Inc., Girl Scouts, National Jewish Welfare Board, National Federation of Settlements, National Council of Y.M.C.A., National Board of Y.W.C.A.; Mrs. William L. Lefferts, Vice-President, N.Y.S. Congress of Parents and Teachers, Inc., Chairman, Parent Teacher Association Recreation Committee, Chairman, Westchester County Recreation Commission. James E. Rogers, Special Field Representative, National Recreation Association; Paul J. Maholchic, Regional Recreation Representative, Office of Community War Services, Federal Security Agency; E. Dana Caulkins, Supt., Westchester Co. Recreation Commission, Chairman, Westchester Co. War Council Recreation Committee; Frank P. Callahan, Chairman, Schenectady City and County War Council Recreation Committee, Industrial Recreation, General Electric Company; Donald A. Campbell, Deputy Director, State Office of Civilian Mobilization, Chairman, the Advisory Recreation Committee.

munities was also solicited. Church and school groups were especially interested in the work of the committee and in many cases councils of social agencies gave effective aid and support to community recreation programs. Clearance with the State Departments of Health, Social Welfare, and Education made certain that no conflicts would be created with the established programs of these departments.

Encouragement was given to the establishment of youth and recreation centers wherever communities felt the need. A questionnaire sent out by the Office of Civilian Mobilization returned 104 reports on individual centers and gave information as to date of opening, number of members, sponsoring groups, sources of finance, type of supervision, and the likelihood of their retention after the war. This information was made available to private organizations and to the Office of Community War Services of the Federal Security Agency. A large number of youth centers was brought into operation as a result of regional conferences held during 1943.

By the early part of 1945 there were seventy-one recreation committees composed of agencies actively operating recreation programs, such as school boards, park committees, churches, municipal commissions, young people's youth service organizations, commercial interests, and supporting groups such as P.T.A., civic clubs, women's clubs, etc. Together in committee, they became aware of each other's programs and were in a position to plan for the social needs of the community as a whole, including social needs of the teen-age group. In 1944, school superintendents were instructed by the Commissioner of Education to integrate their programs with other community programs and where leadership was not forthcoming to provide it themselves. Occasionally, perhaps, out of an exaggerated sense of trusteeship, school boards were reluctant to make their fa-

cilities available for other than strictly school activities. As trustees for the municipalities of tangible physical education equipment, they were quite properly determined to prevent anything happening to it, with the result, however, that it remained unused. The idea that recreation equipment might be expendable took hold slowly. Generally speaking, a recreation program was completely successful only where participation and support were community-wide.

Although "recreation" is in some respects broader than "vacationing," no section devoted to recreation, no matter how brief, should neglect the work of two State Departments in the latter field — the Department of Conservation and the Department of Commerce. To the former, New Yorkers owe large numbers of bathing beaches, State parks, and innumerable attractive forest preserves, camp sites and picnic grounds in the Catskills and the Adirondacks, at Watkins Glen, Letchworth Park, and Niagara Falls. Such locations are beautifully landscaped and well serviced. Since 1942, when it undertook a program to induce New Yorkers to vacation at home, thereby saving gas and tires and relieving congestion on the trains, the Department of Commerce, through its Bureau of Publicity, has been pointing out the innumerable recreational advantages offered in New York to those fortunate enough to enjoy a summer or winter vacation. The Department has recently produced an attractive *Pictorial Map Featuring the Natural Wonders, Scenic Attractions, and Historical Sites in the State of New York.* The map also provides a brief historical description of the evolution of New York "from Colony to Empire State."

To those who could afford it, the State offered unusual opportunities for relaxation, healthful living, and complete enjoyment of the out-of-doors. For those unable to take advantage of these opportunities, State and municipal governments did not provide adequate compensation in terms of a well-rounded community recreation program. This need was underlined heavily by the war, by the return of servicemen and women to civilian life, and by the relocation of families upon leaving defense work.

Although the work of the Office of Civilian Mobilization in forming recreation committees within the local war councils was a step in the right direction, it was felt that possibly results could be secured more quickly if the State would supplement the work of existing departments financially and would create some official body to draft and operate a Statewide coordinated attack.

THE YOUTH COMMISSION

Emmett R. Gauhn, Chairman of the New York State Youth Commission, once said, "The resources of influences which traditionally safeguarded the best interests of our children were impaired during the war. Family life was subordinated to production schedules; draft-riddled social agencies and police departments and understaffed schools struggled along in an atmosphere which was not conducive to academic achievement or wholesome social development." The truth of this statement became increasingly apparent as the war progressed.

As early as the fall of 1943 it was evident to the new Republican administration that precisely because the prevention of juvenile delinquency was "everybody's business" an over-all approach had as yet become "nobody's business." Governor Dewey himself was familiar with "the tragic spectacle of youngsters being put through our criminal courts by a process they did not understand and sent to prison, often to be made worse rather than better." In recognition of this need for a more systematic approach to the prevention and treatment of delinquency, he created in October, 1943, an Interdepartmental Committee to study with his counsel the entire question of

the State's responsibility in the field of juvenile delinquency. This Interdepartmental Committee on Delinquency consisted of the heads of the departments of Correction, Education, Mental Hygiene, Social Welfare, and the Chairman of the State Board of Parole. These were the State agencies most concerned in the matter.

In December, 1944, *Part One* of the committee's *Interim Report* recommended the creation of a Temporary State Youth Service Commission to coordinate the work of the five agencies and to give guidance, leadership, and financial aid for five years to the local units of government in the development of an adequate program for the prevention of delinquency. The report outlined in detail the major functions of such a Commission, asked for adequate funds to put the program into operation, and presented a plan for organizing local resources in each municipality under the direction of a central agency headed by a full-time public official. According to its authors, the development of an effective prevention program required leadership from public officials and others to focus all community forces on a cooperative approach to the problems of young people. Only in this way could the services and activities necessary to meet diversified needs be ensured. The findings and recommendations of this study laid the basis for the far-reaching legislation of 1945.

The work of the Interdepartmental Committee was in part supplemented concurrently by a special committee from the Department of Education. This group pointed out the responsibilities of the schools in a community-wide program for finding and assisting maladjusted youth. It published a plan for the schools, late in 1944, with the title *Schools Against Delinquency*. This was based on the belief that it was possible through multiple-test criteria to spot early those children most likely to get into trouble, and to take steps to ensure a program of activities which would increase the chances that potential difficulties would not materialize. In general this plan complemented the Interdepartment Committee's Report in the area of education.

Pursuant to the recommendations of the Interdepartmental Committee, Chapter 556 of the Laws of 1945 provided for a Temporary New York State Youth Commission with a life of two years. Membership included the Commissioners of Correction, Education, Mental Hygiene, Social Welfare, the Industrial Commissioner, a member of the Parole Board and a member to be appointed by Governor Dewey. Its purpose was to cooperate with public and private agencies for the prevention of juvenile delinquency. Under its supervision State aid was for the first time to be given to cities and counties for (1) youth bureaus and to all municipalities for (2) recreational or (3) educational activities. Financial assistance was to be on the basis of reimbursement for one-half of actual expenditures. The maximum amount of State assistance for youth bureaus was set at $15,000 a year, and for education and recreation projects at $250 per year for every thousand children resident in a municipality. Those municipalities with fewer than four thousand children could still secure a maximum of $1000 in State aid. Loans were also available from the State for the payment of fixed charges and the purchase of equipment. All plans had to be approved by the commission and to maintain its approval.

The major functions of the commission followed the general pattern suggested by the Interdepartmental Committee and may be summarized as follows:

1. To help municipalities help themselves in the solution of the delinquency problem

2. To make studies and analyses of the problems of youth guidance and the prevention of juvenile delinquency

3. To coordinate and unify the child guidance, protective, and welfare services of the various State departments and to stimulate the coordination of children's services within local units of government

4. To render financial assistance to municipalities so that adequate and effective children's services could be locally provided

5. To plan and put into effect a program which would promote the welfare and protection of children

The reasoning behind this new program rested upon certain known facts. Since provision for the needs of children had not kept pace with social and economic changes a thorough reconsideration of children's problems was necessary. The prevention of delinquency should no longer be the by-product of either law enforcement, recreation, housing, or welfare programs. If it were true that "a community deserves the delinquency and crime it has," prevention had better become a major municipal function. The task was to find the child before he got into trouble and put him in the hands of trained people who could solve his problems before they overwhelmed him. The treatment had to fit the child. Prevention was costly, to be sure, but corrective measures were more costly yet, and far less effective. The problem could be solved permanently only by making New York State a better place in which to raise children.

All three of the approaches emphasized in the law represented efforts to attack children's problems in their incipient stages, and were believed to have greater chances of success than the treatment of the individual after antisocial behavior had become crystallized. The administration responsible for the creation of the Youth Commission has frequently been accused of a deficient sense of social responsibility. If fairly examined, the record will not support the charges.

WELFARE

Welfare is a subject of almost infinite ramifications. The weaknesses of society are not concentrated in any one place, nor confined to any single group in the population. Those departments concerned with community welfare in New York State, principally the Department of Social Welfare, but including also those of Correction, Education, Mental Hygiene, and the State Board of Parole, as well as innumerable private agencies, provide a vast range of services. Because there is no system in social need, to the layman these services present a bewildering patchwork. When war came, the outline of the patchwork changed.

Reduced to its simplest terms, social welfare consists, on the one hand, of the relief of economic and physical distress, temporary and chronic, and on the other hand, of guidance, counseling, and moral rehabilitation, individual and collective. In New York State these functions were performed under the general supervision of the Department of Social Welfare by some 1800 welfare agencies, including the 107 local public welfare departments. Public assistance is available through these 107 agencies, for the aged, for the blind, for dependent children, and for other persons in need of financial assistance, and of medical and institutional services. The restoration of men, women, and children to useful and productive lives prevents untold loss to society from the tragic waste of human abilities.

War makes things worse, for it is wasteful of human lives at home as well as on the battlefield. The extreme dislocation produced by the rapid growth of war industries, and the induction of nearly one-tenth of the population into the armed services, greatly accentuated many of the problems with which welfare agencies had already been dealing. Fortunately, increased employment had the effect of partially relieving economic distress, permitting greater concentration of welfare activities in the field of guidance and other noneconomic services. This was especially true in the case of children, young people, and returning servicemen.

As a whole, however, social welfare work increased during the war, and these augmented functions had to be performed with sharply reduced welfare staffs. In 1942, 1445 local staff workers left the agencies as against replacements of only 590. In 1943, there were 1286 separations and only 556 appointments, and for the fourteen-month period ending February, 1945, 1133 local workers were released and 674 taken on. Thus the ranks of New York State's social workers furnished their fair share of recruits to military service, war welfare agencies, and war industries. Declining public assistance caseloads, redistribution of assignments, and other reorganizations made it possible for local agencies to continue their operations in the face of such losses of personnel. This was indeed fortunate in view of the shortage of case workers capable of caring for the high proportion of aged, chronically sick, and other handicapped persons.

Like other State departments, the Department of Social Welfare was conscious as early as 1940-1941 of the accentuation of problems within its sphere of operations. One of the principal war-connected situations that it was anticipated would require extensive efforts on the part of the Department and local public welfare agencies was the potential problem of caring for people affected by enemy action and the potential problem of evacuating large numbers of people from the State's principal target areas. As a result, the commissioner was put in charge of Emergency Welfare Services and Evacuation throughout the State. Under the War Emergency Act, emergency welfare services meant assistance to families and individuals deprived of their livelihood or homes, or otherwise affected by enemy action within the State. These services, to be administered in Red Cross Rest Centers and Emergency Welfare Service Centers, comprised (as pointed out in Chapter IV) a branch of the Office of Civilian Protection of the State War Council. At the close of the program in 1945, local emergency welfare plans in accordance with the Department's master plan had been formulated in practically every county and city, and more than three thousand employees of public welfare agencies and over nine thousand volunteer men and women had been trained for all types of services related to community welfare emergencies.

The role of the department in connection with child welfare had a number of variations during the war. Under the State War Emergency Act, responsibility for issuing permits to all persons and agencies (other than nursery schools) offering day care for three or more children was placed upon the department. Standards of care and protection for children in day care were set by the department, and a system for training volunteer workers established throughout the State. The director of the Department's Bureau of Child Welfare was also a member of the State War Council Committee on Child Care, Development, and Protection. In war production areas, Department supervision of child care agencies and institutions was intensified.

Although problems involved in the prevention and treatment of juvenile delinquency were not new, wartime pressures emphasized the need for renewed efforts and additional machinery for handling maladjusted youngsters. The spasmodic and piecemeal development of existing facilities failed to provide a coordinated program embracing all public and private agencies dealing with delinquency. By the fall of 1943, overcrowding at the State Training School for Boys at Warwick had necessitated a suspension of admissions to that school. This bottleneck was matched by insuffi-

cient New York City court probation services, and its inability to utilize certain available private facilities because the city was unwilling to pay the rates charged. The training schools, whose facilities were being heavily taxed, were not only undermanned, but many of the new staff directly responsible for the care and supervision of the children were less experienced and less skilled than those who had left.

The State Board of Social Welfare conducted a series of public hearings on the causes, extent, prevention, and treatment of juvenile delinquency and published a report of its findings, *The Effects of the War on Children,* which was widely distributed. The department also studied the wartime care of children of working mothers in Elmira and published the results under the title of *Children on the Home Front.* The department contracted with the Children's Village, Dobbs Ferry, to provide care for additional delinquent boys, using these private agency facilities and services as an adjunct to the State school at Warwick. The Governor appointed the Interdepartmental Committee on Delinquency to study the whole field of State services for youth. As a result of this committee's recommendations, the State Youth Commission was created in 1945 and fundamental attacks on juvenile delinquency were launched on two basic fronts — prevention and treatment — with State aid and with the pooling and coordination of State and local resources.

In addition to its regular public welfare activities, the Department of Social Welfare acted as the agency by which the State distributed to localities State aid and Federal public assistance and other funds available under the Social Security Act. This constant and well-established administrative relationship between the State agency and the Federal Social Security Board was utilized to provide a number of emergency forms of assistance. One of these was aid to dependents of enemy aliens, entirely financed by the Federal government. This program was essential at the time aliens were being interned. When the government froze funds belonging to aliens, many of them were without financial means. The Federal Department of Justice kept them under surveillance, and restricted their freedom of movement. Federal funds were, therefore, made available to dependent persons for their support and allocated through the states. In New York State these funds were administered by the State Department of Social Welfare.

The second program developed in cooperation with the Federal government was that of Civilian War Assistance. It was set up in the early days of the war to alleviate distress among persons repatriated to the United States from enemy lands, persons evacuated from United States territory, and among persons injured in civilian war activities.

A third program was developed in connection with Selective Service. Skilled workers from the State and local public welfare departments assisted with the medical survey and screening processes of the Selective Service boards in making a more satisfactory choice of men for the armed forces. Social workers, many with medical and psychiatric training, were well equipped to sift out men with actual or potential physical and personality difficulties. The value and the volume of the work, begun as a volunteer effort on the part of social workers, was officially recognized by the Selective Service authorities and became an integral element of induction. Accordingly, an appropriation was provided for the employment of social workers in Selective Service boards.

In addition, Federal funds were made available to reimburse local agencies for the costs of clearance of information and data concerned with selective service cases. The Department of Social Welfare acted as the transmission agent for these funds.

Dependency status surveys were also made for local Selective Service boards by public welfare agencies, both in the matter of military deferments and military discharges.

For civilians, the department performed a number of other noteworthy services. As indicated in Chapter V, its field staff originally helped the State Office of Civilian Mobilization establish Civilian War Services divisions within the local war councils. It also originated many studies of war problems, such as labor shortages, living costs, housing scarcity, day care for children of working mothers, juvenile delinquency, hospitals, and other current situations. A number of public community surveys on the impact of the war in designated target areas of the State were also made.

Definitive information on benefits and services for veterans and their dependents was compiled and kept current for the use of local welfare agencies. This material was of considerable assistance in guiding veterans to needed sources of assistance. Many of these informational services for veterans were assumed by the State Veterans' Commission upon its creation by the Legislature, March 29, 1944.

Three staff specialists of the State Commission for the Blind were given leaves for service in Federal hospitals receiving war-blinded veterans. In fact, increased effort to prevent blindness became imperative as Selective Service refused large numbers of men for sight impairment and the shortage of eye specialists increased. To meet this need, the State Commission for the Blind augmented its program for early eye examination and medical care. Instruction programs were expanded to inform school nurses and other professional workers responsible for the care of children, youths, and others. The commission also enlarged its programs for home and job teaching of trades and handicrafts, placements of blind persons in jobs, and sale of home and job products. Unusual recognition of skilled and dexterous blind persons in relation to both general and war industry greatly increased their opportunities for job placement, making this section of the Commission's program especially active.

Throughout the war the State Department of Social Welfare and local welfare agencies adapted their operations to the changing patterns of social need and, despite reduction in staffs and increases in certain lines of work, continued to care for human beings in distress.

CHAPTER NINE

New York in Transition: Reconstruction, Reconversion, and Rehabilitation

WARS have always caused dislocations. Historically, modern wars are a deviation from the normal activities of the human race so that terminal as well as initial changes are involved. Disconcerting as most changes are, it may be fortunate that after a war the return of human society to its accustomed ways of living is only approximate. Certainly when peace comes no social, economic, or political clock is ever turned back exactly. In the State of New York, as in the country at large, postwar adjustments presented increasing problems between 1943 and 1946, partly because the return to an approximate normal created new rather than old and familiar situations.

In New York State the inevitability of the postwar changes was foreshadowed early. Veterans discharged from the armed forces in 1943 were probably the first harbingers of the problems of terminal adjustment. The exodus of war workers from certain types of armament factories began as early as 1944, and by the end of 1945 private industry as a whole faced large-scale problems of reconversion. The shortage of housing, especially for veterans, became an acute emergency late in 1945, for the Federal government's solution of which the State could no longer wait. The return of vet-

erans to schools and colleges also raised a critical problem in housing and in the supply of educational facilities. One hundred thousand new businesses replaced a like number that had disappeared; frequently not the same businesses, rarely the same people. Because it was impossible during the war to secure labor and materials for the maintenance of buildings and services, a large share of the State's normal maintenance had to be deferred. Its capital construction ceased altogether. Accordingly, the list of needed construction grew rapidly. After 1942, and partly due to this enforced economy, surpluses mounted in the State treasury. These brought a certain freedom of choice which in itself posed a problem.

Any analysis of the postwar situation in the State of New York must take count of three major factors:

First, there were the people on the homefront — 13 million of them. To those in business, postwar adjustment signified primarily the conversion of wartime industries to the production of civilian goods. If the transition to a peacetime economy were to be rapid and smooth, private initiative would have to play the dominant role in the process. The State, however, could help.

A second powerful factor in the postwar situation was government — primarily State, but local as well. The course of any transition could be smoothed if at the critical time the State and the municipalities would stage simultaneously a full-scale postwar program of public works. It was assumed on the basis of the experience following World War I that within two years from the end of hostilities a period of depression would ensue requiring the best efforts of government to supply an adequate employment cushion. In addition, however, the State could assist industry directly or indirectly through the localities to meet successfully the multifarious problems of reconversion.

Factor number three was the returning veterans — approximately 1.7 millions of them. What, if anything, could the State do to facilitate the rapid and painless transformation of soldiers into civilians? Could it organize the necessary services such as counseling, housing, and education on the local level where the veterans lived? Would New York society be flexible enough to adjust to that part of itself which had been away at war? Careful account of these major factors in the postwar situation was taken by Governor Dewey in coordinating through the State Departments a many-sided program for meeting head-on the problems left on New York's doorstep by the war. Although the program did not spring into being full grown in 1943, the broad outlines were conceived then, and step by step as the need arose details were filled in. The end product made sense.

In the activities of the Postwar Public Works Planning Commission and in the creation of the Postwar Reconstruction Fund the State government, with cooperation from the municipalities, acted alone to strengthen New York's general economic position. Through the activities of the Department of Commerce and of the Reconversion Service Agency the government aided private industry once more to push ahead in a civilian econ-

omy. Through the work of the Temporary Veterans' Commission and of the Division of Veterans' Affairs, through the Emergency Housing Program and the Emergency Program for Veterans' Education, New York acted energetically and effectively for the welfare of its returning veterans. In its plan for soldier voting it kept faith with its fighting men while they were still in service, and in its provision of a cash bonus, however disproportionate to the magnitude of their sacrifices, it supplied a token of the lasting esteem and gratitude of its citizens.

Not only did New York bestir itself early in the game, but its efforts were farsighted, thoroughgoing, and remarkably successful in meeting problems which in their sheer size dwarfed those of any other single state. The remainder of this chapter is devoted to a brief presentation of the record.

THE POSTWAR PUBLIC WORKS PLANNING COMMISSION

One of the earliest systematic statements about postwar adjustments in New York State is found in a 1942 *Report of the New York State Joint Legislative Committee on Industrial and Labor Conditions* headed by Assemblyman, now United States Senator, Irving M. Ives. In this report the committee recommended both a broad and specific approach to problems incident to the end of the war. In particular it recommended "the creation of a temporary state commission for the purpose of both preparing and, through coordination with other suitable State agencies, assisting in the preparation of immediate plans for a gigantic public works program to be begun just as soon as the fighting shall end." Governor Lehman and the Legislature took up the idea and the Postwar Public Works Planning Commission was established May 5, 1942, by Chapter 660 of the Laws of 1942 with an appropriation of $450,000.

Apparently the thinking of many people in 1942 was dominated by the memory of unemployment in the late thirties. To guard against the recurrence of a similar misfortune it was felt the commission should purchase for the State insurance against unemployment by paying part of the cost of plans for additional State public works projects. Later, in 1943 and 1944 the memory of the depression of the early 1920's once more became vivid, and it was assumed that the pattern of events after World War I might very likely be repeated. To prevent if possible the occurrence of a similar disaster following World War II, the original commission was continued by Governor Dewey, its membership revised and its functions expanded.

As originally stated, objectives of the commission were to alleviate unemployment, stimulate private industry, and plan in an orderly fashion the construction work of the State deferred on account of war. Its specific duties were to (a) record all designs in process of preparation by any State agency and all employment possibilities, materials required, and equipment needed; (b) to allot funds for the design of plans for additional State projects; (c) to maintain progress information on the design of postwar projects being prepared by the municipalities of the State; (d) maintain liaison with Federal officials and agencies concerned with postwar planning. No such program had been undertaken either during or following World War I.

In his 1943 Message to the Legislature, Governor Dewey gave full support to the program of the commission, although making it perfectly clear that public works were no substitute for the enterprise of free individuals. In typical fashion, he cut down the membership of the commission to those who by virtue of their office would naturally be concerned with the program. These included the Director of the Budget, the Counsel to the Governor, the State Comptroller, the Commissioner of the Department of Commerce, the chairman and the ranking minority member of the Assembly Ways and Means Committee, and the chairman of the Senate Finance Committee.

The operating principle of the original commission was payment by the commission of one-half the cost of State plans. This was expanded by Governor Dewey to include payment of one-half the cost of preliminary and final plans for municipal projects as well up to 2 per cent of the estimated final cost of construction. Additional payments were authorized for test borings, pictures, renderings, sketches, and models. The significance of this extension was to make it possible, by offering State support for municipal planning, to systematize such planning thereby preventing wild orgies of capital construction with resulting deficits, such as had occurred after World War I. No municipality was allotted funds for the planning of a project the construction of which would place undue hardship on its taxpayers. No funds were allotted to a municipality for projects that would obligate for postwar construction its entire legal borrowing capacity. As a result, the State's refusal to approve a project usually resulted in its being reconsidered by the municipality and upon second thought frequently abandoned.

So great was the interest evidenced by the municipalities in State aid for planning that by V-J Day plans were underway for projects totaling 236 million dollars, of which 58 million dollars' worth had been completed. These consisted largely of sewers, roads, buildings, water lines, and bridges. At the same time State departmental projects calling for an additional 108 million dollars' worth of construction were 35 per cent complete. It was estimated by March, 1946, that more than a full year's planned construction work was available whenever needed. Oddly enough, however, postwar construction and employment conditions were not quite what had been anticipated in 1942 and 1943.

In its fourth interim report, March, 1946, the commission stated that although the postwar period had now arrived and the program of public works was ready for launching, it would be necessary to await the availability of labor and materials in quantities sufficient to permit progress without competing with private demands. This was the first statement recognizing clearly that original estimates as to the timing of the program would have to be revised. The change in tone was the result of bitter headaches incurred by the Joint Emergency Housing Board while pushing the temporary housing program for veterans.

To launch this program now would, we feel, be calamitous. Prices are high, material and labor scarce, and private demands great. A large program of public construction would drive prices higher, accentuate the scarcity of materials and labor, and further delay the needs and wants of the citizens of the State for adequate housing. The public works program must be delayed until both labor and materials are available in sufficient quantities to preclude any chance of undue competition between private and public building.

So the program was held in abeyance. After July 1, 1946, no further applications from the municipalities for State aid for public works planning were accepted. In view of the large backlog of unprocessed applications existing at that time and in view of the crystalization of efficient administrative procedures for the reception and processing of such applications, the commission recommended February 12, 1947, that its labors be terminated April 1, 1947. The administration of the State's own construction program was assigned to the Division of the Budget, together with approval of the plans. Administration of municipal programs was assigned to the Department of Public Works, which also took responsibility for the approval of plans for the administration of the programs of public authorities.

In its final report March 31, 1947, the commission reviewed its achievements. It pointed to the fact that the increasing needs of the State Departments and the needs and interest of the municipalities during the war had made it essential that it be continued year after year. As a result of five years' work and appropriations totaling $15,450,000, the completed program was one of which the State could well be proud. It consisted of (a) 378 construction projects approved for eight State departments, costs of which were estimated at 183 million dollars; (b) 3165 construction projects for 501 municipalities, estimated to cost 294 million dollars; and (c) twenty-five projects for ten public authorities.

As one of its functions the commission had also kept a classified record of the progress of designs for railroad grade-crossing eliminations, highways, throughways, parkways, buildings, and other structures and public housing projects for which planning funds had previously been appropriated to the various State departments. Potential reconstruction and construction in connection with these items totaled $1,532,000,000, on the basis of 1940 costs, subdivided as shown in Table 21.

Table 21. Public Works Projects

Project	Estimated cost
State Departmental construction and reconstruction	$200,000,000
Highways and throughways......	689,000,000
Parkways	72,000,000
Grade-crossing elimination	80,000,000
Veterans' emergency housing.....	70,000,000
Canal improvements	14,000,000
Permanent low-rent housing......	407,000,000
	$1,532,000,000

In the long run probably the most important results of the State's experience with a postwar planning commission lay in the field of public works administration. The several State departments had developed satisfactory methods of advance planning. The State had developed "fundamental machinery for a workable capital budget system on a pay-as-you-go basis." There had also been evolved an equally efficient procedure for investigating requests for State aid for planning from the municipalities and of supervising the development of plans for municipal public works. These methods represented a distinct contribution to better government in New York State, especially since they were the logical and economical outgrowth of normal departmental functions. They could therefore be applied continuously by those departments which had inherited jointly the mantle of the Postwar Public Works Planning Commission.

THE POSTWAR RECONSTRUCTION FUND

It may perhaps be wondered how the State proposed to finance those public works for the construction of which it had assumed sole responsibility. A combination of fortunate circumstances and sound common sense produced the Postwar Reconstruction Fund which became the backbone of the entire postwar public works plan. By March 31, 1948, this fund contained approximately $427,-000,000 — an amount which could be drawn upon during periods of possible reduced employment and shrunken private and public income.

In the spring of 1943 Governor Dewey vetoed six bills earmarking for the postwar planning and capital reserve funds various repayments of advances, unclaimed funds, and unused balances resulting from specific appropriations. At that time he stated that earmarking indeterminable sums of money generally for undefined purposes in the future was bad fiscal practice. Future funds for postwar work, he thought, should be allocated by the Legislature by definite amounts, and all the existing factors involved should be considered at the time of the appropriation. During 1943, the surplus continued to grow. In his opening message to the 1944 Legislature the Governor presented a definite proposal for a Postwar Reconstruction Fund to which should be transferred not only the existing, but any future, cash balances in the General Fund.

Replying to numerous pleasant suggestions that taxes be reduced or that the surplus be devoted to special causes and special groups, the Governor set forth at length the philosophy of his proposal:

Either tax reduction or increased spending at this time would, in my judgment, be unsound and irresponsible. We must never forget that this is not a normal surplus. It does not reflect either normal receipts or normal expenditures. It has come to us out of the hurricane of war. It can be, it must be safeguarded to meet postwar needs. . . .

If we were to dissipate this money now we would be adding fuel to the threatened forces of inflation; we would be wilfully injuring the war effort; we would be contributing to the economic dislocations which may follow the war.

If, on the other hand, we husband these savings against the inevitable rainy day, we can help to finance out of them a postwar program of necessary deferred works. Let us not forget that the stimulus of public spending can be nullified by the burden of taxes and debt erected to finance it. But a postwar program of public works and of rehabilitation financed out of wartime savings can be a real, a healthy and a sound stimulus to our economy. By the proper use of these funds at the proper time we can contribute to the economic and social rehabilitation of the men and women who will return from our armed forces, seeking once more to find their places in a going peacetime economy.

This State Surplus is not ours to spend at this time or to give away in the remission of taxes. It has come to us out of savings and out of the war. As such we hold it only as trustees. It belongs as much, indeed more, to the men who are fighting this war. When they return it must be available to meet the needs of that critical period.

Upon the Governors' recommendation the Legislature enacted Chapter 1, Laws of 1944, creating a Postwar Reconstruction Fund from which appropriations could be made for the specific purposes for which the fund was created. Provision was made in the law for investing these moneys in United States obligations. Once begun, annual surpluses totaling in four years more than half a billion dollars were transferred to the Postwar Reconstruction Fund. Thus, New York State funds, invested in government bonds, helped to win the war, while at the same time they constituted a trust fund for returning veterans and unemployed war workers against a day of reduced employment.

It may seem strange perhaps that at a time when the Federal government was adding rapidly to its burden of public debt, the State of New York should be able to build up a substantial surplus. However, in time of war military expenditures fall primarily on the Federal government, whereas wartime shortages of material and skilled personnel forced the State to defer much of its regular maintenance program and virtually all of its capital construction. An additional explanation of New York's growing surplus was the temporary though rapid increase in revenues from the expanded war incomes of individuals and corporations.

The critical factor in piling up the surplus, however, was the Governor's refusal to entertain the numerous ingenious suggestions for disposing of it. As the Governor said in his 1945 Message to the Legislature: "It would be easy for the administration in power to spend and spend. That is the easy way. The honest way is to keep the State strong and prepared to meet the needs of our people, as 1,500,000 fighting New Yorkers have a right to know we will do." Taxes could have been reduced by even more than the 25 per cent figure set in 1943 without endangering a balanced budget but this was rejected on the grounds that rates

should remain stable and that payment of taxes out of swollen wartime incomes was far easier than it would be during any subsequent business recession. New York State set the example during the war of stable tax rates and thereby allowed businessmen and wage earners to anticipate their obligations to the government. This course was followed by other states and by 450 of its own municipalities.

The policy of firmness under pressure paid other dividends. In four fiscal years, 1944 through 1947, the State debt was reduced from 496 million to 360 million dollars. Savings to taxpayers aggregating 320 million dollars were permitted in regular taxes plus an additional 161 million dollars in unemployment insurance costs. In the same period it was also possible for the State to extend an additional 100 million dollars in State aid to New York City. It was estimated that tax stabilization reserves, created in 1946, would receive an additional 100 million dollars as of March 31, 1947.

In his 1947 Message to the Legislature, however, the Governor predicted that the day of large surpluses had passed. There were a number of reasons. For the first time in history the State would pay individuals for rights-of-way and would also pay the entire cost of construction of arterial highways in the cities, and one-half the cost of land acquisition, an aggregate approximating 110 million dollars. He called attention to anticipated increases in the State debt totaling 700 million dollars from an expanded health and tuberculosis program, authorized low-rent housing subsidies, permanent low-rent housing already authorized, and a probable approval by the people of the constitutional amendment on the soldiers' bonus. In view of the fact that Federal income drawn from the State of New York approximated 8 billion dollars he was unwilling to take from the taxpayers more than the estimated 650 million dollars of State income. Under the circumstances the situation called for careful fiscal planning, and the limits of the State's financial aid to postwar readjustment had virtually been reached.

RECONVERSION AND INDUSTRIAL DEVELOPMENT

Apart from the creation in 1942 of the Postwar Public Works Planning Commission, efforts to anticipate postwar business trends began in 1943. State leadership in this field was exercised through the Department of Commerce, at that time a Division in the Executive Department. From 1943 on, the activities of this agency were divided between the prosecution of the war and the anticipation of postwar trends.

In the spring of 1943, at the instigation of Governor Dewey and the Legislature, a broad postwar development program was begun. This program necessitated a review of the conditions in many industrial communities and joint action with business and labor groups on the municipal level. Four of the present twelve branch offices of the Department of Commerce were opened at Buffalo, Rochester, Syracuse, and New York City. Unanimous legislative approval was a second time secured for the Constitutional amendment creating a full-fledged Department of Commerce. This amendment received popular approval at the November elections in 1943, and the department was created by act of the Legislature in 1944.

The investigation of business conditions conducted in the fall of 1943 revealed a number of interesting facts. Figures indicated that fifty thousand veterans would be looking for jobs by the end of the year. The State's economy would have to provide these from among its 162,000 retail outlets and 44,000 factories.

By September a general plan involving all State agencies was developed for the stimulation of postwar employment. This was set forth in a statement by the Governor printed in a pamphlet entitled *A Man Can't Live on Glory,* which was distributed to more than 100,000 firms throughout the State. The aim of this seven-point program was the creation of a million more jobs than were available in 1940. Among the measures on which the State government was acting in partnership with its citizens were:

1. The program of the Division of Commerce to stimulate high level employment and expand the productivity of the free enterprise system in the State of New York.

2. Practical economy in State operations which would keep taxes at a low level at a time of high Federal taxes to pay for the war and make it possible to accumulate at the same time a substantial State reserve to avert possible tax increases and to finance deferred State construction projects at the end of the war.

3. Development under the stimulus of the Postwar Public Works Planning Commission of plans for deferred and necessary construction projects — both State and local — to afford an important additional source of useful employment immediately after the war.

4. Cooperation of the State's agricultural agencies with the farmers of the State to increase production to meet the food crisis during the war and after.

5. Improvements in housing conditions, highway facilities, and other requirements of modern living through programs of the State's Housing, Public Works, Public Service and Health agencies.

6. Availability of a State unemployment insurance reserve of a half billion dollars to tide New York citizens over a period of unemployment if it occurred. Men returning from the armed services were protected by unemployment insurance benefits which had been secured for them in their absence.

7. A program of vocational training, including special technical education for returning members of the armed forces.

Fifteen separate services to business rendered by the Division of Commerce were also listed, and industry was invited to take advantage of them.

To anticipate accurately trends in postwar business, more information was necessary about what had happened to New York business during the period of the war. With the backing of the Joint Legislative Committee on Industrial and Labor Conditions, postwar employment surveys were conducted in cooperation with the Committee for Economic Development. Research was pushed into the extent of displacement of business activities in boom towns and into the sources of the increase, since August, 1940, in the supply of labor in 135 communities throughout the State.

The Department of Commerce likewise began an industrial-development campaign to attract industry to New York State, to stimulate industrial expansion within the State, and to further the launching of new businesses. A broad survey of aviation was likewise undertaken which in 1945 resulted in the creation within the Department of a Bureau of Aviation. An individual business-record inventory including such information as products manufactured, materials used in manufacturing, total pay rolls and number of employees, was prepared and undertaken in 1943 and completed in 1945. The various items were classified for ready reference in anticipation of inquiries on needed production, potential subcontractors, and other matters.

In 1944 the industrial-development campaign was broadened considerably. A full-scale industrial advertising program was inaugurated and assistance furnished to manufacturers planning more active foreign-trade contacts. In May, at the time of the meetings of the Inter-American Development Commission in New York City, twenty Latin-American delegates were conducted on a tour of New York State industrial centers. Euro-

pean governments were also assisted in making contacts with New York State manufacturers. Also in 1944, the Department published a brochure designed to present New York as a good state in which to do business. Entitled *New York Means Business,* it was profusely illustrated in color and contained testimony from New York manufacturers on the advantages of doing business in the State of New York.

In September the Governor appointed an Advisory Committee on Technical Industrial Development composed of businessmen, engineering college deans, industrial engineers, and labor leaders. This committee rendered increasingly effective assistance in expanding the technical information services of the Department of Commerce respecting new processes, products, and materials available to small businesses.

The year 1945 marked the transition from the peak of war production through the period of reconversion to the pursuits of peace. Since New York had relatively few specialized plants to convert to peacetime use, and since 35.9 per cent of its wartime production had been in fields other than aircraft, ships, and ordnance, there were fewer idle government-owned plants at the end of the war than might have been expected. The State was fortunate that the expansion of existing facilities had sufficed to take care of the greater part of its war-contract work. Thus there were no fundamental dislocations in the State's economy, and the return to peacetime operations was less difficult. This may be clearly demonstrated in a number of ways.

In 1945, the annual index of employment of manufacturing workers based on the 1935-1939 average, declined only slightly to 130.6 from the 1943 peak of 159.7. On the same basis, factory pay rolls, although no longer at their peak, were nevertheless in 1945 still high at 253.7. Following V-J Day, New York employment from August through December dropped only 7.7 per cent against a national drop of 14.3 per cent. Payrolls dropped 6.4 per cent in the first two months following V-J Day against a national figure of 16.4 per cent. Weekly earnings for the same period fell 2.1 per cent nationally against a comparable rise in New York State. Thus in the latter part of 1945 the State's purchasing power was sustained in spite of the drastic cutbacks following the cessation of hostilities.

One reason for this favorable picture was New York's backlog of planned construction. During the weeks following V-J Day, construction contracts awarded increased sharply. By December 31 a peacetime record was set of 1,764 plans filed with the State Department of Labor in a single year. Although the State was fifth in the value of its total engineering construction, its estimated backlog of proposed construction ($4,057,455,000 worth) was far greater than that of any other state. Furthermore the results of a Statewide survey conducted by the New York State Department of Commerce, the United States Department of Commerce, and other public and private agencies, showed that by the end of the year New York's industrial reconversion was 90 per cent complete.

For this rapid reconversion to civilian enterprise the private industry of New York State was primarily responsible. The State government did what it could to assist, but the speed with which the job was accomplished was evidence of the vitality of private enterprise in the State. As long as the need existed New York concerns faithfully turned out war materiel under government contracts. In but few cases, however, did this kind of work prove permanently attractive. Plans for reconversion to civilian production were prepared and kept in readiness for the day when government contracts would no longer be available and labor and materials for non-essential produc-

tion and construction could once more be had. The war brought about a temporary reduction following Pearl Harbor of approximtely 80,000 in the number of New York business firms. The total reached an estimated low point slightly above 400,000 near the end of 1943. Most discontinuances occurred in the retail trade, service and construction industries owing to shortages of labor, materials and merchandise. During the last eighteen months of the war, however, the number of business firms began to increase, and expansion became rapid following V-J Day. This vigorous rise continued for two years, erasing the losses sustained during the war and bringing the State business population to a new high by the middle of 1947.[1]

Although the distribution of firms within specific industries changed considerably during the war, many of the shifts were temporary. Aside from the decrease in total number, the most striking change was the shift from the less essential trade and service industries to manufacturing. Within the field of manufacturing there was also a shift from less essential civilian manufacture to the war industries. Following V-J Day, although the number of non-manufacturing firms rose well above prewar levels, manufacturing retained some of its gain and still remained of relatively greater importance as a source of employment than it was in 1941.

To assist business within the State to reconvert quickly and wisely to civilian production, thereby maintaining the high level of prosperity, Governor Dewey created on August 20, 1945, a State Reconversion Service Agency headed by the State Commissioners of Commerce, Labor, and Public Works. It was assumed that the next few months would be difficult ones and that without being officious or paternalistic the State government

[1] For lack of sufficient data all figures are net and therefore do not indicate the extent of business turn-over during the war.

could make itself useful. The Reconversion Service Agency at once requested the State Labor Department to take a census of the amount and the effects of layoffs in employment in the major industrial centers of the State. This would afford precise information on available manpower. As a complementary move, a telegraphic survey of job offerings was made September 13, revealing one hundred thousand immediate jobs in manufacturing industries and a like number available in the non-manufacturing industries of the State. A survey was also undertaken of 343 principal war contractors accounting for more than half the workers then engaged in war-contract manufacture. Eighty-six per cent of these reported they were reconverting with no serious bottlenecks in materials, and 91 per cent that they were not seriously delayed from lack of vital equipment.

New York State industry was offered all possible assistance by the Reconversion Agency in procuring materials and machinery needed for civilian manufacturing. An announcement was made of the start of a five-year 840-million-dollar public works program, and at the same time thirty new unemployment insurance offices were set up at different points in the State to cushion the expected shock of unemployment due to unavoidable temporary layoffs.

On September 6, Governor Dewey began a series of moves to hasten reconversion to civilian use of forty-one large government war plants built in New York State during the war at a cost of 157 million dollars. These plants, each costing over 1 million dollars and together containing 16 million square feet of floor space had at peak production employed over 200,000 workers. The Governor's letter to John W. Snyder, Director of the Office of War Mobilization and Reconversion, urged the necessity for greater speed in selling these plants to private interests. At the same time, he wrote to the head of each concern operating a government plant strongly advocating immediate decision on their ninety-day option to buy, so that in case his firm was no longer interested in operating the plant, the way would be cleared for its use by other persons anxious to obtain space for peacetime production. A third letter went to chambers of commerce, stating that public interest required the speedy conversion to private ownership of all government-owned war production facilities, and suggesting that these organizations consider forming industrial development corporations to take over plants in their vicinity. Full cooperation, he pointed out, should cut the reconversion time on these plants by many months and make some badly needed floor space available to small businessmen seeking advantageous locations. By July 31, 1947, all but one of the forty-one major war plants were either sold, leased, or under negotiation. Furthermore, of seventy-seven smaller war plants, only thirteen were still available.

Perhaps the most significant aspect of the entire reconversion program was a logical sequence to the expanded role played by women in the war. In June, 1945, a program in the interests of business women had been inaugurated in the Department of Commerce by the appointment of Miss Jane H. Todd, as Deputy Commissioner. She was the first woman in this country to hold such a position in a State Department of Commerce. Considering that over 25,000 women had served in the armed forces from the State of New York; that approximately 275,000 or 32 per cent of the State's war workers had been women and that more than a million women had served on the homefront as volunteers, it was only fair that the State should no longer ignore the importance of women entrepreneurs in its economic life.

Miss Todd was placed in charge of all efforts to secure through government planning greater employment opportunities for women. On October 23, as an advisory group to work with Miss Todd, the Governor appointed a New York State Women's Council whose cooperation with the new Deputy Commissioner in building up a program for the assistance of women in business was an important part of the State's reconversion aid program. Conferences were held in all parts of the State to determine the variety and number of available job opportunities in the fields of housing, transportation, science, food, and domestic service. Studies were made of the kind of small businesses owned and operated by women, and the interest of women students in such fields as child care, decoration, and fashions. Statewide publicity flooded the Albany office with inquiries; the program was obviously filling a long-felt need.

Still another step in the Reconversion Program was an invitation from the Governor to manufacturers in other states, setting forth the advantages of the State as a location for business. Among the inducements listed were moderate taxes, New York's excellent record of labor stability, its unexcelled transportation facilities, and its proximity to the largest retail market in the country. The full support of one of the best equipped Departments of Commerce was promised in providing full and concrete information on available sites. Resulting inquiries were followed up by special representatives of the Department.

As a final step in the Reconversion Program, Governor Dewey formally launched November 8, 1945, the New York State Plan for Small Business Expansion. The war had closed nearly one hundred thousand small businesses in New York alone, and their replacement was essential to the general prosperity. Over fifty thousand returning New York veterans had indicated an interest in starting businesses of their own. Since small businesses comprised 90 per cent of the concerns of the State, and since small businessmen and women were natural leaders in their communities, it was essential following the war either that those who had discontinued operations reenter business themselves or that their places be taken by others. The purpose of the plan was to create new job opportunities through the reestablishment and expansion of the basic structure of the State's private economy. Sound and experienced counsel was made available to veterans and all others wishing to start their own enterprises, as well as to owners of existing establishments desirous of improving their positions. In cooperation with the regional offices of the State Department of Commerce, a field staff was made available to the communities. With the assistance of ten attractively designed booklets giving specific advice, and available for distribution in the number of 1 million copies, these men were able to supply information on such important factors in business success as methods of cost accounting, modern advertising and display methods, market conditions, and technical information as to new products, processes, and materials. Personalized service by members of the department's staff was supplemented by local guidance from community organizations. Over 120 small business advisory committees covering every one of the State's sixty-two counties were in operation by the end of 1946.

Taking everything into consideration reconversion in the State of New York was not only relatively rapid but without major difficulties. According to the State Department of Commerce, "Just as New York's concentration in the manufacture of non-convertible consumer goods limited the State's wartime expansion, the State's concentration in these fields has permitted a more rapid postwar expansion of manufacturing activity."

The distribution of skills on a wartime basis, however, is always different from that required in time of peace. One hundred per cent readjustment takes time. In an economy as closely integrated as that of the United States it was inevitable that the 1946 wave of strikes should affect New York State. However, as against a national figure of 1.4 per cent of all available working time lost due to strikes, New York State suffered a loss of only 0.9 per cent. In this respect the high degree of labor stability and the high plane of industrial relations which contributed so much to the State's record of war production, again came to the aid of the State in the unsettled times of postwar reconversion.

THE DIVISION OF VETERANS' AFFAIRS

We now come to the most human problem in the entire field of postwar readjustment — the returning veteran. Had the State's basic economy been shaky, or its level of employment during the transition period more nearly as originally anticipated, the solution of the veterans' problem would have been far more difficult. This would have been true even though for the first time in the history of the country adequate national planning for the reception of servicemen into the life of the nation took place before the end of hostilities.

New York was the first state to devote its energies to the solution of this complex problem. At a time when many states had done nothing, when others were expecting the American Legion to handle the job, or had a director working through the American Legion posts, and thus had no designated or enforced responsibility, New York had a Commission that was creating an organization and studying the problem as it went along. In 1944 in the larger cities of the country information centers were still uncoordinated, with the result that there was much confusion. Few communities had undertaken surveys of needs or requirements and there was little idea of what there was to do.

In marked contrast, not only did the leaders of the State act early in this matter, but they developed a grass-roots system with a human approach based upon personal contact and interest. For this reason, the New York organization proved extremely effective in helping individual veterans to solve problems incident to their return to civilian life. Instead of regarding the veteran problem in the mass, the Governor and his advisors wisely prepared to deal with a million and a half individuals in their home environment where they were known and honored and where they could be most effectively assisted. The fact that the returning serviceman was young, tough, and adaptable, usually capable of solving most of his problems in his own way, greatly assisted in keeping the task within manageable proportions.

As early as the summer of 1943, servicemen were returning in sufficient numbers to make the various State war council agencies conscious of their presence. These agencies began to combine with local civic organizations, primarily to help servicemen find satisfactory jobs in the immediate vicinity of their families. By the fall of 1943 plans for assistance to veterans were in progress on a State level, and in the 1944 Legislature 120 bills affecting veterans were introduced, of which 49 passed and 32 became laws.

The most important of these last was Chapter 416 of the Laws of 1944, effective March 29, which established a Temporary Veterans' Commission with an appropriation of $100,000. The duties of the commission were (a) to develop plans for assistance to war veterans; (b) to prepare legislation for the creation of appropriate agencies; (c) to coordinate the programs of various State departments represented on the commission in the provision of services and facilities to veterans; (d) to maintain liaison with other public officials and agencies operating along similar lines and (e) to establish a service agency in conjunction with the Division of Military Affairs and other departments, divisions, or agencies of the government, to inform military and naval authorities, members of the armed services, veterans and their families of the existence or availability of services for veterans. Such services and facilities were classified in the law under the headings: (1) educational, training and retraining; (2) health, medical and rehabilitation; (3) provisions of Federal, State, and local laws affecting special rights and privileges to members of the armed forces, war veterans, and their families; (4) reemployment; and (5) others of a similar or related nature.

Members of the commission were the commissioners of Education, Social Welfare, Agriculture and Markets, Mental Hygiene, Health, Commerce, the Industrial Commissioner, the Director of the Budget, the Adjutant General, and the State Commanders of the American Legion and Veterans of Foreign Wars. Lieutenant General Hugh A. Drum (Ret.), Commanding General of the New York Guard, was made chairman. At his request, in July, 1944, Governor Dewey approved the appointment of Colonel Edward C. O. Thomas, Director of the State Office of Civilian Protection, as director (without additional compensation) of the new Veterans' Service Agency. The Office of Civilian Protection facilities and personnel were put at the disposition of the new organization.

As described in the final report of the Temporary Veterans' Commission, February 1, 1945, the Veterans' Service Agency was organized down to the grass roots on the model of the State Office of Civilian Protection described above in Chapter IV. Control by the central office was thereby greatly facilitated. In addition to the State office in Albany, eastern and western districts were set up with Deputy Directors located in Albany and Buffalo.

In July, 1944, on receipt of instructions from General Drum, local directors were appointed by Mayors or Chairmen of County Boards of Supervisors in 108 cities and counties of the State to coordinate on the local level all information and services for assistance to veterans. Local advisory veterans' service committees of from ten to twenty members were also organized from among local representatives, "all those public and private agencies, commercial, professional and labor groups which could contribute to the assistance of the returning veterans."

During the formative period of the organization, the State office was extremely active. In addition to advising the localities on the establishment of local veterans' service agencies, it digested for their benefit all current Federal and State veterans' legislation and collected in book form all New York State laws affecting veterans, members of the armed forces, and their dependents. The plan and organization of New York's Veterans' Service Agency was made available to the Army and Navy separation centers, and through the Washington office of the State Department of Commerce close touch was maintained with veterans' affairs there. A *Monthly Record* devoted exclusively to veterans' affairs in New York State was widely circulated. In December, 1944, regional schools were inaugurated for the briefing of directors and deputy county directors of local service agencies on all problems likely to confront veterans in their localities.

Relations with the Federal Re-Training and Re-Employment Administration were established on the basis of Federal cooperation with the State program as developed under Chapter 416, Laws of 1944, in order to avoid duplication by the Federal Agency of State services already being provided under the law.

The broad program outlined by the Temporary Veterans' Commission in its final report to the Governor, February 1, 1945, was based upon the assumption that (1) the Federal government had assumed a large measure of responsibility for providing initial financial assistance to most veterans; (2) that it had assumed a large share of financial responsibility for rehabilitating the physically and mentally disabled; (3) that it had assumed a large share of the cost to the veteran of educational, retraining, and refresher courses; (4) that it had also assumed permanent responsibility for those veterans totally disabled; and (5) that it would assume the major share of any readjustment compensation. The commission concluded, however, that within this framework of Federal legislation the State of New York had a "major responsibility for the formation of policies and the organization of community forces for the return of its veterans to civilian life."

The commission likewise recognized the importance of general economic factors in any permanent solution. "Profitable and satisfying employment" it concluded would solve most of the problems. At this point private business would have to make the largest contribution and State efforts should be directed toward the maintenance of full private, as well as public, employment. Fortunately, New York's reconversion problem would prove less difficult than that of many other industrial states. Critical areas would exist, but in view of the backlog of private works available at the end of the war, and considering the program of postwar public works currently being planned as an employment cushion, the economic situation appeared hopeful.

Against this favorable economic background State efforts to coordinate national, State, and local authorities providing services and benefits to veterans seemed likely to bring maximum results. The commission criticized policies followed after World War I which it considered to have covered a relatively narrow field, to have been limited to direct financial compensation, and to have

been productive of "uneconomical, temporary, and inefficient results." In contrast, it pointed out the broader scope of the benefits, services, and assistance available after World War II. These it considered would make unnecessary direct financial compensation in addition to that already provided by law.

In the light of such reasoning, the commission proposed a comprehensive veteran program including (1) the establishment of a Division of Veterans' Affairs in the Executive Department (appropriation $2,852,000) to be a focal point for all State activities relating to veterans and with the duty and authority to coordinate the activities for veterans within the State of all agencies — Federal, State, and local; (2) the establishment of a system of local veterans' service agencies under the supervision of the State Veterans' Service Agency (this was actually in process of development); (3) the development of a veteran counseling service administered on a local community level; (4) the development of a Rest Camp program; and (5) development of programs relative to matters such as on-the-job training, education, and psychiatric services.

The Governor incorporated these proposals in a special message to the Legislature, January 29, 1945, and the Condon-Suitor bill introduced at that session passed the Senate and the Assembly unanimously with the support of the American Legion, Veterans of Foreign Wars, Disabled American Veterans, and other spokesmen for veterans. The bill was approved by Governor Dewey on April 11 and became Chapter 763 of the Laws of 1945. Its approval was extremely well received throughout the State by veterans' organizations and the public.

Pursuant to its provisions, on April 26, 1945, Governor Dewey appointed Edward J. Neary to head the Division of Veterans' Affairs. Mr. Neary immediately began setting up a Statewide system of veterans' counselors to go beyond the services of the local veterans' service agencies and to provide veterans with personal information as to their rights, privileges, and benefits available under Federal and State laws. This service was more comprehensive particularly with regard to the benefits rendered by public agencies and private organizations in connection with vocational education, business, personal, and employment matters.

Basic instruction for the veterans' counselors was inaugurated by means of three schools held in the Senate Chamber of the State Capitol in Albany from July 30 to December 14, 1945. Lectures on all facilities, services, special rights, privileges, and benefits available to veterans were delivered by qualified representatives of Federal and State departments. Additional instruction in counseling and interviewing techniques was given by specialists in those fields. The following April, nine senior State veterans' counselors were appointed and trained to provide continuous in-service training for State veterans' counselors. The system of counselors was then virtually completed.

It was well that this was so, for 1946 proved numerically to be the peak year in the handling of veterans' problems. Whereas in 1945, 200,000 veterans had visited the 78 local veterans' service agencies, in 1946, 653,300 veterans and 3,189 veterans' dependents made a total of 914,053 inquiries. The personnel which handled those inquiries included 161 local directors and deputy directors of veterans' service agencies, 166 State veterans' counselors and 33 on-the-job training field representatives. With a load like this to dispose of it was little wonder that continuous emphasis was placed on improving counseling techniques. Two more schools for counselors were conducted in 1946 and three for senior counselors. These latter conducted an average of about thirty local training conferences a month. Weekly bulletins of current information, suggestions, and successful practices were prepared for distribution to local agencies and counselors. In these activities the cooperation of State departments and bureaus and of Federal agencies was an important factor making for marked improvement in services to veterans.

In October, 1945, the Division of Veterans' Affairs assumed the responsibility for making employer contacts in connection with the Federal program of on-the-job training authorized by public laws 346 and 679. This program was designed to offer World War II veterans an opportunity to learn while they earned, through the payment of government assistance in addition to wages during the period of training. The program was soon found to require State cooperation. At the request of the Federal Veterans' Administration, Governor Dewey designated the State Department of Labor as the agency to pass approval on all programs instituted by New York firms. Promotion, however, was likewise needed and for this function the Division of Veterans' Affairs assumed responsibility. It made available as a field force its State veterans' counselors thereby securing complete coverage of the State.

So effective was the program of on-the-job training that by July, 1946, it had grown too large for the counselors to handle along with their primary counseling duties. A separate section was accordingly set up for this purpose within the Division of Veterans' Affairs, consisting of a State supervisor, seven on-the-job training district supervisors, and over fifty field representatives. Districts corresponding to those of the Assistant Industrial Commissioners of the Department of Labor were set up and initial investigation of all inquiries was assigned to the field representatives prior to their approval by assistant industrial commissioners. The total number of programs approved by the Labor Department for the year 1946 was over 13,000.

Perhaps the most colorful part of the New York program for veterans was the Veterans' Rest Camp operated by the Division at Mt. McGregor, New York. On September 27, 1945, Governor Thomas E. Dewey purchased this property for the State from the Metropolitan Life Insurance Company for a cash payment equal to one-fifteenth the original cost. The property consisted of the veterans' rest camp with a model 1600-acre farm. Well staffed and well equipped, thanks to gifts from organizations all over the State, and with a varied recreational program, this model facility was referred to by a prominent official of the Federal Re-Training and Re-Employment Administration as "The finest thing of its kind in this country." The Rest Camp now provides rest and convalescent care for approximately 500 veterans. Total admissions to August 1, 1947, were 2,486; discharges, 2,099.

The effectiveness of any program of assistance to human beings can best be judged by the percentage of those whom it enables once more to walk on their own two economic and psychological feet. After the last war there was a large floating veteran population, even after the depression of the early twenties had passed. One task of the present Division of Veterans' Affairs in New York is to do the best possible job of readjusting the veterans to civilian life now, thereby keeping down relief loads twenty years from now. Because a man's return to civilian life is a permanent thing, it is more important to assist him to make a successful transition than it is to make him a soldier in the first place.

Large numbers of returning veterans needed little, if any, help. Others simply needed encouragement to think through their own ideas and clarify their own opinions. These have successfully gone their own way and the agencies will never hear from them again. On the other hand, as the Division of Veterans' Affairs is well aware, while the number

of inquiries has already passed its peak, the character of those inquiries is changing and the nature of the cases is becoming infinitely more difficult. The Army was a cross section of American society. Unfortunately, there is a percentage in this country of individuals who find it difficult to go through life on their own. Those of this type who were accepted by the armed forces are now more and more in evidence as they return again and again for assistance to the local service agencies. The State of New York is indeed fortunate that as the numbers drop and the cases become more complex, it has an experienced Statewide organization that is devoted to the task of ensuring that this time there shall be no "veteran problem" apart from the normal problems of human welfare.

THE EMERGENCY IN HOUSING

Outstanding as it was, New York's program of assistance to veterans was not originally designed to supply housing or education. One of the most serious of all the wartime crises faced Governor Dewey in the field of housing toward the end of his third year in office. For ten years before 1941, residential and apartment-house building had failed to keep pace with the growth of the population. When the war came private building for all purposes except those of war production virtually stopped. Although a slight reversal in the trend of war-worker migration began in the middle of 1944, the majority of those who left home to enter defense plants remained in the vicinity of their wartime employment to see what the employment situation in the early months of peace would be.

The rather sudden ending of the war and the rapid demobilization of American forces precipitated a large number of returning G.I.'s into the middle of this already tight housing situation. With materials practically unavailable, veterans had to compete for shelter with everyone else. Coming into the situation late, they were at a disadvantage, and it soon became imperative that some form of relief be provided quickly. The nation faced the most severe housing crisis in its history.

The situation in New York State was particularly acute owing to the concentration of population in the large metropolitan centers. Out of an estimated national demand for 2,150,000 new home units, New York was believed to require 230,000. Although the State had embarked in 1938 on a program of low-rent public housing with authorized loan funds of 300 million dollars, progress during the war, had been relatively slight because of lack of material and labor.

The situation in New York City was especially acute. Returning veterans were unable to find adequate shelter for their families. Many of them lived with relatives under extremely crowded conditions; others made homes in abandoned tenements, trucks, or buses, or found temporary shelter in tents. As a result, protests began to reach the Governor in October and November. There were even calls for a special session of the Legislature.

However, as was recognized by the New York State Commissioner of Housing, the war had steadily depleted the stocks of lumber, materials, and other supplies and skilled labor was not plentiful at any time. Under these circumstances, in view of the emergency, permanent housing was no solution. Time was too short. It fell once more to Governor Dewey to take a hand in the situation and under extremely adverse conditions to push through the first State-supported postwar program for large-scale emergency housing for veterans.

Following an intensive investigation by the State Division of Housing, it was decided to make full use of existing buildings whether civilian or military. To prevent the demolition or disposal of housing structures no longer useful to the armed services, Governor Dewey telegraphed Secretaries Patterson and Forrestal, of the War and Navy Departments respectively, requesting the release to the State of New York of the Army Base at Fox Hills, Staten Island, and the Coast Guard Station at Manhattan Beach, Brooklyn. A meeting was held shortly thereafter, at the Pentagon Building in Washington, at which New York was represented by its Commissioner of Housing. The principle of assigning to the State surplus military installations for conversion into temporary dwellings was agreed upon, and within two weeks definite cooperation from the Federal agencies was forthcoming.

On December 5, a nation-wide order was issued by the Surplus Property Administrator making available without monetary considerations Army and Navy installations for housing purposes to State and local governments. On December 21, the Fox Hills cantonment was released to the State, followed by that of Manhattan Beach on the twenty-seventh. With the help of $600,000 supplied December 19 by Resolution No. 475 of the New York State War Council, and an additional $1,250,000 from the State's war emergency lease fund, construction on those projects was begun before the end of the year.

For a period of several weeks in December the housing question was constantly under discussion. Various proposals were carefully considered by the Governor. A request was made for 2,500 trailers to the National Housing Agency. Abandoned schools, prefabricated houses, boarded-up tenements, quonset huts, — even an experimental ocean-going vessel — were all considered as possible solutions to the emergency. It was obvious that many of the municipalities would be unable to cope with their local situations unless materially aided by the State. As the Housing Commissioner pointed out, industrial builders could at the time easily outbid home builders without priorities. The latter were not prepared to meet the demand for low-cost housing in view of the anticipated continued scarcity of materials and the instability of the labor supply. There was no alternative, therefore, but to apply to the Federal government once more for the transferral to the State of additional military and naval facilities.

On December 21, the day of the release of Fox Hills, Governor Dewey requested the transferral of the Syracuse Air Base, Fort Niagara, Pouch Terminal on Staten Island, Camp Shanks, and Madison Barracks. He also requested building materials believed to be at the Army Engineer's subdepot at Saratoga Springs. The next day he sent a telegram to the mayors of cities and villages of more than ten thousand inhabitants, calling attention to the situation, stating measures taken up to that time, and requesting information as to the extent of the emergency in their communities. He offered trailers, provided proper sites could be furnished, and asked whether any schoolhouses or military installations, not previously considered by the State, were available to them. He even sought their views on possible legal proposals to induce conversion of abandoned or partially occupied buildings.

Early in the program the Governor laid down the following stipulations regarding the emergency housing program: temporary construction (1) must not divert undue amounts of building material from permanent housing; (2) must not unduly take from the limited supply of skilled labor men who should be building permanent homes; (3) must not take for temporary shelter an undue share of existing sites suitable for future permanent housing, particularly where streets, water supply, gas, and electricity were already installed and awaited only the building of permanent homes; (4) must not perpetuate present slums or create new ones.

The 1946 Legislature was undoubtedly housing conscious. On January 28, following a special message by the Governor, it passed an emergency housing act incorporating his recommendations. Thirty-five million dollars was made available to provide temporary housing for veterans and an Emergency Housing Joint Board composed of the State Commissioner of Public Works, the State Commissioner of Housing, and the State Commissioner of Standards and Purchase was created to carry out the program.

Long before the legislation was enacted, technicians of the Division of Housing were already busy making research, planning, and cost studies. The State was scouted for all kinds of suitable existing buildings and material. Sketch plans and layouts were prepared. This division, the Department of Public Works, and the Division of Standards and Purchase promptly set up an effective working team. Architects and engineers began planning, designing, and conducting negotiations even before the official go ahead signal could be given. It was not necessary to cut red tape — none was permitted to get in the way. In some instances oral agreements were made with municipalities with regard to sites, with contractors as to supervision, with material men as to supplies, and with others as to the myriad of necessities for an efficient building program, to be reduced to writing at some later, more convenient time. Occasionally sites were being prepared before contracts for building were let. Cooperation was general and no one claimed that an oral agreement was not fully observed.

This has paid dividends in the form of speedily built emergency homes. At Manhattan Beach, Brooklyn, and at Fox Hills, Staten Island, for example, the first veterans' families were able to move in within sixty days after construction started.

Other legislation sponsored by the Governor and enacted by the Legislature included: (1) making available the last 80 million dollars from the 300 million dollar low-rent permanent housing loan fund created in 1938; (2) provision for financing with emergency housing moneys the construction of three emergency colleges and additional facilities at colleges and universities to meet the greatly increased veteran demand for education; (3) giving veterans an eligibility preference in State-aided public housing projects by establishing for them the income-to-rent ratio of 7 and 8 to 1 instead of 5 and 6 to 1, which would otherwise apply; (4) important changes in the multiple dwelling law, to encourage the rehabilitation and reconversion of older buildings and other suitable structures; (5) subject to referendum at the 1946 election, an authorized increase to 9 million dollars in the amount of the maximum annual State subsidy to permanent public housing; (6) the creation of seven new local housing authorities.

By March 2, the Governor's program began to bear fruit. The housing projects on Staten Island and Manhattan Beach were opened to the first contingent of veterans' families on that day. By March 31, thirty thousand applications had been received by the Division of Housing for apartments in State-built temporary housing structures. A little over three months later this figure was up to forty thousand. The need was real.

At this point it became clear that one of the bottlenecks in the new program for Veterans' Education was likewise housing. This will be discussed below with the Educational Program.

All during the summer and on into the fall of 1946 one State project after another was opened for possession by soldiers and their families. Rentals ranged from $27 to $54 per month for one- to four-room apartments, including heat, light, and electricity or gas for cooking. The result was that by March 31, 1947, the State had succeeded in housing nearly 30,000 persons in 214 of its emergency housing and educational projects. These projects were located in 39 communities and in 52 colleges and universities. The State also prepared the sites for 52 Federal college projects. The State's total program was planned to cost approximately 70 million dollars and, when completed, to provide homes for fifty thousand veterans, their wives and children.

Bottlenecks there were, many of them. Exasperating delays for reasons not always clear to those under pressure in New York State to make available quickly the housing so vitally needed. Always, however, it seemed to be the State government which understood these needs first, assumed responsibility, and fought to meet them.

This was, of course, partly due to the fact that State officials were closer to the people and to local problems. But unfortunately Federal thinking seemed predicated on the assumption that housing had best be left to the national government; that states which actively grasped the urgency of the situation and tried to accomplish things on their own initiative were interfering with national policies. This might have been justifiable reasoning had Federal policies in New York proved superior to those of the State. However, the reverse was actually true. As one veteran observer put it: "After today's tour I realize that the rest of the country is dead on their rumps. They're waiting for a public handout — Federal appropriations — instead of getting down to business. New York has done a tremendous job that couldn't have been done under FPHA."

Although the emergency housing program achieved the main results, there were other steps taken in 1946 and 1947 which helped to improve the total housing picture in the State of New York.

In December, 1945, more than six months before the expiration on June 30, 1946, of the Federal emergency price control act, Governor Dewey requested the

Joint Legislative Committee on Commercial Rents in New York City to study rent controls on private dwellings and report to the Legislature, early in the 1946 session, on possible State-aid controls for rentals on private dwellings. As a result, the State's rent control law, Chapter 274 of the Laws of 1946, was passed. This provided a temporary State Housing Rent Commissioner to administer rent controls on private homes, if, and whenever, Federal controls were relaxed. This farsighted piece of legislation was called into operation on midnight of June 30, with the termination of the Federal Price Control Act. When an extension of that act was passed, July 25, the State law was terminated by proclamation of the Governor and the State's Commissioner was authorized to cooperate with the Federal office to reestablish and continue Federal control and regulation of rents. More than one state, caught on June 30, requested copies of the New York law.

The 1947 Legislature also amended the housing law by eliminating statutory rental limitations and permitting the State Commissioner of Housing to determine rentals in new limited dividend housing. The reason for lifting such limitations was to stimulate the construction by private enterprise of limited dividend housing. Under the law, such housing could be built for middle-income families at moderate rentals because certain municipal and State tax exemptions were granted, providing the investors agreed to limit their return to no more than 6 per cent. Within thirty days after the revised limited dividend law was adopted, inquiries relating to more than thirty proposed limited-dividend housing projects were received by the Housing Division.

Although housing is still a long-term problem, the peak postwar demands have been met, and there is no doubt but what the war has greatly accelerated the tempo of the long-range attack on the problem.

Permanent low-rental housing, limited-dividend housing, slum clearance, community planning, and cooperation between State and municipal agencies and private builders, all point the way to a gradual improvement in the situation.

THE EMERGENCY PROGRAM FOR VETERANS' EDUCATION[1]

Supplying adequate educational facilities and instruction for returning veterans became a national problem with the sudden end of the war in August, 1945. The unexpected decision of military leaders, early in 1946, to demobilize the armed services in a matter of months immediately rendered that problem acute. By August, 1946, out of a total of 12 million veterans nearly 1.25 million were receiving educational benefits under public laws 16 and 246. One out of four had applied for a certificate of eligibility for some form of education or training.

Undoubtedly, the passage in July, 1944, of the Servicemen's Readjustment Act, otherwise known as the G-I Bill of Rights was a tremendous factor in heading veterans toward the colleges, but the fact that in World War II 71 per cent of military personnel had gone beyond the eighth grade as against about 20 per cent in World War I was a significant indication that the educational world was familiar and attractive to many. Furthermore, the demands of modern warfare for competent personnel and for advanced technical knowledge had placed during the war an added premium on the possession of an education. This wartime emphasis was not immediately dissipated with the end of hostilities.

As the most populous state in the nation, New York reflected accurately the national crisis. By October, 1946, 120,605 veterans alone were enrolled in its

---

[1] This section is based largely upon the study of Dr. J. Hillis Miller and Dr. John S. Allen of the State Department of Education entitled *Veterans Challenge the Colleges.* King's Crown Press, Columbia University, New York, 1947.

schools and colleges. Prewar enrollments were 104,000 in 1941, and in April, 1943, estimates by the universities placed their maximum postwar capacity at 142,000. Actually, by 1946, they had admitted 180,811 full-time and 88,301 part-time civilians and veterans. How was this magic accomplished?

As Drs. J. Hillis Miller and John S. Allen of the State Education Department have so well stated in their excellent study entitled, *Veterans Challenge the Colleges:*

Everyone expected an increase in college enrollment during 1946 but relatively few expected it to be so rapid and so great an increase as actually proved to be the case. If it had not been recognized in New York State that such an increase was imminent, facilities would not have been ready for so many students, and thus great numbers of veterans and recent high school graduates, who were fully qualified for college admission, would have been denied a privilege to which they were fully entitled.

The expansion of the necessary facilities for the higher education of veterans was such an acute problem by the early part of 1946 that only with the willing and effective cooperation of the colleges and universities, of the several departments of the State government directly concerned, and of agencies of the Federal government, was it possible to develop an adequate solution. That this cooperation was forthcoming was due partly to the knowledge and foresight of the Department of Education itself; partly to the vigorous leadership supplied at the crucial moment by Governor Dewey. Public interest was spontaneous and financial support of the program which was readily accorded by the Legislature was, of course, essential. These factors combined to provide in New York State one of the earliest and considering the short time for preparations one of the most complete programs available.

As early as 1943 it was recognized that one of the important factors in the post-war period would be the return of veterans to the colleges. Various reports, analyses, and surveys were made from 1943 through 1946 by the Federal government, by foundations, and by the New York State Department of Education. However, at the time many of these were undertaken a sudden ending to the war was not anticipated, nor was it certain that World War I precedents would be followed. The abrupt termination of hostilities in August, 1945, came as a surprise. The decision to demobilize five hundred thousand New York veterans between January 1 and July 1, 1946, however, was the principal fact which first brought home to certain members of the State Education Department a realization that the crisis would be even greater than they had anticipated.

Generally speaking, up to that time the leaders of the profession in New York had done what they could to prepare for the veterans' return. Early in 1944, on the initiative of the Department of Education, college administrators had met and agreed to standardize credits for military experience, thereby hoping to avoid undesirable competition among institutions following the war. The results obtained were approved by the Board of Regents in April, 1944, and became accepted policy for the State. Following the passage of the G-I Bill of Rights the Education Department supplied the Veterans' Administration with a list of approved schools, and a special committee within the Department coordinated all work on veterans education. Guidance bulletins were prepared and made available to the Veterans' Administration, the State Division of Veterans' Affairs, school administrators, and separation counselors of the armed services.

Secondary school administrators were likewise busy studying the situation that would face them in 1946. Arrangements had been made for veterans who were planning a college course to finish high-school work on the campus of the college of their choice. In the fall of 1945 six regional conferences of secondary-school administrators considered all aspects of the veteran problem. By the spring of 1946 the enrollment of veterans in New York State high schools was over ten thousand.

That conditions in the colleges were getting serious, and, if nothing further were done, would soon become unmanageable, is revealed by Table 22 which gives college enrollments in New York.

During the period of the war, it is true, a number of developments of a nonemergency character had taken place which helped to increase the State's capacity to provide higher education. On its own initiative, the Department of Education liberalized regulations in certain State-supported institutions so as to expand enrollment quotas. It had sanctioned the establishment of two new degree-granting institutions, the State Maritime Academy and the School of Industrial and Labor Relations at Cornell University. It also chartered fifteen new privately supported institutions and amended charters of a number of others already in existence. In 1946, the State Legislature authorized the establishment of five new Institutes of Applied Arts and Sciences offering two-year terminal programs above the secondary level. According to Drs. Miller and Allen, "not since the early years of the growth and development of our society had higher education, under private auspices, shown such capacity for rapid expansion."

In spite of these efforts and in view of the new demobilization policy, it became apparent in February, 1946, that further expansion of educational facilities would be necessary beyond the estimated maximum capacity of 142,292 students reported by the degree-granting colleges and universities. Calculations indicated that a figure nearer 200,000 was likely and that permanent facilities to care for 58,000 additional students would, at the current rate of $3,198 per full-time student, cost over 185 million dollars. Prices in 1946 would have doubled that figure. Financially, therefore, permanent facilities were out of the question, even if it had been possible, which it was not, to find materials and complete construction before the fall of 1946.

In this emergency the Education Department turned to Governor Dewey who, on March 7, called a conference of eighty-six college and university presidents to consider how best to meet the needs of New York State veterans for higher education. The Governor was well aware of the crisis in housing as he had been largely responsible for the passage of Chapter 3, Laws of 1946, appropriating 35 million dollars for emergency housing. In his letter to the presidents, February 15, he called attention to the fact that housing was one of the principal bottlenecks preventing colleges from serving all veterans and high-school graduates who were qualified for admission. The Governor called for a temporary expansion of educational facilities "by at least 26 per cent" and of housing

Table 22. College Enrollments, New York State

	Fall 1944	Fall 1945	Spring 1946	Fall 1946
Veterans	2,811	14,308	50,778	120,605
Nonveterans	130,317	127,626	137,707	148,507
Men	47,768	57,243	97,600	170,600
Women	85,360	84,691	90,885	98,512
Full-time students	75,438	71,721	109,483	180,811

SOURCE: Miller and Allen, *Veterans Challenge the Colleges.*

facilities "by 30 or 35 per cent." His letter outlined a detailed agenda for discussion and concluded with these words:

Education in our State faces a monumental task. I realize full well that it is made all the more difficult by continuing absences of teaching staff in the armed services and by the temporary nature of the enormous increase in students. It is a challenge arising from the war, however, and if it is met in the spirit of completing our wartime job in building for the peace, I am sure the challenge can be met.

In his opening address to the Conference, March 7, Governor Dewey said that while the State was in general well prepared, or preparing, for the problems of postwar adjustment in such fields as industrial reconversion, veterans' counseling, and veterans' housing, one major need still remained — that was education. He pointed out that in view of additional information available since February 15, his figure of a needed 26 per cent increase in educational facilities had had to be revised upward to 40 per cent and that institutions of higher learning in the State would probably have to take care of as many as 60,000 students above their 142,000 estimated maximum. Under these circumstances, he said, it was fortunate that New York had eighty-six colleges and universities. It would thus be in a better position than most states to meet individual variations, and to spread the housing problem over a wide area. He defined the problem before the universities as, first of all, one of classrooms, educational facilities, and instruction; and second, one of food, shelter, medical service, gymnasiums, and similar services. It was in connection with the second group that the State could be of the greatest help, and the Governor made the specific suggestion that efforts be made to convert the military installations at Sampson and Plattsburg for educational purposes.

The final decisions of the conference were summarized the following day by President Case of Colgate University. "Success," he declared, "would depend heavily upon a high measure of cooperation among all agencies of government and the colleges and universities in making effective provision for housing, classroom and laboratory facilities and transportation, as well as necessary clearances for the prompt procurement of equipment and staff." As a result of the two-day discussions it was thought possible with State help to expand on-campus enrollments to about 173,000. Primary emphasis would be placed on this program. The presidents had also agreed that it might be necessary to sponsor a two-year college program in former military installations to the possible extent of 19,000 additional students. If such were the case, it was agreed on behalf of the eighty-six colleges that a small group of institutions consisting of Colgate University, Cornell University, Hobart and William Smith Colleges, and the Universities of Rochester and Syracuse would operate collectively on a nonprofit basis an experimental institution located at the Sampson Naval Training Center offering the first two years of college. If these two measures proved insufficient, emergency extension college centers could be established to take care of ten thousand more on the Freshman and Sophomore levels. The whole program would, of course, require legislative authorization, additional facilities, and financial assistance.

The results of this conference were unique in that for the first time a specific group of college presidents were aware of the dimensions of their task. No other state had gone so far in developing a coordinated program of such proportions. Not only had the problem itself been recognized at an early stage, but decisive action had been taken by the Governor to effect a solution. Legislative support was immediate and unqualified. "It was this relatively early recognition of the problem, and the early development of plans to meet it that placed New York State in the forefront of all other states in providing for the higher education of veterans."

Implementation of these plans followed quickly. The Governor recommended and the Legislature passed additional appropriations to take care of classrooms, laboratories, educational equipment, eating facilities, housing for the faculty, textbooks, and books for the libraries. Emergency housing funds appropriated under Chapter 3, Laws of 1946, were also made available for other than housing facilities. The State Education Department was authorized by law to underwrite operating losses by the emergency institutions. Transportation in lieu of additional housing was authorized at State expense, and income received from emergency housing and educational projects was permitted to apply toward the emergency collegiate program.[1]

By dint of hard work and a cooperative spirit administrative procedures were successfully developed by the fall of 1946. Total expenditure finally authorized by Federal and State agencies and by the colleges themselves amounted to $41,-637,408. As against a total of 2,811 veterans enrolled in New York State colleges in November, 1944, the number rose by October, 1946, to 120,580 of which 74.3 per cent were full-time students. Expansion of such magnitude represented an heroic achievement on the part of New York's educational institutions. It was the main part of the program but it was not in itself quite enough. On the basis of study as to the need of different centers of the State, nine colleges also cooperated that fall in carrying out the third and final part of the emergency program — the establishment and administration of off-campus collegiate centers for an initial total of 3,550 students.

The most colorful part of the emer-

gency program for the higher education of veterans was the establishment of not one, but three, colleges located at the former military installations of Plattsburg, Rhoads, and Sampson. A temporary charter was granted by the Board of Regents May 17, 1946, incorporating the presidents of ten colleges and universities individually as members of a Board of Trustees. One comment on this Board of The Associated Colleges of Upper New York, runs as follows:

There probably has never been a similar Board of Trustees for a college in the history of higher education in America. Each board member is a successful administrator of a college or university. Each one has had considerable experience in the field of higher education, but none of them had ever founded a college before, and as trustees of the Associated Colleges of Upper New York they were expected to found three colleges and have them in operation in less than five months.

To make sure they would have some students in the fall a quick survey of five thousand veterans rejected by existing colleges was made by post card. Of these, 95 per cent, faced by the choice of an emergency junior college or no college at all, indicated their willingness to attend college in a former military institution. Apparently there would be students.

The Board of Trustees selected its officers, appointed an experienced administrator as president of the three institutions, and proceded to build an organization. Each college was assigned its own resident dean, and faculty were hired with the help of such organizations as the National Roster of Scientific and Specialized Personnel, American Association of University Women, Placement Offices of Graduate Schools, the State Department of Education, and even a broadcast by Lowell Thomas. By the end of September four hundred faculty and administrative officers had been hired. Because of its permanent facilities Champlain College at Plattsburg, New York, required less construction and opened

---

[1] Chaps. 680-681, Laws of 1946.

first, on September 23, with 1,047 students. Mohawk College, located at the former Rhoads General Hospital at Utica, opened October 16 with 1,281, and Sampson College, located at the Naval Training Station at Sampson, October 23 with 2,785. Governor Dewey and President Asa S. Knowles made addresses on all three occasions.

In his opening address the Governor dedicated these three institutions, which had sprung from a "sense of accrued liability" for the welfare of "G-I Joe," "in the name of those who gave their lives that we might be free and that others might go forward in liberty and enlightenment to create a better and happier world." By radical action at high speed, New York was able to provide educational facilities for all veterans wishing to exercise their rights under the G-I Bill, thereby avoiding what would undoubtedly have been a social tragedy of the first magnitude.

One supplementary program should be mentioned briefly at this point. Prior to January, 1944, no Federal provisions had been made for assisting veterans wishing to continue their education following discharge from the armed services. The G-I Bill of Rights of July, 1944, had not yet been passed by Congress. In New York State, however, many veterans had already sought technical or vocational training, special courses, or the traditional college and university careers. Upon recommendation of the Governor the 1944 Legislature provided twelve hundred war service scholarships, each paying tuition and fees up to $350 a year for four years. A similar number were created in each of the three succeeding years making a total of forty-eight hundred. When no longer taken up by veterans, these were to be transferred to the class of Regents Scholarships. By raising the amount of the three hundred existing Regents Scholarships from $100 to $350 each in 1946, these were placed once

again in line with the increased cost of college and university tuitions.

With all its shortcomings — diminished staff, oversized classes, inadequate facilities — the entire emergency program for veterans' education accomplished in two years what it had taken a full century to accomplish prior to that time. Changes of such magnitude unquestionably provided one of the highlights of the period of postwar adjustment.

SOLDIER VOTING

The major items in New York's postwar program have now been examined. Two others, however, should be mentioned as affording additional insight into the attitude of the State toward those of its citizens who served with the armed forces. These are the soldier ballot and the veteran's bonus.

Voting by members of the armed forces from the State of New York was provided in Article II, Section 1 of the State Constitution. In 1942, in accordance with the Constitution, the New York State Legislature passed a law guaranteeing to members of the armed forces both within and without the continental United States the right to execute a full ballot for State and municipal offices. A bipartisan War Ballot Commission was created to administer the law. Virtually the same law was reenacted in 1943.

In these two elections, however, the soldier vote in New York State was small both numerically and by per cent. The procedure under the law proved impossible of effective operation owing to lack of cooperation from the heads of the armed forces. With them, security and administrative reasons were properly dominant and the State Commission's request for the names and addresses of New York service men was not granted. Consequently, State ballots could be sent only to those soldiers whose addresses were given by interested persons or were obtained from local selective service boards, or local newspaper lists, or if the soldiers themselves voluntarily mailed in State or Federal applications requesting ballots. The total servicemen's vote in 1942 and 1943 was 27,281 and 41,103 respectively.

In 1944, the question arose early as to how an effective soldier vote could be secured in the crucial national elections of that year. Without Congressional action the armed services had not been willing, or able, to cooperate with the states. Congress put a different face on the matter by providing an acceptable all-purpose postcard application blank and an unacceptable short-form ballot for Federal candidates only. In its zeal to ensure in all of the forty-eight states an effective voting system in time for the November elections, Congress was inclined to disregard the importance of voting for state and local candidates even though such a procedure was specifically provided for in state constitutions such as that of New York.

Since, under the New York Constitution, a short-form ballot omitting the names of candidates for State and local offices would have amounted to a partial disfranchisement of New York's soldiers, it was clearly illegal. Governor Dewey had no choice but to work out a procedure for getting to New York soldiers overseas a full ballot comparable to the standard absentee ballot available within the continental limits of the United States to all New York voters including soldiers. This ballot had to meet War and Navy Department specifications, and could not be dependent for its delivery upon securing from the services prior lists of New York voters in the armed forces.

Under the New York Law, Chapter 183, Laws of 1944, the serviceman overseas simply signed the Federal post card giving his home and military addresses. Upon receipt and checking of his postcard application, he was mailed a full ballot identical with that used by voters at home, containing the names of all candidates. Accompanying the ballot was a self-addressed, postage-free envelope. All the voter had to do was sign a simple oath, mark his ballot, put it in the envelope, seal it, and give it to his voting officer. For the soldier, voting was easy; for State officials back home it meant considerable work. The plan, however, proved effective despite dire predictions from political opponents.

New York's total effective soldier vote of 422,698 was approximately 46.6 per cent of the eligible New York voters in service, and almost double the vote cast in the second largest state, Pennsylvania. It also represented the highest percentage recorded in any of the ten most populous states.

In contrast, the Federal ballot was used entirely overseas and authorized by only twenty states. From these states only 5.3 per cent of the soldiers of voting age executed the ballot, a total out of 7.6 million ballots distributed of only 98,823, or less than one-fourth the total overseas vote of New York alone. In a subsequent report to Congress, the Secretary of War described the Federal balloting procedure as "excessively complex" and criticized it for imposing upon the armed services "burdens disproportionate to any resulting utility."

Whereas New York has made permanent its servicemen's vote law, the Federal system has been discontinued.

THE VETERANS' BONUS

With the end of the war and the approach of the 1946 legislative session all sorts of proposals were broached in the interest of veterans. On recommendation from the Governor that the Legislature take these matters out of the realm of partisan politics and consider them on their merits, the State Legislature, by joint resolution, January 15, created a Joint Legislative Bipartisan Committee to Consider Proposals on Veterans' Benefits. Senator William F. Condon of Yonkers was appointed chairman; Daniel Flynn of New York City, vice chairman; and Brigadier General William F. Donovan, counsel.

On February 12, the committee held a public conference in Albany to which were invited representatives of numerous veteran, union, civil service, and other groups and organizations. An excellent cross section of prevailing opinion was thereby secured on questions concerning veterans' benefits. At the conference the two most discussed subjects were a veterans' bonus and veterans' housing. A list of the subjects brought up and the number of proposals made regarding each follows: the bonus (38); housing (24); repayment of pension contributions of civil service veterans (12); veteran education (12); loans (7); employment for veterans (6); civil service preference for veterans (5); tax exemption (2); miscellaneous (13).

For three weeks the committee considered all aspects of the problem including precedents from World War I. At that time the State had paid a cash bonus of $10 for each month of service up to a maximum of $150. The total cost of the original 45 million-dollar loan amortized over a period of twenty-five years came to 70 million dollars. It was felt the amount of the individual payments could be increased and that the number of annual interest payments could be cut to ten. On March 6, the committee recommended the payment of a cash bonus to veterans of World War II with payments apportioned as follows:

$50 for service of 60 days or less within the United States

$150 for service of more than 60 days within the United States

$250 for overseas service of any duration

Eligibility requirements included:

1. Service in the armed forces during the period from December 7, 1941 to September 2, 1945

2. Residence within the State for six months immediately prior to entry into service and residence at the time of application for the benefits

3. Honorable discharge if separated from the service

In the case of those who died while on active duty, or since September 2, 1945, payments would go to their next of kin.

Assuming a total of 1.7 million veterans for New York State, the committee estimated the State would have to borrow 400 million dollars to pay the loan. Cutting the amortization period from twenty-five years to ten would save a large sum in interest.

The New York State Constitution prohibits the borrowing of funds by the State for making gifts to private individuals. For that reason one early bonus law, 1920, had been declared unconstitutional. After a delay of four years it was found necessary to pass a Constitutional amendment providing specifically for the borrowing of moneys to pay the bonus. In the light of the earlier experience, the committee finally recommended a concurrent resolution of the Legislature proposing an amendment to Article VII of the State Constitution to authorize a bond issue in the exact amount of 400 million dollars for payment of a soldiers' bonus. The amendment was made as specific as possible to give voters a clear program on which to vote. The concurrent resolution was passed by the Legislature in 1946 and 1947, and approved by the people at the November elections. Certainly no bonus can compensate veterans for their sacrifices but it can at least express a people's sense of gratitude.

CHAPTER TEN

The New York State War Council Organization

O NE of the chief criticisms of the democratic form of government after World War I was that it was unable to function quickly in a crisis. Only dictatorships, it was claimed, could solve problems with thoroughness and dispatch. If the Second World War did nothing else, it has successfully dispelled the illusion upon which this charge is based. A true democracy can act swiftly and surely in a crisis and can also delegate power of action to a small number of its citizens without fear that power, so delegated, may be used to destroy the democratic character of the very society from which it derives authority. The operation of the New York State War Council from August 1, 1940, to April 1, 1946, furnishes one of the best modern examples of this process of the centralization of power in the hands of a few and of its effective use under proper direction.

In the Second World War, to arrange a close buyer-seller relationship between the Federal government and a few of the larger units in private industry was not enough. Total war was being waged abroad and total mobilization of American resources and manpower became essential. Such total mobilization brought to New York State definite problems of organization and procedure. The leaders at Albany felt that they owed to the people a certain responsibility beyond that accepted by the Federal government,

and that they must be prepared to act on war-connected problems without the delay entailed in waiting for directives from Washington. Local problems must be met by local authority, but under war conditions, with time at a premium, the routine of legislative action was considered too slow. By 1940, it became an accepted fact that some agency equipped to deal swiftly with emergencies was required. For emergency service the Legislature, a part-time body with time-consuming procedure, was obviously unsuited. The time had come to delegate authority.

In New York State, instead of delegating emergency powers to the Executive, virtually eliminating the Legislature from the governing process, a compromise was developed in the form of a War Council under which the Governor shared responsibility for quick action with other elective officers, the leaders of the Legislature, and a number of members appointed by the Governor. This dual participation of the Executive and the Legislature in policy making, with the retention of the annual legislative session, proved an effective solution.

Like most emergency political devices the New York State War Council, with its 108 local war councils, did not spring into being fully matured; its final form was achieved only after some two years of trial and error. Fortunately, the formative period was largely over when war came, the testing had come while the country was still at peace, and the severe demands put upon the War Council from 1942 to 1945 were met with efficiency and a minimum of friction. The fact that it was completely liquidated in form and substance, April 1, 1946, (except for winding-up details) and that the regular legislative and executive processes of the State were maintained throughout the period of wartime emergency, is a tribute to the wisdom and moderation of the political leaders of both parties, and an outstanding example of the flexibility of democratic government in America. It was not necessary, as some had feared, that in order to triumph in a war against dictatorships democracy must itself become totalitarian.

Just as credit goes to one Governor for the initial creation and early development and expansion of the War Council, so should credit go to his successor for the rapid extension of its functions in the fields of food production and nutrition, child care, antidiscrimination, postwar services to youth and to veterans, industrial reconversion, and emergency housing, as well as for its gradual and orderly liquidation when the need for its services ceased to exist.

ORIGINS AND EARLY EVOLUTION

The origins of the New York State War Council date from 1940, when defense problems became too numerous and too complex for the Governor to handle unaided. This development came earlier in New York State than elsewhere largely because of the interest that Governor Lehman took in national defense, and partly because of his early conviction that war with the dictatorships was inevitable. To a degree, this interest and conviction of the Governor may be explained by his close association with President Roosevelt, his wide personal and business connections, and his experiences in the First World War. However, various moves by the Federal government during 1940, the inauguration of the defense-production program, the induction of the National Guard into Federal service, and the passage of the Selective Service Act forced new and varied problems upon the executives of all states.

The appointment on July 1, 1940, of Lieutenant Governor Charles Poletti as State Coordinator of National Defense reflected this intensification of administrative problems in the sphere of national defense. The appointment of the Defense Council as an advisory body to the Governor, August 1, reflected the growing complexity of the decisions that the Governor had to make. The fact that the council's membership consisted originally of representatives of industry, labor, agriculture, the utilities, transportation, and banking is evidence that the initial problems were primarily economic and were connected with war production. It is significant that during its entire existence no department head, with the exception of the Attorney General, was appointed to the War Council.

The State War Council was the product of rapid development. At the time of the original appointments, the Governor and his advisors had for guidance very few precedents from the First World War. There had been a State Defense Council in 1917 and 1918 and extraordinary powers had been granted the Governor, but very little detailed information on their operation was available, and what was known appeared unsuited to the 1940 situation. Lacking both a blueprint and an inclination on the part of the Executive to venture upon any initial large-scale organization, expansion of the council's operations took place by stages and only following demonstrated necessity. This was true both of the Headquarters staff and of the Statewide War Council organization. As time passed and problems raised by the defense programs became increasingly complex, the realization grew that their solution was a matter too involved for a mere executive committee. What had begun as a side line in the executive chambers had assumed an importance which demanded the political and financial support of the Legislature. During the formative period of 1941, New York's Legislature was Republican while the Governor was a Democrat. The influence of this situation upon the development of the council is difficult to assess. Whatever that influence may have been, the Legislature of that year placed the organization upon a statutory basis.

Meanwhile, the need for organizing the local communities had become apparent. Only a month and a half after the original appointment of the council, the Governor, in attempting to achieve decentralization of responsibility as well as of administration, had requested that the cities and counties appoint local defense councils. This request met prompt compliance in the populous centers, but in rural areas the response was less rapid, and to effect a complete coverage of the State considerable urging and a number of visits from the War Plans Coordinator and others were required. For a short time during late 1940 and early 1941 the lack of specific functions for the local councils raised the question as to whether their interest could be maintained. However, following the passage of Chapter 22 of the Laws of 1941, and with the acceleration of the defense program, request after request began to reach the local councils from Albany, resulting in local recognition that their duties were important and their existence essential.

As previously stated, Chapter 22 of the Laws of 1941 effected a basic change in the formation of the council. The Advisory Defense Council became a statutory temporary commission composed not alone of the Governor's previous appointees, all of whom were now given blanket approval by the Legislature, but

also of the four principal legislative leaders. Henceforth, the council was to include the Governor as chairman, the Lieutenant Governor, the temporary President of the Senate, the Speaker of the Assembly, and the minority leaders of the two chambers. The Governor was authorized to designate a member of the council as vice-chairman, and all appointed council members were to serve during his pleasure.

This same chapter stated specifically that the general purpose of the council was:

To promote State and national security by formulating and assisting in the execution of plans for the mobilization and efficient utilization of the resources and facilities of the State, and for the coordination and direction of State and local activities related to State and national defense.

The law did not make mandatory the establishment of defense councils by cities and counties, but once established local councils were under obligations to cooperate with the State Council in the performance of its duties. These local councils were provided, within their respective jurisdictions, powers and duties exactly parallel to those of the State Council, and the cities and counties were authorized to appropriate the necessary funds for their purposes. It was specifically recommended that to avoid expensive duplication of existing facilities both State and local councils should utilize as far as possible the services and facilities existing in State and local governmental agencies.

Although in 1941 the country was still at peace, the alarming success of Axis forces and a growing sense of danger from both east and west made it relatively easy to secure the popular support needed to make effective the policies initiated by the council. To be sure, even in 1941 there were still those who asked, "Why do we need all this? We are not going to get into war." Had not both presidential candidates tacitly underwritten this sentiment during the 1940 election? As 1941 wore on, however, more and more individuals became convinced that inevitably America would become involved.

The transition from peace to war, a change which came suddenly early in December, resulted in a marked change in the tone of comunications from Albany. Typical is the following telegram which Governor Lehman sent to all defense councils the day following Pearl Harbor:

In order to minimize confusion you are hereby *directed* to enroll all civilians wishing to volunteer in either Civilian Protection or community services through the volunteer offices connected with your council. If you have not already established a volunteer office according to standards set by the State Council of Defense, *proceed to do so immediately*.[1]

For exercising the authority essential to meeting the emergency, the composition of the council was excellent. Within its circle it now included the leaders of both the executive and the legislative branches of the State government. When war came, the council was organized and operating, and from December 7 it could feel secure in assuming powers with which it became officially endowed only following the passage of the comprehensive War Emergency Act of April, 1942. The passage of this act marked the crystallization into law of the previously established organization of the New York State War Council. The earlier statute, Chapter 22, passed February 19, 1941, occupied but two and a quarter pages in the War Council's first Annual Report. At that date, no flight of the imagination could have projected the War Council organization in detail. The Act of 1942 ran to thirty-five pages in describing those features established and functioning at the end of 1941. As is generally true of law, the detailed provisions were based on prior experience.

---

[1] Italics by the author.

MEMBERSHIP AND POWERS OF THE STATE WAR COUNCIL UNDER THE WAR EMERGENCY ACT

The War Emergency Act of 1942 produced a number of changes in the membership and powers of the State War Council. Its title was changed from Defense Council to War Council, and its membership limited to twenty, of whom but ten[1] were to be appointed by the Governor. Upon the resignation of one of the original members, recognition was given to the importance of the problem of racial discrimination by the appointment to the vacancy of an outstanding Negro. Ten members of the Council were specifically named by the War Emergency Act which, in addition to those already on the council, added the Attorney General, the Majority Leader of the Assembly, and the Chairman of the Ways and Means Committee of the Assembly.

While Herbert H. Lehman was Governor he presided over the meetings of the War Council, many of which were held at his home in New York City. In 1943, with a change in administration, Lieutenant Governor Thomas W. Wallace, who was Coordinator of State War Plans, presided. Upon his death, active chairmanship of the council was assumed by Governor Dewey. In November, 1943, Lieutenant Governor Joe R. Hanley was designated as vice-chairman and Speaker Oswald D. Heck as Coordinator of War Plans. The War Council met periodically, at first twice a month, then once a month, and finally as organization improved, as the end of the war approached, and with it the development of a smaller number of pressing problems, meetings were held only at the call of the Governor.

The State War Council was essentially a policy-forming body in line with its general commission under the War Emer-

---

[1] Changed to twelve by Chap. 171, Laws of 1943.

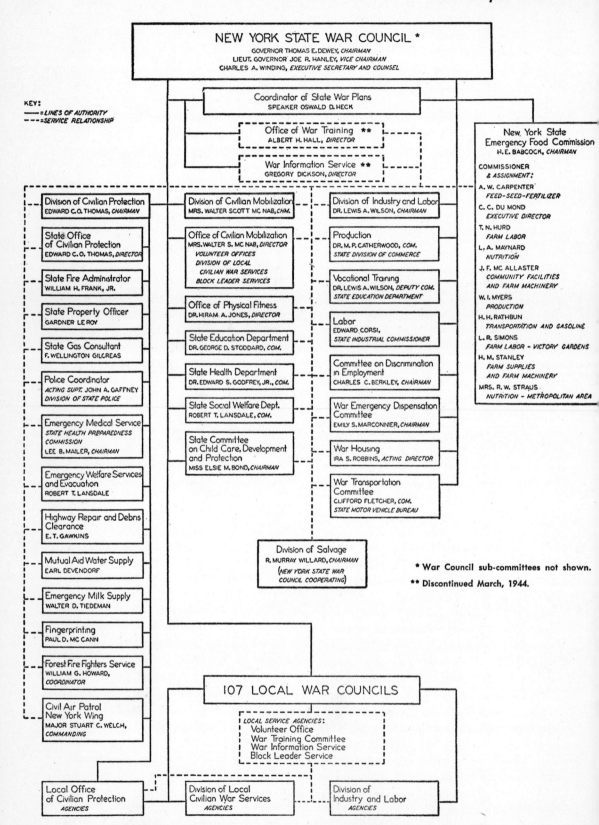

KEY:
— = LINES OF AUTHORITY
--- = SERVICE RELATIONSHIP

NEW YORK STATE WAR COUNCIL *
GOVERNOR THOMAS E. DEWEY, *CHAIRMAN*
LIEUT. GOVERNOR JOE R. HANLEY, *VICE CHAIRMAN*
CHARLES A. WINDING, *EXECUTIVE SECRETARY AND COUNSEL*

Coordinator of State War Plans
SPEAKER OSWALD D. HECK

Office of War Training **
ALBERT H. HALL, *DIRECTOR*

War Information Service **
GREGORY DICKSON, *DIRECTOR*

New York State
Emergency Food Commission
H. E. BABCOCK, *CHAIRMAN*

COMMISSIONER
& ASSIGNMENT:
A. W. CARPENTER
FEED-SEED-FERTILIZER
C. C. DU MOND
EXECUTIVE DIRECTOR
T. N. HURD
FARM LABOR
L. A. MAYNARD
NUTRITION
J. F. MC ALLASTER
*COMMUNITY FACILITIES
AND FARM MACHINERY*
W. I. MYERS
PRODUCTION
H. H. RATHBUN
TRANSPORTATION AND GASOLINE
L. R. SIMONS
FARM LABOR - VICTORY GARDENS
H. M. STANLEY
*FARM SUPPLIES
AND FARM MACHINERY*
MRS. R. W. STRAUS
NUTRITION - METROPOLITAN AREA

Division of Civilian Protection
EDWARD C. O. THOMAS, *CHAIRMAN*

State Office
of Civilian Protection
EDWARD C. O. THOMAS, *DIRECTOR*

State Fire Administrator
WILLIAM H. FRANK, JR.

State Property Officer
GARDNER LE ROY

State Gas Consultant
F. WELLINGTON GILCREAS

Police Coordinator
ACTING SUPT. JOHN A. GAFFNEY
DIVISION OF STATE POLICE

Emergency Medical Service
*STATE HEALTH PREPAREDNESS
COMMISSION*
LEE B. MAILER, *CHAIRMAN*

Emergency Welfare Services
and Evacuation
ROBERT T. LANSDALE

Highway Repair and Debris
Clearance
E. T. GAWKINS

Mutual Aid Water Supply
EARL DEVENDORF

Emergency Milk Supply
WALTER D. TIEDEMAN

Fingerprinting
PAUL D. MC CANN

Forest Fire Fighters Service
WILLIAM G. HOWARD,
COORDINATOR

Civil Air Patrol
New York Wing
MAJOR STUART C. WELCH,
COMMANDING

Division of Civilian Mobilization
MRS. WALTER SCOTT MC NAB, *CHM.*

Office of Civilian Mobilization
MRS. WALTER S. MC NAB, *DIRECTOR*
*VOLUNTEER OFFICES
DIVISION OF LOCAL
CIVILIAN WAR SERVICES
BLOCK LEADER SERVICES*

Office of Physical Fitness
DR. HIRAM A. JONES, *DIRECTOR*

State Education Department
DR. GEORGE D. STODDARD, *COM.*

State Health Department
DR. EDWARD S. GODFREY, JR., *COM.*

State Social Welfare Dept.
ROBERT T. LANSDALE, *COM.*

State Committee
on Child Care, Development
and Protection
MISS ELSIE M. BOND, *CHAIRMAN*

Division of Industry and Labor
DR. LEWIS A. WILSON, *CHAIRMAN*

Production
DR. M. P. CATHERWOOD, *COM.*
STATE DIVISION OF COMMERCE

Vocational Training
DR. LEWIS A. WILSON, *DEPUTY COM.*
STATE EDUCATION DEPARTMENT

Labor
EDWARD CORSI,
STATE INDUSTRIAL COMMISSIONER

Committee on Discrimination
in Employment
CHARLES C. BERKLEY, *CHAIRMAN*

War Emergency Dispensation
Committee
EMILY S. MARCONNIER, *CHAIRMAN*

War Housing
IRA S. ROBBINS, *ACTING DIRECTOR*

War Transportation
Committee
CLIFFORD FLETCHER, *COM.*
STATE MOTOR VEHICLE BUREAU

Division of Salvage
R. MURRAY WILLARD, *CHAIRMAN*
*(NEW YORK STATE WAR
COUNCIL COOPERATING)*

* War Council sub-committees not shown.
** Discontinued March, 1944.

107 LOCAL WAR COUNCILS

LOCAL SERVICE AGENCIES:
Volunteer Office
War Training Committee
War Information Service
Block Leader Service

Local Office
of Civilian Protection
AGENCIES

Division of Local
Civilian War Services
AGENCIES

Division of
Industry and Labor
AGENCIES

Chart of the New York State War Council, November, 1943

gency Act "to formulate and assist in the execution of plans for the mobilization and efficient utilization of the resources and facilities of the State, and for the coordination and direction of State and local activities related to civilian protection and to State and national defense." In addition to its general functions, it had power to allocate for specific purposes monies generally appropriated to it by the Legislature. It also had power to "adopt, promulgate, and make effective plans, rules and orders with respect to any matter deemed by the State War Council essential to the war effort." Similar powers were granted with respect to civilian protection, provided State action did not conflict with rules and orders of the Army or of the Navy.

Official action by the council generally took the form of the promulgation of an order or a *resolution*, the latter being the vehicle for rules and regulations, financial allocations, and commendatory action. Its *orders* were in the nature of administrative legislation. Most of these dealt with transportation matters, such as regulation of speed limits, use of buses, and prohibition of racing. One provided for the enforcement of Office of Price Administration regulations in State courts, another provided similar enforcement for the so-called brown-out order of the War Production Board, and others supplied legal authority when statutory law was silent on the subject.

Certain specific powers granted the War Council under the War Emergency Act reflected the rapid expansion of its functions in 1941. In addition to establishing and defining anew the powers of the State and local war councils, the act created a Civilian Protection organization. As part of this organization it included the Police Mobilization Plan, the Mutual-aid Plans for Fire Defense, Highway Repair and Debris Clearance, specific financial procedures, administration of emergency relief, regulations developed in 1941 for closing or restricting the

use of highways or waterways, for the posting of property, and the establishment of emergency health and sanitation areas. Separate laws provided for the Water Supply Coordination Plan and for the Emergency Milk Plan. The War Emergency Act also provided for granting dispensations from limitations imposed by the labor laws upon hours of work and the age of workers, and it included a section on the manufacture and sale of prison-made articles and materials necessary for the prosecution of the war, pursuant to which such articles were manufactured for agencies of the United States.

Implicit in the War Emergency Act were three fundamental principles of organization. The first was the separation of all civilian protection activities, enumerated in Chapter IV, from the more miscellaneous group of programs designated as Community War Services. This separation was achieved by establishing a Statewide civilian protection organization under the authority of a State director. The second principle was the creation of a single command within this organization on both State and local levels. Just as the State director of civilian protection had authority over all civilian protection programs, and in time of emergency over all individuals, so on the local level did the local director of civilian protection have similar authority over all community defense organizations in time of attack. This director, who was appointed by, and could be removed by, the mayor of his city or chairman of his board of supervisors, was in time of emergency the essential coordinating agent for defense in the municipalities.

The third administrative principle in the act was the establishment of a line of authority from the State to local governments. Just as in the sphere of national defense the State took its orders from the Federal government, so, henceforth, the communities would act pursuant to

Statewide policies determined by the State War Council. With war a reality, it was no longer possible to run the home front on the basis of volunteer cooperation, successful though volunteer action proved up to that time. In the presence of an emergency, an established command was essential.

POLICY-MAKING FUNCTIONS OF THE COUNCIL

The functions of the State War Council underwent a very definite evolution. During the period 1940-1941 almost every new problem confronting the Governor was taken to the War Council, whereas in the latter part of Governor Dewey's administration, the council became essentially a policy-making body concerned only with matters of the utmost importance. This statement requires one modification in that, under the War Emergency Act, there were certain functions such as approval of dispensations, extensions of orders, and allocations of money that the War Council was required to perform. Otherwise, however, once a policy had been determined, the individual or committee responsible was supposed to administer his program without bringing minor questions back to the council for determination. Such methods placed greater freedom in the hands of individual administrators who were carefully chosen and, within the framework of policy determined by the council, were held strictly accountable for the results.

In the earlier period centralization of policy and administrative decisions were unavoidable. In 1940, before the appointment of the council, the Governor made most of the decisions. As problems increased in number, the administration and coordination of the defense effort were entrusted to Lieutenant Governor Poletti, who took over more and more the duties of chairman of the War Council. As questions of policy became ever more complex, it was found necessary

not only to appoint an advisory State Council of (National)[1] Defense, but also, after January 1, 1943, to require it to delegate certain decisions on policy to some of its own members, especially when the council did not have sufficient information upon which to base a decision. The chairman would then appoint a subcommittee or the executive secretary, or both, to study the problem and report. Following the submission of the report, the council would make its decision. Examples of study committees were the two subcommittees on Physical Fitness and those on Office of Price Administration Egg Regulation, and the Interim Committee on Living War Memorials. Occasionally, the council investigated its own agencies to determine their usefulness and the extent to which the functions of two or more agencies might overlap. These investigations were made by individual members, by committees, and at times by the executive secretary.

At least four of the council's subcommittees, however, became important operating committees.

1. The Attorney General served as a committee of one to report on applications to close highways or post properties pursuant to Article 6 of the War Emergency Act. His recommendations were invariably followed.

2. The Subcommittee on Child Care, together with the executive secretary and the director of child care, conducted the Child Care Program and constituted collectively the machinery by which grants of aid were given to child care projects. As the policy of the War Council became more definite in child care matters, the committee and finally its chairman, Speaker Oswald D. Heck, were given more power.

3. The Committee on Dispensations from the Labor Laws was perhaps the

[1] The word "National" was soon dropped, and the term "State Defense Council" adhered to until the passage of the War Emergency Act.

best example of the evolution of a "recommending" committee to the status of an "operating" committee. It was first appointed to make recommendations to the War Council as to the disposition of applications for dispensations pursuant to Section 82 of the War Emergency Act. The committee consisted of two labor leaders, two industrialists, and one legislator, all being members of the War Council, who acted only by unanimous vote. At first the committee made recommendations to the War Council, and after approval of such recommendations, an order was issued to carry the recommendations into effect. Because of the comparatively long periods of time between War Council meetings, it was determined in November, 1943, that since policy had become defined, the committee could act for the War Council but subject to ratification. The committee met regularly and authorized the issuance of orders which were invariably ratified by the council. When committee members were unable to agree, or when new problems arose requiring the deliberation of the War Council, the matter was brought before the council at its next meeting and determined. Finally, because the Dispensation Committee had developed a clear policy, the executive secretary was authorized to grant orders on behalf of the council as to applications falling within the framework of such established policy. This authorization was given in March, 1945, and reduced the time required for the consideration of cases to approximately forty-eight hours.

4. The Committee on Prison Industries had the task of considering requests of Federal authorities for work to be done by prison industries. It was to make certain that no competition occurred with any industry that could produce the item or items desired by the Federal authorities. In practice, once determinations of policy — mostly legal — had been made, it was not necessary for the committee to function, except occasionally, as the director of the program found it possible to make his own decisions within the established legal framework and policies.

The extent to which operating committees and temporary commissions created by the War Council, such as the Emergency Food Commission, returned to the council periodically for determinations of policy varied considerably. Particularly under Governor Dewey, a distinct effort was made to free the War Council from as many administrative details as possible. A good example of this was the Emergency Food Commission created in the spring of 1943. From its inception, this commission determined policy in the field of agriculture, returning to the War Council mostly for budgetary considerations. The Committee on Prison Industries functioned independently. The Child Care Committee, however, partly because its chairman was War Plans Coordinator and partly because of all fields entered by the War Council that of child care was the most difficult to reduce to any clear administrative pattern, returned most often to the council for full discussion and determination of policies. For this reason, its story stands out in the War Council minutes. Another subcommittee, that on Migrant Labor, actually worked from committee recommendation directly to Legislature. With the exception of its first report which was submitted to the War Council, the committee's subsequent recommendations for legislation went directly to the Governor and to the Legislature. It may be said that problems in the latter half of the war period were handled administratively rather than by discussion in the War Council, a policy consistently pursued under Governor Dewey of deliberately allowing administrative heads of programs to execute their assignments within the broad policies established for them by the council. This left the Governor and the War Council free to give full consideration to major matters and the careful selection of key personnel.

In the case of the committee to investigate Migrant Labor Camps, ameliorative legislation resulted. The committee was appointed in March, 1945, to study conditions in migrant labor camps and following its first report in June, 1945, it was directed to continue its efforts. It brought together State departments interested in aspects of the migrant labor camp program, such as the State Departments of Health, of Labor, and of Social Welfare. The second report, made in February, 1946, recommended the enactment of two laws. These recommendations were accepted by the Legislature and became Chapters 501 and 502 of the Laws of 1946. Chapter 501 amended the Labor Law to require persons who imported migrant laborers to register with the Industrial Commissioner and to furnish him with information regarding wages and working conditions. This information also was to be furnished to all out-of-State employees at the time either of their recruitment or of their entrance upon the job. Chapter 502 of the Laws of 1946 provided the State Department of Health with adequate legal authority and machinery by which it could enforce health and sanitation orders in camps housing migrant laborers.

Any discussion of the policy-making functions of the War Council would be incomplete without reference to the position occupied by that body in relation to the executive and legislative branches of the State government. In both relationships the policy of decentralization was clearly in evidence, although there was a difference in its form and character. As has already been pointed out, when decisions became too difficult and too numerous for the executive head of the State, he was forced to secure advice on major policies and help in matters of administration; hence, a War Council and a War Plans Coordinator, represent-

ing in effect an increase in personnel to handle problems falling specifically within the province of the Executive. The process of decentralization in the legislative sphere of government was influenced primarily by the time factor. Here, there was no dearth of personnel for the Legislature was perfectly adequate to make decisions. However, when it was in session, like all large bodies, it proceeded slowly. Furthermore, it remained in session for less than four months, leaving the State without a legislative body for the remainder of the year. This state of affairs, while satisfactory in time of peace, when the time factor was of relatively minor importance, could under no circumstances be tolerated in time of war when time was so essential to military victory. Decisions involving appropriations and legislation had to be made quickly at all times of the year and had no War Council been created, some form of Interim Committee of the Legislature would have become essential. This need was fully met by the inclusion in the membership of the council of the principal legislative leaders who, although in no position to bind the Legislature legally, were nevertheless in practice able to supply for all War Council decisions a virtual guarantee of subsequent legislative approval. Thus the Legislature met the needs of the moment by delegating its functions to a small group of its leaders, while retaining ultimate control through its power of appropriation and the device of annual extensions of the War Emergency Act.

One other aspect of the policy-making functions of the War Council should be noted. The success of a government of 13 million people oftentime depends upon the quality of personnel and upon personal relationships among that personnel. From this standpoint, the internal operations of the War Council as reflected in the minutes make interesting reading. Both Governor Lehman and Governor Dewey presided at meetings, and each conducted discussions within the council so as to allow full play for differences of opinion and adequate time for thorough understanding of the subject at hand. Neither attempted to dominate the discussions. Some of the early programs attempted by the council did not accomplish everything that had been hoped and, together with a number of agencies which had fulfilled their original purposes, were subsequently dropped. In general, however, the attitude prevailed that if money or personnel were really needed for a purpose which could in any way be regarded as aiding the war effort, and which was not being achieved by an existing department, assistance should be provided by the council.

That discussions were conducted on a high plane, and in a spirit of informal give-and-take, speaks well for the membership of the council and for the nonpartisan attitude which prevailed throughout its existence. Mention has already been made in Chapter III of the importance in private industry of Messrs. Morgan, Wilson, and Hancock. A desirable link with the policies of the Federal government was provided by Mrs. Anna Rosenberg, a "trouble shooter" in the fields of health, welfare, and labor. As Regional Director for both the Federal Security Agency and the War Manpower Commission, she was in a position to give the council, informally, advance information on national manpower policies. Dean Carl E. Ladd, of the New York State College of Agriculture, was a prominent authority in the field of agriculture and nutrition and was in constant touch with officials in Washington. The labor leaders, Gustave A. Strebel, and his successor on the council, Louis Hollander, both chairmen of the State Congress of Industrial Organizations, and Thomas J. Lyons and his successor, Thomas A. Murray, both presidents of the State American Federation of Labor, were in close touch with their national organizations. At no time was there disagreement

in the council over the necessity of protecting fully the position of labor. All relaxations of labor laws were clearly understood to be temporary. Regardless of the emergency, no one wanted the war situation used to promote unsound practices, and, as pointed out in Chapter III, in New York State labor relations remained excellent throughout the war. Within the council one might say that there developed mutual understanding and respect among the leaders of labor and the representatives of industry. Each group leaned over backward in an effort to be strictly fair on all questions, and each applied the same adjectives, "realistic," "sensible," "practical," "honest" to the other. At all times the *needs* of the situation came first.

Elmer Carter, a Negro member of the council, made two significant comments on the membership of the council. In speaking of one of the other members, who was president of a large manufacturing concern, he said:

He is a very frank person ... Mr. .... is a very frank and a very honest person, and once he makes up his mind on the course of action and that course is right, he never hesitates, and not only that, but Mr. ...., who is a southerner, a North Carolinian, has tremendous interest in the Negro, to such an extent that he was selected to lead the Negro College Fund Drive this year.

Speaking of his own membership on the council, Mr. Carter said:

This was a very enriching experience for me, because for the first time I came in contact with representatives of the whole State, and of every interest in the State, — agriculture, industry, commerce and labor as well as legislators, and in a united effort — a cooperative effort — to prepare this State and keep it prepared for war and for the conditions which war brings. I say it was an enriching experience for me because it demonstrated to me the ability of men of widely divergent interests and opinions to work together under pressure towards a common end. It gave me a great deal of encouragement, particularly since my experiences have been that in certain problems it was almost impossible to achieve that sort of cooperative effort.

Not only did the industrialists and the labor leaders on the council make an honest effort to view all questions in the larger perspective, but their efforts were ably seconded by the members of the council who represented the Legislature. As one put it, "Politics were out, they did not have any meaning." There was some "kidding," but at no time were patronage considerations allowed to obstruct the work of the council. In one case where the service of a recent appointee had left much to be desired, a member of the council who came from the same district undertook to handle the situation and did so, to the satisfaction of all concerned. In fact, the willingness of the legislators on the council to do what was generally regarded as the wise thing, even though they might later on have trouble in securing the support of the Legislature, was a matter of considerable marvel to a number of their more tough-minded business colleagues. All of this goes to show that under certain circumstances and certain pressures, people of widely diverse backgrounds and interests can and will cooperate for the common good.

In no better way can the nonpartisan attitude of the council be exhibited than by quoting certain remarks made at the last meeting of the council presided over by Governor Lehman. Part way through the session, the Governor addressed the members as follows:

As you gentlemen know, I am resigning the office of Governor tomorrow. I cannot tell you how much I appreciate the support and encouragement which I have received from you. I lay down this work with a very heavy heart. Mrs. Lehman joins with me when I say that we regret that we are leaving Albany.

You men have been of the greatest assistance to me. We were the first state to under-

take defense and civilian protection work. I think that we have done a very valuable and constructive job. I need not tell you how grateful I am. Your terms continue until July 1, 1943. I know what is in Charlie's[1] mind. He feels as I do. He has been our Vice-Chairman and our Coordinator of War Plans. I do not know what is in the mind of the incoming Governor. But I bespeak your support for him just as you have supported me. This Council has been a great help and I hope he will see fit to continue it and that all of you will remain as members of the Council for the terms of your office. . . .

To which Speaker Oswald D. Heck replied:

Governor Lehman, not only as a member of this Council but also as a member of the opposition party, I want to say, on behalf of the members of this Council and the members of the opposition party, that we are very sorry to see you go. . . . In spite of our differences, when we came to your office and to the Mansion as members of the State War Council that was all put aside. No politics ever intruded in our deliberations. And that goes for everybody no matter what party they represent, Democratic, Republican, or American Labor. At no time has politics been permitted to intrude in our deliberations and I think it is a matter of great credit to this War Council and particularly to you, Mr. Governor, for having appointed members as efficient and nonpartisan as are the members of this Council.

I say this — I agree with you when you characterize the members of this War Council as members who have worked cooperatively and well in order to further our State war effort. I am going to do everything that I can to see to it that members of this War Council continue as members of this Council after their terms expire. This is a promise which it is unwise for me to make, but I think we have worked so well and have made such a great reputation in the State that we should continue. . . .

The change of administration, January 1, 1943, made no change in the mem-

---

[1] Lieutenant Governor Charles Poletti.

bership of the council. Governor Dewey kept the council exactly as he had received it. Normal loss of personnel from death and resignations, however, effected a gradual lessening in the familiarity of members with the original purposes behind the programs. Those who became members of the council at later dates were never quite able to begin where their predecessors left off. This had both beneficial and detrimental effects: salutary in that it was possible for newcomers to assess objectively the value of programs without being unduly influenced by sentimental or, more accurately, parental attachment; detrimental in that they sometimes failed to appreciate the purposes and achievements of established agencies, having missed the discussions leading to the council's original action in setting them up.

One situation inherited by the new regime in 1943 was promptly dealt with. A breach apparently existed between the State of New York and the Second Service Command over the matter of signals for air-raid warnings. The signals in New York were at variance with those in other northeastern states and the reason appeared to be a clash of personalities between the State and Army officials. This problem was solved upon the appointment of Colonel Edward C. O. Thomas, of Nassau County, as State Director of Civilian Protection. He immediately adopted the Army signals, whereupon relations between Civilian Protection and the Second Service Command became, and remained thereafter, entirely harmonious.

OPERATIONS OF THE STATE WAR COUNCIL ORGANIZATION: PRINCIPLES OF ADMINISTRATION

The two officials most closely connected with the administration of the thirty-odd War Council agencies and programs were the War Plans Coordinator and the Executive Secretary of the War Council. At the beginning, and until the death of Lieutenant Governor Wallace, the coordinator was chief of operations on both State and local levels. He was primarily responsible for the Statewide details of War Council programs. He supervised the creation of the original Statewide machinery of local councils and State War Council agencies. Within the broad framework of the War Council policy, he exercised freedom of choice. Whenever the head of a department or agency confronted a problem on which he needed advice, the coordinator was the man to see. It was the responsibility of the coordinator to establish each program quickly and see that it operated smoothly in accordance with War Council policy. In cases where agencies of the War Council were supplementing the work of regularly established State departments, it was his task to set boundaries to their functions, avoid overlapping, and secure cooperation. So burdensome did his duties become that, in May, 1942, it was found necessary to bring in as assistant coordinator Dr. Maurice F. Neufeld, who had recently wound up the affairs of the State Bureau of Rationing.

As the first coordinator, Lieutenant Governor Poletti occupied a strategic position in the evolution of War Council organization. The initiation of programs in 1941 and 1942 was largely his doing. He was in constant touch with groups and organizations throughout the State. Letters and visitors flooded his office, and in turn he spoke constantly on matters of defense and later of the war effort. A continual interchange of ideas occurred between the people of the State and their leaders. Liaison between the War Council and the communities was close. Proposals of every sort were screened through the coordinator and his assistant so that everyone was heard, but only suggestions of importance reached the Governor and the War Council.

The necessity for clear thinking in the

field of administration was recognized early. Modest as had been the beginning, from the spring of 1941 the growth of Statewide programs, both within existing departments and outside, was rapid. Speaking in February, 1942, the coordinator emphasized as a ruling principle of the War Council the *maximum use of existing facilities,* both State and local. Application of this policy appeared in (1) the designation of the Committee on Health Preparedness as the Medical Section of the War Council; (2) the recognition of the Committee on Agricultural Defense as the initial body to form State policy in the field of agricultural production; (3) the assignment to the Commissioner of Social Welfare of responsibility for Statewide plans for evacuation of the populous centers; (4) the delegation to the State Education Department of all programs for vocational and defense training; (5) the appointment of the Industrial Commissioner to head a new committee, established within the Department of Labor, for the study and prevention of discrimination in employment; (6) the establishment of officials from appropriate departments as responsible heads for each of the plans for mutual aid: an officer of the Department of Health as Coordinator of Water Supply, an officer of the Highway Division of the Department of Public Works to head the program for highway repair and debris clearance, and a committee of firemen to plan for defense against fire.

It was natural, however, that certain problems should arise in World War II where this method did not prove feasible. Some of these could not have been anticipated, and on account of their scope no State department was in a position to handle them. Under the circumstances, the creation of new agencies for certain specific tasks was inevitable.

The principle of *decentralization* has already been discussed in connection with policy making. Its application in

the field of administration was equally essential. Just as Washington could not administer national programs without the help of the states, so Albany found it impossible to administer State programs without the help of the localities. This was recognized early and the local war councils became essential cogs in the State War Council organization. As the coordinator put it on one occasion:

Fundamentally and in the last analysis, the job must be done and can only be done on the local level. . . . We must have decentralization and recognize that the most important units of all are on the local level of government.

The only practical limitation that was placed upon this principle was the designation of city and county defense councils as the ruling units of local administration. Town and village councils recognized only in Westchester County were made responsible to the county councils.[1]

A third administrative principle was that of *close integration of all war activities on the local level.* In actual operation, this was not always fully achieved. Theoretically, however, it was sound. Just as the State War Council, through the coordinator, maintained close supervision over the operation of State agencies, so it was intended that the local war councils should be the coordinating force in the communities. The original idea was to have volunteer offices act as a central clearing-house for all volunteers, and to ask every local committee to cooperate with the war council and with the volunteer office. Time and again it was pointed out to enthusiastic correspondents who wished to start a new committee that it would be much better to work through the volunteer offices on existing community committees instead of forming additional ones. While this idea of a central coordinating direction on the local level was a sensible one, for

---

[1] War Emergency Act, Section 10.

a number of reasons it was only partially attained. The degree of success depended somewhat upon the harmony that existed within the local war council, and this in turn depended upon personalities and the absence or presence of cliques in the community. Local war councils were frequently no better than the spirit of cooperation which had existed in the community prior to their creation. Furthermore, in many instances, instead of concentrating upon a well-coordinated community program, many localities found it virtually impossible to prevent organizations from placing primary emphasis upon communications proceeding from State or national headquarters. This was true no matter whether the organization was Civilian Protection, Civilian Mobilization, or one entirely outside the War Council such as the Red Cross. In other words, vertical and horizontal lines of authority were bound to get mixed whenever personalities became involved or insight into the needs of the situation was lacking. Integration of local activities on a community basis was, therefore, far from complete.

The placing of final command of all civilian defense organizations in the hands of a single Director of Civilian Protection has already been emphasized in Chapter IV and in the discussion of changes in the War Council organizations effected by the enactment of the War Emergency Act.

A fifth administrative principle, which applied primarily to the State level, was *the grouping on June 15, 1942, of the thirty-three War Council agencies and programs under three main divisions: Civilian Protection, Civilian Mobilization and Industry, Agriculture and Labor.* Those grouped under the Director of Civilian Protection have been mentioned in Chapter IV. All social, health, nutrition, and allied activities were first brought together in the Division of Civilian Mobilization under the chairman-

ship of Mrs. Clarice L. Pennock. Agencies and committees concerned with war production, war workers, war transportation, war housing, and war work training, both industrial and agricultural, were placed in the Division of Industry, Agriculture, and Labor under Dr. Lewis A. Wilson, Deputy Commissioner of the Education Department.

The programs and services of these groups were sufficiently alike to justify an attempt to coordinate their activities in the areas where interests and objectives were similar. While the principle undoubtedly had theoretical merit, in actual operation it proved too difficult to make of the periodic meetings more than a series of individual reports. These were informative, but except for Civilian Protection, where the director had statutory authority over all branches of the organization and an adequate budget, the chairmen were unable to bring about any sustained connected effort on a divisional basis. With the change of administration, the attempt at coordination was dropped.

Coordination within the field of agriculture, however, became so essential that in 1943, Governor Dewey, with consent of the War Council, created the Emergency Food Commission financed with War Council funds. The success of this organization depended partly upon three factors not present in the case of two of the three divisions mentioned above, i.e., legal powers, adequate funds, and a relatively homogeneous field of operations such as the production and preparation of food.

Two service agencies, in addition to the Office of Civilian Mobilization described in Chapter V, were the Office of War Training and the Office of War Information. The work of the Office of War Training was largely, although not entirely, in the field of civilian protection and has been described in connection with the training programs mentioned in Chapter IV. The Office of War

Information was originally designed to aid all War Council agencies with publicity. It never dealt with the local councils, however, and remained a centralized publicity bureau for the State agencies. In March 1944, it was discontinued, and the publication of its fortnightly bulletin of directives was transferred to Headquarters Office under the able editorship of Henry B. Kraft, Director of the Division of Public Relations. Its form was altered to that more nearly resembling a newspaper. Mr. Kraft also arranged speaking engagements and radio and television appearances for key War Council personnel, edited the *Annual Reports,* and performed other duties in connection with public relations.

The task of maintaining smooth operations in this far-flung organization with its many branches, interests, and varieties of conditions and personnel required infinite patience and tact. Misunderstandings and differences of opinion were inevitable, both horizontally at each of the State and local levels, and vertically between State and local groups. There were also occasional difficulties between the State and Federal governments. The problem of maintaining close liaison between all three levels, Federal, State and local, was constantly present and could never be regarded as having been permanently solved. In relations of this character, the quality of the personnel was all-important.

THE EXECUTIVE SECRETARY AND THE HEADQUARTERS OFFICE

In 1941 and 1942, it was the coordinator and his assistant who were in close touch with War Council operations. Since they had the facts at hand, they made most of the proposals at War Council meetings, whereas the executive secretary figured but slightly in making policies.

Under the Dewey administration, this system continued, although in modified form until the death of Lieutenant Governor Thomas W. Wallace. Upon the death of Mr. Wallace, his successor at his own request was relieved of the position of coordinator. These functions passed instead to the Speaker of the Assembly, Oswald D. Heck, a very busy individual. The inevitable result was that greater administrative responsibilities were delegated to Charles A. Winding, the executive secretary and counsel of the State War Council. From 1943 to 1945, this official became in fact an assistant coordinator, and his importance was considerably heightened. He was forced into close association with the details and personnel of the Statewide War Council organizations, and the maintenance of essential liaison between Albany and the local communities gradually devolved upon him. Consequently, it was he who came to present and explain to the War Council the majority of matters on the agenda, and he whose judgment was more and more relied upon in matters of administrative detail. Under the supervision of the executive secretary, the Headquarters Office of the War Council developed from a centralized financial office to an office which had general administrative supervision under the War Plans Coordinator of all programs of the War Council.

In addition to shouldering some of the duties of the coordinator, Mr. Winding found that the change of emphasis in 1943 from protective to civilian war service activities added substantially to both the legal and administrative functions of his office. Among other duties, he was required as Counsel to render legal advice on all War Council activities and programs. By resolution of the council, the executive secretary was designated to act with the War Council Subcommittee on Child Care, and with the Director of Child Care, Miss Elsie M. Bond, in making State grants to child care centers. Not only did he supervise the entire Child Care program, but he was empowered, after appropriate investigation, to make grants for individual child care projects. The granting of dispensation orders involved him in further work, for he assisted the Dispensation Committee and drew the necessary dispensation orders. He was likewise available to an increasing extent to all local war council agencies for advice and consultation, and was frequently called upon to speak before groups within and outside the State on aspects of the war effort. The evolution in the functions of this individual and of the personnel of the office under his supervision kept pace with the steadily increasing number of duties assigned to him. As a result, Headquarters developed into a collection of minor agencies, each a separate functioning unit of the Headquarters staff under the supervision of the executive secretary.

The Headquarters Office served as the secretariat for the War Council and the executive secretary was ex-officio secretary of the council's subcommittees. This phase of the duties of the office included the preparation of the agenda, the scrutiny and preparation of budgetary requests, the drafting of numerous resolutions and orders for council meetings, and subsequently the preparation of the final minutes. The executive secretary was also frequently called upon to make studies and to conduct investigations of War Council programs, either alone or as a member of a small committee, and to prepare reports based upon them for the Council.

On a number of occasions the personnel of the secretariat was mobilized for a specific task. One of the best examples of this function occurred in January, 1945, during the transportation crisis caused by high winds, heavy snow, and a partial Federal embargo on the shipment of items other than munitions.[1] To cope with emergency conditions and to

avert suffering in various areas Governor Dewey appointed an Emergency Committee of which Dr. Harold H. Schaff, successor to Mr. Winding as executive secretary of the War Council, was a member. His first task was to obtain reports from all local war councils on the fuel, feed, and food needs in their particular areas. He also obtained from the major railroads operating in the State detailed accounts of their most pressing operating requirements. As a result of telegrams to all directors of local offices of Civilian Mobilization and to directors of local offices of Civilian Protection, reports were immediately received from approximately 95 per cent of the localities. On the basis of this information, estimates were made of available manpower and of the sections of the State where such was needed. From January 29 to February 3, 1945, the office of the executive secretary worked day and night collecting information from all over the State. When a complete picture of the transportation situation brought about by the weather had been obtained, it was turned over to the chairman of the Emergency Committee. On the basis of this information, Dr. Schaff and Earl Foster, executive secretary of the New York State Emergency Food Commission, were directed to arrange for the largest possible number of trucks with which to distribute feed and food during the embargo. As a result of this, privately owned trucks and vehicles of the State Department of Public Works were placed in trucking pools and made available where their services were most needed.

Prior to the appointment of Dr. Schaff, the executive secretary of the War Council was a lawyer with the full title, Executive Secretary and Counsel. The Headquarters Office was thus the central point from which the State and local war council agencies obtained advice and assistance on problems having legal ramifications. These problems grew in number and complexity and because of his many

---

[1] See Chapter VI, section on Transportation, p. 173.

other duties, Mr. Winding required assistance. Accordingly, in 1943, Milton Alpert was employed to handle legal matters, subject to Mr. Winding's supervision. Soon after Dr. Schaff became executive secretary Mr. Alpert's status was changed and his title became Counsel to the Executive Secretary. Thenceforth, all agencies looked to him for legal advice and he furthermore prepared and analyzed legislation and undertook research in connection with legal and other problems. He assisted in the preparation of proposed resolutions and orders, analyzed dispensation recommendations, and compiled the 1944 and 1945 editions of the War Emergency Act. These functions were extremely important, as upon his performance depended the smooth operation of both State and local war council agencies. Upon Dr. Schaff's death, the council designated Mr. Alpert as acting executive secretary and its work was eventually terminated under his direction.

The disbursement of all War Council funds required the loan from the Comptroller's Office, June 5, 1941, of George E. Mireault, an experienced finance officer. Working under the supervision of the executive secretary, Mr. Mireault established a centralized clearance of appointments, budgets, payrolls, purchasing, and expense accounts. The financial system of the Comptroller's Office, then operating in all departments, was adopted and the usual accounting procedures established. The preparation of all financial items for the agenda of the council, the analysis of the budgets of child care projects, and the payment of grants to such projects were likewise in his hands.

The rapid growth of the War Council organization after Pearl Harbor led to a thorough examination of the finance unit by experts from the Department of Audit and Control. In a memorandum drawn up by Mr. W. J. Dougherty, executive assistant to the comptroller, a complete plan — a large part of which was already in operation — was outlined. This plan called for:

1. Fixed administrative procedure controlling the creation of committees and of the agencies through which the functions of the council were performed.

2. Organization of a finance unit operating under the executive secretary in which would be centralized the control of budgets, personnel appointments, purchasing, property accounting, and other fiscal matters.

3. Adoption of annual budgets conforming to council allocations for each committee or agency of the council.

4. Organization of a headquarters or central information unit operating under the executive secretary in which would be concentrated all records on the activities of the council and its committees.

Besides personnel in the finance unit, numerous additions to the staff occurred from time to time, and by the spring of 1945 fifteen people were working at the Headquarters Office.

It is interesting to note that at the high point of War Council activities in the summer of 1944, the Headquarters staff handled financial transactions for approximately 325 permanent employees and 450 part-time or seasonal employees, the latter connected largely with the work of the Emergency Food Commission. Thus in size this organization compared favorably with some of the smaller State departments. The fact that the total cost of operation for Headquarters was less than 4 per cent of the total expenditures for the War Council programs demonstrates efficient management, and in view of the over-all achievements of the War Council represents money well spent — actually a remarkably cheap investment.

In the field of public relations, principally liaison with local war councils, the evolution of the Headquarters Office was broken in 1942. In Chapter V reference was made to the appointment of two field men to work out of War Council Headquarters in connection with the establishment first of local war councils, and then of volunteer offices. For a number of reasons this embryonic field staff was not only not further extended, but was actually completely discontinued. Instead, as one War Council agency after another was created, each requested and secured as instruments of their immediate purposes field men whose duties were to make contact with the appropriate committees of local war councils. Consequently, a direct channel of communication between the Headquarters Office of the executive secretary and the local councils was never established. No field man, whether from Civilian Protection or Civilian Mobilization, could speak with authority to the local chairmen on war council matters as a whole. This situation was a permanent source of confusion to the local councils. To supply this lack of a direct link with Headquarters, the first two executive secretaries who served under Governor Dewey, Charles A. Winding and Dr. Harold H. Schaff, seriously injured their health trying to perform the combined duties of executive secretary and field representative for headquarters. The latter's death, in August 1945, was in a measure brought about by his strenuous devotion to this back-breaking task.

Prior to the death of Lieutenant Governor Wallace, in July, 1943, the State War Plans Coordinator had performed most of those functions falling within the field of public relations. In 1942, Lieutenant Governor Poletti had been ably assisted by Dr. Maurice F. Neufeld, and the heads of a number of War Council agencies, such as Clarice L. Pennock, Helen Nolan, General Charles F. Haskell, Lewis A. Wilson, R. C. Georger, and others. Following the death of Lieutenant Governor Wallace, and in view of the failure to develop a field staff directly responsible to headquarters, essential liaison work devolved upon the executive secretary. Prior to its termination in March, 1944, publicity of a nonpersonal character had been in the hands of the War Council's Office of War Information. Subsequent to that time, these functions were curtailed and entrusted to the Director of Public Relations, Henry B. Kraft, whose office was transferred to Headquarters.

One of the principal projects engaged in by the headquarters staff as a whole was in the field of public relations. In the early fall of 1944, the work of the State War Council and its agencies was exhibited to more than a quarter of a million persons at four large county fairs held at Mineola, Cobleskill, Elmira and Trumansburg. As an added feature, motion pictures were shown by the War Council's Film Division. Each phase of War Council activities was depicted. By working day and night, headquarters personnel were able to give scheduled performances in spite of destruction of much of the original material in a hurricane that struck Long Island and flooded the fair grounds.

Following the termination of the Office of War Training, its Film Division, which maintained one of the largest film libraries in the country, was continued as part of the headquarters organization. The work of the division consisted primarily in the distribution of sixteen-millimeter sound motion pictures, the acquisition of suitable films, and the promotion of their exhibition among responsible groups and organizations in the State. Ten film exchanges in various cities in the State were coordinated in 1944 under the Film Division for more effective distribution. Films were obtained from Federal agencies, from foreign governments, and from private sources. A few were made by the War Council agencies. The total wartime audience ran in the neighborhood of 4.5 million residents of the State. In connection with the Seventh War Loan Drive, special war bond promotional films were distributed through the division's facilities and the Director, Edward J. Mallin, served on the Executive Committee of the National sixteen-millimeter War Finance Committee, representing more than three hundred distributors throughout the nation. The accomplishments of this division were considered sufficient to justify its transfer and absorption on April 1, 1946, by the State Department of Commerce.

A completely new function was assumed by the Headquarters Office July 1, 1945. At the 1945 legislative session, the War Emergency Act was amended to authorize the War Council to provide a uniform method for the care, custody, control, and disposition of local war council records. Order No. 23 was issued by the council authorizing the executive secretary to carry out this program. Dr. Karl D. Hartzell, Assistant Professor of Social Studies, Geneseo State Teachers College, was selected to execute this program which, with the advice and cooperation of the Division of Archives and History of the State Department of Education, was designed to inventory and prepare for permanent storage all records created under the War Emergency Act. The records of local communities were deposited at county seats, public libraries, or with historical societies; those of the principal War Council agencies with the Division of Manuscripts in the State Library; those of most of the regular State departments with their departmental files. As a result of this program, there is on deposit with the State Library in the State Education Building, Albany, a Statewide inventory catalogue showing the location and type of records created under the War Emergency Act, together with a considerable part of the historically valuable records of the War Council programs. Henceforth, it will be possible to conduct historical research into the home front activities of the State of New York during World War II with the knowledge that ample reference material is available. This material is located primarily in Albany, at Cornell University in Ithaca, in the Municipal Reference Library in New York City, and in the communities in which local war councils operated.

MAJOR ACHIEVEMENTS OF THE WAR COUNCIL: SHIFTS IN EMPHASIS

It is difficult to assess judiciously the relative importance of the achievements of the War Council. An examination of the total allocations for the council's ten major fields of action shows the relative costs of the programs. It is also easy to arrange these fields of action chronologically according to the occurrence of their acute stage, and to point out the shifts in emphasis as indicated by the periods in which the greatest expenditures on each program took place. If, however, a choice has to be made as to the program through which the council made its greatest single contribution to the winning of the war, the number of factors involved makes a decision extremely difficult.

When placed in descending order of total allocations, the list of major War Council activities was as follows:

From the figures in Table 23 it is evident that over half (57.8 per cent) of the total expenditures of the War Council during its sixty-eight months of existence was devoted to keeping the individual citizens of the State adequately fed, healthy, and able to carry on the war effort. The individual human being is the basic unit of society and in time of crisis his efficiency and well-being are essential. It is the clear recognition of this fact by democratic governments that distinguishes them fundamentally from the dictatorships.

Assuming March 31, 1943, the end of the 1942-1943 fiscal year, to be the dividing line between the Lehman and Dewey administrations, the War Council was under Governor Lehman for exactly thirty-two months, and under Governor Dewey for thirty-six.

Table 23. Allocations, Major War Council Activities

Major fields of war council activity	Total allocations	Percentages allocated after March 31, 1943
Maintaining the Working Efficiency of the Individual.....	$2,654,510.81	97.8
Agricultural Production and Nutrition....................	1,640,433.34	93.2
Defense of Civilian Property and Personnel...............	988,594.22	46.0
War Production...	810,865.79	58.3
Post War Problems — Reconversion and Emergency Housing	650,000.00	100.0
Mobilization and Direction of Civilians..................	274,290.51	57.3
Headquarters Organization..............................	243,366.22	79.1
Support of Federal Programs............................	168,740.00	52.5
War Transportation.....................................	166,630.00	61.6
Publicity and Information...............................	165,682.00	50.5
TOTAL	$7,763,112.89	

With the sole exception of Civilian Protection, whose activities were curtailed after the invasion of the Italian mainland and the subsequent armistice on September 3, the greater part of the funds made available by the Legislature to the War Council were allocated by it to the various programs after March 31, 1943. The percentages range from 50.5 per cent for Publicity and Information to 100 per cent for the postwar problems of emergency housing and reconversion. The most stable operations, and those which reflect most nearly the greater duration of War Council functions under Governor Dewey, without at the same time showing any noticeable increase in functional scope, are: (1) the Support of Federal Programs, whose 52.5 per cent is largely due to the slow increase from 1943 to 1945 in the work of the State War Bond Unit, (2) the Mobilization and Direction of Civilians (57.3 per cent), (3) assistance to the war production program through aid to the Departments of Commerce and of Labor (58.3 per cent), and (4) the Office of War Transportation (61.6 per cent). The items which reflect not only the longer period of operation but a rapid expansion in functions are the expenditures for (1) the headquarters organization incident to the expansion of the pay roll, which continued until late in 1944, and the transferral to it of the residual functions of the two Offices of War Information and War Training, (2) the Emergency Food Commission under which were grouped the activities of the council in the twin fields of agricultural production and nutrition, and (3) the maintenance of the working efficiency of the individual. The size of this last item is due to the extent to which the State, through the War Council, finally entered into the program of support for child care centers. The appropriations for these centers alone amounted to more than 80 per cent of the entire cost of this item.

Table 23 does not, however, indicate the order in which the major war problems arose. In some respects this is of primary importance as the very sequence of these problems is an index to the points at which the impact of war may sometime be felt again. A list of the programs in order of the chronological occurrence of their acute stage would run somewhat as follows:

1. War Production
2. Defense of Civilian Property and Personnel
3. Mobilization of Volunteers
4. War Transportation
5. Food Production and Nutrition
6. The Maintenance of the Efficiency of the individual
7. Postwar Problems

By the end of 1941, war production had ceased to be a major concern of the War Council proper, as the general direction of the program had been successfully taken over by the Division of Commerce. By the middle of 1943, as the balance of war swung in America's favor and the danger of attack from across the ocean diminished, civilian protection also ceased to be a major concern of the council. The mobilization and direction of volunteers, which became essential by the middle of 1941, remained a constant preoccupation of the council until the spring of 1945, as the Office of Civilian Mobilization figured prominently in programs of community health, welfare, recreation, salvage, and rationing. The War Transportation program was another constant, for wartime controls over trucks, autos, and buses remained necessary until the spring of 1945, and few of the orders were actually repealed before the following September.

The major fields of activity which proved most expensive, agricultural production and nutrition, and the maintenance of the efficiency of the individual, steadily increased in importance from the spring of 1943. As farm labor became scarce and farm machinery wore out, it became imperative that new sources of agricultural labor be found and that everything possible be done to maintain in working order the machinery remaining on the farms. In the face of diminishing resources, production had to be increased to meet the needs of civilians, soldiers, and distressed populations abroad. In the allied field of nutrition, as certain types of food became scarce

and were placed on ration lists, the importance of efficient utilization of the right foods grew correspondingly. It was no easy task to modify the dietary habits of an entire state nor, in the face of growing demands upon human energy and intelligence, was nutrition alone the only means necessary to keep the individual operating at top efficiency. Adequate exercise, careful supervision of working conditions, and personal health were also necessary. The recruiting and training of additional nurses became essential. As the importance of employing women workers in factories increased, greater attention was focused upon the problem of caring for children of working mothers. While the State entered this field ostensibly to provide additional war workers, once child care projects were undertaken the fact that they were related to a whole set of community problems became obvious, and in the course of approximately three full years of operation Governor Dewey and his advisors became convinced of the need for maintaining child care centers for a period beyond the war.

The chronological sequence in which the State's major problems arose undoubtedly presented a fairly typical pattern of the strains placed upon any civilian economy by war. After production had been geared to war, after precautionary measures had been taken against possible attack, after the use of transportation facilities had been rationed in the interests of production, and the energies of the average citizen had been harnessed to the war effort, an adequate food supply and the health and efficiency of the people stood out as factors fundamental to success in a long war. By 1943, emphasis was being placed squarely upon programs designed to maintain at peak levels the production and utilization of food and the health and stamina of the general public.

Between V-J Day and the end of the fiscal year, March 31, 1946, the State War

Council performed an important service by providing interim authorization and financial support for necessary postwar activities which could not wait for the Legislature. At its September meeting the council authorized the appropriation of funds for the Reconversion Program set up within the Department of Commerce. In December, it made available considerable sums for the emergency veterans' housing program in New York City.[1] It likewise carried the program of the Emergency Food Commission until the Legislature could decide which of its component parts were to be abolished, which assigned to Cornell University, and which to the State Department of Agriculture and Markets. Similarly with the Child Care Program, it carried the entire Federal program from March 1 to March 31, 1946, in addition to that supported by the State until the new Youth Commission was in a position to assume direction of operations. Such functions, while not spectacular, were extremely valuable in helping preserve for permanent operation those parts of the wartime program most needed in time of peace.

In assessing from all angles the successful record of New York State in World War II, four or five factors stand out. First in point of time, and a prerequisite from the standpoint of organization, was the creation of the State War Council and the local county and city councils. This organization was fundamental to the entire State picture and was an achievement of both branches of the State government. A second remarkable accomplishment was the tremendous New York production of munitions of war. Credit here belonged fundamentally to both management and labor, and initially to the foresight and energy of the Defense Council and its primary agent, the Division of Commerce. To the last two was due in large measure the early

expansion of the State's war production facilities. A third achievement of equal importance, although coming in 1943, was the creation by Governor Dewey of the Emergency Food Commission, which successfully mastered the interrelated problems of agriculture at the time they were most pressing.

All other problems were in essence subsidiary to the production, either of war materials or of food. In this connection, a fourth factor, namely, the work of the State Office of Civilian Mobilization, which assumed responsibility for direction on the local level of innumerable community war services and the guidance of countless volunteers, was absolutely essential. Still a fifth, the organization of the civilian protection forces, might very well have become all important had the State been subjected to air attack. To say that New York State had a good record in practically every phase of home-front activity is an understatement. Many programs were exceptionally well handled, and in many instances were inaugurated in advance of the rest of the country. To discuss a complete list at this period, however, would serve no useful purpose. In some lines of activity, such as labor relations, and the regulatory services and functions of the State departments, the War Council played little or no part. In spite of personnel shortages, these were maintained uninterrupted throughout the war. In other directions, however, activities that included the care of children of working mothers, the development of an agency to combat discrimination in employment, the building of an up-to-date physical fitness program for young and old alike, the enforcement by State courts of Office of Price Administration regulations, and many others of equal importance were due to leadership by the War Council. When one considers the relatively small expenditure for the activities of this temporary commission from 1940 to 1946, as compared with the total State budget, the

---

[1] Both of these programs have been described briefly in Chapter IX.

Table 24. Allocation of Funds by the New York State War Council, August 1, 1940 – March 31, 1946

SUPPORT OF FEDERAL PROGRAMS	August 1, 1940 to May 1, 1942	May 1, 1942 to March 31, 1943	April 1, 1943 to March 31, 1944	April 1, 1944 to March 31, 1945	April 1, 1945 to March 31, 1946	TOTALS
State Bureau of Rationing	$50,000.00	$9,000.00	......	......	......	$59,000.00
Mental Data of Selectees	2,700.00	3,300.00	$3,600.00	$6,275.00	$5,460.00	21,335.00
State Automotive Rationing Bureau	......	7,000.00	......	......	......	7,000.00
War Bond Unit (Dept. of Audit & Control)	......	8,000.00	21,300.00	23,300.00	25,655.00	78,255.00
Salvage Division	......	......	......	2,200.00	950.00	3,150.00
	52,700.00	27,300.00	24,900.00	31,775.00	32,065.00	168,740.00
DEFENSE OF CIVILIAN PROPERTY & PERSONNEL						
State Office of Civilian Defense	119,500.00	162,132.10	142,800.00	101,935.00	35,803.78	562,170.88
Fire Defense Training Program	35,000.00	6,873.00	......	......	......	41,873.00
became						
Office of War Training	......	125,300.17	101,073.30	6,900.00	......	233,273.47
State Fire Defense Committee	15,000.00	......	......	......	......	15,000.00
became						
Committee on Fire Defense	......	20,000.00	......	......	......	20,000.00
became						
State Office of Fire Mobilization	......	4,875.00	2,283.33	......	......	7,158.33
Administration of Explosives Laws	2,500.00	300.00	......	......	......	2,800.00
Governor's Committee on Evacuation	......	778.54	......	......	......	778.54
Fingerprinting — Correction Department	......	36,000.00	31,925.00	24,540.00	2,400.00	94,865.00
Health Zone Coordinators	2,500.00	2,790.00	......	......	......	5,290.00
Health State Water Coordinator	......	......	3,500.00	1,300.00	585.00	5,385.00
	$174,500.00	$359,048.81	$281,581.63	$184,675.00	$38,788.78	$988,594.22

WAR PRODUCTION (*Training, Vocational, Labor, Housing*)

Civilian Defense Training Program (Education)	40,000.00	58,000.00	28,069.00	18,575.00	8,520.00	153,164.99
Defense Housing	28,000.00					28,000.00
Division of Housing		36,662.50	22,550.00	4,765.00		63,977.50
Committee on Discrimination (Labor)	15,000.00	58,500.00	44,414.96	50,375.00	14,940.00	183,229.96
Priorities, Sub-contracting (Commerce)	16,000.00	30,575.00	39,650.00	39,700.00		125,925.00
War Emergency Dispensation (Labor)		24,933.34	37,793.00	55,590.00	29,745.00	148,061.34
Aid to Industries (Commerce)		30,000.00	38,950.00	38,690.00		107,640.00
Prison Industries — Rebuilding Army Shoes (Correction)				867.00		867.00
	$99,000.00	$238,670.84	$211,427.96	$208,562.00	$53,205.00	$810,865.79

AGRICULTURAL PRODUCTION AND NUTRITION

State Nutrition Committee	10,000.00	4,986.92				14,986.92
became						
Office of War Nutrition Services		28,210.85	3,578.31			31,789.16
Agricultural Statistical Records	1,200.00	1,100.00	1,200.00			3,500.00
became						
Food Inspectors and Agricultural Statistics				19,495.00	17,805.00	37,300.00
N.Y.S. College of Home Economics at Cornell		15,811.58				15,811.58
School of Nutrition at Cornell University		2,615.68				2,615.68
County Agricultural Agents		18,850.00				18,850.00
Farm Machinery Repair Program		15,250.00	60,500.00	51,595.00	45,515.00	172,860.00
Food Inspection (Agriculture & Markets)		13,750.00	17,500.00			31,250.00
Victory Garden Council			500.00			500.00
Office of Farm Manpower			39,200.00	32,625.00	28,210.00	100,035.00
Office of Farm Manpower — Farm Cadet Victory Corps			100,000.00	86,725.00	78,430.00	265,155.00
New York State Emergency Food Commission —			61,975.00	54,200.00	20,130.00	136,305.00
New York State Emergency Food Commission — Upstate Nutrition Division			149,225.00	106,825.00	92,975.00	349,025.00
New York State Emergency Food Commission — New York City Nutrition Division			100,000.00	101,350.00	56,570.00	257,920.00
New York State Emergency Food Commission — Victory Garden Council			30,515.00	21,145.00	22,725.00	74,385.00

Table 24. Allocation of Funds by the New York State War Council, August 1, 1940 – March 31, 1946 – Continued

	August 1, 1940 to May 1, 1942	May 1, 1942 to March 31, 1943	April 1, 1943 to March 31, 1944	April 1, 1944 to March 31, 1945	April 1, 1945 to March 31, 1946	TOTALS
Health – Emergency Milk Supply	. . . . . .	. . . . . .	275.00	125.00	65.00	465.00
N.Y.S. College of Agriculture – Extension Service –						
Farm Manpower	. . . . . .	. . . . . .	3,335.00	20,000.00	16,800.00	40,135.00
School Lunch Program (Department of Education)	. . . . . .	. . . . . .	5,100.00	12,600.00	21,730.00	39,430.00
Walkill Prison – Canning – (Correction Department)	. . . . . .	. . . . . .	. . . . . .	1,275.00	1,700.00	2,975.00
Agricultural Extension Work	. . . . . .	. . . . . .	. . . . . .	18,940.00	25,400.00	44,340.00
Local Canning Centers (Department of Education)	. . . . . .	. . . . . .	. . . . . .	. . . . . .	800.00	800.00
	$11,200.00	$100,575.03	$572,903.31	$526,900.00	$428,855.00	$1,640,433.34
MOBILIZATION AND DIRECTION OF CIVILIANS						
Division of Volunteer Participation	25,000.00	. . . . . .	. . . . . .	. . . . . .	. . . . . .	25,000.00
became						
Office of Civilian Mobilization	. . . . . .	69,591.34	66,358.33	52,567.50	27,740.00	216,257.17
Section on Citizen Morale	. . . . . .	22,500.00	. . . . . .	. . . . . .	. . . . . .	22,500.00
became						
Section on Citizen Unity	. . . . . .	. . . . . .	10,533.34	. . . . . .	. . . . . .	10,533.34
	$25,000.00	$92,091.34	$76,891.67	$52,567.50	$27,740.00	$274,290.51
WAR TRANSPORTATION						
War Transportation Committee	. . . . . .	40,000.00	44,450.00	37,200.00	19,980.00	141,630.00
War Transportation Committee – Traffic Control Stations	. . . . . .	25,000.00	. . . . . .	. . . . . .	. . . . . .	25,000.00
		$65,000.00	$44,450.00	$37,200.00	$19,980.00	$166,630.00

						Total
MAINTAINING THE WORKING EFFICIENCY OF THE INDIVIDUAL CITIZEN						
Physical Fitness Program	.....	36,000.00	47,736.00	56,930.00	33,412.54	174,078.54
Health — Purchase of Surgical Instruments and Equipment	...	8,043.45	......	......	......	8,043.45
Committee on Child Care, Development and Protection	...	12,758.32	48,200.00	55,350.50	51,090.00	167,398.82
N.Y.S. Health Preparedness Commission — War Nursing Program	...	......	12,000.00	20,565.00	24,525.00	57,090.00
Child Care Program — Department of Education	...	......	15,230.00	33,150.00	42,420.00	90,800.00
State Aid — To cover the State's share of costs of operations of such Child Care Centers as may be approved by the State War Council	...	......	1,000,000.00	860,000.00	150,000.00	2,010,000.00
Sanitary Inspection of Farm Labor Camps (Health)	...	......	......	......	22,000.00	22,000.00
Comm. on Child Care, etc. — State Aid for Rent, Repairs or Equipment for Child Care Projects	...	......	......	......	100,000.00	100,000.00
Comm. on Child Care, etc. — State Aid for Foster Day Care of Infants and Young Children	...	......	......	......	25,000.00	25,000.00
		$56,801.77	$1,123,166.00	$1,025,995.50	$448,447.54	$2,654,410.81
HEADQUARTERS ORGANIZATION						
Headquarters	25,000.00	18,500.00	44,025.00	73,785.00	72,981.22	234,291.22
Department of Law	.....	2,800.00	......	......	......	2,800.00
Division of Standards and Purchase	.....	2,700.00	......	......	......	2,700.00
Division of the Budget	.....	1,575.00	1,900.00	......	......	3,475.00
Division of Standards and Purchase for type. repairs	.....	100.00	......	......	......	100.00
	$25,000.00	$25,675.00	$45,925.00	$73,785.00	$72,981.22	$243,366.22
POSTWAR PROBLEMS						
Division of Housing	.....	.....	.....	.....	100,000.00	100,000.00
Reconversion Service Agency	.....	.....	.....	.....	50,000.00	50,000.00
Department of Public Works — To Provide Emergency Housing	.....	.....	.....	.....	500,000.00	500,000.00
					$650,000.00	$650,000.00

Table 24. Allocation of Funds by the New York State War Council, August 1, 1940 – March 31, 1946 – Concluded

	August 1, 1940 to May 1, 1942	May 1, 1942 to March 31, 1943	April 1, 1943 to March 31, 1944	April 1, 1944 to March 31, 1945	April 1, 1945 to March 31, 1946	TOTALS
PUBLICITY AND INFORMATION						
Defense Information Committee........ became	20,000.00	......	......	......	......	20,000.00
Office of War Information Service......	......	52,916.67	78,163.33	5,602.00	......	136,682.00
Defense Exposition.................	8,700.00	......	......	......	......	8,700.00
Victory Garden Exhibit in New York City......	300.00	......	......	......	......	300.00
	29,000.00	52,916.67	78,163.33	5,602.00		165,682.00
GRAND TOTAL	$416,400.00	$1,018,079.46	$2,459,408.89	$2,097,062.00	$1,772,062.54	$7,763,112.89

conclusion is inescapable — that leadership of a high order was purchased at a remarkably small cost.

In reviewing these achievements, however, it should not be forgotten that occasionally mistakes were made and valuable time was lost. It is difficult at this distance to realize the atmosphere in which the early meetings of the council were held. To recapture it, some of the subjects to which much time and thought were given deserve brief review. Until the invasion of North Africa, it was considered quite possible that the east coast, especially New York City and the more important industrial target areas, would be bombed. Under this apprehension the council spent much thought upon the evacuation of New York City and the purchase of identification tags. A special committee investigated various types of tags and the administrative problem involved in distributing them. The accidental discovery that the tags were inflammable and consequently valueless should any large area be destroyed by fire was one of life's minor ironies. Negotiations dragged on over the question of identification until after the invasion of North Africa, when the committee recommended the matter be dropped.

The sense of danger which pervaded the State in 1942 is reflected by the insuring of State buildings and property against damage from air bombing and sabotage. As this was a venture entirely new, a War Council Committee on War Insurance put much thought into estimating the value of State property and investigating the types of insurance available. At the July 21, 1942, meeting, it was finally resolved:

That the State War Council authorize the said Committee on War Insurance to obtain insurance against damage from enemy air attack up to ninety per cent of the value of such property owned by the State, as is considered by said Committee to be vulnerable to such attack, and to obtain insurance against sabotage on the canal system of the State; and be

it further resolved, that any commissions or fees earned by any person or corporation through the placement of such insurance on State property shall be turned over to the United States Service organizations or to some war relief agency.

This insurance was not renewed in 1943.

An even greater expenditure, which subsequently proved needless, was that for civilian protection, but in view of the uncertainty as to the outcome of the war, this expenditure represented the best possible insurance the State could have secured. The War Council had to act with all possible eventualities in view, and there had been so many examples since 1939 of "too little and too late" that foresight and preparation were at the moment prime virtues.

One problem with which Governor Dewey alone had to deal was that of tapering off the operations of the council as the need for the work performed by various agencies declined. It is to his credit that he allowed no agency to continue once it had outlived its usefulness. In the fall of 1943 there came numerous suggestions that certain War Council functions be cut down. As has already been noted, several agencies were terminated May 1, 1944. At the same time, budget decreases were voted for Civilian Protection, Civilian Mobilization, and War Nursing. Thereafter, problems of what agency to terminate, and when, became more and more prominent, and more and more difficult. In the summer of 1944, nearly two years before its actual termination, there was already some anticipation of the final closing of the council. On the whole, there was very little effort to keep the various agencies alive despite the fact that there had developed during the period of their existence so remarkably high an esprit de corps that one employee expressed the general sentiment when he said, "It was the most interesting job I have ever had or ever will have." The work was enjoyable and because people felt they were performing a needed service to the State as a whole, morale was on an exceptionally high level.

The quality of an organization is best measured by the quickness with which it recognizes problems, and the speed and wisdom with which it provides the proper solutions. If a body's mere existence is essential, were its performance only indifferent it would still be a success. The New York State War Council, however, was composed of extremely able and experienced men. It was fortunate in having two unusually gifted Governors as chairmen. Its record, consequently, stands comparison with that of any wartime state agency in the country. It was the council's task to anticipate trouble before it became acute and to find the proper remedies in time to maintain unhindered the progress of the State's war effort. That it did this with unqualified success was evident from the statistics given in previous chapters regarding war production, civilian protection, food production, salvage, child care and public health, and many other phases of the State's war effort.

It is no detraction from the regular departments, which performed additional wartime services with depleted staffs, to say that had there been no council to take up each war problem as it came along and decide what to do about it, the entire war effort of the State would have been jeopardized by hopeless confusion. Not only would the State departments have needed guidance, but there would have been no direction whatsoever of the individuals in the communities who were anxious to do something to help with the war. Some coordinating body representative of the highest authority of the State was essential to cope successfully with these fundamental questions. The answer was found in a temporary commission uniting in itself two of the three traditional branches of political sovereignty, the executive in the person of the Governor as chairman, and the leg-

islative in the persons of the principal leaders of the Senate and Assembly.

The institution and operation of this original political instrument was, by no means, the least significant wartime achievement of the people of New York. Two or three decades ago it was extremely fashionable to speculate upon the possibility that the machine age was rapidly producing a society so complicated that one day the wit of man would not be able to cope with it. This willingness to sell human wisdom short, when matched with the problems of a man-made environment, was a counterpart of that prewar spirit, referred to at the beginning of this chapter, that upheld the matchless efficiency of the totalitarian state and so proudly proclaimed the weaknesses of democracy. The significance of the New York State War Council lies in its utter refutation of this pessimistic thesis. No problem produced by the dislocations of the war proved impossible of solution as long as it was (1) attacked from all sides at once, and (2) attacked in a spirit of cooperation; as long as (3) the attack was led by both the executive and legislative branches of the government, (4) as long as it was joined by both political parties, and (5) as long as all groups and classes of the population united to give it wholehearted support. It was the principal contribution of the War Council that it served as a spearhead for the energies of 13 million people, that it was able to furnish unquestioned leadership in a crisis, and to focus the best brains of the State upon solving each new problem raised by the war.

Although this formula was developed under the pressures of war and proved effective in the solution of problems far more complicated and far more pressing than are those of peace, it would be unfortunate if this blueprint were to be completely forgotten with the end of the emergency. The extent of cooperation from all segments of the population of the State which it prescribes may be unattainable in time of peace, may even, if not supplied voluntarily, be undesirable in a democracy that protects the right of disagreement with the majority. Nevertheless, the fact that New York State demonstrated that in a crisis it could work out a successful pattern for emergency government, which avoided the delegation of complete legislative authority for an unlimited period of time, was a clear indication of a high level of political maturity.

CHAPTER ELEVEN

Contributions and Problems
of Special Areas

THE impact of war is not the same on any two areas, because no two areas are ever exactly alike. Secondary social and economic problems bulk larger in small areas where rapid war expansion brings a greater percentage of population increase and a more extensive dislocation of the entire community than occurs in large cities. Variations in location affect problems of transportation and housing, cause diversity in types of industry, and influence the composition of the labor force. The population density and size of an urban community likewise affect its transportation, housing patterns, and the composition of the labor force as a result of immigration and the consolidation of national and racial minorities. The history and evolution of an urban community likewise accounts for its character; upon the character of a community often depends the efficiency of its government and the nature of its industries. In this connection, historical accidents have occasionally produced far-reaching consequences. The presence of large industries evolved over a considerable period of time has often exerted a very strong influence upon the skills of the local population through what might almost be called a process of natural industrial selection. With as many variables as these determining the character of municipalities in New York State, it is little wonder that the war raised special problems in nearly every one. The accidents of the war period added to the multiplicity and variety of local problems through the location in various parts of the State of large war plants and Army or Navy installations. To give in brief compass a survey of the major types of war impact, which is the purpose of this chapter, it is necessary to adopt a sampling method and deal only with representative examples.

The examples which have been selected are New York City, Buffalo, Rochester, Syracuse, Schenectady, Binghamton, Geneva, and Sidney. New York City was included for obvious reasons. It was the largest metropolis in the world and its very size presented special organizational problems. It was also the country's largest port and the principal embarkation point for the European theater of war. As a labor market it was also unique, being consistently the only surplus labor area in the State.

Buffalo, aside from being the number two city, was chosen among other reasons because of the tremendous development of its aircraft industry, because of its unusual transportation problem, and because of the fact that during the entire period of the war it was the only area of acute labor shortage.

Rochester was selected as an example of an efficiently operated, remarkably stable industrial community which produced war materials classified primarily in the miscellaneous category. It also

Air Raid Warden's Vigil

An air raid warden, with arm band showing, stands by for action in New York City's Times Square area before one of many practice blackouts during the war.

employed highly skilled labor, of which an especially large percentage was composed of women.

Aside from its concentration upon heavy industry, Syracuse was included because of its outstanding capacity to organize itself on a community-wide basis for the performance of such important wartime tasks as salvage, the sale of war bonds, and the recruitment of female labor. The progressive character of the city's leadership was also reflected in the postwar studies of its Chamber of Commerce and of its Postwar Planning Council, for which aid was secured from nationally known publishers, manufacturers, and professional organizations.

Schenectady was selected as a city whose main production efforts went into the output of two key producers of heavy war equipment, the General Electric Company and the American Locomotive Company. The contributions of these two companies are told in some detail as typical examples of American ingenuity and productive capacity.

The Binghamton area has been included as representative of the smaller manufacturing centers of the Southern Tier with special geographical and transportation problems, and for a city of its size an unusual assortment of contracts for vital war materials. Geneva was an outstanding example of a small city whose way of life was radically altered during the war by the location in its vicinity of two large Federal war facilities. Sidney was included as a typical example of what can happen to a small town in a rural setting when its one industrial plant suddenly mushrooms into a large producer of highly critical war materials.

Undoubtedly other examples might have been chosen to illustrate the impact of war upon communities in New York State. There were also variations from the major types which have not been covered. Space, however, does not permit an exhaustive enumeration, although it is hoped that municipalities whose war experience is deemed by them sufficiently noteworthy will invest time and energy and the necessary funds to produce a reasonably full account of what took place.[1]

To be sure, all communities had certain war activities in common. All were subject to selective service and rationing, and all played their full part in the salvage drives and in the purchase of war bonds and stamps. The only variation among these four was in the nature of scrap available in certain regions, and in the methods used by different communities to procure scrap and sell bonds. The purpose of civilian protection was everywhere the same, and to a large extent its organization was built up around the local fire, police, and highway departments and the private medical and local welfare organizations.

Variation consisted primarily in the complexity of the problem of organization as between cities like New York, Buffalo, or Rochester, and the rural areas of the State. The mobilization of volunteers was a universal problem, varying only with the personality of the leaders in charge, the strength of local social agencies, and the personal relations between the leaders of the local war councils and the directors of civilian mobilization and volunteer offices. The larger the city, the more definitely institutionalized were the volunteer offices. Elsewhere, in the smaller towns and rural counties, instead of one or two floors of offices the volunteer center was to be found in a small rented room, in the private office of the person in charge, or in his own home.

In many respects, the programs that dealt with individuals retained a certain similarity. Child care centers had the same purpose, the same type of clientele,

---

[1] Cf. the history of the Buffalo War Council written by Dudley M. Irwin, Jr., Vice-President of the Manufacturers' and Traders' Trust Company.

and frequently the same type of location. The shortage of nurses was not confined to the larger cities, nor were problems of health and welfare. Recreation, however, was a greater problem in the larger cities, particularly for those who worked second and third shifts. In general, however, these problems were common to the State as a whole.

The biggest contrast between the city and the country was to be found in the two major war programs — production of munitions and materials of war, and the production of food. Essentially, production for war was a problem of the larger centers, although there were numerous examples of large war plants located in small towns and villages. On the other hand, apart from victory gardens and nutrition information and education for consumers, the production and preservation of food was a rural problem. In this chapter attention will be centered upon varying examples of war impact from New York City to the small rural town of Sidney.

NEW YORK CITY

The contribution to the war effort made by New York City was in keeping with its size and its position as the number one port and banking center of the country. Although not generally recognized as a manufacturing city, New York also had the largest volume of war contracts of any city in the State. While only one-third of its labor force was in war work, the total was larger than the total labor force employed in war and nonwar industries in the second largest city — Buffalo. At the same time, it furnished from its surplus labor pool tens of thousands of workers for war production plants in states as far west as the Pacific coast. Because of the concentration of banking and insurance facilities in Manhattan, the city was likewise responsible for the purchase of more than 85.6 per cent of the State's entire total of war bonds. Furthermore, as a shipping center,

despite changes in the volume and direction of its foreign and coastwise trade forced upon it by the menace of Axis submarines, the volume of its foreign trade, both exports and imports, for the peak year, 1944, was 23.8 per cent of the national total.

Any city capable of compiling such a record in the prosecution of the war might be expected to have been seriously affected by wartime changes. Actually, however, because of its huge size and the character of its economy and society, the impact of the war upon New York was unique. Because of the presence of 7.5 million people, and because of its extremely varied economic life, the war had less effect upon New York than upon any other city in the State. Its diversified industrial pattern as well as its balanced economy, distributed evenly between the services, manufacturing, and trade, protected it against violent dislocations. The fact that manufacturing in New York City was concentrated in the nondurable consumer goods field, and that so many positions were available in the services and trade, meant that what conversion to war production took place affected but a small segment of the city's economy. Despite the shortage of labor in certain lines, the fact that throughout the war there was a total surplus for the city as a whole meant that it was classified by the War Manpower Commission as a group four, or surplus, labor market. In New York there was no great influx of war workers. In fact, exactly the reverse occurred, and for that reason no building boom resulted. School facilities and, until the return of substantial numbers of veterans, housing accommodations were adequate. The transportation network was unexcelled and the other municipal services were characteristic of a modern metropolis.

War Production, Unemployment, and the Labor Market. New York City's principal war industries were shipbuilding and repair (including government yards),

DOLLAR VOLUME PER CAPITA OF WAR CONTRACTS FOR SUPPLIES AND FACILITIES IN THE 15 LARGEST INDUSTRIAL AREAS JUNE 1, 1940 — MARCH 31, 1942

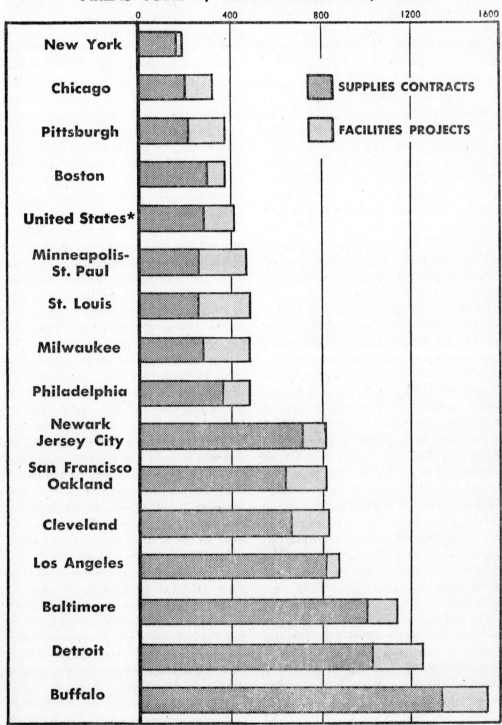

Source: War Production Board and Bureau of the Census
*Relative position, U. S. total per capita

aircraft and parts, electrical machinery, professional and scientific instruments, ordnance, and accessories. War supply contracts for the metropolitan area for the period, June, 1940 – June, 1946, totaled 9.36 billion dollars, or 43.5 per cent of the total awarded the State. Of the New York City total, 35.2 per cent was in aircraft and 22.9 per cent in ordnance. Because of her position as the country's foremost seaport, employment in the metal and machine groups including shipbuilding and repairing, which at that time were primarily war industries, expanded both relatively and absolutely more in the city than in any other large area of the State. Employment in the shipyards jumped from 25,000 to 100,000, including 75,000 for the Brooklyn Navy yard which built the *Missouri* and repaired the *Ben Franklin*. In 1943, the tremendous requirements for the support of the North African and Italian campaigns brought about the largest expansion of employment in "services allied to transportation not elsewhere classified (including companies engaged in freight forwarding, packing, services auxiliary to water transportation such as dock operation and stevedoring, etc.) ."

However, despite the fact that New York City had the largest number of workers of any city in the State employed in war production, total employment covered by workmen's compensation insurance rose only 17 per cent to the November, 1943, peak. Manufacturing employment alone did not reach its wartime peak until January, 1944, while in all upstate areas, except Rochester, peaks were reached between November, 1942, and November, 1943. One reason for this low percentage lay in the fact that an unusually large number of those employed in the city were in service or nonmanufacturing employment such as banking, finance, trade, transportation, hotels, and building construction and maintenance. Even among manufacturing employees it was estimated that 66 per

cent were connected with industries not extensively required in war production, and consequently not likely to receive any large number of war contracts. Over 40 per cent of these workers were in clothing and allied industries, many of which made women's garments and were consequently not suited for filling war contracts. Still a third reason for the small proportion of war contracts awarded the New York City area was the high proportion of manufacturing industries which, though generally considered more closely allied with war production, were nevertheless not easily adapted to war production under the procurement policies of the Federal government. Because of costs geared to the production of a quality product, it was difficult for certain industries to compete on a price basis for war orders. Taken together, these factors explain the fact that as late as June 1, 1942, there was a labor reserve in the city of three hundred thousand persons who were seeking work.

The persistence of sizable unemployment in New York City became one of the principal problems of Governor Lehman's last year in office. As a result of his efforts and those of Mayor LaGuardia, the cooperation of President Roosevelt was secured and several conferences were held in the summer of 1942 with the principal leaders of the national government for the purpose of bringing about more extensive utilization for war work of the available labor reserves and unused plant facilities of the city.

Information collected at the time by the State Division of Commerce and the United States Employment Service not only showed the extent of unemployment but the relatively small volume of war contracts awarded firms in New York City. To balance a decrease in nonessential employment owing to cutbacks in the manufacture of civilian goods, the Federal government from June 4, 1940, through March, 1942, had awarded the area a total of 1.6 billion dollars worth of war supply and facility contracts. This sum represented the lowest per capita ratio of any leading urban area in the country. As a result, only a relatively small portion of the city's manufacturing facilities were being employed in war production. Contracts for industrial and nonindustrial facilities were also lower on a per capita basis than for any other leading urban area, a fact largely accounting for the consistently low employment among the city's construction workers. The submission of this information to Federal authorities together with a series of recommendations developed jointly by the State Division of Commerce and the United States Employment Service produced substantial results. Thanks to Federal cooperation, employment in New York City rose steadily in the last half of 1942 and throughout 1943 to a peak in January, 1944.

There were, however, certain peculiarities about the New York labor market which did not show up in the figures, and which actually indicated a tighter situation than at any time appeared on paper. Although throughout the war Queens and Staten Island were classified as group two areas by the War Manpower Commission, Brooklyn, Manhattan, and the Bronx were always classified as group four, and because they outweighed the other two, New York City as a whole received a group four rating. Nevertheless, despite this rating and despite the effect of its excellent transportation system in rendering relatively mobile its large labor supply, the New York City area was actually extremely tight in all classes of labor required for war work. This was true though the number employed in wholesale and retail establishments and in the services was double that employed in essential war work, a situation in the city exactly the reverse of that common in upstate areas.

The failure of the New York City unemployment figures to reflect accurately these conditions of labor stringency was due to a number of factors. Part of the paper surplus of labor included a hypothetical availability of women which did not develop. Although there was a definite surplus of clerical workers, which was figured as part of the total labor surplus, these individuals were little suited to war work and were not readily convertible to it. A shift from less essential occupations to more essential war work was likewise counted upon. This did not develop, however, as it was impossible to force some people who were in nonessential work, such as fur workers getting $3 an hour, into essential work where such a shift involved a large financial cut. In fact at this point New York was exceptional in that the better paying jobs were not in war work, a condition by no means typical of the State as a whole, where wages in war plants were much higher than the average for civilian work. For these reasons it is understandable that New York City developed a shortage of foundry workers, tool mechanics, and other branches of skilled labor, which could be met only by extensive training programs. To fill the demand in these categories training-within-industry was successfully employed on a large scale together with apprenticeship training. In fact, the whole program of war production training inaugurated and carried through by the State Department of Education proved exceptionally effective especially in Nassau County.

Because of the difficulty of administration in a city the size of New York as well as on account of the comparative looseness of its labor supply, manpower control measures were not applied as completely as elsewhere. The priority referral program of the War Manpower Commission covered only male workers from eighteen to forty-five years of age. Essential firms were permitted to hire directly, and authority to refer workers to essential industry was also granted to

unions and to nonprofit employment
agencies.

Despite its relatively confused manpower situation, one of New York City's
outstanding contributions to the war
effort was the great number of men and
women sent to other areas. Trainload after trainload left for the west coast.
When an outstanding Pacific coast ship-
builder came to the city advertising for
twenty thousand workers, he received so
many that he had to stop hiring temporarily in order to catch up on his absorption process. As many as ten thousand
persons a month left the city and the
exodus averaged one thousand a week
for a considerable period. Many unions
handled placements for their own membership and did an excellent job. The
largest number of workers went to Connecticut and New Jersey, a flow which
was assisted by the United States Employment Service. Workers were sent to
Hawaii and other bases such as Bermuda
and Newfoundland. The United States
Employment Service recruited for the
aircraft plants in southern California
and for the Manhattan District project.
In the case of the latter, many took jobs
without knowing any more than that it
was the most important job to which
they could possibly have been sent.
Friends would sign up together in a
spirit of adventure, or solely to make
their skills available where they would
do the most good. Many of them, upon
appeals from their unions, took less pay.
One electricians' union, in particular,
accepted the Navy rate of $1.25 per hour
instead of much higher pay on local short
construction jobs. Minority groups carried through beautifully. The city which
had the highest proportion of foreign-
born of any of the large cities of the
country experienced no strikes or sabotage of any significance during the war.
In this connection, the work of the State
Mediation Board, of the Labor-Management Committee of the United States
Employment Service, and also of the

Labor Officers assigned by the Army and
Navy Air Forces was especially to be commended. Patriotic motives were everywhere predominant.

Activities of the Port of New York. In
addition to its value as the largest producer of war equipment in the State, and
as a source of labor for other sections of
the country, the nation's largest seaport
was also the gateway for shipments to the
fighting fronts in Europe and Africa. As
such it played a vital role in mounting
the trans-Atlantic attack upon the Axis.
For this task New York's 700 piers, 650
miles of developed waterfront, 122 square
miles of lower bay and extensive floating
equipment, including 500 tugs, enabled
it to dispatch during the war an average
of one ship every fifteen minutes, and to
accommodate in the harbor at the peak
of the war effort a daily average of 400
ships.

Prior to the war, the Port of New York
was increasing rapidly both the volume
and the value of its foreign trade. From
1938 through 1941, the total value rose
over 2 billion dollars, an increase of
more than 100 per cent, while the total
tonnage rose nearly 15 millions, very
nearly a 100 per cent increase. In 1941,
the volume of the country's foreign trade
rose 19.5 per cent, (96.2 million long
tons in 1940, 115.1 million in 1941),
while for the same period the volume of
foreign trade at the Port of New York
rose 44.5 per cent (21.8 million long tons
in 1940, 31.5 in 1941). At the same time,
the port accounted for a substantially
higher percentage of the value of the
total United States foreign trade than it
did of the volume — in 1941, 50.4 per
cent of the value, 27.4 per cent of the
volume — an indication of its preemi-
nence as a port for mixed merchandise
general cargo as compared with bulk cargoes of ore or petroleum. Under these
circumstances it was natural that the substantial expansion in the volume of export and import cargoes moving through
the port prior to Pearl Harbor should

stimulate those agencies responsible for its operations, such as the Port Authority, the United States Army and Navy, the Maritime Commission, the Office of Defense Transportation, and local government agencies and transportation companies, to bend every effort to keep the port in a liquid condition. With the repeal of the Neutrality Act, November 5, 1941, and the declaration of war, December 8, a shift from a peacetime to a wartime basis was effected in all phases of port operation.

The entry of the country into the war had an adverse effect upon the trade of the port which lasted throughout 1942 and as long as the Axis submarine campaign remained effective. Figures for the volume of United States and New York City foreign trade in that year are not given, but the total number of foreign and American vessels entering and leaving the port with cargo in 1942 dropped 34 per cent from the 1941 figure. The greatest decline, 57 per cent, came in American vessels entering the port with cargo. This situation lasted but a short time, however, and with the exception of foreign vessels entering with cargo, both the number of vessels and the total tonnage picked up rapidly from 1943 on.

For each of the last three years of the war, 1943-1945, the volume of exports topped the 1941 figure. The peak year for export tonnage at the port was 1944, in which the volume was approximately 62 per cent higher than in 1941. That this reflected the height of the war effort in Europe, and the extraordinary dependence of the high command upon the facilities of the port, is borne out by the fact that in 1944 the increase over 1943 of 5.2 million tons in national exports occurred almost entirely (5.1 million tons) at the Port of New York. Furthermore, as reported by the War Shipping Administration for 1944, New York's 2,277 ship sailings represented 46.7 per cent of all sailings from Atlantic coast

ports and accounted for 44.3 per cent of the total tons of dry cargo loaded.

The New York Port of Embarkation in Brooklyn was a primary military facility employing during the war years an average of 55,000 men and women. Total personnel embarked from it during the years 1941-1945 were 3,283,678; total personnel debarked, 2,150,065. Tonnage (measurement tons) shipped overseas from its wharves in the same period came to 38,244,302. Some 3,171,922,000 pieces of incoming and outgoing first-class mail to and from men overseas were also handled by its Postal Terminal.

A further idea of the importance of the port of New York as a war facility may be gathered from a breakdown of the volume of exports through the port for 1944 and the first six months of 1945 — the peak war months. Of the total dry cargo shipped during those months, 28 million long tons, Army cargoes totaled 9 million, Lend-lease 8.3 million, and Navy 2.4 million. Tanker cargo (petroleum products) totaled 30.6 million tons, of which Lend-lease was 17.8 million and the combined Army, Navy and United States government shipments were 12.8 million. Of the combined total of dry and tanker cargo shipped, 58.6 million tons, Lend-lease shipments comprised 44.6 per cent, Army, Navy, and United States government tanker shipments, 41.3 per cent, and general commercial shipments approximately 14 per cent.

The persistent decline in the percentage of the value of New York imports in relation to the national total — 47.1 per cent in 1941, 33.3 per cent in 1944, and a similar decline in the ratio of their volume — 39.7 per cent in 1941, 23.9 per cent in 1944, reflected the war-caused drop in exports to this country from Europe and the Middle East which previously had entered through the Port of New York. This development was confirmed by the consistently low number of foreign vessels entering the port with cargo throughout the war, despite the

Table 25. Value and Volume of Foreign Trade, Port of New York and United States,
1938-1946

	VALUE (All Foreign Trade) (Thousands of Dollars)			VOLUME (Waterborne Foreign Trade) (Long Tons)		
Cal. Year	United States	Port of New York	Per cent N.Y. of U.S.	United States	Port of New York	Per cent N.Y. of U.S.

EXPORTS AND IMPORTS

1938	5,044,064	2,109,778	41.8	88,430,269	16,692,912	18.9
1939	5,453,275	2,442,846	44.8	92,518,381	19,354,700	20.9
1940	6,561,802	3,186,713	48.6	96,275,843	21,801,412	22.6
1941	8,369,108	4,217,692	50.4	107,725,591	31,554,170	29.3
1942	10,848,802	4,774,986	44.0	77,886,475	14,431,463	18.5
1943	16,346,255	6,173,367	37.8	88,328,375	26,830,915	30.4
1944	18,177,972	7,243,039	39.8	102,044,026	32,505,787	31.9
1945	13,941,816	5,540,882	39.7	103,708,921	28,254,085	27.2
1946	14,648,377	6,393,452	43.6	121,525,492	24,266,340	20.0

EXPORTS

1938	3,094,440	1,126,260	36.4	55,612,107	5,969,772	10.7
1939	3,177,176	1,293,846	40.7	55,087,100	7,104,489	12.9
1940	4,021,146	1,944,885	48.4	55,296,642	9,433,248	17.1
1941	5,147,154	2,699,821	52.5	54,828,686	12,209,771	22.3
1942	8,079,517	3,804,147	47.1	52,291,688	7,482,324	14.3
1943	12,964,906	5,016,094	38.7	54,698,268	14,696,021	26.9
1944	14,258,702	5,938,435	41.6	62,099,738	19,774,639	31.8
1945	9,805,875	4,023,035	41.0	62,744,786	16,332,821	26.0
1946	9,739,482	4,017,685	41.3	77,604,688	10,949,554	14.1

IMPORTS*

1938	1,949,624	983,518	50.4	32,818,162	10,723,140	32.7
1939	2,276,099	1,149,000	50.5	37,431,281	12,250,211	32.7
1940	2,540,656	1,241,828	48.9	40,979,201	12,368,164	30.2
1941	3,221,954	1,517,871	47.1	52,896,905	19,344,399	36.6
1942	2,769,285	970,839	35.1	25,594,787	6,949,139	27.2
1943	3,381,349	1,157,273	34.2	33,630,107	12,134,894	36.1
1944	3,919,270	1,304,604	33.3	39,944,288	12,731,148	31.9
1945	4,135,941	1,517,847	36.7	40,964,135	11,921,264	29.1
1946	4,908,895	2,375,767	48.4	43,920,804	13,316,786	30.3

*VALUE — United States figures show imports for consumption, 1938-1942 (Immediate Consumption
and Warehouse Withdrawals).
New York figures, same as above for years 1938-1942.
United States and New York figures show general imports for years 1943-1945 (Immediate Consumption and Warehouse Entries).

VOLUME — United States figures show general imports for years 1943, 1944, 1945.
New York figures show general imports for years 1943, 1944, 1945.
United States and New York figures — The Grouping of Imports (How Grouped)
Unknown for Years — 1938-1941.

SOURCE: Port of New York Authority.

Table 26. Number and Net Registered Tonnage of American and Foreign Vessels Cleared and Entering in Ballast and with Cargo in the Foreign Trade of the United States, 1941-1946. (Thousands of Tons)

Custom District		In ballast				With cargo			
		Number		Tons		Number		Tons	
		Cleared	Entering	Cleared	Entering	Cleared	Entering	Cleared	Entering
1941									
New York	Amer.	439	49	1,773	160	1,502	1,431	5,189	5,740
	For.	672	908	2,505	3,830	2,265	1,871	6,916	5,257
GRAND TOTAL	Amer.	6,164	5,029	6,916	3,949	5,995	7,846	14,954	16,991
	For.	10,900	8,412	9,143	16,759	14,965	16,548	31,583	21,362
1942									
New York	Amer.	188	208	810	819	906	609	3,152	2,462
	For.	202	923	826	3,617	1,984	1,162	5,958	3,415
GRAND TOTAL	Amer.	3,777	4,995	3,087	4,614	5,104	5,036	13,267	8,997
	For.	8,508	7,999	4,373	16,146	13,117	13,328	26,979	14,185
1943									
New York	Amer.	560	1,408	2,645	6,201	2,175	1,355	9,666	6,041
	For.	240	1,470	1,427	7,249	2,153	987	9,024	3,472
GRAND TOTAL	Amer.	5,013	6,695	6,360	13,233	7,893	7,306	27,322	16,059
	For.	9,068	8,052	4,248	18,225	13,941	14,587	28,786	13,567
1944									
New York	Amer.	591	2,845	2,935	13,569	3,083	1,504	14,571	6,720
	For.	355	1,623	1,608	8,456	2,375	1,101	11,188	4,121
GRAND TOTAL	Amer.	5,026	8,478	9,482	24,931	11,191	8,368	43,567	23,137
	For.	10,410	8,379	5,793	9,583	13,690	15,609	28,545	14,207
1945									
New York	Amer.	832	2,394	4,088	11,131	2,286	1,660	10,173	7,281
	For.	365	1,359	1,730	6,613	1,804	986	7,946	3,697
U. S.	Amer.	6,721	11,215	14,050	32,845	11,714	9,422	47,410	28,531
	For.	14,525	12,069	6,490	19,405	13,250	15,612	26,608	13,241
1946									
New York	Amer.	1,022	1,604	4,959	7,514	1,801	1,677	7,677	7,166
	For.	315	430	1,144	1,773	1,354	1,218	5,417	4,846
U. S.	Amer.	6,573	11,208	13,771	28,840	9,245	8,580	35,330	24,202
	For.	16,590	10,909	6,068	12,750	12,061	17,385	22,093	14,463

SOURCE: U. S. Department of Commerce, Bureau of the Census.

decline in the submarine menace, as well as by the steady rise from 1943 to 1945 in the number of American and foreign vessels entering the port in ballast. Not only was the North Atlantic crossing the most dangerous of all shipping routes, but Europe and the Middle East were producing less for export to the United States.

From these figures it may be concluded that the effect of the war upon port commerce and employment was less a loss in over-all volume than a marked change in the character of cargoes moving through the port. Port ships and cargoes were forced out of the usual channels, as typified by the 66 per cent drop in tonnage of coastwise receipts at New York harbor for the first year of the war (34.2 million tons in 1941, 11.6 million tons in 1942). As shown above, exports were almost entirely specialized movements of materiel to armed forces overseas and to our allies. Imports were almost exclusively priority commodities. Most shipping was carried on under military or other government (WSA) supervision, the result being a highly concentrated operation centered at a few terminals, such as the Army's Port of Embarkation in Brooklyn, or the installations of the Third Naval District. Under these circumstances, neither labor nor facilities were employed on as broad a scale as would normally have been the case in time of peace. Furthermore, because of submarine activity, Federal authorities in the spring of 1942 diverted to New Orleans and other gulf ports shipping services normally plying between the Port of New York and the Caribbean, Central, and South American ports. Consequently, commercial shipping activities at New York dropped to a record low, and severe unemployment of longshore and other port labor resulted. This situation improved steadily, however, after 1942 owing to the decline in the submarine menace and the increase in tempo of the war in Europe.

The principal effects of the war upon New York City as a manufacturing center and as a port were bound to be reflected in traffic changes between Manhattan and Staten Island and the New Jersey shore. These changes were carefully measured by the Port of New York Authority on the interstate facilities which it operates between the States of New York and New Jersey. Created in 1921 by compact between the two states, the Port Authority operates among other facilities the Holland and Lincoln Tunnels, the George Washington, Bayonne, Goethals, and Outerbridge Crossing Bridges, and the Union Railroad Freight Terminal. Curiously enough, although vehicular traffic over these facilities declined from the 1941 high of 30.6 million vehicles, which partly reflected an increased volume of trucks carrying munitions of war to piers for shipment overseas, to the 1943 low of 22 million vehicles, nevertheless, despite this curtailed automobile usage and owing to increased use of rail and bus facilities, more people crossed the Hudson in 1942 than in 1941. Until 1945, the total number of buses to use the facilities annually increased steadily throughout the war. From a low point of 4.35 million trucks in 1942, the number using Port Authority facilities rose steadily each year to a high of 5.54 million in 1945. (See Table 27.)

Besides, the character of traffic changed considerably. The week-end peaks of pleasure-car travel were eliminated, and the proportion of essential to total traffic rose rapidly. There also occurred a partial reversal of week-day peak hours owing to large-scale movements of war workers from homes in the various boroughs of the city to factories west of the Hudson. Throughout the period of rationing, total traffic losses on Port Authority crossings were relatively less percentagewise than the decline in general motoring, thus reflecting the comparatively heavy use of these facilities by essential (approximately 60 per cent B

Table 27. *Traffic on Port of New York Authority Facilities, 1941-1945*
(Number of Vehicles)

	Passenger Cars	Buses	Trucks	Other	Total
1941	24,114,183	1,824,360	4,637,462	24,562	30,600,567
1942	18,607,150	2,021,860	4,356,546	24,289	25,009,845
1943	15,341,887	2,067,434	4,558,365	18,827	21,986,513
1944	19,835,723	2,122,846	5,251,524	24,668	27,234,761
1945	22,382,565	2,122,327	5,542,693	25,030	30,072,615

SOURCE: Port of New York Authority.

and C book holders) motorists. In line with the extensive use of the port as a war facility, the number of trucks using the Port Authority facilities returned to the 1941 level in the latter part of 1943, with the result that the annual totals for 1944 and 1945 exceeded the 1941 figures by 13.1 and 19.4 per cent respectively. Traffic in the Lincoln Tunnel showed an especially heavy increase. The strategic importance of the bridges and tunnels thus evidenced fully warranted the protection given them during the war.

Two important steps in the expansion of Port Authority facilities took place during the war. Owing to the rapid increase of vehicular traffic in the south tube of the Lincoln Tunnel, construction was resumed on the north tube which was opened February 1, 1945. With its opening, a total of eight lanes of underwater crossing of the Hudson River became available. A second step was taken May 1, 1944, on the recommendation of Governor Dewey. The Port Authority accepted from the State of New York transferral of the Gowanus Grain Terminal, a 2-million-bushel elevator, with pier and other property, situated on Gowanus Bay, Brooklyn. Empty and in disrepair when taken over, its subsequent operation as a major Port Authority facility for the delivery of railroad as well as Barge Canal grain filled the structure to capacity and placed it on a paying basis.

The use of the word "reconversion" in connection with the operations of the port may sound a bit peculiar, but it definitely applies to part of the planning for New York's postwar development begun by the Port Authority in 1943. These plans, part of which were already in the construction stage by 1946, included: (1) measures designed to restore to the port merchant shipping diverted elsewhere during the war by the submarine menace along the Atlantic coast; (2) increased facilities for air-borne commerce designed to enable the port to compete successfully for what it is estimated will be an increasing amount of air-borne high-grade freight and passenger traffic; (3) the construction of a union marine grain terminal, union bus and bulk commodity terminals, and a reorganization of the produce terminals; (4) the cheapening where possible of local costs of transportation in order to prevent the slow strangling of the commerce of the port by higher costs incident to extensive metropolitan developments.

This planning program for a "cheaper, faster, and surer port" is evidence that the Commissioners of the Port Authority understand current needs and within their power will do everything to promote the welfare of its citizens. Basically, however, the future of the port depends upon the resumption of a free flow of foreign commerce, and since one out of every ten persons gainfully employed in the metropolitan area depends upon the port for a livelihood, and since the total investment in port facilities represents several billion dollars, the economic well-being of a large section of New York is vitally dependent upon a revival of foreign trade. The responsibility for such a revival, however, rests primarily upon the national government.

Protection of the City. Because of its size and its importance to the military and naval strategy of the United States, New York City was target number one for any Axis attempt at transatlantic bombing. The protection of 7.5 million people, located on islands and peninsulas, was a gigantic task involving the organization of an unprecedented number of civilian defense volunteers, and the erection of a system of communications unparalleled in extent and complexity. Because of the unique character of the measures required to protect the city, a somewhat detailed description of the organization and functions of the New York City protective services seems justified at this point.

President Roosevelt's proclamation of an unlimited national emergency, May 27, 1941, was followed the next day by a proclamation from Mayor LaGuardia stating that New York City would cooperate with the civilian defense agencies of the Federal government. Two weeks later, the Mayor appointed Police Chief Lewis J. Valentine as Police Defense Coordinator to set up an air-raid warden service and an auxiliary police force. Enrollment of volunteers began June 20, 1941, and the organization was developed on the basis of police precincts, which in turn were subdivided by zones of fifty thousand, precinct sectors of five thousand, and posts of five hundred inhabitants. Training was inaugurated June 30, and instructors were drawn from the Police Department, the United States Army, nearby colleges and universities, and the American Red Cross. Through the cooperation of NBC, tele-

vision equipment was set up in each police station house, and 428 television broadcasts for selected air-raid wardens were given between February, 1942, and December, 1943. Since England was America's big practice incident, although real enough in itself, sixteen films were shown depicting actual air raids on that country.

At its peak in September, 1943, the Air Warden Service numbered approximately 290,000 volunteers, with a constant turnover bringing the total enrollment for the duration up to 400,000 — of which 80 per cent were men. Within the headquarters of the Air Warden Service, subdivisions were set up consisting of the Staff Bureaus of Personnel, Information and Planning, Operations and Training, communications including the Messenger Corps, Light Duty Rescue Squads, the Emergency Taxi Corps, and the Bureau of Supply. Practice incidents involving part or all of the following civilian protection services — Police Emergency Division, Fire Emergency Division, Public Works Emergency Division — were staged periodically from 1942 through 1944. The Air Warden Service likewise performed additional duties in connection with parades, rescue work during the hurricane of September 14, 1944, speaking engagements with the Civilian Defense Volunteer Office, and the donation of blood to the Red Cross.

As was true for the rest of the State, the air-raid warning system was activated from the Army Information Center of the Second Service Command. Warnings were sent to New York City Police headquarters over direct telephone lines, and were then relayed by teletypewriter network to all police station houses, report centers, control centers, and fire headquarters. From these they were in turn relayed by telephone to key people in the city administration, and by radio to police patrol cars. Fire headquarters relayed the warning to all local firehouses by telegraph. From each police station house the warning was further relayed to nearby schools, hospitals, public utilities, and defense plants by means of a push button that activated a wire network furnished by the telephone company. Fifty-seven separate networks were provided, one for each telephone central office building, and thus approximately 1600 locations were served. Upon receipt of the signal, report centers telephoned their operating staffs to report for duty and called the warden zone headquarters. From there, the signal was telephoned to warden sector headquarters, where telephoning ceased. From that point on, wardens' posts and individual wardens were alerted by the ringing of doorbells and other means. The staffs of control centers, police and fire headquarters, and other communication centers were summoned by telephone, as in the case of the report center. The public at large, however, was alerted by a total of 454 sirens installed on the roofs of police station houses, firehouses, elevated railroad stations, and other strategically located buildings, and activated by push buttons generally located in police stations and firehouses. In sections of the city where the sound did not penetrate with sufficient volume, sirens on some five hundred police radio patrol cars effected the remaining coverage.

As was true for other cities, the fundamental protective services were furnished by the logical municipal departments, augmented to perform emergency operations. Six principal departments were involved — those of Police, Fire, Welfare, Public Works, and the Departments of Hospitals and Health. As part of the city's civilian protection organization they were given five special designations — Police Emergency Division, Fire Emergency Division, Public Works Emergency Division, Medical Emergency Division, and Welfare Emergency Division. The heads of these services formed the Mayor's War Cabinet, and an advisory committee of representatives of both the Congress of Industrial Organizations and the American Federation of Labor was appointed to advise on the important contributions which the unions could make to the defense of the city. A brief discussion of each of the protective services follows:

The Police Emergency Division included the 18,000 police officers of the peacetime force, 3800 City Patrol Corps members, and the entire Air Warden Service of over 200,000. A central Bureau of War Operations was established at police headquarters and the existing police facilities in the seven borough and sixteen division offices were supplemented with additional wire communications. All bureau, division, and precinct commands were linked by telephone, teletypewriter, and radio. The peacetime communications system was augmented for civilian defense purposes by the establishment in the Criminal Courts Building of an alternate police headquarters. During an air raid, each precinct maintained a chart showing men and equipment on hand and dispatched to incidents, and reported this information to the Division Office periodically. Consolidated reports were passed on through the Borough Command to the Bureau of War Operations.

The services rendered by the New York City Police Department in the war effort were varied and important. It was largely instrumental in training the personnel of the Air Warden Service and the City Patrol Corps. It likewise trained Military Police and Shore Patrol for the Army and Navy, as well as personnel that handled bombs, mines, and unexploded shells. It also gave physical and mental instruction to the Army, Navy, and State Guard. The police investigated unregistered aliens, deserters, escaped prisoners of war, black market Office of Price Administration violators, subversive elements, and violators of the Selective Service Act. They had charge of the enforcement of the dimout and blackout regulations, of Office of Price Administration regulations, and after December 8, 1941, confiscated cameras and radios from enemy aliens. They were on hand as guards at parades, rallies, piers, bridges, shipping, foreign consulates, meetings of foreign nations, control centers, and, in the beginning, at defense plants. They escorted officials of the Army and Navy, shipments of gold, pay rolls, vehicles transporting explosives, and naval vessels in the harbor. They maintained a Harbor Patrol, fingerprinted volunteers, operated the television sets installed and maintained for the instruction of air wardens, and generally performed valuable war services as the watchful eyes of the city government. The City Patrol Corps, composed of three thousand men and eight hundred women, was organized under the Police Commissioner to supplement and assist the City Police wherever possible. Its early task was considered to be the prevention of sabotage, but later it turned its attention primarily to the prevention of crime.

The Fire Emergency Division consisted of the city's local fire-fighting forces and equipment — 10,000 men, 261 regular pumpers, 130 additional hose wagons, 131 hook-and-ladder trucks, 10 fire boats, and 26 other equipment including water towers, searchlights, and chemical engines. These forces were located in 265 firehouses throughout the five boroughs and were augmented during the war by 50,000 volunteer firemen, 700 auxiliary fire pumpers, 17 auxiliary fireboats, and 375,000 feet of hose. The regular communication system in Manhattan, typical of that in use in the other boroughs, was the fire department's telegraph system which provided two-way communication between 1700 alarm boxes and Borough Alarm Headquarters, and between the latter point and 85 firehouses. If the telegraph system was overloaded or inoperative, dispatching would be carried on by telephone. The fire department's radio system supplemented wire facilities, and provided an alternate means of communication.

The regular forces, however, were not considered adequate by themselves. The experience of European cities was an object lesson in the need for training auxiliary fire fighters. Accordingly, the city sent a deputation of trained fire-fighting men to London to secure information on the latest fire-fighting methods of the British. Others were sent as observers to the United States Army Training Centers at Edgewood and Raritan Arsenals. The observations thus recorded, plus standard New York City fire-fighting practices, became the basis for subsequent courses designed to build up in the fire department an Emergency Auxiliary Corps. Inaugurated June 27, 1941, and federalized April 29, 1942, the corps reached an all-time high of 55,000 volunteers, 11,000 of whom were trained to handle incendiary explosives and war gases. First-aid courses were given to all personnel by authorized American Red Cross instructors, and heavy emphasis was placed upon communications such as messengers, motorcycles, radio, roof watchers, street patrols, and telephones. Plans were also made for emergency water-supply connections and auxiliary fire stations.

The Welfare Emergency Division included the Department of Welfare, the American Red Cross, the Salvation Army, the American Women's Volunteer Service, and other social agencies with a total personnel of over eleven thousand. Seventy-three Emergency Welfare Centers were located throughout the city, prepared to meet the needs of persons requiring care, clothing, food, rehousing, or other aid in an emergency, and to give counsel to those in distress. In addition, the Red Cross selected over eight hundred locations in schools, churches, and clubs for Rest Centers. Care in these centers was available for forty-eight hours, after which the Welfare Centers would provide further assistance. All communications were handled directly between the seventy-three Emergency Welfare Centers and Headquarters. During an alert, one or more representatives were stationed in each police station house to report on conditions in the area and to care for people coming into the station house for assistance. Representatives were also attached to the Borough and Civic Control Centers from which, in cooperation with the Medical and Police Departments, a central registration bureau would be operated following an air raid to facilitate the reuniting of families, friends, or relatives, and the location of the injured or dead.

The Public Works Emergency Division, created by the Public Works Department, was composed of equipment and personnel from that department, from several other city departments, and from over one hundred private organizations such as building contractors, plumbers, trade groups, public utility companies, etc. The air-raid responsibilities of this division included demolition of bombed buildings, the clearance of streets, the restoration of utility services by the appropriate companies, and decontamination of gas areas in order to permit the earliest possible resumption of civilian activities. Personnel totaled 31,000, of whom 2000 were engineers, architects, chemists, and technicians. Equipment included cranes, bulldozers, power shovels, automatic drills, trucks of all kinds, shoring lumber, and the repair equipment of the utilities companies.

The working unit, known as a Battery, was a complement of men and equipment varying in size and type depending upon the work assigned. These were mobilized upon an alert at four hundred emergency depots, such as garages, repair headquarters, emergency stations, and points regularly used by private or municipal organizations. Additional telephone facilities were generally not required at the Emergency Depots. When damage to electric cables, gas, steam, and water mains was reported, a Public Works officer was dispatched from the Report Center to the scene of the damage and his findings telephoned to the Public Works Room of the Borough Control Station. There, dispatch of the required Battery was arranged. Unlike the fire and medical services, the greater part of the repair work was not to be undertaken until sometime after cessation of the air raid.

The Medical Emergency Division included eight thousand physicians and fourteen thousand nurses and nurses' aides, and was based upon the twenty-one municipal and sixty-four private hospitals, each of which maintained an Emergency Field Unit. The average unit consisted of six teams, each team composed of a doctor, a nurse, two nurses' aides, and two stretcher bearers. Arrangements for 550 casualty stations were made in public buildings, schools, churches, and clubs. These were to be activated when required by a medical team. First-aid posts would be established in sheltered locations at the incident and serve as a base of operations for medical personnel. Plans were likewise developed for augmenting the ambulance service by panel delivery trucks from commercial organizations and by other private vehicles. The eight District Control Hospitals referred to above each controlled ten casualty hospitals from which ambulances and medical teams would be dispatched. Authority for dispatching medical services was in the hands of the Borough Medical Chief operating the Borough Control, thus relieving the Report or Control Centers of the performance of a highly technical duty.

The Gas Defense Service was set up in August, 1942, under the City Commissioner of Health as Gas Protection Coordinator. Courses in defense against chemical attack were given to employees of city departments, and to physicians and nurses by members of the Chemical Warfare Service. In January, 1943, a gas training laboratory was equipped and used to train approximately four hundred Gas Reconnaissance Officers. Decontamination Squads were also developed within the Public Works Emergency Division. One incident requiring the actual mobilization of Gas Defense Service occurred June 1, 1944, when chlorine gas was drawn into a Brooklyn subway by action of the trains, and considerable numbers of people were temporarily incapacitated.

More or less independent, yet thoroughly integrated with the other five emergency protective services, was the War Emergency Radio Service, established September 24, 1942, in accordance with rules of the Federal Communications Commission. In all, 324 sending and receiving units were donated to the city by amateur radio operators and utilized to supplement telephone and telegraph communication systems. Some of these units were fixed. Others were in cars, and about one hundred were on portable packs. The sets were manned by nearly six hundred licensed radio operators. The Service was used twice — once in particular during the 1944 hurricane when several precincts and the Flushing Hospital were cut off but for a mobile War Emergency Radio Station. All licenses were cancelled November 15, 1945, and equipment returned to the original owners.

Although the system by which New York City's 7.5 million citizens were warned of impending air raids has been described, together with the protective services which in such an event could be mobilized to control and minimize damage from air raids, no reference has yet been made to the system of communications established for the purpose of notifying these services of the number, location, and type of incidents requiring their presence and assistance. This New York City Civilian Defense communica-

tions system, the most highly organized system in the country, was the work of a Communications Staff headed by an official of the New York Telephone Company as Communications Coordinator.[1] A Communications Staff operated under the direction of Arthur W. Wallander, Chief of Staff of the New York City Civilian Defense Organization.

This staff worked out the plans and trained the personnel with the result that the extensive system of Report and Control Centers bound together into a functioning unit the entire Civilian Defense Organization — the Civilian Defense Air Warden organization, and the five branches of the city's regular protective services consisting of the Police, Fire, Medical, Public Works, and Welfare Departments. To cope with the possibility that in time of air attack disaster would be dispersed over many areas, the communications system was based upon the necessity for dispatching the protective services to many locations simultaneously. Communication operations were thus decentralized and, in addition, alternate communications centers were established for use in the event of telephone service failure. To supplement telephone service, a plan was developed to utilize radio and messenger service. The procedure for mobilizing Police, Fire, and Welfare Departments followed closely the pattern of their peacetime operations, but in the case of the Medical and Public Works Departments, special coordinating arrangements proved necessary.

To tie together the Civilian Defense Air Warden organization and the five protective services, seventy-one Report Centers, each manned by volunteers and serving a single precinct, were established in police precinct houses. Air-raid damage reports from the wardens were relayed by these Report Centers to the

---

[1] This is not to be confused with the air-raid warning system described above.

Nation's Largest Combat Plane Factory

The Buffalo Municipal Airport was selected by Curtiss-Wright Corporation as the site for construction of the largest combat airplane plant in the United States.

Borough Control Centers of which there was one for each of the five boroughs. The dispatch of emergency services to the incident, at first placed with the Report Centers, was ultimately taken over by the Borough Control Centers. Coordinating the five Control Centers was the New York City Control Center which functioned for the city as a whole.

The control Centers were the protective nerve centers of the city, located with reference to central telephone office loads, protection from bombs, and the availability of volunteers and of city employees to man the centers. Each consisted primarily of a telephone room, a room for each of the five protective services, and one for the Office of the Director. Reports of incidents received in the telephone room were duplicated for each of the Service Rooms which maintained maps and prepared periodic status reports of the personnel and equipment available at the various Service Depots. A combination picture of air-raid damage was thus possible on short notice, and the pool of resources available to the center could thus be tapped as needed. A typical Control Center, like that of Manhattan, had a total of sixty-three telephone lines, thirty-five in the telephone room, twelve for Public Works, three for Police, one for Fire, four for Medical, three for Welfare, and two for the Control Center Director. The Control Center for the entire city had a somewhat larger number and the other boroughs varied in proportion to their requirements.

Two alternate means of communication were developed to supplement telephone service. The War Emergency Radio Service has been discussed above. The Messenger Service, an integral part of the Air Warden Service, consisted of more than twenty thousand trained volunteers, usually boys between sixteen and eighteen years of age, thoroughly familiar with primary and alternate routes of travel between their respective centers

and the Report Centers, and the twenty-six locations at which telephone wardens were stationed.

In addition to integrating the Center forces with the city's five protective services, the Communications Staff greatly expanded facilities for each of the five services. Telephone communication was important in the Police Emergency Division, which included the Air Warden Service, the City Patrol Corps, and the regular uniformed police. The operating unit of the Warden Service was the sector which had from eighty to one hundred wardens serving about five thousand people. In organizing service, coin telephones were installed for the duration of the war at some 1560 sector headquarters, and over 4500 existing telephones were selected by the New York Telephone Company and police officials as auxiliary communication points. Each of these posts was manned by a Warden, and the posts were usually located in the lobbies of office buildings, restaurants, garages, residences, and other places where access could be obtained day and night. The Communications Staff gave instructions in the technique of reporting air-raid incidents to the Report Center, to the Police Lieutenants assigned as Precinct Warden Commanders, and to the seventy civilian volunteers. Wardens were then trained locally in the Report Centers and at Sector Headquarters.

In the case of the Fire Emergency Division, the communications staff was concerned principally with the establishment of three alternate fire-alarm headquarters for use in case the Fire Department's telegraph system was rendered inoperative, or became overloaded, and also the supplementing of existing telephone facilities at fire-alarm headquarters and in individual houses.

Since in New York City there were twenty-one municipal and sixty-four large private hospitals, the Emergency Medical Division consisted of an over-all integration of these two groups into a single unit designed to carry the Medical Service load for Civilian Defense. Originally set up on a borough basis, it was subsequently slightly decentralized so that reports from the seventy-one Report Centers were channeled to eight strategically located district control hospitals equipped with the necessary telephones, maps, and control boards. The hospitals furnished the operating personnel for the communications system and training was given by the communications staff.

In connection with the Public Works and Welfare Divisions, the communications staff assisted in the layout of the communications centers for these services and in the development of procedures and forms. Assistance was also given in the training of volunteer instructors for the Welfare Department.

For a period of over eighteen months, official communications exercises were held in which various sections of the city were activated on a rotating basis. Each exercise involved from six to eighteen Report Centers and the reporting of 250 to 500 incidents. However, men and equipment were not actually dispatched. These exercises tested the system, supplemented the training, helped the morale, and encouraged cooperation among the protective services.

In general, the entire communications system attracted volunteers who were conscientious and capable in their work and highly responsive to good leadership. The work itself was of the utmost importance to the protection of the community, and its many interesting features appealed strongly to volunteers, despite its lack of glamour and the relative anonymity of the personnel.

The Civilian Defense Volunteer Office. The Civilian Defense Volunteer Office, in operation from 1941 through 1945, was an official war agency of the City of New York. During that period, more than 260,000 volunteers were associated with the office, and more than a million workers were recruited for civilian de-

fense and other war activities. This work was entirely voluntary and was carried out with the same "dedication, loyalty, discipline and selflessness" as that displayed by soldiers in the armed forces. In 1941 (before the creation of the CDVO, complete priority was given to the recruitment of the protective services. A coordinated program was developed at the same time with the American Red Cross for the training of thousands of nurse's aides. By December 7, a large portion of New York City's inhabitants had been trained to meet the impact of war.

As the immediate danger of attack decreased, services other than protective were developed concerning primarily the welfare of communities. Among these may be listed child care, health and welfare, consumer education, and services in support of the Federal war programs. Since the maintenance of adequate defense services would depend upon availability of volunteer manpower recruited from the civilian population of the city, the Mayor created, in October, 1941, the Civilian Defense Volunteer Office and charged it with the recruiting, training, and placing of volunteers in the war services. Chairmen for each borough and one for the entire city were appointed to organize, direct, and put into operation the functions of the volunteer office.

The city-wide Civilian Defense Volunteer Office was nonoperational, its functions being to determine policy, to direct, advise, suggest, and promote. Operational activities, largely the responsibility of the borough offices, were later further decentralized among sixty-eight branch offices. Although the borough offices had opened for business before the Japanese attack on Pearl Harbor and before all the protective services were established and could be listed for volunteer recruiting, not all volunteers were willing to accept protective jobs. Since other types of services had not yet been developed, and many volunteers were apathetic to the probability of war, all that could be done was to take their names and indicate they would be called when their services were required.

The Japanese attack changed this situation over night and on Monday morning, December 8, 1941, every local CDVO office was swamped by long lines of volunteers — civilians who wished to serve their country on what had suddenly become the home front. Throughout the month of December, 1941, training in interviewing, recently given the personnel of the offices, was strained to the utmost as there were many more volunteers than there were jobs.

In 1942, the protective services continued to take precedence, but the impact of war upon New York City was beginning to raise other problems which demanded volunteer manpower for additional services. Hospitals, health centers and child care centers were rapidly losing professional personnel, and the principal Federal programs necessary to a successful prosecution of the war were rapidly being developed and calling in their turn for volunteer manpower. There was also a developing need for consumer education.

As a result, a rapid expansion in the organization of the Civilian Defense Volunteer Office occurred on the city-wide and borough level and within particular fields. Not all services required a separate division. The Division of War Service Opportunities and Placement, uniformly established in each borough, was charged with the listing of all services and the recruitment and placement of volunteers. Many fields, however, were highly specialized, such as Child Care and Youth Services, and required direction from people familiar with this type of work.

The question of training arose early, and to avoid any possibility of opportunism a Training Division, capable of analyzing and approving the best of the many available training courses,

was organized. Public relations was another essential, and speakers were in constant demand on every conceivable subject. Organizations and groups wishing to enroll as a body with the Civilian Defense Volunteer Office were handled by the creation on a city-wide level of a Division of Group Activities. The need for an Information Division, capable of supplying correct war and home-front information, arose practically at the start. Each borough developed its own Information Service, and early in 1942 an Information Center was established at Pershing Square for the entire city. In this building were also housed the Division of Group activities, and representatives of other wartime agencies. A Music Division was likewise created in response to the desire of artists to give their talents. This division gradually became one of the most effective of the Civilian Defense Volunteer Office programs, especially in connection with the veterans' hospitals.

In 1942, it became apparent that decentralization on a neighborhood or precinct basis was necessary, especially in the nonprotective services affecting community welfare. Following a survey in each borough, local Civilian Defense Volunteer Office branch offices to the number of 68 were created in each borough. These did the bulk of the volunteer recruiting and the success of the CDVO programs and campaigns was in a great part due to the existence of these offices. Expansion of the organization, however, placed a heavier burden upon the city-wide office, with the result that sub-divisions had to be established. These were charged with directing and guiding their counterparts in the boroughs and, in turn, they received reports from them on the operation of the services in which they were engaged. A full list, including those cited above, comprised the Block Service Organization, Child Care and Youth Services, Consumer Services, Film Bureau, Group

Activities Division, Music Unit, Neighborhood Representatives, Public Relations Division, Salvage Division, Speakers Bureau, Training Division, Victory Gardens, War Bonds and Stamps Division, and the War Service Opportunities and Placement Division.

Early in 1942, in recognition of the tremendous contribution the labor unions were making in manpower defense, education, program execution, and campaign successes, representatives of the American Federation of Labor and of the Congress of Industrial Organizations were appointed by their respective unions to the city-wide Division of Group Activities and later to the Civilian Defense Volunteer Office Executive Committee.

On June 6, in accordance with requirements of the State War Emergency Act, the Mayor appointed the New York City War Council. By the end of 1942, a far-reaching organization of volunteer services was in operation with over 100,000 volunteers placed in war work. Wartime programs and campaigns had already been successfully carried out. By the spring of 1943, although the protective services still claimed priority, the needs and number of the nonprotective services had grown so steadily that the borough and branch offices found it necessary to keep open one or two, and sometimes more, evenings a week. In March, 1943, the New York City War Council passed a resolution designating the Civilian Defense Volunteer Office its official agency

For recruiting and placing of volunteers for civilian protection, community services and other activities to promote the war effort — for

Coordinating and controlling the volunteer activities in relationship to rationing, conservation of food and essential materials, health and hospital service, neighborhood and block organizations, salvage and other activities to promote the Civilian War Serv-

ices in such manner as the Mayor may direct or request — requesting and obtaining such cooperation, assistance and data from any department, board, bureau, commission, agency or official of the City of New York as may reasonably be required for the consummation of the work of the Civilian Defense Volunteer Office (CDVO) .[1]

The year 1943 was a time of tremendous expansion in all Civilian Defense Volunteer Office activities. Simultaneously, however, hospitals, health and welfare agencies, child care and youth services were suffering acutely from depletion of personnel, and their need for volunteer replacements was rapidly rising. Increasing scarcities of food and materials made conservation through consumer education a vital necessity, and consumer centers for the promulgation of consumer education and the distribution of explanatory materials were created throughout the city. Federal agencies became more and more dependent upon intelligent volunteer interpretation of their purposes and even for the execution of their programs. The number of war service opportunities for which the Civilian Defense Volunteer Office was recruiting more than doubled, and outside agencies were constantly appealing for more extensive aid.

It is impossible, in a study of this sort, to go into the number of drives and activities. The following partial list for 1943 will give some idea of the extensive character of the office's operations:

War Bonds and Stamps Division (Third and Fourth War Loans)

CDVO Recruitment Drive

Victory Garden Division

36,000 Volunteers for the distribution of Ration Book 3

New York War Fund (American Red Cross Drive)

---

[1] *History of the Civilian Defense Volunteer Office of the City of New York*, 1941-1945, p. 17.

Victory Book Campaign

Consumer Division in Home Canning

Block Leader and Neighborhood Representatives

CDVO — WPB Programs (Salvage)

Owing to the progress of the 1944 campaigns in Europe, New York City was by far the most important coastal city in the country. The troops, guns, ammunition, and supplies which sailed from its harbor rendered it "Enemy Target Number One." The possibility that leakage of information vital to the enemy might occur led the Army, the Navy, and the Federal Bureau of Investigation to request the Civilian Defense Volunteer Office to put on a city-wide campaign for safeguarding military information. This was done through newspapers, radio broadcasts, posters, and signs. The entire city was warned against careless talk, and speakers and volunteers carried the campaign by word of mouth. The success of this effort, which was one of the most important of 1944, earned the unstinted praise of the armed forces.

Other far-reaching programs for that year included the "At Home Vacation" program, supported by railroads and bus lines in cooperation with the Office of Defense Transportation. The many attractions of the city were pointed out by posters, car-card signs, and pamphlets, and a master file listing sports, educational material, entertainment, recreation, historic places and trips, and park facilities was prepared by the City Home Office and distributed to the five borough offices under the War Information Center.

With the return of increasing numbers of wounded to the military and naval hospitals, the Music Division instituted a program which became a regular part of rehabilitation activities in all hospitals. The increasing number of questions asked by discharged servicemen also led to the development of an information file for veterans, which was made available in all Civilian Defense Volunteer Offices throughout the city.

By 1945, the organization had achieved full growth and was functioning smoothly as a cohesive whole. The annual campaigns for the Treasury, the New York National War Fund, and additional drives, such as the United National Clothing Collection which netted 7 million pounds of clothing, were handled as matters of routine. With the end of the war, the Civilian Defense Volunteer Office as a wartime city agency was officially terminated September 30, 1945. It continued its services, however, as a private agency under the New York National War Fund until the conclusion of that Fund's last drive and the termination also of the United States Treasury Victory Drive. Its doors closed at last on December 29, 1945.

As in the case of the other volunteer offices of the State, the end of the organization and the cessation of such widespread activity seemed unfortunate, as the energy which had gone into wartime service would never again be so completely devoted to the welfare of the city. Nevertheless, in the nation's largest metropolis, as everywhere else in New York State, was clearly demonstrated the tremendous capacity of a democracy, in the face of an external threat to its existence, to develop and coordinate its manpower reserves in the achievement of its own protection. It was this unaccountable and intangible elasticity in a democratic society, so completely overlooked by its opponents and so little recognized and understood by its own citizens, that in the final analysis constituted its margin of superiority over other forms of social and political organization.

BUFFALO[1]

Buffalo, the second largest city in the

---

[1] The section on Buffalo consists in very large measure of material furnished through the courtesy of Mr. Dudley M. Irwin, Jr., Vice-President, Manufacturers' and Traders' Trust Company.

State, was before the war the largest milling and grain storage city in the country and the second largest railroad transportation center. Together with the adjacent industrial areas in Erie and Niagara counties, it faced, during the war, a number of problems quite different from those encountered by New York City. In addition to being the only area in the State with an early and constant critical labor shortage (classified by WMC as group one), Buffalo had a difficult transportation problem to solve. Rapid industrial expansion likewise brought a number of social problems to the fore which persisted into the period of reconversion. On the whole, these problems were recognized and well handled by alert War Councils which cooperated well with State and Federal officials.

The Niagara Frontier area, which included the cities of Niagara Falls and Lockport as well as Buffalo, was the largest center of military aircraft production in the State, and almost equaled New York City in the manufacture of iron and steel products. Other important war industries were the manufacture of machinery (air compressors, radar equipment), basic chemicals, automotive equipment (heat-transfer units), and ordnance (shells and small arms). Specific products included aircraft, machine guns, self-sealing tanks, proximity fuses, marine engines, radio communication equipment, parachutes, Pratt and Whitney motors, and precision instruments. From June 1, 1940, to June, 1945, this area received prime war supply and facility contracts of $5,337,147,000. It was sixth in the United States in value of war contracts (third among inland cities) and third in value of aircraft contracts, which amounted to $3,929,825,000. In the value of its war contracts, Erie County was fourth among all the counties of the country. Subcontracts of Buffalo-area manufacturers were valued at approximately one-half of prime war contracts or nearly 3 billion dollars additional to $5,337,147,000.

In reaching these tremendous quotas this area, which in 1940 contained 7 per cent of the State's population, experienced many typical wartime dislocations. To cite one case: Bell Aircraft and Curtiss Wright, at peak production (Curtiss Wright producing more than 15,000 P-40s in addition to several hundred P-47s and C-46s), employed close to 85,000 people; a few years before this, their total employment was less than 2000. Expansion of this sort was bound to have drastic repercussions. Few areas of the nation and none of the major cities of the State were more affected by wartime industrial changes than the Niagara Frontier and the City of Buffalo.

The demand for manpower during the war was tremendous. Employment in the area increased from 329,570 in 1940 to approximately 500,000 in 1945. In addition, about 100,000 persons were supplied to the armed forces. In general, the needed manpower was secured from the following sources: (1) approximately 70,000 from the unemployed, including those on government emergency work; (2) an estimated 30,000 migrant workers from other areas; (3) an estimated 100,000 women from those not normally in the labor forces; and (4) additional numbers from the young, the handicapped, and the aged.

Throughout the war, the principal bottleneck was men capable of doing heavy common labor in the steel plants, foundries, and other basic industries. Shortages of male workers appeared earlier in Buffalo than in other areas of the State because of the unusually rapid expansion of the aircraft industry. Since heavy industry was the backbone of Buffalo's economy, the city could ill afford to have these plants denied additional contracts and perhaps threatened with extinction because of a migration of workers to the aircraft plants. The community therefore strongly supported a campaign initiated by the War Manpower Commission to bring thousands of additional women into the labor market to fill the aircraft jobs and to stimulate able-bodied men to leave less essential work and take on the heavy, dirty jobs of the foundries and mills. Organized labor and contractors in the building industry contributed labor and materials to build the widely publicized "Cape Cod Cottage" in Lafayette Square as recruitment headquarters for the campaign. Public-spirited women, undertaking responsibility for the campaign, devoted their full-time efforts to enlisting women for jobs and through affiliated committees extended their efforts to Lockport, Niagara Falls, and the Tonawandas where there were similar serious manpower shortages. This united community effort and the willingness of Buffalo industry to submit itself to the most stringent manpower controls in July, 1943, a full year before it became effective elsewhere — Buffalo was one of the guinea pigs for the entire country for "controlled referral"[1]— made it possible for the city to meet its wartime production commitments and to come through the war with a healthy well-balanced industry.

Buffalo furnished an excellent example of the way in which rapid expansion of production due to war brought in its train a number of severe secondary problems. The impact of the tremendous increase in employment put a terrific strain upon the mass transportation system. This was made worse by the creeping obsolescence of private cars, shortages of tires, and gasoline rationing. The recruitment of women to supplement critical labor markets brought with it the problem of daytime care of children of working mothers. Shortages of critical materials, a need for additional housing for war workers, occasional threats to the city's food supply — these and many other

pressing problems faced the leadership of the community.

Within the Niagara Frontier area there were a number of city and county war councils, all of which did excellent work in coping with the problems brought to their communities by the war. Since, in a volume of this character, it is not possible to do justice to all of them, and since for that reason a sampling policy is being followed in the chapter as a whole, the ensuing discussion has been focused upon the Buffalo City War Council, whose history and organization largely parallel those of the larger cities other than New York City, and whose problems were in general representative of the area of which it was the center.

The City of Buffalo responded to the request from Governor Lehman that a local defense council be appointed by creating such a body, October 7, 1940. At the organization meeting, called by Mayor Thomas L. Holling, discussion centered largely around the protection of power, water and other utilities, and general plans for organizing the city. The next meeting, May 19, 1941, saw the appointment of an executive committee, a full-time Defense Administrator (General O'Ryan had been appointed State Director of Civilian Protection on May 8) and provision for offices in the City Hall. For the first year (1941), the work of the Council was concerned primarily with

1. Cooperating with Federal and State governments in the National Defense Program.

2. Starting the difficult and ramified task of coordinating all community efforts pertaining to national defense in Buffalo with the activities of the Defense Council.

3. Attempting to conserve community effort by undertaking only those problems which had been recommended and endorsed by Federal and State agencies.

---

[1] See Chapter III, pp. 61-62.

The Defense Council was active in the field of preliminary machine-tool surveys and other studies in connection with the expansion of the defense production program. The first large-scale defense production clinic designed to speed sub-contracting was held there in the spring of 1941. Buffalo was active in sponsoring "Civilian Defense Week" November 11-16, and stimulating its citizens to an awareness of the need for civilian defense with the theme "the only effective answer to total war is total defense." The program devoted special days to conservation and salvage, enrollment in air-raid warden and fire-warden organizations, health and welfare, and other phases of the defense preparations.

The first meeting of the Buffalo War Council, successor to the Defense Council, was held May 7, 1942 under the new mayor, Joseph J. Kelly. One of Buffalo's most distinguished citizens, the Honorable Daniel J. Kenefick, although over seventy at the time, was appointed Chairman of a Council of which more than three-fourths of the members were new. An executive committee of seven met once a week and the War Council once a month. Fifteen committees, including those on Transportation, Salvage, Child Care, and Discrimination from the former Defense Council were organized and operating inside of a month. Six were grouped under a chairman of Civilian War Services; five under a chairman of the Division of Industry, Agriculture, and Labor, while the Division of Civilian Mobilization (Volunteer Office) served all the committees of the War Council and, in addition, provided volunteers for the Office of Civilian Protection. A staff of ten people was assembled, including the executive secretary, Dudley M. Irwin, Jr., a full-time head of the Victory Garden Committee and three secretaries in the Office of Civilian Mobilization. Annual expenses averaged in the neighborhood of $20,000 a year.

While the Office of Civilian Protec-tion operated independently of the War Council, there was, nevertheless, a cooperative relationship. Many officials of the Office of Civilian Protection were members of the War Council and though the former reported direct to the State Office of Civilian Protection and received its orders from them, a form of "interlocking directorate" existed between the two.

The personnel of the War Council committees was hand picked and took their duties and responsibilities seriously. The time and care given to the city's collective war effort by so many varied groups of citizens was an inspiration to all who had occasion to work with them. Committee meetings were attended by the executive secretary or his assistant to coordinate activities, answer questions, and consistently guard against the development of overlapping functions. To further unify the efforts of committees, a quarterly "Digest of Committee Activities" was published by the Committee on Public Information and distributed to every member of the War Council organization. With so much to be done on so many different fronts, there was no room for any waste and confusion that might arise from duplication of effort.

One of the outstanding committees of the Buffalo War Council was that on War Transportation, first organized in the middle of January, 1942. It was responsible for making recommendations to the Council on all matters pertaining to conservation and improvement of transportation including mass transportation. It worked for larger gasoline allocations to Buffalo, carried on an aggressive and persistent "Share-the-Ride" campaign, and worked closely with the State and Federal Transportation authorities in ironing out traffic problems within the city limits.

Early in 1942, the committee began a study of railroad belt lines surrounding Buffalo, and another of inter- and intra-city truck operations. A careful check was made on car occupancy among employees of the larger industries and official war transportation maps of the Niagara Frontier were prepared for the Army, Military Police, State Highway Police, and City and County highway agencies. It also gave serious thought to the need for staggered hours and the extension of city bus operations, with the result that its principal contribution to the war effort of the city was the development in cooperation with the Transportation Committees of the City of Lackawanna and the County of Erie, of a staggered hours plan to solve the transportation problems of the Metropolitan area.

Since war conditions in Buffalo doubled public-transportation demands in 1942, and since further demands were anticipated with the imposition of gasoline rationing in the Niagara Frontier area on August 22, and with the progressive wear and tear on tires and automobiles, the War Transportation Administrators of the war councils of Buffalo, Lackawanna, and the County of Erie requested a Transportation Technical Committee, headed by Bertram D. Tallamy, then Chief Engineer of the Niagara Frontier Planning Board, to prepare a plan to provide adequate public bus transportation within the Buffalo metropolitan area. Together with other technical assistants and consultants, the committee consisted of

> Niagara Frontier Planning Board
> Division of Safety, City of Buffalo
> Buffalo City Planning Association
> Buffalo Chamber of Commerce
> International Railway Company
> Buffalo Transit Company
> Wooley Bus Lines, Inc.

On August 18, 1942, upon recommendations of its Transportation Committee, based upon advices of the Technical Committee, and as a first step in its overall staggered hours program, the Buffalo

War Council changed the school hours for public, vocational, and academic high schools.

To aid in the analysis of this most serious problem, Buffalo was divided into three zones consisting of three concentric circles — Zone 1 being the downtown area, Zone 2 the next area, and Zone 3 extending to the perimeter of the city. By November, 1942, the Buffalo War Council had established rules governing factory shifts of one hundred or more persons, and certain other rules as follows:

Zone	Classification	Work Hours
3	Heavy industry — factory shifts on an 8 hour work span (with 100 or more on a shift)	7:30 — 3:30
3	Heavy industry — factory shifts on 8½ hours or longer work span (with 100 or more on a shift)	7:30 — 4:00
1	Downtown industry —	
	8 hour work span	8:30 — 4:30
	8½ hour work span	8:30 — 5:00
1	Downtown retail stores	10:15 — 5:45
	All city schools — day sessions in public and parochial schools, vocational schools and academic undergraduates and business colleges	9:30 — 3:30
	All city entertainments and other nonessential gatherings of 200 or more persons at noncontinuous shows, exhibitions, rodeos, parades, circuses, sport events, conventions, social gatherings, and similar events and meetings should not terminate between on week days	4:00 — 6:30

By early spring of the next year, the third and last step in the over-all staggered-hours plan was adopted by the War Council, approved by the State War Council, and filed with the City Clerk — thus becoming an official rule:

Quitting Time	Business Classifications
4:15 or 6:00 P.M.	Government Agencies
4:45	Banking
5:15	Accounting, Auditing, Legal Architects, Artists, Engineers, Contractors and Surveyors
5:30	Retail Services, Insurance, Real Estate, Mortgage, Social Service, Associations, Societies, Councils
5:45	Utilities and Transportation
6:15	Sales and Distribution Agencies, Dealers' Offices

In the survey on "Working Hours for Downtown" was outlined the factual information on the working hours, the business classification and the modes of transportation of approximately forty thousand persons whose work brought them daily into downtown Buffalo, Zone 1. Particular attention was directed to the large number of persons using public transit who quit work at 5:00 P.M. It was realized that the drastic changes in living and working habits necessitated by the emergencies of war and war-caused transportation shortages would take careful interpretation and wise administration in order to enlist the complete support of the community. The War Council appropriated close to $2000 to its Committee on Public Information to properly publicize and officially notify the public of these changes as they took place. The police force cooperated in warning the few who were slow to conform to the rules and, fortunately, it was not necessary to prosecute violators. Through the operation of this plan for staggering the hours of work, it was possible for available transportation facilities to handle successfully for the duration the peak morning and afternoon traffic loads.

Although salvage operations were universal throughout the State, Buffalo had an especially fine record. The War Council Committee, under energetic leadership, met weekly from May, 1942, to September 30, 1945, with each member in charge of a specific branch of the program. For the period August 1, 1942, to April 11, 1945, the city's tonnage of tin cans salvaged was 3316. In the salvage of waste fats and grease, it led the country for metropolitan areas with a total of over 6.25 million pounds, or approximately 11.5 pounds per capita. During October, 1942, the scrap-metal drive, sponsored by the press, salvaged over 5 million pounds, and this total was raised to 68.8 million pounds, or 120 pounds per capita, by the middle of May, 1943. The entire program was so successful that Buffalo was awarded a War Production Board pennant for outstanding work in this field.

The Office of Civilian Mobilization, also known as the Volunteer Office, was organized in October, 1940, from among the volunteer groups of the Catholic Charities, Jewish Federations Joint Charities and Community Fund, the Junior League, and the Buffalo Chapter of the American Red Cross. At the end of 1941, the offices were moved to the City Hall, and under the new War Council the primary purpose of the organization was to cooperate with and assist the various committee activities of the War Council, and to recruit, enroll, and train volunteers and place them where they were needed. After Pearl Harbor, the recruiting, registering, training, and placing of men, women, and children volunteers as nurses aides, air-raid wardens, fire wardens, clerks, etc., skyrocketed. Over 2000 volunteers were registered on December 11, 1941, and in less than two years the total reached 51,000. The Volunteer Office supplied volunteer help to almost all committees of the War Council as well as many Federal, State, and local agencies, such as the First Fighter Command, Treasury Department, United States Army Induction centers, Selective Service boards, various rationing boards, hospitals, Office of Price Administration, etc. If these workers had received payment at the nominal rate of $.50 per hour, close to $11,000 would have been paid out in clerical help alone for the months of December, 1942, and January, 1943.

An outstanding contribution of the Office of Civilian Mobilization was its block leader organization. There were about three thousand block leaders in the seventeen city precincts. These assisted in almost all the activities of the War Council and its committees as well as of the agencies named above. They conducted surveys for the Child Care Committee, gathering information regarding numbers and ages of children of working mothers requiring daily care. Tabulation of these statistics and compilation of reports therefrom were handled by volunteers of the Office of Civilian Mobilization, and proved invaluable to the establishment of child care centers. Block leaders also conducted surveys for the Victory Garden Committee and for the Nutrition Committee, and demonstrated methods of food preservation. When rationing came into effect, they explained to householders the mysteries of the point system. The Army requested their aid in a recruiting campaign for WACS. However, their most effective work was done in the tin-can salvage drives, and contributed greatly to the success of these campaigns. They made house-to-house calls, telephone reminder calls, distributed literature and posters, and organized the assistance of school children and Boy and Girl Scout troops into efficiently working teams.

Early in June, 1942, the Family Security, or Child Care Committee surveyed the need for daytime care of children of working mothers not only for the purpose of providing much needed manpower, but also for protecting the health and welfare of the children. Industrial plants in the area were supplied with cards on which to indicate the number of children under fifteen years of age, the specific ages of such children, and whether the mother desired to have them cared for during her working hours. Where care was desired, the mother was given a pamphlet containing a list of existing Works Progress Administration nurseries. By the end of January, 1943, the 16 cooperating industrial plants reported employment of 1143 women involving 2232 children. Of these, 145 women with 290 children specifically requested care for their children.

Realizing the need for child care centers, the committee designated the Board of Education to take charge and conduct the existing Works Progress Administration nursery schools, which were to be closed with the withdrawal of Works Progress Administration funds. It was also to lay plans for the establishment of an extended school program for children beyond the nursery-school age. On February 23, 1943, the Board of Education made application for Lanham Act funds to operate the nursery schools. This was approved by the Federal Works Agency, and on May 1, 1943, the board also filed application for funds to operate the extended school centers. These were opened shortly after the first of July. The responsibility of the committee did not end there. It continued its endeavors by obtaining support of the community and industry, and by recruiting children for the centers through the interpretation of the program to parents in the Buffalo area.

In April, 1943, representatives of sixteen or eighteen of the larger industries in the area undertook formation of a membership corporation, which all war industries were invited to join, and whose purpose was to lend financial and other assistance to whatever child care program was legally established or recognized under the auspices of the Buffalo War Council and other duly established war councils in the Niagara Frontier. This corporation was known as the Buffalo Victory and Child Care Association, Inc. For the remainder of the war period, the Buffalo Child Care Program, although closed on two separate occasions by outbreaks of infantile paralysis, maintained its staff intact and kept its facilities in full use.

The migration of war workers into the Buffalo area, resulting from the letting of huge contracts for materiel of war, brought in its wake many dislocations to the community. Not the least of these was the difficult and complex problem of discrimination with which the local War Council concerned itself throughout the war. A local Committee on Discrimination in Employment was appointed in November, 1941, by Governor Lehman, as a subcommittee of the State committee. It was the only local committee so appointed during the emergency. On May 1, 1942, the Buffalo War Council officially designated this as one of its committees to operate under the joint jurisdiction and authority of the New York State War Emergency Act and the Civil Rights Law. The committee included representatives of minority groups, employers, labor, placement, training, social services, and civic organizations. In an effort to combat, reduce, and eliminate discrimination in war plants, the committee concentrated on a three-point program: (1) a general campaign of education, (2) direct contact with employers and labor unions, and (3) the handling of all alleged and actual complaints of discrimination.

Out of a population in 1940 of 575,000 Buffalo had a large foreign-born section 50 per cent of whom were Poles, Italians, Germans, and Irish, as well as 20,000 Negroes. On the whole, relations between labor and management in the majority of plants were good. In some, especially where the policies of management were arbitrary, there was some suspicion between labor and company authorities. However, most of the complaints handled by the committee revolved around the questions of upgrading Negro work-

ers, many of whom held porter jobs, and alleged discriminatory practices in physical tests for colored people. There were a few complaints of discrimination against other minority groups, but these were shortly settled or at least not brought to the attention of the committee.

By means of friendly persuasion of nonconforming employers most of the complaints were remedied; in the more obstinate cases the committee recommended to the State that these companies be penalized under the Civil Rights Law. Fortunately, however, it was unnecessary to appeal to the Industrial Commissioner except in the rarest instances. Believing that a comfortable and happy worker was a good worker, the committee concerned itself to a great degree with housing problems of discriminated-against groups. Here again, as in employment circles, it was successful in obtaining the cooperation of various existing local agencies.

Early in the spring of 1942, at the instance of the United States Secretary of Agriculture, a Victory Garden Council was organized. On March 16, 1943, it became a Committee of the Buffalo War Council, with a full-time secretary employed in the War Council offices. Its purpose was to formulate a broad coordinated program for enlisting interest in and guiding a campaign to encourage home and community gardens as a defense measure. It conducted surveys to locate existing gardens, available garden space, and need for space. Through its efforts, city-owned and privately owned land were made available to gardeners. Among the problems confronting the gardeners of Buffalo were the matter of obtaining seeds and seedlings, the location of tools for preparation of the soil, soil testing to determine whether fertilizer was needed, whether the soil was suited for vegetables, and if so, what kind, and various other related problems. The committee acted as a clearinghouse for all the above and, in addition, provided literature on methods of gardening, speakers on planning, culture, and care of gardens for clubs and various gatherings, as well as newspaper articles, regular talks on the radio, and forums.

With the planting of gardens came a new challenge to the committee — to do something about the rat menace. The committee formulated and set in motion an extensive Rat Control Program. Another menace — vandalism — was also effectively controlled through the efforts of this committee and the close cooperation of the police department and social agencies.

As a part of its program to "feed the city," the committee worked in close cooperation with the Nutrition and Farm Labor Committees on a Food Preservation Program — participating in demonstrations in canning, drying, and storage of garden produce.

A Committee on Public Information, consisting of a group of advertising and sales-promotion men, was organized toward the end of July, 1942. Its functions were to develop special publicity programs from time to time to publicize the need for various drives, restrictions, and recruiting campaigns. In practically every case these projects were requested by the State War Council, and/or Federal agencies which had already cleared with the State War Council before moving in. The committee also acted as a clearinghouse for all committees on matters of publicity, such as news releases to the press, radio broadcasts, and related media. One of the outstanding jobs done by this professional group was the handling and promotion of the highly successful tin-can salvage campaigns. Another was announcing, publicizing, and interpreting to the people of Buffalo the need for staggered hours and the "share-the-ride" campaign. The committee was also responsible for preparing, publishing, and distributing the quarterly *Digest of Committee Activities,* and for establishing an Information Center to dispense authentic information regarding all war activities in Buffalo.

Early in 1943, after several weeks or preliminary study, the Rumor Clinic — a subcommittee of the Information Committee — was organized, with the active aid and cooperation of the Junior Chamber of Commerce. This group, made up of leading educators, newspapermen, Federal and police officials, representatives of the armed forces, professors of psychology, and representatives of all racial groups, did an expert undercover job of counteracting false rumors that gained circulation and impeded the community's war effort. Upon advice of Federal law-enforcement agencies and the Office of War Information, their work was largely of a confidential nature. Only on rare occasions did they find it necessary to publish general denials of rumors in the press. This well-qualified and experienced group of citizens investigated and focused the spotlight of truth on over a hundred false rumors.

Other committees of the Buffalo War Council performed important services to the city which, for lack of space, cannot be detailed here. Their contributions, however, will be covered in the local history now in process of preparation by the city.

One important wartime occasion was sponsored by the Buffalo War Council. On the 25th of June, 1943, the Council arranged a community-wide mass meeting to hear former Ambassador Joseph C. Grew speak to the citizens of Buffalo on "Our War With Japan." Buffalo was one of several key cities picked by the National Office of Civilian Defense in cooperation with the Office of War Information and the State Department for Mr. Grew's itinerary. The meeting took place at Kleinhans Music Hall before an overflow audience of more than three thousand people. Several hundred heard the proceedings outside through a public-address system. Before the meeting was formally opened by the Mayor, and before the Ambassador was introduced by the chairman of the War Council, a contingent of WACS and 250 Air Cadets sang with the Coast Guard Band. In the foyer of the auditorium were set up recruiting tables for the Office of Civilian Mobilization, Red Cross, WACS, WAVES, Marines, and for selling war bonds, all manned by volunteers in their respective uniforms. A table was furnished with War Council materials: the latest issue of the *Digest*, organization manuals, and several thousand copies of *You and the War*, which were given out to each person by the ushers. The ushers were members of the Volunteer Office (Office of Civilian Mobilization) in uniform. Part of the address was broadcast, and the net effect on the morale of the city was excellent.

The protection of the Niagara Frontier area against the possibility of bombing, while less complicated than the problem presented by a city the size of New York, was, nevertheless, of sizable proportions. Buffalo's importance as a center of aircraft production made her one of the prime targets of the northeast, and the measures which had to be taken to protect the larger plants were as elaborate as those developed anywhere else in the State. Of particular interest and of unusual character were the arrangements worked out in Niagara Falls to guard against possible disaster to the population in the vicinity of the large plants which were then manufacturing war gases and basic chemicals. For lack of space, however, the description of the New York City Civilian Protection organization, together with the details of the State organization outlined in Chapter IV, will have to suffice. The special features present in each local civilian protection organization will, it is hoped, be brought out in brief monographs on the order of those now available for Syracuse and Rochester.

Generally speaking, Buffalo, like the other war production areas of the State, successfully met the challenge of total war. The city was thoroughly organized for all eventualities and handled her principal problems promptly and with ability.

ROCHESTER[1]

Rochester, a city of diversified, highly technical industries, situated five miles from the mouth of the Genesee River and sixty-five miles east of Buffalo, felt the impact of war long before the attack on Pearl Harbor. Armament contracts began to stimulate industrial activity in 1939, thus setting the wheels in motion and making possible the efficient production of the war years. A total of $1,-215,145,000 in war supply contracts, fourth largest in the State, was placed with Rochester and Monroe County firms between June, 1940, and June, 1945. This was a large order in itself, but more significant because of the specialized character of the products. The Rochester area was the leading center in the State in the manufacture of professional and scientific instruments, photographic apparatus, and optical equipment. Other important products were electrical machinery, machine tools, and ordnance. The apparel industry, particularly men's clothing firms with war contracts for uniforms, was also a leading manufacturing group. Many companies shared in the task of producing for war. The achievements of thirty-four were recognized by Army-Navy "E" awards, twenty of them receiving fifty-six additional citations.

This notable record sprang from the contributions of many citizens and agencies. A Production Clinic held by the Chamber of Commerce in May, 1941, while not the first in the State proved eminently successful in stimulating subcontracting and in other ways marshal-

[1] Except for one or two slight additions, the section on Rochester was contributed entirely by Dr. Blake McKelvey, Assistant City Historian of the City of Rochester.

ling the full industrial potentiality of the area. The manpower needs were met in large part by a full enlistment of the personnel already resident in the area. This was only accomplished by the patriotic efforts of women as well as men, including part-time workers. Although the turnover among women was higher than for men, the ratio of women to total workers employed — 40 per cent — remained higher in Rochester than in any other area of the State. This was primarily because light precision work, in which employment was relatively stable, was especially suited to them. Stability of employment was a prime characteristic of the Rochester-Monroe County area, even in 1944 and 1945. With 3 per cent of the State's population, this community led the State in the proportionate use of part-time workers in manufacturing industries, and in addition had the lowest turnover and lowest absentee rates among manufacturing industries in the State.

The following will give some idea of the measure of each of these factors. In 1940, at the time of the census, women comprised 27.5 per cent of all employees in Rochester manufacturing industries. By July, 1945, this ratio was 42 per cent. Separation rates for all employees in manufacturing industries fluctuated during the war period between 3.0 and 5.4 per 100 employees. The peak in the use of part-time workers was reached in July, 1945, when they comprised approximately 5 per cent of all employees in manufacturing industries. Absenteeism rates in manufacturing industries in the area fluctuated between 5 and 6 per cent of total man days of labor scheduled for work.

That the war was to be a supreme battle of wits was clear in Rochester from the outset. A primary concern at the local office of the War Manpower Commission and other agencies responsible for the mobilization of the labor force was to make it available at critical points in the production schedule. Throughout the war, Rochester, with urgent shortages of male workers — predominantly professional and technical workers — was classified as a Group II labor market. In Rochester, employment ceilings covered both male and female employees.[1] Priority referral, however, was limited to male job applicants only. Permission to hire or refer directly was granted by the War Manpower Commission to the larger war plants, to unions, to some private employment agencies, and to firms in outlying districts.

That priorities on available skills would not be enough was recognized early, and Vocational Education for National Defense classes were organized in seven high schools. The program was continued with noteworthy vigor, matching the industrial and scientific research projects which did much to ensure and speed victory. Indeed, the city's most carefully guarded secret was the nature and purposes of the Manhattan laboratory, later revealed as engaged in research connected with the medical aspects of atomic warfare. Rochester could keep a secret when desirable, but the city likewise made a unique contribution toward the development of war publicity. Among the many remarkable uses of Kodak film, none was more widely appreciated than the V-mail developed and distributed by the Eastman Kodak Company.

In its corporate capacity, Rochester was likewise alert to the need for an intelligent approach to the problem of defense. The decision of the City Council was that the responsibility for civilian protection should be taken by the city authorities rather than by amateurs, and accordingly Louis J. Cartwright, the city manager, was made Director of Civilian Protection. The close cooperation between the municipal authorities and Rochester's unusually far-sighted and ex-

---

[1] For Federal Manpower Controls, see p. 61.

perienced group of civic and industrial leaders was well illustrated in connection with the War Council's Committee for the Conservation of Critical Resources and in the case of its Civilian Protection organization. Careful watch was kept by the Conservation Committee over the city's supplies of water, gas, electricity, coal, and oil, as well as upon the increased load placed by the war upon the telephone service. Representatives of each industry appointed by the Mayor met regularly with the Director of Civilian Protection and others prepared to recommend to the War Council all conservation measures that appeared to be necessary.

The protection of the city as a war production center required protection of the facilities of the public utilities. In the beginning, city officials were especially worried about its long water supply line, and the vulnerability of the spillway. Other important points were the Ontario Pumping Station, the reservoir at Hemlock Lake, and the ammonia plant at Kodak Park which, if hit, could have blanketed a large part of the city. Although initial protective measures were taken by the industrial plants themselves or by the police forces, unheralded visits by Army representatives showed the city was wide open from a sabotage standpoint. As a consequence, the city promptly put on a large number of police and guards, and placed wire netting around the principal utilities, bridges, and other facilities. A plant protection school was opened with the help of the State Office of War Training, and after taking initial responsibility for protecting most of the city's war plants, the Army turned two-thirds of them over to the Rochester Civilian Protection authorities.

The protection of utilities and war plants was but a part, although a major one, of the general protection program upon which Rochester spent in the neighborhood of a quarter of a million

dollars. Few of the many thousand volunteers in the several civilian protection units were ever called upon for the emergency service for which they were enrolled and trained, yet their faithful preparation to meet possible emergencies on the home front supplied confidence for other aspects of the war effort. Outstanding among the training programs connected with defense precautions was the Fire College, established in April, 1941, a month prior to the appointment of a State Director of Civilian Defense. Soon the much larger program of the School of Civilian Protection Services was launched and a number of detailed manuals were issued, manuals which attracted wide attention as useful guidebooks. In addition to the usual courses for air-raid wardens, training was provided for a gas defense unit and for auxiliary police. Those trained by the Red Cross as hospital aides found ample scope for practical service throughout the war.

The carefully drawn plans for action in case of an emergency rivaled the training courses in importance. An elaborate evacuation program, including welfare and shelter provisions, was worked out. Among the precautionary programs was a mutual-aid plan adopted by the city and the surrounding towns under which the fire-fighting equipment of each municipality would be available at any point of danger — a program which has since proved its usefulness at a number of area fires. This mutual-aid plan has been continud by contracts with the outlying towns. The Fire College has been continued, as has also the training of the volunteer firemen of Monroe County.

The Emergency Medical Service, established early in 1942 as part of the Civilian Protection Services, did face a real test in August, 1943, when a food-poisoning incident occurred at Kodak Park. In less than an hour from the first alarm, forty-eight of the more serious

Recruiting Women for War Work

In recruiting women for wartime work, the Syracuse Victory Center uses a novel display in the volunteer office simulating actual processes in war plant operation.

cases among the two hundred workers afflicted were removed to hospitals. Speedy and intelligent treatment brought early recovery, and the poison was quickly traced to an infected finger of a cafeteria worker, thus dispelling fear of an enemy agent. In like fashion, the prompt action of the protection authorities in dispatching blood plasma to the scene of the Wayland railroad wreck helped to meet that emergency, and two years later the wreck of the Wolverine in the heart of the city brought all emergency services promptly into action.

As the war strategy of the democracies shifted from the defense to the attack, Rochester's protection program gave place to salvage drives, war bond campaigns, and appeals for relief. The Civic Exhibits Building, which had served as headquarters for the Civilian Protection Services, was turned over to the government in 1943, and behind a cloak of absolute secrecy a vital industrial plant was soon turning out thousands of the newly developed proximity fuses for use in blasting V-bombs and rockets from the sky. The skill with which the police guarded this and hundreds of other key plants, sifting the records of more than forty thousand applicants for war jobs, and otherwise safeguarding the war effort, is best indicated by the lack of incident in this field.

Rochester's traditional generosity as organized by the Community Chest assured a ready response to urgent calls for relief. Much could be said about the clothing and other collections as well as the cash donations which flowed forth to needy folk in Europe and Asia. Rochester, for example, gave 2655 watches, nearly a third of all contributed by the entire country, in response to an urgent appeal from Russia for these essential aids in its effort to mount a coordinated drive against the Axis early in 1943. The Rochester Chapter of the Red Cross not only exceeded its quotas in each financial drive and fulfilled its obligations in the preparation of surgical kits, but also enrolled over 500 nurses and 163 other men and women for service in the field. Its 110,000 blood donors contributed 303,397 pints of blood and won three Army-Navy "E" citations.

However, the program which will be remembered longest, at least by those Rochester families who took part, was that instituted by the Eastman Company when it brought to Rochester 156 of the children of its British employees. The several years these youngsters spent in Rochester homes have established lasting ties. Most of them have returned to their folks in England, but one young lass has recently come back to Rochester as the bride of a local GI and thus proposes to perpetuate the spirit of union engendered by the war.

A lasting benefit resulted from the Child Care Program developed during the war. Rochester was one of the first cities to apply for Federal aid for child care. Its program was well organized under the Board of Education and steadily expanded until it became the largest of the up-State programs. Generally speaking, Rochester's recognition of the need for this service for school-age children and its success in this program were outstanding. Another good feature of the Rochester program was the consultant service provided for the mothers through the Rochester Child Care Committee, a type of service that was not generally provided in other cities.

In several of these fields the city's contribution as a corporate entity was slight, but its example and leadership were frequently important. Thus in the war bond drive, volunteers carried the brunt of the labor and citizen response was of course private in character. Yet city officials took part with other citizens and the authorities hastened to cooperate whenever official action was necessary. The erection of the Liberty Bridge over Main Street, equipped with a Liberty Bell and a loud speaker, in June,

1944, was one such instance, while the "U. S. Flattop" and the string of Pacific Islands strewn down the center of that principal thoroughfare a half year later was another example. The popular attention focused on the Fifth and Sixth war bond drives by these unusual features may not have accounted for the success of these campaigns, but they at least contributed a colorful and musical touch to Rochester's Main Street scene and helped to unify and dramatize the community's war effort.

SYRACUSE[1]

The City of Syracuse lies in the center of the State eighty miles east of Rochester. Together with Onondaga County, of which it is the industrial nucleus, it contains 2 per cent of the State's population. During the war, machinery manufacture, including communication and electrical wiring parts, generators, air conditioning, and business equipment, was the leading war production group. Next in order of importance was ordnance (munitions, shells, and guns), while other important war industries were the manufacture of iron and steel products, including alloy and tool steel, iron castings, motor vehicle parts, aircraft parts, and basic chemicals. With one of the highest concentrations of heavy manufacturing in the State, it was natural that before the war Syracuse should make little use of women. During the war, however, labor jobs traditionally considered only for men became so tight that more women had to be recruited. It was found they could handle many of these positions. By late 1943, the period of peak employment, women comprised 35 per cent of the total number of employees in war industry. Thanks to the extremely able recruiting program maintained throughout the

[1] Material for the section on Syracuse was largely supplied through the courtesy of the Syracuse Chamber of Commerce and the Volunteer Center, Inc.

war by the Volunteer Office — Victory Center, Syracuse was consistently classified as a Group II labor market, although the labor supply was much tighter than that classification would indicate. With the exception of the stabilization program, the priority referral and employment ceiling policies of the War Manpower Commission applied only to men.

Because of the concentration of heavy manufacturing in the area, much of Syracuse industry was able to turn to war production without the problem of conversion, its normal production being essential to the prosecution of the war. Another unusual feature of the Syracuse situation was the fact that industrial employment more than doubled without any importation of outsiders. By strenuous efforts the Syracuse area furnished its own workers from service and less essential industries, and from among other residents of the city and of Onondaga County.

The Civilian Protection organization of Syracuse and Onondaga County was complete and efficient. One unusual feature was the fact that the Chamber of Commerce through its many contacts was able to set up the organization and enlist the personnel. The city was divided into twenty-one sectors based upon the fire districts, and the membership of the Chamber was asked if it would volunteer for protective work.

Another feature of civilian protection was the creation shortly after Pearl Harbor of a women's air-raid warden organization parallel to that of the men and known as the Personnel Officer's Division. The primary reasons for organizing this unit were that men were not always available in the event of daylight raids; many were constantly being called into the armed services; those in industry were faced with increasing working hours and responsibilities. Women, on the other hand, were better qualified to perform certain disaster tasks, such as reclamation of lost property, provision of consolation and assistance to bereaved, and maintenance of records. There was also an increasing need for a thorough coverage of the city and county for purposes of surveys and training. The Women's Personnel Division developed a block coverage which antedated by nearly a year the inauguration by the Federal Office of Civilian Defense of the national block plan. Ultimately the Personnel Officer's Division, or Block Plan as it was later called, became separate from both the Volunteer Office and from Civilian Protection. In June, 1942, the leaders of the Syracuse Block Plan were called to Washington and used as guinea pigs for testing out through their organization the interpretive program to induce housewives to use more cheese, flour, and milk. Under vigorous, careful, and educative leadership the organization developed an *esprit de corps* and habit of being successful that proved useful in numerous important city-wide drives.

The early Personnel Officers made the civilian protection survey of families for evacuation purposes. Members of this organization enlisted as "Liberty Belles" in the war bond campaigns. A date was set during the campaign when each household might expect a call from one of the "Belles," at which time they were to be ready to purchase their bonds or show a receipt of purchase made. The household then received a handsome display poster as evidence of its participation. In one of these canvasses over 30 million dollars worth of war bonds was bought or counted in three hours. In fact the city either possessed before the war, or developed during the war, a remarkable spirit of efficient community cooperation in the performance of necessary war services.

Another form of assistance rendered Uncle Sam by the citizens of the Syracuse area was the salvage work. The Syracuse salvage operations were excep-

tional. The entire county was organized on a pseudo-military basis with generals, majors, captains, lieutenants, and privates — an organization of about five hundred in which everyone had a command. As a result, the primary need of the early days for scrap iron was met with a total amount sufficient to fill a solid trainload, eighty miles in length or the distance from Syracuse to Rochester. Every industrial plant, home, and farm was canvassed, abandoned equipment such as old bridges and trolley tracks was gathered up, and at the end of the scrap-iron campaign it was estimated that in the entire county fewer than five hundred tons remained uncollected. Following the national call for rubber, it took four months to ship out the mountainous piles that resulted from the campaign collections. In the latter phase of the war when paper and tin became the number one necessities, Syracuse compiled an equally fine record. With the exception of certain communities in California, Syracuse led all cities of its size in the salvage of tin cans. As for paper it had the highest per capita amount saved and sent to war of all cities in the United States. Collections were made approximately every six weeks, and at the peak of the operations seventy-two carloads were loaded in a single day. An outstanding and unique feature of the paper salvage was that all waste paper shipped out was sent to six mills in New York State that made paper board; those mills returned to Syracuse paper-box factories an equal tonnage of paper board to supply containers for Onondaga County industries with war contracts, thereby making sure that paper saved in that county actually went to war. All labor used in collecting the paper was paid at the rate of $.70 per hour and at the end of the war there was a surplus of over $37,000.

The salvage record was fully matched by perhaps the most active and successful civic recruitment campaign in the entire State. The spearhead of the campaign was the Volunteer Center, an outgrowth of a private Volunteer Office begun back in 1934, which from January, 1942, to November 19, 1943, was financed by the Onondaga County War Council. In November, 1943, when the Volunteer Office - Victory Center was opened in new rent-free quarters, the increased operating costs were partly defrayed by the United War Fund. The purpose of the Victory Center was to act as a central office for the recruitment, interviewing, and referral of women to any war job, volunteer or paid, including Red Cross and other volunteer jobs, paid employment, WACS, WAVES, Marines, SPARS, and nursing services. In February, 1944, the Personnel Officers' Division of the War Council with its executive secretary moved into the center.

In 1944, the Volunteer Center conducted 11,336 interviews of which 589 were for volunteer service, 146 for Red Cross work, 383 for service in the armed forces, 66 for nursing service, 10 for preinduction information, and 10,142 for paid employment. Of these latter 6154 were referred to paid employment and 2704 were hired. The Placement Department reported a total of 3194 volunteers referred, 2120 for temporary jobs and 1074 for permanent jobs. So effective had its methods proved that in June the Manufacturers' Association asked the Victory Center to participate in the drive for war workers to prevent Syracuse from being declared a number one critical labor area. Funds for additional staff in the Employment Department were supplied by Syracuse war industries. Results — in four and a half months of the drive, out of 6665 women interviewed for paid employment, 4178 were referred to war jobs and 2376, or 57 per cent of those referred, were hired. On September 28, 1944, the Victory Center participated in the celebration marking the presentation to the City of Syracuse of the second War Manpower Commission flag ever awarded

in the country. It was the first flag to be given to a city for the recruitment of war workers.

In 1945 the Employment Department, until its closing on August 31, conducted 8726 interviews. Of these essential referrals were 4571, essential hires 2637, less essential referrals 1047, and less essential hires 415. From March 18 through July 7 a special campaign was conducted for the recruitment of women war workers. A group of manufacturers contributed $15,000 for a twelve-week period and followed it up with $4000 more for a continuation period of four weeks. Early in the year, the job of recruiting and referring women to war jobs was still so imperative that the manufacturers' Association initiated a system of taxing member war plants $6 for each hire resulting from a Victory Center referral. From these funds, the Center was given $900 a month to finance promotion and the costs of the Employment Department. By June, sufficient funds for the support of the Employment Department had been secured and the Board of Directors of the Victory Center requested that the Manufacturers' Association discontinue the tax for hires. With the end of the war, the need for war workers ceased and the Employment Department closed August 31, 1945.

Primary reasons for the success of the Syracuse Volunteer Office and of its Victory Center were the capacity for promotion displayed by its directors, the close relations maintained with the Chamber of Commerce and the Manufacturers' Association, both of which obviously respected the business ability of those in charge of the Center, and the willingness of its management to cooperate in any way possible with agencies in the city engaged in war activities. There was no question but that the Center carried out its assignments satisfactorily on all occasions, so much so that it became the focal point for a wide variety of campaigns.

In May, 1944, it put on a training course for 150 volunteers in the recruiting of women reserves of the armed services. Ten days later the Victory Center Honor Roll, dedicated to the women in service from Syracuse and Onondaga County, was designated the official women's honor roll by the mayor and the chairman of the Board of Supervisors. Later on a series of events was staged to assist the recruiting of women for the armed services including two highly successful fashion shows of women's uniforms and dress fatigues. Receptions were also held in honor of those families who had girls in the service, and their names were placed on the honor roll. Asked to participate in the campaign for the sixth war loan, the Center put on a contest in which bonds were purchased in honor of girls in the armed services. The total of "E" bonds ran over a quarter of a million dollars. In 1944, the reputation of the Center was such that it was visited by Mrs. Franklin D. Roosevelt and by the associate editor of *McCall's*. The latter gathered on-the-spot information about the Center for an article which appeared in the April issue.

In 1945, the Center was active during the city's greatest snowfall and resulting coal shortage by furnishing volunteers who manned telephones in the control center for a total of 720 hours. It was headquarters for the official City of Syracuse Victory Parade in September, and in October, with the increased shortage of housing, conducted a house-to-house canvass in an effort to locate housekeeping accommodations for returning veterans and their families. It provided working space for sixty volunteers on the United War Fund drive and provided the necessary volunteer assistance. The work performed for all sorts of projects by its "production" department in typing minutes, letters, and postcards, cutting stencils, running them off on mimeograph machines, folding, stuffing, stapling, and mailing was astounding. On September 25, 1945, the center was visited by General Jonathan M. Wainwright, hero of Bataan, and a scroll bearing the names of women who had taken war jobs in his honor, during his imprisonment, was presented to the General at that time. So important had the place of the Victory Center become in the life of the City of Syracuse that with the end of the war it was incorporated as the Volunteer Center and its activities continued. The year ended with plans being discussed with the State Department of Commerce whereby the center would become the test case in its projected program for establishing information and referral centers for women in the larger industrial communities of the State.

It was perhaps natural that a city which manifested such outstanding ability to organize itself during the war in the interests of war production, self-protection, salvage, recruitment, and other war activities should also display unusual foresight in planning for its postwar future. In the opinion of nationally recognized experts, the Syracuse and Onondaga County Postwar Planning Council made the most comprehensive and far-reaching studies in this field of any city in the country. Valuable assistance with this work was given by such organizations as *Time, Life, Fortune,* and the *Agricultural Forum* magazines; the International Business Machines Corporation; the Automotive Safety Foundation; the National Safety Council; the American Society of Planning Officials; the National Association of Housing Officials; the National Housing Agency; Survey Midmonthly; and the New York State Department of Education. Surveys were not limited to the purely physical planning phase but went into the fields of educational and cultural services, social and religious planning, recreation, employment, and rural and urban land use.

One unique feature of the study was the census taken in 1943 with Civilian Protection personnel supervised by Syracuse University, assisted by the Committee for Economic Development and the International Business Machines Corporation. This complete census gave the Postwar Planning Council accurate and comprehensive data on employment, social conditions, health, education, and other subjects. It also enabled Syracuse to make the best possible estimate of postwar employment possibilities and enabled industry and business in general to prepare for postwar conditions. The methods by which postwar possibilities were estimated was adopted by the War Production Board as a model to be used in other cities throughout the United States. The results were thoroughly digested, reduced to concrete proposals, and set forth in an attractively printed "Program for Progress." The keynote to the entire atmosphere of the city was struck by a brief paragraph in the introduction:

Many of the proposals contained in the *Postwar Report* may be pigeon-holed, modified, discarded. The important thing is not the survival of any single project. Rather, it is the establishment of the machinery for continuous, coordinated, community-wide thinking and action — backed by the enlightened interest of all of us.

SCHENECTADY[1]

Sixteen miles northwest of Albany lies Schenectady, one of the principal divisions of the Albany labor market and war production area, which included Albany, Troy, Rensselaer, and Schenectady. During the war, this area with 4 per cent of the State's population was the chief up-State center of electrical machinery construction including radar

---

[1] Material for this section on Schenectady has been very kindly furnished by Thomas E. Hanigan, Esq., with the assistance of the American Locomotive Company and the General Electric Company.

and radio equipment, a field in which the General Electric Company held a virtual monopoly. The manufacture of ordnance (cannon), transportation equipment (locomotives and tanks), and textiles and government warehousing and distributing were also important war and war-supporting industries. At Schenectady the four main employers of labor in September, 1942, were the General Electric Company with 39,000 employees, the American Locomotive Company with 9000, the United States Army Depot with 3500, and the United States Navy Depot with 2500.

Although the area as a whole was classified by the War Manpower Commission in Group II, and the supply of women was always theoretically sufficient to meet war demands, the recruiting of an adequate labor force especially in Schenectady encountered a number of difficulties. The need for experienced manual laborers was greater than the available supply. It was likewise a difficult problem to get women to work. Although wages were high in Schenectady and the patriotic appeal counted heavily with women, it was not always possible to place them in suitable jobs. By 1944, however, approximately 34 per cent of the total number of employees in the area were women.

A further difficulty arose from the very fact of an influx of such a large number of war workers as to cause a shortage of housing. This became particularly acute in Schenectady. To meet that need the local Office of Civilian Mobilization operated an exceptionally fine Rooms Registration Bureau, whose services were in continual demand well into the period of reconversion. The transportation problem likewise was a hindrance to recruiting workers from any distance. Nevertheless, despite these difficulties, individuals were able to find rides for themselves, and workers were drawn from a radius of fifty miles. At one time, 3200 workers on the maximum shift at

General Electric lived outside of Schenectady. These used mass transportation where possible, or joined a car pool. Some came from as far away as Rutland, Vermont.

In view of the essential character of the war work being turned out, employment ceilings and priority referral programs applied in the area to both men and women, and with but few exceptions employers required the direct consent of the United States Employment Service to take on additional labor. Occasionally, loans or transfers of various types of workers urgently needed for specific tasks were arranged by the War Manpower Commission. Supplementary labor was likewise brought in from Jamaica for work in the foundries and forges and from Mexico for work on the railroads.

In Schenectady, as elsewhere in the State, it was apparent to many far-seeing men long before Pearl Harbor that America could not escape being drawn into the fast-developing world conflict. As early as the spring of 1940, many residents envisioned their city as a vital war production center and commenced discussion of plans for defense against possible aerial attack and sabotage. With Europe aflame in the summer of 1940, Schenectady took its first official action toward a forward-looking program of civilian defense — a program that was destined to develop into widespread home-front activities in support of the war effort, and one which was to enlist the active volunteer participation of some 20,000 men, women, and young folk of the community. It was in July, 1940, that Mayor Mills Ten Eyck started forming a local Citizens Committee on National Defense, making Schenectady one of the first cities in the State to organize a local defense council. From this early start in organizing for defense, the city continued to pioneer in many of the subsequent wartime activities that were set up as a part of the State program. In several instances, its wartime agencies were used as models in the development of Statewide programs, especially in the Division of Civilian Mobilization and Civilian War Services. Such widespread attention was attracted to Schenectady's Civilian Protection organization that the State frequently used Schenectady as the meeting place for schools of instruction and demonstration.

The Schenectady County Consolidated War Council planned and encouraged such a comprehensive program of home-front war activities in active support of State and Federal programs that the major portion of the population was drawn into some form of active participation. Union College, under the celebrated Dixon Ryan Fox, sponsored a series of informative weekly radio broadcasts under the heading, "The Empire Town Meeting of the Air." He also headed a group of distinguished educators and businessmen known collectively as the Conference on Democratic Processes, from whose activities emerged the Section on Citizen Morale of the State Office of Civilian Mobilization. With such a heavy demand in the city for women workers in industry, the child care program developed rapidly into one of the major upstate projects. The city also had an active Civic Youth Council.

With this background of widespread community activity, it was natural that Schenectady should become a center for the development of methods to handle the special problems concerned with winning the war. As the home of the General Electric Company and the American Locomotive Company, the city became one of the nation's vital war production centers in which were developed some of the secret weapons that turned the tide of battle. In many ways the stories of the contributions of these two companies are indirectly descriptive of the efforts and hopes of the citizens of the Schenectady area during the war. For this reason, and because it seemed wise at some point in this volume to give a few typical examples of American industrial enterprise as applied to war, the achievements of these two companies have been given somewhat fuller treatment than that accorded similar concerns in other cities, whose contributions to the war effort might have been cited with equal justification.

During World War II, the General Electric Company, whose general offices and largest manufacturing plant are located in Schenectady, was called upon to produce a greater variety of complex war equipment and to solve a greater diversity of difficult technical problems than any other manufacturing concern in the country. This was a natural result of the employment of electricity by the combatant forces on a much greater scale than in any previous war. When the National Defense Program was first announced in 1940, the company volunteered to do its share. Then little by little, and more and more, it was drafted for war work. What began as a part-time job turned into a full-time job with overtime. Twelve years' production was crowded into four. In the aggregate, the company turned out 4 billion dollars of war equipment, ranging from giant turbines for battleships to delicate instruments for airplanes and mass spectrometers for the atomic bomb project.

A large part of the complex war equipment produced by General Electric was made at the Schenectady works — the largest electrical workshop in the world. In these buildings many of the difficult technical problems of the war were handled by the company's research and engineering laboratories. The expansion of these unique activities distinguished Schenectady from other cities in its contribution to ultimate victory and influenced to a marked extent the whole trend of community life throughout the period of the war.

Biggest of the General Electric Company's wartime job was building the propulsion machinery to drive more than 1700 of the United States Navy's fighting ships and the vessels of the greatly expanded Merchant Marine. Altogether, three-quarters of the Navy's total propulsion and auxiliary turbine horsepower built during the war period was produced directly by General Electric, or built by others to its design. The company had been building propulsion equipment for the Navy for many years, but never on a scale remotely approaching that demanded by World War II. Under the pressure of the nation's greatly expanded naval construction program, the company supplied turbines for 6 of the 10 new battleships, 37 of the 43 new cruisers, 10 of the 27 new aircraft carriers, and 200 of the 364 new destroyers. In addition, General Electric provided turbine-electric drive machinery for 255 destroyer escorts, as well as turbine equipment for some 300 naval auxiliary vessels and more than 800 ships of the Merchant Marine. The company was entrusted with the production of 60 per cent of the electric drive machinery for the wartime submarine fleet.

General Electric plants in a number of cities participated in the manufacture of ship propulsion equipment, with Schenectady playing a major part. All of the propulsion turbines for battleships were built at Schenectady, as were nearly all of those for aircraft carriers. About half of the cruiser turbines were also built there, as well as some for destroyers and naval auxiliary vessels. Construction building of the electric-drive machinery for submarines was also a Schenectady project.

Another of the wartime activities in which the Schenectady works had a major part was the production of radar and radio communication equipment. Radar, the art of radio detection and ranging, probably contributed more to the success of the United Nations than any other single device. Since the 1920's engineers of the General Electric Company had been experimenting with radio as a means of detecting the presence of aircraft and surface objects. When the tremendous expansion of American defense activities in 1940 demanded large-scale production of radar equipment, General Electric decided to freeze all its existing commercial radio types and concentrate the work of its engineers on radar. The company was the first to go into quantity manufacture of radar for the Navy. As the war progressed, the use of radar was extended from being simply a warning service to being a means of actually aiming antiaircraft and ships' guns quickly and accurately at distant, fast-moving targets. This was the key to the Allies' success in beating Germans' much-talked-of secret weapon, the V-1, or "buzz bomb." It was also the key to the Navy's extraordinarily effective gun-fire in many engagements with the Japanese. Huge quantities of both search radar and fire-control radar were produced by General Electric. Before the war was over, the company had participated in the design and manufacture of more than fifty different kinds of radar sets for the armed services. This was a tremendous assignment, amounting in terms of money to about a million dollars a day.

Less spectacular, but not less important, was General Electric's production of radio communication equipment. To assure unity of action among the diverse and fastmoving elements of the fighting forces, many new types of radio equipment were needed, particularly those designed for voice operation. Working in conjunction with the Signal Corps, the Army Air Forces, and the Navy, the company participated in the design and manufacture of a prodigious amount of this equipment.

Closely associated with the development of radar was the development of the Navy's gun directors. When, in the 1920's, electricity came to play an im-portant part in naval fire-control, the General Electric Company became the first commercial manufacturer to build the highly complex equipment required. During the war, the company produced thousands of gun directors for the main batteries on cruisers and the five-inch guns on battleships, carriers, cruisers, and destroyers. The complexity of this apparatus is indicated by the fact that in the manufacture of a single gun director there are more than eleven thousand mistakes that could be made in the wiring.

General Electric also built the hydraulic power drives for the sixteen-inch main batteries on battleships and developed an hydraulic drive system for the Navy's dual-purpose five-inch guns. The reliability and accuracy of this drive was so outstanding that the company was required to produce these units in large quantity, even though it was necessary to put up and equip a huge new building for the purpose.

Shortly before Pearl Harbor, the Army Air Forces asked the General Electric Company to design a remotely controlled gun turret for its big new bomber, the B-29 Super-fortress. Similarly, Schenectady participated in the development of the radically new jet engine for airplanes and the "prop jet," a combination of jet engine and a turbine-driven propeller.

Besides these special jobs, the Schenectady works produced enormous quantities of other war equipment, especially large motors, generators, and other apparatus. A number of floating power plants were built for service in Europe and the islands of the Pacific. Generating equipment for power-driven trains was built for the Navy and for the Russian government. The steadily growing volume of war work meant ever-increasing demands for plant facilities. Prior to the war, the Schenectady works had about 6 million square feet of floor space. Every bit of it was already crowded to capacity before Pearl Harbor. To meet the enormously increased demands placed upon the company after the United States became an active participant in the war, the capacity of the Schenectady works was expanded by nearly a third. Huge new buildings were constructed for the manufacture of radio tubes, gun controls, and turbines, bringing the total plant floor area up to about 8 million square feet.

In the years immediately before the war, about 24,000 persons were employed at the Schenectady works and in the company's general offices. At the height of the war activity, the number was approximately 47,000. But that does not tell the whole story. At the same time that the company was increasing its Schenectady force by some 23,000, it had to find replacements for about 10,000 who entered the armed forces, and many hundreds of others whose services were lost through death, retirement, or other causes.

The tremendous increase in the number of employees at the Schenectady works placed a heavy burden on the city's transportation facilities. The situation was helped somewhat by the fact that many of the company's manufacturing operations were on a twenty-four-hour basis with three shifts, thus spreading the transportation requirements over several different periods of the day. Hours of the general office workers were altered so that their transportation requirements came at times different from those of the shop workers.

Some of the new employees were part-time workers. Men and women who were employed in the company's offices during the daytime went into the shops and put in a short shift of extra work in the evening. Lawyers, real-estate agents, insurance salesmen, clerks in stores, and many others did factory work after hours. When the afternoon dismissal bell rang in Schenectady schools, many teachers and students hurried down to punch the time clock at the General Electric works. One minister of a nearby church worked the night shift at the plant, taking Saturday as his night off each week so that he would be fresh to preach to his congregation on Sunday.

As the war continued, women were put to work in increasing numbers, not only in the offices but in the shops as well. Former music teachers, ex-newspaper writers, a retired headwaitress, numerous grandmothers, and hundreds of housewives helped turn out war equipment at the Schenectady works. In 1940, women comprised about 20 per cent of the company's employees. In 1944, they constituted 40 per cent.

The great increase in the number of General Electric workers was a major factor in creating a labor scarcity in the Schenectady area. This was felt with respect to all types of labor, but it was most acute with respect to experienced mechanical and electrical workers needed for the many war production jobs requiring a high degree of skill. It was acute also with respect to draftsmen and engineers needed for design work. This is shown by the fact that the number of workers in the General Electric's Engineering Laboratory increased from 312 before the war to 850 at the peak of the war effort. In the company's Research Laboratory the increase was from 322 to a maximum of 630. Training the company's new wartime employees was a tremendous undertaking. Months are required to make a passable soldier, but it takes even longer to make a good mechanic. To train its new workers and retrain its older employees, the General Electric Company set up a program of instruction in which the workers were taught quickly to perform certain specific jobs. While this type of training did not produce all-around mechanics, it proved to be an excellent solution of the war emergency problem. Somewhat similar training courses were conducted for women. As most of them worked on light assembly lines, however, it was usually possible to make these courses shorter than those for machine operators.

Altogether, the war production job of General Electric's Schenectady works was one of huge proportions. It was not alone a job of numbers of workers or quantities of equipment. It was also a job of constantly seeking and finding ways to improve that equipment. The company's successful accomplishment of these difficult tasks was a preeminent feature of Schenectady's contribution to the war effort.

Equally busy and successful in inventing and developing weapons of victory was the Schenectady plant of the American Locomotive Company. It too contributed secret weapons that helped change the course of history. When, in the summer of 1942, Nazi armored columns in North Africa had smashed great gaps in Allied defenses and were rolling eastward to threaten Egypt, Field Marshal Rommel's panzer divisions, supported by the Germans' powerful 88 millimeter self-propelled gun, seemed like an unbeatable military machine. Suddenly an Allied army, reinforced with new weapons and equipment, struck. Rommel's forces reeled back, to be decisively defeated on November 2 at El Alamein in a bloody battle that historians have described as the turning point of the African war.

Months before, on the drawing boards and in the shops of the American Locomotive Company, one of the new weapons which helped turn the tide of battle was taking shape. It was the M-7 "tank killer," a swift, hard-hitting 105-millimeter howitzer, mounted on a medium tank chassis. The M-7 poured deadly accurate fire into the surprised Nazi column, destroying German armor and proving more than a match for the enemy's feared 88-millimeter gun. While production of the M-7 was probably the Schenectady plant's most spectacular contribution to the Allied war effort, a year earlier the same plant had turned out the first accepted medium tank ever built by private industry. It was the M-3, popularly known as the General Grant, which was built in April, 1941. A twenty-eight tonner, the General Grant mounted 75-millimeter and 37-millimeter guns, four machine guns, and had 14,000 separate parts. As tank design improved with battle experience, ALCO went into production of the M-4 or General Sherman medium tank. Still later came the production of heavy tanks and the M-36 tank killer, an improved version of the original model, which mounted a 90-millimeter gun and full armored hull.

The total output for the Schenectady plant during the war period was 7211 vehicles, of which 6301 were new and 910 reconditioned. This was the war record of 10,000 ALCO "soldiers of production," who toiled long hours to meet requirements of the fighting forces and who carefully guarded the secret of the M-7 and other allied weapons until a surprised enemy met them on the battlefield.

The story of the M-7 began in the spring of 1942 when American Locomotive officials met with high Army officers in Washington. So urgent was the Army's need for more powerful weapons to combat the Nazis that work on the tank killer started on the following day. Shop workers stayed at their benches and remained on the erecting floor for long hours. The first M-7 came off the line in nineteen days. Two days later it was given exhaustive tests at the Army's Aberdeen Proving Ground in Maryland, and from that point on production was rushed for the surprise assault at El Alamein. In April, 1943, on the anniversary of the first M-7, high-ranking representatives of the British and American armies visited Schenectady to pay tribute to the workmen who built the tank killer and carefully guarded its secret.

However, everywhere in the plant's busy shops locomotive production went right along with tank production. One of the big locomotive jobs completed during the war was the manufacture of many "Big Boy" locomotives which were to play such a conspicuous part in the railway war job for the Union Pacific. The largest ever built anywhere, these locomotive giants were 132 feet long and weighed 596 tons.

As the flow of Lend-Lease goods and later war materials grew to a huge volume, the Schenectady plant put forth the greatest effort in its near 100-year history to supply power plants for the nation's vast railroad network. From a depression low, locomotive production was up to 42 units a year in 1934, and by 1941 it had increased to 236. This figure jumped to 520 locomotives in 1942, jumped again to 986 in 1943, and by 1944 production reached an all-time company high of 1414 locomotives.

In late 1942, the plant converted 57 Diesel-electric locomotives to haul essential war goods over the Trans-Iranian line to Russia. To keep these locomotives going, the American Locomotive Company sponsored and helped organize an Army battalion, including many of its own shop employees and workers from other railroad equipment plants. The unit became the 762d Railway Shop Battalion and went overseas thirty days after it was organized.

While Schenectady's inventive genius and skilled workers were presenting to the Army, Navy, and Air Forces many of the tools of victory, certain civilian problems unique to this city were pressing for solution. The influx of thousands of workers to the war plants created critical housing and transportation problems. Conversion of one- and two-family dwellings into multiple dwelling units was backed by the Federal Housing Administration, while the State of New York supported the construction of Lincoln Heights and Steinmetz Homes — developments designed primarily for rental to war workers. A campaign to open private homes to war plant employees was launched. All these plans aided, but the housing shortage continued acute throughout the war period.

This pressure for living space brought in its wake a new problem — rent control. The Federal Office of Price Administration on March 2, 1942, declared Schenectady a defense rental area and three months later moved in to open a rent division office. This Schenectady office was the first Federal Rent Control Office to open physically in the United States. Thus, this city became the focal point of national interest in the highly controversial debates over rent control. As other rent control offices were to be opened in various rent control areas of the country, Federal fieldmen and directors were sent here for a course of training, since the setup and operation of the local office had become the early model of this new experiment.

Other unique problems growing out of wartime stress involved the "staggering of hours of employment around the clock" at the war plants. The resultant changes in bus and trolley transportation schedules made it necessary to restrict shopping hours in the stores, as well as to change public school schedules so that school travel would not interfere with industrial travel. Furthermore, it was urged by the State Public Service Commission that all bus riding "by persons not directly involved in the war effort" be eliminated during certain specified "rush" hours. A "share the ride" automobile plan was developed to help move war workers in and out of the city. Thousands joined this movement, not only locally, but throughout a fifty-mile radius of Schenectady. It proved a real aid when transportation difficulties were further aggravated through automobile, gasoline, and tire rationing.

Because an industrial city like Schenectady suddenly became an almost 100 per cent war work community, it was faced with problems unique in its civic, economic, and social life. To the credit of its citizens be it said that they accepted conditions the way they found them as a price that had to be paid by any community that unreservedly went to war.

BROOME COUNTY— THE BINGHAMTON AREA[1]

War was pursued on the home front of Broome County with vigor and effectiveness from the earliest defense preparations until the final end of hostilities. The local pattern of civilian defense and war organization in most instances followed well-defined State and national regulations, and needs no elaboration. But in several realms of activity definite departures were made in order to meet the special requirements of unique situations. In certain other cases, local genius initiated new techniques. This record covers only such features as seem to be of special interest or value from the historical viewpoint or as a precedent to be followed in any future work.

Local Conditions. The natural terrain, the industries, and the social setup of Broome County were the factors which determined its principal war pattern, so far as anything out-of-the-ordinary is concerned. There is no other New York State community just exactly like it, and we can briefly describe its salient features. The county, as a whole, may be considered a single cohesive unit, centering upon the Binghamton-Johnson City-Endicott valley (called the Triple Cities), as its dominating element. Elsewhere, except in one far-eastern township, the populace was largely integrated with the industrial setup of the Triple Cities and may be considered a metropolitan district. The rural and suburban population within this area was mainly

a mixed agricultural and industrial group. About 80 per cent of the families outside the Triple Cities urban section consisted of factory workers, many of whom had formerly been farmers and still drew some subsistence from the land. During the war, of approximately 15,000 rural residents of Broome County, nearly 900 worked at the Scintilla plant in Sidney, New York. About one-third of the total war-plant population of the Triple Cities lived in the rural parts, with several hundred more coming in from outside the county. Out of 45,000 essential war workers in Broome County, not counting those in other businesses and professions, more than 25,000 required transportation to and from work. There were only 2000 self-sustaining farms in Broome County, yet many people helped to sustain themselves on their own land.

The industrial valley of the Triple Cities was formed as a narrow ribbon, about fourteen miles long and two miles wide, distorted by rivers and flood plains and having only two main traffic arteries running lengthwise through it. Several small creek valleys, coming in from the hills, furnished access to the hinterlands where many people dwelt. Urban conditions were confined to the valleys along the rivers, and the population in Binghamton and Endicott was relatively dense. There were about 120,000 people in the various urban centers and about 50,000 in the outer periphery constituting the rural areas. As a labor market the Binghamton area was classified in Group III, one exception being that of skilled male workers capable of heavy labor of which the supply never equaled the demand. In 1940, the area contained 1 per cent of the State's population. Out of slightly more than 41,000 workers in 1944, 36 per cent were women. The labor turnover for both men and women in 1944 was among the lowest in the State, falling from 4.1 per cent in January to 3 per cent in December. War Manpower Commission priority referral and em-

---

[1] Material on the section on Broome County and the Binghamton area has been supplied by members of the Broome County War Council.

ployment ceiling programs applied to all firms and to all male workers or applicants.

The war setup in Broome County was greatly influenced by these physical features, as well as by special and industrial factors. The pattern of highways limited approach. The many rivers and bridges, plus the concentration of factories in contiguous areas, made vulnerable targets for enemy attack. Likewise, the county's position as a natural air crossroads put the region in line of possible enemy attack. The presence in the community of a very large industry which had been 90 per cent German-owned and operated was a very disquieting factor, too, in the early part of the war. Moreover, natural forces, in the form of river floods and inaccessible roads in the hilly parts, made war problems difficult. Finally, the industries themselves were highly essential to the success of the war and required uninterrupted operation.

In no community were more vital kinds of war materials manufactured than in Broome County. For aerial warfare, Link Trainers, including the large one for celestial navigation, were made there. Numerous instruments of precision, including the Ansco sextant, Driftmeter, Collinator, aerial photographic films, papers, printers, and color film, plus Ozalid papers and Impellors for aircraft motors; the big twenty-millimeter aircraft cannon, the M-1 Carbine, three-inch gun parts, Browning guns, fire locks, hand-grenade parts, and vast quantities of bomb-tail fuses, as well as parts for amphibious and half-track vehicles and trucks, big flexible shafting for the Navy, valves, ship parts, and debarkation ladders were all made there. So also were Army and Navy shoes of all kinds, including those for specialized services, as well as Navy pants, Army combat suits, jackets, knit goods and squad tents, felting, spools, tow ropes and parachute cords, chemicals, insecticides, machine tools, and lumber products. A huge amount of elaborate tabulating equipment was turned out for the armed forces. The United States Army Medical Depot for New York was also located there and served as a highly important base for medical supplies and equipment shipped to Europe via Atlantic ports.

Under the War Emergency Act, two War Councils were established in Broome County, one for the City of Binghamton, and one for the rest of the county. On the whole, this proved cumbersome, and while the two Councils never consolidated several of their subgroups found it necessary to combine. The first agency to assume combined city and county functions was the War Nutrition Committee which had previously been known as the Broome County Nutrition Committee. It was authorized to take over combined functions under the chairman of the county committee. When the city and county War Transportation Administrators were appointed in June, 1942, they both perceived that unified action was necessary because of the fluidity of transportation and traffic. So a consolidated War Transportation Committee was formed on the over-all level. Later Civilian War Services were reorganized on a combined basis under one chairmanship. City and County Civilian Protection remained apart.

War services in Broome County had to be tailored to fit the special needs. Many set rules were inapplicable here, and the wisdom of certain State officials, who were willing to permit the use of special methods to serve local conditions, became clearly apparent before the war was over.

War Transportation. In no branch of the war services was this more obvious than in war transportation. At the outset, it was said that the transportation problems facing Broome County, because of the poor local facilities for mass transportation, were potentially more serious than elsewhere in the State. When the war began, there were only seventy-six transport omnibuses in Broome County, plus a few converted school coaches on rural routes. In an average community of like size, one would have expected the number to exceed three hundred transport buses. But because the industrial population had been stable and well-paid for many prior years, people owned their own cars and almost no mass transportation facilities had ever developed. Moreover, the hilly terrain restricted omnibuses to valley routes. And there were between twenty-five and thirty thousand essential war workers requiring daily transportation, up and down the long ribbonlike valley and coming in from the rural areas. This meant that the prevailing pattern adopted for war transportation had to be based upon group-riding and the sharing of privately owned automobiles. Only in special cases, where the use of traction facilities was possible, could the recommended procedures of staggered hours and leveling of the peak load be followed. Generally, the factories had to open and close at the same hour to accommodate employees who lived in the same neighborhood and had to ride together.

Despite their small number, the traction coaches performed valiant service. It should be recorded that, although experiencing a huge overload for four years of war, the Triple Cities Traction Corporation kept all of their coaches in service until the last shot was fired. This was accomplished by almost unbelievable efforts and constitutes a record which, it is believed, is unmatched for a community of like size in the East. It was done only by vigilance in repair and management.

For group-riding on a large scale, plant transportation committees were organized in sixty-six industrial establishments. This included all plants employing more than twenty people. All industries of any size cooperated with the County War Transportation Com-

mittee without a single exception, which it is also believed is something of a record. Comprehending the importance of transportation the management of the larger industries employed special transportation staffs who gave full time to war-worker transportation problems. High officials of Endicott-Johnson, International Business Machines, Ansco, and Link became members of the County War Transportation Committee, along with other outstanding citizens and public officials. The success of this work was largely due to the strength of its personnel. A high mark for ride-sharing was ultimately reached by International Business Machines Corporation with an average of over four riders per car.

Special techniques were developed in connection with this transportation work. Monthly meetings, called by the combined City and County Transportation Committee were attended by representatives of the leading industries, the rationing boards, the OPA, local and State police officials, school superintendents, the farmers' committee, and State War Transportation field agents. These meetings served as great coordinating media and clearing houses for many acute problems.

Some twenty self-dispatch ride-sharing stations were set up in rural sites where neighbors could file registration cards and make up carloads of group-riders. This technique was initiated in Broome County and copied elsewhere in the State. Destination cards, to be affixed to sun-visors of cars, were printed and distributed. One side carried the work destination, with the home destination printed on its reverse. This enabled drivers to pick up casual pedestrians at the curb. It was not greatly used by the public. The block system canvass was used briefly for transportation, but it availed little.

In 1943 the County War Transportation Administrator was called upon to settle a "wildcat" traction strike, which he did successfully after government and city officials had declined to intervene as mediators. He found the strikers essentially patriotic, but misguided as to facts by ill-informed persons.

The unusually large percentage of private automobiles which were necessarily kept in service created huge demands upon gasoline supplies in Broome County, with the result that critical shortages were felt upon two occasions, and a complete breakdown of transportation was narrowly averted. The Director of the State War Transportation Committee was invaluable during these crises.

Civilian Protection. The administration of the Civilian Protection program was assigned to the County Planning Board as it was thought best equipped to carry on this work because of its expert knowledge of the geographical features of the county and because of its facilities, such as maps showing locations, widths, and carrying capacities of bridges, condition of roads and highways, traffic and population density charts, and other essential engineering data.

The response of the public to the call for volunteers was spontaneous, and as a consequence 7142 workers were enrolled in the various groups. The Civilian Protection staff occupied three large offices on the fifth floor of the County Office Building, consisting of the director's office, the administration office and the main Control Center which was equipped with a network of telephones reaching out to sixteen subcontrol centers and forty-two report centers stationed throughout the county. More than three hundred men and women participated in maintaining twenty-four hour service in the main Control Center, the hours being divided into four shifts. Thoughtful consideration was given to those who served on these control centers, and furnishings, such as comfortable

chairs, books, magazines, daily newspapers, checkers, playing cards, dominoes, and a radio receiving set were provided.

The County Civilian Protection office erected, equipped, and maintained twenty-eight observation post shelters for the Aircraft Warning Service. These buildings were completely equipped with electric lights, stoves, chairs, tables, telephones, coal bins, and lavatory facilities.

Two unique units of Civilian Protection were the "Emergency Defense Reserve Corps" and the "Minute Men," organized during the early preparation for home defense. The former consisted of one hundred men recruited from various parts of Broome County and the latter, with a personnel of seventy-five men, was organized by the American Legion of Johnson City. These two units were uniformed and were comprised of Veterans of World War I. Their equipment included two ambulances, each fitted with stretchers and medical supplies for first aid, and rescue trucks equipped with floodlights, flashlights, picks, shovels, crowbars, sand pails, rope, and ladders. The men were instructed in home defense by ex-army officers and in efficient methods of rescue work by competent structural engineers.

During the early months of the year 1942, a motorcycle squad of thirty-two men and machines was organized to provide messenger service. The squad operated from the main Control Center under direct orders from the Headquarters staff.

Anticipating the possible necessity of traveling over rough terrain and wooded country in order to by-pass bridges destroyed by enemy action, a horse-mounted unit was organized in February 1943, comprising seventy horses and riders. This unit was trained to carry messages and transport medical supplies to isolated districts made inaccessible to other means of travel.

M-4 Tank

Completed M-4 Combat Tank rolls out of the Schenectady plant of American Locomotive Company for a run on the proving ground before shipment overseas.

In Broome County, outside of the boundaries of the villages of Johnson City and Endicott, fire departments in the majority of cases were comprised of volunteers, and before the war there were eight towns with no organized fire protection. As a result of Civilian Protection activities during the war these eight towns formed volunteer fire companies, raised money by popular subscription, purchased fire apparatus, and erected buildings in which to house the equipment.

The protection of school children during an air raid was of vital concern to the civilian protection administration and a very unique plan of evacuation of children in the lower grades was worked out by the school safety committee. One of the things every school teaches children in the lower grades is to identify colors; so using this as a basis for their plan, different colored disks twenty-four inches in diameter were tacked to one of the walls of the gymnasium or assembly hall ten feet above the floor. Each pupil was assigned a color according to the neighborhood in which he lived and instructed to go to the hall indicated and line up under the disk which corresponded with the color assigned to him. Each group, guided by a teacher, was then marched from school over a predetermined route so that each child could be brought to his own home.

The Triple Cities nestle deep in a valley surrounded by high, sparsely wooded hills. The Chenango and Susquehanna rivers, fed by many small streams, flow through this valley, and in the spring of the year when the ice and snow melt too rapidly these rivers and streams overflow their banks and homes adjacent to these streams are surrounded by water.

In the spring of 1943, the valley was visited by a serious flood, and it was necessary to rescue people marooned in their homes. The Civilian Protection organization immediately went into action. Boats, boots, pumps, and other needed

equipment previously mobilized were put into use. Crews composed of air-raid wardens rescued people from the affected area, auxiliary police guarded property against vandalism, evacuation units set up cots in the American Legion clubhouses, and the Food and Housing group took over the job of providing and serving food. Trucks and vans evacuated household goods. All of these activities were directed by the headquarters control center in cooperation with the subcontrol centers.

In September of 1942, a mobile instruction unit was organized and under the direction of the Chief Incident Officer and Chief Air Raid Warden a miniature knockdown model of the main control center and a miniature model of a typical city or village with streets, houses, public buildings, hydrants, telephone and light poles, and lines with street traffic (autos, trucks, buses, and pedestrians) were constructed and taken into each town and village of the county, where lectures were given on "What To Do and What Not To Do in an Air Raid," the models being used to illustrate the talks. Some of the model buildings were so constructed that they would collapse coincidence with a firecracker explosion, simulating a bombing attack. This exhibit proved very popular.

As the war progressed an increasing number of service men and women passed through Broome County, coming from or returning to their service bases after furloughs at home, and a plan was developed to assist them in securing free transportation to their destinations.

A "Free Rides for Military Personnel" campaign was sponsored by the County Civilian Protection Administration with the splendid cooperation of the local newspapers, a radio station, and USO. Twenty "Registration and Pick-up Stations" were established throughout the county located on the main highways. Double-face wood signs four by five feet in size, lettered in red against a white background, worded "FREE RIDES FOR MILITARY PERSONNEL — REGISTER HERE" were located in front of each station. In addition to these signs, and with the financial assistance of local manufacturers, seven hand-painted signs, size twenty-five by forty feet, were erected on the seven main highways entering the city. These carried large images of a soldier, a sailor, and a marine, and urged motorists, when traveling to any point out of Binghamton, to register at the USO and there offer a ride to a serviceman or woman.

The names of motorists offering rides to military personnel were entered on a large blackboard in the USO headquarters indicating their destination, time of leaving, and the number of passengers they could accommodate. To be approved for such transportation, applicants were required to show their furlough papers. Permanent records were made of the names of the motorist and of his passengers. Under this plan thousands of rides were provided for servicemen and women. Connections with distant points were established and some riders were routed to destinations as far distant as California.

Civilian War Services. As elsewhere in the State, various segments of home-front activity, which eventually came under the aegis of Civilian War Services, arose sporadically as the war proceeded. The Mobilization Office, with branches, was an early feature and functioned effectively. Late in 1942 Civilian War Services for the two War Councils of Binghamton and Broome County were merged under one head. This proved the only effective method.

Ultimately, the volunteer offices in Johnson City, Endicott, and Deposit, plus the CWS office in Binghamton and similar committee setups elsewhere, became nuclei around which local work of a routine nature centered. These were contact points for the rank and file of citizens. The energy that went into these undertakings was tremendous, their accomplishments were prodigious, and no brief account can adequately portray their importance. Yet so much of the work done was of a routine nature, or the local application of programs projected on a Statewide basis, that little can be said here beyond this mere statement concerning the zeal and effectiveness of the people who did the work. Besides general citizen support, certain preexisting groups, such as the Red Cross, the nutrition committee, and the volunteer health and welfare agencies, adapting themselves to a wartime basis, became a part of the picture. On several fronts, the county was covered with extreme thoroughness. The Johnson City Volunteer Office was especially active, and it was there that the first 5000-hour service ribbon in New York State was granted for individual volunteer effort.

Courses of many kinds were offered and specialized training given. Surgical-dressings classes, nutrition, canning, canteen emergency driving, nurse's aides, and similar courses were available through the various CWS committees, plus those given under Civilian Protection. The program, in general, followed State and national patterns. There were, however, a few unique or noteworthy features and these only will be specifically mentioned.

The Broome County War Nutrition Committee combined both city and county functions from the outset. More than fifty professionally trained nutritionists were enlisted in this group, plus several scores of trainees. Broome was the first county in New York State to place a fully organized and trained canteen service into action on the home front. Red Cross methods were employed for the canteen service. When food rationing began, the entire county was covered by lecturing nutritionists who used locally devised educational charts for graphic presentation of data. Information centers were set up in grocery stores throughout the county and staffed by specially trained lay members of the Nutrition Committee. Actual demonstrations of the use of low-point and low-priced meats and other available commodities were made on a countywide basis. In addition, the usual routine classes and demonstrations were held as elsewhere. A closely allied activity was the canning campaign of the Victory Garden Council which secured by gift a completely equipped trailer, called the Canning Caravan, which toured the county giving curb-side demonstrations of food canning methods. The Victory Garden Council also functioned in obtaining garden plots and having them plowed, the volunteer offices and county headquarters acting as clearing houses for the project.

The Committee for Child Care began work by conducting a comprehensive questionnaire survey which touched every school child in city and county. The resulting huge amount of data concerning needs and conditions was presented to the War Council with recommendations. A counseling office was then set up, staffed by volunteers, to which persons might come and referrals be made to various agencies. This volunteer arrangement proved inadequate, but no more elaborate setup was installed, however, because a local pattern already existed which had applied to the industrial population for some years previous and which, with no large influx of wartime newcomers into the community, still continued to function. Some information of lasting value was derived from the survey.

Although the Red Cross handled blood donations for the military services, a Civilian Blood Plasma Bank, operating through the CWS, functioned with splendid success and has developed into permanency with the close of the war.

The Committee on Physical Fitness followed in a broad way the State and national programs. The most significant feature of this work is that a considerable number of recreation centers set up by the Physical Fitness group have worked into permanency. Along the same line, it should be noted that a Youth Center, originally set up by the Civilian War Services in Johnson City, has now become an important and permanent institution.

One of the more spectacular outgrowths of the Civilian War effort was the formation of permanent Community Councils. At the suggestion of the State, the Broome County War Council joined with certain civic groups and sponsored a community conference on postwar planning in 1943. Other conferences were subsequently held. Shortly there emerged a countywide executive committee of key persons, most of whom had been active in civilian war work and each of whom represented a certain special segment of community interest. Behind this group were committees and organizations within the various segments. The new organization was called the Broome County Community Council and its objective was community planning in all phases. While it started as a postwar planning group, it soon became apparent that most postwar planning must also embrace community planning for permanency. Similar local units were formed throughout the county on a town, village, or neighborhood basis, their purpose being to serve as citizen-interest groups in such matters, both official and unofficial, as might affect the common good. Where the movement has expanded very slowly, it has persisted, and the county organization has published a brochure, held public "clinics" on current problems and, on the local level, given stimulation and study to specific projects. Time alone will tell whether this movement is worthy of survival, but it exists in Broome County, at present, as the most enduring and tangible end product of the home-front war.

GENEVA[1]

The City of Geneva, at the head of Seneca Lake, was radically influenced by the location of the Sampson Naval Training Station and the Seneca Ordnance Depot on the east bank of the lake about fifteen miles to the south. The latter project was begun July, 1941, and the Training Center in June, 1942. At its peak, construction of these two military facilities involved some 25,000 workers, most of whom were recruited from cities such as New York, Detroit, Buffalo, Rochester, Syracuse, and Auburn. The problem of securing a sufficient number of skilled workers for these two projects dominated the entire Geneva labor market area, which included smaller towns within a radius of fifty miles of the naval base. In the face of this terrific competition, the local industries in Geneva, Canandaigua, Newark, and Seneca Falls experienced considerable difficulty in securing adequate supplies of skilled labor with which to meet government contracts for war materials.

Since the population of the area in 1940 was little more than 110,000, the influx of such a large number of nonresidents, of whom over 7000 were Negroes from New York City, required major readjustments. Many farmers were uprooted from their lands in the towns of Romulus and Newark. Transportation, housing, eating, and recreational facilities were greatly overtaxed. Small diners fed as many as 2400 a day and required police supervision to guard against overcrowding. In order to meet the competition of higher wages in war plants and facilities, restaurants had to pay their help on the same scale as war workers, and accordingly raised their prices to patrons. Quite naturally, servicemen were not too happy about this.

Banks handled long lines of depositors which extended around the block. Services and facilities generally were taxed beyond capacity.

Housing and transportation for workers were major problems. The construction contractors opened their own housing offices in Geneva to register rooms available for their employees. They were also forced to make arrangements to equalize transportation costs within a radius of fifty miles of the bases. Despite these difficulties a sizeable labor force was recruited. The United States Employment Service office in Geneva placed 1700 in 1940, 14,500 in 1941, and over 23,000 in 1942. Turnover, however, was heavy, with over 4000 Negroes disappearing in 1942 over Labor Day.

In the face of the labor shortage, local concerns that wanted to expand on war contracts had a difficult time. The fact that they paid relatively low wages proved a handicap in meeting not only competition from the bases but from industries in Auburn, Syracuse, Rochester, Ithaca, and elsewhere. As a result of the limited supply of available labor, employers' specifications were greatly reduced. Very young people were accepted. Restaurant help was at a premium and chefs could name their own terms. Both public and private employers were willing to take women and put them on the same level with men because of high turnover among the latter. At the Ordnance Depot and at the Training Station, the requirements were citizenship and age between eighteen and seventy. By 1942 competition had raised wages perceptibly in local nonessential industries. This was possible because all but two of the principal private companies in the area were by that time engaged in 100 per cent war work. War production training facilities were not utilized to any great extent because of lack of trainees. Men were scarce, and the major contractors resorted to extensive use of radio and newspaper publicity in their

[1] Material for the section on Geneva has been secured from Mr. C. M. Britt, now of the New York State Youth Commission, and from reports of the United States Employment Service.

recruiting programs, as well as to the facilities of the United States Employment Service.

The influx of between 15,000 and 20,000 additional workers greatly taxed housing facilities which were barely adequate before the war. In 1940, six of the surrounding counties had approximately 9000 vacant dwelling units. By February, 1942, a survey in Seneca County showed a vacancy ratio of 0.1 per cent. Only 16,000 available rooms were reported in the thirty-six communities within a forty-mile radius of the Sampson Training Station. Under such circumstances, to keep rents from soaring, rent control was imposed in 1943. Limited, large-scale housing was also made available in the form of temporary dormitory units — 100 at Seneca Ordnance and 500 at Sampson — 550 units at the CCC camp at Watkins Glen, 150 at the Glens Spring Hotel, and 400 in dormitories at Hobart. By the end of 1943 a Federal housing project of 250 units was completed in Geneva, but too late to help out with the peak load of construction workers.

By 1943, bus transportation had been equalized at twenty-five cents per person within a forty-mile radius, and the Lehigh Valley Railroad was supplying the Seneca Ordnance Depot from such towns as Geneva, Auburn, Waterloo, and Seneca Falls. The termination of construction did not by any means end the housing problem, as the housing of permanent personnel succeeded it. Transportation for between two to four thousand permanent operating personnel became a problem, since funds were not available to pay for buses.

The effect upon the farm labor force of the surrounding area was, as might be expected, drastic. Over 20 per cent of the available labor supply was lost to construction projects, with the result that workers were brought in from Florida, Georgia, Virginia, Pennsylvania, and New York City. Here again, however, inadequate wages and lack of housing proved a handicap in placement. Many farmers were able to help themselves financially, and the war effort as well, by working in war plants in the wintertime after the harvest was over.

In 1943 training of workers on the job was developed extensively because upgrading seemed to be the only way to secure higher skills. Employment remained tight all during the spring and summer of 1944. On July 1, 1944, the War Manpower Commission introduced its manpower stabilization plan, especially the priority referral system. The Geneva area was one of the three in the Rochester district to have the plan tried out. Despite the tight labor market, one local manufacturer received a 7 million-dollar contract for airplane motor parts in August, 1944. The labor supply remained relatively stable for the rest of the year, thanks to the fact that the supply of women remained adequate. There were, however, few withdrawals from the labor market and no significant transfer of workers from nonessential to essential industries. In September, 1944, a Veterans' Service Agency was set up to anticipate the needs for employment of returning veterans.

In 1945, in spite of the fact that a larger number of veterans were returning, there was a shortage of all types of workers. Three industries in the locality were given a No. 3 labor priority rating because they were not meeting their schedules. The demand for labor continued good until the termination of a large number of government contracts following V-J Day. For a short period thereafter those laid off were absorbed readily, but by December the supply of labor greatly exceeded the demand.

The proximity of Geneva to the Sampson Naval Training Station and to the Seneca Ordnance Depot, and the sudden expansion and contraction of the labor force required to build these installations, produced in the city a number of secondary social problems which required for their solution all the ingenuity its leaders could command. Essentially there were two periods in the wartime history of Geneva. The first period began and ended with the appearance and disappearance of the construction workers who built the two large war facilities. The second began with the coming of the naval trainees at Sampson.

During the first period construction workers lived where and how they pleased. Most of them were fortunate to find places in which to live. The contractors recruited labor from all over the country. The contractors had little control over their men after hours and the police of Geneva had the task not only of handling the town's own population, but also the additional working population. The result was that until the construction work had been finished police protection and supervision were inadequate. The problem was actually area-wide as the labor force was spread throughout the countryside. Men from as far away as Penn Yan now commuted to Dresden and then were ferried across the lake. Many local war councils besides that of Geneva endeavored to meet the housing problem by bringing house and room hunters into contact with those who had vacancies to fill.

With the coming of the sailors and the exit of most of the workers, the situation improved rapidly. Relations between the city and the Federal government were good. The latter understood the situation and allowed only a limited number of sailors off duty at any one time. Furthermore, the Navy policed its own men and had them under control. It even arranged to have attendance at the motion-picture houses staggered so that residents of the town could find seats. In short, with the coming of the sailors who were under discipline, order in Geneva was once more restored.

One of the outstanding USO clubs was organized under sponsorship of the Geneva War Council. The club was located at one of the main intersections in the city and became one of the main off-campus bases for sailors with free afternoons. Its patronage was more constant than in the case of USO clubs in the large cities, where men on furlough and in transit were the principal patrons. Because in Geneva there were few other places to go, except for the theaters, restaurants, and bars, the Sampson men were more dependent upon the USO Club, and its services were, therefore, essential. The Ontario County Civilian Mobilization Office operated a cookie jar at the USO which was always kept filled with the best the farmers' wives knew how to bake. The sheriff regularly picked up fresh supplies from farms in the neighborhood.

In some respects the high-school boy was at a definite disadvantage in Geneva. His natural companion, the high-school girl, was courted by the sailors. The surplus of men was so tremendous that the uniform and superior age and sophistication of the servicemen provided unnaturally stiff competition. This was secretly and sometimes openly resented. Although too young to compete with the sailors on even terms, groups of high-school students sometimes took matters into their own hands. The community made intelligent efforts to handle the situation and received substantial Federal cooperation. Dances and other forms of recreation were held for teen-age groups from which servicemen were excluded. As would be natural under the circumstances, rumors were rife concerning relations between the sexes. These stories were very largely exaggerated. What little basis they had, in fact, lay in the appearance of women professionals at the time of the earlier influx of the unsupervised construction workers.

Like other cities, Geneva engaged in the usual war activities such as salvage operations and the sale of war bonds. An active Volunteer Office was established on the main street which became headquarters for the bond drives. A child care project and a block leader system were also established.

In two other respects, however, the experience of Geneva did not fit into the usual pattern. The fact that all the telephone calls to the Naval Training Station went through Geneva meant a tremendous expansion in the Geneva exchange. Telephone girls were brought in from far and wide and the importance of the Geneva office rose to a position on a par with those in the larger up-State cities.

The war conditions in the Geneva area also affected adversely the labor supply of the large canneries located in the city. These relied for their raw material upon the farmers of the general vicinity who were themselves having a difficult time securing labor. The problem of an adequate supply of farm labor for the canneries was finally met by the location in the vicinity of a camp for prisoners of war.

Thus in many respects the wartime experience of Geneva was, for the size of the town, even more dislocating and nerve-racking than that of the larger centers of the State.

SIDNEY AND SCINTILLA[1]

The town of Sidney, in the northeast corner of Delaware County, is situated in the valley of the Susquehanna River on the main line of the Delaware and Hudson Railroad. Oneonta, the nearest large community, is twenty-five miles to the northeast, and Binghamton, the nearest metropolitan center, is forty miles southeast. At Sidney was located the Scintilla Magneto Division of Bendix Aviation Corporation, an essential war plant. Because of its remote location, Scintilla was faced with many problems uncommon to plants in urban areas,

while the rapid expansion of its working force from less than 1000 in 1939 to more than 8500 employees in 1943 exerted a profound influence upon the entire life and development of the town of Sidney.[2]

From humble beginnings in 1925, Scintilla gradually developed its line of aircraft ignition equipment to the point where its products became essential to the Army and Navy, as well as to private airlines. When, in 1939, war broke out in Europe and the allied nations began to expand their air forces, Scintilla received military orders which necessitated expansion well before the entrance of the United States into the war. American participation occasioned still further expansion as Scintilla then became a large-scale supplier of vitally needed equipment for the military purposes of this country.

Principal products manufactured by Scintilla during the war were aircraft ignition equipment consisting of magnetos, switches, sparkplugs and harnesses for radio shielding; magnetos and switches for tanks and tank destroyers; various types of industrial magnetos for power plants, industrial engines, and other similar applications, magnetos and distributors for PT boats; Diesel fuel injection pump equipment for seagoing tugs, mine sweepers, net tenders, freighters, floating drydocks, portable power plants, and auxiliary power plants on larger ships; millions of spare parts, including plastic subassemblies of special design and material composition for high-altitude operations. Military demands for Scintilla products were so heavy that subcontracting had to be instituted to ensure an uninterrupted flow of critical equipment.

On Pearl Harbor Day in 1941, approximately 3900 employees were on the Scintilla pay roll. With the United

---

[1] Information on Sidney and the Scintilla Company has very largely been furnished through the courtesy of the Scintilla Company.

[2] Scintilla received three Army-Navy "E" Awards for efficiency in the production of war materials.

States' entrance into the war, it became increasingly urgent to expand the working forces within the plant. The rise and decline of employed personnel from January 1, 1939, through December 31, 1945, is shown briefly in Table 28.

Table 28. Employees, Scintilla Magneto Division, Bendix Aviation Corporation

Date	Total employees
Jan. 1, 1939	750
July 1, 1939	900
Jan. 1, 1940	1100
July 1, 1940	1700
Jan. 1, 1941	2200
July 1, 1941	3100
Jan. 1, 1942	3900
July 1, 1942	3500
Jan. 1, 1943	8600
July 1, 1943	7700
Jan. 1, 1944	7200
July 1, 1944	5600
Jan. 1, 1945	4700
July 1, 1945	4200
Dec. 31, 1945	1678

A brief glance at the above table indicates that from January 1, 1939 to January 1, 1943, the employed personnel total expanded from 750 to 8600 persons. When it is remembered that Scintilla was located in a semirural area, nearly devoid of experienced industrial workers, the size of the employment problem becomes evident. The principal source of labor, from which the plant continued to draw as it instituted first two and then three shifts, was the homogeneous native-born American population of the small towns in the nearby vicinity. Through careful planning, persistence, and cooperation between the company's industrial relations department, the schools, the general public, and various local, State, and Federal agencies of government, the company's needs for both skilled and unskilled labor were successfully met.

Representatives of Scintilla's employment section were constantly in touch with various labor sources. Employment agencies in numerous cities were combed for experienced technical and mechanical workers. Newspaper and theatre advertising were utilized to focus public attention on employment requirements. Special defense schools in neighboring localities provided preliminary training to prospective employees. Of the graduates from these schools, Scintilla hired over 90 per cent. Valuable assistance in obtaining applicants was received from the USES. The Vocational Training Program, sponsored by the State Department of Education and operated in the Sidney High School on a twenty-four-hour basis, was of major importance in supplying trained defense workers. The New York State Department of Labor helped greatly, especially by assisting the company to obtain dispensations from certain labor-law restrictions, thereby expediting the company's personnel expansion.

In order to convert inexperienced yet trainable labor into productive employees, Scintilla concentrated its attention primarily upon the problem of training. New employees underwent an indoctrination training program to familiarize them with the working knowledge applying to their specific jobs. Through special arrangements with the high schools in Sidney and Oneonta, courses in shop training and related subjects were instituted. Employees selected for these courses were paid while attending the classes, which were of two weeks' duration, eight hours daily. Experienced employees received two weeks of training in shop practice in the Scintilla plant school on company time. Visual education methods were used in many phases of the training program, as it was found that motion pictures provided an ideal medium of instruction. As a result of this sysem of on-the-job training, the company was able to upgrade a larger number of its own employees. By subdividing other jobs, it was able to employ additional unskilled workers.

Courses were provided to meet special departmental requirements, for example, courses in magneto theory, motion analysis, office procedure, etc. The engineering department established a drafting class to train employees in the rudiments of drafting. A number of those completing the course were then employed in various capacities in the drafting room. The company also arranged for a stenographic course to be taught at the Sidney High School to provide stenographic training for a selected group of Scintilla's female employees.

Supervisory training also was included in the Scintilla program, featuring classes in job methods, job relations, and job instruction training. Special classes were held for supervisors for the purpose of interpreting labor contracts and industrial relations. In this way it was possible to produce enough men who could train other men, thus enabling the company to inaugurate its third shift in the summer of 1942.

Under direction of the service manager, a separate school was set up for members of the armed forces. Candidates for this school were drawn from the United States Army and Navy and from the military personnel of the allied nations. They received intensive training in the servicing and proper maintenance of Scintilla equipment used in the armed forces. During its existence, a total number of approximately seven hundred service members were graduated from this school, which was highly acclaimed by military circles.

The outstanding feature of Scintilla's training program was its flexibility. Although courses were planned for application to general groups, every effort was made to provide instruction for specialized groups when the need for such training became obvious.

Most of the plant operations called for production and inspection skills. Although workers were obtained from various parts of the country, the large majority came from the countryside lying within a forty-mile radius of Sidney. Without its training program, Scintilla could not have built an efficient production organization, because the labor material available was almost totally unfamiliar with industrial skills and procedures. Although many younger workers attracted by the relatively high wage scale came from farm communities, skilled farm workers were not encouraged to leave their essential farm jobs. This did not prevent, however, considerable dislocation of farm labor in the vicinity.

Selective Service complicated the manpower situation by its continual draining of skilled men from the Scintilla pay roll. The problem was solved by training replacements, many of whom were women, who by natural ability and temperament were found to be well adapted to performing numerous precision operations. At one period during the war, women employees constituted about 40 per cent of the total Scintilla pay roll.

While the wartime emergency required considerable expansion of physical properties, every effort was made to avoid overexpansion. It is expected that Scintilla will utilize for civilian production the major portion of the buildings erected by the Defense Plant Corporation during the war.

While, at the beginning of the war, the village of Sidney was not prepared to meet the wartime boom or the host of secondary social problems which followed in its train, the village, nevertheless, made rapid strides in adjusting itself to the situation. Although the great majority of Scintilla employees, at the peak of employment, were commuting daily from their homes in outlying areas, it soon became evident that the village was faced with a housing problem. Fortunately the President designated Sidney a special defense area which enabled the Federal Housing Administration to underwrite 90 per cent of the cost of its housing project. After 1940, housing facilities were provided as follows: 200 permanent units and 160 temporary units erected by the Federal Housing Administration, and two dormitories with accommodations for 100 workers, also built by the same agency; 150 new houses erected by other means; an estimated 150 old houses reconverted to multiple dwelling units; and an estimated total of about 500 rooms made available in private homes. A housing coordinator was employed by the company's industrial relations department to assist employees in obtaining housing facilities.

The Federal Housing Project also was equipped with a firehouse and fire-fighting equipment and a new sewage disposal plant. In order to release women for work at Scintilla, a day nursery school subsidized by the State War Council was established on the project grounds to care for small children. The salary of the nursery school's director was paid by Scintilla. Playground facilities were also provided for the children of project residents, and the Sidney Library extended its services to project families through the medium of a branch library located on the grounds.

During the war a new wing was added to the Sidney Central High School, and a new building was erected to house the industrial arts activities. In order to accommodate the increased enrollment in the grade-school section, the old school building which had previously been abandoned was reconditioned and restored to active service.

As the population increased, recreation became more of a problem. Through cooperation of village and Scintilla officials, a USO Recreation Center was established in a building formerly utilized as a silk mill. The building was completely renovated and decorated, and a recreation program instituted under the guidance of a paid director. Cost of the renovating and decorating was borne

jointly by Scintilla and by public contributions. When the USO withdrew following the end of the war, the village of Sidney purchased the building and retains it as a Community Recreation Center with a salaried director. The population of the village of Sidney was listed as 3013 in the 1940 census. According to recent survey figures, the 1946 total was about 5500.

In common with most war plants in isolated areas, Scintilla was faced with the ordeal of providing transportation for its employees. Early in the war a transportation coordinator was employed by the industrial relations department of the plant to help provide transportation. Eventually, in addition to group-riding facilities, the company arranged for bus transportation for employees who were unable to obtain suitable commuting facilities. At the peak of employment, between fifty and sixty buses were transporting employees. Finally it became necessary to obtain special train service on the Ontario & Western Railroad from Cadosia and from Norwich to Sidney to complete the transportation service.

When it became apparent that tire and gasoline rationing were becoming a major problem in the busy lives of Scintilla employees, a ration board was installed in the plant. This made it possible for employees to obtain their tire and gasoline allotments without the inconvenience of contacting local ration boards. Work-shoe ration coupons also were made available through the plant-site ration board.

It is difficult to draw conclusions as to how any future problem such as that created by the rapid growth of an industrial plant in a small rural community should be handled. However, experience has proved that an emergency can be met and overcome by close cooperation between industry and the agencies representing local, State, and Federal governments.

CHAPTER TWELVE

Impact of the War Upon Individuals and Communities

WAR brings about many changes — not only in things but primarily in people. Yet all changes are not experienced equally by everyone. The degree of change varies from locality to locality, and from person to person. Some experiences are shared widely; others only by a few. For example, every community contributed men and women to the armed services; every community felt the shortages of civilian consumer goods, suffered audibly under rationing, and shared in the decline from the normal peacetime standard of living. Every profession and every craft suffered from losses of personnel, and those who remained behind, of necessity, worked harder and longer to supply the needs of the community in which they lived. In the literal sense of the phrase, dentists, doctors, nurses, automobile mechanics, utilities service men, and countless others became public servants. Vacations were shortened; teachers and students, not obligated for summer school, worked in factories and on farms. According to the State Department of Commerce, approximately one hundred thousand small businesses in New York State alone were forced to close for lack of goods and lack of help.

In countless ways the reality of war was brought home to every family. For most, the four years of war were years of disorganization. For many a wife and mother, the everyday problems of maintaining a home and family had to be faced in a manless world. Storm windows, screens, lawns, furnace tending, and all the innumerable household repairs had somehow to be met without the aid of the man of the house. There was the disciplining and putting to bed at night of children. No longer could mothers maintain order by threatening, "Just wait until your daddy comes home tonight." Daddy simply was not coming home that night or for many nights thereafter.

Human mobility was in a semifrozen state — shorter distances, less frequent trips at a slower pace, became the rule. For the first time, many families took vacations within their own state. Others learned the art of living without benefit of the car or of night clubs. There was little place for social life in a seven-day work week. Many had to live with themselves for the first time and like it. Neighbors became important; so did one's furniture, and the arrangement of the living room, and the regularity with which housework was done.

Economic changes were legion and the resulting social changes were by no means uniform. The war intensified markedly the normal social migration from rural to industrial areas. The exodus from the countryside was on the whole relatively uniform, whereas the emigration to the urban areas depended largely upon the location of the major war industries. As a consequence, economic and social phenomena were one thing in rural areas, and quite different things in the cities and large towns. In the smaller towns, for lack of retail merchandise, small businesses closed their doors. Many of the services likewise ceased for lack of help and transportation. Economic security disappeared as the maze of government regulations made it impossible for business men to plan in advance. Personal contact by telephone became the only safe way to get results, and even that method proved precarious. Many an individual enjoyed a standard of living for the first time high enough to enable him to purchase an adequate diet. Some had more money than they knew what to do with. Ten years from now, these will be thankful that Uncle Sam persuaded them to save a portion of their income. Others had never before been in a position to save and welcomed the experience with a fierce satisfaction.

In the larger cities, employers wrestled with the necessity of curtailing or completely closing down their normal lines of production or operation. The loss of great commercial services made jobless overnight huge blocks of workers, who were then faced with the trying situation of retraining themselves, late in life, for other occupations. In many lines, conversion to war production finally brought a happy ending to the hectic period of indecision, pending the successful termination of the quest for a government contract. The problems of reconversion were left to take care of themselves.

Immediate social aspects of economic changes presented problems in their own right. Moving a family to the vicinity of a war plant was a tremendous gamble. All too often, housing was inadequate, high-priced, or nonexistent. School and recreational facilities for the children were overcrowded. Many a mother and father sat by helplessly while a teen-age son or daughter contracted an early marriage whose future was rendered uncertain by the fortunes of war and the continuing evolution in the character of the parties concerned. While in many cases increased wages kept pace with rising costs, for those with fixed salaries the rising cost of living represented a steadily increasing cut in the purchasing power of the family income. It is little wonder that wives and mothers gave favorable attention to the appeals of manufacturers that women enter industry. Many mothers, prompted by patriotic motives and economic need, responded to this call of industry and were faced with the problem of caring for their children during working hours. Thus arose a new problem to take the place of the one employment had solved. War made social changes fully as inevitable as economic changes.

COMMUNITY OF PERSONAL LOSS AND SACRIFICE

In the English language, the word "community" means more than the visible collection of houses and stores that make a small town or village. It means the less tangible sharing of common experiences and attitudes. In this sense, the war produced among the 13 million people of New York an invisible community of personal loss and personal sacrifice just as real as any of the visible communities of the State. People sacrificed quietly in countless ways and were glad that they could, for such sacrifices gave them the feeling of having a part in the war. Nights, Sundays, holidays, and odd hours were put in on a hundred and one forms of community service connected immediately or remotely with some activity vital to the war programs of the Federal government, the State, or local authorities.

Shortages of personnel cut two ways. Doctors, nurses, mechanics, laundry men, and almost everyone who remained behind in one service or another worked overtime — not primarily for the money but because only by so doing could he come anywhere near to meeting the needs of the community in which he lived. Furnace men worked nights and Sunday mornings and were on call equally with physicians. The other side of this picture is represented by the interminable waiting for services to be performed. Two hours in doctors' offices, an hour in the dentists', weeks for the repair of a clock, an electric iron, or a heater, months for parts for the car or truck. Everything seemed to be in slow motion.

The shortage of consumer goods increased with every month. For a while this was a novelty and furnished excellent topics for conversation across the dinner table, at cocktail parties, barber shops, and grocery stores. It was a minor triumph to discover an unexhausted source of supplies. Close friends were grateful for tips. Time, however, put an end to that particular sport. Shortages came to stay, and for the first time many Americans began to value and care for the things which collectively helped to make their standard of living. The experience of having to care for possessions, with the knowledge that if broken or destroyed they could not be replaced for love or money, taught many people a lesson they had failed to learn as children. The old New England expression had never been truer than in World War II, "Make it do, use it up, wear it out." People to whom $5 meant nothing began to save string, paper bags, leftovers, vegetable juices, bacon fat, to say nothing of the standard salvage materials demanded by the War Production Board. The word "prewar" once again took on a magic sound — whether it referred to rubber, woolens, electrical equipment, toys, or the last bottle of Scotch. If you had not saved, you did without and envied your neighbors or accepted with alacrity invitations from your more fortunate friends. It was all in the interest of victory, however, and

most people took minor irritations in stride.

Of course, many shortages were major ones. Hospital facilities became crowded; reservations for maternity cases had to be made in advance; male teachers, especially of physical education, were hard to find; war production areas were without sanitary facilities or the normal business services.

Consumer goods disappeared, as if America had suddenly lost fifty years and returned to living in the preelectrical era. For some, this shortage of consumer goods meant far more than personal inconvenience. As many retail merchants said, "When you don't have goods, you can't sell," and all over the State of New York, from 1942 to 1946, thousands of small businesses disappeared, and thousands of businessmen took jobs in war plants. Thousands of middle-class home owners struggled to hang on to their homes and maintain their social standing in the community. Everywhere a war economy upset the normal civilian economy and caused hardship among retailers and among consumers with fixed incomes.

Most of all, however, it was the absence from the home of those in the service that meant loneliness for civilians, no matter how hard they worked to forget it, no matter how often they strove to write the things that could not be said face to face. From practically every home, someone was missing. Anxiety was a constant companion that could not be shaken. To all appearances life went on just the same, but many, numbed by fear, were merely going through the motions until the war could be brought to an end and the family reunited.

There was a still smaller community, composed only of those who had suffered the tragic loss of dear ones through death in the service of the country. Among these there was a common experience and understanding that no outsiders, no matter how close or sympathetic, could fully comprehend or share. Only time, and the knowledge and pride that the Creator in His infinite wisdom had deemed their home worthy to share in the ransom required for the continued freedom of their country could in any way compensate for such loss or dull the anguish and heartache.

COMMUNITY OF WORK

If one were to ask the question, "How did America play such an important role in winning World War II; what were the factors that underlay the ingenuity of her engineers and the skill and energy of her workers?" the answer would be difficult indeed. Perhaps the greatest amount of initiative was displayed by the business and industrial leaders of the State, who accepted government contracts and sweated to get them out on time and according to specifications. In the adaptation of means at their disposal to the achievement of the government's requirements, in practical judgment, and in reliance upon themselves, these men displayed the personal qualities which have always lain at the foundation of America's greatness. In a literal sense, the future of the country rested upon the character of its citizens.

One of New York's outstanding industrial leaders, in commenting upon a State program designed to aid manufacturers to train workers for skilled positions, set forth a philosophy of the responsibility of the employer for the performance of this contract. According to him, the immediate motive power behind the war production effort, apart from patriotism, was the contract with the government. In order to receive such a contract, the individual employer assumed an obligation to perform a service. He put it this way:

The government says, "Here! We're going to do this and we want you to do that." Well, that idea was opposed to the idea, that if the government went to that same contractor and said, "Now, in order to help you do that service we are willing to train some people for you, we are going to rent some space for you, we are going to the banks and borrow some money for you." Well, then, what does the employer become — nothing. The government would be much better off to go and do it itself. You are taking away from the employer the necessity of achieving something. I mean you are relieving him of something — so to speak — that is probably going to interfere with his acomplishing his part of the deal. So my point in many of the things that came up . . . was that they were the responsibility of the contractor. If he cannot perform, well let him default, and give the contract to somebody else.

This philosophy of the responsibility of the individual employer for carrying out his contract with the government was shared by the majority of New York's business fraternity. In this respect, the war brought about a community of understanding — although, to be sure, a community of headaches and anxieties — among businessmen operating under contracts with the Federal government. If, because of the headaches and anxieties involved, these men had been unwilling to produce at top speed, the arming of America could not have been achieved so rapidly or with such overwhelming superiority in equipment. If ever this willingness to assume responsibility for the performance of a contract in time of war — regardless of the amount of ingenuity, engineering skill, and patience required — should begin to decline, i.e., if management should ever strike, the country would find itself on the road to defeat.

What has been said above regarding management applies equally to labor within its own sphere of responsibility. Americans have a priceless heritage of mechanical skill. It is this background that has enabled the average citizen to undertake and master quickly new procedures of manufacturing. To be sure, wages in war plants were phenomenally high, but there comes a point in human endurance beyond which additional cash cannot compensate for chronic fatigue, loss of weight, and the monotony of the job. It took the will to win the war — reinforced by the belief that the survival of this country not only depended upon them, but also that it was immediately important to each of them and to their children's future — to keep millions of war workers operating on their jobs at top speed. In New York, as pointed out in Chapter III, labor cooperated 100 per cent in the war production program, and there is little doubt but that its wartime record of patriotic devotion to the job, its reasonableness in the face of wartime conditions and hours of work that were far from ideal, were very largely responsible for the tremendous volume of war contracts awarded to industries in the Empire State.

In its effect upon people in communities, war is like nothing else under the sun. War synthesizes the conflicting purposes of a community. Fear and the general sense of danger act like a magnet on iron filings and point all community efforts in one direction — that of winning the war. The general will of the community becomes clear in wartime, and all efforts to assist in the struggle have community sanction. Making war becomes everybody's business. In a very real sense, we have priority of purpose, a single criterion by which all human actions are tested.

At no other time is the obligation of the individual to make the most of his talents so great, nor is such dependence placed by the community upon previous preparation for leadership. It is tragic, yet true, that war still gives leadership its best chance — far better than peace has ever afforded it. The man who can lead his fellows is in demand and, suddenly, communities all over the state discover new men and women who are able to perform the countless tasks found to be necessary.

In New York State, as elsewhere, wartime activities were superimposed upon the normal functions of the communities. In carrying out these wartime programs there developed among volunteers an unparalleled community of work, the cessation of which following the war became a matter of regret to many farsighted, public-spirited citizens. Fortunately, elimination of the wartime organization was not entirely complete. Even where organization ceased to exist, the memory of it lingered on, leaving a consciousness of civic opportunity and duty which continues to bear fruit in public service by individuals.

The performance of their common wartime tasks drew the members of the community closer together. There was hardly anyone in the State, even among those in the larger cities, who was not conscious of this warmer feeling—a feeling of comradeship in an enterprise participated in and approved of by all. Salvage and scrap drives, war loan drives, knitting and bandage-rolling for the Red Cross, and the entire Civilian Protection organization with its observation posts, warning stations, control rooms, and air-raid wardens required the thought and energies of well over a million volunteers throughout the State. Hundreds of individuals will never forget the hours they put in at the ration boards nor the decisions they had to make as members of the Selective Service boards. Victory gardens vied with consumer shortages as an inexhaustible topic of conversation wherever two or three people gathered together. The possession of a car in working order was an opportunity to prove one's generosity and neighborliness. Friendliness and an informal camaraderie were in the air, born of a common preoccupation with war-connected tasks and war-connected problems.

The purposes of social life, sometimes so confusing in time of peace, became clearer and more easily understood in time of war. War threw a spotlight upon the weak spots in the community. The connection between the welfare of the community and its efficiency in the production of goods and services, while by no means self-evident, nevertheless received widespread acknowledgment. Some understood that a healthy community was primarily composed of individuals working with a minimum of friction, both among themselves and within themselves. The efficient society was after all the just society, and the importance of the priority which democracy placed upon persons and their welfare received additional confirmation from the necessities of the war. It was demonstrated that individual welfare was best advanced, not by coddling, but through the provision of an opportunity for work useful to the community. The release of pent-up human energies brought about by Pearl Harbor was a psychological mass phenomenon comparable only to the release of an individual's energies in support of a suddenly acquired ambition. The by-product of this sort of action is morale of a high order based upon the conviction that what is being done is right and socially useful not only in the eyes of the individual, but in the eyes of his community, state, and nation. Wartime priorities were not confined to the realm of economics or to material things.

It was fortunate that in New York State the War Council organization was sufficiently flexible to allow the smaller units of government to initiate worthwhile war activities. In addition to the support that they loyally accorded Federal and State programs, cities, towns and villages developed programs of their own that they felt would help prepare the country for all eventualities, or, following the attack on Pearl Harbor, would help with the State's war effort. The variety of these local programs was extensive, but most of them would fall under one or another of the following headings:

1. Civilian Protective Services, including assistance in the event of natural and accidental disasters
2. Civilian Mobilization activities including
   A. Services to the sick, to housekeepers, and to veterans
   B. Services to soldiers — Blood Bank of Red Cross
   C. Community recreation and care for youth
   D. Services to war workers — rooms registration
   E. Information and morale — Speakers bureaus
   F. The provision of volunteers for:
      (1) The production of food on farms
      (2) The ration boards
      (3) Training classes in first aid, auto mechanics, nutrition, and the conservation of food
3. Transportation

In connection with civilian protection, unusual ingenuity was displayed locally in furnishing control rooms, preparing control boards that would give at any moment the exact position of fire-fighting and medical equipment, and of miniature model equipment with which training in fire fighting could be conducted. Any number of war councils, both large and small, did an excellent job along these lines as well as in the training of the civilian protection personnel.

The services rendered locally took an infinite number of forms. One unusual service for veterans was inaugurated by the Utica War Council at the Rhoads Hospital. By an unusual arrangement with the telephone company, boys who were unable to leave their beds were permitted to telephone, without cost, once a month to their wives, mothers, or other relatives. The telephone company installed plugs between the beds and loaded telephones on portable wagons which could be moved from bed to bed and plugged in. Funds to pay for the cost of the calls were contributed by people of the city. More than one war council appointed an advisory committee for returning war veterans to coordinate the efforts of existing organizations attempting to handle the problem. In Delaware County, a letter was sent to each serviceman explaining the purpose of the committee, and asking what assistance from the county each would desire upon his return to civilian life. The Albany War Council, in cooperation with such private welfare agencies as the Department of Public Welfare and the Red Cross, established a Visiting Housekeeper Service under the supervision of the Visiting Nurse Association. Three full-time housekeepers were kept busy constantly taking care of any home where the mother was ill, and where there was no one to take care of the children. The problem was especially acute with so many fathers away in the Army, and the program was eminently successful in meeting a real community need.

Services to inductees and to servicemen overseas were numerous. Preinduction Information Centers, one of the earliest of which was established in Albany in 1943, were approved throughout the State by the Army, the Marine Corps, the Navy, the Office of Civilian Defense, the local draft boards, and boards of education. At no time were servicemen absent from the thoughts of the communities they had left. Cookies were baked periodically for the boys in nearby Army camps by the housewives in Ontario County. Various groups knitted sweaters and made other garments for servicemen and their families on the order of Bundles for Britain. The work of the Ithaca Camera Club, which took photographs of families of servicemen and sent them abroad, was another example of community service. Local USO Centers, Red Cross canteens, and information centers were operated for servicemen all over the State.

Recreation activities were legion. In Albany, a Youth Service Committee of the War Council, under the leadership of a local clergyman, devoted itself to increasing recreational facilities in the city. In Gloversville, during the five-day business closure incident to the Fuel Conservation Program in February, 1945, snow sculpturing contests were conducted as a recreational project and prizes given for the best figures. Also, in Gloversville, the Civilian Training Corps was used in the policing of block parties, coasting areas, playgrounds, community sings, and public gatherings of all sorts. The Buffalo Recreation Committee worked with servicemen and also conducted a community recreation program with special emphasis upon recreation for war workers. It was instrumental in securing commercial recreation facilities for men on the night shifts, and it sponsored open-air concerts and dances in Delaware Park, near the Albright Art Gallery.

Probably the field in which the largest number of local projects fell was that of information and morale. In Schenectady, a radio program, "Speaking of Slavs," was conducted through the summer of 1942 for the purpose of bolstering the morale of some forty thousand citizens of Slavic origin in the Schenectady area during the crisis of the Stalingrad campaign. Broadcasts were also designed to inform Americans about the nature and customs of Slavic people and thereby to create a better understanding between the two groups. Surveys of active community organizations were also made in Schenectady, revealing over 950 conducted by Americans, 19 by Europeans, and 1 by Asiatics. In Buffalo, the Consumer Information Center and the War Information Board were particularly active. The work of the War Information Division in Albany included the preparation by a special artwork shop of posters, store-window displays, exhibits, puppet shows, and five radio programs weekly. The Division also edited a weekly news bulletin and conducted war information forums. It also had the signal honor of being chosen by the Federal Office of Civilian Defense to help set the national pattern for the Security of Military Information Campaign.

In Westchester County, an extensive "Warfair" was held early in the war to illustrate how the typical American home could live most efficiently. The vital contribution that the restricted civilian economy of the State was making toward the all-out military effort was visually and dramatically presented. All branches of the Westchester War Council participated, along with public and private organizations.

High-school essay contests on all subjects were held throughout the State. One at Oneida City set as the subject, "How Can the High School Student Best Prepare for the Duties Inherent in Full United States Citizenship?" The title was picked to counteract emphasis upon "our rights," and students pointed out that every right has a corresponding duty.

In Buffalo and Syracuse, the war councils sponsored unusually successful Rumor Clinics. In each city a group composed of leading educators, newspaper men, Federal and police officials, representatives of the armed forces, and professors of psychology performed an excellent undercover job of counteracting false rumors that had gained circulation and were impeding the communities' war effort by undermining confidence and spreading hatred and suspicion. Upon advice of Federal law-enforcement agencies and the Office of War Information, their work was largely of a confidential nature, and some day, when written up, will furnish an interesting chapter of the State's war effort.

Community-wide mass meetings, such as those addressed by Ambassador Joseph C. Grew at Syracuse in 1942, and at Buffalo in 1943, were widely attended and served to focus attention on the nature, strength, and weaknesses of our wartime Asiatic enemy. In fact, all during the war, speakers were in demand on every conceivable phase of the European and Asiatic campaigns. The people of the State were hungry not only for news but also for the basic facts by which they could interpret the news for themselves. Nowhere except in this country would people have been able to satisfy so adequately this thirst for knowledge of happenings at home and abroad.

The role of the communities in supplying labor on farms and in the canning factories has already been described in Chapter VI. Local initiative and organization proved of great assistance to the State's Farm Manpower Program. There were other programs, however, which were strictly local. The Glens Falls Chamber of Commerce developed a startlingly different plan to help with food production. It offered to sell a live pig to any boy or girl between the ages of twelve and eighteen years, if the buyer would feed the pig properly and promise not to kill it without consent of the chamber until the pig had attained the live weight of approximately 250 pounds.

In Buffalo, as a result of damage inflicted by rats on victory gardens planted within the city limits, the War Council appointed a Rat Control Committee which made a survey of damages and proposed a vigorous and continuing rat-control program for the entire city. The plan was supervised by the Rodent Control Division of the Fish and Wild Life Service of the United States Department of the Interior. City officials and a citizens' committee cooperated to make the program a huge success.

In the field of transportation, the plans for staggered hours involved an unusual amount of cooperative planning on the part of war plants, department stores, public utilities, and city officials.

In some of the smaller communities, great pains were taken to draw up maps, such as the one prepared in Fulton County which showed the location of each war worker's home, time of travel, the particular war plant in which he was employed, the time of his shift, and the route he habitually traveled to reach the plant. This map enabled the highway officials to gauge the transportation needs of the area at any time of day or night. In Utica, a group of women mechanics called "War Mandos" were mobilized to help meet the shortage of mechanics and repairmen in local garages.

Any account of programs originating in the municipalities and applying locally would be incomplete without a brief mention of those activities which were caused by natural and accidental disasters. The work of the Emergency Medical and Civilian Protection authorities in connection with the Wayland wreck, outlined in Chapter IV, was a striking example of this service. Any emergency, regardless of its nature, demanded prompt local action, and the record of the Civilian Protection forces in over twenty incidents during the course of the war reflected great credit upon the quality of the personnel and the thoroughness of their training. Coal shortages, feed shortages, hurricanes along the seacoast, and problems of snow removal in the up-State areas taxed facilities, plans, and personnel on occasion, but at no time were the local or State services unable to cope successfully with these emergencies.

In no small measure was World War II won in the hearts and minds of the American people who supported to the fullest extent of their power the sons and daughters they sent to fight for this America.

COMMUNITY OF SPIRIT

There is a famous saying current among European historians that the French Revolution of 1789 was accomplished before it occurred, meaning that before the storming of the Bastille a radical change had taken place in the hearts and minds of a large number of Frenchmen. War produces a curious spiritual paradox. On the fighting fronts, it unleashes the gates of hell; on the home front, it lifts people out of themselves and transmutes the human spirit in the service of the high cause of national self-preservation. In loyalty to this cause, individuals forget themselves and become bigger people through participation in the total effort of the community. A service-station owner is reported as saying, "Many gas stations will soon have to close up. There's no way out, and it's too bad. But the main job is to win the war. We have to win it come hell and high water for us. Nothing else matters." An automobile dealer, after discussing the fate of his enterprise, adds this, "But if we can win the war, to hell with my business."[1]

Actually, there occurred on the home front a psychological phenomenon approaching mass therapy as a result of intensive work by individuals in a cause bigger than themselves. One member of the State War Council, in commenting upon the reservoir of latent energies that was suddenly tapped in 1940 and 1941 by the approaching shadow of the European struggle and the shock of Pearl Harbor, said that he saw in it one of the finest examples of democracy in action that he ever hoped to witness. In fact, he said, "a lot of people were hurt because they could not be allowed to help as much as they wanted to. They were falling all over each other in their eagerness to be of help." Another member of the council remarked, "People wanted to participate. They wanted to help and they were all cheerful." Still a third

---

[1] Quoted in, *Economic Impact of the War Upon Ameriton, U.S.A.*, a sociological study by members of the faculty of Hobart and William Smith Colleges.

member of the council thought he saw in the spontaneous outburst of the volunteer movement a renaissance of the American spirit of pioneer days with which cabins were built, crops harvested, and defenses prepared by the community as a whole.

In fact, communities became more friendly. The circle of acquaintanceship widened to include many a former stranger or newcomer. Individual loneliness declined. All were engaged in a common enterprise. Each person's motives were understood and approved because they were shared by everyone else. Understanding was common to all. There was a new measure of citizenship and of importance in the life of the community. It was no longer where you lived, with whom you associated, or how much you had in the bank. It was what you were doing to help win the war, the amount of time you were willing to put in on that job, and the amount of ability you could bring to it. Many regretted they could not give as much time as they would like. It was the golden opportunity for those who had retired, yet were still in possession of health, vigor, and the respect of their fellows. The autumn years of many a life were crowned by outstanding services to the community in civilian protection, community war services, or service on the war council, ration, or Selective Service boards.

Had war not furnished this opportunity for action in a common cause, the strain of constant anxiety over the fate of loved ones in the armed services would have been almost unbearable. Anxiety was always present. As time wore on, and more Americans became prisoners of war, a common bond sprang up among families who had not heard from the European or Asiatic fronts in weeks or months. Any scrap of news, no matter by whom received, was relayed to those to whom it would mean everything. Perfect strangers became close friends, and the bond of sympathy seemed to include everyone. Loss and grief, whether fully understood by others or not, became a family's open sesame to the heart of the community. Old feuds were forgotten in the recognition that in one respect at least a family had rendered a service to the entire community for which there could be no recompense. Those with children, children who might at some future date be called upon to serve their country, realized dimly what other parents were going through, and they appreciated in varying degrees the debt they owed for the preservation of the freedom that they were still able to enjoy.

Community of spirit is a fundamental reality in time of war, but because it is partly based upon tragedy and fear of disaster, which human beings try to forget, its original vividness fades rapidly. When life is full, and the present impinges sharply upon an individual's consciousness, the memory of intangibles is difficult to keep fresh. Nevertheless, a record of the heights and depths of human experience, however inadequate it may be, should be preserved if only to prevent the subsequent growth of skepticism regarding the honesty and disinterestedness of human motives in the recent national struggle. These emotions of satisfaction and sorrow, shared so deeply by so many at the time, let no man hereafter call in question!

CHAPTER THIRTEEN

Results and Conclusions

ANY period which lasts for as considerable a length of time as five years, and during which so many changes have to be made in the habits and occupations of individuals, is bound to leave behind it a permanent imprint. Society does not go back to the prewar normal after a war, no matter how many of its members consider that "a consummation devoutly to be wished." Although in New York State, the War Council itself, the 108 local war councils, and the various war council agencies went out of existence, a number of the war council programs were continued as activities of permanent State departments, or, in a number of cases, under the auspices of permanent or temporary State commissions. Those war-created activities which have now taken their place with the normal State services will be indicated in the order in which they have previously received treatment in this volume.

Enforcement in New York State courts of Office of Price Administration orders and regulations, originally required by order of the State War Council, was provided for by the Legislature in Chapters 404 and 405 of the Laws of 1946. While in itself not a permanent result of the war period, as an example of State support of Federal legislation it will undoubtedly be of significance as a precedent for future action along this line. Personnel of the War Council War Bond Unit, which operated the Payroll Savings Plan, was absorbed by the State Department of Audit and Control, and the principle of payroll savings was contributed as a peacetime service to State employees.

The rapid development of the personnel and facilities of the State Department of Commerce was a wartime phenomenon. It was during the war that the department proved itself to be the one agency best capable of helping New York business. It has consequently established for itself a permanent position among the services rendered its citizens by the government of the State. Especially noteworthy was the establishment of the department's Washington office. This will undoubtedly prove to be a development of long-range significance in the business life of the State through the provision of on-the-spot contact with agencies of the Federal government. The Industrial Reconversion Program, for which funds were initially allocated by the State War Council, was absorbed by the Department of Commerce as an important phase of its program for the postwar development of business. The war also brought about a revival of mining operations in the Adirondack area and elsewhere. In all likelihood the titanium and iron-ore mines in the Adirondack region will be continued due to the increased interest on the part of the Legislature in the development of the State's natural resources.

Another important wartime development was the creation within the Executive Department, pursuant to Chapter

118 of the Laws of 1945, of the permanent State Commission against Discrimination. The critical need for an expanded labor supply called attention forcibly to the waste of human energies occasioned by discriminatory employment practices, and furnished an unusual opportunity not only for studying the evils of discrimination, but for developing a State organization to cope with them. The War Council Committee on Discrimination in Employment was discontinued July 1, 1945, to make way for the permanent State Commission against Discrimination. The essential contribution of the original committee must be given full recognition because, as a member of the present commission has well stated,

The economic and social forces which shaped the Ives-Quinn Bill had their genesis in the activities of the War Council Committee against Discrimination. It was out of the experience of this committee that the threat of discrimination on the basis of race, creed and color became fully and completely apprehended, and it was out of the experience of this committee that the philosophy of approach expressed and developed in the Law against discrimination was tested and found to be wise.

The passage of this law was a courageous act on the part of Governor Dewey, Assemblyman Irving M. Ives, and the State Legislature. Common-sense administration, requiring equal amounts of courage and tact, has shown that the basic policy was sound.

Instead of suffering from the war period, labor standards have received further support from many employers who had experience with the wartime Dispensation Act. When this act was first passed there was a great deal of apprehension on the part of many that the long-fought-for labor standards of the State would be lost because of the relaxation of the law. The opposite, however, seems to be true. Because careful consideration was given to each application for dispensation, in practically every case during the war it was possible to take a broad educational point of view. This has borne fruit in changed attitudes.

Through the conference method, it was possible to convince employers that long hours were unproductive, and that by limiting the length of the working day the law regulating hours of work actually contributed to better production and in so doing protected the employer as well as the workers. Many employers repeatedly stated that the philosophy back of labor legislation had never been very much a part of their thinking until it was pointed out in this graphic way. The moment the war was over, employers were glad to go back to legal hours of working, and, as many of them stated, they appreciated the law in a way that they never had before. Through the administration of the Dispensation Act, it was possible to drive home the old philosophy of fatigue and efficiency, namely, that production falls off when hours are lengthened. Relying at first on the British experience, gradually our own experience was built up so that employers in New York State now have their own experience and records to show that long hours are unproductive. As the result of efforts by the State Department of Labor to keep hours relatively short, employers found themselves working out all sorts of ingenious schedules in order to meet production demands. This planning, according to employers, will stand them in good stead for the future. Many of the old haphazard methods of production which had to be discontinued during the war will never reappear. Many employers actually, because of the Dispensation Act, were legislated into efficiency.

The granting of a dispensation involved far more than a request for a dispensation and an investigator's report. Problems between workers and employers arose in a large number of cases which had to be ironed out. To this end the War Emergency Committee held hundreds of conferences of workers and representatives of management before dispensations were granted. Problems and schedules were freely discussed between the two sides, and often schedules were worked out which had not been originally requested but which were far more useful to the employer and acceptable to the workers. The War Emergency Committee acted as a mediator between the two sides. This method was not only successful in the emergency period, but will undoubtedly have a good effect within plants themselves and has taught management and workers that the Labor Department is ready and able to help iron out differences.

At the start of the war, New York had perhaps the most comprehensive safety legislation of any state in the union. As a result of the war, however, one new standard was developed. This was Industrial Code Bulletin No. 37 relating to the manufacture of military pyrotechnics, which became effective June 1, 1943.

Permanent results of the civilian protection organization were the incorporation of the various mutual-aid plans into the pattern of State organization. The mutual-aid plans covering Police Mobilization and Activities and Fire Mobilization and Control, which originated as part of the War Council program, were transferred by Chapter 834 of the Laws of 1946 to the newly created State Division of Safety. As a result of the inventory of fire-fighting equipment available in the State, which was made by State Fire Administrator William H. Frank, Jr., the total quantity and kind of equipment on hand are now a matter of record. By Chapter 729 of the Laws of 1946, the Mutual-aid Water Supply Plan was made permanent within the Department of Health. Provision of equipment for the State Police was also rapidly improved in 1943 and 1944. The addition of five new radio stations provided State-wide short-wave police radio coverage. The scientific laboratory was moved from Schenectady to superior quarters in Albany by order of the Governor, and its equipment improved and expanded.

Undoubtedly, the most extensive carry-over of an organization and activities built up during the war occurred in the field of food production and nutrition. Most of the activities of the Emergency Food Commission were assumed either by the Colleges of Agriculture and Home Economics at Cornell, or by the State Department of Agriculture and Markets in Albany. The activities assumed by the college included the Farm-Machinery Repair Program, a reduced upstate Nutrition Program, which is being continued in cooperation with municipalities, and some of the activities under the supervision of the Victory Garden Council. The activities assumed by the State Department of Agriculture and Markets included the work of the commission in relation to feed, fertilizer, and machinery supply, the Farm Manpower Office, and the Farm Cadet Victory Corps.

The Interdepartmental Committee on Migrant Labor, of which Dr. T. N. Hurd was chairman during the war, was reappointed by Governor Dewey in 1946 as a peacetime clearinghouse for study and action in that field. The membership of this committee, under the continuing chairmanship of Dr. Hurd, included the following State agencies; Health, Social Welfare, Agriculture and Markets, Labor, Education, the Youth Commission, and the State Police. Mention also should be made of the continuing State Farm Labor Operating Committee, which serves as the policy and program-making body in the field of agricultural labor. Membership of this committee includes private, State, and Federal organizations, such as the New York State Association of Canners, the Extension Service, the State Departments of Agriculture and Markets and of Labor, and the United States Employment Service.

Among the permanent contributions that the Emergency Food Program made to New York producers and consumers were:

1. The establishment of a force of Extension Agricultural Engineers, each of whom is to continue intensive work on the Farm-Machinery Repair Program in an especially assigned group of counties.

2. The development of a long-range postwar program for food and farming in New York, referred to in Chapter VI, which was designed to guide consumers, farmers, farm organizations, and government in their attack on farm problems.

3. The inauguration of a vast additional research program needed in the field of food production, processing, and distribution to improve diets, health, and productivity.

4. The initiation of intensive research and extension in farm labor, a field which had been generally overlooked and neglected before the war.

5. Expansion of the work of the Extension Service of the State Colleges of Agriculture and Home Economics into numerous counties not previously completely organized, and for the first time into the New York City metropolitan area.

As a result of the research program (mentioned in item 3 above) which was developed by the commission in 1944, a temporary Agricultural Commission, recommended by Governor Dewey, was authorized by the 1945 Legislature. Originally headed by Assemblyman Irving M. Ives, upon his retirement from the Legislature the commission was headed by Senator Austin W. Erwin of Geneseo. The purpose of the commission is best given in the words of the Governor's Message to the Legislature, January 3, 1945:

The problems and needs of agriculture in the postwar period relate particularly to the conditions of production, marketing, processing and consumption of all types of agricultural products, in industry as well as in the home. Economic practices, such as pricing, affecting milk and milk products, poultry, fruits, vegetables and many other farm and forest products, affect producers no less than consumers.

We need in the State a marketing system which is fast, efficient and honest for the handling of fresh food such as fruits and vegetables, eggs and milk. Both farmers and consumers have a vital stake in such a system. Neither can afford to leave its development to chance. The normal processes of food production and food marketing are now upset by the impact of war. Consumers, especially in our larger towns and cities, are being forced daily to make drastic and sometimes unhealthful adjustments in their diets.

It is high time to appraise the whole food situation in the State. The objectives of this appraisal should be, first, to determine what adverse conditions can be corrected immediately; second, to lay a broad foundation for a long-time State program of food production, marketing, and diets, designed to keep the farms of the State profitably employed and to supply the people of the State with the best possible food from these farms at reasonable prices. To this end I recommend the creation of a Temporary Commission to make this vital survey.

In the field of nutrition, the work of the Emergency Food Commission has likewise left permanent results. Considerable expansion of personnel took place in both urban and agricultural counties to continue permanently nutrition services temporarily provided during the war. The Test Kitchen established by the Food Commission at Ithaca became a permanent part of the College of Home Economics. The Food Information Service at Ithaca, which supplied information about markets, market conditions, and available food supplies to newspapers and radio stations was also continued. The early activities of the industrial nutritionists of the service demonstrated the need for a continuing program in group feeding. This service was expanded with the help of State and university funds to support a specialist and three field workers. In addition to work in industry, the nutritionists also gave attention to resort and tourist-home operators, organization camps, and small public institutions.

Another less tangible contribution of the Food Commission in the field of nutrition was the development of new methods and new materials for the use of regular State agencies. Among these were various information centers, short colorful leaflets on many nutrition subjects, exhibit materials, motion pictures, slides, enlarged photographs, radio write-ups, and news letters. In this way, the Extension Service and other agencies working in the field of nutrition, such as Red Cross nutrition committees and public health workers, gained increased prestige and the ability to reach many more people. Efforts of the commission along these lines succeeded in making citizens of the State, particularly those in cities, conscious of the importance of the right kind and amount of food needed for health.

In contrast to the carry-over in the fields of agriculture and human nutrition, there was very little of a permanent character in the work of the War Transportation Committee. Most of its activities were discontinued late in 1945. One, however, the power to grant permission to institute emergency bus service pursuant to Subdivisions 5 and 6 of Section 63-I of the Public Service Law, was temporarily administered by the State Traffic Commission. Later on, in Chapter 614 of the Laws of 1946, this power was given to the Public Service Commission. As a result of efforts by the Interdepartmental Committee on Farm Labor, headed by T. N. Hurd, a new section of the Vehicle and Traffic Law, Section 88, paragraph 11, was added by Chapter 570 of the Laws of 1945. This paragraph forbade owners or operators of trucks to transport persons more than five miles while more than one-third of the passengers were standing unless seats, a tail gate, and three-foot side racks were pro-

vided. Although none of the organizational pattern of the War Council's War Transportation Committee survived, experience gained from coping with the transportation problems of the war undoubtedly proved of value to the director and staff of the Traffic Commission, upon whom fell the lion's share of the activities of the War Transportation Committee.

One wartime program, instead of being abandoned, was transferred in its entirety to a new temporary commission. The Child Care Program was transferred from the War Council to the Youth Commission by Chapter 298 of the Laws of 1946. Chapter 445, which, with certain exceptions, repealed the War Emergency Act, not only authorized the State and local war councils to wind up their affairs, but it authorized the transfer for child care purposes of unexpended local funds which had been appropriated for war council purposes. This was done in view of the fact that the State Child Care Program had been transferred to the Youth Commission, and consequently there was a possibility in some localities that no local funds would be available for child care purposes sponsored by that commission.

One program which was vitally connected with the later stages of the war period was that dealing with the needs and problems of returning veterans. Its administrative aspects bore no causal relationship to the actual winning of the war, nor did the State War Council function with respect to this program. Nevertheless, the State Division of Veterans' Affairs with its local Veterans' Service Agencies and its comprehensive approach to the problem of rehabilitation was created to meet a wartime need. Not only will it be a permanent addition to the ranks of the State's administrative agencies, but its organization and methods constitute a significant advance in governmental handling of a vital social problem.

The 1946 Legislature established upon an experimental basis and until August 31, 1951, five State institutes of applied arts and sciences to be located in Binghamton, Buffalo, New York City, Utica, and White Plains. The courses were to include two-year courses in applied arts, crafts, aeronautics, retail business management, subprofessions, and technical skills.

By Chapter 680 of the Laws of 1946 the Commissioner of Education was authorized to contract for instruction in higher education of World War II veterans and other students with trustees of an institution chartered by the Board of Regents on a temporary basis to meet the emergency created by the lack of college facilities, and to pay costs not covered by receipts from Federal, State, or other sources. Pursuant to this authorization, three colleges were organized at Sampson, Plattsburg, and Rhoads General Hospital. These were intended primarily for veterans. Enrollment was first restricted to veterans only and later opened to others. Consequently, these colleges commenced to function with veterans composing the largest percentage of their student bodies. State warservice scholarships for veterans increased to the number of 1200 were also available.

The related problem of emergency housing for veterans has been touched upon in Chapter III. In addition to the provisions of Chapter 3 of the Laws of 1946 appropriating 35 million dollars for an emergency housing fund, Chapter 681 provided that real and personal property could be acquired and converted into classrooms, libraries, laboratories, offices, restaurants, and other facilities for transfer to a college or university for emergency housing and education purposes. Pursuant to this latter authorization many facilities were built for existing institutions and thus these were enabled to expand their enroll-

ments for the benefit of veterans seeking higher education.

Chapter 298 authorized the State Youth Commission to furnish care for children whose fathers were in the United States armed forces or in the maritime service. This was the Child Care Program previously administered by the State War Council.

These provisions relating to the interests of veterans in the fields of guidance and counseling, housing, education, and child care, not to mention many other measures of a similar sort in other fields which for lack of space must be omitted here, furnish some idea of the extent of the postwar veterans' problem and of the efforts of the State of New York to handle it in a businesslike fashion.

On April 1, 1946, aid to the War Nursing Program was discontinued by the War Council, but the State Nursing Council planned to continue as a private organization with coordinating and informational services of a Statewide character in the field of nursing.

The Physical Fitness Program was absorbed by the State Education Department's Bureau of Health and Physical Education.

The Community Recreation Program, developed under the Office of Civilian Mobilization, was transferred to the Department of Commerce and continued by that department.

Two of the war activities of the State Department of Social Welfare, performed by it pursuant to the War Emergency Act, were continued by legislation in 1946. Chapter 735 authorized continuation of the Civilian War Assistance Program to help repatriates, and Chapter 266 authorized the State Department of Social Welfare to continue to conduct dependency and other investigations for Selective Service boards.

The creation of the Youth Commission was undoubtedly accelerated by the war. Although the problems with which it must deal are not new, it was because they had been intensified by the social dislocations proceeding from the war that in October, 1943, Governor Dewey created the Interdepartmental Committee to go into the entire matter with his counsel. The report of this committee carried weight with the Legislature, inducing it to provide in Chapter 556 of the Laws of 1945 for the Temporary Youth Commission. This was another occasion similar to the appointment of the Emergency Food Commission and of the Commission Against Discrimination, in which the State was placed squarely behind a well-rounded program to deal with a definite set of problems. Regardless of the length of life of the Youth Commission, the experience to be gained from its operations can be used in the solution of other social problems of a related nature.

RESULTS ON THE LOCAL LEVEL

In the communities it is more difficult to point to permanent changes of an organizational nature. In practically all cases no effort was made to continue the local war councils, although a need for some form of over-all community planning was felt by many of those who had had a part in the war council activities. On the other hand, the phrase, "It took a war to do it," has been used in a number of instances to indicate the effective solution of a long-recognized community problem. There are various examples of war-caused changes which should be mentioned at this point.

A few of the major benefits from the Civilian Protection Program in one of the major upstate cities were listed in a report as follows:

1. The establishment of the Mutual Aid Fire Plan, which functioned effectively on six actual calls and which, in the opinion of city and town firemen, is a practical guarantee against a major fire disaster anywhere in the county.

2. A per capita fire loss of $1.08, the second lowest in the city's history, together with a marked drop in false alarms, both of which were results of the Fire Training Program, which directly affected thousands of citizens.

3. A record-high degree of industrial safety resulting from participation by war industry personnel in the Fire College Program.

4. First hand knowledge of the interior construction of all major buildings by battalion chiefs assigned to the areas in which the buildings were located. The inspections were made by the Chiefs, acting as Deputy Plant Protection Officers of the Plant Protection Unit.

5. Personnel in hotels, office buildings, theaters and retail stores trained to meet emergencies as the result of participation in the Plant Protection School.

6. Thousands of trained citizens ready to act whenever an emergency should strike, regardless of its source.

Benefits of this sort, while applicable primarily to large cities, nevertheless furnish a general indication of the long-range value of the Civilian Protection Program as applied to defense against fire.

It likewise took a war to make possible the interconnection of municipal water systems provided for under the Mutual Aid Water Supply Plan. Examples of the operation of this plan during emergencies were given in Chapter IV.

Although in most communities all traces of wartime organization have disappeared, there remains the volunteer personnel itself with identified skills and a wider understanding of community needs. The war thus brought about in a general way mass training in community service. It is conceivable that later, after individuals have recovered somewhat from wartime fatigue and the psychological slump known to follow closely upon the emotional tension of war, the memory of their wartime activities will serve to spur many to further constructive participation in community life.

Although Community Councils appeared during World War I, they were not so highly developed, nor, because there was no longer any authority for their existence, did they persist once the war emergency had passed. It is, nevertheless, of interest to quote Newton D. Baker, Chairman of the Council of National Defense in 1919, who said, in speaking of the Community Councils of that period,

Community Councils, however, are of more than present value. The community organization which they have initiated is a permanent need of the United States, and permanent provision should be made for it by legislation. A community organization will bring into our national life a much needed element of cooperative endeavor and civic orderliness which will go far to make our government both democratic and efficient in public service. The organization of all communities will develop a new community consciousness, fellowship, and pride, and a new means of community action.[1]

This quotation illustrates the strange fact that although in time of war, because of an overwhelming necessity, it is relatively easy to comprehend the value of a broad-based, popular support of community activities, it becomes more and more difficult as the wartime necessities fade into the past to keep this realization fresh. Apparently, the peacetime needs of society do not yet seem to require systematic focusing of attention on the part of large numbers of citizens. Yet the fact remains that knowledge acquired by one generation through experience in the field of social organization is often forgotten and seldom transmitted, while knowledge acquired in the field of the sciences is written down and utilized as a foundation for further achievement by subsequent generations.

Undoubtedly, there will be many changes in the pattern of community life in the fields of transportation, victory gardens, housing, and recreation. Although many traffic lights have been restored to full operation, some which were never needed even before the war

have not been replaced. Certain local patterns of traffic flow evolved during the war have been retained. This does not include, however, the staggered-hours programs which pretty generally have been abandoned. In many instances, it looks as though the small private garden has come to stay, especially with prices of farm commodities at present levels. The housewife's knowledge of food preservation will be a contributing factor, as will be the general expansion in the public's understanding of the basic principles of nutrition, such as the importance of fresh vegetables. Likewise of permanent value was the greatly increased emphasis upon recreational facilities for young people. The provision of this particular service in communities which had previously been without it should create a permanent demand through acquaintance with its benefits.

Then, too, the war has undoubtedly changed the living habits of a large number of those who migrated from the rural areas to the cities. These individuals and, in the case of war impact areas, municipal officials generally, have become more housing conscious. The present general housing shortage and the hardships that it has imposed upon returning veterans has focused attention on the need for an extensive expansion in the field of low-cost public and private housing. The high price of building materials is likewise serving as a stimulus to research in new building products and methods.

The war had its effect upon the State's labor force. Many women who first entered industry during the war undoubtedly will remain permanently. An increase in the family income, or greater personal freedom and security, have proved more attractive than the previous life in the home. Furthermore, women demonstrated unusual skill and ability in work requiring finger dexterity, and by accepting training in employment during the war they revealed still further

---

[1] Office of Civilian Defense Publication 4228, p. 2.

evidence of their capacities and adaptability. Although it took a war to reduce the public assistance or relief load, the extensive training of industrial workers carried on in industry and through the facilities of public schools should help to prevent for some time to come its rise to the prewar level.

The Vocational Training Program developed under the exigencies of war played an important part in promoting common understanding between industry and the vocational and high schools of the State. The value of the training program in providing industries with more intelligent, skilled, and efficient workers was clearly demonstrated, whether training was carried on in the plants themselves or in the schools. Out of the war experience came opportunities for increased contact with people and with industries. Not only did the ivory in the ivory tower diminish in quantity, but the value of the State's educational system in helping to promote better human relations and more enlightened and skilled workers became more apparent to the general public.

The principal effect of the war upon the educational program in the secondary schools was to change the orientation of instruction. This may not prove entirely permanent. In time of war, young people were destined to play a part in their country's war program. Since many of the boys were going into the Army or Navy or into war industry, war-related jobs, or work on the farms, and since many girls were going into nursing or auxiliary branches of the services, it was felt that the schools should provide courses in the curriculum with a practical wartime application. Not only that, but since schools were obligated to educate young people for society and an active citizenship, and since in America that society was at war, the educational program should be adapted to general wartime implications.

These twin objectives were accomplished in two ways. Since war was preeminently a technical operation, and since the Second World War required from the average soldier more technical knowledge than had ever before been necessary, the secondary schools hastened to alter their curricula to supply the needed scientific information and skills. The war thus placed a terrific demand upon the high schools for more widespread and more effective teaching of science. Likewise, in order to bring out the general implications of the second world conflict in twenty-five years, material of value in understanding the fundamental war aims of America and her allies as well as the characteristics and purposes of our opponents was woven into the curriculum wherever possible.

To secure the most efficient results in as short a time as possible an extensive survey was made of Army educational methods. Army instructional materials were examined and State syllabi in mathematics, science, and other subjects were in turn reviewed by Army School authorities. An extensive revision of State instructional materials was then carried out in 1942 in line with requirements of Army School authorities. Revisions of this sort were most extensive in mathematics, in physics, and in those social studies courses into which a wartime consumer-education program was inserted. Such changes may be classified under the general heading of preinduction training, although they should not be confused with special instructions for selectees furnished by members of the armed forces and civilian guidance counselors on the requirements of army life.

The efforts to adapt programs to immediate war needs brought the schools closer than before to the communities in which they were located. Schools had to assume leadership not only in education but in many other things as well. School people — teachers and pupils alike — participated in community drives, in the sale of war bonds and stamps, and in furnishing help to ration boards. In some places school facilities were made available after hours for adult recreation programs. Luncheons and dinners, lectures, exhibits, and meetings of all kinds were held in school buildings. People developed a habit of looking to the schools for information and guidance. In countless ways the schools showed themselves to be integral parts of community life, continually responsive to local interests and demands. As a result, their prestige has never been higher.

Several functions of a slightly different character were also performed increasingly by educational institutions. In view of the extraordinary number of opportunities for the use of talents in the war, and the necessity for boys and girls to arrive at decisions for careers while still in high school, the guidance function of the school was developed far beyond anything that could be imagined before the war. Interest in guidance work among school administrators increased, and pupils were urged to look ahead and plan ahead as far into the future as possible.

The importance of keeping the schools in close touch with the training needs of the community was realized as a result of demands from industry and the armed services for special types of training. Under the necessity of war, it was shown that to develop competence, training need not be extended over a long period of time. One implication of this discovery was that greater opportunity could be afforded for general education in the schools, and that intensive specific training could be presented later. In effect, the war shook the schools from established ways of doing things and helped teachers and communities alike to a clearer perspective on possibilities latent in the educational process. As in other lines of endeavor, the stimulus of the war produced in a few years progress which would normally have taken much longer.

The three years of operation of the School Lunch Program by the Department of Education netted valuable experience in the operation of school cafeterias. As a result of the federally supported program, school administrators in New York State became increasingly aware of the need for a good feeding program. It took some persuasion to overcome the feeling on the part of boards of education against anything federal. However, the interest of administrators and parents was such that in New York State applications for Federal funds with which to maintain School Lunch Programs were so numerous as to exhaust the allocations for that purpose made to the State by the United States Department of Agriculture.

Three years' experience in the operation of the program demonstrated the need for trained personnel — cooks and managers — additional nutrition education, and better menus to fit the needs of children, the nature of the local food supplies, and the type of available facilities. Up-to-date equipment was in great demand at the end of the war, but purchasing and arrangement required technical advice. Although the program had by no means reached its natural limits, many schools were already doing an excellent job of feeding their youngsters at noon.

Medical gains from five years of war were too extensive for treatment in a volume of this sort. One general statement, however, seems warranted. The average man became more conscious of the importance of health. Health frequently was not appreciated until an individual had worked to the limit of his endurance in the war plant, the office, or on the farm. Furthermore, the failure of individuals to pass the Army and Navy physical examinations called attention to the general physical condition of the population. As a result, considerable improvement in personal health, either on the initiative of the individual or that of his family, developed during the war. This outcome was closely connected with the widespread increase in dietary knowledge.

Familiarity with the value of blood plasma and increased knowledge of its uses on the part of the medical profession were likewise a war result. The public became familiar with it through widespread blood donations and the extensive publicity surrounding its use both at home and abroad. Publicity on the efficient use of foods, of leisure time, and on avoiding accidents in the home and on the road also contributed to the general welfare. During World War II, if military casualties are omitted, despite longer hours and harder work the United States enjoyed a lower death rate than in time of peace. Here again, as in practically everything else, the stimulus of the war brought progress more rapid than would have occurred under normal circumstances.

In a brief study it is not possible to exhaust a subject of this sort. However, one or two intangible results of the war may prove of far-reaching importance. The bottleneck in a community is sometimes a lack of comprehension on the part of its leading citizens of the more immediate economic and social needs. The new Citizens' Council organized by leaders in the original Citizens' Unity Section of the Office of Civilian Mobilization has become an influential Statewide organization in the field of community services. It has drawn together a progressive group of educators, State officials, businessmen, and community leaders who are interested in keeping alive after the war an interest in economic and social planning on the local level. Through an annual series of regional institutes, it has reached a representative group of business and professional people and serves to channel ideas in both directions between the State and the communities. Although its chief interests are economic and social questions of importance to the State of New York, its meetings generally run the entire length and breadth of the social sciences, including State and national politics, social psychology, and religion. Since it draws its strength from professional and business leaders in the cities, the degree of its success will be a partial index to the postwar survival of the community spirit engendered by the war.

While the war has had practically no effect upon the form of local government, there are indications that certain intangible results have accrued. The interest of city and town governments in recording the activities of the local war councils and the production record of their principal war plants has been widespread. Instead of throwing away all traces of the war efforts of their citizens, thereby cutting them off from their own past, cities, towns, and villages generally, realizing the historical importance of the war records, are taking the trouble to see that they are placed in permanent safekeeping. Evidence of this sort indicates on the part of political leaders a greater appreciation of the importance of popular participation in the wartime life of the community. It may also be possible, as one county official has indicated, that in the rural counties the war induced a greater willingness on the part of supervisors to consider on their merits new business methods and new types of social services. Such changes of outlook are difficult to assess, but the impact of a total war is universal, and the greater cohesiveness which it forced upon American communities will undoubtedly have permanent results in terms of quickened community consciousness.

LEADERSHIP IN A DEMOCRACY

A society which frustrates cannot prevent the rise of leaders for the frustrated whose warped vision focuses to the exclusion of all else upon the welfare of the underprivileged group from which they spring. Thence come social aggression and class war.

A society which is free, on the other hand, generates leadership with a broader view. When relations between individuals are fluid, those with superior gifts are conditioned to exercise them for the good of all. If the social context within which leadership receives its basic training and direction is free and permeated with faith in the supreme worth of human personality, that leadership will retain its concern to preserve the freedom of association between minds to which it is accustomed and the forward thrust which that freedom generates.

It is America's good fortune that the areas in civilian life where individual relations are fluid, and where careers of usefulness await men of talent, still outnumber those areas in which relations are now being frozen or are already fixed, routinized and stultifying. The major problem is to prevent this situation from deteriorating.

Although a democratic society provides opportunity for intelligent leadership, of all forms of government it is also most in need of such leadership. It is precisely because of its atmosphere of free enterprise and association that it is the fastest moving, fastest changing society yet evolved. The widespread application of science to technology, so characteristic for example of America, has induced rapid social transformations. It is these changes in the complexion of society which lie at the root of our political problems. In dealing with such problems government operates constantly on the frontier of social evolution, continually mediating between conditions as they are and the ideas of the electorate as to how these conditions can best be improved. This discrepancy between fact and desire is the essence of all problems whether individual or collective, of peace or of war.

It was the experience of the people of New York that within their midst, frequently unknown to but a small circle of personal friends, were men and women capable of shouldering the special burdens of the war and rendering unique services to their State and Nation. No matter what the task, people could be found in this democratic microcosm possessed of the vision of what was needed, and of the energy and enthusiasm to transform that vision into substance.

In every municipality in the State, latent capacity for leadership existed in abundance and in the vast majority it was given a chance. In the business world, industrial management faced squarely such problems as government controls and government contracts, additional capital investments, re-tooling, new products, personnel expansion, double and triple shifts and housing, — grappled with them and came out on top. In communities, retired business men stepped back into harness; society women dropped their bridge; busy executives took on another job; school teachers and college professors applied themselves to immediate problems; clergymen pulled their weight and engineers, merchants and countless others contributed special skills and experience. New York municipalities were thus beneficiaries during the war of individual talents nurtured in the soil of a free society.

Of this condition the State's two wartime administrations took full advantage. With the New York State War Council and its thirty-odd agencies giving direction to approximately two million volunteer men and women, the quality of that leadership became a matter of supreme importance. No people on earth — British, Russian, German, French, Chinese or American — have been better than the top leadership which they habitually choose for themselves. New York has enjoyed in the past a long line of able executives — among others Grover Cleveland, Theodore Roosevelt, Charles Evans Hughes, Alfred E. Smith and Franklin D. Roosevelt. Herbert H. Lehman and Thomas E. Dewey were cast in the same tradition. Regardless of inherited abilities, varying social origins, and the special character of early public services, the membership of these men in the citizenry of this country, and their experience with the spirit of its laws and institutions, predisposed each to a deep-seated faith in the fundamental rightness of individual freedom and personal accountability, and in the wisdom of meeting squarely, rationally and *early,* the political, economic and social problems of his time.

Under Governor Lehman New York was one of the very first States to mobilize industrially in support of the national re-armament program. It was in the vanguard with its civilian protection and civilian mobilization programs, and in the establishment of a Council of Defense. Under Governor Dewey the accumulated shortages of the later years were dealt with vigorously and effectively and the problems of the transition period were faced early and realistically.

From the experience of the war and post-war years, there has emerged in New York State a system of administration and a philosophy of government that have proved their worth under severe test. While much of this thinking is old, important aspects are new, and the whole represents a consistent set of principles applicable to all levels of government, local, State or national. The basic ideas are given below in the form of a simple creed. They represent aspiration — something to shoot at — rather than absolute achievement. Their embodiment in practice, however, has been attempted by the present Executive and the Legislature. The results speak for themselves.

A Political Creed. He who governs should have: —

1. A sense of responsibility for the public welfare which accepts hard work as part of the business of government.

2. An interest in governing so profound that tough situations are welcomed and met squarely because they provide opportunities for working out answers to fundamental problems.

3. Skill and integrity in administration, — not only ability to pick the right man, willingness to delegate authority and to fix responsibility, but capacity to get at the facts personally and courage to follow the logic of the situation they reveal.

4. A social understanding that springs from continual application to the problems of an ever-changing society.

5. Foresight — perception of what it is that gives the present a future.

6. Wisdom to resolve conflicting purposes, and courage to resist on behalf of the public welfare, pressure from special interests whether of left or right.

7. Respect for the power of public funds to nurture well-being and misfortune alike; integrity and imagination to use them to achieve the former.

8. Faith in the capacity of the American people to make their political institutions serve the general welfare.

He should believe that: —

9. Responsibility begins with the individual, continues with the municipality and the State, and should never be usurped by a superior political unit where administrative competence demonstrably exists on the local level.

10. Social or economic problems can best be solved by the unit of government closest to them, and should be met with all available resources before aid is sought from a higher political unit.

11. To achieve local self-sufficiency, municipal initiative is to be encouraged wherever possible, and obstacles to its free exercise such as legislative curtailment of the legal rights of municipalities in favor of the State or Federal government is not to be permitted.

12. Taxation by the State and Federal government must be kept to a minimum to enable public funds to remain close to the problems for which they can be spent most effectively.

13. To each generation falls the task of transmitting intact the freedom which it inherits.

The first eight items are essential personal qualifications for the exercise of leadership in a democracy. The last five reflect a trend away from the glorification of the centralized state and a sorely needed emphasis upon the responsibility of the individual citizen as the fundamental prerequisite of a democratic society. If this State and Nation are to maintain themselves, their basic unit, the private citizen, cannot dodge his obligation to keep house and community in order. Only those, however, who habitually make the most of their opportunities, will appreciate, when in positions of leadership, the importance of providing opportunity for others.

Index

T

X

Y

Date Due

	PRINTED	IN U. S. A.